The Effects of Imprisonment

Cambridge Criminal Justice Series

Published in association with the Institute of Criminology, University of Cambridge

Published titles

Community Penalties: change and challenges, edited by Anthony Bottoms, Loraine Gelsthorpe and Sue Rex

Ideology, Crime and Criminal Justice: a symposium in honour of Sir Leon Radzinowicz, edited by Anthony Bottoms and Michael Tonry

Reform and Punishment: the future of sentencing, edited by Sue Rex and Michael Tonry

Confronting Crime: crime control policy under New Labour, edited by Michael Tonry

Sex Offenders in the Community: managing and reducing the risks, edited by Amanda Matravers

The Effects of Imprisonment, edited by Alison Liebling and Shadd Maruna

The Effects of Imprisonment

Edited by

Alison Liebling
Shadd Maruna

WILLAN
PUBLISHING

Published by

Willan Publishing
Culmcott House
Mill Street, Uffculme
Cullompton, Devon
EX15 3AT, UK
Tel: +44(0)1884 840337
Fax: +44(0)1884 840251
e-mail: info@willanpublishing.co.uk
website: www.willanpublishing.co.uk

Published simultaneously in the USA and Canada by

Willan Publishing
c/o ISBS, 920 NE 58th Ave, Suite 300
Portland, Oregon 97213-3644, USA
Tel: +001(0)503 287 3093
Fax: +001(0)503 280 8832
e-mail: info@isbs.com
website: www.isbs.com

Hardback first published 2005
Reprinted 2006, 2008
ISBN 10: 1-84392-093-X
ISBN 13: 978-1-84392-093-9

Paperback edition 2006
Reprinted 2006, 2007
ISBN 10: 1-84392-217-7
ISBN 13: 978-1-84392-217-9

British Library Cataloguing-in-Publication Data

A catalogue record for this book is available from the British Library

Project management by Deer Park Productions, Tavistock, Devon
Typeset by GCS, Leighton Buzzard, Beds
Printed and bound by T J I Digital, Padstow, Cornwall

Contents

The Editors dedicate this book to Distinguished Professor Hans Toch, the patron saint of prison effects research and our cherished friend.

A. Liebling
S. Maruna

List of tables and figures

Tables

Figures

Notes on contributors

Helen Arnold is a PhD student at the University of Cambridge Institute of Criminology and has been working and conducting research in prison for the last eight years. After completing the MPhil in Criminology at the Cambridge Institute in 1999 she was a research assistant for two years on two projects: 'An Exploration of Decision-Making in Discretionary Lifer Panels', and 'Measuring the Quality of Prison Life', before beginning her doctorate titled 'Identifying the High Performing Prison Officer'.

Pat Carlen is a freelance sociologist and Honorary Professor of Criminology at Keele University. She has written extensively on the relationships between crime and social justice and in 1997 was recipient of the American Society of Criminology Sellin-Glueck Award for international contributions to criminology.

Elaine Crawley is a Lecturer in Criminology at Keele University. She has conducted extensive prison research both with prisoners and uniformed prison staff. Her most recent research includes a two-year study of elderly men in prison and an ethnographic study of prison officers at work. In July 2004 she published the findings of her research into the lives of prison officers in a book called *Doing Prison Work* (Willan, 2004).

Ben Crewe is a Senior Research Associate at the Institute of Criminology, a Nuffield Foundation New Career Development Fellow in the Social Sciences, and a Research Fellow at Robinson College, Cambridge. He has recently conducted an ethnographic study of everyday life in a UK prison, titled 'The New Society of Captives'. He has also written on masculinity and media culture.

Linda Durie was a research assistant in the Institute on Criminology, Prison Research Centre, responsible for organising before and after surveys, conducting interviews with prisoners and staff, and carrying out observation on an evaluation on a safe local prison initiative. She has conducted several research projects in prisons, and has worked for the Prisons Inspectorate.

Tomer Einat received a PhD in Criminology from the Hebrew University and is a lecturer of criminology at The Jordan Valley College (Israel). His main interests are penology, prisons, prisoners' subculture, alternatives to imprisonment and criminal fines, areas of study where his work has made a significant impact. He served as the co-chairperson of the International Prison Initiative.

Adrian Grounds is a University Senior Lecturer in Forensic Psychiatry at the Institute of Criminology, University of Cambridge, and Honorary Consultant Forensic Psychiatrist in the Cambridgeshire and Peterborough Mental Health Partnership Trust. His research interests are in services for mentally disordered offenders, and the effects of wrongful conviction and imprisonment. He is also currently a Sentence Review Commissioner and Life Sentence Review Commissioner in Northern Ireland, and a Trustee of the Prison Reform Trust.

Craig Haney received his PhD (in Psychology) and JD degrees from Stanford University in 1978. One of the principal researchers on the 'Stanford Prison Experiment' in 1971, he has been studying the psychological effects of living and working in actual prison environments since then. His work has taken him to dozens of maximum-security prisons across the United States and in several different countries where he has evaluated conditions of confinement and interviewed prisoners about the mental health consequences of incarceration. His scholarly writing and empirical research have addressed a wide range of crime and punishment-related topics, including the causes of violent crime, psychological mechanisms by which prisoners adjust to incarceration, and the adverse effects of prolonged imprisonment, especially under severe conditions of confinement (especially in solitary or 'supermax' facilities). His forthcoming book about prison conditions in the United States will be published by the American Psychological Association in 2005.

Joel Harvey completed his MA (first class honours) in Psychology at the University of St Andrews in 1997 and his MSc in Forensic Psychology at the University of Kent in 1998. He completed his PhD in Criminology at the Institute of Criminology, University of Cambridge, in 2004. Joel has worked for the New South Wales Police Service, The University of New South Wales, and HM Prison Service on various research projects. Currently, he is training to be a clinical psychologist at the University of Manchester.

John Irwin After serving a five-year sentence (1952–1957) in a California prison, John Irwin attended college and eventually received a PhD in Sociology from the University of California, Berkeley. His PhD dissertation was on the career of the felon, which was published in 1970 as *The Felon*. In 1967, he joined the sociology faculty of San Francisco State University where he taught for 27 years. During his career as a sociologist he continued studying prisons and jails and wrote *Prisons in Turmoil*, *The Jail*, and *Its About Time*, the latter with James Austin. He recently published a new book on the modern American prison, *The Warehouse Prison: The Disposal of the New 'Dangerous Class'*. He also was highly active in prison reform during his professional career. He was a member of a 'working party' organised by the American Friends Service Committed and helped write the influential *Struggle for Justice* (1971). With other activists he organised The Prisoners Union, which was highly active in prison reform in the early 1970s. He continues to work on prison reform and at present is participating with a group of criminologists, lawyers and law professors on a sentencing reform pamphlet.

Ruth Jamieson is currently a Lecturer in Criminology and Criminal Justice in the School of Law at Queen's University, Belfast. Prior to joining the Institute of Criminology and Criminal Justice at Queen's in 2004 she taught at Keele University from 1995–2004 and worked for the Canadian Department of Justice on the research and evaluation of Federal/Provincial Legal Aid and Access to Justice Programs. She has also published in the areas of war and crime and transnational crime. She is currently involved in research on topics such as the effects of long-term imprisonment, and gender and resilience in armed conflict.

Yvonne Jewkes is Reader in Criminology and member of the International Centre for Comparative Criminological Research at the Open University. She has published widely on various aspects of imprisonment and is the author of *Captive Audience: Media, Masculinity and Power in Prisons* (Willan, 2002) and editor of the forthcoming *Handbook on Prisons* (Willan).

Robert Johnson is a Professor of Justice, Law and Society at the American University in Washington, DC. He is the author of several social science books, including *Condemned to Die*, *Death Work*, and *Hard Time*, as well as a collection of original poems, *Poetic Justice*. Johnson has testified or provided expert affidavits before state and federal courts, the US Congress, and the European Commission of Human Rights, and is a Distinguished Alumnus of the Nelson A. Rockefeller College of Public Affairs and Policy, University at Albany, State University of New York.

Roy D. King is Senior Research Fellow at the Institute of Criminology, Cambridge. Before that he was Professor of Criminology and Criminal Justice at the University of Wales where he established the Centre for Comparative Criminology and Criminal Justice. He has published several books on prisons and his continuing research interests are in the proliferation of supermax custody, and international comparisons of prisons and imprisonment. He is currently working on prisons and imprisonment in Brazil.

Candace Kruttschnitt is a Professor in the Department of Sociology at the University of Minnesota. She has published extensively on the subject of female offenders, including both reviews of research pertaining to gender differences in aetiology and primary analysis of criminal court sanctions. She recently completed a book with Rosemary Gartner on women's imprisonment (*Marking Time in the Golden State: Women' Imprisonment in California*. Cambridge University Press, 2005). She also chaired the National Research Council's Workshop on Violence Against Women. She was Vice President of the American Society of Criminology, and a council member of the Crime, Law and Deviance Section of the American Sociology Association. She received her BA degree from the University of California, Berkeley, her MPhil, MA and PhD degrees in sociology from Yale University.

Alison Liebling is a Reader in Criminology and Criminal Justice at the University of Cambridge, and a Fellow of Trinity Hall. She is the Director of the Cambridge Institute of Criminology's Prisons Research Centre. She is the author of *Suicides in Prison* (1992), *The Prison Officer* (2001, with David Price), and *Prisons and their Moral Performance* (2004).

Shadd Maruna is a Lecturer at the Institute of Criminology, University of Cambridge. His book, *Making Good: How Ex-Convicts Reform and Rebuild Their Lives* (American Psychological Association Books, 2001), was awarded the American Society of Criminology's Prize for Outstanding

Contribution to Criminology in 2001. More recently, he co-edited *After Crime and Punishment: Pathways to Offender Reintegration* (Willan, 2004). In 2005 he begins a new position as a Reader in Law and Criminology at Queen's University Belfast.

Joseph Murray is completing his doctoral dissertation on prisoners' children at the Institute of Criminology, Cambridge University. Previously he researched neighbourhood poverty at the Social Exclusion Centre, London School of Economics. He was awarded the Manuel Lopez-Rey prize at the Institute of Criminology, Cambridge University, 2002. His main research interests are in longitudinal studies and the social and psychological effects of imprisonment.

Barbara Owen is a Professor of Criminology at California State University, Fresno. She earned her PhD in Sociology from UC Berkeley in 1984. As an ethnographer, she continues to work in the areas of feminist criminology, gender-responsive policy, substance abuse treatment and prison culture for women.

Sonja Snacken is Professor of Criminology and Penology at the Vrije Universiteit Brussel and the University of Gent (Belgium). Her research concentrates on sentencing and the implementation of sanctions and measures, including the causes and consequences of penal inflation, prisoners' rights, prison regimes and prison violence, sentencing and human rights.

Richard Sparks is Professor of Criminology at the University of Edinburgh. Prior to taking up his present position he worked for thirteen years at Keele University where the research reported in this volume (with Elaine Crawley) was undertaken. Richard's research interests lie mainly in the areas of the sociology of punishment, especially imprisonment, penal politics and public sensibilities towards crime and criminal justice.

Annick Stiles was a Research Associate at the University of Cambridge Institute of Criminology; Prison Research Centre, responsible for quantitative data analysis. Since completing the project, Annick has left the Institute to take up a career in landscape gardening.

Sarah Tait was educated at the Universities of McGill in Montreal (BA Women's Studies) and Toronto (MA Criminology). She was a research assistant, in the Prison Research Centre, University of Cambridge, responsible for conducting interviews with prisoners and staff, and carrying out observation. She is a PhD student at the University of Cambridge, Institute of Criminology, studying gender, culture and care among prison officers.

Hans Toch is Distinguished Professor of Criminal Justice at the University at Albany, State University New York. A social psychologist working in criminology and criminal justice administration, Hans Toch is a prolific author whose books include *Living in Prison* (Free Press, 1975), *Violent Men* (Aldine, 1969), *The Disturbed Violent Offender* (with Ken Adams, Yale, 1989), *Police as Problem Solvers* (with J.D. Grant, Plenum, 1991), *Mosaic of Despair* (A.P.A. Books, 1992), *Police Violence* (with William Geller, Yale, 1996), *Corrections: A Humanistic Approach* (Harrow and Heston, 1997) and *Acting Out* (with Ken Adams, APA Books, 2002). Hans Toch is an elected Fellow of the American Psychological Association and the American Society of Criminology, and in 1996 he served as president of the American Association for Forensic Psychology. He was a member of the Governor's Task Force on Juvenile Violence and a consultant to the National Commission on the Causes and Prevention of Violence. His book *Men in Crisis* won the Hadley Cantril Memorial Award and he is co-recipient of the August Vollmer Award from the ASC.

Acknowledgements

Like its predecessors in the *Cambridge Criminal Justice Series*, this collection is an outgrowth of a Cropwood Conference at the University of Cambridge, the International Symposium on the Effects of Imprisonment (14 and 15 April 2004). Cambridge's Institute of Criminology has been receiving support from the Barrow Cadbury Trust since 1968 to underwrite the convening of Cropwood Conferences on a variety of criminal justice related topics. The Trust also supports the Cropwood Fellowship Programme, which enables Fellows, selected in a competitive process, to spend up to three months in Cambridge working on a research-related project, advised by a member of the Institute's academic staff. The Institute is enormously grateful to the Barrow Cadbury Trust and to Barry Mussenden and Sukhvinder Stubbs from Barrow Cadbury in particular, for their support of the Cropwood Programme.

The International Symposium on the Effects of Imprisonment received additional funding from the Prisons Research Centre and the Institute of Criminology.

We are also grateful to all the participants at the conference for their lively contributions (see list in the Appendix), and especially to Andrew Coyle for so ably chairing the event. Robinson College staff were excellent hosts. We would also like to thank Helen Griffiths for her most efficient work in organising the conference and preparing papers, and Ann Phillips for her very valuable assistance with the preparation of the manuscript for publication.

Foreword

Andrew Coyle (Professor of Prison Studies, King's College, London)

In their introduction to this book Liebling and Maruna ask whether the world really needs another book on the effects of prison. That is a question which deserves an answer.

During all the years that I worked in prisons I never ceased to ask myself why I did so. This was not because of obsessive uncertainty about my chosen career. Rather, it came from a desire never to lose sight of the reality of what I was doing. Shorn of all subtleties and rationalisations, my task was to deprive other human beings of their liberty. I tried to ensure that I did so in the most decent and humane way possible. I attempted to reduce the pain of imprisonment for those men who were under my care. I did my best to provide them with opportunities to make positive use of their enforced time in captivity. But in doing all of those things it was important always to remember that prison is by its very nature a debilitating experience. That is why in any decent and democratic society the imposition of imprisonment should always be an instrument of last resort, only to be used when there is no other option.

In a number of countries, especially in the Western world, that principle is no longer observed. The number of people in prison in the United States has gone from half a million to over two million in just over 20 years. In England and Wales the prison population has risen in the last 15 years from 45,000 to 75,000. In neither case has there been anything like comparable rises in the crime rates or in detection rates. Put simply, courts now send more offenders to prison and impose longer sentences than they did before. One explanation for this is that society has become more punitive and courts are simply responding to the demands of the public and the media. This is partly true.

It seems to me that there is also another dangerous influence at work and that is the proposition advanced by some people who work in and around the prison system that good can come out of imprisonment; that it can be an important method of changing the behaviour and attitude of those who are sent there, so that they will come out better people and much less likely to commit crime as a result of their experiences in prison. This is what Nils Christie has called 'the denial of existence strategy':

> Study after study has shown how penal measures and long-term incarceration have been made more acceptable to society if they were disguised as treatment, training or pure help to suffering individuals in need of such measures. (Christie 1978: 181)

As a result, in England and Wales many prisoners are now required to undergo 'programmes' in an attempt to change their behaviour; the number of women in prison has increased four times within a very short period; in some parts of the country drug addicts can get better treatment in prison than in the community; and it is now claimed that some difficult children are better off in prison service custody than in a welfare environment. Duguid (2000: 230) has characterised this phenomenon, which of course is not new, as treating the prisoner as 'object rather than subject', someone whose only role is to co-operate with decisions made by others, rather than someone to be encouraged to take control of his or her own life.

In a similar context, one of the dangers when studying criminology is that one can come to view the prisoner as an object rather than a subject, engaging in dispassionate and supposedly neutral analyses of whether human beings suffer 'pain', or indeed are affected in any way, by the experience of imprisonment. In so far as this is the case, the answer to the editors' initial question is that the world does not need another book on the effects of imprisonment; certainly prisoners do not.

Fortunately, the contributors to this volume have not fallen into that trap. As they demonstrated during the two days they gathered in Cambridge in 2004, they care deeply about the humanity of prisoners and about the effects which imprisonment has on those who suffer it and on their families. As a consequence, this book is not an arid scholastic treatise. It has rigorous academic foundations but the conclusion which cries out from it is that prison should have a very limited role to play in a modern society. In that respect it is a fitting tribute to Hans Toch, to whom it is dedicated.

References

Christie, N. (1978) 'Prisons in Society or Society as a Prison', in J. Freeman (ed.) *Prisons, Past and Future*. London: Heinemann.

Duguid, S. (2000) *Can Prisons Work? The prisoner as object and subject in modern corrections*. Toronto: University of Toronto Press.

Chapter I

Introduction: the effects of imprisonment revisited[1]

Alison Liebling and Shadd Maruna

Offenders emerge from prison afraid to trust, fearful of the unknown, and with a vision of the world shaped by the meaning that behaviours had in the prison context. For a recently released prisoner, experiences like being jostled on the subway, having someone reach across him in the bathroom to take a paper towel, or making eye contact can be taken as a precursor to a physical attack. In relationships with loved ones, this warped kind of socialization means that problems will not easily be talked through. In a sense, the system we have designed to deal with offenders is among the most iatrogenic in history, nurturing those very qualities it claims to deter.

(Miller 2001: 3)

Florence Nightingale (1859) famously argued that the first principle of the hospital should be to do the sick no harm. A recent history of prison standards (Keve 1996: 1) begins by arguing that Nightingale 'undoubtedly would have expressed a similar principle for prisons'. It seems that she actually did – or at least argued that we should do more research into whether or not prisons caused harm. In a letter to the *Manchester Guardian* in 1890, Nightingale laments the fact that 'criminology is much less studied than insectology' and argues that: 'It would be of immense importance if the public had kept before them the statistics, well worked out, of the influence of punishment on crime or of reformatories and industrial schools on juvenile offenders.' Armed with such knowledge, she believed, no rational society would support a system of 'reformation' that made its subjects more likely to offend upon their release than they were prior to admittance.

Since Nightingale's time, the discipline of criminology has grown immensely (surely by now eclipsing entomology at least in terms of undergraduate interest levels) and recidivism statistics of the type she described have become one of the discipline's most essential products (see Baumer *et al* 2002; Beck 2000; Kershaw 1997). However, the prison has remained and indeed reliance on imprisonment as a means of social control has increased substantially over the last 20 years in the United Kingdom and especially in the United States. We rely on imprisonment by remaining blind to the falseness of our assumptions about its role and effectiveness. As Garland (1990) has argued, restricted to its technical functions, imprisonment does not work, and there are other institutions far better placed to deliver goods such as 'repair', 'inclusion' or 'correction'. Yet, presumably, the public consent to the increasing use of imprisonment based at least in large part on these narrow, technicist and unproven grounds (Useem *et al* 2003).

Where did Nightingale's remarkable prognostic abilities go wrong? Perhaps we human beings are not as rational as she gave us credit for being. Or else, more optimistically, perhaps criminology has simply failed to make the case that prisons do not 'work'. The study of the effects of prison has a distinguished history within criminology, yet the debate has gone stale in recent decades (partially indicated by how few investigations of this nature have been supported by criminal justice research councils in recent years). Haney and Zimbardo (1998: 721) have argued that although social scientists contributed significantly to the intellectual foundations on which the modern prison was developed, over the last 25 years, we have 'relinquished voice and authority in the debates that surround prison policy'. This absence has created 'an ethical and intellectual void that has undermined both the quality and the legitimacy of correctional practices', they argue.

In recent years, the reigning paradigm in the prison effects literature, voiced by Zamble and Porporino (1988) and others, is that incarceration is akin to a 'behavioral deep freeze' (see Oleson 2002 for an ingenious parody of this finding). In other words, the adaptational styles and capacities of offenders are basically invariant and largely impervious to effects of imprisonment. In this framework, incarceration simply acts to put a person's pre-existing propensities on hold until renewed opportunities are presented for these propensities to be freely exercised in the future. Essentially, Dostoevsky's tragic optimism that humans must be creatures who can 'withstand anything' – earned the hard way after he spent four years in a Siberian prison camp – has become the dangerously taken-for-granted assumption in contemporary thinking about prison effects.

The logical conclusion of this 'deep freeze' argument is not so much that 'nothing works', but essentially 'nothing much matters'. Prisons can become as harsh and inhumane as desired – and imprisonment does not get much more inhumane than the conditions in so-called 'supermax' confinement widespread in the United States (see Haney, this volume) – and no real damage will be done to their unfortunate inhabitants. Among the shortcomings of this argument is the narrowness by which it defines 'harm'. The contemporary effects literature lacks a sufficient affective dimension. Fear, anxiety, loneliness, trauma, depression, injustice, powerlessness, violence and uncertainty are all part of the experience of prison life. These 'hidden', but everywhere apparent, features of prison life have not been measured or taken seriously enough by those interested in the question of prison effects. Sociologists of prison life knew these things were significant, but have largely failed to convince others in a methodologically convincing way that such 'pain' constitutes a measurable 'harm' (see Liebling 1999). Yet, 'pains' have consequences, however indirect. The petty humiliations and daily injustices experienced in prison (as in our communities) may be suffered in silence, but as they accumulate and fester these hurts can return as hatred and 'inexplicable' violence (see Gilligan, 1999). After all, if the consequence of injustice and rejection is hatred (Storr 1991: 49; Parker 1970: 84–6) or resentment (Barbalet 1998) and the product of this pain is violence (de Zulueta 1993), we are surely obliged to avoid these unwanted and unintended effects.

Our dissatisfactions with the state of the existing literature, and our recognition that important work challenging the 'deep freeze' paradigm was beginning to emerge, provided the rationale for the conference out of which the following chapters emerged.[2] Our admittedly ambitious aim in assembling this collection of chapters from leading international scholars is to redirect the conversation among academics, policy-makers and professionals regarding the effects of imprisonment. We define this topic broadly to include the social, psychological, behavioural and emotional impacts of the incarceration experience on prisoners (during and after their captivity); as well as the impact of imprisonment on prisoners' families (see Murray, this volume); and on those working in the institutions themselves (see e.g. Arnold, this volume; Carlen, this volume); and, indeed, the impact that the institution of the prison has on a society (especially in the present times of mass incarceration in the US and elsewhere).

These are far from mere academic issues. For instance, there may be justice implications if apparently objective measures of punishment, calibrated in chunks of time, have radically different subjective effects on recipients (von Hirsch 1993; Liebling 2004). Understanding the true effects of imprisonment is necessary if we are to appreciate what goes on in prisons as well. As Sykes argued, the deprivations of prison life provide the energy for the system of action that characterises the prison (Sykes 1958). There is even a relationship between the effects debate and prison design: reflecting on assumptions about the impact of prison over time helps us to make sense of the varied and apparently contradictory penal estate in England and Wales, for example.[3] Finally, of course, an understanding of the intended and unintended effects of imprisonment has serious implications for the treatment of offenders and the reduction of recidivism. One reason for the null findings of so many of the best designed interventions may be that the positive impact of interventions such as education or job training may be systematically undermined by the negative effects of the incarceration process itself.

The account below presents a selective review of the debate over the effects of imprisonment over the last 50 years or so, and shows some of the limitations of the argument to date. We begin with the post-war consensus regarding the dangers of total institutions like prisons on the mental health and personality of the individuals they hold captive. Then, we review the shift in the 1980s to seeing imprisonment as a largely neutral experience with little lasting impact, good or bad. We conclude with some of the new issues that have emerged in recent years and which inform this collection.

The post-war consensus on prison effects

The first major critiques of imprisonment and its effects came from sociologists critical of institutions *per se* (e.g. Goffman's 1961 classic *Asylums*). In the UK, Barton (1966) brought together several studies showing detrimental effects of institutionalisation under the heading 'institutional neurosis'. This was:

> ... a disease characterised by apathy, lack of initiative, loss of interest more marked in things and events not immediately personal or present, submissiveness, and sometimes no expression of feelings of resentment at harsh or unfair orders. There is also a lack of interest in the future and an apparent inability to make practical plans for it, a deterioration in personal habits, toilet and standards generally, a loss of individuality, and a resigned acceptance that things will go on as they are – unchangingly, inevitably, and indefinitely.
>
> (Barton 1966: 14)

There were several overlapping factors associated with its aetiology: loss of contact with the outside world; enforced idleness and loss of responsibility; the authoritarian attitudes of medical and nursing staff; the loss of personal possessions and friends; prescribed drugs; and loss of prospects outside the institution (p. 63).[4]

Around the same time, other, more specific reservations about the effects of imprisonment were being expressed from various sources in the UK, including a report of the Advisory Council on the Treatment of Offenders on Preventive Detention (Home Office 1963). It was clear from research (e.g. West 1963) that very long sentences were being inappropriately given to socially 'inadequate', repeat offenders and that such prison terms only reinforced the cycle of dependency, institutionalisation and crime (West 1963: 106–7; Home Office 1963). Tony Parker's *The Unknown Citizen* powerfully illustrated this critique:

> Imprisonment neither reforms nor deters me. It confirms and completes the destruction of my personality, and has now so conditioned me that I am almost totally incapable of living outside. A prison has become the only place in which I can exist satisfactorily, and it has become a kindness on your part to return me to it since the strain of living outside is so painful and intense.
>
> (Parker 1963: 156)

In a landmark study of prison environments,[5] Gresham Sykes (1958) used the language of the 'pains of imprisonment'. In his sociological study of a maximum security prison in Trenton, Sykes identified five main pains of imprisonment. They were:

- the loss of liberty (confinement, removal from family and friends, rejection by the community, and loss of citizenship: a civil death, resulting in lost emotional relationships, loneliness and boredom)

- the deprivation of goods and services (choice, amenities and material possessions)

- the frustration of sexual desire (prisoners were figuratively castrated by involuntary celibacy)

- the deprivation of autonomy (regime routine, work, activities, trivial and apparently meaningless restrictions – for example, the delivery of letters, lack of explanations for decisions)

- the deprivation of security (enforced association with other unpredictable prisoners, causing fear and anxiety; prisoners had to fight
for the safety of their person and possessions) (Sykes 1958: 63–78).

According to Sykes, prisoners lost society's trust, the status of
citizenship and material possessions, which constituted a large part
of their self-perception. The minutiae of life were regulated with a
bureaucratic indifference to individual need and worth:

> Imprisonment, then, is painful. The pains of imprisonment,
> however, cannot be viewed as being limited to the loss of physical
> liberty. The significant hurts lie in the frustrations or deprivations
> which attend the withdrawal of freedom, such as the lack of
> heterosexual relationships, isolation from the free community,
> the withholding of goods and services, and so on. And however
> painful these frustrations or deprivations may be in the immediate
> terms of thwarted goals, discomfort, boredom, and loneliness, they
> carry a more profound hurt as a set of threats or attacks which
> are directed against the very foundations of the prisoner's being.
> The individual's picture of himself as a person of value ... begins
> to waver and grow dim. Society did not plan this onslaught, it is
> true, and society may even 'point with pride' to its humanity in the
> modern treatment of the criminal. But the pains of imprisonment
> remain and it is imperative that we recognise them, for they provide
> the energy for the society of captives as a system of action.
>
> (Sykes 1958: 78–9)

These deprivations threatened the prisoner's sense of worth and self-
concept. They provided the energy for the 'society of captives' to act
collectively, in order to mitigate their effects. They caused prisoners to
generate alternative methods of gaining self-esteem.

The post-war literature, then, has represented the power of institutions
as dangerous and damaging, including the fear of breakdown (Cohen
and Taylor 1972), and hopelessness about the future. This tradition
might be best captured in a more recent study by Gallo and Ruggiero
(1991). They describe prisons as 'factories for the manufacture of psychosocial handicaps': 'Even the most modern, comfortable and 'humane'
regimes provide forms of destruction which are built into the normalcy
of incarceration' (Gallo and Ruggiero 1991: 278). They argue that the
two most common types of behaviour found in prison were aggression
and depression. Prisoners in the research described the distress caused
by trying to keep their own distress under control as one of the harshest

pains of imprisonment. Their survival techniques, adopted to survive imprisonment, damaged them. As one prisoner said:

> I found myself giving precedence in a queue to 'respectable' prisoners; shaking hands with some and ignoring others; mocking one inmate and being respectful and subservient to another. Everybody complied with these unwritten rules. If you didn't, you were looked at with suspicion; you were regarded as someone to shun, sometimes to punish.
>
> (ibid.)

Gallo and Ruggiero describe prisons as worlds of 'de-communication' (see Johnson, this volume), where prisoners either lived in a state of constant anxiety, or 'disengaged' in a form of psychological absenteeism encouraged by the availability of drugs. In prison, they argued, 'it is possible to speak using a hundred words' (ibid.: 285).

Two landmark psychological studies provided considerable support for this anti-institution consensus in sociology: Milgram's obedience study and Zimbardo's model prison experiment. Both studies remain important, despite significant and well-documented methodological shortcomings.[6] With some exceptions (e.g. Shover 1996), contemporary penology neglects these studies and tends to consider them discredited. However, our view is that both studies (and the controversy they provoked) provide important theoretical and empirical insights which have considerable relevance to the contemporary prison experience.

Milgram and obedience to authority

> Arendt's conception of the banality of evil comes closer to the truth than one might dare imagine. The ordinary person who shocked the victim did so out of a sense of obligation – a conception of his duties as a subject – and not from any peculiarly aggressive tendencies.
>
> (Milgram 1974: 6)

How are personal morals overcome in the face of autocratic authority? How do individuals shake off their own responsibility for unacceptable actions? What is the psychology of 'ordinary cruelty'? Stanley Milgram conducted a series of experiments in the 1960s intended to investigate readiness to obey morally wrong and physically dangerous acts (Milgram 1974; see also Asch 1951 on conformity). Motivated by curiosity about the cooperation of thousands of Germans with the systematic destruction of the Jews and others during the 1930s and 1940s, Milgram conducted his experiments at Yale University under the title, 'the effects of punishment on learning'.

In the now infamous tests, he persuaded duped volunteers to administer shocks of increasing severity to a 'student' who gave wrong answers to a series of learning tests. The experiment was conducted under the strict guidance of the experimenter, who encouraged the subjects to continue. Many participants showed signs of distress, and some eventually refused to go on. However, levels of conformity far exceeded expectations. Sixty-five per cent of the subjects administered shocks of what they thought were as high as 450 volts, apparently endangering the life of the actor who masqueraded as the student.

The level of blind obedience in such behaviour varied, of course. When the experiments were repeated at a less prestigious location, the number of subjects willing to deliver these levels fell to 50 per cent. When the subject was in the same room as the 'student' instead of being the other side of a glass partition, obedience levels dropped to 40 per cent. When other 'teachers' left the room during the experiment in protest (providing support for refusing to obey), obedience levels dropped to 10 per cent. If the experimenter left the room, obedience dropped to almost zero, and many participants administered lower levels than required (while assuring the experimenter that they were obeying his instructions). When subjects could enlist another person to actually deliver the shock for them, obedience levels rose to 95 per cent.

The participants expressed serious reservations about their own behaviour once the experiment was over. Milgram concluded in his Epilogue, drawing on other examples of real atrocities, that 'we find a set of people carrying out their jobs and dominated by an administrative, rather than a moral, outlook' (p. 186). Other related studies showed that ordinary citizens were more likely to obey an instruction if it was given by someone in uniform, even if the instructor subsequently left the scene. Nurses would deliver dangerous levels of drugs to patients if instructed to do so by an unknown doctor over the telephone. Behaviour was transformed under instruction from a legitimate authority.

Milgram concluded that his studies revealed 'the capacity for man to abandon his humanity ... as he merges his unique personality into larger institutional structures' (p. 188). He claimed that morally wrong behaviour can be viewed as a product of transactions with an environment that supports such behaviour, and that social institutions contain powerful forces (including authority structures) which can make good men engage in evil deeds. Individuals experience strain during these activities, but many resolve this strain through avoidance or denial, and continue with their work (Milgram 1974: 156–64). As the world of prisons becomes increasingly managerial and bureaucratic, the threat of this sort of interpersonal masking of evil actions as legitimate ('just doing my job') takes on increased urgency. Likewise, the exposure of the extraordinary treatment of captives by British and American soldiers in Iraq in recent years is a grim reminder of the truth behind Milgram's basic findings of the human capacity for evil in the line of duty.

The Zimbardo experiment

The Zimbardo 'Simulated Prison' experiment was another, classic illustration of the dangers of institutional roles in influencing human behaviour. Haney, Banks and Zimbardo (1973) conducted an experiment in which subjects role-played prisoners and guards in a simulated prison. Subjects were selected after careful diagnostic testing of a large group of volunteer, male college students. Participants were randomly assigned to act as either prisoners or guards in an experiment designed to last two weeks.

The experiment was cut short, however, as the researchers became startled and concerned by what they were seeing. The authors reported that the 'prison' became a 'psychologically compelling environment', eliciting unexpectedly intense, realistic and often pathological reactions from the participants. The prisoners seemed to experience a loss of personal identity and reacted profoundly to the arbitrary control of their behaviour. This resulted in a syndrome of passivity, dependency, depression and helplessness. Alternatively, most of the guards experienced gains in social power, status and group identification, which made their role-playing rewarding. Half the prisoners developed an acute emotional disturbance. A third of the guards became more aggressive and dehumanising than predicted. Importantly, few of these reactions could be attributed to pre-existing personality traits. The authors concluded that imprisonment destroys the human spirit of both the imprisoned and their keepers. They argued that the brutality of prison stems not from the characteristics of individual guards and prisoners (the 'dispositional hypothesis'), but from the 'deep structure' of the prison as an institution.

They concluded that 'harmful structures do not require ill-intentioned persons to inflict psychological damage on those in their charge' (Haney and Zimbardo 1998: 721). Evil can arise out of powerful social forces, and situational variables shape even the most unethical social behaviours, overriding personality traits. Personality traits, by themselves, did not predict who survived, resisted and broke down under extreme stress, although they may have operated as moderator variables:

> We feel there is abundant evidence that virtually all the subjects at one time or another experienced reactions which went well beyond the surface demands of role-playing and penetrated the deep structure of the psychology of imprisonment.
>
> (Haney *et al* 1973: 91)

The authors suggested that power was self-aggrandising. The most hostile guards moved into leadership positions, making decisions which were rarely contradicted. Rights were redefined as privileges, to be earned by obedience. Everyone in the experiment came to despise lack of power in others and in themselves. The prisoners showed disbelief, followed by rebellion and self-interest. Some sided with the guards and tried to win approval. The model prisoner reaction was passivity, dependence (or learned helplessness) and flattened affect. The loss of personal identity, and the experience of arbitrary control, forced them to allow others to exercise power over them. The prisoners believed that guards had been selected on the basis of their larger size. In fact, there was no difference between the groups in average weight or height.

The conclusion was clear: 'Like all powerful situations, prisons transform the worldviews of those who inhabit them, on both sides of the bars' (Haney and Zimbardo 1998: 721). The risks of bureaucratic practices, and of barely visible uses of power, were higher than we commonly assume. Among the important implications of the research were clear lessons for the training of prison officers (see the interview with Zimbardo by Cheliotis; 2004: 48). Shortly after the study was completed, there was a spate of killings at San Quentin and Attica prisons. These incidents emphasised the urgency of reforms which recognised the dignity and humanity of both prisoners and guards (Pallas and Barber 1972).

The emergence of a new consensus

Beginning in the 1970s, however, these studies alleging the dangers of institutions were subjected to methodological criticism and accusations of ideological bias and selectivity (Sapsford 1978; Walker 1987). The 'pains' identified by these studies were largely unsubstantiated by more carefully designed psychological research, leading a number of psychologists to conclude that the effects of imprisonment were largely minimal (Banister *et al* 1973; Bolton *et al* 1976; Bukstel and Kilmann 1980; Walker 1983, 1987). Walker (1987) argues that 'research – chiefly by psychologists – has done much to deflate the sweeping exaggerations – chiefly by sociologists – about the ill effects of normal incarceration'.

Research in the 1970s and 1980s suggested that prisoners coped surprisingly well (Richards 1978; Sapsford 1978, 1983),[7] despite an initial period of disorientation, and anxieties about family and friends. Empirical studies concluded that ex-prisoners were able to resettle after an initial period of restlessness upon release (Coker and Martin 1983). This psychological research characterised the experience of imprisonment as little worse than a period of 'deep freeze' (Zamble and Porporino 1988; and see comments by officers in Crawley 2004: 97). Research such as the Durham study (e.g. Banister *et al* 1973) seemed to many to largely close the heated debate of the effects of imprisonment in favour of a conservative, new consensus (see e.g. Bukstel and Kilmann 1980).

How is it possible to reconcile these apparently 'neutral' findings of psychological research on the effects of long-term imprisonment with earlier, and alternative, accounts of the nature of the prison experience? During the late 1980s, psychological studies continued, but broadened, and began to include the concept of *coping*. This concept allowed for individual differences and environmental conditions to be considered in more detail, and led to a richer stage in the study of prison and its effects (see e.g. Toch *et al* 1989). For instance, prisoners who made suicide attempts were found to differ in significant ways from other prisoners, showing poorer coping strategies and suffering from a greater degree of background disadvantage. The prison experience was far more difficult for those prisoners who were not able to find their way into jobs, activities and social networks in prison (see Liebling 1992). Imprisonment seemed to be most distressing for vulnerable groups who were least able to cope with the demands made by an unresponsive and depriving environment (Liebling 1999).

In other words, the psychological resources and individual circumstances of prisoners had been insufficiently examined in the prison effects research. Prison can be extremely, and differentially, painful depending on one's psychosocial background and particular experiences inside, and yet this apparently obvious fact was not being reflected in the research of the 1970s and 1980s. In the most comprehensive review of the prison effects literature to date, Gendreau *et al* (1999: 18)[8] conclude that:

> The sad reality that so little is known about what goes on inside the 'black box' of prisons and how this relates to recidivism … Only a mere handful of studies have attempted to address this matter … Analogously, could one imagine so ubiquitous and costly a

procedure in the medical or social services fields receiving such cursory research attention?

At the beginning of the 1990s, Hay and Sparks nicely characterised the 'effects debate' as 'sterile' (Hay and Sparks 1992: 302). The measurement of harm was poor, and the focus of most of the research was on long-term prisoners because of an assumption that any harmful effects – if they existed – would be curvilinear, increasing with length of time in custody. There are several flaws in this argument. The impact of custody is often most negative at the earliest stages. This is reflected in suicide rates, absconding figures and in several research studies (for example, Ericson 1975; Sapsford 1983; Gibbs 1987; Liebling 1999; and see Harvey, this volume). Prisoners who die by suicide do not appear in these 'long-term' samples, nor do those who leave prison by other means, for example, by transfer to psychiatric hospital. At the end of a long period of imprisonment, only the survivors appear in research samples.

Additionally, there are few substantial longitudinal or developmental studies of the effects of imprisonment (but see Jamieson and Grounds, this volume). Most studies rely on short follow-up periods (e.g. Zamble and Porporino 1988) or on cross-sectional samples, comparing groups of different prisoners who have served different lengths of time. Further, research has concentrated on prisoners during the period of custody, when important effects may manifest themselves after release from prison. The few studies that have examined long-term prisoners after release (e.g. Coker and Martin 1983) have focused on general measures of social adjustment, rather than more subtle, hidden kinds of psychological and emotional disability (Grounds 2004).

Prison is not a uniform experience. Studies have tended to take undifferentiated samples and to look for general patterns. These general studies neglect the experience of particular groups and individuals, such as women, the young, the old, prisoners segregated for their own protection, those spending long periods of time in segregation units for other reasons, and so on (see Kruttschnitt; Crawley and Sparks; and King, this volume). Moreover, assumptions about 'harm-as-deterioration' (e.g. in IQ) are seriously limited. Suicide does not require a permanent drop in measurable psychological constructs such as IQ. Pain is a harm which psychological scales have so far failed to reflect (see Haney 1997). Damage may be immediate, or cumulative, and independent of time spent in custody. Repeated short periods of custody may engender at least as much pain as one long sentence serving to 'exacerbate psychological vulnerabilities and emotional difficulties' (Porporino and Zamble 1984).

In short, the real effects of imprisonment, when understood in a broad context, appear to be anything but a 'deep freeze'. As the British Home Office wrote in the 1991 White Paper, *Custody, Care and Justice*, following the Woolf Report:

> ... [Prison] breaks up families. It is hard for prisoners to retain or subsequently to secure law-abiding jobs. Imprisonment can lessen people's sense of responsibility for their actions and reduce their self-respect, both of which are fundamental to law abiding citizenship. Some, often the young and less experienced, acquire in prisons a wider knowledge of criminal activity. Imprisonment is costly for the individual, for the prisoner's family and for the community.
>
> (Home Office 1991: para 1.16)

New directions in the effects debate

The next generation of research on prison effects needs to focus on issues such as mental and physical health (including addiction issues), the possibility of post-traumatic stress disorder (PTSD), the developmental health and well-being of prisoner families, and the impact of imprisonment on the ability to successfully desist from crime. The failure of research to pursue these crucial other harms of imprisonment has resulted in the sterility to which Hay and Sparks (1992) refer.

Mental and physical health

Imprisonment can be detrimental both to the physical and mental health of prisoners, and this is a particularly urgent issue with regard to long-term and aged prisoners (see Jewkes; Crawley and Sparks, this volume). While many prisoners receive medical treatment in prison that would be unavailable to them outside (see Jones 1976), the health risks of imprisonment are high, uneven and specific to the conditions of confinement.

For instance, research by Gore *et al* in Scottish prisons has demonstrated the increasing risk of HIV transmission in prisons (Gore *et al* 1995; Taylor *et al* 1995; and Crofts *et al* 1995 on Australian prisoners) where the random sharing of injecting equipment is common. Rates of hepatitis B and C are increasing in prison, particularly among injecting drug users. Crofts and colleagues argue that:

> ... [s]everal risk behaviours for transmission of HIV and hepatitis B and C occur in prison, including the injection of illicit drugs and tattooing with inadequately disinfected equipment as well as unprotected sexual intercourse, including male to male anal intercourse. One Australian study estimated that 36 percent of prisoners had injected themselves intravenously, and twelve percent had participated in anal intercourse at least once whilst in prison.
>
> (Crofts *et al* 1995: 285)

The authors also found that the high rate of continuing exposure to hepatitis B in male prisoners aged less than 30 years who inject drugs suggests that this is a group in whom 'spread of HIV must be considered to be simply a matter of time' (ibid.: 287).

The Crofts study found that injecting drug use was more common amongst women prisoners (ibid.: 286) and that exposure to hepatitis B and C was more frequent. Recent Inspectorate reports have condemned particular female establishments in the UK for turning 'shoplifters' into 'drug addicts', arguing that as many as 80 per cent of Styal Prison's female prisoners were injecting drugs (HMCIP 1995). In the above studies, risk of transmission of viruses relating to intravenous drug use was found to be high both during custody and immediately after release. Many prisoners begin their injecting habit while in custody, although those who inject daily outside prison do so less frequently whilst in custody (Taylor *et al* 1995: 290–91) and some regular drug users stop while in prison (ibid.: 292). The sharing of needles by injecting drug users is however, far more common in custody than outside, and the cleaning methods used by prisoners (rinsing with water, bleach or hairdressing liquid) are more ineffective than those typically used on the outside. Taylor and colleagues conclude that 'various studies of behaviour and prevalence of HIV in injecting drug users have shown that a period of imprisonment is an independent predictor of being positive for HIV' (ibid.: 291).

Their study of an outbreak of HIV infection in a Scottish prison, which was initiated following a cluster of cases of acute hepatitis B infection, demonstrates that transmission may occur during a period of custody as a result of high-risk behaviours practised by prisoners. All of the infected prisoners had shared injecting equipment within the prison.

A follow-up study of the prevalence of HIV infection and of drug-injecting behaviour in the same establishment one year later concluded that 'the arrival of a carrier of hepatitis B or HIV within any of the needle-sharing networks common within British prisons is all that is required to start such an outbreak' (Gore *et al* 1995: 295). A quarter of known injecting drug users in the prison (18 of 72) had started injecting while in custody. Between a quarter and a third of the men who injected drugs between January and June 1993 became infected with HIV while in custody (Gore *et al* 1995: 296). Over a quarter of the prison's population were injecting drug users.

The authors note that:

> The predilection of prison populations for blood-borne virus infections is not a new observation. Because of a more than 10 times higher prevalence of previous hepatitis B infection and carriage rates among prison inmates in the UK Blood Transfusion Services ceased donor sessions in prisons in the early 1980s.
>
> (Gore *et al* 1995: 296)

Yet the policy climate in the UK supports the use of prison to reduce drug use. Detoxification programmes are proliferating, voluntary and mandatory drug testing programmes are widespread, and prisoners themselves sometimes rely on a short prison sentence to 'get themselves clean' (see Crewe, this volume).

Post-traumatic stress

Research on the psychological effects of trauma has been shown to apply to certain groups of prisoners who have been found to develop symptoms of PTSD in medico-legal assessments. Such symptoms can have debilitating effects and are associated with difficulties in restoring and maintaining relationships. High levels of anxiety, disturbed sleep, chronic depression, withdrawal from others and persistent feelings of being 'different' from others and from one's previous self are described by clinicians working with former prisoners. For instance, in a series of assessments of men who had served long prison terms after wrongful convictions, Grounds (2004) found strong evidence of severe and disabling psychological morbidity. Similar symptoms have been found by other prisoners released after long prison sentences, particularly, for example, where they have witnessed violence. Characteristic symptoms of PTSD include restlessness, irritability and severe difficulties in forming or restoring close relationships, fear and distress in response to reminders of the traumatic event, avoidance behaviour, diminished interest or participation in significant activities, feelings of detachment and estrangement from others, loss of motivation and a restricted range of affect (for example, an inability to feel warmth), and anxiety and depression. There may also be physical symptoms: increased physiological arousal, outbursts of anger, difficulties in concentration and hyper-vigilance. Such symptoms can be associated with increased alcohol and drug use.

Adrian Grounds has argued that such symptoms can be regarded as an 'enduring personality change'. This is manifested as 'inflexible and maladaptive characteristics that impair interpersonal, social and occupational functioning' and which were not present before, such as 'a hostile or mistrustful attitude towards the world, social withdrawal, feelings of emptiness or hopelessness, a chronic feeling of threat, and estrangement' (Grounds 2004, forthcoming; and see Jamieson and Grounds, this volume). Prolonged trauma can lead to major problems of relatedness and identity which are only manifest in close relationships, attitudes to themselves and sense of purpose (Grounds, forthcoming). These shifts, in one's sense of time and identity, and in the capacity to build or sustain social connections, can make coping with the demands of everyday life extremely difficult. The psychosocial and psychiatric effects associated with imprisonment could be much more widely understood as a result of these analyses.

Research on prisoners' families

Finally, there is little research emphasis on the effects of imprisonment on prisoners' families (see Lanier 2003; and Murray, this volume). As Light (1993: 322) argued, a term of imprisonment affects not only the person remanded or sentenced. 'The inmate's family and dependants are all too often the ones who suffer most'. Shaw (1992) further points out:

> It is a sobering thought that, in spite of the increasing attention being paid to the children of broken and bereaved families, no government in Europe, North America, or elsewhere appears to know how many children within its jurisdiction are affected by the imprisonment of a parent.

Despite considerable progress in understanding the immediate and long-term effects of separation trauma upon children (see especially, Hendriks *et al* 1993; and Rutter 1982), the impact of imprisonment upon the children of prisoners has been slow to appear in the literature on the effects of imprisonment. The effects of separation and loss on children include increased behaviour disturbance and later delinquency, depression and feelings of low self-esteem (Richards 1992). The apparent failure to apply the findings of research on separation to our understanding of imprisonment is particularly surprising, given the inevitability of distress when one or both parents are imprisoned, in some cases for an offence against the other parent (see Hendriks *et al* 1993). Additionally, criminologists have amassed considerable evidence relating to the damaging effects of early loss on child development and later antisocial and destructive behaviour:

> For children, imprisonment of adults may result in sudden separation from a parent. Young children who lose parents are likely to show separation anxiety, anger, behavioural disturbance and deterioration in school performance. In their later lives they may have more difficulties in forming satisfactory relationships, lower than expected occupational status and increased incidence of psychiatric illness.
>
> (Grounds, forthcoming)

The links between research on the effects of divorce upon children and the effects of imprisonment upon children have barely been drawn. This link has been established by those concerned with the development of children or with prisoners' families rather than by commentators on prison life and its effects. The vulnerability engendered by trauma and loss in childhood, which is so common in the histories of the imprisoned, plays a crucial role in the pattern of anger, misery and mistrust which characterises violent offending (de Zulueta 1993). It may be exposed by the rejecting and isolating experience of imprisonment. Shaw referred to the pain and harm inflicted on children by the imprisonment of a parent as 'institutionalised child abuse' (Shaw 1987) and to the children themselves as 'the orphans of justice' (Shaw 1992).

These issues may be even more acute when the imprisoned parent is the mother (see Kruttschnitt, this volume). There is some evidence that keeping small babies in mother and baby units can have temporarily damaging effects on development (see Catan 1992), and that a variety of factors connected with their mother's imprisonment (such as poverty, unstable relationships and living arrangements, etc.) may have longer-term detrimental effects (see also Woodrow 1992).

Imprisonment and desistance from crime

The study of desistance from crime has received an increasing amount of attention in recent years (see Burnett 2004; Laub and Sampson 2003), yet little of this work has focused on the role of the correctional system in this process. Indeed, something of a passive consensus has been reached among desistance scholars (like the 'deep freeze' school of prison effects) that the experience of imprisonment is somewhat irrelevant to the process. Farrall (1995: 56) writes, 'Most of the research suggests that desistance "occurs" away from the criminal justice system. That is to say that very few people actually desist as a result of intervention on the part of the criminal justice system or its representatives.' As a result, prison effects researchers have largely ignored the growing body of research on desistance from crime. This is more than a little ironic due to the fact that desistance and recidivism (the outcome variable favoured in prison effects research) are arguably two sides of the same coin.

Fortunately, a number of studies have sought to reverse this trend and marry prison-recidivism research with studies of desistance from crime (see Burnett and Maruna 2004; Bushway *et al* 2003; Hosser 2004; Petersilia 2003). In particular, much of this research draws on Robert Sampson and John Laub's influential theory of informal social control, which suggests that social bonds (in particular, employment and marriage) may inhibit offending. Their longitudinal research on crime over the life course suggests that the experience of imprisonment reduces opportunities to achieve relational and economic stability and, therefore, increase re-offending (see also Laub and Sampson 2003). Imprisonment weakens these (already vulnerable) bonds, and makes them difficult to re-establish, hence severing a significant source of legitimate or law-abiding behaviour. Imprisonment thereby becomes part of the cycle of delinquency and crime.

Although early offending behaviour precedes imprisonment, Sampson and Laub show that those offenders with the 'most to lose' by offending had the best chance of positive recovery or change. Imprisonment in youth and early adulthood had a negative effect on later job and relationship stability, which were 'negatively related to continued involvement in crime over the life course' (Sampson and Laub 1993: 248). This was related to length of incarceration and could not be explained by individual differences such as previous criminal history, excessive drinking, etc. These indirect but powerful criminogenic effects of imprisonment on life course transitions are significant as 'the effect of confinement may be indirect and operative in a developmental, cumulative process that reproduces itself over time' (ibid.: 168).

Imprisonment and prison staff

Research on the effects of prison work upon staff has also been sparse. The Zimbardo experiment found that power (especially its overuse) had dehumanising effects (Haney *et al* 1973). Other studies have documented the destructive effects of power cultures (e.g. Gibbs 1991; Marquart 1986) and the culture of masculinity characteristic of prison staff on prison officers (Sim 1994). The features of prison life which may exacerbate such conditions are greatly under-researched.

A significant contribution has recently been made to this literature by Elaine Crawley, who has focused attention on the emotional dimensions of prison work and on the power of 'feeling rules' to keep emotions in check. She applies the notion of a 'spoiled identity' to prison staff, and suggests that this effect is extended to prison officers' families (Crawley 2004). Helen Arnold's work on 'identifying the high performing prison officer' is also taking this agenda further. Via a participant observation study of new entrant prison officers undergoing training, and a follow-up study, she finds that the process of becoming a prison officer brings with it a range of emotions, and new emotion-management techniques. Some of these techniques can lead to hardening, distancing and distrust. The process of adaptation could lead to enduring changes in their character and family life – to cynicism and a preparedness to respond to danger (Arnold, this volume).

The road ahead

We hope that the chapters in this book stimulate renewed reflection on the contemporary nature of imprisonment. In recent years, the management of prisons has been radically transformed (Carlen, this volume; Irwin and Owen, this volume), its operation reinvented (King, this volume), and claims about its effectiveness have increased. Additionally, there is a growing dissonance between an increasingly connected world and the particular capacity of prisons to 'cut off' (Johnson, this volume). As John Irwin and Barbara Owen argue, loss of agency and a sense of unfairness constitute two of the significant harms caused by the prison (see Irwin and Owen; Snacken, this volume). Other potential harms include social dislocation, drug addiction, loss of authenticity, threats to safety, mental illness and suicide (Liebling *et al*, this volume).

Despite these harms, and the apparent pains of prison life, one of the paradoxes of modern penal life is the apparent lack of organised protest among prisoners in newly configured, mega-institutions. Control is finely calibrated, new forms of power are in operation, and prisoners seem disconcertingly compliant in their behaviour, while expressing deep discomfort with their own predicament and the failure of the prison to show them a future (Irwin and Owen, this volume). As images of the prison become increasingly benign, its use continues to grow rapidly, and its damaging effects seem to be of little interest to practitioners or criminal justice research agencies.

Craig Haney (this volume) suggests that we need to reconsider the problem that if criminal behaviour has roots in social/family background and current social contexts, then a system that targets individuals is by its very nature self-limiting. The current approach to crime control is, in this sense, irrational. If the goal is crime reduction, we should pay more attention to the contexts from which prisoners come, and into which they are released.

The aim of this volume, like the conference on which it was based, is to re-open the debate about prison effects in this new climate, and to stimulate renewed research effort and collaboration in this area. A second aim is to pay tribute to the work of Hans Toch, in recognition of his major contribution to this field, and of his rigorous and humanistic research approach (see e.g. Toch 1975, 1992, 1997, 2002). As Andrew Coyle suggested in his opening comments at the conference, we believe the best compliment we can pay to Hans Toch is to firmly restate the limitations of the prison in accomplishing either criminal or social justice.

Before proceeding, however, we need to ask whether the world really needs another book on the effects of prison. It seems obvious to us, like Nightingale before us, that if we want to reduce the harms (and the use) of imprisonment, we need strong, careful research evidence exploring different penal systems and practices, documenting not just 'what works', but 'what hurts', and uncovering means of alleviating these harms. Yet, conducting research of this kind does carry some risks, as we have discovered in past reactions to our own work. For instance, do we as prisons researchers not lend legitimacy to an institution thought by many to be broadly illegitimate? After all, why focus research efforts on making imprisonment less painful when we should be using our energy to tear prisons down altogether?

Over 20 years ago, writing in *The Pains of Imprisonment* (Johnson and Toch 1982), one of the most important predecessors to the present collection, Toch himself wrestled with these ethical tensions inherent in putting together a collection of this sort. Acknowledging that congested, undersupplied, 'warehouse' prisons are morally indefensible, Toch (1982: 41–2) asks, 'Then why do we stipulate them? Are we gilding the lily on the corpse of civilised society? Do we compromise with evil when we talk of "coping", "adaptation", "amelioration" in prisons?'

In response to these hypothetical criticisms, Toch argues eloquently that there are two, basic justifications for studying prison effects:

One is that as inmates must cope, society must cope. While prisons exist it does no good to cry without effect in the wilderness of unresponsive public opinion. Assertive responding means doing what we can with as much effect as possible ... Prisons are not an abstraction. They are a painful, tangible reality for ... inmates [and] their keepers ... These fellow humans are stressed now, and must be helped to survive.

(pp. 41–2)

Essentially, then, the first justification for researching prison effects is to lessen the pains suffered by prisoners. Toch writes, 'Given the obvious hurt of prison pains, the most plausible argument for this research ... is the potential it offers for amelioration through insight' (p. 41). Zamble and Porporino (1988: 2) go one step further than this, arguing: 'In order to be sound and reasonable, the design and operation of prisons should be based not on any particular theory or ideology, but on some fundamental understanding of how imprisonment affects individuals.' This ideal of designing prisons on the basis of empirical evidence on the effects of imprisonment is, of course, a long way from being realised. Yet, research on the effects of imprisonment is one of the few remaining defences against a complete 'race to the bottom' in corrections, and, in theory at least, should set limits on penal policies. If prisons are to exist (and they do not seem to be going anywhere anytime soon), criminology cannot simply stand back and wish them away. More research *is* needed, and, as Nightingale argued 100 years ago, we need to continue to push our findings under the noses of anyone who will read them. Quoting Stan Cohen (2001: 296) in a different context, the known harms of imprisonment 'should be regular and accessible' to the average citizen, 'rolling in front of our eyes like the news headlines on the screens in Times Square'.

Toch's second justification for studying prison effects is perhaps less immediately obvious. He writes:

The second issue is existential ... Though prisons be adjudged evil, human survival must be good. There are those – Frankl (1959) and Bettelheim (1960) for example – who surmounted the unspeakable evil of Nazi death camps. Such victories are monuments to human resilience. They are worth studying and emulating. Inmates too can conquer evil (ours and theirs) and they must do so if the race – with its cruelty to itself – is to survive.

(p. 42)

Thus, the point of studying prison effects is not just the need to understand the potentially brutalising aspects of institutional living, but also to document and learn from examples in which prisoners, like Dostoevsky, have overcome these substantial social forces. Toch's dual reality of the pains of confinement and the enduring potential of human transcendence characterises our own work (see e.g. Liebling 1992; Maruna 2001) as well as the diverse contributions to this volume. Hence, it is most appropriate that we are dedicating this collection (as we did the conference that proceeded it) to Professor Toch and his legacy of humanistic inquiry into the effects of imprisonment.

Notes

1 Some of the ideas developed in this chapter have appeared in an earlier form in Liebling 1999; Liebling and Price 2001; and Maruna and Toch, in press.
2 Like the previous books in Willan's *Cambridge Criminal Justice Series*, this volume has grown out of a two-day symposium at the University of Cambridge sponsored by the Cropwood Trust. This particular Cropwood Conference received additional funding from Cambridge's Prisons Research Centre.
3 An illustration of this general point is the use of stately homes or army camps as prisons after the Second World War in England and Wales. As a view that 'you can't train men for freedom in conditions of captivity' came to prominence, Victorian prisons began to be seen as unacceptable for the delivery of a 'treatment and training' ideology.
4 Suggested remedies included purposeful work, activities and events; participatory regimes; staff job satisfaction and positive staff attitudes (Barton 1966: 63).
5 Sykes' analysis provides the framework for several of the chapters to follow (see Crewe; Einat; and Jewkes, this volume).
6 Jones and Fowles (1994), for example, argued that the Zimbardo experiment was biased, and structured in a way that made the results inevitable.
7 On the other hand, specific concerns such as overcrowding were investigated in some detail, and high degrees of sustained overcrowding were indeed found to contribute to higher levels of disciplinary infractions, illness complaints, deaths in custody and recidivism (Farrington and Nuttall 1980; Cox *et al* 1984; Gaes 1985).
8 Synthesising the findings from 50 prison effects studies dating from 1958 involving over 300,000 prisoner subjects, Gendreau and colleagues argue that there is no evidence that longer prison sentences could reduce recidivism through specific deterrence, and substantial evidence that the relationship works the other way around. Indeed, they found the higher the quality of the study (including two randomised designs), the more likely it is to find

a strong positive correlation between time spent in prison and likelihood of recidivism (Gendreau *et al* 1999).

References

Adams, K. (1992) 'Adaptation and maladaptation in prison', in M. Tonry and N. Morris (eds) *Crime and Justice: An Annual Review of Research*, Volume X. Chicago: University of Chicago Press.

Asch, S.E. (1951) 'Effect of group pressure upon the modification and distortion of judgments', in H. Guetzkow (ed.) *Groups, Leadership and Men*. Pittsburgh: Carnegie Press.

Banister, P.A., Smith, F.V., Heskin, K.J. and Bolton, N. (1973) 'Psychological correlates of long-term imprisonment. I: Cognitive variables', *British Journal of Criminology*, 13, 312–322.

Banks, C., Mayhew, P. and Sapsford, R. (1975) *Absconding from Open Prisons* (Home Office Research Studies, Vol. 26). London: HMSO.

Barbalet, J.M. (1998) *Emotion, Social Theory, and Social Structure: A Macrosociological Approach*. Cambridge: Cambridge University Press.

Barton, R. (1959; 2nd edn 1966) *Institutional Neurosis*. Bristol: Wright Publishing.

Baumer, E., Wright, R., Kristinsdottir, K. and Gunnlaugsson, H. (2002) 'Crime, shame, and recidivism: The case of Iceland', *British Journal of Criminology*, 42 (1), 20–39.

Beck, A.J. (2000) *State and Federal Prisoners Returning to the Community: Findings for the Bureau of Justice Statistics*. Washington, DC: Bureau of Justice Statistics.

Bennett, W.J., DiIulio, J.J. and Walters, J. (1997) *Body Count: Moral Poverty and How to Win America's War Against Crime and Drugs*. New York: Simon and Schuster.

Bettleheim, B. (1960) *The Informed Heart: A Study of the Psychological Consequences of Living Under Extreme Fear and Terror*. New York: The Free Press.

Bolton, N., Smith, F.V., Heskin, K.J. and Banister, P.A (1976) 'Psychological correlates of long-term imprisonment. IV: A longitudinal analysis', *British Journal of Criminology*, 16, 38–47.

Bowker, L. H. (1980) *Prison Victimization*. New York: Elsevier.

Bowlby, J. (1965) *Child Care and the Growth of Love*. Middlesex: Penguin.

Bukstel, L.H. and Kilmann, P.R. (1980) 'Psychological effects of imprisonment on confined individuals', *Psychological Bulletin*, 88 (2), 469–493.

Burnett, R. (2004), 'To reoffend or not to reoffend? The ambivalence of convicted property offenders', in S. Maruna and R. Immarigeon (eds) *After Crime and Punishment: Pathways to Offender Reintegration*. Cullompton: Willan Publishing.

Burnett, R. and Maruna, S. (2004) 'So, "prison works" does it? The criminal careers of 130 men released from prison under Home Secretary Michael Howard'. *Howard Journal of Criminal Justice*, 43, 390–404.

Bushway, S.D., Brame, R. and Paternoster, R. (2003). 'Connecting desistance and recidivism: Measuring changes in criminality over the lifespan', in S. Maruna and R. Immarigeon (eds) *Ex-Offender Reintegration: Pathways to Desistance from Crime*. Albany, NY: SUNY.

Catan, L. (1992) 'Infants with mothers in prison', in R. Shaw (ed.) *Prisoners Children: What are the Issues?* London: Routledge.

Cheliotis, L. (2004) 'Interview: Professor Philip Zimbardo', *Prison Service Journal*, 155, September, pp. 47–50.

Clarke, R.V.G. and Martin, D.N. (1971) *Absconding from Approved Schools*. (Home Office Research Studies, Vol. 12). London: HMSO.

Clemmer, D. (1940) *The Prison Community*. New York: Holt, Rinehart and Winston.

Cohen, S. (2001) *States of Denial*. Cambridge: Polity Press.

Cohen, S. and Taylor, L. (1972) *Psychological Survival*. Harmondsworth: Penguin.

Coker, J. and Martin, J.P. (1983) *Licensed to Live*. Oxford: Blackwell.

Cox, V.C., Paulus, P. and McCain, G. (1984) 'Prison crowding research: The relevance for prison housing standards and a general approach regarding crowding phenomena', *American Psychologist*, 39 (10), 1148–1160.

Crawley, E. (2004) *Doing Prison Work: The Public and Private Lives of Prison Officers*. Cullompton: Willan Publishing.

Crofts, N., Stewart, T., Hearne, P., Ping, X.Z., Breschkin, A.M. and Locarni, S.A. (1995) 'Spread of bloodborne viruses among Australian prison entrants', *British Medical Journal*, 310 (6975), 285–289.

Ericson, R.V. (1975) *Young Offenders and their Social Work*. Massachusetts: Lexington Books.

Farrall, S. (1995) 'Why do people stop offending?', *Scottish Journal of Criminal Justice Studies*, 1, 51–59.

Farrall, S. (2002) *Rethinking What Works with Offenders: Probation, Social Context and Desistance from Crime*. Devon: Willan Publishing.

Farrington, D.P. and Nuttall, C.P. (1980) 'Prison size, overcrowding, prison violence, and recidivism', *Journal of Criminal Justice*, 8, 221–231.

Frankl, V. (1959) *Man's Search for Meaning*. New York: Washington Square Press.

Gaes, G.G. (1985) 'The effects of overcrowding in prison', in M. Tonry and N. Morris (eds) *Crime and Justice: An Annual Review of Research*, Volume 6. Chicago: University of Chicago Press.

Gallo, E. and Ruggiero, V. (1991) 'The immaterial prison: Custody as a factory for the manufacture of handicaps', *International Journal for the Sociology of Law*, 19, 273–291.

Garland, David. (1990) *Punishment and Modern Society: A Study in Social Theory*. Chicago: University of Chicago Press.

Gendreau, P., Goggin, C. and Cullen, F. (1999) *The Effects of Prison Sentences on Recidivism*. A report to the Corrections Research and Development and Aboriginal Policy Branch, Solicitor General of Canada, Ottawa.

Giallombardo, R. (1966) *Society of Women: A Study of Women's Prison*. Chichester: Wiley.

Gibbs, J.J. (1987) 'Symptoms of psychopathology among jail prisoners: The effects of exposure to the jail environment', *Criminal Justice and Behaviour*, 14 (3), 288–310.

Gibbs, J. (1991) 'Environmental congruence and symptoms of psychopathology: A further exploration of the effects of exposure to the jail environment', *Criminal Justice and Behaviour*, 18, 351–374.

Gilligan, J. (1999) *Violence: Reflections on our Deadliest Epidemic*. London: Kingsley.

Goffman, E. (1961; 2nd edn 1968) *Asylums*. London: Penguin.

Gore, S.M., Bird, A.G., Burns, S.M., Goldberg, D.J., Ross, A.J. and MacGregor, J. (1995) 'Drug injection and HIV prevalence in inmates of Glenochil prison', *British Medical Journal*, 310 (6975), 285–289.

Grounds, A. (2004) 'Psychological consequences of wrongful conviction and imprisonment', *Canadian Journal of Criminology and Criminal Justice*, 46 (2), 165–182.

Grounds, A. (forthcoming) 'Research on the effects of long term imprisonment', in M. Tonry (ed.) *Crime and Justice*.

Gunn, J., Maden, T. and Swinton, M. (1991) *Mentally Disordered Prisoners*. London: Home Office.

HMCIP (1995) *Inspectorate Report on HMP Styal*. London: Home Office.

Haney, C. (1997) 'Psychology and the limits to prison pain: Confronting the coming crisis in the Eighth Amendment Law'. *Psychology, Public Policy and Law*, 3/4, 499–588.

Haney, C., Banks, W. and Zimbardo, P. (1973) 'Interpersonal dynamics in a simulated prison', *International Journal of Criminology and Penology*, 1, 69–97.

Haney, C. and Zimbardo, P. (1998) 'The past and future of U.S. prison policy: Twenty-five years after the Stanford prison experiment', *American Psychologist*, 53, 709–727.

Hay, W. and Sparks. R. (1992) 'Vulnerable prisoners: Risk in long-term prisons', in A.K. Bottomley, A.J. Fowles and R. Reiner (eds) *Criminal Justice: Theory and Practice*. London: British Society of Criminology.

Hay, W. and Sparks. R. (1991) 'What is a prison officer?' *Prison Service Journal*, 83, 2–7.

Hendriks. J.H., Black, D. and Kaplan, T. (1993) *When Father Kills Mother: Guiding Children through Trauma and Grief*. London: Routledge Press.

von Hirsch, A. (1993) *Censure and Sanctions*. Oxford: Clarendon Press.

Home Office (1963) *Advisory Council on the Treatment of Offenders in Preventive Detention*. London: HMSO.

Home Office (1991) *Custody, Care and Justice: The Way Ahead for the Prison Service in England and Wales*. London: HMSO.

Hosser, D. (2004) *'The Hanover Prison Study'*, paper presented at the European Society of Criminology Conference, Amsterdam.

Howard, M. (1996). 'Protecting the public', *Criminal Justice Matters*, 26, 4–5.

Johnson, R. and Toch, H. (1982) *The Pains of Imprisonment*. Beverly Hills, CA: Sage Publishing.

Jones, D.A. (1976) *The Health Risks of Imprisonment*. Massachusetts: Lexington Books.

Jones, K. and Fowles, A.J. (1994) 'Haney, Banks and Zimbardo: The experimentalists', in K. Jones and A.J. Fowles (eds) *Ideas on Institutions: Analysing the Literature on Long-term Care and Custody*. London: Routledge and Kegan Paul.

Kershaw, C. (1997) 'Reconvictions of those commencing community penalties in 1993, England and Wales', *Home Office Statistical Bulletin*, 6/97, 1–27.

Keve, P.W. (1996). *Measuring Excellence: The History of Correctional Standards and Accreditation*. Lanham, MD: American Correctional Association.

Kreitman, N., Carstairs, V. and Duffy, J. (1991) 'Association of age and social class with suicide among men in Great Britain', *Journal of Epidemiology and Community Health*, 45, 195–202.

Lanier, C.S. (2003). 'Who's doing the time here, me or my children? Addressing the issues implicated by mounting numbers of fathers in prison', in J.I. Ross and S.C. Richards (eds) *Convict Criminology*. Belmont, CA: Wadsworth.

Laub, J.H. and Sampson, R.J. (2003) *Shared Beginnings, Divergent Lives: Delinquent Boys to Age 70*. Cambridge, MA: Harvard University Press.

Laycock, G.K. (1977) *Absconding from Borstals* (Home Office Research Study, Vol. 41). London: HMSO.

Liebling, A. (1992) *Suicides in Prison*. London: Routledge Press.

Liebling, A. (1994) 'Suicides amongst women prisoners', *Howard Journal*, 33 (1), 1–9.

Liebling, A. (1999) 'Prison suicide and prisoner coping', in M. Tonry and J. Petersilia (eds) *Prisons, Crime and Justice: An Annual Review of Research*, Vol. 26, pp. 283–360.

Liebling, A. (2004) *Prisons and their Moral Performance: A Study of Values, Quality and Prison Life*. Oxford: Clarenden Press.

Liebling, A. and Krarup, H. (1993) *Suicide Attempts in Male Prisons*. London: Home Office.

Liebling, A. and Price, D. (2001) *The Prison Officer*. Leyhill: Waterside Press.

Liebling, H. (1990) 'A study of anxiety levels in female prison officers working in different levels of security and female hostel staff', unpublished MPhil thesis. University of Edinburgh.

Liebling, A., Muir, G., Rose, G. and Bottoms, A.E. (1997) *An Evaluation of Incentives and Earned Privileges*. Final Report submitted to the Home Office, London.

Light, R. (1993) 'Why support prisoners' family-tie groups?' *Howard Journal*, 32 (4), 322–329.

McCain, G., Cox, V.C. and Paulus, P.B. (1980) *The Effects of Prison Crowding on Inmate Behaviour*, Washington, DC: National Institute of Justice.

McGurk, B.J. and McDougal, C. (1986) *The Prevention of Bullying among Incarcerated Delinquents*. (DPS Report, Series 11, No. 114, Restricted circulation), London.

Marquart, J.W. (1986) 'Prison guards and the use of physical coercion as a mechanism of prisoner control', *Criminology*, 24 (2), 347–366.

Maruna, S. (2001) *Making Good: How Ex-convicts Reform and Rebuild their Lives.* Washington, DC: American Psychological Association Books.

Maruna, S. and Toch, H. (in press) 'The impact of incarceration on the desistance process', in J. Travis and C. Visher (eds) *Prisoner Reentry and Public Safety.* New York: Cambridge University Press.

Milgram, S. (1974) *Obedience to Authority.* London: Tavistock Publishing.

Miller, J. (2001) 'American Gulag'. *Yes Magazine* (6 February 2001).

Nightingale, F. (1859) *Notes on Hospitals.* London: Parker and Son.

Oleson, J.C. (2002). 'The punitive coma', *California Law Review*, 90, 829–901.

Pallas, J. and Barber, B. (1972) 'From riot to revolution', *Issues in Criminology*, 7 (2), 1–19.

Pallone, N.J. (1991) *Mental Disorder Among Prisoners: Toward an Epidemiological Inventory.* New Jersey: Transaction Publishers.

Parker, T. (1963) *The Unknown Citizen.* London: Hutchinson Press.

Parker, T. (1970) *The Frying Pan: A Prison and the Prisoners.* London: Hutchinson Press.

Petersilia, J. (2003) *When Prisoners Come Home: Parole and Prisoner Reentry.* Oxford: Oxford University Press.

Porporino, E.J. and Zamble, E. (1984) 'Coping with imprisonment', *Canadian Journal of Criminology*, (Special Issue), 26 (4), 403–422.

Richards, M. (1978) 'The experience of long-term imprisonment', *British Journal of Criminology*, 18, 162–169.

Richards, M. (1992) 'The separation of children and parents: Some issues and problems', in R. Shaw (ed.) *Prisoners Children: What Are the Issues?* London: Routledge.

Rutter, M. (1982) *Maternal Deprivation Reassessed.* Harmondsworth: Penguin.

Rutter, M. and Smith, D. (1995) *Psychosocial Problems in Young People: Time Trends and Their Causes.* Chichester: Wiley and Sons.

Sampson, R.J. and Laub, J.H. (1993) *Crime in the Making: Pathways and Turning Points Through Life.* Cambridge, MA: Harvard University Press.

Sapsford, R (1978) 'Life sentence prisoners: psychological changes during sentence', *British Journal of Criminology*, 18 (2), 128–145.

Sapsford, R. (1983) *Life Sentence Prisoners.* Milton Keynes: Open University Press.

Shaw, R. (1987) *Children of Imprisoned Fathers.* London: Hodder and Stoughton.

Shaw, R. (ed.) (1992) *Prisoners Children: What Are the Issues?* London: Routledge.

Shine, J., Wilson, R. and Hammond, D. (1990) 'Understanding and controlling violence in a long-term young offender institution', in N.L. Fludger and I.R. Simmons: *Proceedings From Psychologists Conference 1989* (DPS Report Series I, No. 34, pp. 115–32). London: Directorate of Psychological Services.

Shover, N. (1996) *Great Pretenders: Pursuits and Careers of Persistent Thieves.* Boulder, CO: Westview Press.

Sim, J. (1990) *Medical Power in Prisons: The Prison Medical Service in England: 1774–1989*. Milton Keynes: Open University Press.

Sim, J. (1994) 'Tougher than the rest? Men in prison', in T. Newburn and E.A. Stanko (eds) *Just Boys Doing Business? Men, Masculinities and Crime*. London: Routledge.

Sparks, R., Hay, W. and Bottoms, A. (1996) *Prisons and the Problem of Order*. Oxford: Clarendon Press.

Storr, A. (1991; 1st edn 1972) *Human Destructiveness: The Roots of Genocide and Human Cruelty*. London: Routledge Publishing.

Sutton, N. (1995) *Bruno Bettleheim: The Other Side of Madness*. London: Duckworth Publishing.

Sykes, G. (1958) *The Society of Captives*. Princeton: Princeton University Press.

Taylor, A., Goldberg, D., Emslie, J., Wrench, J., Gruer, L., Cameron, S., Black, J., Davis, B., Macgragor, J., Follett, E., Harvey, J., Basson, J. and McGavigan, J. (1995) 'Outbreak of HIV infection in a Scottish prison', *British Medical Journal* 310 (6975), 285–289.

Thornton, D., Curran, L., Grayson, D. and Holloway, V. (1984) *Tougher Regimes in Detention Centres: Report of an Evaluation by the Young Offender Psychology Unit*. London: HMSO.

Toch, H. (1975) *Men in Crisis: Human Breakdowns in Prisons*. New York: Aldine Publishing.

Toch, H. (1982) 'Studying and reducing stress', in R. Johnson and H. Toch (eds) *The Pains of Imprisonment*. Beverly Hills, CA: Sage Publishing.

Toch, H. (1992) *Mosaic of Despair: Human Breakdowns in Prisons* (revised edition). Easton: Easton Publishing Services.

Toch, H. (1997) *Corrections: A Humanistic Approach*. Guilderland, NY: Harrow and Heston Publishers.

Toch, H. (2002) 'The life of lifers', in R.A. Silverman, T.P. Thornberry, B. Cohen and B. Krisberg (eds) *Crime and Justice at the Millennium: Essays by and in Honor of Marvin E. Wolfgang*. Boston: Kluwer Academic Publishers.

Toch, H., Adams, K. and Grant, D. (1989) *Coping: Maladaptation in Prisons*. New Brunswick, NJ: Transaction Publishing.

Useem, B., Liedka, R.V. and Piehl, A.M. (2003) 'Popular support for the prison build-up'. *Punishment and Society*, 5, 5–32.

Walker, N. (1983) 'The side-effects of incarceration', *British Journal of Criminology*, 23, 61–71.

Walker, N. (1987) 'The unwanted effects of long-term imprisonment', in A.E. Bottoms and R. Light (eds) *Problems of Long-Term Imprisonment*. Aldershot: Gower Publishing.

Walmsley, R., Howard, L. and White, S. (1991) *The National Prison Survey 1991: Main Findings*. London: HMSO.

West, D.J. (1963) *The Habitual Prisoner*. Cambridge Studies in Criminology. London: Macmillan.

Woodrow, J. (1992) 'Mothers inside, children outside: What happens to the dependant children of female inmates?', in R. Shaw (ed.) *Prisoners Children: What Are the Issues?* London: Routledge.

Zamble, E. and Porporino, E.J. (1988) *Coping, Behaviour and Adaptation in Prison Inmates*. New York: Springer-Verlag.

de Zulueta (1993) *From Pain to Violence: The Traumatic Roots of Destructiveness*. London: Whurr Publishers.

Part I

The Harms of Imprisonment: Thawing Out the 'Deep Freeze' Paradigm

Chapter 2

Release and adjustment: perspectives from studies of wrongly convicted and politically motivated prisoners

Ruth Jamieson and Adrian Grounds[1]

Time held me green and dying
Though I sang in my chains like the sea

These lines from the end of Dylan Thomas' poem, 'Fern Hill', were brought to our attention by one of our interviewees.

The purpose of this chapter is to provide some reflections on time in relation to imprisonment. These arise from three small-scale interview-based studies we have been carrying out. The studies involve distinctly different groups of ex-prisoners, but are linked methodologically and in the framework of interpretation we have adopted. We will be focusing particularly on the phenomena of post-release experience, and their implications for the ways in which we think about imprisonment effects.

We are outsiders in the field of prison research, and our routes into it have been different and unanticipated: RJ is a criminologist with an interest in the sociology of war and war veterans, and AG is a forensic psychiatrist whose work includes clinical assessment and aftercare of long-term prisoners. The first study to which we will refer arose out of AG's clinical work. Fifteen years ago he was asked to carry out psychiatric assessments of a few individuals who had been released on appeal following miscarriages of justice, and he has seen a slowly accumulating number of others since. This has become an ongoing descriptive clinical study, for which the clinical literature on responses to chronic psychological trauma has been especially relevant (Grounds 2004). The discussion at the end of this chapter is drawn from the latter paper (Grounds 2005). The second study originated in a request to both of us in 1999 to advise and assist a non-aligned support group for predominantly Republican ex-prisoners in Ireland and Northern Ireland (ExPac[2]) who wished to research the post-release adjustment difficulties of released prisoners and their families (Grounds and Jamieson 2003). The interview schedules used for this drew on the biographical, phenomenological framework of clinical interviewing used in the first study. The third, and most recent, study has been jointly developed by RJ and colleagues in the UK and Canada[3] and uses the same approach in interviews with a sample of released Canadian life-sentence prisoners. We will briefly summarise the three studies and then discuss some possible implications arising from them.

Effects of imprisonment on the wrongly convicted

The study of imprisonment effects among the wrongly convicted arose from requests to carry out psychiatric assessments of five individuals from the 'Guildford Four' and 'Birmingham Six' for the purpose of their compensation claims. They have consented to their cases being described. Since then psychiatric assessments of fourteen other men released by the Court of Appeal have been completed, most of whom had been wrongly convicted of non-terrorist murder. The duration of the wrongful imprisonment ranged from nine months to nineteen years. Their average age on entry to prison was 30, and their average age on release was 41.

All but five of the total group of nineteen had been released for two years or more at the point of assessment. Each man was interviewed over one or two days. Partners and other relatives and friends who had known the man before and after the period in prison were separately interviewed, except in one case where they refused. There was a wide range of documentary material provided by the men's lawyers. Self-completion diagnostic questionnaires for post-traumatic stress disorder and depression were administered where possible.[4]

Before the first assessments were done it was anticipated that psychiatric morbidity would not be found because it was broadly accepted that the research literature on the effects of long-term imprisonment had concluded that there was little good evidence of psychological deterioration in custody.[5] The clinical findings, however, were unexpected. Most of the men changed in personality in ways that caused distress to them and their families. They had marked features of estrangement, loss of capacity for intimacy, moodiness, inability to settle and loss of a sense of purpose and direction. They were withdrawn, unable to relate properly. Families consistently said the men had changed – they were not the people they used to be. For example, two mothers said of her sons:

He is like a stranger to you…He always used to be affectionate. Now he can't express emotion, he can't sit and talk. He jumps about, he is unsettled. Prison has changed him. His personality has changed.

Sometimes he doesn't seem like my son. He's like a complete stranger. I don't understand him at all.

The wives of two other men described how their husbands used to be warm, family men, but when they came out of prison:

We were really shocked … It's very distressing … he is not the same person … he just was not able to fit into family life.

He is very different. He's nervous, fidgety, not really looking at me. I find it upsetting.

Other relatives and friends commented:

To see how he was before he went into jail, and to see him now, it's a shame … He was the kind of person who would carry your bags, run errands and help people. Not now – now he just doesn't want to be bothered with anybody…He's totally changed. I feel sorry for him.

[He is] very much more reserved…Less able to talk to other people…I've never heard him laughing and joking or anything like that.

In fourteen of the nineteen cases the personality change caused significant impairment and fitted the diagnostic category of 'enduring personality change after catastrophic experience' (F62.0 in the ICD-10 (World Health Organisation 1992)). This is defined as enduring and disabling personality change with characteristics which were not previously seen, such as a hostile or mistrustful attitude towards the world, social withdrawal, feelings of emptiness or hopelessness, a chronic feeling of threat, and estrangement.

Thirteen of the men had severe post-traumatic stress symptoms, usually relating to specific events of extreme threat or violence following arrest or in prison. They met the ICD-10 diagnostic criteria for PTSD. Examples of their symptoms were repeated nightmares of assaults in prison and panic attacks in response to police sirens. Others described being constantly on edge, and apprehensive when out in public places, fearful of being attacked or constantly feeling they were being looked at malevolently and talked about.

There was evidence of additional disorders in sixteen of the nineteen cases, particularly depressive disorders both during and after imprisonment. Additionally, after release most had chronic difficulties in sleeping, and moodiness and irritability that made them very difficult to live with. Some had unremitting feelings of bitterness, loss and inability to come to terms with what had been done to them. All were changed in a way that one person perfectly captured when she said there was a permanent loss of joy. Generally these were people without previous psychiatric histories, and in all cases the psychiatric conditions appeared to be directly attributable to the wrongful arrests, convictions and imprisonment.

Their difficulties after release were particularly striking. All the men were released suddenly and without even the limited preparation and supervision from statutory services that are normally provided for long-term prisoners. After being in prison for years they were typically taken to the Appeal Court, the decision was given and they were released with a small amount of money and a bag of possessions to their waiting families and the media.

They had marked and embarrassing difficulties in coping with ordinary practical tasks in the initial days and weeks, for example, crossing busy roads and going into shops. Some had more persistent difficulties, not knowing, for example, how to work central heating, TV remote controls, videos, credit cards, cash points at banks; and experiencing shame which prevented them asking for help. One said: 'It's like when someone has a stroke; you have to be taught how to do things again.' He felt humiliated by his lack of ability and the fact that his wife had to teach him elementary skills. Some men had little sense of the value of money, could not budget, spent recklessly and got into debt.

Many found it difficult, after living in the predictable, ordered environment of a prison cell, to tolerate living in a household where others would keep moving possessions and household items. Others habitually felt they remained in a prison regime. Some kept their room arranged like their prison cell. At a deeper level the men had learned to deal with emotional pressures and stresses in prison by blocking off painful feelings, avoiding communication and isolating themselves.

They continued to use similar strategies of withdrawal, self-isolation and uncommunicativeness after release. They would avoid social contact and shut themselves away for hours. While this may have been adaptive in a prison context, it was maladaptive in a family, and relatives found it upsetting and bewildering. It was particularly notable that the men reported that they did not talk to families or partners about their prison experience.

In relation to their social circumstances, eight of the men were living alone. Some had tried and failed to resume living with previous partners who had supported them throughout the sentence, and these break-ups were particularly tragic. Most of the men had lost hope and sense of purpose for the future. They felt unsettled, could not find a sense of direction and were troubled by having lost years that could not be put back. All described estrangement from other people because of their prison experience that others would not understand. For those who had found a sense of purpose, it typically came from working to help others in the same position.

While it may be argued that many of these outcomes may have been due to the specific circumstances of being wrongly convicted, which differ from those of most prisoners, there were also adjustment problems that were a function of long-term detention *per se*. First there were losses: while the men were in prison, parents died, family funerals and weddings were missed. On release the families had adapted to living without the men and substantial problems and conflicts could arise when they tried to return to family households. The men related to their children in ways that were appropriate to the age the children had been at the time of arrest. Those who had been in for many years had difficulty coping with cultural changes that had taken place, for example in attitudes to the role of women in families. There were also adjustment problems that have to be understood in terms of a person's developmental life history. On release these men were dislocated in time. They found little in common with their peers who were now at a different stage of life. For two men from a minority community with powerful bonds of family life this was particularly distressing. They were embarrassed and ashamed because their young children, born since the men's release, were not similar in age to their cousins, but to their cousins' children. The men felt out of synchrony themselves with their families, but they were also troubled that this would adversely affect the place and self-esteem of their children in the next generation.

All the released men talked of feeling on release psychologically the age they had been on entry to prison. As one said: 'I'm 35 but I'm 20 in my head.' Some of the single men embarrassed themselves by trying to buy clothes that were out of keeping with their age or going to social venues for a younger age group. Such phenomena are common to other long-term prisoners. Lifers interviewed by Tony Parker (1990) in his book *Life after Life* describe this phenomenon, and Zamble and Porporino (1988: 153) talk of the prisoner being 'frozen developmentaly', that is, he is unable to learn through the accumulated social experience of normal life. For others there was a more disturbing sense of loss of direction and of their lives being foreshortened; they were too old for the period of time they felt they should have to live.

All described difficulties in family and close relationships; after release the men and their families found they no longer properly knew each other. One man's daughter reported, for example, that at the time of her father's release everyone in the family thought that feelings of closeness would be instantaneous, 'But no one realised how distant we would be. My sister broke down – she found it hard to call him dad because she'd never had a dad.'

Another man's wife commented: 'When he came out we were like two strangers. I did not know him and he didn't know me. Yet, I'd stood by him ... The children think that their father doesn't care. He does care but can't show it.'

One of the men said: 'There is something lacking – I think it's the bonding. I'm separated from the wife and family. I don't have feelings of love.' He described having 'a big void' inside himself. Another described having a 'big gap' inside him:

> You keep looking for it and all you know is that you're never going to get it, you can't get the time back ... It's like an invisible wall, emptiness; there is nothing there ... I just don't think about it because if you do you get wound up like a spring.

These acknowledgements that they no longer had feelings of closeness towards those who had stood by them were difficult to admit to and a source of guilt.

The accounts given by the men and their families indicated that this estrangement had gradually developed over the years in prison and the way they handled prison visits may have been significant in leading to the gulf in mutual knowledge that separated them. Characteristically, on visits the men and the families avoided disclosing to each other the difficulties they were experiencing. Partners did not want to worry the men by disclosing their own anxieties, such as lack of money, children being ill; and the men would similarly hide their problems. This continued throughout the sentence. As one man remarked:

It plays havoc with your life. You just seem cut off from one another. It's a very emotional thing; you've had no family life, no emotional links. After sixteen years of visits it's just disastrous.

Thus, over the years there developed mutual incomprehension and lack of knowledge about what they had each gone through. In the end they were in a true sense strangers to each other.

For the families there were other forms of hardship and loss, and the pattern of their lives changed irrevocably. For years their weekends were spent in long journeys for prison visits. After the celebration of release they often then discovered permanent estrangement in the family relationships. The children's accounts of this echoed those given by the children of the 1940s, for whom the arrival home of the 'stranger' was a recurring theme in the memories of those whose fathers were away in the war. In Turner and Rennell's book, *When Daddy Came Home*, one described how the family was taken on holiday after their father returned, and it was a disaster, a wretched time. She recalled:

We returned sick and exhausted with the money gone and nothing to show for it. The fragile relationships within the family could not withstand even trivial anxieties, like the non-arrival of a train ... The 'bonding' that was meant to occur, the coming together of one happy family on holiday, with Daddy safely back in charge, did not happen. Nor could it ever happen.

(Turner and Rennell 1995: 76)

The forms of suffering and damage experienced by these wrongly convicted men were numerous; they interacted and compounded one another. They led to secondary problems. The life courses of those involved were permanently changed. They suffered losses, of relationships, prospects and years of their expected life history. The harms extended over time and generations.

The research literature that most closely describes the adjustment and relationship difficulties in these cases is the psychiatric literature on war veterans. It documents both the characteristic clinical syndrome that may follow chronic psychological trauma and the difficulties of adjustment among soldiers returning home. The literature of the 1940s describes how many soldiers returned from the Second World War with an unrealistic, idealised view of the family, but experienced restlessness, irritability and severe difficulties in restoring intimate relationships (Newman 1944; Rollin 1948). The post-Vietnam literature also describes this (Kulka *et al* 1990), as does the more recent war-veteran literature. For example, Solomon (1993) gave a detailed account of these problems in her follow-up study of Israeli soldiers who had fought in the Lebanon war. She wrote:

> Especially problematic for the PTSD veteran is the resumption of the more demanding and intimate roles of husband and father. Most PTSD casualties are removed and detached from their families…Many neither talk nor listen. Wrapped up in their continued suffering, they describe being unfocussed, cut off, or in a world of their own…
>
> The family often remains bewildered by the veteran's unusual behaviour, whereas the veteran, locked in his silence, becomes even more detached and cut off. He deprives himself of the emotional support his family could potentially give, and deprives his family of the emotional connection and involvement that is their due.
>
> (Solomon 1993: 109–11)

The relevance of the war-veteran literature is not surprising insofar as we know that widely differing kinds of traumatic experience can lead to a common clinical picture. What is surprising is the lack of reference to these phenomena in the 'prison effects' literature, despite the fact that many of these problems are vividly conveyed in prisoners' own accounts of their return to life on the outside.

Effects of imprisonment on Republican ex-prisoners

The second study, carried out with Republican ex-prisoners, also focused on post-release experience and adjustment. It drew on the first study in using semi-structured interviews exploring the same areas of psychological experience, following a biographical format and using questioning derived from psychiatric history-taking. Our approach to interpreting the material was influenced by the interest we had developed, from our contrasting academic backgrounds, in the literature on war trauma. This also had resonance for the interviewees, who had seen themselves as involved in politically motivated military conflict.

Interviews were completed with eighteen Republican ex-prisoners from communities across Northern Ireland. Most had served most or all of their sentences in The Maze in Northern Ireland. All had been released before the Good Friday Agreement of 1998: the interviewed men were part of a cohort of Republican prisoners who served their sentences during the most intense and stressful period (1976–82) of prison protests in Northern Ireland, culminating in hunger strikes that resulted in the deaths of ten men (Beresford 1987; McKeown 2001). In four cases additional interviews were completed: with a partner and close relative in two cases, and with a close relative only in two cases. There were few of these additional interviews because sometimes a partner or close relative was unavailable, some declined to participate, and sometimes it was the ex-prisoner's preference that only he should be interviewed. The interviews were tape-recorded and transcribed and a thematic content analysis of the verbatim transcripts was carried out. At the time of our fieldwork the eighteen interviewed men had been released for an average of eleven years (range 5–18 years). Most had been young on entry to prison (mean age 20). Typically they came out of prison in their early 30s and had lost over a decade of life outside.

Previous research in Northern Ireland by McEvoy *et al* (1999) indicated that the fact of being politically motivated did not insulate prisoners and families from having to face substantial emotional, practical and emotional pressures.[6] Shirlow (2001) described complex, long-lasting negative effects of imprisonment on family relationships and children, and major problems in relation to employment. He also suggested that features of post-traumatic stress disorder may be common but unrecognised among ex-prisoners.

It was impossible to convey in any adequate way the nature of the prison experience in our sample. Most men were in prison at the time of the Blanket Protest and Hunger Strikes, and this was recollected as an intensely distressing and difficult time. Some recalled it as a time that changed them irrevocably.

Typically, the psychological coping strategies used in prison involved blocking out emotions and thoughts about the future, hiding feelings of depression, suppressing problems, avoiding disturbing thoughts about the family, and maintaining pride:

> You do find yourself developing strategies to get yourself through and you do suppress your own feelings or problems ... or try to minimise them, and emotionally you are stunted, there's no doubt about it. You are never really encouraged to show any sort of emotions, as I say, because you would show weakness ... In that situation you were really vulnerable and you had to show a certain facade to it all...

One of the men described how he would just 'sit out' unwanted emotions: 'I hoped they would go away and they did.' Such strategies were necessary for the social group as well as the individual:

> When you were mixing normally [with others] you couldn't really express what was going on [emotionally] because it had a domino effect on other people. You know, if someone's marriage is breaking down if someone is getting a hard time, it was, sorry to hear that, but you had to switch off.

Maintaining reminders of outside family life could also make prison life emotionally harder:

> Now I came across about three if not four different reactions. One reaction was to turn religious. Some men manage to get through their time praying obsessively and I don't know if they made it; another group of people attempted to create cosy images, and they had family portraits in their cell and come Christmas they'd put tinsel in the cell as if they weren't inside, and those people I found invariably found life in prison the hardest, they are the people who done their time the hardest, because they were constantly trying to take something that wasn't there. The religious people ... survived better than the day dreamers. And there was a group with a certain amount of austerity. I would avoid listening to the music that I had been familiar with before I was arrested because it tended to remind me. It was upsetting, Irish ballads, country and western music ... The better course of action was to start to concentrate on learning, reading, coping with what we will do, what we can do ... Looking back I practised a regime of austerity. And rather than have the walls decorated with the family photos ... the illustrations that I did have on the wall were political ...

Like the wrongly convicted, on visits the men would hide their worries and difficulties and reassure visitors that everything was all right; and the families on visits would do likewise. Ironically this was done in the mistaken belief that it helped the maintenance of family ties:

> We were glad to see them. But we put on a front too. There was a bit of a culture of deceit. We didn't actually convey how you were or how things were happening. We didn't want to upset them. We didn't want the visits to be upsetting. We only had half an hour to try and maintain that family continuity and to strengthen all these ties because of our separation ... So that's what we used the visit for.

Some men described a growing emotional detachment from loved ones over time.

> Earlier years, always looking forward to them and very disappointed if I had missed a visit. But gradually, and more so in the Blocks phase of the imprisonment, I was having longer and longer time-outs from the family. I think I was drifting away ... and I found that I was turning more into a loner really.

> I couldn't wait to get back into the routine again, and if I had bad news on a visit and it had impacted on me, my way of dealing with that was to go straight into training, run around the yard, back into the shower and block it out. That is the way I did it.

The nature of the emotional dilemma was starkly stated by one interviewee: 'I didn't have any bad visits because I wasn't in love.'

These forms of relating were functional for coping with imprisonment, but became dysfunctional for coping after release. Some ex-prisoners described a strong sense that they were not understood by their families, and they felt closer to other ex-prisoners:

> No, [my family have] no conception of what it's like ... I don't think they understand the emotional pressure of long-term imprisonment; that's the thing they don't understand.

Yerkes and Holloway (1996) described similar responses among returning veterans from the Persian Gulf War, and noted the self-defeating consequences of the claim that civilian others can never understand. It maintains isolation, and within families, 'With few shared ... experiences between them, each is seen as a stranger in the other's world' (Yerkes and Holloway 1996: 37).

Families of the ex-prisoners described how the modes of coping in prison could be maladaptive outside:

> [They] have an actual added set of problems and it's called *pride*. It's a huge thing and they don't crack up. They don't have drug addictions, alcohol addictions. They're the tough men ... and then once all this gets down to the nitty gritty of living they're not qualified, they're not trained, they're too old for the physical labour, they're not physically fit to do it. There's just nothing there for them, there is no support for them. Yet they're afraid to be seen

to crack up. They're afraid to say, 'Listen, my wife doesn't want me back'; the children won't [listen] – 'Where have you been for 12 years? You're not going to ask me where I'm going at night. Don't tell me this skirt's too short'. They're afraid to admit they're having these problems.

After prison the major obstacle to successful resettlement was finding and keeping meaningful work. Although four-fifths had qualifications, more than half the men were unemployed. Social integration was also problematic. The initial welcome and celebration on returning home was often short-lived. It became clear that although part of the community they were different. Their peers had moved on and had lives that the ex-prisoners were not part of. The interviewed men described being distant and estranged from other people. They also found it difficult to make plans, and to regain a sense of purpose, a sense of having a future:

I didn't fit in anywhere. [Others]...had moved on big time...had established roots, that was the main pattern...they were solid, secure, they were in employment. They seemed to be coming to the end of something that I was only beginning...there was no common ground between us...I would say to myself, how the f... am I going to manage all this; where do I go now? Going crazy to get out of prison, [then] here I am standing in my own living room, looking out through the window saying what will I do now? And everyone seemed to be a stranger. And even though the conflict was still going on I felt that I just didn't fit in anywhere...

It was hard to converse with people...[they] knew you but you didn't know them. They were the sons of somebody you once knew.

I couldn't relate to them. There was people coming up to you and saying to you, 'Do you remember...' and I'd say, 'Aye', just for the sake of conversation, 'I remember you.'...[I remembered] their names but not their faces. Someone else says, 'You call me...', and I'd say, 'You lived at the top of the street', and that was the end of the conversation. I didn't want to talk to them.

It's a gap that can't be filled. They went different ways, lived different lives, had different experiences. I don't know how to live their lives. This was another world to me. They lived in other worlds. We lived in the one world; we lived in the one-dimensional world of prison. There was a multi-dimensional world of normal life experience – going on holidays, getting jobs, settling down, planning a family, that was their world. Our world was the prison, tied into the political situation – always – that determined everything.

Some prisoners described a troubling and persisting loss of closeness and intimacy with families after release:

When I arrive up home it is all polite, the same old talk. It is almost like a visit again and the closeness it's gone, it is not the same. And I have found more and more the distance is getting greater rather than smaller. I would always feel that maybe they don't understand me or I them, I always feel there is a big communication gap somewhere.

The effects on family relationships could be profound. Ex-prisoners and their families did not anticipate how much they each had changed during the years of custody. For some men the chances of starting a family and a career at the normal time had gone. Others lost the years in which their children had grown up and these relationships could never be recovered:

When you go to hold someone and you know that the warmth has gone and there's a coldness there ... obviously I'd been away for so long and the kids didn't know who I was, so they knew an image of me, certainly I felt that. I understand it now, why that gap's so wide, why that coldness, why that reluctance is there. I think most ex-prisoners' kids are like this ... I felt hurt by it. I didn't feel resentful towards the children for it, but I understood it. I understood it and thought that it was very sad.

There could be major problems in relationships with children, especially boys. Families could find the ex-prisoners were institutionalised and, as one relative put it, they lacked a concept of how to conduct daily life in a family. They could be demanding and arrogant, for example. There had also been no negotiation about what would happen after the long-anticipated homecoming. As one relative recalled:

[His] mother was convinced that she was finally getting her son home and nothing could tell her she wasn't. [His] mother and father had so much emotionally invested in him coming home ... [They hoped] he was going to stay. But the point is – and I don't think our family's any worse than any other family over this – nobody discussed it. It was like going into a marriage not knowing whether your partner wanted children or if they ever wanted to be tied down with a mortgage or what part of Dublin or what part of Ireland they want…nobody had discussed their expectations. I don't think they knew that they had to do it. But you're this person over there with one set of dreams and another person here with another set of dreams and somebody with their other ideas. It was a marriage with no dialogue.

There was also a range of other psychological phenomena. On release men described guilt at leaving fellow prisoners behind. They felt overwhelmed by new experiences of being outside, for example the vivid colours and the traffic. They had difficulty in mixing socially with others, particularly engaging in small talk. Some experienced delayed mourning for family deaths that had occurred during the years in prison. Over half described problems of depression, at least two had post-traumatic stress disorder, and others described alcohol misuse. They reported changes in personality; typically the men had become more introverted and closed:

Yes, I'm introvert now. I do not show emotion very well…I find it hard to relate to people initially…I used to be very friendly with people but now I find it very hard to get to know people properly.

I don't think I could go back to the way I was. Even if I tried, I don't think I could. I think it would be a false sentiment. I don't think I could get close to people.

They said that they felt they had gained in intellectual development but lost in emotional development. Some were preoccupied with the issue of how to evaluate the past, and with troubling questions about whether the sacrifices had been worth it.

The study had clear limitations and was modest in scale. It is of note, however, that similar findings are reported by McEvoy *et al* (2004) in their much larger study of over 400 politically motivated ex-prisoners in Northern Ireland.

As in the first study of wrongly convicted men, the range and depth of the post-release difficulties among the interviewed Republican ex-prisoners would not have been anticipated from the psychological research literature on imprisonment effects. The findings are additionally remarkable because this group is likely to have entered prison with fewer psychological problems than would be expected among ordinary long-term prisoners, and they would have received a higher level of mutual support.

Effects of imprisonment on Canadian lifers

The third study extends the same methodology to a sample of released life-sentence prisoners in Canada. These interviews follow the same biographical, narrative format used in the study of Republican ex-prisoners, adapted for ordinary prisoners in the Canadian correctional context. To date, in-depth interviews with seven former long-term prisoners (six men and one woman) and two of the men's partners have been completed, and another round of interviews will be conducted in the near future. The summary that follows will refer only to the findings on the men.

The Canadian ex-prisoners were slightly older on arrest (22 compared to 20), had spent more time in prison (20 compared to 11 years), were older on release (43 compared to 32) and had been out in the community for less time (7 compared to 11.5 years) than the men in the Irish sample. All of the Canadian men interviewed had been out of prison for two or more years on full parole at the time of interviews (one has since had his licence revoked and is back in custody). The duration of imprisonment prior to release on life licence ranged from 10 to 34 years.

All of the interviewed Canadian men had been incarcerated in a cluster of federal correctional institutions in Ontario and Quebec where there had been serious upheaval and violence during the period of their imprisonment (the 1970s through early 1990s). This violence included major disturbances, hostage takings and mutilations, the murder of one prison officer, assaults on prisoners by prison staff and dogs, serious inmate-on-inmate assaults and a spate of inmate-on-inmate homicides. The worst period was between January 1983 and March 1984, when there were thirteen inmate homicides in the Ontario region alone.[7]

There were social differences between the small group of Canadian lifers and the Republican ex-prisoners. The Canadian men tended to have less stable backgrounds, and none had returned to their communities of origin. Those who had formed new families tended to keep their distance from others in the community and tried to avoid revealing their pasts. Some had non-association conditions as part of their parole and needed to avoid contact with their former friends. Parole conditions that prohibited drinking alcohol were also common.

All but one of the men were living in their own accommodation. Four men worked for ex-prisoner support groups or in the voluntary sector. One did casual work while studying and one was self-employed.

Experiences of serious violence in prison, either as witnesses or victims, still troubled some of the men, and were referred to as important turning points in the men's perception of themselves:

> So I guess always being in the frame of mind that what you got sent here for [homicide] is maybe something you're going to have to do while you're in here too. But a much more conscious and deliberate decision. It's like it's a total lack of respect for anybody. In the sense that life is cheap and it's treated cheaply in there … [Of] all my experience in prison that's the one [I] … hate the most and I don't know if I'll ever lose it. I'm not sure that I want to sometimes.

The accounts of some of the interviewees suggested that they adopted similar strategies to the other groups in selective avoidance of emotionally disturbing thoughts in prison:

> It's a mind world. The physical environment contains you. You know you can only walk so far so many times round the yard, and so on, or walk from one cell to another. You're contained in that space; it's a spatial thing. It's a terrible thing because you're confined as well. But when you come out you [continue to] live in the mind.

> So you did, you could train your mind to look at things or not look at things or you would sift things in or sift things f…ing out – do you know what I mean? You're not unrealistic; otherwise you would become sort of mad wouldn't you, in a world of your own.

One interviewee described this as a process of 'removal' that he continued to use after release:

> Removal is one of the strange things. It's like, where I really don't want to talk about the situation; I really don't want any input into it; I wanna kind of wrap my own head around it first. And, at first, my wife would be very inquisitive: 'What's wrong?' You know, 'Lets talk about it' … And I'd be like, 'No, I don't want to talk about it.' She'd take that somewhat personal. Now she understands that, no, it's ok … It's the way *I* deal with things.

Rebellion could also enable emotional isolation and avoidance:

> No, I blocked out the outside completely. And, I was a complete rebel, and so I did a lot of time in 'the hole,' I did a lot of time in the special handling units, I did a lot of time in segregation; and it served my purpose because I was further away from people.

> I didn't feel like I belonged, I didn't care, I seen no-one emotionally because I didn't deal with emotions. I guess I did, but it was all attack, and there was no love ... It was mostly hate and bitterness; and it helped me cope in that if I was negative, I was blocking everything out and it was much easier for me to do my time. I found it much more easier because the people would leave me alone: the guards and the whatever, would leave me alone ... Everybody else was running around having visits and, you know, like if I had a visit it was very uncomfortable ... I found more friendship with a weight bar or a weight machine, where it never spoke back to me, it never asked me any questions, and if anything, it helped me physically and took away the stress or whatever.

> You know, I stayed away from personal relationships where people could know more about me; I blocked them off right away: strike out of it.

The Canadian interviewees also described similar experiences of estrangement and loss of closeness to others after release. When asked about this, one responded:

> Yep. I think so. I think also I don't know how to resolve those kind of issues. That's because in jail you can't let anything get to you. It's tearing up inside but you've got to keep that mask on, and so even out here I keep that mask on it, still. It's easier not to try and deal with it. I have to process it inside you know and I don't know how to do that.

> You build a wall while you're in there ... There's not that many people I let get close. I have lots of friends, lots of relationships but in terms of somebody that can get inside of me, I don't allow that very much.

> For the most part as that wall got built it stayed there for the rest of it. I was in there and whatever was going on outside was not

going to come in. Like this was my life, this was what I needed to do to survive and I can't afford to let anything else in. That's kinda how I went on.

One of the partners described her husband's persisting difficulty with expressing closeness:

He has a hard time showing emotions: any emotion. I don't know if that's from being in prison 20 years or if it's the way he was before ... I'll go to sit next to him and he'll go to the other end of the couch ... The affection is not there anymore.

The men reported substantial losses and changes in relationships with children:

The other ones [children of pre-prison relationship] I hadn't seen in such a long time ... I mean, they were important but they are strangers. Definitely.

Well my son has had a lot of problems, and ... My son probably took over where I ... where I started. Like, abandoned, being abandoned: their mother committed suicide and here I'm in jail and ... So, there was a heavy situation like that. Especially when there's two males, and I come from the 'fifties' and the 'forties' where you never show your emotions and you never show your true feelings and, you know, you work and do what you gotta do ... I'm not home; whether I'm in jail or whether I'm on the street, I'm not home because I just hang around and do what I want. I was on parole and everything, but I got him to live with me and we all got arrested, and he got arrested; and that was the last time I seen any of my kids.

There could also be a more pervasive sense of estrangement from others:

I feel like I don't belong, and as much as I can do, I just don't feel like I belong: I feel more like one of those animals at the zoo, that people are interested in because of their past, you know, and not interested in the person themselves, you know.

Some men recognised permanent changes in their personalities:

I think I'm a lot colder, a lot less compassionate sometimes ... and I think that has a lot to do with the maturing in a prison environment. I can become very, very remote very quickly, and it doesn't bother me as much as it bothers other people.

However, there were also differences between the Irish and Canadian men in the ways they construed the experience of change. The former tended to see changes in themselves as negative in relation to emotional capacities for trust, intimacy and sociability. They saw it as positive in relation to education, intellectual development and their ability to judge situations and people. The Canadian men described the same emotional losses, but talked about change as positive in relation to reform, greater insight and self-control. Some observed that they had changed through maturation, becoming less impulsive, less aggressive and more reflective. Although one or two of the men interviewed discussed changes in themselves in terms of the correctional vocabularies of 'reform', most attributed their greater self-awareness and psychological survival to being able to find support and understanding in the few close friendships they had formed with other prisoners. In summary, there were several strands woven into their discussion of change, including the enduring influence of traumatic events, avoidance of painful emotion, detachment from emotional ties, positive change or reform through intellectual development or self-examination, and the processes of maturation and ageing.

Time and prison experience

Academic writing on prisons and personal narratives about the experience of imprisonment both use time as an organising metaphor, for example, *Dead Time* (Rives 1989), *Doing Time* (Matthews 1999), *Undoing Time* (Evans *et al* 2000), or *Out of Time* (McKeown 2001). The prisoners' experience of imprisonment tends to be framed in terms of managing time: inmates 'serve time', 'do time', do 'hard time' or 'easy time', they 'kill time' or get through 'dead time'. They have a dual sense of time passing and standing still. In the words of one man: 'Time had stopped in my head.'

There are vivid accounts of how prisoners accomplish the doing of time, how they manipulate, 'consciously toy, bend, and mould' time in order to survive (Scarce 2002: 306). A pervasive theme in the accounts of the former prisoners we spoke is that, 'Prison is about survival: everyday, 24/7.'

Cohen and Taylor (1978) stress how acutely felt the problem of survival is for long-term prisoners:

> We began to realize that the whole business of getting through each day, let alone each month, or year, or decade of their sentence, was a far more precarious and problematic journey than we had ever taken it to be. The central question was about how to accommodate to prison life. In what ways should one resist or yield to its demands in order to make life bearable, in order to preserve some sense of identity? And behind this question lay their greatest anxiety – the consequence, as it were, of failing to solve the accommodation problem – the sense of imminent deterioration.
>
> (Cohen and Taylor 1978: 13)

> The prisoners who faced thirty years did not find their vision blurred by an immediate visible web of developing processes but instead could stare right across the void of their sentence into the eyes of death itself. For them death and deterioration had suddenly come into perspective and they wrestled with ways in which they might again be placed at the periphery of consciousness.
>
> (ibid.: 17)

Both *Psychological Survival* (Cohen and Taylor 1972) and *Escape Attempts* (Cohen and Taylor 1978) deal with the problem of doing time and the necessity of developing strategies of 'resistance' in order to counter the 'insidious processes that attack personal identity'.[8] Understanding and mapping different modes of resistance also inevitably involved Cohen and Taylor in touching on two related and fundamental existential issues, although they did so through a symbolic interactionist perspective. The first of these issues is how prisoners dealt with the problem of being in the world, i.e. how could they maintain affective relationships with others in the world. The second issue concerned how the prisoner might maintain authenticity of the self (for Cohen and Taylor 'identity') in the confrontation with temporality, finitude, and his 'being-towards-death'.[9]

This is in marked contrast to the liberal perspective on imprisonment which conceives of the pains of imprisonment as series of losses or deprivations, e.g. loss of liberty, loss of autonomy and deprivations of important material, physical comforts and emotional attachments (Sykes 1958). The pains of imprisonment are taken to be those things that are taken away from the prisoner. But surprisingly, the prisoner's time (lost out of a finite life span) is not counted among these pains or losses.

Similarly, Foucauldian commentaries on imprisonment see prison as a site of domination that targets 'the soul', or 'knowable man', but which also encompasses the control and regulation of time, space and material and human resources (Smart 1983: 70). For Foucault, time is a modality of disciplinary power exercised through the punctuation of activity by a timetable (a 'factory-monastery' framework) and the imposition on the individual of a collective and obligatory rhythm for activity (Foucault 1979: 151–2). Both the liberal and Foucauldian perspectives conceive of time spent in prison as an accumulation of 'the linear time of successive "nows"' (Baugh 2000: 75) and not as a depletion of something that is finite, unique and might be forever lost to the prisoner. Neither takes account of the temporality of imprisonment from the perspective of prisoners' being-towards-death. This may be, in part, because prison is usually the experience of young men; however, as the duration of imprisonment lengthens, this perspective assumes greater significance.

These small studies of the outcomes of long-term imprisonment among three very different groups of men across different correctional contexts found a remarkably consistent and shared set of psychological effects. The unifying theme among these is time – the men's irrevocable loss of time and life history, the dislocation in time and reduced future after release, and the enduring nature of the changes in close affective relationships with others.

> We lost a part of ourselves in jail, we lost our youth. But that's a consequence of being in jail and being involved in the struggle. And I think we're still growing up; even though I'm 40, and I was in jail from when I was 19, I think I'm still growing up. So when you come out you're not re-born, you just have to start again.

> You build a wall when you're in there... You were living in a different world as far as I was concerned. There were different rules. Whatever rules there were on the outside meant nothing there... People getting stabbed near you, ball battered and anything else... you witness all this stuff and you have no avenue to let this out. You bury it, you hide it and you don't show your feelings over it ... I stop people from getting inside of who I am with it.

And after release the time in prison can not be put in the past but stays in the present: 'I can't get away from it. There is no way out of it... Those things have not gone – they are still in me.'

There are common thematic concerns with time, self and change that connect our findings with the current work of Elaine Crawley and

Richard Sparks on older prisoners (e.g. this volume). The themes of temporality and enduring change suggest we should rethink the assumption that the pains or losses of imprisonment end with the end of sentences.

Re-evaluating the 'prison effects' literature

The preliminary findings in these small studies would not have been anticipated from the bulk of research on the effects of long-term imprisonment. There is a general acceptance that well-designed psychological studies have failed to demonstrate that long-term imprisonment has substantial detrimental effects, notwithstanding the 'pains of imprisonment' and the forms of adaptation to prison culture described by Sykes (1958) and Clemmer (1958). Psychological research has shown little evidence of deterioration in personality, intellectual functioning, attitudes and psychiatric morbidity associated with long-term custody (Banister *et al* 1973; Heskin *et al* 1973; Bolton *et al* 1976; Sapsford 1978; Rasch 1981).[10] Later work, however, has shed more light on the complexity of the issue, with studies illustrating the variety of responses among prisoners (Bukstel and Kilmann 1980; Adams 1993), changes during the course of custody (Zamble 1992), and the pathways to prison suicide (Liebling 1999). There is also a growing understanding of heterogeneity among prisons: quality of life varies in different establishments and this differentially impacts on prisoner distress (Liebling 2004).

The lack of reference in the prison effects literature to the psychological and adjustment problems described above may reflect limitations in previous research. A critique of the prison effects literature suggests it has five principal limitations.

Firstly, there is a lack of substantial longitudinal studies in which prisoners are followed up for very long periods of time. Most studies have either used cross-sectional samples, or periods of follow-up have been relatively short. Zamble and Porporino's longitudinal study of 133 prisoners in Ontario, Canada had a follow-up period of one year (Zamble and Porporino 1988), although a smaller group of 25 long-term prisoners from their sample was subsequently followed up five years later, by which time they had been in prison for seven years on average (Zamble 1992).

Secondly, studies of the effects of long-term imprisonment have almost exclusively been carried out on prisoners during the period of custody. However, what is of most importance and relevance is how the effects of long-term imprisonment are manifested after release from prison. Studies that have examined long-term prisoners after release have tended to focus on recidivism and general measures of social adjustment, rather than more subtle, hidden kinds of psychological and emotional disability (e.g. Waller 1974; Coker and Martin 1985). Likewise, such problems tend not to feature in the content of prisoner re-entry programmes (Petersilia 2003).

This second limitation has both practical and theoretical implications. As noted above, changes during long-term imprisonment that are perceived as adaptive in the prison environment may not be adaptive for the outside environment. It has been observed, for example, that over time prisoners tend to exercise more control over their thoughts and become more self-contained (Zamble and Porporino 1988). They become more engaged in structured routines and withdrawn from emotional and social entanglements in prison (Zamble 1992); and they increasingly value environmental stability, order and predictability (Toch 1977). From the research perspective of changes during custody, these findings are seen as functional in enabling the prisoner to cope (Flanagan 1995), and as evidence of improved maturity and adaptation. They are seen as counter-evidence against previous beliefs that long-term imprisonment is harmful (Wormith 1984; Zamble 1992). However, the right comparator for evaluating such changes would be how the prisoner functions in the post-release environment. This changed perspective could alter the way in which the effects of imprisonment are interpreted. It is possible, for example, that the above psychological changes could be dysfunctional for coping with the demands of family life. Withdrawal, self-containment and loss of engagement in ordinary social experience may not be particularly problematic while the prisoner is in custody, but may have a disabling impact when the prisoner is facing the tasks of resuming relationships and establishing a normal life after release.

Thirdly, research has used measures that appear to be inadequate to the task. This is not a criticism of individual empirical studies: the efforts to improve the design and methodological rigour of psychological research on imprisonment have yielded major advances. However, as others have observed (e.g. Flanagan 1995), there remains a troubling discrepancy between the negative findings of formal experimental psychological research and the vivid accounts in case studies of difficulties experienced by long-term prisoners (e.g. Cohen and Taylor 1972). This at least suggests that the empirical psychological studies have failed adequately to capture and characterise the kinds of distress that are reported by long-term prisoners. The way forward, however, is not to revisit arguments between protagonists of quantitative and qualitative methods, but to consider how research measures could be more sensitive and appropriate, and whether new theoretical paradigms are needed for the design of future work.[11]

Fourthly, research has lacked a developmental and 'life history' perspective. Long-term prisoners, who typically may serve between ten and fifteen years before release, enter a different world from the one they left. They may have lost key relationships in the outside world, and a substantial segment of their life history – the decade or more of adult life when they would normally have been establishing themselves in their occupations, lifestyles, relationships and bringing up young families. But in their psychological development they may feel as they did on entry into prison. Moreover, the outside the world they left has changed in their absence. On release they may wish to resume the life they left but this cannot be done, and they are dislocated and out of synchrony with the peer group and social and family networks in which they previously belonged.

The importance of these developmental issues and the difficulties to which they may give rise need to be recognised. As noted above, it is important to have the right frame of reference. The research findings on how individuals change within prison need to be evaluated from the perspective of their past and future outside life. Zamble and Porporino (1988, 1990) found that prisoners' coping abilities, which were commonly very poor and dysfunctional before they came into prison, remained essentially unchanged while they were in custody, and this led the authors to conclude:

> ... we were led to summarise what happens during imprisonment as a 'behavioral deep freeze' in which a person's set of outside world behaviors are stored until his release.
>
> (Zamble and Porporino 1990: 62)

However, this does not necessarily imply that imprisonment has not had adverse effects. While the prisoner's coping skills may not deteriorate over time, the outside world will be increasingly changing as custody lengthens, and there will be accumulation of the challenges the prisoner will face in coping and coming to terms with the altered environment and his personal losses.

The need for correct perspective is illustrated in an example cited by Sapsford (1983) of lifers who,

... go through the prison day mechanically, saving all their spare time and mental energies for keeping in touch with their families, writing letters, making models and toys for the children, and remain husbands and fathers who happen to be in prison rather than prisoners who happen to be married.

(Sapsford 1983: 96)

Sapsford interprets this as an example of how prisoners can construct positive roles imported from the outside world as a means of maintaining self-respect; a means of coping with prison time that is, 'an interruption of life, not part of it, like a form of cryogenic suspension' (ibid.: 76).

Viewed from the perspective of how prisoners cope in custody, such behaviour may seem constructive in relation to post-release prospects. Viewed from the perspective of the world outside, this may be an illusion: children and families will be growing older and adapting to paternal separation and absence. In reality the father's behaviour is increasingly and painfully irrelevant.

The fifth limitation is that many psychological studies do not locate their work in a wider context of relevant research. Cohen and Taylor (1972) argued that the material in psychological and sociological studies of prison life was not sufficiently sophisticated and subtle to characterise the experience of long-term prisoners, and it was necessary to turn to other studies examining how individuals deal with stress produced by massive disruption in their normal lives.

We were looking at the ways in which men in general might react to an extreme situation, a situation which disrupted their normal lives so as to make problematic such every day matters as time, friendship, privacy, identity, self-consciousness, ageing and physical deterioration.

(Cohen and Taylor 1972: 51)

[A long-term prisoner] ... faces up to two decades inside, two decades away from home, wife, children, job, social life and friends. He cannot reassure himself that each of these domains is merely being held in cold storage until his return – a life cannot be reassembled twenty years after its destruction.

(ibid.: 53)

> Without a full consciousness of the way in which the every day world has been broken for the long term prisoner, we can underestimate the pains he experiences and assume that his apparent ease represents a natural adaption to prison conditions, and not one which has been personally constructed as a solution to intolerable problems.
>
> (ibid.: 54)

Like Toch (1992), Cohen and Taylor found studies of victims of disaster more relevant because such studies are similarly concerned with the consequences of sudden and overwhelming dislocations that affect the individual's total life.

Implications for future research

In relation to the wider field of research on psychological effects of imprisonment, the above critique suggests that new approaches are needed in future work. Longitudinal studies should seek to examine the consequences of custody from initial reception until after release. They should include parallel study and follow-up of families so as to map comprehensively the effects on them of the imprisonment.

A new research perspective is needed based on an appreciation of the individual's developmental life history. Thus the effects of imprisonment should not only be considered in terms of change and adaptation within prison; two other comparisons are relevant. First, the consequences of imprisonment should be considered in relation to the individual's circumstances and likely life prospects prior to arrest. In other words, if the individual had not been imprisoned, how his life would have been likely to progress, and how the experience and outcome of imprisonment differ from this expected life course. Second, the consequences of imprisonment should be considered in relation to the changing outside context. How does the individual's pre-arrest world – family, work and social setting – change during the period of imprisonment, and what are the consequences and effects of those changes? Such questions are formidably difficult to answer but they provide perspectives that better match the complexity of prison experience. They may also provide a means of reconciling the discrepancy between the findings of previous case studies and experimental research.

New theoretical paradigms for such studies might usefully draw on trauma theory, particularly research on responses to chronic trauma, and disruption of the assumptive world (Parkes 1971; Kauffman 2002). Attachment theory (Parkes *et al* 1991) may also provide valuable approaches for investigating the consequences of separation among prisoners, families and children. The research methods and measures in such studies would need to be clinically informed, sensitive and appropriate for assessing changes in emotional life, family dynamics and attachments.

The use of interview schedules drawn from experience of psychiatric history-taking may also be useful to facilitate clear and detailed description of the complex subjective experiences at issue. Such interviews follow a biographical format and involve exploration of the interviewee's psychological life in the phenomenological tradition articulated by Jaspers (1963) and influential in clinical psychiatry since his time. Phenomenology, according to Jaspers, provides, 'a concrete description of the psychic states which patients actually experience and presents them for observation' (Jaspers 1963: 55).

By means of biographical enquiry we try to understand the individual's psychological life as a temporal whole, so that, 'Every good history grows into a biography' (Jaspers 1963: 671).

These research interviews are also narratives of personal experience. Narratives serve to bind us to our culture and enable us to communicate our lives to others around us (Craib 2000; Brunner 1990; Crossley 2000); but this does not imply that they are just theoretical or ideological constructions of meaning. The narratives given in the research interviews are direct accounts of experience, of psychological trauma, loss and change.

Implications for penology

If it is the case that long-term imprisonment leads to demonstrable psychological harms that extend beyond custody, this would pose a challenge for notions of proportionality in penal sanctions. In *Principled Sentencing*, von Hirsch (1998) discusses what the basis should be for gauging the severity of punishments. He argues that the test should not be subjective, that is, how unpleasant the experience of the penalty is. Rather, the severity of punishment should be gauged by reference to an interests analysis – that is, penalties should be ranked according to how much they typically affect a person's living standard interests – the means and capabilities that ordinarily assist people in living a good life, such as freedom of movement, earning ability, etc. This is not just an abstract notion but has empirical reference: the test is actual impact on ordinary lives.

Proportionality means that a punishment should not be disproportionate: at the appropriate point in time the punishment should cease to adversely affect the individual's interests or living standard. However, the above studies suggest that long-term imprisonment may entail losses of life history that cannot be reconstituted, and the possibility of lasting impairments of psychological capabilities. If this is correct, the adverse effects on the individual's living standard interests do not cease but continue beyond the term of the penal sanction.

If a more accurate view of long-term imprisonment is that it permanently alters the life courses of those involved and removes part of their expected life history (and that seems to be the psychological reality of it), and if furthermore, it causes positive harms and impairments that extend beyond sentence, then a theory of proportionate penal sanctions becomes very difficult to sustain, insofar as it has empirical reference to impact on offenders' lives.

Notes

1   The authors would like to thank Kieran McEvoy for his helpful comments on this paper.

2   The Ex-Prisoners Assistance Committee, 59, Glaslough St, Monaghan, Ireland. The study was developed with and commissioned by ExPac and was supported by a grant from the European Union Special Support Fund for Peace and Reconciliation in Ireland. Other advisors in the study were Dave Wall (then Chief Executive, NIACRO), Nuala Kelly (Co-ordinator of the Irish Conference for Prisoners Overseas), and Bernadette McAliskey (founder member of the H-Block Armagh Committee). The fieldwork was co-ordinated by Eugene Byrne on behalf of ExPac. The study report was published by ExPac (Jamieson and Grounds 2002).

3   The Canadian interviews were funded under the Canadian High Commission's Institutional Research Programme, 2002, as part of a joint project (Ruth Jamieson, Keele University; Elaine Crawley, Keele University; Adrian Grounds, University of Cambridge; and Bill Noble, University of Sheffield) entitled 'Older Prisoners in Custody and on Release: Lessons from the Canadian Experience'. We would also like to acknowledge the assistance of Prof. Bob Gaucher, University of Ottawa, who was instrumental in both the design and facilitation of the Canadian ex-prisoner interviews. We would like to thank Bob Gaucher, Elaine Crawley and Kieran McEvoy for their very helpful comments on this paper.

4   The *Traumatic Life Events Questionnaire* (Kubany *et al* 2000), the *Purdue PTSD Scale Revised* (Lauterbach and Vrana 1996), the *Revised Civilian Mississippi*

Scale (Norris and Perilla 1996), the *Beck Depression Inventory* (Beck *et al* 1979), and the *Beck Hopelessness Scale* (Beck *et al* 1974).

5   Haney (this volume), 'The contextual revolution in psychology and the question of prison effects'.

6   Nevertheless, the high level of solidarity among Irish political prisoners and their determined resistance to criminalisation provided them some protection from the more destructive effects of prison. The capacity to resist the stigma of criminalisation also appears to have mitigated – but not eliminated – the effects of imprisonment for conscientious objectors (see Brock 2004) and this appears to be an important difference between the experiences of the political and 'ordinary' prisoners we interviewed. Similarly, campaigns for justice by the wrongfully convicted may also represent an important focus of resistance. For a detailed account of paramilitary imprisonment in Northern Ireland, see McEvoy (2001).

7   See Culhane (1984), McNeil and Vance (1978) and Porporino and Marton (1983).

8   See also the vivid accounts of prisoners' fears of deterioration in Hassine (2002).

9   Both are central ontological concerns of existential philosophers, most often associated with Heidegger's theory of existence or being-in-the world (*dasein*) and being-towards-death expounded in his early book *Being and Time* (1927).

10 The research findings are not uniform. See for example Lapornik *et al* (1996), who reported significant decline in concentration and memory performance tests in their sample of prisoners tested on two occasions 42 months apart.

11 See Haney, this volume, for a discussion of the influence of psychological individualism on prison effects research.

References

Adams, K. (1993) 'Adjusting to prison life', in M. Tonry (ed.) *Crime and Justice: A Review of Research*, Volume 16. Chicago: University of Chicago Press, pp. 275–359.

Banister, P.A., Smith, F.V, Heskin, K.J. and Bolton, N. (1973) 'Psychological correlates of long-term imprisonment: I Cognitive variables', *British Journal of Criminology*, 13, 312–323.

Baugh, B. (2000) 'Death and temporality in Deleuse and Derrida', *Angelaki – Journal of the Theoretical Humanities*, 5, 73–83.

Beck, A.T., Weissman, A., Lester, D. and Trexler, L. (1974) 'The measurement of pessimism: The hopelessness scale', *Journal of Clinical and Consulting Psychology*, 42, 861–865.

Beck, A.T., Rush, J., Shaw, B. and Emery, G. (1979) *Cognitive Theory of Depression*. New York: Guildford Press.

Beresford, D. (1987) *Ten Men Dead*. London: Grafton.

Bolton, N., Smith, F.V., Heskin, K.J. and Banister, P.A. (1976) 'Psychological correlates of long-term imprisonment: IV A longitudinal analysis', *British Journal of Criminology*, 16, 38–47.

Brock, P. (ed.) (2004) *These Strange Criminals: An Anthology of Prison Memoirs by Conscientious Objectors from the Great War to the Cold War*. Toronto: University of Toronto Press.

Brunner, J.S. (1990) *Acts of Meaning*. Cambridge, MA: Harvard University Press.

Bukstel, L.H. and Kilmann, P.R. (1980) 'Psychological effects of imprisonment on confined individuals', *Psychological Bulletin*, 88, 469–493.

Clemmer, D. (1958) *The Prison Community*. New York: Holt, Rinehart and Winston.

Cohen, S. and Taylor, L. (1972) *Psychological Survival: The Experience of Long-Term Imprisonment*. Harmondsworth: Penguin.

Cohen, S. and Taylor, L. (1978) *Escape Attempts: The Theory and Practice of Resistance to Everyday Life*. London: Pelican Books.

Coker, J.B. and Martin, J.P. (1985) *Licensed to Live*. Oxford: Basil Blackwell.

Craib, I. (2000) 'Narratives as bad faith', in M. Andrews, S.D. Sclater, C. Squire and A. Treacher (eds) *Lines of Narrative: Psychosocial Perspectives*. London: Routledge, pp. 64–74.

Crossley, M.L. (2000) *Introducing Narrative Psychology: Self, Trauma and the Construction of Meaning*. Buckingham: Open University Press.

Culhane, C. (1984) *Still Barred from Prison: Social Injustice in Canada*. Montreal: Black Rose Books.

Evans, J., Santiago, J.B. and Haney, C.W. (2000) *Undoing Time: American Prisoners in Their Own Words*. Boston: Northeastern University Press.

Flanagan, T.J. (1995) 'Adaptation and adjustment among long-term prisoners', in T.J. Flanagan (ed.) *Long-Term Imprisonment: Policy, Science and Correctional Practice*. Thousand Oaks, CA: Sage, pp. 109–116.

Foucault, M. (1979) *Discipline and Punish: The Birth of the Prison*. London: Penguin.

Grounds, A. (2004) 'Psychological consequences of wrongful conviction and imprisonment', *Canadian Journal of Criminology and Criminal Justice*, 46, 165–182.

Grounds, A. (2005) 'Understanding the effects of wrongful imprisonment', in M. Tonry (ed.) *Crime and Justice A Review of Research*, 32. Chicago: University of Chiacago Press, pp. 1–58.

Grounds, A. and Jamieson, R (2003) 'No sense of an ending: Researching the experience of imprisonment and release among Republican ex-prisoners', *Theoretical Criminology*, 7, 347–362.

Hassine, V. (2002) 'Monochromes from over a prison's edge', in B. Gaucher (ed.) *Writing as Resistance: The Journal of Prisoners on Prisons Anthology 1988–2000*. Toronto: Canadian Scholar's Press, pp. 272–286.

Heidegger, M. (1927) (trans. by J. Macquarrie and E. Robinson, 1978) *Being and Time*. Oxford: Basil Blackwell.

Heskin, K.J., Smith, F.V, Banister, P.A. and Bolton, N. (1973) 'Psychological correlates of long-term imprisonment: II Personality variables', *British Journal of Criminology*, 13, 323–330.

Jamieson, R. and Grounds, A. (2002) *No Sense of an Ending: The Effects of Long-Term Imprisonment amongst Republican Prisoners and their Families*. Monaghan: Seesyu Press.

Jaspers, K. (1963) *General Psychopathology* (trans. J. Hoenig and M.W. Hamilton). Manchester: Manchester University Press.

Kauffman, J. (2002) *Loss of the Assumptive World: A Theory of Traumatic Loss*. New York: Brunner-Routledge.

Kubany, E.S., Haynes, S.N., Leisen, M.B., Owens, J.A., Kaplan, A.S., Watson, S.B. and Burns, K. (2000) 'Development and preliminary validation of a brief broad-spectrum measure of trauma exposure: The traumatic life events questionnaire', *Psychological Assessment*, 12, 210–224.

Kulka, R.A., Schlenger, W.E., Fairbank, J.A., Hough, R.A., Jordan, B.K., Marmar, C.R., Weiss, D.S. and Grady, D.A. (1990) *Trauma and the Vietnam War Generation: Report of Findings from the National Vietnam Veterans Readjustment Study*. New York: Brunner/Mazel.

Lapornik, R.M., Lehofer, M., Moser, G., Pump, S., Egner, C., Posch, G., Hildebrandt and Zapotoczky, H.G. (1996) 'Long-term imprisonment leads to cognitive impairment', *Forensic Science International*, 82, 121–127.

Lauterbach, D. and Vrana, S. (1996) 'Three studies on the reliability and validity of a self-report measure of PTSD', *Psychological Assessment*, 3, 17–25.

Liebling, A. (1999) 'Prison suicide and prisoner coping', in M. Tonry and J. Petersilia (eds) *Prisons, Crime and Justice: A Review of Research*, Volume 26, Chicago: University of Chicago Press, pp. 283–360.

Liebling, A. (2004) *Prisons and their Moral Performance. A Study of Values, Quality and Prison Life*. Oxford: Clarendon Press.

Matthews, R. (1999) *Doing Time: An Introduction to the Sociology of Imprisonment*. Basingstoke: Macmillan.

McKeown, L. (2001) *Out of Time: Irish Republican Prisoners, Long Kesh 1972–2000*. Belfast: Beyond the Pale, BTP Publications Ltd.

McEvoy, K. (2001) *Paramilitary Imprisonment in Northern Ireland: Resistance, Management and Release*. Oxford: Clarendon Press.

McEvoy, K., O'Mahony, D., Horner, C. and Lyner, O. (1999) 'The home front: The families of politically motivated prisoners in Northern Ireland', *British Journal of Criminology*, 39, 175–197.

McEvoy, K., Shirlow, P. and McElraith, K. (2004) 'Resistance transition and exclusion: Politically motivated ex-prisoners and conflict transformation in Northern Ireland', *Political Violence and Terrorism Studies* (in press).

McNeil, G. and Vance, S. (1978) *Cruel and Unusual*. Toronto: Deneau and Greenberg.

Newman, P.H. (1944) 'The prisoner-of-war mentality: Its effect after repatriation', *British Medical Journal*, 1, 8–10.

Norris, F. and Perilla, J. (1996) 'The Revised Civilian Mississippi Scale for PTSD: Reliability, validity, and cross-language stability', *Journal of Traumatic Stress*, 9, 285–298.

Parker, T. (1990) *Life after Life: Interviews with Twelve Murderers*. London: Secker & Warburg.

Parkes, C.M. (1971) 'Psychosocial transitions: A field for study', *Social Science and Medicine*, 5, 101–115.

Parkes, C.M., Stevenson-Hinde, J. and Marris, P. (1991) *Attachment across the Life Cycle*. London: Routledge.

Petersilia, J. (2003) *When Prisoners Come Home: Parole and Prisoner Re-entry*. Oxford: Oxford University Press.

Porporino, F.J. and Marton, J.P. (1983) *Strategies to Reduce Prison Violence*. Ottawa: Ministry of the Solicitor General of Canada, Programs Branch, and Research Division.

Rasch, W. (1981) 'The effects of indeterminate detention: A study of men sentenced to life imprisonment', *International Journal of Law and Psychiatry*, 4, 417–431.

Rives, J. (1989) *Dead Time: Poems from Prison*. Hamilton, Ontario: Mini Mocho Press.

Rollin, H.R. (1948) 'The psychological problems of the repatriated prisoner of war', *Medical Press*, 220, 301–304.

Sapsford, R.J. (1978) 'Life-sentence prisoners: Psychological changes during sentence'. *British Journal of Criminology*, 18, 128–145.

Sapsford, R.J. (1983) *Life-Sentence Prisoners: Reaction, Response and Change*. Milton Keynes: Open University Press.

Scarce, R. (2002) 'Doing time as an act of survival', *Symbolic Interaction*, 25, 303–321.

Shirlow, P. (2001) *The State They Are In: An Independent Evaluation*. Coleraine: University of Ulster Social Exclusion Research Unit.

Smart, B. (1983) 'On discipline and social regulation: a review of Foucault's genealogical analysis', in D. Garland and P. Young (eds) *The Power to Punish: Contemporary Penality and Social Analysis*. London: Heinemann.

Solomon, Z. (1993) *Combat Stress Reaction: The Enduring Toll of War*. New York: Plenum Press.

Sykes, G. (1958) *Society of Captives: A Study of a Maximum Security Prison*. Princeton, NJ: Princeton University Press.

Toch, H. (1977) *Living in Prison: The Ecology of Survival*. New York: Free Press.

Toch, H. (1992) *Mosaic of Despair: Human Breakdowns in Prison*. Washington, DC: American Psychological Association.

Turner, B. and Rennell, T. (1995) *When Daddy Came Home: How Family Life Changed Forever in 1945*. London: Hutchinson.

Von Hirsch, A. (1998) 'Seriousness, severity and the living standard', in A. von Hirsch and A. Ashworth (eds) *Principled Sentencing: Readings in Theory and Policy* (2nd edn). Oxford: Hart, pp. 185–190.

Waller, I. (1974) *Men Released from Prison*. Toronto: University of Toronto Press.

World Health Organisation (1992) *The ICD-10 Classification of Mental and Behavioural Disorders: Clinical Descriptions and Diagnostic Guidelines.* Geneva: WHO.

Wormith, J.S. (1984) 'The controversy over the effects of long-term incarceration', *Canadian Journal of Criminology*, 26, 423–437.

Yerkes, S.A. and Holloway, H.C. (1996) 'War and homecomings: The stressors of war and of returning from war', in R.J. Ursano and A.E. Norwood (eds) *Emotional Aftermath of the Persian Gulf War: Veterans, Families, Communities and Nations.* Washington, DC: American Psychiatric Press, pp. 25–42.

Zamble, E. (1992) 'Behaviour and adaption in long-term prison inmates: Descriptive longitudinal results', *Criminal Justice and Behaviour*, 19, 409–425.

Zamble, E. and Porporino, F.J. (1988) *Coping, Behaviour and Adaption in Prison Inmates.* New York: Springer-Verlag.

Zamble, E. and Porporino, F.J. (1990) 'Coping, imprisonment and rehabilitation: Some data and their implications', *Criminal Justice and Behaviour*, 17, 53–70.

Chapter 3

The contextual revolution in psychology and the question of prison effects

Craig Haney[1]

Not long ago I was driving to a federal penitentiary in the Midwestern United States, in connection with a legal case on which I was working. Like many maximum-security prisons in the United States, this one is located in a rural area, surrounded by farmland and little else. After you leave the interstate highway and travel down several country roads, you turn onto an even smaller road that leads directly to the prison grounds. Just at the corner where you make this last turn to enter the prison sits a small, white church – quaint and picturesque. It is a kind of landmark relied upon by people like myself who only travel there sporadically. 'Make sure you look for the white church', more experienced visitors always tell you, knowing that, if you miss it, you may be lost for quite some time before you make your way back to the prison.

Like many churches nowadays in the United States, this one has a sign out front proclaiming a religious message or aphorism. On my recent visit to the prison, as I slowed to make the turn at the church, just as everyone who goes to the penitentiary does, I noticed for the first time the name of the congregation that worships there: 'The Free Will Baptists'. And then I read these startling words of wisdom on the sign out the front: 'Compassion in the face of evil is no virtue.'

I confess that the sign took me aback. I stopped in the church car park to reflect on its meaning. It certainly led me to wonder about the particular theology to which Free Will Baptists subscribed, and how much of it was reflected in this statement.[2] I have always thought that the extension of compassion was a long-standing Christian virtue; the Free Will Baptist aphorism reminded me that I am hardly an expert on theology. Of course, I also wondered about the effect that the daily reading of this message might have on the guards and other employees who passed by it each day on their way into the prison, presumably to administer to the needs of the persons locked inside.

But it also occurred to me that this aphorism expressed a belief that has been at the core of much prison policy in the United States for several decades now: the belief that evil is a tangible thing that inheres inside persons who have done bad, reprehensible things. Once identified, evil requires condemnation rather than compassion. Since, by this model of crime and punishment, the free will of perpetrators and nothing else accounts for the bad choices they have made, there is no need to attempt to understand how, for example, the dire circumstances of their lives may have contributed to the things they have done – one starting point of compassionate justice.

Indeed, whatever suffering may have preceded their ignoble acts (and perhaps helps to account for them), this doctrine holds that evildoers deserve to experience more suffering, administered at the hands of a vengeful state. Thus, there is no reason to inquire into the conditions of their punitive confinement, at least not with an eye towards ameliorating the harshest or most destructive aspects or minimising the adjustment problems prisoners will experience upon release. In the political atmosphere that has prevailed in my country over this recent period in the history of corrections, anyone who fails to appreciate the logic of this tough approach to crime and punishment not only lacks virtue (as the Free Will Baptists suggest) but wisdom, common sense, and courage as well.

This punitive belief system is supported by more than just a unique form of religious fervour and the expedient use of law-and-order sloganeering in campaigns designed to propel political candidates past their more nuanced and complex thinking competitors. For more than a century, one or another version of it has been shored up by the invocation of some brand of science – especially my own discipline, psychology. In this chapter, I want to briefly review the role of psychology in supporting harsh prison policies and then, at greater length, explore this irony: during the course of the imprisonment binge that has overtaken many advanced societies over the last three decades, the discipline of psychology has undergone a revolution in thinking that, among other things, has drastically changed our perspective on the causes of crime and the psychological implications of the pains of imprisonment.

Thus, for the first time in the modern history of corrections, contemporary psychology stands in direct opposition to (rather than in support of) the basic notion that intelligent (let alone humane) crime control policies should entail little more than apprehending and isolating the individuals responsible for wrongdoing. Moreover, modern psychological theory directly contradicts the notion that what happens to people in prison does not much matter. Instead, the discipline of psychology now acknowledges, and has empirically documented the extent to which, context – past and present – matters dearly. Readers trained in more structurally oriented disciplines are no doubt thinking, 'I should say, it is about time'. So it is, but that time has finally come.

Thus, although we are latecomers to these basic insights about human nature, we now know that past context can profoundly shape future behaviour, including future criminal behaviour. We know that traumas inflicted at earlier times in someone's life – whether by structural forces like poverty and deprivation, more direct forms of mistreatment like parental neglect and abuse, and even institutional forces like the effects of incarceration in uncaring or brutalising juvenile justice facilities – are more than just regrettable; they also can be deeply criminogenic. Moreover, not only can social and institutional *histories* shape criminal behaviour – so that addressing contextual causes of crime must be made at least an equal priority in crime control policies – but *immediate* criminogenic circumstances and contexts matter too. And we know that, if context matters, then the *institutional* context of prison itself must be carefully examined on the basis of its potentially harmful effects on those exposed to it. That is, the pains of certain forms of imprisonment, far from being merely unpleasant, can transform prisoners, permanently impede their development, undermine their present and future well-being, and shape and affect their potential for post-prison adjustment.

These insights sit uneasily at best against the backdrop of contemporary prison policy. Indeed, the nature and amount of prison pain that has been inflicted over the last several decades – at least in the United States, whose prison systems are my main reference points – have pushed us to the brink of a genuine crisis, one with social, legal and even moral dimensions. An unprecedented amount of pain has been inflicted in the name of crime control (and the belief that compassion in the face of evil is no virtue). In too many instances, it has been inflicted with the widespread and sometimes enthusiastic support of many persons who lack real knowledge about the nature and consequences of the punishments imposed in their name.

The distribution of this pain has been facilitated by the rise of what some have termed a modern 'prison industrial complex' that now wields unprecedented political and economic influence in our society.[3] The pain also has been exacerbated by the actions of the mass media, which has significant interests in 'making crime pay' by amplifying politically charged and sensationalised stories that perpetuate many myths about crime and criminals (see Beckett 1997).

Crisis-level proportions have been reached in part because so few countervailing forces remain in our society to act as restraining edges against punitive excess. The intense politicising of the question of prison pain has meant that many courts in the United States have simply abdicated their regulatory function, apparently in deference to explicitly popular and political pressures. As a result, few legal limits remain to what can be done in the name of 'corrections', even as our criminal justice systems have abandoned any hope of ever correcting anything.

The sad irony is that this crisis developed during a time when there was a growing body of knowledge that underscored the wrongheadedness of the policies that were being pursued. Specifically, insights derived from contemporary psychological research and theory – in the midst of a significant 'contextual revolution' – should have played an important role in the critique and restraint of these excesses. Indeed, the aggressive and painful prison policies that have been implemented over the last several decades are based on what is now understood to be a faulty conception of human behaviour, one better suited to the 19th century in which it became so influential than the 21st century where it still shapes criminal justice policy. I will argue in this chapter that the excessive and unprecedented over-reliance on imprisonment stems from what is now understood to be a faulty model of behaviour; it is flawed public policy not least because it is based on bad science.

Psychological individualism in traditional prison policy

To put this discussion in a somewhat larger framework, let me say a few words about the history of the relationship between psychology and prison policy. As a number of historians have noted – usually in an accusatory tone – psychological theory was implicated at all levels in the process by which the institution of prison was made part of the natural order of things in modern society. In fact, Michel Foucault and Michael Ignatieff both have suggested that 'human sciences' like psychology were in large part responsible for the notion that human behaviour could and should be controlled by the state and, hence, contributed directly to the proliferation of prisons that took place in the late 18th and early 19th centuries (Foucault 1977; Ignatieff 1978). As Ignatieff put it, the 'premise that men could be scientifically described and understood was immediately translated into institutional strategies of control and reform' (1978: 218).

Although state power certainly had been used to dominate and subdue troublesome citizens long before the human sciences came on the scene, it is difficult to dispute the notion that these disciplines and the perspective on human nature they helped to formalise greatly influenced the nature of social control that followed. A detailed discussion of the nature of this influence during various historical periods is beyond the scope of this chapter, but allow me to pick just a few illustrative examples.

The general notion that lawbreakers should be rounded up, taken to centralised locations and forced to submit to some kind of systematic regimen or 'correctional' experience was necessarily based on some particular view of human nature. Beyond the simple 'otherness' of criminals (that many have argued was facilitated by the fixation of psychological science on the classification of persons, especially those regarded as deviant or different), there were a number of additional psychological components to what would eventually come to be called 'corrections'. For one, prison reflected a view of the human psyche as at least in some ways malleable – capable (in the minds of those who undertook the task) of being improved or perfected. This notion, in turn, was part of an emerging perspective known as 'materialist psychology', different from the understanding of human nature that had preceded it. John Locke was among the first to challenge the previously accepted notion that ideas and dispositions were innate, contending instead that character was formed by experience (Locke, 1954). By this view, material conditions had direct effects on persons exposed to them. Eventually, prison advocates argued that penal institutions could be properly structured to effectively change the character of prisoners.

For example, materialist psychology influenced prominent 18th-century English prison reformer John Howard, who relied on it as the basis of his claim that 'men's moral behaviour could be altered by disciplining their bodies' (cited in Ignatieff, 1978: 67). It is worth noting that Howard's scathing critiques of prison mismanagement and inhumane practices were expressly 'scientific' in nature. That is, he was deeply devoted to data collection, and recorded the precise physical dimensions and nature of the institutional regime of every prison he studied. In fact, his descriptions were so detailed that, as Michael Ignatieff reported, 'the Royal Statistical Society in the 1870s … laud[ed] him as a father of social science'. In any event, the materialist psychology on which he and others relied was the basis of the belief that '[t]hrough routinisation and repetition, the regiments of discipline would be internalized as moral duties'.

Historian Herman Franke observed that psychological individualism was reflected in another aspect of the prison policy that prevailed during this period: the extensive use of solitary confinement that began at the outset of the 19th century (Franke 1992). As he noted, the enthusiasm for this form of prison punishment – which occurred in comparatively liberal European nations as well as in the United States – is connected to 'the highly individualistic concept of sin and evil avowed by the confessional politicians and members of the societies of for moral improvement of prisoners'.

In the 19th century, the emerging discipline of psychology certainly contributed to the idea that confinement was an appropriate mechanism of social control and, in this sense, helped solidify the prison form. In the century and a half that has passed since imprisonment became the predominant response to criminal deviance in the United States, psychological concepts – and sometimes the discipline of psychology itself – have played an important practical and functional role in determining the shape and manner of prison operations.

Of course, the rise of imprisonment during the 19th century was entirely consistent with the emphasis on individualism that was en-shrined in the American legal system during the same period. Like the amateur social scientists of the day who employed the paradigm of independent and autonomous human agency in most of their causal attributions, lawyers and judges went about the task of finding and applying the common law with much the same perspective. Roscoe Pound's broad but accurate generalisation captured the legal spirit of these times: '[T]he common law knows individuals only...And this compels a narrow and one-sided view' (Pound 1905).

In the course of the 19th century, the prison form came to dominate the criminal justice landscape in the United States and elsewhere. Although initially reflecting the core premise of materialist psychology that persons were shaped and influenced by their surroundings, it came increasingly to embody the staunchly individualist view that the causes of behaviour were internal. Albeit roughly and imprecisely, prison policy reflected a popular and increasingly professional consensus about the causes of crime, woven together with strands of religiously based free-will doctrine as well as, at times, seemingly inconsistent beliefs in biological determinism. Nonetheless, prison continued to be the place where putatively damaged persons were taken to have their defects addressed.

As the century progressed, 'prison science' drew increasingly from the loose set of ideas that were being formalised under the rubric of psychology and the science of human behaviour. Of course, the 'science' was metaphor at best. Although the prison advocates had scientific aspirations and pretensions, they relied for most of the century on primitive and unsupported theories and engaged in crude forms of prison treatment. Even in the case of esteemed penologists like Zebulon Brockway, ostensibly noble intentions and supposedly enlightened scientific techniques quickly degenerated into outright mistreatment when their prisoner-changing programmes failed to produce the expected results.[4]

There were at least four early 20th-century innovations – the juvenile court, indeterminate sentencing, the parole system and the use of probation officers – that were designed to make more extensive and explicit use of psychological information in criminal justice decision-making. They also represented examples of the way in which the science of behaviour and the psychological individualism it embodied were closely joined with an emerging technology of social control. One historian has noted that the crucial changes in the public mood and style of life that occurred in American society during the 1920s were reflected in what once again came to be known as 'the new psychology' of the times. This time it was a psychology that 'provided information about the instincts, drives, and wants of men' and, therefore, was thought to provide insights into 'new ways in which they might be controlled' (Burnham, 1968). Criminal justice reforms during this period reflected an awareness of the new psychology and the range of its potential applications.

Eventually, however, the early decades of the 20th century brought a new vision to bear, one that was seemingly more humane and empirically valid. The human sciences had matured into genuine professions with a host of techniques and approaches to treatment that could be evaluated and scientifically supported or discarded as appropriate. That did not mean that there was a harmonious melding of the prison form and the helping professions: far from it. But it did add to a growing sense that, to the extent prison systems genuinely committed to the idea of rehabilitation and invested in its logic, there was a body of scientific knowledge on which to draw.

Mental health and programme-oriented staff rarely, if ever, attained sufficient power to significantly transform the standard operating procedures of the penal institutions in which they worked. Yet the professional orientation of persons trained to see themselves as helpers or caregivers was incompatible with the norms of an institution premised on pain. At times this tension served to establish humane limits in prison environments where they had been lacking. Prison might still have been primarily about punishment but, to the extent prison advocates entertained the purpose of providing opportunities for positive change, there were now formal disciplines and trained personnel from organised professions that could provide them with some amount of assistance. It also meant that, as scientific ideas evolved and the logic of rehabilitation was extended to encompass new and broader perspectives on the causes of crime, prisons eventually would be pressed to modify and transform their approaches to treatment and their relationship to crime control policies.

However, for largely political reasons, these otherwise promising trends were abruptly reversed in the mid-1970s. Although I have addressed the nature and implications of this reversal in more detail elsewhere, see Haney and Zimbardo (1998) suffice it to say that prison policies were implemented that were based on politics rather than valid theory or empirical data. Among other things, the alleged failure of prison rehabilitation programmes was used to renew a 19th-century argument that criminality was an intractable trait and that the predisposition to offend was unyielding in the face of even the most powerful and well-designed correctional treatment. In essence, advocates of increasingly harsh prison policies contended that criminals were too innately bad to be changed for the better, no matter how potent the new circumstance or situation in which they were placed. Prisoners were portrayed as much worse and tougher than the penal institutions to which they were being sent. Politicians and policy-makers implied that since prisoners' bad characters were too resilient to be changed for the better in these settings, they could not be harmed by them either. That is, as the roots of criminal behaviour were increasingly portrayed as residing in the extraordinarily strong and unmodifiable character of prisoners, 'liberal' concerns over the potentially harmful effects of prison conditions came to be seen as exaggerated and misplaced.

This new model of intractable criminality was also used to imply that social and economic circumstances outside of prison were irrelevant to the control of crime. Criminal behaviour was once again seen as the exclusive product of internal rather than external causes. Thus, rather than wasting time on what were portrayed as futile and irrelevant attempts to transform criminogenic environments, what really mattered was to identify, contain, incapacitate and punish as many of these criminally disposed misfits as possible. The emphasis in the American criminal justice system shifted rapidly and decisively to do just that.

The next several decades brought a vigorous campaign of incarceration, pursued in the name of punishing and incapacitating wrongdoers, with a corresponding lack of concern over the environments from which they had come and the particular conditions of confinement to which they were being sent. Even though, as always, the overwhelming majority of prisoners eventually would be released from these harsh places, little or no thought was given to the potentially harmful consequences of long-term incarceration within them. However, these broad punitive policies – and the unquestioned enthusiasm with which they were supported over the remaining decades of the 20th century – came about in spite of what was being learned in psychology and related disciplines about the origins of criminality and the long-term effects of incarceration. I will examine some of these issues in greater detail in the following section.

The contextual revolution in psychology

The pervasive individualism that has characterised prison policy over much of the previous two centuries and which, over the last three decades, turned especially pessimistic and harshly punitive is now markedly at odds with contemporary psychological theory (see Haney 1982; 2002). At the outset of the era of over-incarceration, Albert Bandura noted that prevailing individualistic theories of moral action typically assume an internalisation of behavioural standards that, in turn, create a permanent control mechanism within the person that governs future behaviour. This internal mechanism is assumed to operate as an enduring control that restrains reprehensible or illegal conduct irrespective of context. But Bandura also observed, '[t]he testimony of human behaviour … contradicts this view' (Bandura 1974: 7). Even earlier (specifically, see the editors' introductory chapter of this volume), Stanley Milgram (1965) provided classic demonstrations of the power of social settings to elicit extreme behaviour, concluding that '[u]nder certain circumstances, it is not so much the kind of person a man is as it is the kind of situation in which he is placed that determines his actions'.

Indeed, the entire intellectual framework in which psychological individualism once flourished has shifted radically. A dramatically increased and continuing recognition of the importance of the situational and contextual determinants of behaviour has emerged throughout many different areas of contemporary psychology and, as I will show in the final section of this chapter, it has enormous implications for crime control and prison policy.

Thus, many basic operating assumptions have changed within the discipline of psychology. For example, 'explaining the behaviour of particular individuals' is now understood to require 'not only psychological theory but also situational, biographical, and historical information' (Manicas and Secord 1983). More recently, social psychologists Lee Ross and Richard Nisbett (1991) have written that 'what has been demonstrated through a host of celebrated laboratory and field studies is that manipulations of the immediate social situation can overwhelm in importance the type of individual differences in personal traits or dispositions that people normally think of as being determinative of social behaviour'.

In fact, virtually every area of empirical psychology now recognises the importance of social context and situation in making sense of the phenomena once studied in sterile laboratory settings. The shape of contemporary cognitive psychology has been changed by prominent researchers like Ulric Neisser who now emphasise the importance of examining human memory in everyday situations and 'natural contexts', and one of them has even been led to declare that 'context is everything' in the study of memory and cognition (Engel 1999; see also Neisser and Hyman 1999).

The important influence of social context on cognitive processes is recognised by numerous researchers in other areas of psychology who study a wide range of related topics. For example, psychologists who specialise in cognitive development increasingly emphasise the importance of social and cultural context in setting the broad but crucial parameters within which children learn to think and develop intellectually (see Rogoff 1990). Psycholinguist Raymond Gibbs has argued that our use of metaphors to structure concepts is strongly shaped by how we 'culturally conceptualise situations' and 'by our interactions with social/cultural artefacts around us'. He observed that 'the cognitive models we create surely extend beyond the individual' (Gibbs 1999).

Similarly, a recent collaboration between distinguished law professor Anthony Amsterdam and revered cognitive psychologist Jerome Bruner examined the categorising, narrative and rhetorical practices of law and lawyers. Underscoring a fundamental social contextualist point, the authors chose to begin by noting that 'everything that human beings do … is in some sense specialized, reflecting the particular roles people are playing, the specific aims they are pursuing, the context-dependent position they occupy in their society. In that sense, one can give no general account of human pursuits' (Amsterdam and Bruner 2000). And they ended their analysis by observing that '[t]here always remains the wild card of *all* interpretation – the consideration of *context*, that ineradicable element in meaning-making'.

Even in personality psychology – for obvious reasons, likely to be one of the last bastions of psychological individualism – Walter Mischel's thoughtful and balanced summary of the current state of the field

(Mischel, 1990) conceded that 'context sensitivity and discriminativeness across situations' are 'the rule rather than the exception for most social behaviour'. In fact, Mischel is as clear about this now as he was more than a generation ago: '[O]ne of the core conclusions that needs to be drawn from 50 years of research is that the situation of the moment plays an enormously powerful role in the often automatic activation and regulation of complex human social behaviour' (Mischel 1997).

The attention now devoted by psychologists to the study of the life course reflects awareness of what one researcher has termed 'the reality imperatives – situational demands, opportunities, and barriers' that shape our lives (Moen, 1995). Few contemporary psychologists would disagree that human behaviour must be examined in context because '[i]ndividuals are embedded in a changing social, cultural, and economic environment, as well as being products of a life history of events, beliefs, relationships, and behaviour'. In addition, the work done in a branch of psychology known as 'developmental contextualism' has greatly increased our understanding of the importance of social context in shaping the individual life course: '[A] given organismic attribute only has meaning for psychological development by virtue of … its relation to a particular set of time-bound, contextual conditions' (Lerner and Kauffman 1985; see also Bronfenbrenner 1979, 1989; Lerner 1984; Lerner and Lerner 1989).

In ways that have direct application to a wide range of law-related behaviours, '[r]esearch exploring the effects of living in certain neighbourhoods on individuals, families, peer groups, and other social networks has mushroomed in the last several years. Scholars are increasingly recognizing that neighbourhoods matter' (Elliot *et al* 1996; see also Leventhal and Brooks-Gunn 2000). Indeed, there is now widespread recognition of the fact that what one scholar has termed the 'contexts of maltreatment' have profound and long-lasting effects over the life course of persons exposed to them (Belsky 1993; see also Briere 1992; Dutton and Hart 1992; Masten and Garmezy 1985), and beyond (Doumas *et al* 1994). In fact, the emerging field of 'developmental criminology' has relied upon this and other contextual and social historical insights to analyse the origins of criminal behaviour (see particularly Loeber 1996; also Rowe and Farrington 1997), make recommendations about fairer and more just sentencing practices in death penalty cases (for example, Haney 1995, 1997a, b), and suggest more effective policies to address crime control (as outlined by Welsh and Farrington 1998).

Indeed, situational structure is now recognised as exerting a powerful influence over behaviour in a wide range of social settings

(Baumeister and Tice 1985; Furnham and Argyle 1981; Magnusson 1981). Psychologists have also demonstrated that the cognitive representations of the settings in which people act exercise an important effect on the consistency of their actions (see for example, Krahe, 1986). Contemporary psychological research has provided convincing empirical support for the powerful influence of situational characteristics on various forms of psychopathology, including depression (Hammen 1990), and on behaviour as diverse as altruism (Darley and Batson, 1973; Holahan 1977), coping (McCrae 1992), cheating (Leming 1978), and even a police officer's decision to take someone into custody (Worden 1989).

We also know that variations in the immediate nature of social settings and contexts play an extremely important and direct causal role in the incidence of criminality, aggression and violence, homicide, and even torture that occurs within them. As Anthony Mawson states: '[T]ransient criminality is largely the result of stressful events combined with the simultaneous absence or destruction of social bonds. The suggestion is that transient criminality is due more to environmental influences than enduring characteristics of the person' (Mawson 1987). Similarly, situational analyses of misconduct and violent behaviour in prisons themselves underscore the importance of social context in influencing behaviour in institutional settings (Bottoms et al 1995; Deroches 1983; Pfefferbaum and Dishotsky 1981; Steinke 1991).

Thus, there is widespread recognition of the causal role of both past and present situations and social contexts in shaping present behaviour, including criminal behaviour (Bandura 1978; Veroff 1983; Mischel 1979). Although most contemporary social scientific analyses of social behaviour are 'interactional' in nature and take personal characteristics explicitly into account (Duke 1987; Ekehammar 1974; Georgoudi and Rosnow 1985), it is also undeniably true that situation, context and social structure have attained an empirical and theoretical significance that they did not have several decades ago. The problems of crime and violence – formerly viewed in almost exclusively individualistic terms – are now understood through multi-level analyses that grant equal if not primary significance to situational, community and structural variables (see for example Hepburn 1973; McEwan and Knowles 1984; Sampson and Lauritsen 1994; Toch 1985; Wenk and Emrich 1972; Wright 1991). Prison behaviour, including the way we understand the effects of incarceration, must be understood through the lens of this new contextual framework.

The implications of the contextual revolution for limiting prison pain

Modern psychological theory, in the form of the now indisputable proposition that 'context matters', thus contains several powerful lessons for contemporary criminal justice and penal policy, virtually all of which have been overlooked, ignored or disregarded in the recent trends toward ever-increasing rates of imprisonment and the delivery of heightened levels of prison pain. In summary form, they include the following:

1 Exclusively individual-centred approaches to crime control (like imprisonment) are self-limiting and doomed to fail unless they simultaneously address criminogenic situational and contextual factors. This fact argues in favour of redirecting crime-fighting resources and strategies away from nearly exclusive reliance on prisons and into ones that emphasise preventative programmes and interventions that are designed to reduce the structural causes of crime.

2 Prison environments are themselves powerful and potentially damaging situations, whose negative psychological effects must be taken seriously, carefully evaluated, purposefully regulated and controlled and, when appropriate, changed or eliminated. This fact argues in favour of creating and enforcing more realistic and effective legal limits to the nature and amount of prison pain that is dispensed inside these institutions.

3 The long-term effects of exposure to powerful and destructive situations, contexts and structures means that prisons themselves can act as criminogenic agents – in both their primary effects on prisoners and secondary effects on the lives of persons connected to them. Thus, high rates of imprisonment paradoxically may serve to increase the amount of crime that occurs within a society. This fact argues in favour of not only relying on incarceration more sparingly than we presently do but also taking direct and forceful steps to limit or reduce its criminogenic effects on the people and communities it touches most.

4 Programmes of prisoner change cannot ignore the situations and social conditions that prevail after prisoners are released if they are to have any real chance of sustaining whatever positive growth or gains were achieved during their imprisonment. This fact argues in favour

of viewing crime control as a continuum of programmes that address the structural and contextual causes of crime in community settings before and after imprisonment, as well as institutional conditions and prison treatment during the period someone is incarcerated.

All of these implications derive from a critical but more realistic context-based perspective on the nature and effects of imprisonment. Similarly, the logic of these theoretically driven insights pushes us clearly and inevitably in the direction of developing and implementing more psychologically informed limits to the amount of prison pain that we are willing to inflict in the name of social control. I say this in full recognition of the fact that the powerful forces that pushed so hard and so effectively in the opposite direction over the last quarter of the 20th century and that brought us to our current level of incarceration have not abated. And I say it despite the unfortunate fact that the traditional mechanisms once employed to limit prison pain have become less useful and engaged in the struggle to bring reason back into the debate over how much imprisonment is too much. As Nils Christie put it, we are squarely within an era of 'democratic crime control by the voting majority. To this there are no natural limits, as long as the actions do not hurt that majority' (Christie 1993).

But here is precisely where the lessons of modern psychological theory must be interposed in the debate. Because exclusively punitive models of crime control are out of synch with what we know about the social-historical and social-contextual roots of criminal behaviour, they are likely to do as little for the long-term reduction of crime rates as for the promotion of a broad and enduring framework of social justice. Moreover, as I have suggested, these popular but painful strategies are ill advised and hurtful to the point of being debilitating, destructive and even criminogenic.

Let me elaborate on some of the things that would have to change if these psychological insights about the importance of social context were taken seriously in our criminal justice and prison systems.

Current doctrines of legal responsibility, crime control strategies and prison policies still depend heavily on individualist assumptions about human nature. In perhaps no other areas of law do these individualistic assumptions continue to operate with more persistent force and effect. As Clarke aptly summarised it: 'The essential background assumption of responsibility is that of the autonomous individual whose decisions are not to be explained by reference to anything other than [himself]' (Clarke 1975). Obviously, fully embracing contemporary psychological theory and recognising the importance of context and situation would have potentially profound consequences for the way we attribute legal culpability, approach the task of crime control and view the importance of prison and prison conditions in the lives of incarcerated persons.

As I noted in the preceding section, we know that criminogenic social contexts substantially increase the likelihood that persons exposed to them will engage in crime, and that these contexts include a variety of forces and factors that individual offenders have little or no control over, including structural inequalities (Cole 1996) and racial discrimination (Harris 1997), as well as a range of developmental 'risk factors' that are related to serious violent crime (as explored earlier in Haney 1995, 1997a, b). By demonstrating the various ways in which criminal behaviour arises from a psychologically potent combination of traumatic social histories and criminogenic present circumstances, modern psychological research and theory cast doubt not only on the way existing methods of allocating legal blame are structured but also on approaches to crime prevention and assessments of the severity and ultimate fairness of legal sanctions.

A psychologically informed model of criminal justice would require revised standards of culpability that accounted for the power of certain contexts and situations to strongly influence and even control behaviour. Legal decision-makers would need to reflect on whether and when justice was being served by holding persons fully responsible whose primary distinguishing characteristic was their presence in a crime-producing or criminogenic situation. Indeed, legal decision-makers who understood how much context mattered would concentrate less exclusively on defective properties of the person and more on situational pathologies. That is, a modern, psychologically informed criminal law would more carefully weigh the effects of environmental stressors that may have significantly altered a defendant's psychological state and it would take into explicit account those situational pressures that may have undermined or precluded the 'mature reflection' that, in the past, has been presumed to precede action. In appropriate cases, these inquiries could lead to: reductions in the amount of moral turpitude attached to defendants' criminal acts, modifications in the nature and amount of punishment meted out, and greater attention being given to the environmental or contextual causes of crime. Referring to Stanton Samenow's (1984) book, we would become far less preoccupied with looking 'inside the criminal mind' and much more interested in being taken into criminogenic situations and contexts in order to change them.

This aspect of recognising how much context matters is similar to the approach advocated by Angela Harris in a provocative 1997 article, where she suggested that many traditional criminal justice questions could be recast in 'environmental justice' terms:

> The traditional conservative perspective on crime sees it as a moral problem: crime results when individuals turn to evil instead of good, either because they have evil in their hearts or because they have been brought up without proper moral training. An environmental justice approach to crime, in contrast, would see it as inextricably intertwined with larger social and economic issues.
>
> (1997: 23)

She also saw this as a way to increase pressures to reform the larger context in which crime occurs: 'An environmental justice perspective on criminal justice suggests greater attention to the social and economic practices within which crime is committed, and less emphasis on exposing prejudice within the existing justice system: transformation, not accommodation' (1997: 28).

Similarly, de-contextualised and de-contextualising diagnostic labels like 'antisocial' and 'psychopathic personality' would be dislodged from their current prominence in forensic settings. The atheoretical shortcomings of these kinds of diagnostic labels force us to describe the behaviour of individuals in truly asocial and, therefore, alienating and stigmatising ways, 'but does not enable us to understand them', as Hans Toch recognised. Thus, embracing the notion that context matters means that clinicians would be encouraged to view behaviour in the larger context in which it occurs, with reference to 'studies of such subjects as social learning, psychological maturation, levels of cognitive and moral development, the sociology of delinquent subcultures, the psychoanalytic literature on the formation of egos and superegos, and the criminological literature on violent delinquency' (Toch 1998).

Because the prison is a concrete-and-steel embodiment of the individualistic belief that the social problem of crime is to be solved primarily through the identification and punishment of the persons who have engaged in it, the modern contextual model of behaviour represents a persuasive argument for crime control policies that are far less dependent on prison as a solution to the crime problem. From this perspective, criminal behaviour can only be significantly reduced when the contextual, situational and structural forces that produce it are addressed more directly. Rather than continuing the harsh policies of the past several decades, especially the over-reliance on imprisonment, modern psychological theory, represents a statement in favour of preventive approaches to crime control, ones that target criminogenic risk factors in the developmental histories and immediate social contexts of persons convicted of criminal offences and also of ex-convicts attempting to make the transition from prison to home (for example Travis and Waul 2003).

Recognising the degree to which context matters means that social structural and situational factors would be seen not only as significant causal elements to be taken explicitly into account in legal decisions about criminal responsibility and as primary targets in any effective programme of crime control, but also in assessments of the effects of institutional conditions themselves. That is, violence, disruptive behaviour and disciplinary infractions inside prisons and jails would be more routinely understood in social contextual terms. We would recognise, as James Gibbs put it, that:

> [T]here has been an overemphasis on person-centred approaches for explaining and dealing with the problem of psychological problems among jail inmates. Person-centred thinking creates a conceptual bind that limits options for dealing with psychologically disturbed jail inmates. Different frameworks or models must be applied to the situation to develop new solutions.
>
> (Gibbs 1991)

More generally, problematic prisoner behaviour would be more commonly seen as the product of variously problematic institutional conditions that promote it (Bottoms *et al* 1995; see also Steinke 1991). This would mean that the current correctional trend toward solitary and 'supermax' confinement (which reflects the explicitly individualistic view that prison disturbances are best addressed by not only segregating but socially isolating those individuals who are involved in them) would be reversed. Furthermore, incorporating a contextual view of behaviour into prison policy would lead us to more carefully weigh and thoughtfully consider the harmful long-term consequences of placing prisoners in debilitating conditions of confinement like these (Haney 2003; Haney and Lynch 1997).

Of course, prison policy premised on modern psychological theory that emphasised the importance of context in shaping and influencing behaviour would acknowledge that no programme of prison 'rehabilitation' is likely to be effective if little or nothing is done to change criminogenic contexts in the future life of the prisoner.

Thus, we would begin to recognise more explicitly the futility of returning offenders to precisely the communities from which they came, and the short-sightedness of moving them directly from the confines of prison back into the free world without having been given transitional experiences and other resources with which to buffer them from the criminogenic forces they almost inevitably will encounter.

The insight that changes in behaviour can only be stabilised and sustained through changes in the context in which they occur would be introduced into a panoply of parole, post-prison and community-based crime control policies as well. Indeed, McElhaney and Effley (1999) have shown the recent trend towards community-based violence reduction programmes is based implicitly on the new-found understanding that exclusively individual models of the causes of criminal behaviour are not up to the task of effectively reducing it. These and similar programmes would be increased in number and complexity.

Community risk factors – the social context of crime – have already become the focus of crime reduction efforts in some places. Modern psychological theory argues in favour of intensifying and expanding these efforts. A broad range of social conditions, including families, peers, schools, as well as the larger community, would be increasingly targeted in meaningful violence-prevention efforts (Becker and Rickel 1998; Seydlitz and Jenkins 1998). Formerly narrow and *post-hoc* approaches to crime control that have relied so exclusively on the imprisonment of individuals would be increasingly supplanted by future-oriented programmes of 'integrated developmental and situational crime prevention' (Welsh and Farrington 1998).

Similarly, in looking closer at Borduin *et al* (1995), we see that the use of so-called 'multi-systemic' therapies could be implemented to acknowledge and address the causes of antisocial behaviour that often reside in the offender's 'natural ecology', and thus include them as an important part of the context of therapeutic change. Because these newly emerging public health approaches to violence prevention acknowledge that 'the "social disease" entities responsible for violence are multiple' and that 'certain "social circumstances" appear to be fertile breeding conditions for violence', the multi-systemic therapies they bring to bear 'are individually tailored to ameliorate those factors within and across the various systems or subsystems (i.e., family, peers, school, community) contributing to antisocial behaviour' (Henggeler *et al* 1996: 49–50).

Of course, this new model of behaviour has implications for prison reform. Historians have acknowledged the way in which the tendency to focus on individual shortcomings rather than grapple with the implications of failed legal policy or structural impediments to justice have limited, delayed and sometimes prevented meaningful reform. Prisons have been no exception. Using Rothman (1980) for an example, as evidence began to mount in the late 19th century that prisons were failing to achieve the lavish claims of reformation that had been made on their behalf, reformers were prone to conclude that 'incompetence and abuse were not the inevitable result of institutionalisation, but the fault of one particular warden or guard; failure reflected individual inadequacy, not a flaw in the concept of the penitentiary ... [T]he problem rested with one or another administrator.'

However, reforming prisons in a system that recognised how much context matters would concentrate upon structural and situational rather than personal (or, personnel) change. It certainly would recognise that under certain conditions, even 'good' people do 'bad' things (Bersoff 1999), and that biased, abusive, capricious and even unethical behaviour cannot be purged from law-related contexts, processes or proceedings merely by attempts to refine the 'purity' of persons who occupy key legal and judicial roles. Even the most elaborate screening and training procedures promise to effect little improvement if the relevant situations – the working environments of legal personnel – continue unaltered, with their most powerful negative influences unabated.

We now know that prison is itself a powerful social context that can have destructive, even criminogenic consequences on the persons confined there. In fact, one of the problematic legacies of our dependence on psychological individualism – the belief that persons matter much more than contexts – has been its tendency to deflect attention away from the destructive effects of imprisonment. This 19th-century view of behaviour allowed prison advocates to account for the failures of their early carceral regimes in terms of the intractable character of their captives rather than inhumane conditions of confinement. The devastating effects of prison life could be discounted or ignored because of a willingness to assume that the deteriorated state of the prisoners was a result of their pre-existing depraved or pathological natures.

However, as the importance of social context in influencing behaviour is acknowledged more fully, prison conditions and the pains of imprisonment must be taken more seriously and analysed more carefully. Among other things, this perspective sensitises us to the ways in which the setting of prison and the nature of prison life can shape prisoner behaviour. Adapting to the realities of prison life may change prisoners' habits of thinking and acting in ways that will persist long after their incarceration has ended. What we have learned about the psychological pains of imprisonment should guide the reform of those potentially harmful aspects of this context, especially those aspects that have criminogenic effects on those who pass through it.

A more modern, psychologically informed jurisprudence would also encourage much more active involvement of the legal system in ensuring the *implementation* of structural reform once it has been decreed. Thomas Pettigrew and I once wrote about the way legally mandated prison reform often loses momentum in the course of translating legal decisions into real-world institutional change (Haney and Pettigrew, 1984; see also Yackle, 1989). This pattern seems to stem in part from the tendency to underestimate the power of contexts in general and institutional contexts in particular. The notion that widespread behaviour change will result from verbal directives alone – for example, that institutions will change merely because of abstract legal rulings that order them to – without an overarching set of systematic and specific changes in the immediate context of behaviour, is now seen as bad social engineering.

The restructuring of a powerful situation or social context, which virtually all legally ordered institutional change entails, requires sensitivity to what are basically social-psychological dynamics – how to modify a social setting so that behaviour changes accordingly. Acknowledging how much context matters would create an impetus to cultivate and teach such expertise among persons charged with the responsibility of implementing and monitoring prison reform orders. It would remind us that the implementation of any legally mandated institutional or structural reform may be the most challenging and important stage of law reform, and that this kind of change must utilise a contextualist framework to achieve broad-based and long-lasting behaviour change.

Conclusion

Prison is a supremely individualistic response to the social problem of crime. It is a clear reflection of a longstanding belief in our culture that crime should be addressed almost exclusively by identifying and incarcerating those responsible for committing it (Haney 1982). It was during the 19th century that the emerging discipline of psychology and the dominant paradigm of individualism on which it was based helped to shape a prevailing cultural ethos and political world view in which people were seen as the exclusive causal locus of behaviour. This perspective reached its pinnacle in the United States at virtually the same time that prisons proliferated throughout the country. Indeed, it was a time when what was then regarded as the highly developed 'American prison form' was being studied and emulated by nations throughout the world. But modern psychological theory now brings a new perspective to bear in understanding the causes of social behaviour, one that places our dependency on traditional forms of imprisonment in a fundamentally different light.

The reformulation in prison policy that would be brought about by the integration of modern psychological theory I have advocated here is badly needed. This is not just because, as some have observed, the current harsh and expensive policies we have been pursuing mortgage the future of our young against the astronomical social and economic costs of runaway incarceration – costs that threaten to bankrupt state governments, siphoning away monies intended for health care, education and other critically important social welfare programmes. Equally important, in my view, is the fact that the imprisonment binge that has consumed us over the last quarter-century flies in the face of what good data and theory teach us: it is doomed to fail because it is based on behavioural premises that are invalid. There is no compelling evidence that the spreading of prison pain is capable of accomplishing its alleged purpose – a sizeable reduction of crime that is commensurate with the resources we have invested in the policy of mass imprisonment. Thus, perhaps the most powerful argument against this recent overdependency on prison is that, in the long run, it simply will not and cannot work.

Indeed, viewed from the perspective of modern psychological theory, prison itself can be seen as a powerful and potentially debilitating social context, one that shapes behaviour now and in the future. It can, therefore, have long-term criminogenic effects on prisoners once they are released, increasing rather than decreasing the likelihood that they will engage in crime in the future. The psychological costs of placing vast numbers of people in harsh correctional institutions for such long periods of time are now entirely predictable; they raise profound moral and practical questions about the wisdom of the policies that many nations began to pursue over the last several decades.

The issue of whether psychologists owe their intellectual origins to the birth of the prison or not is debatable; the fact that psychological justifications have been offered throughout history for prison policies in general and for particular penal practices in specific is not. Moreover, despite this historical connection – having helped give birth to the prison form and contributed to its proliferation – the discipline at times has abdicated responsibility for the way psychological theories and perspectives have been used (and sometimes misused and distorted). Especially over the last quarter of a century, many psychologists have remained passive while penal systems and prison policies were used in a terribly inhumane, exceedingly expensive, and in the long run, I believe, very dangerous political tug-of-war over who can lock up the most people for the longest amount of time.

With apologies to the Free Will Baptists with whom I began this discussion, modern psychological theory now, finally, recognises the extent to which the roots of evil – at least as evil is thought to be manifested in criminal behaviour – are found in more than simply the morally blameworthy free choices of equally autonomous individuals. Instead, crime more often stems from exposure to traumatic social histories, immediate criminogenic circumstances, and even to confinement in the very institutions designed to reduce such behaviour. As social philosopher Martha Nussbaum reminds us, a compassionate society 'is one that takes the full measure of the harms that can befall citizens beyond their own doing', including 'the cost of social hierarchy and economic deprivation' (and, I would add, confinement in unduly harsh and sometimes brutalising prison environments). In this sense, 'compassion thus provides a motive to secure to all the basic support that will undergird and protect human dignity', in our communities as well as inside our prisons (Nussbaum, 2001). Acknowledging these facts helps us to appreciate the way in which extending compassion to wrongdoers – by easing the pains of imprisonment and responding to crime with policies that address its real causes – is not only a virtue but a form of wisdom as well.

Notes

1 A more elaborate discussion of some of those issues appears in my forthcoming book, *Reforming Punishment: Psychological Limits to the Pains of Imprisonment*, to be published later this year by the American Psychological Association.

2 I later learned that the Free Will Baptists are a very large denomination, comprising over 2,400 churches throughout the world. Among their Articles of Faith is the belief that '[t]he human will is free and self controlled...'. National Association of Free Will Baptists website: www.nafwb.org (accessed 15 July 2004).

3 The term 'prison industrial complex' was first coined in the 1980s to describe a phenomenon that has grown considerably since. Indeed, the cover story of the *Multinational Monitor* described the spreading of prison pain as one of

the 'new growth industries' in the modern multinational economy. See Eric Lotke (1996).

4 For a sobering account of the 'new penology' that was carried out at Brockway's Elmira Penitentiary, describing the 'extremely severe corporal punishment...administered to force conformity and maintain order', see Pisciotta (1983: 626). See also Rafter (1997).

References

Amsterdam, A. and Bruner, J. (2000) *Minding the Law*. Cambridge, MA: Harvard University Press.

Bandura, A. (1974) *Behavior Theory and the Models of Man*. Presidential Address given at the meeting of the American Psychological Association, New Orleans (August, 1974, p. 7).

Bandura, A. (1978) 'The self system in reciprocal determinism', *American Psychologist*, 33, 344–358.

Baumeister, R. and Tice, D. (1985) 'Toward a theory of situational structure', *Environment & Behavior*, 17, 147–192.

Becker, E. and Rickel, A. (1998) 'Incarcerated juvenile offenders: Integrating trauma-oriented treatment with state-of-the-art delinquency interventions', in T. Gullotta, G. Adams *et al* (eds) *Delinquent Violent Youth: Theory and Interventions*. Thousand Oaks, CA: Sage.

Beckett, K. (1997) *Making Crime Pay: Law and Order in Contemporary American Society*. New York: Oxford University Press.

Belsky, J. (1993) 'Etiology of child maltreatment: A developmental-ecological analysis', *Psychological Bulletin*, 114, 413–434.

Bersoff, D. (1999) 'Why good people sometimes do bad things: Motivated reasoning and unethical behavior', *Personality & Social Psychology Bulletin*, 25, 28–39.

Borduin, C., Mann, B., Cone, L. and Henggeler, S. (1995) 'Multisystemic treatment of serious juvenile offenders: Long-term prevention of criminality and violence', *Journal of Consulting & Clinical Psychology*, 63, 569–578.

Bottoms, A., Hay, W. and Sparks, R. (1995) 'Situational and social approaches to the prevention of disorder in long-term prisons', in T. Flanagan (ed.) *Long-term Imprisonment: Policy, Science, and Correctional Practice*. Thousand Oaks, CA: Sage Publications.

Briere, J. (1992) *Child Abuse Trauma: Theory and Treatment of the Lasting Effects*. Newbury Park, CA: Sage Publications.

Bronfenbrenner, U. (1979) *The Ecology of Human Development*. Cambridge, MA: Harvard University Press.

Bronfenbrenner, U. (1989) 'Ecological systems theory', in R. Vasta (ed.) *Annals of Child Development – Six Theories of Child Development: Revised Formulations and Current Issues*. Greenwich, CT: JAI Press.

Burnham, J. (1968) 'The new psychology: From narcissism to social control', in J. Braeman, R. Bremmer and D. Brody (eds) *Change and Continuity in Twentieth Century America: The 1920s*. Columbus, OH: Ohio State University Press.

Christie, N. (1993) *Crime Control as Industry: Towards Gulags, Western Style?* London: Routledge.

Clarke, M. (1975) 'The impact of social science on conceptions of responsibility', *British Journal of Law & Society*, 2, 32–44.

Cole, D. (1996) 'What's criminology got to do with It?', *Stanford Law Review*, 48, 1605–1624.

Darley, J. and Batson, D. (1973) 'From Jerusalem to Jericho: A study of situational and dispositional variables in helping behavior', *Journal of Personality and Social Psychology*, 27, 100–119.

Deroches, F. (1983) 'Anomie: Two theories of prison riots', *Canadian Journal of Criminology*, 25, 173–190.

Doumas, D., Margolin, G. and John, R. (1994) 'The intergenerational transmission of aggression across three generations', *Journal of Family Violence*, 9, 157–175.

Duke, M. (1987) 'The situational stream hypothesis: A unifying view of behavior with special emphasis on adaptive and maladaptive personality patterns', *Journal of Research in Personality*, 21, 239–263.

Dutton, D. and Hart, S. (1992) 'Evidence for long-term, specific effects of childhood abuse and neglect on criminal behavior in men', *International Journal of Offender Therapy & Comparative Criminology*, 36, 129–137.

Ekehammar, B. (1974) 'Interactionism in personality from a historical perspective', *Psychological Bulletin*, 81, 1026–1048.

Elliot, D., Wilson, W., Huizinga, D., Sampson, R. and Rankin, B. (1996) 'The effects of neighborhood disadvantage on adolescent development', *Journal of Research in Crime and Delinquency*, 33, 389–426.

Engel, S. (1999) *Context Is Everything: The Nature of Memory*. New York: Worth.

Foucault, M. (1977) *Discipline and Punishment: The Birth of the Prison*. New York: Vintage Books.

Franke, H. (1992) 'The rise and decline of solitary confinement: Socio-historical explanations of long-term penal changes', *British Journal of Criminology*, 32, 125–143.

Furnham, A. and Argyle, M. (eds) (1981) *The Psychology of Social Situations: Selected Readings*. Oxford: Pergamon.

Georgoudi, M. and Rosnow, R. (1985) 'Notes toward a contextualist understanding of social psychology', *Personality and Social Psychology Bulletin*, 5–22.

Gibbs, J. (1991) 'Environmental congruence and symptoms of psychopathology: A further exploration of the effects of exposure to the jail environment', *Criminal Justice and Behavior*, 18, 351–374.

Gibbs, R. (1999) 'Taking metaphor out of our heads and putting it into the cultural world', *Current Issues in Linguistic Theory*, 175, 145–166.

Hammen, C. (1990) 'Vulnerability to depression: Personal, situational and family aspects', in R.E. Ingram (ed.) *Contemporary Psychological Approaches to Depression: Theory, Research, and Treatment*. New York: Plenum Press.

Haney, C. (1982) 'Criminal justice and the nineteenth-century paradigm: The triumph of psychological individualism in the "Formative Era"', *Law and Human Behavior*, 6, 191.

Haney, C. (1995) 'The social context of capital murder: Social histories and the logic of capital mitigation', *Santa Clara Law Review*, 35, 547–609.

Haney, C. (1997a) 'Mitigation and the study of lives: The roots of violent criminality and the nature of capital justice', in J. Acker, R. Bohm and C. Lanier (eds) *America's Experiment with Capital Punishment: Reflections on the Past, Present, and Future of the Ultimate Penal Sanction*. Durham, NC: Carolina Academic Press.

Haney, C. (1997b) 'Psychological secrecy and the death penalty: Observations on "the mere extinguishment of life"', *Studies in Law, Politics, and Society*, 16, 3–69.

Haney, C. (2002) 'Making law modern: Toward a contextual model of justice', *Psychology, Public Policy, and Law*, 7, 3–63.

Haney, C. (2003) 'Mental health issues in long-term solitary and "supermax" confinement', *Crime & Delinquency*, 49, 124–156.

Haney, C. and Lynch, M. (1997) 'Regulating prisons of the future: A psychological analysis of supermax and solitary confinement', *New York University Review of Law and Social Change*, 23, 477–570.

Haney, C. and Pettigrew, T. (1984) 'Civil rights and institutional law: The role of social psychology in judicial implementation', *Journal of Community Psychology*, 14, 267–277.

Haney, C. and Zimbardo, P. (1998) 'The past and future of U.S. prison policy: Twenty-five years after the Stanford prison experiment', *American Psychologist*, 53, 709–727.

Harris, A. (1997) 'Criminal justice as environmental justice', *Journal of Gender, Race and Justice*, 1, 1–45.

Henggeler, S., Cunningham, P., Pickrel, S. and Schoenwald, S. (1996) 'Multisystemic therapy: An effective violence prevention approach for serious juvenile offenders', *Journal of Adolescence*, 19, 47–61.

Hepburn, J. (1973) 'Violent behavior in interpersonal relationships', *Sociological Quarterly*, 14, 419–429.

Holahan, C. (1977) 'Effects of urban size and heterogeneity on judged appropriateness of altruistic responses: Situational vs. subject variables', *Social Psychology Quarterly*, 40, 378–382.

Ignatieff, M.A. (1978) *Just Measure of Pain: The Penitentiary in the Industrial Revolution, 1750–1850*. New York: Pantheon.

Krahe, B. (1986) 'Similar perceptions, similar reactions: An idiographic approach to cross-situational coherence', *Journal of Research in Personality*, 20, 349–361.

Leming, J. (1978) 'Cheating behavior, situational influence and moral development', *Journal of Educational Research*, 71, 214–217.

Lerner, R. (1984) *On the Nature of Human Plasticity*. New York: Cambridge University Press.

Lerner, R. and Kauffman, M. (1985) 'The concept of development in contextualism', *Developmental Review*, 5, 309–333.

Lerner, R. and Lerner, J. (1989) 'Organismic and social contextual bases of development: The sample case of adolescence', in W. Damon (ed.) *Child Development Today and Tomorrow*. San Francisco: Jossey-Bass.

Leventhal, T. and Brooks-Gunn, J. (2000) 'The neighborhoods they live in: The effects of neighborhood residence on child and adolescent outcomes', *Psychological Bulletin*, 126, 309–337.

Locke, J. (1954) *Essays on the Law of Nature* (edited by W. von Leyden). Oxford: Clarendon Press.

Loeber, R. (1996) 'Developmental continuity, change, and pathways in male juvenile problem behaviors and delinquency', in J.D. Hawkins *et al* (eds) *Delinquency and Crime: Current Theories*. New York: Cambridge University Press.

Lotke, E. (1996) 'The prison industrial complex: The new growth industries', *Multinational Monitor*, November, p. 17.

McElhaney, S. and Effley, K. (1999) 'Community-based approaches to violence prevention', in T. Gullotta, S. McElhaney *et al* (eds) *Violence in Homes and Communities: Prevention, intervention, and treatment*. Thousand Oaks, CA: Sage.

McEwan, A.W. and Knowles, C. (1984) 'Delinquent personality types and the situational contexts of their crimes', *Personality & Individual Differences*, 5, 339–344.

McCrae, R. (1992) 'Situational determinants of coping', in B.N. Carpenter (ed.) *Personal Coping: Theory, Research, and Application*. Westport, CT: Praeger/Greenwood.

Magnusson, D. (ed.) (1981) *Toward a Psychology of Situations: An Interactional Perspective*. Hillsdale, NJ: Lawrence Erlbaum.

Manicas, P. and Secord, P. (1983) 'Implications for psychology of the new philosophy of science', *American Psychologist*, 91, 399–413.

Masten, A. and Garmezy, N. (1985) 'Risk, vulnerability and protective factors in developmental psychopathology', in F. Lahey and A. Kazdin (eds) *Advances in Clinical Child Psychology*. New York: Plenum.

Mawson, A. (1987) *Situational Criminality: A Model of Stress-Induced Crime*. New York: Praeger.

Milgram, S. (1965) 'Some conditions of obedience and disobedience to authority', *Human Relations*, 18, 57–76.

Mischel, W. (1979) 'On the interface of cognition and personality: Beyond the person-situation debate', *American Psychologist*, 34, 740–754.

Mischel, W. (1990) 'Personality dispositions revisited and revised: A view after three decades', in L. Pervin (ed.) *Handbook of Personality: Theory and Research*, New York: Guilford Press, p. 130.

Mischel, W. (1997) 'Was the cognitive revolution just a detour on the road to behaviorism? On the need to reconcile situational control and personal control', in R. Wyer (ed.) *The Automaticity of Everyday Life. Advances in Social Cognition*, Volume 10. Mahwah, NJ: Lawrence Erlbaum, p. 183.

Moen, P. (1995) 'Introduction', in P. Moen, G. Elder and K. Luscher (eds) *Examining Lives in Context: Perspectives on the Ecology of Human Development*. Washington, DC: American Psychological Association.

National Association of Free Will Baptists www.nafwb.org (accessed 15 July 2004).

Neisser, U. and Hyman, I. (eds) (1999) *Memory Observed: Remembering in Natural Contexts*, 2nd edn. New York: Worth.

Nussbaum, M. (2001) *Upheavals of Thought: The Intelligence of Emotions*. New York: Cambridge University Press.

Pfefferbaum, A. and Dishotsky, N. (1981) 'Racial intolerance in a correctional institution: An ecological view', *American Journal of Psychiatry*, 138, 1057–1062.

Pisciotta, A. (1983) 'Scientific reform: The new penology at Elmira, 1876–1900', *Crime & Delinquency*, 29, 613–630.

Pound, R. (1905) 'Do we need a philosophy of law?', *Columbia Law Review*, 5, 339–353.

Rafter, N. (1997) *Creating Born Criminals*. Urbana, IL: University of Illinois Press.

Rogoff, B. (1990) *Apprenticeship in Thinking: Cognitive Development in Social Context*. New York: Oxford University Press.

Ross, L. and Nisbett, R. (1991) *The Person and the Situation: Perspectives of Social Psychology*. New York: McGraw-Hill.

Rothman, D. (1980) *Conscience and Convenience: The Asylum and its Alternatives in Progressive America*. Boston: Little, Brown.

Rowe, D. and Farrington, D. (1997) 'The familial transmission of criminal convictions', *Criminology*, 35, 177–201.

Samenow, S. (1984) *Inside the Criminal Mind*. New York: Times Books.

Sampson, R. and Lauritsen, J. (1994) 'Violent victimization and offending: Individual-, situational-, and community-level risk factors', in A.J. Reiss Jr. and J.A. Roth (eds) *Understanding and Preventing Violence, Vol. 3: Social Influences*. Washington, DC: National Research Council. National Academy Press.

Seydlitz, R. and Jenkins, P. (1998) 'The influence of families, friends, schools, and community on delinquent behavior', in T. Gullotta, G. Adams *et al* (eds) *Delinquent Violent Youth: Theory and Interventions*. Thousand Oaks, CA: Sage.

Steinke, P. (1991) 'Using situational factors to predict types of prison violence', *Journal of Offender Rehabilitation*, 17, 119–132.

Toch, H. (1985) 'The catalytic situation in the violence equation', *Journal of Applied Social Psychology*, 15, 105–123.

Toch, H. (1998) 'Psychopathy or antisocial personality in forensic settings', in T. Millon, E. Simonsen, M. Birdet-Smith and R. Davis (eds) *Psychopathy: Antisocial, Criminal, and Violent Behavior*. New York: Guilford.

Travis, J. and Waul, M. (eds) (2003) *Prisoners Once Removed: The Impact of Incarceration and Reentry on Children, Families, and Communities*. Washington, DC: Urban Institute Press.

Veroff, J. (1983) 'Contextual determinants of personality', *Personality and Social Psychology Bulletin*, 9, 331–343.

Welsh, B. and Farrington, D. (1998) 'Assessing the effectiveness and economic benefits of an integrated developmental and situational crime prevention programme', *Psychology, Crime & Law*, 4, 281–308.

Wenk, E.A. and Emrich, R.L. (1972) 'Assaultive youth: An exploratory study of the assaultive experience and assaultive potential of California Youth Authority Wards', *Journal of Research in Crime & Delinquency*, 9, 171–196.

Worden, R. (1989) 'Situational and attitudinal explanations of police behavior: A theoretical reappraisal and empirical assessment', *Law & Society Review*, 23, 667–711.

Wright, K. (1991) 'The violent and victimized in the male prison', *Journal of Offender Rehabilitation*, 16, 1–25.

Yackle, L. (1989) *Reform and Regret: The Story of Federal Judicial Involvement in the Alabama Prison System*. New York: Oxford University Press.

Chapter 4

Harm and the contemporary prison

John Irwin and Barbara Owen

Both during incarceration and upon release, the experience of imprisonment does considerable harm to prisoners in obvious and subtle ways. Continuing beyond the prison term, these ongoing harms create significant obstacles to successful community reintegration, extending the harm of imprisonment and, for most prisoners, diminishing life chances. Some of this harm is directly related to the intended 'pains' that are inherent in imprisonment. Much of the harm, however, stems from other features of imprisonment which do not overtly intend harm. We will examine some of the main sources of harm in the contemporary prison, based on our fieldwork in California prisons.

The official purposes of imprisonment do not include harming prisoners. However, as Todd Clear, a student of imprisonment, points out, imprisonment invariably does harm: 'Professionals in the field of corrections are loath to admit that they are bureaucrats whose jobs it is to implement judicially decreed harm' (Clear 1994). Robert Johnson, on the other hand, believes that the harm is unintended:

> There is much value in Clear's book, but it is, in my view, misleading to say that we as a society seek to harm or damage offenders when we punish them. Pain and suffering need not produce damage and, indeed, can be a source of moral education ... Moreover, the general thrust of modern prison practice is to minimize pain and suffering and in my view, to avoid inflicting damage on offenders. Pain has become, in other words, a necessary evil we aim to minimize, not a policy of choice.
>
> (Johnson 2002)

Articulating the dimensions of harm experienced by imprisoned women and men provides a foundation for understanding and eventually addressing damages created by the contemporary prison. While the immediate injury to incarcerated women and men has specific implications for daily life in the prison, we suggest that this harm creates long-term damage in constricting the life chances of released prisoners. This chapter discusses harms created by the existing medical care delivery; social processes that shape psychological processes; the conditions which fuel anger, frustration, and a sense of injustice; and the overall impact of imprisonment on prisoners over time. We conclude by arguing that these harms must be minimised in order to increase the released prisoners' ability to achieve economic and social viability, satisfaction and respect when returning to the free world.

Health and disease

For those prisoners with few health problems, the modern prison is a good place to maintain general health due to the consistent routine, adequate diet and absence or great restriction of many common deleterious activities such as drug and alcohol use and cigarette smoking. Many male prisoners exercise regularly; some of them follow a strict workout routine. This is less true for women, given the high-calorie diets and a less developed exercise ethic. But for those who do, the contemporary prison provides a structure for pursing healthier activities.

However, the prison is a terrible place in which to cope with a serious ailment. The main reason for this is that the prison system does not have adequate staff or resources to deal with major health problems such as heart disease, AIDS/HIV, hepatitis C, or tuberculosis (TB). Because so many prisoners have histories of risky health behaviour, including intravenous (IV) drug use, HIV/AIDS and hepatitis C infections are rampant in prison.[1] Within the prison, sexual practices – particularly among male prisoners – and tattooing spread HIV/AIDS and Hepatitis C, and crowded living promotes the spread of TB.

State governments are unwilling to allocate funds to combat these prison epidemics because the convicts with such medical conditions rank at the bottom of the state's priorities. Julia Lusky, in an article on prison plagues, including hepatitis B and C, HIV/AIDS, TB and sexually transmitted diseases, notes that:

[T]he high level of disease among prisoners when they enter the correctional system presents the authorities with two clear options:

intervene to treat those who are ill and to arrange for treatment to continue when the person leaves prison – or let the infections fester and spread.

(Lusky 2002)

The inadequate prison medical delivery system creates often insurmountable barriers to obtaining adequate medical treatment. Initially, prisoners with all levels of health problems must first get past a screening process to see a doctor. In California, prisoners must first see a medical technical assistant (MTA), a correctional officer with a small amount of special training in medical issues who acts as a screening agent. Most MTAs share the general prison staff's cynicism regarding prisoner motivations and honesty and automatically deflect most prisoners' requests for medical attention. As one male prisoner recently interviewed by Irwin put it: 'Man, you can't get by those motherfucking MTAs. They think everyone is trying to bullshit them and you have to be fallen down, half dead, before you can get by them.'[2]

Legal Services for Prisoners with Children (LSPC) describes in compelling detail the health problems of women prisoners in California.[3] They describe the minimal training of MTAs who are the gatekeepers of the system and suggest that MTAs demonstrate a custodial approach to medical care rather than a health-professional approach. Other common problems include cancellation of sick call, the $5.00 co-payment now required of all prisoners, and delays in receiving regular medication.

If prisoners with a serious medical problem succeed in obtaining an appointment with one of the prison's physicians, the chances that they will not receive adequate medical treatment are still great. A Pelican Bay (California) prisoner confided, 'I kept complaining about my hernia and the best they would do is give me a hernia belt that I never got'.[4] There are several reasons for this, all related to the fact that prisoners' health is a low priority in the state administration's list of concerns, and there is insufficient funding. Many prison physicians are not as highly trained, current in their medical knowledge, or as dedicated to their practice as physicians practising on the outside. Prison doctors are frequently older, retired military doctors who are neither highly motivated, highly trained nor current with medical advances. Moreover, these physicians are more likely to be general practitioners than specialists. If a specialist is required, access to one is limited.

In addition to issues of medical treatment quality, availability and costs, in the face of escalating problems in prison, i.e. HIV/AIDS, TB, and hepatitis B and C, the California Department of Corrections (CDC) has greatly restricted some treatments offered to prisoners. In 2001, they stopped treating many prisoners infected with hepatitis C with interferon and ribervarin because of the tremendous costs.

Imprisoned women have particular and perhaps more serious healthcare problems. LSPC argues that inadequate medical care is one of the most pressing problems facing women prisoners. They demonstrate that women in custody have an increased incidence of chronic health problems, including asthma, gynaecological disease, nutrition and convulsive seizure disorders, often a result of their exposure to violence. While men also suffer from irregular preventive care, women suffer in terms of their gendered diseases (see Bloom *et al* 2003). LSPC states that many reproductive cancers, such as breast and uterine cancers, go undiagnosed and untreated because there is no systematic plan in place to provide for regular pap smears and mammograms. They also document that women prisoners seeking medical assistance for tumours or chronic pain are likely to experience delays at every step in the process: access to a doctor, tests and follow-up care or surgery. In California – and elsewhere – there is little preventive healthcare education that would allow women to learn how to manage their own medical problems. Care is provided with an eye to reducing costs and is based upon the military model, which assumes a healthy male. LSPC concludes that medical care for women in California prisons is woefully inadequate. These problems and conditions occur across the nation.

It is probably true that many male and female prisoners with serious medical problems would not have received better medical care in the community. Most of them were poor and living chaotic lives on the outside, conditions related to medical neglect. However, in prison they have no other means to acquire medical help, so when they are denied treatment, they feel trapped and hopeless.

Psychological damage

Imprisonment can offer individuals a psychologically beneficial 'respite'. Irwin (1980) argued, in *Prisons in Turmoil*, that most prisoners:

> were caught in somewhat destructive social webs or were being swept along out of control, careening and ricocheting through the days. Imprisonment affords these persons a respite from their involvements, during which they can extricate themselves from destructive dynamics, sort through their values and beliefs, pull themselves together, and make new plans and preparations for

a new effort at life. The longer the respite lasts, the more likely it becomes that prisoners drift into special prison-nurtured belief systems and lose subtle skills required to function in the outside world.

In addition to the well-recognised consequences of imprisonment labelled 'prisonisation', long imprisonment assaults and disorganises the personality in other insidious and subtle ways, including loss of agency, assaults on the self and damage to sexual orientation.

Loss of agency

Agency is 'the capacity, condition or state of acting or exerting power'.[5] Prisoners steadily lose their capacity to exert power and control their destiny as they serve time in prison. Prison life is completely routinised and restricted, with few opportunities to make decisions or exert choice in their daily routine. As described by one lifer in a California prison, the prisoner's day is laid out for him or her:

	Weekday
6:00 a.m.	Breakfast
6:30–7:00 a.m.	Stand in front of education building, waiting for work
7:00–10:30 a.m.	Work
10:30–11:00 a.m.	Break-time on the yard
11:00–11:30 a.m.	Lunch in the cell
11:30–2:00 p.m.	More work
2:00–3:30 p.m.	Recreation (yard or dayroom)
3:30–6:30 p.m.	Lock-up
6:30–7:00 p.m.	Dinner
7:00–8:00 p.m.	Lock-up
8:00–8:45 p.m.	Night yard or dayroom
8:45–9:30 p.m.	Dayroom or lock-up
9:30 p.m.	Lock-up until breakfast
	Weekend
6:30–7:00 a.m.	Breakfast
7:00–8:30 a.m.	Lock-up
8:30–12:00 p.m.	Yard or dayroom
12:00–1:30 p.m.	Lock-up
1:30–3:30 p.m.	Yard or dayroom
Rest of day	Same as weekday

This type of routine is followed week after week, month after month, year after year, with occasional deviations. A prisoner may go to the library and wait his/her turn to use its limited facilities, go to sick call, or to an occasional visit. By and large, however, the lives of most prisoners follow repetitive and restricted courses that dull their senses and corrode their abilities:

> The innocuous taste of my world, devoid of any emotional nourishment, is gradually overpowering. Bleak and colorless walls, insipid disgusting meals, and phlegmatic, timeworn daily routines, staked upon overcrowding; unadulterated trivia by unwarranted and irrational guardian harassment all collaborate to numb my faculties. In tiny surreptitious doses, anaesthesia is dripped into my heart – a formerly complacent heart that is slowly beginning to resemble my dreadful surroundings.
>
> (Hairgrove 2000)

Prisoners are also trapped in a maze of rules which further erodes agency. Each prisoner is provided with a copy of 'Title 15', the manual containing the rules that govern all facets of institutional activities in California prisons which is 189 pages long. Many 'acceptable' practices are spelled out in fine detail. For example, the following describes required grooming style:

3062. Inmate Grooming Standards.

(a) An inmate's hair shall be clean, neatly styled, and groomed, as specified in these regulations, when he/she is away from the immediate area of his/her quarters.

(b) An inmate's hair shall have no lettering, numbering, or designs of any kind cut, shaved, dyed, painted or in any way placed in the hair or on the scalp of the inmate.

(c) An inmate shall not alter the appearance of his/her hair by changing its natural color.

(d) An inmate shall not possess a wig or hairpiece unless deemed medically necessary by the Chief Medical Officer and authorized, in writing, by the appropriate institutions Division's Regional Administrator.

(e) A male inmate's hair shall not be longer than three inches and shall not extend over the eyebrows or below the top of the shirt collar while standing upright. Hair shall be cut around the ears, and sideburns shall be neatly trimmed, and shall not extend below the mid-point of the ear. The width of the sideburns shall not exceed one and one-half inches and shall not include flared ends.

(f) A female inmate's hair may be any length but shall not extend over the eyebrows or below the bottom of the shirt collar while standing upright. If hair is long, it shall be worn up in a neat, plain style, which does not draw undue attention to the inmate.

(g) A female inmate may possess and use hair-holding devices (such as but not limited to, barrettes, pins, clips, and bands). If used, hair-holding devices shall be unadorned, transparent, or similar in color to the hair. Beads or similar ornaments are not authorized for use in the hair.

(h) An inmate's face shall be clean shaven at all times, except as follows:

(1) Mustaches are permitted for male inmates and shall not extend below the top of the upper lip, and shall extend to the corner of the mouth but not more than one-half inch beyond the corner of the mouth.

(2) An exemption from shaving shall only be authorized by the appropriate Institutions Division's Regional Administrator and only when an exemption is deemed medically necessary by a physician. Such exemption must not exceed ninety days. If the condition persists, another exemption request shall be submitted. Facial hair permitted by such an exemption, shall not exceed 1/4 inch in length.

(California Department of Corrections 2000)

Years of following repetitive, restricted routines and of being regulated by an extensive and somewhat rigidly enforced body of rules steadily erodes the skills prisoners will need to cope with life in the outside world with its relatively rapid pace, lack of structure and vast number of choices.

Assaults on the self

The ongoing human enterprise of maintaining the self as a functional entity requires a balance of social interaction and privacy. Prisoners, many of whom arrived at the prison with deeply damaged or dysfunctional psyches, could greatly benefit by regular contacts with sympathetic and 'wise' others for emotional sustenance and empathy and for assistance in understanding of their surroundings. Hans Toch (1977) lists this as one of the essential 'needs' of prisoners. In the contemporary prisons, they are regularly jammed together with other prisoners who are more threatening than supportive and more immature or ignorant than wise. Moreover, they are closely supervised by unsympathetic, even hostile, staff who are also mostly unwise. This is not the type of human interaction that helps individuals construct a more viable orientation for the future.

Prisoners – like all human beings – have a great need for privacy for reflection, a time during which to arrange and integrate the confusing multitude of feelings and ideas that steadily impinge on their consciousness. These must be sorted out if one is to have a sufficiently cohesive concept of self – a requirement for getting by in the world. Prisoners require privacy to plan reasonable, productive, and rewarding courses of action and projects, and to perform many personal functions.

In contrast, some forms of imprisonment afford too much privacy and not enough interaction with others, at least with helpful, insightful and sympathetic others. In other forms, such as in the dormitory sections of warehouse prisons, there is almost a total lack of privacy. In one male institution, more than half of the Level II prisoners are jammed together in dorms, dayrooms, and the yard, where they live 24 hours a day in a crowd with no privacy. Level III prisoners are housed in small double cells, which offer more privacy. However, for about fourteen hours every day, they are squeezed into an 8 by 12 foot area with their 'cellie,' whom they may or may not like or get along with, and in the presence of whom they must defecate, urinate, belch and masturbate. All in all, such a prison may be one of the worst places to keep or get one's self 'together'.

In prison, as well as the free world, women have a larger expectation of privacy than men. Perhaps relating to biological needs (such as sitting down to urinate) but more likely tied to social proscriptions about modesty and the need to hide from the male gaze, recent court decisions have held that women have a greater expectation of privacy in the prison (Bloom *et al* 2003). While older prisons may continue to use group showers or unprotected toilets, the modern prison for women typically has more private shower and toilet areas. 'Modesty panels', covering the 'average' woman from shoulder to knee, provide somewhat more privacy. Women can be afforded such shielding because, unlike men, security is less of a concern due to the lower level of inmate-on-inmate violence in women's prisons. The potential for violence among male prison populations precludes such privileges.

But, with these few exceptions, prison design works against expectations of privacy. In the contemporary prison, privacy is an ever decreasing, and greatly desired, resource. For women, more so than for men, the lack of physical and psychological privacy becomes one of the pains of imprisonment due to one central fact: women in prison rarely escape the male gaze. In most women's prisons, males make up the majority of correctional staff. While privacy is eroded by crowded conditions, shared housing units and the need for surveillance, the presence of male staff undermines one's ability to attend to personal hygiene and grooming without the scrutiny of men. Male staff supervise housing units, observing showers, toilets and areas where women dress.

Damage to sexual orientation

The involuntary celibacy of imprisonment is not only painful but has a more or less permanent impact on prisoners' psychological orientations. Gresham Sykes, in his seminal study of the prison, *The Society of Captives* (1958), lists this as one of the major pains of imprisonment. Robert Johnson identifies two problems of living in the prison mono-sexual milieu:

> One is the pressure toward homosexual satisfaction of one's sexual needs, which provokes anxiety in many prisoners. The other is the tendency for traditionally male personality traits such as toughness to become exaggerated in the absence of the moderating effect of persons of the opposite sex (women in men's prisons, men in women's prisons), thus distorting in psychologically painful ways the image of manliness (in the men's prison) and womanliness (in women's prison).
>
> (Johnson 2002)

Most (particularly male) prisoners are uncomfortable with or made anxious by prison homosexual patterns, not so much because they feel 'pressure toward homosexual satisfaction of one's sexual needs', but because they are regularly confronted with and disturbed by the complex and unique prison homosexual activities. In addition to the recognised prison homosexuals – the punks and queens – many heterosexually oriented prisoners, particularly those who have grown up in prisons (such as state-raised prisoners) or have spent many years in prison, engage in sex with other prisoners. As Edward Bunker put it in his novel *Animal Factory*, which is an insightful ethnography of prison life in the 1970s:

It was a jocular credo that after one year behind walls it was permissible to kiss a kid or a queen. After five years it was okay to jerk them off to 'get'em hot'. After ten years, 'making tortillas' or 'flip-flopping' was acceptable, and after twenty years anything was fine. So the banter said. It was not a true reflection of the ethos, which condemned anything that didn't ignore male physiology. It did, however, reflect a general cynicism about roles played in the privacy of a cell.

As Bunker hints, most male prisoners do not engage in homosexual behaviour, but they are nervous about it. Always present are prison sexual predators in search of new victims they can seduce or rape. Additionally, prisoners, in humour or intimidation, regularly impute homosexuality to others. The following exchange, a typical example of the 'dozens' carried on constantly by convicts in the Big House, demonstrates the style of homosexual imputation engaged in by most prisoners:

Two convicts approach a third, who is known by one of them. One introduces the third to his companion, 'Tony, this is Charlie', and he adds in an afterthought, 'He's my kid' (punk or prison homosexual). Charlie quickly retorts, 'I got your kid hanging, you punk'.

(Irwin 1980)

Consequently, all male prisoners are alert to the issue of homosexuality, about which there is constant tension. The result is that many prisoners experience considerable discomfort regarding their sexual identity and develop an inordinate distaste for homosexual practices and dislike of homosexuals.

Another lasting effect of involuntary celibacy is a distortion in prisoners' sexual tastes and desires. Irwin wrote about the impact of living in the mono-sexual prison world:

Being a convict was making voyeurs out of us. Pictures of women became powerful stimulants. One day I was walking down the tier and glanced down at a newspaper lying on the floor. I spied a picture of a women's face that grabbed my attention. I stopped, picked up the discarded newspaper and stared at the face. There was something about her, the smile, the eyes or something. She was overwhelmingly beautiful to me. But then the ache set in, deep in my gut. The possibility of being close, getting to know, romancing a woman like this was completely absent, not that my chances would have been that much greater if I was on the outside. But on the outside, there would be some small chance and this small chance would change the subjective experience considerably.

(Irwin, unpublished manuscript: 275)

Because of these prison-induced distortions – exaggerated 'machismo', homophobia, and distorted sexual preferences – released male prisoners have special problems adapting to outside social arrangements and relating to conventional members of the opposite sex.

'Homosexuality' is a less obvious problem for female prisoners. While there is some recent evidence that sexual coercion has been under-counted within women's prisons, most data agree that there is minimal physical and psychological danger among women prisoners in the mono-sexual environment (see Struckman-Johnson and Struckman-Johnson 2002). Staff sexual misconduct represents a much greater danger to women in this world.

Anger, frustration and the sense of injustice

Though rehabilitation has not been a stated purpose of imprisonment since the onslaught of penal conservatism, the public continues to express its desire that prisoners come back into the society prepared to live an 'honest' life and not to pose a threat to public safety. It has been well documented that current rehabilitation programmes are weak. Beyond not being educationally or vocationally prepared for life on the outside, prisoners are ill-prepared to achieve the goal of rehabilitation because the prison experience incites their anger, resentment and sense of injustice towards the conventional society. As Irwin argued in his earlier study of the career of *The Felon* (1970):

Adult criminals have felt some sense of injustice for various reasons for many years. This feeling stemmed, first, from their perception of the inequality in the social circumstances in which they were born, grew up, and competed as adults. Second, they perceived inequality and unfairness because of corruption and class bias in the way they were handled by law enforcement agencies and the courts.

In the 1970s, California prisoners' anger and sense of injustice was focused on the indeterminate sentence system. Today, this anger and sense of injustice is aroused because they are being forced to live by arbitrarily enforced, restrictive, and 'chicken-shit rules'; by pervasive degradation by staff; and by their economic exploitation.

'Chicken-shit rules'

In the contemporary prison, prisoners are governed by a vast and pervasive set of rules. These rules frustrate and anger prisoners because of the extensive and arbitrary manner in which they are enforced. It is difficult to know all the rules, much less comply with them. Beyond that, many of these rules intrude into prisoners' ordinary practices and significantly interfere with their attempts to carry on their already excessively reduced life routines. These rules are seen as 'chicken shit'. Dannie Martin, a prisoner in Federal Prison at Lompoc during its shift to a new, more regulated regimen, comments on the new rules:

> As the saying goes, it's the little things that make a house a home. To those who face the mind killing boredom of long prison sentences, small changes take on large significance in this our home-away-from-home.
>
> He [a new warden] also managed to curtail most of the small liberties enjoyed by the convict population. Before his arrival, we had been permitted to wear our own clothes. Now we were to wear strictly tucked-in and buttoned-up government issue. And our recreational opportunities and food went from bad to worse. No sooner did the warden close the yard than we lost our chairs, and that hurt. For as long as most of us can remember, we've had our own chairs in the TV rooms as well as in our cells. There's little enough in here for a man to call his own, and over the years these chairs have been modified and customized in an amazing degree – legs bent to suit the occupant, arm rests glued on, pads knitted for comfort. And the final personal touch is always the printing of a name on the back.
>
> (Martin 1989)

A lifer interviewed at a California prison revealed his anger at the succession of restrictive rules passed by the administration over the last few years: 'I don't know what it would take to get us to stand up to them. They took away our family visits. They took away our weights. They made is shave our beards and cut our hair. Next they'll tell us to bend over, so they can fuck us in the ass'.[6]

Many, perhaps most, prisoners find it impossible to obey all the new rules, and they put themselves in regular jeopardy of receiving 'beefs' (disciplinary actions). For example, if prisoners followed the rules governing smoking, they would not be able to smoke for ten to twelve hours at a stretch. Many rules also require subjective interpretation. For example, there is a rule prohibiting disrespect towards employees (as well as other prisoners). After the introduction of female guards into the prison, the problem of male prisoners making sexual gestures, comments and approaches to these guards arose. Some female guards are particularly sensitive to actions they interpret as sexual harassment. This led to an infraction the prisoners refer to as 'reckless eyeballing', which is a highly subjective interpretation of disrespect.

Women in prison commit fewer violent offences while incarcerated, but, ironically, women tend to receive disciplinary infractions at a greater rate than men. Researchers have found that women prisoners are cited more frequently and punished more severely than males. The infractions committed by women are overwhelmingly petty and the result of more stringent social control over their everyday lives in the prison (McClellan 1994). The patriarchal patterns of social control that propel women into the prison may also be responsible for the differential rule-enforcement patterns between male and female institutions.

More importantly, the rules are enforced with considerable in-consistency and arbitrariness. One of the best examples of this is the appeals procedure, which is elaborately spelt out in six pages of the CDC Operations Manual. The description of the procedure begins by stating that 'Any inmate or parolee under the department's jurisdiction may appeal any departmental decision, action, condition, or policy which they can demonstrate as having an adverse effect upon their welfare' (California Department of Corrections 2002: 530). The regulations go on to describe how appeals are to be submitted, the time limits for the prisoner to submit them and the administrators to rule on them, the grounds for rejection or denial of appeals, restrictions and punishments for 'abuse' of the appeal procedure, and, importantly, 'exceptions to the regular appeal process'.

The appeal process has the appearance of a legitimate, due process system. However, in reality, it fails to conform to basic standards of due process and renders arbitrary and biased decisions. The main reason for this is that the process remains internal. If an appeal is denied and the prisoner pursues it, it passes up the through the levels of the prison bureaucracy. An appeal must be reviewed informally by the staff involved directly in the issue. If the appeal is not resolved to the prisoner's satisfaction at this level, it is passed up to an 'appeals coordinator' at the institution. If resolution is not achieved there, the appeal is passed on to the 'institution head or their designee'. Lastly, it is reviewed by a 'designated representative of the director'. There is no eventual appeal to an outside, impartial decision-maker, such as an ombudsman, which many organisations, including prison systems, have employed.

Any appeal process that does not eventually shift to an impartial adjudicator is invariably subject to systematic abuse. The overseeing staff, bosses, administrators or chiefs who make the final decisions always have considerable incentive for ruling in favour of 'their side'. This is particularly true in the prison bureaucracy in which the appellants are convicts, individuals deemed less than trustworthy, and in which the decision-makers strongly believe there is a need to maintain solidarity in their ranks. A lifer, who has worked for years as a clerk handling the appeals paper work, commented on the processes:

I can't remember when a convict outright won an appeal. First of all, it takes months to get through the process. They just stall everyone. Then the most they ever get is to be found guilty but no punishment. That means the administration *knew* the convict was right but they wouldn't rule against the cops.[7]

In sum, to get by in prison, prisoners must skip around the complex obstacles of excessive rules enforced inconsistently and arbitrarily by 'cops', who more or less despise and distrust them. Over the years, coping in this way instils a sense of powerlessness as well as frustration and anger.

Degradation

Degradation ceremonies, which are part of the processes of arrest, incarceration, adjudication and eventual imprisonment of felons, have been thoroughly examined by students of criminal justice. The degradation begins the moment a prisoner enters the jail: 'Prisoners receive much more than the treatment required to introduce them to the jail and hold them there. They are impersonally and systematically degraded by every step in the criminal justice process, from arrest through detention to court appearance' (Irwin 1985). Other degradation ceremonies, such as regular strip searches and humiliating confrontations with staff, extend throughout a prisoner's sentence. However, the most persistent and insidious degradation is the hostility and contempt directed at them by police officers, deputies and other criminal justice functionaries.

Treating prisoners with contempt and hostility and persistently and systematically casting them as ill-worthy, harms prisoners in complicated and somewhat unexpected ways. Many are psychologically scarred. More reject their rejecters, turn away from conventional society and embrace an outsider, usually criminal, viewpoint. Pete Earley relates the following statements made by a state-raised 'habitual criminal':

> As the years go by and you get older, you realize more and more that your life is considered a failure by society's standards … You are a jailbird. You don't have any money, no house, no job, no status. In society's eyes you're a worthless piece of shit. Now, you can buy into what society says and decide you really are a piece of shit or you can say, 'Fuck society, I'll live by my own rules'. That's what I did. I decided to live by my own standards and rules. They aren't society's but they are mine and that's what I've done. In your society, I may not be anybody, but in here, I am.
>
> (Earley 1992)

For women, degradation occurs in gender-related ways. Clothing policies provide one small but significant example. Generally, clothes and styles of dress have more meaning for women than men. However, all California prisoners – female and male – wear a 'uniform of the day', generally blue denim pants, baseball-style caps, long-sleeved cotton t-shirts, and state-issued shoes. Few of these clothing items were specifically designed for women: women at most US prisons are issued shirts and shoes made for men. In California, women are also issued 'muu muus', recycled underwear and bras. Until recently, female prisoners in California were allowed to wear 'street clothes', usually sent by their families or others on the outside, during non-programming times. As the clothing and grooming rules for women become more in-line with those for men, these more expressive arrangements seem to be decreasing.

While these clothing and grooming standards do not, at first glance, appear to be an onerous aspect of imprisonment, these regulations are a subtle but corrosive aspect of the demeaning nature of the prison. Women are accused of not being 'feminine', but they are required to wear male clothing. Another charge against women prisoners is that they often do not act like responsible adults. The female state-issued clothing is anything but empowering. Although muu muus look like house dresses, women are required to wear them in public places. Walking around in a house dress does little to promote feelings of adulthood and, in our view, further serves to demean women. Another demeaning aspect of the muu muu as a garment is found at post-release. If a prisoner does not receive a 'going home package' with street clothes to wear at release or does not have personal clothing, the inmate (female and male) is required to purchase their 'state-issue' clothing. Women with few resources often choose to purchase the muu muu because it is the least expensive item. Wearing a muu muu home, appearing in a house dress in public, is a very discouraging experience. It has been reported that drug dealers hang out at the bus station, targeting these recently released women wearing muu muus as potential customers.

A small but significant indignity suffered by women relates to material needs created by menses. Some women have resources that allow them to purchase sanitary supplies in the prison canteen, or to have them sent from home in quarterly packages. Those without such resources must ask staff (who are frequently male) for these products, standing in line in the housing unit to make this request. In one instance, Owen observed male staff responding to such a request by saying, 'I just gave you a pad an hour ago. Why do you need another one?'

For both women and men, imprisonment can be an undignified environment. For women, however, much of this indignity occurs though assaults on their definitions of self, specifically as women. Imprisonment does little to raise one's sense of self-worth. Even among some of the most progressive prison managers, the habit of calling adult women 'girls' remains. While calling these women 'girls' conveys the patriarchal subtext of women's imprisonment, more demeaning names occur. While much rarer than the ubiquitous 'girl' reference, female prisoners report that staff refer to women as 'bitches' and 'whores'.

Economic exploitation

Many prisoners believe that the California prison system operates as a big business and the profit motive guides important decisions.

> It's all just business. I've watched it. Whenever there are a few empty beds around here, you wait. You'll see a bunch of guys getting violated. They got to keep the place full. They get paid by the convict. You watch it. They fill the place up by bringing guys back in, then they go to legislature and get more money to build a new prison.[8]

Though the prisoners' view of how the system works is somewhat distorted, it is based in reality. Prison systems are big businesses and many groups, such as guards' unions, architects, construction companies, prison hardware manufacturers and prison professionals, have an economic interest in expanding prison populations. Prisoners understand this and have developed a profoundly cynical view of the operation, which they see as corrupt and unjustly exploitative and oppressive.

There are some profit-making practices in the prison operation that directly affect prisoners and are seen as particularly corrupt and exploitative of them and their families. The most blatant of these is the telephone policy. In California prisons, pay telephones are located in all housing units and are readily available to prisoners. Prisoners may only make collect calls from these phones, which are installed and maintained by a private company, which charges an extra fee of $7 per call. This fee is paid by the person (usually a family member) receiving the call. The fee is split by the private company and the CDC. The CDC's share goes into the state's general fund. In the year 2000, California earned $36 million from this source.

Prisoners feel that this is gross exploitation of them, their friends and their families, who are usually poorer people and less able to pay this fee. Several prisoners told Irwin that they believe that the CDC unscrupulously delays their mail to encourage telephone use. At present, a letter may take as long 21 days to be delivered to a prisoner.

Moreover, prisoners must pay an added 10 per cent fee for every item they purchase through the canteen or any other source. This fee goes into the Inmate Welfare Fund along with any other money prisoners possess. The fund totalled $10,100,000 in 1998, at which time some California prisoners sued the state to receive the interest from this money. The state informed the courts that the money held in the Inmate Welfare Fund had not been deposited in interest-earning accounts. Litigation continues on this issue, and prisoners in other states have filed similar suits. Regardless of the outcome of these cases, California prisoners feel the state has cheated them or has earned money on their money. As the California prisoners' attorney, Herman Franck, views it, the state is stealing from the prisoners, and though each convict is losing only a few dollars, when you consider the vast number of prisoners, '150,000 small thefts becomes one big, fat theft' (Franck 1999). In addition to aggravating prisoners' sense of injustice, these practices corrode the administrators' claims of moral superiority and reduce prisoners' sense of moral inferiority and responsibility.

Other problems related to gender

Separation from children

Women prisoners react differently from men to the separation from children and significant others. Most research describes the importance of family, particularly children, in the lives of imprisoned women (Owen 1998). National surveys of women prisoners find that three-quarters were mothers, with two-thirds having children who were under the age of eighteen (Greenfield and Snell 1999). For mothers, separation from their children is the most painful aspect of incarceration. Bloom and Chesney-Lind (2000) stated that the distance between the prison and the children's homes, lack of transportation, and very limited economic resources compromise a woman prisoner's ability to maintain these relationships. Slightly over half of the women responding to Bloom and Steinhart's (1993) survey of imprisoned mothers reported never receiving visits from their children. Lord (1995), a prison warden in New York, has stated that while men in prison 'do their own time', women 'remain interwoven in the lives of significant others, primarily their children and their own mothers'. Connections to the free world can make it much harder to 'do time', particularly for those with a long time to serve. As one woman serving her third prison terms comments:

> You cannot do your time in here and out on the streets at the same time. That makes you do hard time. You just have to block that out of your mind. You can't think about what is going on out there and try to do your five, ten [years] or whatever in here. You will just drive yourself crazy.
>
> (Owen 1998)

Pregnant women

Although their numbers are small, the presence of pregnant women in the women's prison population reminds others of the separation from their children. For the majority who are mothers, the presence of a pregnant woman is a reminder of loss and reinforces their feelings of separation and guilt at leaving their children. Most women in this housing unit do not participate in prison programmes; instead, they are 'medically unassigned' and many do not earn the 'good time credits' that reduce time in prison. At delivery, women are taken to a community hospital under escort by the correctional staff. After the baby is born, the inmate stays in the hospital only one or two days. Some women make arrangements for a relative, usually a mother or sister, to pick up the baby. If there are no prior arrangements made, the county social service agency provides foster care for the child.

Physical and psychological safety

Compared with prisons for men, almost all women's prisons are physically safer. Physical violence between female prisoners is infrequent, with serious assaults involving weapons even more so. Verbal threats and loud arguments are more typical expressions of conflict. Physical fights do occur, but typically take place in the context of a personal relationship or, less often, as a result of a drug deal or other material conflict. Organised conflicts related to gangs and ethnic strife have not been reported in the research literature. Women prisoners strike or scratch each other, but usually do not inflict serious injury. Occasionally, women will resort to a 'lock in a sock' as an improvised weapon. The extremely rare stabbing may occur with a pair of scissors or a tool in a spontaneous fight. Riots and other collective disturbances are also atypical. Isolated reports of sexual assaults between female prisoners have been made but prison sexual assaults are many times more likely in a male facility. In 2003, the Congress passed the 'Prison Rape Elimination Act', designed to address the problem of prison sexual assault and few separate provisions for women are described. In fact, the concept of gender is largely absent in the legislation.

Women prisoners, like women in the free community, are at a much greater risk of violence and sexual assault from males. Multiple reports of staff sexual misconduct have been released from Human Rights Watch (1996), Amnesty International (1999), and other women's rights advocates, such as Smith (2001) and Moss (1999). In *All Too Familiar: Sexual Abuse of Women in U.S. Prisons*, Human Rights Watch examines this serious problem. In their review of sexual abuse in selected prisons, the Human Rights Watch investigators identified four specific issues: the inability to escape one's abuser; ineffectual or nonexistent investigative and grievance procedures; lack of employee accountability (either criminally or administratively); and little public concern. They bluntly state that 'Our findings indicate that being a woman in U.S. state prisons can be a terrifying experience'.

Prisonisation

Donald Clemmer, in his classic 1958 study, *The Prison Community*, recognised that prisoners take on, 'in greater or less degree', the 'folkways, mores, customs, and general culture of the penitentiary'. Prisonisation occurs on several levels. The first is the 'taken for granted' set of deeply embedded interpretations and responses that prisoners acquire through living in the unique, routinised prison world in spite of any conscious effort to avoid acquiring them. Months or years of getting up at a certain time to certain signals, going about the day in a routine fashion, responding to certain commands, being among people who speak a certain way, and doing things repetitively inures prisoners to a deeply embedded set of unconscious habits and automatic responses. An example of an unthinking act performed by a parolee in the first week after his release reveals the operation of this effect of prisonisation:

> I was coming out of a theatre and I came to this guy standing at the front entrance with a uniform. He was an usher or something. All the sudden I was standing there with my hands up above my head waiting for the guy to frisk me, like they do every time you pass through some gate in prison.[9]

The next level of prisonisation consists of the special values, beliefs and habits most prisoners carry or practise and impart to others. In previous eras, there tended to be a single, overreaching convict code. This code has fragmented and weakened considerably due to the growing heterogeneity and conflict among prisoners. However, there still is a pervasive set of prison attitudes, beliefs, mannerisms and speech habits that most prisoners acquire. These include attitudes toward authorities (represented by guards and other prison staff), stool-pigeons, sexual deviants, particularly child molesters, and other races. Regrettably, many persons who had no racial prejudices prior to incarceration acquire them in prison where they have to cope with the racial hostilities and threats of racial violence that prevail in the prison.

Prisonisation also includes acquiring a special vocabulary (with words like 'car', which are indigenous to the prison), a set of prison mannerisms, and grooming styles (prison tattooing being the most manifest example). These characteristics will obtrude into actions and relationships prisoners attempt to take or form on the outside.

Many prisoners become deeply involved in some of the prison criminal subcultures, such as those of various drug users, 'gangstas', or 'outlaws', and acquire a full-blown deviant identity. There is evidence that this may not be the case for women prisoners, most of whom begin their prison term with a less committed deviant identity. Finally, there is the identity of the 'old con':

The final level of the perspective of the convict is that of the 'old con'. This is a degree of identification reached after serving a great deal of time, so much time that all outside-based identities have dissipated and the only meaningful world is that of the prison. The old con has become totally immersed in the prison world.

The old con tends to carve out a narrow but orderly existence in the prison. He has learned to secure many luxuries and learned to be satisfied with the prison forms of pleasure – e.g., homosexual activities, cards, dominoes, handball, hobbies, and reading. He usually obtains jobs which afford him considerable privileges and leisure time.

(Irwin 1970)

With the growing number of lifers serving very long sentences, this level of prisonisation is becoming increasingly prevalent. At the extreme end of the spectrum are 'LWOPs'– prisoners serving life without the possibility of parole. Ernest Patrick, a lifer, wrote in Johnson and Toch's *Crime and Punishment: Inside Views* (2000):

The lifers who have no hope of pardon or parole to look forward to, have to face the hardship of doing time. If they have no hope for release, they must start to think of the alternatives to doing time, such as suicide or escape. Given these deadly choices, maybe they can find it in themselves to cope with the rest of their life in prison.

When Irwin asked a group of lifers how they did their time, one said, 'I'm not doing time, this is my life'.[10]

Conclusion

Many aspects of imprisonment hamper prisoners' preparation for life after prison. They are coerced into repetitive, excessively reduced routines and trapped in an ongoing state of extreme control formed by an extensive body of rules inconsistently, arbitrarily and prejudicially enforced by guards and other administrators. This situation is extremely frustrating and painful because prisoners view these overseers who exercise complete control over them as benign, disinterested overseers at best, or as arbitrary and insidious enforcers at worst. For prisoners serving short sentences, less than two years, this routine of imprisonment is relatively less deleterious than imprisonment in former times or in more punitive states than California. Some of these short-termers, particularly young state-raised convicts, gangbangers and thugs, are a volatile and disruptive force: they get into trouble, escalate their legal problems and their prison classification scores, and thereby worsen their imprisonment situation. Women in particular suffer from their tenuous ties to their children and their families. While most short-termers float through their sentences with little damage to their persons or impact on prison society, the numbers of those serving longer terms is increasing. In one California prison for men, 60 per cent of the population are serving sentences of more than five years and 27 per cent are serving more than fifteen years. For long-termers, the new situation of doing time, of enduring years of suspension, deprived material conditions, crowded living without privacy, reduced options, arbitrary control, disrespect and economic exploitation is excruciatingly frustrating and aggravating. Anger, frustration and a burning sense of injustice, coupled with the crippling processing inherent in imprisonment, significantly reduce the likelihood of prisoners pursuing a viable, relatively conventional, non-criminal life after release from prison.

Taken together, the harm of the contemporary prison creates human beings that are less equipped to deal with post-release realities. Each of the harms described here – existing medical care delivery; social processes that shape psychological processes; the conditions which fuel anger, frustration and a sense of injustice; and the overall impact of prisonisation on prisoners over time – reduces the released prisoners' ability to achieve economic and social viability, satisfaction and respect when returning to the free world. Decreasing recidivism and breaking the cycle of repeated incarcerations requires more humane prisoner management, and realistic preparation for release through acknowledging, and ultimately reducing, the harm of imprisonment.

Notes

1   The estimated HIV infection rate among prisoners runs from 30 to 60 per cent. According to Sasha Abramsky, author of 'The shame of prison health' (2002), experts estimate the rate of infection of these contagious diseases among prisoners to be ten times as great as in the population as a whole.
2   Interview, Solano Prison, spring 2000.
3   Accessed at http://www.prisonerswithchildren.org/ 18 January 2004.
4   Letter from prisoner in Pelican Bay, Oct. 1999.
5   *Webster's Third New International Dictionary* (Springfield, MA: G. and C. Merriam Co., 1971), p. 40.

6   Interview with prisoner, Solano, spring 2001.
7   Interview with prisoner, Solano, April 2001.
8   Interview with prisoner, Solano, March 2001.
9   Interview with parolee, San Francisco, 1967.
10   Solano, autumn 2001

References

Abramsky, S. (2002) 'The shame of prison health', *Nation Magazine*, 1 July.

Acoca, L. (1998) 'Defusing the time bomb: Understanding and meeting the growing health care needs of incarcerated women in America', *Crime & Delinquency*, 44 (1), 49–70.

Amnesty International USA. (1999) *Not Part of My Sentence: Violations of the Human Rights Watch in Custody*. New York: Amnesty International.

Babcock-Grove, P. (1971) *Webster's Third New International Dictionary*. Springfield, MA: G. & C. Merrriam Co.

Bloom, B. and Chesney-Lind, M. (2000) 'Women in prison: vengeful equity', in R. Muraskin (ed.) *It's a Crime: Women and Justice*. Upper Saddle River, NJ: Prentice-Hall.

Bloom, B., Owen, B. and Covington S. (2003) *Gender-Responsive Strategies: Research, Practice, and Guiding Principles for Women Offenders*. Washington, DC: National Institute of Corrections.

Bloom, B. and Steinhart, D. (1993) *Why Punish the Children? A Reappraisal of the Children of Incarcerated Parents*. San Francisco, CA: National Council on Crime and Delinquency.

Bunker, E. (1977) *Animal Factory*. New York: Viking Press.

California Department of Corrections (2000) *California Code of Regulations: Title 15; Crime Prevention and Corrections*. Sacramento, CA.

California Department of Corrections (2002) *Operations Manual*. State of California. Sacramento, CA.

Clear, T. (1994) *Harm in American Penology: Offenders, Victims, and their Communities*. Albany, NY: State University of New York Press.

Clemmer, D. (1958) *The Prison Community*. New York: Rinehart.

Earley, P. (1993) *The Hot House*. New York: Bantam Books.

Franck, H. (1999) 'Inmates go to court to earn interest on prison accounts', *The Wall Street Journal*, 17 November, California.

Greenfeld, L. and Snell, T. (1999) *Special Report: Women Offenders*. Washington, DC: US Department of Justice.

Hairgrove, D. (2000) 'A single unheard voice', in R. Johnson and H. Toch (eds) *Crime and Punishment: Inside Views*. Los Angeles: Roxbury Publishing Co.

Human Rights Watch Women's Rights Project (1996) *All Too Familiar: Sexual Abuse of Women in U.S. State Prisons*. New York: The Ford Foundation.

Irwin, J. (1970) *The Felon*. Englewood Cliffs, NJ: Prentice Hall.

Irwin, J. (1980) *Prisons in Turmoil*. Boston: Little Brown.

Irwin, J. (1985) *The Jail*. Berkeley, CA: University of California Press.

Irwin, J. (in progress) *Rogue*. Unpublished manuscript.

Johnson, R. (2002) *Hard Time*. Belmont, CA: Wadsworth.

Johnson, R. and Toch, H. (eds) (2000) *Crime and Punishment: Inside Views*. Los Angeles: Roxbury.

Legal Services for Prisoners with Children (Retrieved 18 January 2004). Accessed at http://prisonerswithchildren.org

Leonard, E. (2002) *Convicted Survivors: The Imprisonment of Battered Women who Kill*. Albany, NY: State University of New York Press.

Lord, E. (1995) 'A prison superintendent's perspective on women in prison', *Prison Journal*, 75 (2), 257–269.

Lusky, J. (2002, Summer/Fall) 'The plagues of prison', *New Letter of the Western Prison Project*, 8.

McClellan, D. (1994) 'Disparity in the discipline of male and female inmates in Texas prisons', *Women and Criminal Justice*, 5, 71–97.

Martin, D. (1989) 'The Gulag mentality', *San Francisco Chronicle*, 19 June, Sunday 'Punch' section, p. 5.

Moss, A. (1999) 'Sexual misconduct among staff and inmates', in P. Carlson and J. Garrett (eds) *Prison and Jail Administration: Practice and Theory*. New York: Aspen Publishers.

Owen, B. (1998) *In The Mix*. New York: State University of New York Press.

Patrick, E. (2000) Meaning of 'Life' in prison', in R. Johnson and H. Toch (eds) *Crime and Punishment: Inside Views*. Los Angeles: Roxbury Publishing.

Singer, M., Bussey, J., Song, L. and Lunghofer, L. (1995) 'The psychosocial issues of women serving time in jail, *Social Work*, 40 (1), 103–114.

Smith, B.V. (2001) 'Sexual abuse against women in prison', *Criminal Justice*, 16 (1), 30–38.

Struckman-Johnson, C. and Struckman-Johnson, D. (2002) 'Sexual coercion reported by women in three Midwestern prisons', *Journal of Sex Research*, 39 (3), 217–218.

Sykes, G. (1958) *Society of Captives*. Princeton, NJ: Princeton University Press.

Teplin, L., Abraham, K. and McClelland, G. (1996) 'Prevalence of psychiatric disorders among incarcerated women', *Archives of General Psychiatry*, 53, 505–512.

Toch, H. (1977) *Living in Prison: The Ecology of Survival*. New York: Free Press.

Chapter 5

The effects of supermax custody

Roy D. King

In a volume devoted to considering the effects of imprisonment it is important to examine what is known about the effects of the most extreme form of lawful confinement – the use of supermaximum custody, or 'supermax', as it has come to be called. For the purposes of this chapter, I shall try to consider four types of possible effect – albeit with diminishing degrees of certainty about the data at my disposal: the effects upon prisoners, the effects upon staff, the effects upon prison systems and the effects upon society. The data reported here were mainly collected under the auspices of two research projects funded by ESRC[1] and Leverhulme;[2] but I shall also draw upon experiences in the course of advising HM Prison Service on the feasibility of supermax, and the development of the system of Close Supervision Centres,[3] as well as investigations conducted in the United States at the request of Amnesty International.[4]

Throughout I shall use the definition of supermax I developed elsewhere (King 1999) based upon that used by Chase Riveland for the National Institute of Corrections survey of supermax facilities (NIC 1997). There are three essential elements:

- accommodation which is physically separate, or at least separable, from other units or facilities, in which
- a controlled environment emphasising safety and security, via separation from staff and other prisoners and restricted movement, is provided for
- prisoners who have been identified through an administrative rather than a disciplinary process as needing such control on grounds of

their violent or seriously disruptive behaviour in other high-security facilities.

It is important to bear in mind that the NIC definition specifically excluded units designed for the routine housing of prisoners for disciplinary segregation or protective custody, although some administrators have defended the use of supermax on grounds that it provides better conditions than old-style segregation units (Hershberger 1998), and it seems likely that the effects – on prisoners at least – of long-term housing in, or rotation through, segregation units might be similar. In England and Wales, there has long been concern about the regime in segregation units, and about the historical process of rotating prisoners through them in what officials described, euphemistically, as the Continuous Assessment Scheme, but known to staff and prisoners alike as the merry-go-round or the magic roundabout (King and McDermott 1990). Officials now argue that the English system of close supervision centres – which operate to a very different philosophy from American supermax but which deal essentially with the same target groups of prisoners – have done much to change the patterns of thinking in segregation units for the better[5] (though as yet there is no research to support this).

There are at least two other elements which might have been included in the definition and which may exacerbate or ameliorate the effects upon prisoners and upon staff. The first of these concerns prison design. The NIC did not embrace considerations of prison design, allowing for both retro-fitted accommodation provided within existing prisons and new design/build facilities. But design arguably matters both for staff, whose working environment this will be, and for prisoners for whom this may constitute 'home', 24/7, year after year. California's Pelican Bay, whose living units, known as 'pods', have bleak concrete walls adorned only by notices saying that there will be NO WARNING SHOTS, and H-Block at Oklahoma State Penitentiary, artificially covered in earth so that the only natural light has to filter from central skylights, and penetrate various barriers, before it can seep through the internal windows in cell doors, are clearly designed to give out a particularly negative message to prisoners, staff and the outside world, emphasising what is no longer possible. The message from Oak Park Heights in Minnesota, where every cell has a window to the outside, and overlooks territories to which prisoners have easy, albeit controlled, access is decidedly more positive – and intended to be so.

The second element concerns the regime. Most jurisdictions laying claim to supermax facilities stress the lock-down qualities of their regime, offering no or minimal programming opportunities for prisoners. Some, Oak Park Heights in Minnesota being by far the best example, stress the importance of programming, and have continued to offer substantial opportunities for prisoners even in the severe penological climate that has prevailed over the last fifteen years. Several states acknowledge the importance of programmes, if only in terms of providing 'step-down' facilities, recognising the potential difficulties of releasing prisoners from the most severely restricted environment direct to the community on the expiry of their sentences. There is, undoubtedly, a need to rank supermax facilities along a continuum which measures the availability and take-up of programming opportunities if we are to know anything more precisely about their effects. In the course of my research it was clear that the majority of programming opportunities, where they existed, were provided either individually but on a non-contact basis at cell fronts or else remotely through closed circuit television.

At this juncture it is important to draw attention to one crucial point which marks out Oak Park Heights as essentially different from the run-of-the-mill supermax facility in the United States. The NIC definition of supermax insists that prisoners are managed in a way whereby they are kept separate from staff and other prisoners. The majority of supermax facilities in the United States favour a scheme (to use the jargon) of remote podular supervision, whereby staff in a central security bubble have 180 or 270 degree visual surveillance over prisoner living unit pods[6] which are strictly separated from staff areas. Staff only enter the pods for the purpose of 'cell extractions' where prisoners are removed from their cells through the planned use of force,[7] or to escort prisoners to showers, visits or to use the telephone, or more generally when staff have overwhelming superiority of numbers. The operational philosophy of Oak Park Heights, by contrast, involved direct podular supervision which specifically required staff and prisoners to share communal spaces: for each living complex (a somewhat more human description than 'pod'), policy and procedure documents prescribed one member of staff in the security bubble (surveilling and with access to back-up) and two members of staff on the floor, i.e. mixing with the 50 prisoners or so in the complex. In the English Close Supervision Centres, separate areas for staff and prisoners have never been a serious consideration. If this element in the definition were crucial, neither Oak Park Heights (OPH) nor English Close Supervision Centres (CSCs) could be considered as supermax facilities. Yet Minnesota self-defined Oak Park Heights as a supermax facility in its response both to the NIC survey and to my research.[8] There can be no doubt that both OPH and the English CSCs represent their respective jurisdictions' response to what are deemed to be their 'worst of the worst' prisoners. Intriguingly, the facility at Vught in the Netherlands, perhaps the only European example of the implementation of an American supermax philosophy, strictly separates staff and prisoner worlds and seems to have suffered some of the same problems that are alleged to have bedevilled the American supermax.[9]

The structure of the chapter is as follows: I shall deal with each of the four levels of effects – on prisoners, on staff, on prison systems and upon society – in turn, first exploring what appear to be the main claimed effects of supermax custody and what is known about them, before presenting data or observations based upon my own work, and then setting out what needs to be done in an agenda for future research.

Effects on prisoners

It would be astonishing if prolonged detention in the most impoverished of secure prison environments, reducing human contact with relatives, other prisoners and staff to the barest minimum, had no effects upon prisoners. Clearly the supermax experience is intended by those authorising its use to have the most direct effects upon prisoners, both through incapacitation and individual deterrence, such that they do not 'cause trouble' either while in supermax or when returned to the general population or lower-security facilities. Longer-term effects – in terms of law-abiding post-release behaviour – are rarely explicitly sought because, as the NIC definition makes clear, supermax is regarded as an administrative response to problems of internal order within the prison system. Insofar as longer-term effects have been addressed, this appears to be only in belated recognition of the problems of releasing some prisoners directly to the community who may have become embittered by an experience which may also have deprived them of requisite social skills. Such adverse effects had been previously, and to a large extent still are, disregarded or discounted by advocates of the supermax solution, which is intended to allow the remaining prisons in the system to attend to managing their populations effectively. Impacting upon post-release behaviours through what is left of the rehabilitative ideal is at best a residual in what Feeley and Simon (1992) have called the 'lowered expectations' of the 'new penology' within which supermax has flourished.

Incapacitation effects

Were it not for the unfortunate deaths of some prisoners at the hands of others – in both Colorado State Penitentiary and Vught in the Netherlands staff watched helplessly, unable to intervene either because of the physical barriers, or because of inappropriate procedural guidelines, while a prisoner was murdered – it might seem pointless even to discuss the incapacitative effects of supermax custody. After all, when one is locked alone in an individual cell, and one has to back up to what is now called the cuff-port[10] to be handcuffed and leg-ironed before leaving the cell, and then only when escorted by two or more prison officers, it is hard to do damage to staff or other prisoners or even to prison property (although the possibility of self-harm is never completely eradicated). Misbehaviour in these circumstances tends to be confined to verbal abuse between groups of prisoners or between prisoners and staff (so-called 'door wars'), once prisoners have exhausted the possible methods of spitting or otherwise projecting bodily fluids and solids at staff who have developed their defences to these assaults. It is hard not to see such obscene ritual interactions as directly resulting from the deliberate reduction of environmental stimulation to the absolute minimum. The incapacitative effect of supermax involves essentially the same philosophy as might be deployed by a gardener who solves the problem of unwanted weeds by turning his garden into a concrete courtyard. But those unfortunate deaths have occurred, and they occurred when the concrete lid has been lifted sufficiently to allow prisoners some communal interactive activity. As Ward and Breed (1986) once noted in their report to Congress on the Marion lock-down, the problem with lock-down situations is that sooner or later they have to be lifted. In his recent writings, Ward has been the principal author, with Norman Carlson, the former Director of the Bureau of Prisons (Ward and Carlson 1995), and Thomas Werlich, the in-house research analyst first at Marion and then at Florence ADX which replaced Marion (Ward and Werlich 2003), upholding the efficacy of the individual deterrence effect of supermax – at least in the federal system.

Individual deterrence effects

Although Ward and Werlich (2003) do not use the terminology of individual deterrence – rather presenting their data as refutations of some of the hypothesised inmate reactions to supermax confinement, including embitterment and rage leading to revenge attacks against staff or prisoners, further violent offending on release, and breakdown of mental health – it is mainly as a possible vindication of the individual deterrence effect that I shall consider their work here. Ward and Werlich (2003) report that only 3.1 per cent of their sample of 520 Alcatraz inmates were returned to 'The Rock' for disciplinary reasons once they had been transferred to other federal institutions, and none for killing another prisoner or killing or seriously injuring a member of staff. Only 16 per cent of the 1,020 prisoners who served time at Marion between October 1983 and June 1994 were returned to Marion from the prisons to which they had been transferred. If they could be taken at face value, these are impressive findings and may well indicate a strong individual deterrent effect. However, one would need to know more about the prisoners' actual behaviours and misbehaviours, the length of period at risk, and what alternative sanctions were available to the authorities before one would know how to interpret this. One also needs to know about the behaviours and misbehaviours of those prisoners who were not returned to supermax conditions and the context in which those took place. In either case it is possible that just as the original decision to send prisoners to supermax involved a subjective administrative judgement rather than due process and will have depended upon an assessment of a number of contemporary factors, so subsequent decisions might reflect an administrative view either that the new misbehaviours were 'containable' or that since supermax had not succeeded in impacting upon their subsequent behaviour then alternative measures might now have to be found.

British experience of the small units set up following the Control Review Committee and their successors, the Close Supervision Centres, suggests that prisoners may behave quite differently in different environments (Home Office 1984; Bottomley 1995; Clare and Bottomley 2001). The simple fact of return or non-return to supermax is not a sufficient criterion of success without a good deal of other information. Finally, there is evidence that for some prisoners supermax custody constitutes a sought-after haven, away from the stress and dangers of other high-security prisons where they constantly have to look over their shoulders (Lovell *et al* 2000; Toch 2001). For such prisoners post-supermax behaviour would presumably depend upon the dangers currently experienced in the prisons to which they were returned. Ward and Werlich demonstrate that the outcomes were not simply a function of the ageing process and draw attention to the important caveat that before one could conclude that these results provided evidence of a deterrent effect one would need to know how these (or, presumably, a control group of similar prisoners) would have responded over time had they not been subjected to supermax conditions in the first place.

It is equally difficult to interpret the reported findings that 50 per cent of Alcatraz prisoners never returned to any prison, state or federal, once released to the community, and that 49 per cent of the first 80 prisoners to have been released after serving time in Marion were returned to prison within 36 months of release, in part because it is hard to know what comparator group would be appropriate. The similarity of the findings suggests continuity between Alcatraz and Marion, but since both indicate a lower success rate than that for a sample from the Level 5 facility at Leavenworth, of whom only 37 per cent returned to custody, this does not appear to demonstrate a powerful long-term effect. In the absence of data about the further offences committed by the 50 per cent who did come back to prison, or ways of linking those offences back to experiences in custody, there seems to be insufficient evidence to draw a conclusion about the specific effects of supermax custody on post-release behaviour.

Unwanted negative effects

The literature on potentially unwanted negative effects of solitary confinement is too extensive to be reviewed here in detail, and hardly any of it pertains directly to supermax custody. Chief among critics claiming negative consequences from confinement in supermax custody are Craig Haney (Haney 1997; Haney and Lynch 1997; and Haney, this volume) and Stewart Grassian (1983).

Grassian (1983) provided clinical observations on fourteen of fifteen prisoners who brought a lawsuit against the Commonwealth of Massachusetts for the conditions they experienced in periods of solitary confinement, which ranged from eleven days to ten months, in Walpole, the state maximum-security facility. The conditions he described closely resemble the deprivations experienced in modern supermax facilities (and Walpole was identified as such in response to my survey of supermax some fifteen years later). Because of the circumstances in which the evidence was collected and the purposes to which it was put, Grassian's account falls short of the requirements for a normal scientific research publication; however, the results were indicative of what many other writers were subsequently to find. Most prisoners initially put up a front of unconcern, only to reveal fantasies about revenge, fears that guards would identify weaknesses that could be exploited, or fears that they might be driven insane. Grassian identified a number of perceptual changes, including hypersensitivity to noise and other external stimuli; affective disturbances of shortness of breath, headaches and tachycardia; difficulties with thinking, concentration and memory; disturbances of thought; and problems with impulse control. However, Grassian also reported that when prisoners were taken out of solitary confinement for at least 24 hours every fifteen days, as required under Massachusetts statute, all reported a rapid diminution of symptoms (although not stated, it is presumed that the symptoms returned with a return to solitary confinement).

Grassian reported that his findings were congruent with most of the literature then extant, apart from the sole experimental study using prisoners which was conducted by Walters *et al* (1963). That short-lived experiment (four days) used prisoner volunteers and found no deterioration of mental or psycho-motor functioning among those in solitary confinement. Haney and Lynch (1997), however, referring to the same study, note that some psychological changes were identified in the isolated subjects, who showed significantly increased levels of anxiety.

Haney and Lynch (1997) comprehensively reviewed the literature on the effects of solitary confinement from early laboratory experiments on sensory deprivation, through the use of seclusion among psychiatric patients, to studies of torture victims. They concluded that 'distinctive patterns of negative effects have emerged clearly, consistently and un-equivocally from personal accounts, descriptive studies, and systematic research on solitary and punitive segregation' (p. 530). They claim that there is no study of solitary confinement wherein non-voluntary confinement lasting longer than ten days failed to produce negative psychological effects (p. 521). Those effects included 'increases in negative attitudes and affect, insomnia, anxiety, panic, withdrawal, hypersensitivity, ruminations, cognitive dysfunction, hallucinations, loss of control, aggression, rage, paranoia, hopelessness, lethargy, depression, emotional breakdowns, self-mutilation, and suicidal impulses' (p. 530). It is a long list and not easy to discount. In response to Bonta and Gendreau (1995), who argue that until research on solitary confinement employs genuinely experimental methods definitive conclusions cannot be reached, Haney and Lynch (1997: 495) retort that such arguments have implicitly authorised the increased use of solitary confinement and that genuinely experimental data are virtually impossible to obtain. They cite the early experiment by Haney *et al* (1973) as the only true experiment of prison-like environments, although it should be noted that trenchant criticism has been directed at that 'experiment' by Jones and Fowles (1984) and many other commentators, including Liebling and Maruna in their introduction to this collection, as unrealistic and unethical.

Ward and Werlich (2003) appear to dismiss the writings and clinical judgements of Grassian and of Haney on the grounds that their direct experience has largely been gained in the context of acting as expert witnesses in court cases brought by prisoners (both were involved in one of the landmark cases, *Madrid* v *Gomez*, in California in 1995 concerning conditions at Pelican Bay – of which more below). They argue that work carried out in such circumstances, or on behalf of Human Rights Watch and Amnesty International (which they characterise as prisoners' rights groups), will not be regarded as credible by prison authorities, which probably tells us more about the lack of openness of prison authorities than anything else (cf. the response to criticism of the Close Supervision Centres in England and Wales discussed below).

Ward and Werlich do not appear to have the same reservations about the clinical judgements of psychiatrists employed by the Federal Bureau of Prisons, although they do acknowledge that prisoners are unlikely to be cooperative in their assessments. Clinical decisions regarding transfer to Springfield Medical Centre for Federal Prisoners are accepted as the threshold for evidence of mental illness. They report that only 8 per cent of the 1,550 prisoners in Alcatraz were clinically diagnosed as manifesting psychosis, of whom two-thirds were transferred to Springfield. Among the transferees a quarter were deemed to have brought their mental health problems with them from the outside. On those figures, leaving aside 40 or so prisoners who were apparently diagnosed psychotic and not transferred, I calculate that about 63 prisoners over a 30-year period developed their psychotic symptoms while on the Rock. For Marion, the figures would be somewhat higher – 32 prisoners developing symptoms during the eleven-year period since the lock-down. Of course, we shall never know how many would have developed a psychosis anyway or whether they developed it as a result of their supermax custody experience; nor how many developed mental health problems that fell short of the rather high threshold of full-blown psychosis. It is worth pointing out that it is estimated that about 2 per cent of the prison population in England and Wales suffer from dangerous and severe personality disorder (HMIP 1999), and that three-fifths of male and half of female sentenced prisoners suffer from lesser personality disorders (Singleton et al 1998). In England and Wales 7 per cent of sentenced males and 14 per cent of sentenced females suffered from functional psychoses, with even higher proportions in the remand population. More than a sixth of the prison population suffered co-morbidity exhibiting four out of the five conditions assessed – personality disorder, functional psychosis, neuroses, and drug and alcohol addiction (Singleton et al 1998). One wonders, therefore, whether similar problems in the federal system may be going undiagnosed. Ward and Werlich (2003) make no mention of matters that are now seriously discussed in England and Wales, namely whether some of the behavioural problems exhibited in prison, and which bring prisoners to the attention of the authorities, might be attributed to their personality disorders or other mental health problems, and if so whether current policies and procedures make those problems worse or better. This writer would certainly not subscribe to the view that problems of difficult or dangerous prisoners can be explained away by the characteristics of offenders alone. But in the complex world of analysing the effects of imprisonment, it is an element that cannot be ignored.

Madrid versus Gomez (1995)

After hearing extensive testimony about conditions – and outright abuse – in Pelican Bay Special Housing Unit (SHU), and the psychological impact of those conditions upon prisoners, the Federal District Court determined that '(c)onditions in the SHU may well hover on the edge of what is humanly tolerable for those with normal resilience, particularly when endured for extended periods of time' (1280). However, the court did not rule that those conditions breached Eighth Amendment protections against cruel and unusual punishment because it had not been demonstrated that they created 'a sufficiently high risk to *all* inmates of incurring a serious mental illness' (1267, emphasis added). Although the Madrid court did rule that it would be unconstitutional for prisoners who were already suffering from mental illness, or who were identified as being at serious risk of becoming mentally ill, to be housed in the SHU, the judgement appears to have set a legal standard for Eighth Amendment rights which would be extremely difficult to meet. So far as I am aware, no respected authority has yet argued in favour of using such extreme punitive conditions for mentally ill prisoners. Nor has anyone seriously argued, human nature being what it is, that any environment would have the same effects on all persons experiencing it. In the real and reasonable world we are, or ought to be, talking about probabilities and proportionality, about balancing the costs and benefits of various outcomes. The question is, or should be, whether the psychotic symptoms unambiguously developed in almost 100 prisoners while in Alcatraz and Marion (using the calculations based on Ward and Werlich's data above) are a price worth paying for whatever benefits were achieved.

It is important to note, as Ward and Werlich (2003) point out, that the federal system presents a special case which should not be taken as typical of state systems. The Federal Bureau of Prisons would not be expected either to encourage or condone abuse by its staff members in the ways that undoubtedly happened in Pelican Bay. And the Federal Bureau, with its facility at Springfield, could be expected, better than most state systems, to be able to screen out prisoners with actual or potential mental health problems.[11]

Before leaving the issues of mental health consequences it is worth referring to the Report of Her Majesty's Chief Inspector of Prisons on the Close Supervision Centres in August and September 1999 (HMIP 1999). At that time in the evolution of the CSCs particular concern was expressed about one centre – A wing at Woodhill, which operated the most basic regime among the various CSCs – as well as D wing, which served as the segregation unit for the CSC system. These units contained nine prisoners at the time of the inspection, and had accommodated a total of 53 prisoners over the history of the system, with an average stay of eight months and a range from 27 days to eighteen months. They were locked down in isolation for 23 hours a day, and were greeted by five members of staff dressed in full control-and-restraint uniform (riot gear) whenever the cells were opened. The Inspectorate briefly reviewed some of the same literature as discussed above, and interviewed the prisoners concerned, many of whom expressed fears of 'losing their minds'. Citing the first of the United Nations Body of Principles 1988, which requires that all 'persons under any form of detention or imprisonment shall be treated in a humane manner and with respect for the inherent dignity of the human person', the Chief Inspector concluded that the conditions amounted to sensory deprivation and were unacceptable other than in emergency situations. The Inspectorate recommended immediate changes, including greater psychiatric support for staff as well as prisoners, and a clearer and more independent role for the Advisory Group (of experts from outside the prison system). To the credit of the Prison Service, those changes have been implemented and prisoners are routinely unlocked without a show of force, by staff in shirtsleeves rather than riot gear.

Most writers would agree with HMCIP that the effects of segregation – or any other environmental stimulus or lack of stimulus – will vary from person to person, depending upon a variety of factors. The Madrid court took the view that prisoners of 'normal resilience' could just about survive at the limits of human tolerance in Pelican Bay, although mentally ill persons could not. Ward and Werlich (2003) suggest that Alcatraz and Marion 'convicts' were resilient and took pride in standing up to whatever was thrown at them, and so were able to leave with their self-respect intact. At the time when it was first mooted that Nelson Mandela might be released, I was repeatedly asked by journalists what shape he would be in. I replied that I thought his belief in his cause would have enabled him to survive with his strength of character and sense of purpose undamaged. Even I was surprised by his extraordinary capacity for forgiveness. In promoting his memoirs, Bill Clinton spoke of how the world's most celebrated prisoner had advised him in his hour of need that it was necessary to let things go and move on or risk being destroyed from within.[12] But the point is made: prison conditions must be expected to have differential effects, and it is important to explore them. The reality is that at the end of all reviews we know little enough with any certainty. It is to some of those possible differential effects that I now turn on the basis of my own research in American supermax prisons.

Differential effects

The data reported here are derived from completed interviews conducted with 42 prisoners in Oak Park Heights and 37 interviews with prisoners in Colorado State Penitentiary.[13] It is not my intention in this chapter to make comparisons between the two institutions – although I will be doing that in subsequent publications. Nor do I propose to try to draw conclusions as to the relative weights to be attached to the various reactions. Rather, I aim to illustrate some of the main effects which prisoners reported and to try to link those, where possible, to the experiences which prisoners had and to which they attributed causality. I have therefore amalgamated the two groups for present purposes. About a dozen interviews were also conducted with prisoners in Pelican Bay, but the circumstances in which the interviews were conducted left much to be desired and so they have not been included in the formal analysis but will be referred to as appropriate.[14]

No one should expect that the complex interaction between the biography of prisoners, their respective ego strengths, and the impact of even the most severely restricted of prison regimes will be straightforward to disentangle. Beyond a doubt, the science will be intricate and the possible interactions will be complex and sometimes counter-intuitive. Hans Toch (2001), by no means an advocate of supermax custody, noted that: 'Discomfort can be a regenerative experience. It can be particularly regenerative for irresponsible hedonists who have done what they like at other people's expense, and who must learn to control themselves'. In light of this observation I was prepared for some counter-intuitive results, but not quite to the extent that I found them. I did not start my investigation with a search for clinical symptoms but with enquiries as to the costs and benefits of supermax custody. Somewhat to my surprise, over half of the prisoners I interviewed reported at least some positive feedback on their experience in supermax: it had given them time to think and reflect, and in so doing they had learned patience and control, or had been given an opportunity to turn themselves around away from the influence of their peers. In some sense, at least, some of them could conceive that they might come out of the experience the better for it. It has to be said that this result was quite heavily skewed by the responses of prisoners in the programming units at Oak Park Heights – in itself, perhaps, an indication that any balance of advantage in supermax is to be found more at the positive end of the continuum than in the purely punitive response. But it is important to stress that the overwhelming majority of prisoners I interviewed in both establishments reported multiple effects, and that for most prisoners who reported benefits these were embedded in a wider framework of perceived effects many of which were negative – including many of the psychological consequences reported in the literature, and listed by Haney and Lynch (1997). What this seemed to show, in other words, was that it was perfectly possible for prisoners to gain in behavioural terms and at the same time to suffer potential psychological damage.

At the other extreme, about a fifth of the sample believed, and continued to maintain under repeated questioning, that the experience of supermax had made them so much worse that they would come out, if at all, more bitter and vengeful. This group was heavily concentrated in Colorado State Penitentiary and in the non- programming SHU and Segregation Units at Oak Park Heights. A significant number of these prisoners found it extremely difficult to bring themselves to talk about their experience. In a manner reminiscent of concentration camp victims as reported, for example, by Jorge Semprun (1997), they felt that they could only share these experiences with others who had gone through the same experience and who could truly appreciate what they were talking about. After considerable persistence some prisoners came to regard a researcher from another culture, who treated them with respect and clearly wanted to learn, as an acceptable proxy and began to open up. It was clear that for some of these prisoners supermax was the most vivid experience of their lives, and one which had come to define their very being. It was from among this group that prisoners told me of their retreat into fantasy worlds, of their thoughts of waiting for that moment when a guard would fail to pay attention and revenge could at last be exacted, or of their determination once released to die resisting arrest rather than return to what they regarded as inhumane and unjustifiable conditions. As I talked to a prisoner in a dog-run exercise yard at Pelican Bay it became clear that I was the first person with whom he had had sustained human contact for years. In a reciprocal gesture he tried to empathise with what he supposed would be my concern at the death of Princess Diana, before breaking down into tears at his own forlorn situation. Recovering his composure he explained that he was defined as a gang member and thus part of a Security Threat Group, largely on grounds that he came from the same community and hung out with friends among whom some were gang members. He refused to 'roll over' and give information about other gang members in part because he had little to say. And if he did have anything to say, saying it would simply provide him with a passport into protective custody. He could see no way out of this stalemate, but was concerned that his frustration would lead to violence. This should be seen as one of what Ward and Werlich (2003) also describe as the multiple realities of prison experience. The prisoners concerned may or may not live out their fantasies. The probability is that most won't and some will. The question is how we might better understand these effects and how we might encourage positive outcomes and discourage negative ones.

Among those reporting positive effects, most prisoners felt those effects could have been achieved in other ways and without the level of deprivation sometimes involved. The value of separation was often acknowledged, but this did not have to involve loss of programming, nor did the separation have to last so long. Some of these prisoners already benefited from programmes and argued that by extending programmes to other prisoners, they too would be likely to experience positive effects.

It is a commonplace of the prison literature that prisoners have a profound sense of justice and fair play. As indicated by the prisoner in Pelican Bay, the most frequent causes for complaint, apart from the actual conditions themselves, were the procedures through which one gets into supermax and the procedures through which one might get out. The suggestions, beloved by politicians that supermax is for the 'worst of the worst' and that 'bad behaviour gets you in and good behaviour gets you out', are simply stated but fraught with difficulties in practice.

Many prisoners felt themselves to be victims of injustice over their transfer to a supermax facility and criticised the administration for transferring them despite the fact that they did not meet the expressed criteria. From my check of prisoner records there was, indeed, sometimes little evidence on file that the prisoner met the formal criteria. In Colorado, several prisoners complained, for example, that they had been transferred to supermax because of a riot at another establishment, despite the fact that they had not themselves been involved. One prisoner, at a case management meeting which I attended shortly after his arrival, insisted that the video evidence of the riot would clearly show that he had not participated and asked that this be viewed. He was simply told that the video could not be made available except in prosecutions and that he had to accept that his transfer was justified on the evidence provided by staff at the sending institution. It would not be surprising if there were considerable numbers of prisoners in supermax facilities who did not meet the formal criteria, or who would not if there were no 'catch-all' criterion such as having committed multiple disciplinary offences. Prisoners transferred on those grounds would likely be 'nuisance' prisoners of precisely the kind that the NIC (1999) indicates should not be in supermax. It is, in my view, inevitable that there will be prisoners in supermax to whom the soubriquet 'worst of the worst' could not reasonably be applied. In Minnesota, where 60 new supermax places were being provided, no informed person to whom I spoke could think of more than nine or ten prisoners in the system who could possibly merit being sent there. In Colorado, the supermax facility provided 5.6 per cent of all prison places for the state – only three states had a higher proportion of supermax places.

Beds, once provided, will likely be filled unless there is strong central oversight determined to keep usage for its intended purpose and to overcome the problem that each sending institution will judge its worst prisoner against its own population, not that of the system as a whole (see the discussion in King and McDermott, 1990, of differential identifications of difficult and dangerous prisoners in England and Wales, before the advent of close supervision centres and the creation of a strong central committee controlling admissions). In Wisconsin, the Commissioner of Corrections told Amnesty International[15] that having a central committee to control admissions to the controversial new supermax at Boscobel would undermine the authority and judgement of wardens as to who needed to be transferred. After pressure from Amnesty International and local politicians, however, the practice of placing juveniles in the facility ended (Amnesty International 2001). In England and Wales, the Prison Service has had the courage to leave places in special security wings empty because there are no exceptional (escape) risk prisoners at present in the system, and keeps the numbers of (control risk) prisoners in the close supervision centres to a minimum through a strong central committee which vets all recommendations. The Federal Bureau of Prisons uses its supermax facility more parsimoniously than most state systems, but still more than five times as much as England and Wales.

Getting out may sometimes be as hard as it was easy to get in. There is a serious question as to what constitutes good behaviour in a state of complete lock-down – not masturbating in cell? Not responding to knock-backs by kicking the cell door? There are few, if any, situations of trust. There may be many provocations. Judgements about good behaviour may be made by junior front-line staff in whom considerable discretion may be vested. In Colorado, for example, prisoners were expected to progress from Quality of Life Level I, the entry level with minimum privileges, through to Level III before passing on to the Progressive Reintegration Opportunities Unit at Levels IV and V (the step-down unit) before being released or transferred back to an ordinary prison. Policy dictates that prisoners are reviewed after fixed periods in each level, but may be retained at any level 'indefinitely if their behaviour warrants'; and may be regressed at any stage after a review of 'negative chrons' – negative reports on the daily chronological log kept by front-line staff. It was well known that some staff wrote many more negative chrons than others, and that new staff wrote more negative chrons than established staff. I do not single out Colorado State Penitentiary for special criticism. In many ways its policy and procedures, and the professionalism of staff, rivalled Oak Park Heights – but even in a carefully run system the scope for human misjudgement by staff and consequent sense of injustice experienced by prisoners, who perceived themselves to be in a profoundly consequential game of snakes and ladders (McDermott and King 1988), is considerable.

To unpick the inter-relationships between these various factors which might account for the differential effects of supermax custody will not be easy. It will require longitudinal research which follows prisoners from their point of entry and through their supermax career, back to normal population and onwards to eventual release. Ideally, it would involve comparative work in different jurisdictions and the use, as far as is practical, of control groups of prisoners whose behaviour might have got them into supermax but in the event did not. In the absence of experimental design (ethically unacceptable in this context, although see Farrington and Joliffe, 2002, for a feasibility study of a randomised control to evaluate treatment programmes in a high-security prison), research along these lines would be the best that we could hope for. It would be important for the research to include psychological and psychiatric assessment using standardised instruments upon reception to be repeated at intervals thereafter. It would require systematic monitoring of prisoners' experiences and careful descriptions of the regime to which they are subjected, a review of chronological logs and case reviews, an analysis of adjudications and reports of good and bad behaviours and, of course, eventually measures of final outcomes. Only then would we be in a position to assess the true impact of supermax custody on prisoners.

Effects on staff

Although there are now a number of studies of prison officers in the literature (Kauffman 1988; Crawley 2004; Liebling and Price 2001; and Arnold, this volume), I know of none which specifically explores the effects of working in supermax institutions or even of working in different types of prisons. In my own studies I asked prisoners for their views of staff on a variety of dimensions and also interviewed a number of staff directly. Although the numbers of staff interviewed were too small to warrant systematic analysis, it is possible to draw some inferences both from these and from discussions about staffing in the existing research literature and what has emerged in court cases or public enquiries, to develop some tentative hypotheses.

Although politicians, prison officials and the public might be sceptical about placing too much weight on prisoner assessments of staff, research has shown that prisoners can be surprisingly fair and reasonable in their judgements (King and McDermott 1995) and it certainly provides a sensible starting point for analysis. Prisoners in Colorado State Penitentiary and in Oak Park Heights rated their staff more or less equally in terms of their professionalism: staff were smartly dressed and well turned out, they did not abuse prisoners, they well understood the philosophy behind their respective institutions and could clearly articulate that in discussion with prisoners, researchers and the public. Thereafter, there were consistent differences between the two institutions, with staff in Oak Park Heights being rated as more helpful, more likely to be fair and consistent and less likely to be racist than their counterparts in Colorado State Penitentiary. Some years ago, I was able to report the findings of a comparative study of Oak Park Heights and the English maximum-security prison, Gartree (not a supermax), in which in response to the same questions staff in Gartree were consistently rated as better than staff in Oak Park Heights (King 1991). At the time, that result seemed counter-intuitive because on virtually all other measures Oak Park Heights offered better facilities and more and better programmes, health services and so on than did Gartree. However, for present purposes it is possible to put forward a hypothesis that might account for these findings and which might be tested elsewhere. In Colorado, most staff–prisoner contacts were necessarily specific and in formal settings, because for most of the time prisoners were locked down and staff were behind barriers. In Oak Park Heights, there was much more generalised and informal contact with staff because two officers were always present in the complexes when prisoners were out of cells. In Gartree there were no physical barriers to separate staff from prisoners and the opportunities for staff–prisoner interaction were much higher. Thus one might hypothesise that in situations where potential contact between staff and prisoners in public settings is higher, staff will experience a greater strain towards behaving in helpful, fair, consistent and non-racist ways. By extension, such a hypothesis would explain why, when there is a less clearly articulated philosophy, a lack of professionalism on the part of staff who may be inexperienced or untrained, and a lack of interest or oversight by a Department of Corrections, the kinds of abuses which were seen at Pelican Bay can occur.

In informal interviews with staff in a variety of supermax institutions in the United States and with staff working in close supervision centres in Woodhill and Durham in England, one very striking difference emerged. Virtually without exception staff dealing with the 'worst of the worst' prisoners in England and Wales – prisoners who had killed others while in custody, taken staff or other prisoners' hostage – found their job stressful. Not surprisingly: they were in daily face-to-face contact and had to learn how to deal with extremely difficult situations. Almost equally without exception, staff in American supermax facilities had no such problems with stress: quite the reverse, because those with experience of working in other prisons found their duties in supermax the least stressful they had done. Indeed they found the work rather boring – again, not surprising. When your most difficult and dangerous prisoners are locked away in cells and staff are behind their physical or electronic barriers there is little to disturb one's equilibrium, and when prisoners are escorted anywhere they are (except at Oak Park Heights) at a minimum, handcuffed before leaving their cells. Staff felt safe and in control. Staff in Oak Park Heights did admit to some occasional anxiety but basically they felt safe because they knew everything could be seen by a colleague in the bubble and that back-up could be quickly summoned.

However, there are wider, and potentially very far-reaching, effects arising from the different ways of managing the most difficult and dangerous prisoners. The way in which stress among staff is managed lies at the heart of the matter. Arguably, supermax facilities were developed because staff had become increasingly fearful for their safety following the murder of two prisoners in the Marion Control Unit in 1983. Staff anxieties were dealt with by attempting to remove the causes, by identifying the 'worst of the worst' prisoners and placing them in lock-down facilities where their only contact with staff would be when prisoners were restrained and staff were present in superior numbers. But there is a sense in which this could serve to de-skill prison officers and so create a vicious circle whereby the numbers in lock-down facilities are more or less bound to increase in the face of unreasonable demand. If staff in ordinary prisons are encouraged to think that they need not deal with the more difficult management problems because they can transfer them to supermax, then they are no longer encouraged to acquire the skills required for managing difficult prisoners *in situ*. Moreover, whatever skills they may have had may atrophy for lack of use. In future, they may become more likely to lower the threshold at which prisoners are identified as bad enough to be among the worst of the worst and so demand more places in supermax facilities. The problem is compounded because the staff working in supermax facilities, for the most part, will not acquire skills in dealing with difficult prisoners either, other than by locking them up, restraining them and creating ever more social distance between such prisoners and staff, let alone normal society. These reactions are understandable: managing dangerous prisoners is not an easy job; but it can be done. And unless one is to contemplate a future in which more and more prisoners are locked down, alternative methods need to be nurtured.

Earlier in this chapter, reference was made to the critical report of Her Majesty's Chief Inspector of Prisons on the close supervision centres. In A and D wings at Woodhill, prisoners and staff were in daily confrontation and staff would only open up cells if they were 'suited up' and outnumbered prisoners five to one. With training and counselling and some changes to the rules and careful management, it has been possible to row back from that situation and to resist demands for greater lock-down. This costs time, money, effort and ingenuity, but the confrontations have subsided, and while staff still experience the job as stressful, they have developed a new confidence in their skills and those of their colleagues. Moreover, the spiral effects here are likely to increase skills throughout the system. By maintaining the CSCs as a scarce resource, to be used parsimoniously, staff in other prisons are encouraged to deal with management problems locally and to develop the skills to do so. Meanwhile, those dealing with the most difficult and dangerous prisoners in the CSCs develop real skills which can potentially feed back into training schemes for the benefit of staff throughout the system.

Effects on prison systems

One of the most frequently cited justifications for the establishment of supermax facilities, put forward by correctional officials, is that they serve to relieve the rest of the prison system of its control problems, thereby enabling the system to achieve stability and order. Such a thesis seems to rest on a number of assumptions: that disorder in prisons is a function primarily of a number of 'bad apples' who can be easily identified and removed; that once removed, the supermax experience will operate an individually deterrent effect so that they do not offend again when returned to the mainstream; and that the reputation of supermax and the threat of being sent there will be sufficient to deter other prisoners from following in their footsteps. We have already seen that there is reason to believe that some Departments of Correction do not operate careful enough procedures to ensure that the population in supermax facilities conforms to the selection criteria. I have written elsewhere that, once one moves beyond a rather small number of prisoners who have committed murder while in prison, or taken hostages, or led riots, there are considerable uncertainties and inconsistencies in identifying 'control problem prisoners' in the English context (King and McDermott 1990). Moreover, the point has been well taken by the prison authorities in England and Wales that bad behaviour in prison is a function not just of the characteristics of individual prisoners, but the way in which they are treated by staff and the opportunities available within the prison regime. Twenty years ago, the Prison Service clearly recognised that prisoners who were difficult to manage in one setting behaved perfectly reasonably when transferred to another, without the need to resort to punitive regimes (Home Office 1984). It is fair to say, however, that the authorities in England and Wales, apart from a brief flirtation with the idea of control units in 1974–5, did not seriously contemplate developing regimes so extreme in their deprivation that they could have a profound deterrent effect. It is clear from the discussion of the Report of the Chief Inspector above that without a change in the climate of opinion it would not be possible for the Prison Service to develop such a regime.

The situation is very different in the United States. Although the regime in a facility with high programme content such as Oak Park Heights would probably not be regarded as much of a deterrent, there seems little doubt that Pelican Bay, operating on the threshold of what people with normal resilience could tolerate, might have considerable deterrent effect. Indeed, arguably such a prison might have a deterrent effect regardless of whether the selection procedures were operated in a precisely targeted way.

Although reports and news releases from Departments of Corrections often refer to the impact that opening a supermax facility has had on the state of order in the rest of the system, there has been remarkably little independent research. Establishing a convincing research design, using meaningful conceptions of what constitutes order and stability which could be simply operationalised, would not be easy, not least because it would require substantial baseline data before the supermax were established with which comparisons could subsequently be made. The only study that systematically bears on this that I am aware of is by Briggs et al (2001), although Clare and Bottomley's (2001) evaluation of Close Supervision Centres in England and Wales included an attempt at assessing the impact on the rest of the dispersal (high-security) estate. Briggs and colleagues used a sophisticated quasi-experimental multiple interrupted time series design to test the impact of supermax in three states – Arizona, Illinois and Minnesota.[16] Data had to be collected retrospectively from the official records and thus were limited to recorded data on inmate–inmate assaults and inmate–staff assaults as the index for order. Separate impact assessments of SMU I and SMU II revealed no mitigating impact on levels of institutional violence elsewhere in the Arizona system: some increases in violence suggested that, if anything, there may have been a net harmful effect. In Illinois the opening of Tamms had no impact upon assaults on inmates but was followed by a small reduction in assaults on staff: from 62 a month to 60 a month, significantly less dramatic than the halving of the assault rate claimed by the Department of Corrections. In Minnesota, the opening of Oak Park Heights had no impact on subsequent inmate assaults but paradoxically was followed by an increase in assaults on staff. These results must be regarded as tentative. The problem of order and stability in prisons is complex and cannot simply be reduced to assaults on inmates and staff, important though those are, and conducting research retrospectively leaves the data and definitions in the hands of officials rather than researchers. Nevertheless, the results do not give much sustenance to the hypothesis that establishing a supermax facility is a good way of stabilising the rest of the system. In England and Wales, Clare and Bottomley (2001), on the basis of post hoc interviews and analysis of recorded data, found it virtually impossible to calculate the independent effect of the new CSC system given the number and diversity of other initiatives going on at about the same time. However, staff in the dispersal prisons felt that there had been a reduction in serious incidents, there were fewer prisoners in either long-term segregation or being transferred to other prisons on the 'magic roundabout', and in some but not all dispersal prisons there had been fewer assaults in the three years after CSCs were introduced than in the three years preceding their introduction. Although these results were suggestive, neither prison staff nor researchers linked them directly or unequivocally to the introduction of the CSCs.

Effects on society

If the evidence about the effects of supermax on prisoners, staff and prison systems becomes progressively more tentative, then by the time one comes to consider the effects upon society, clinical or scientific evidence is nonexistent and it is hard to know just what would qualify. And yet it is not something to be ignored. Short of the death penalty and various forms of bodily mutilation, prison represents the ultimate power of the state against its citizens.

High hopes surrounded the introduction of the first prisons. The Reverend Finley may have indulged in hyperbole when he suggested that '(c)ould we all be put on prison fare, for the space of two or three generations, the world would ultimately be better for it. Indeed, should society change places with the prisoner, so far as habits are concerned' then the grandiose goals of peace, right and Christianity would be furthered (cited in Rothman 1971: 84–5). But if few would now see prison as a model for the future of civil society, for much of the late 19th and most of the 20th centuries there has been widespread consensus that prisons reflect the values of the societies in which they are found. Nelson Mandela is perhaps the most distinguished person in recent years to echo the sentiments expressed by so many others before him, including Dostoevsky and Winston Churchill: 'no one truly knows a nation until one has been inside the jails. A nation should not be judged by how it treats its highest citizens, but its lowest ones' (Mandela 1994). There is little doubt that what we do in our prisons makes some kind of moral statement about what we think both of our society and our citizens.

When the Federal Court for the Northern District of California ruled that what went on in Pelican Bay was at the outer limits of what normal human beings could endure, yet did not breach Eighth Amendment Rights precisely because some people could endure it, then in effect it legitimated that regime on behalf of the American people. And it did so in the knowledge that an age of mass imprisonment impacted disproportionately on an underclass of minority American citizens. When Her Majesty's Chief Inspector of Prisons determined that what went on in A and D wings at Woodhill was unacceptable, then it made clear, on behalf of the British people, that such (lesser) practices were not legitimate.

In their comprehensive review of supermax and solitary confinement, Haney and Lynch (1997) devote some discussion to the evolving jurisprudence on Eighth Amendment protections against cruel and unusual punishment. They note Chief Justice Warren's famous observation, in 1958, that the Eighth Amendment was not static but must 'draw its meaning from the evolving standards that mark the progress of a maturing society'. There seems little doubt that Warren expressed a hope, if not a faith, that mature societies developed more civilised standards and court judgements have to reflect that. My teacher and mentor, Norbert Elias, the great sociologist and social psychologist and author of *The Civilising Process* (1978), instilled in his naive and eager students a recognition that the civilising process was not a march of progress: how right he was.

In September 2001, just two weeks after the attack on the twin towers, I attended a conference on supermax at Seattle. After expressing my condolences to my friends and colleagues, I said that this was a peculiarly appropriate time to be considering supermax. I expressed my fears that the apparent legitimation of such extreme forms of punishment for 'normal' American citizens boded ill for the fate of those who might become suspected of terrorist offences; and that the future treatment of suspected terrorists might retrospectively justify, and further ratchet up, measures that might be taken against convicted American felons. In less than a year Guantanamo Bay was established.

Notes

1   *The Origins and Operation of Supermax,* under Grant No R000236769, involved visits to sixteen supermax facilities in nine states: Southport and Marcy Correctional Facilities in New York, Camp Hill and Greene in Pennsylvania, Tamms in Illinois, Oak Park Heights in Minnesota, the Wynne, Estelle and Terrel Units in Texas, Red Onion and Wallens Ridge in Virginia, Special Management Units I and II in Arizona, Pelican Bay, Corcoran and Valley State in California, and the Colorado State Penitentiary.

2   *The Proliferation of Supermax* involved study visits to Belgium, Germany, the Netherlands, Romania, Russia and Sweden to explore the extent to which supermax ideas had been imported from the United States.

3   The Feasibility of Supermax Project Team was established following the escapes from Whitemoor and Parkhurst to consider the implications of the recommendation by Learmont (Home Office 1995) to build two supermax facilities in England and Wales.

4   Particularly concerning death row in H Unit at Oklahoma State Penitentiary (Amnesty International 1994) and Boscobel, Wisconsin (Amnesty International 2001).

5   The suggestion is that as the use of the continuous assessment scheme has been discouraged and as experience of dealing with difficult and dangerous prisoners in close supervision centres has accumulated, so staff

in segregation units within the high security estate have been encouraged to apply the lessons learned. This remains an important area for future research.

6 It is tempting to make the cross reference to Bentham's panopticon and few writers on supermax have resisted it. To do so ignores the fact that Bentham's ideas placed work at the centre – a mill to grind rogues honest – and Bentham, had his scheme ever been adopted, would have reaped the profits. Few supermax facilities make provision for prisoners to work. And whereas Bentham, in an abortive bid to persuade Parliament to adopt his scheme, felt constrained to offer compensation should his inmates suffer suicides or other problems greater than those to be found in the general population outside, such safeguards are rarely offered – or contemplated – by modern Commissioners of Corrections.

7 Cell extractions most commonly occur when a prisoner has refused to return a meal tray. Often a five-man team will be assembled dressed in riot gear, and after one or more warnings will enter the cell to remove the prisoner. Four staff members may be assigned to the prisoner's limbs and the fifth to the prisoner's head. A sixth staff member might video the proceedings and the whole process might be overseen by a senior member of the uniformed staff. Often a prisoner will be sprayed with mace or pepper spray before the extraction team go in. Sometimes the team will be armed with stun shields. During fieldwork at Pelican Bay, I observed a 'pod extraction' where a prisoner was removed from the pod because, having refused to return to his cell from exercise in a solitary exercise yard, he was deemed to be 'holding the pod to ransom'. On that occasion the prisoner was subdued first through being shot with rubber pellets from a 37mm gas gun, and then sprayed with a chemical agent.

8 At the time of my latest visit to Oak Park Heights building work had just commenced to provide 60 additional lock-down spaces and an extension to the mental health facility. At the time of writing it is not known whether the same operational policy applies to them.

9 Both Colorado State Penitentiary and Vught have experienced the death of a prisoner at the hands of another either because there were too many barriers for staff to cross to make a timely intervention or because there were insufficient staff on duty to intervene under the policy guidelines.

10 In many prison designs cell doors often have a hatch at waist height through which meals may be passed. In Oklahoma State Penitentiary this hatch was known as the 'bean hole'. Many years ago a prisoner attempted to stab a member of staff through the beanhole. In the new H Block at the penitentiary the doors were redesigned with the bean hole at knee level so that staff would be less at risk from such incidents. Most supermax facilities now have a cuff port (which might also still be used for the passing of meal trays) in the centre of the door. Before leaving their cells prisoners are required to back up to the cuff port and put their hands through to be handcuffed. Only then do staff enter the cell to place the prisoner in leg

irons and a belly chain before escorting the prisoner to wherever he needs to go outside the cell.

11   However, it should also be noted that Ward and Werlich acknowledge that no psychologist or social worker was ever employed at Alcatraz and diagnoses were made by outside specialists, presumably only after referrals by non-expert prison staff; and that although psychologists and psychiatric consultants were available at Marion they were regarded with hostility or suspicion by the prisoners.

12   There are those who might have wished Clinton would have reflected beyond his personal torment over the Lewinsky affair or at the hands of the special prosecutor to consider the plight of the several hundred thousand people added to federal and state prison populations during his administration.

13   I would like to record my thanks to Minnesota and Colorado Departments of Corrections for granting permission for the research, to Jim Bruton and Gene Atherton the respective wardens and their staffs for all the help and support extended to me personally. In my experience, these two prisons were the easiest in which to conduct research. I have repaid them poorly in being extremely tardy in providing feedback, although I hope to do better in future. Lastly, I need to thank all the staff and prisoners who shared their experiences with me so openly. Thanks are also due to the the California DoC and the warden of Pelican Bay for permitting me to observe the prison during the Madrid Enforcement phase of its existence. In the nature of the situation this was not an easy prison to research. It was the only prison where I was routinely required to wear a flak jacket, for example.

14   In Oak Park Heights, prisoners were drawn equally from programming units and non-programming units and all interviews were conducted in privacy in a small office at the end of each living unit, except for prisoners in segregation when interviews were conducted at a table in the day space within sight, but not hearing, of staff. In Colorado State Penitentiary, prisoners selected in approximately equal numbers from each of the six pods were brought to me under escort, handcuffed and shackled, to the non-contact visiting booths. In Pelican Bay it was not possible to arrange a formal interviewing programme. 'Interviews' were conducted on the hoof, as and when they were possible, with the researcher standing on the walkway above the exercise yard while prisoners were taking exercise. Since it was necessary to speak loudly, sometimes exchanges would be within the hearing of staff and were necessarily guarded.

15   In an interview with the present author who was acting as expert advisor to Amnesty International. Intriguingly, although I was offered access to Wisconsin facilities in my capacity as a researcher I was denied access as an advisor to Amnesty.

16   It will be recalled that the supermax facilities in all three states were visited by me in my own research – Units SMUs I and II in Arizona, Tamms in Illinois and, of course, Oak Park Heights in Minnesota.

References

Amnesty International (1994) *Conditions for Death Row Prisoners in H-Unit, Oklahoma State Penitentiary*, AMR 51/35/94. London: Amnesty International.

Amnesty International (2001) *Boscobel – News*, AI Index AMR 51/072/2001 and AMR 51/108/2001. London: Amnesty International.

Bentham, J. (1791) 'Panopticon: or The Inspection House', in J. Bowring (ed.) *Works*, vol. 4, 37–172, London: Simpkin Marshall and Co.

Bonta, J. and Gendreau, P. (1995) 'Re-examining the cruel and unusual punishment of prison life', in T. Flanagan (ed.) *Long-Term Imprisonment: Policy, Science and Correctional Practice*. Thousand Oaks, CA: Sage Publications.

Bottomley, A.K. (1995) *CRC Special Units: A General Assessment*. London: Home Office.

Briggs, C.S., Sundt, J.L., Castellano, T.C. and Vaux, A. (2001) 'Supermaximum security prisons and institutional violence: An impact assessment'. Paper presented at the Conference on Best Practices and Human Rights in Supermax Prisons: a dialogue, September 28–29, Seattle, Washington.

Clare, E. and Bottomley, A.K. (2001) *Evaluation of Close Supervision Centres*. Home Office Research Study 219. London: Home Office.

Crawley, E. (2004) *Doing Prison Work: The Public and Private Lives of Prison Officers*. Cullompton: Willan.

Elias, N (1978) *The Civilising Process*. Oxford: Blackwell.

Farrington, D.P. and Joliffe, D. (2002) *Feasibility study into using a randomised control trial to evaluate treatment pilots at HMP Whitemoor*. Home Office Online Report 14/02 (www.homeoffice.gov.uk/rds/onlinepubs1.html).

Feeley, M. and Simon, J. (1992) 'The new penology: Notes on the emerging strategy of corrections and its implications', *Criminology*, 30 (4), 449–475.

Grassian, S. (1983) 'Psychological effects of solitary confinement', *American Journal of Psychiatry*, 140 (11), 1450–1454.

Haney, C. (1997) 'Infamous punishment: The psychological consequences of isolation,' in J.W. Marquart and J.R. Sorensen (eds) *Correctional Contexts: Contemporary and Classical Readings*. Los Angeles: Roxbury Publishing Co, pp. 428–437.

Haney, C., Banks, C. and Zimbardo, P. (1973) 'Interpersonal dynamics in a simulated prison', *International Journal of Criminology and Penology*, 1, 69–97.

Haney, C. and Lynch, M. (1997) 'Regulating prisons of the future: A psychological analysis of supermax and solitary confinement', *New York University Review of Law and Social Change*, 23, 477–570.

Hershberger, G. (1998) 'To the max', *Corrections Today*, American Correctional Association, 59, 1.

HMIP (1999) *Inspection of Close Supervision Centres, August–September 1999. A Thematic Inspection*. London: Home Office.

Home Office (1984) *Managing the Long-term Prison System: the Report of the Control Review Committee*. London: HMSO.

Home Office (1995) *Review of Prison Service Security in England and Wales and the Escape from Parkhurst Prison on Tuesday 3rd January 1995* (The Learmont Inquiry), Cm. 3020. London: HMSO.

Jones, K. and Fowles, A.J. (1984) *Ideas on Institutions: Analyzing the Literature on Long-Term Care and Custody.* London: Routledge and Kegan Paul.

Kauffman, K. (1988) *Prison Officers and Their World.* London: Harvard University Press.

King, R.D. (1991) 'Maximum security custody in Britain and the USA: A study of Gartree and Oak Park Heights', *British Journal of Criminology*, 31, 126–152.

King, R.D. (1999) 'The rise and rise of supermax: An American solution in search of a problem?', *Punishment and Society*, 1 (2), 163–186.

King, R.D. and McDermott, K. (1990) 'My geranium is subversive': Some notes on the management of trouble in prisons', *British Journal of Sociology*, 41 (4), 445–471.

King, R.D. and McDermott, K. (1995) *The State of Our Prisons.* Oxford: Clarendon Press.

Liebling, A. and Price, D. (2001) *The Prison Officer.* Rugby: Prison Service Journal.

Lovell, D., Cloyes, K., Allen, D. and Rhodes, L. (2000) 'Who lives in supermax custody?', *Federal Probation*, 64, 33–38.

McDermott, K. and King, R.D. (1988) 'Mind games: Where the action is in prisons', *British Journal of Criminology*, 28/3, 161–176

Madrid versus Gomez (1995) No.C90-3094-THE, Class action: findings of fact, conclusions of law, and order, US District Court for the Northern District of California, January.

Mandela, N. (1994) *Long Walk to Freedom.* London: Little Brown.

NIC (1997) *Supermax Housing: A Survey of Current Practice.* Longmont, CO: US Department of Justice, National Institute of Corrections.

NIC (1999) *Supermax Prisons: Overview and General Considerations.* Longmont, CO: US Department of Justice, National Institute of Corrections.

Rothman, D. (1971) *The Discovery of the Asylum: Social Order and Disorder in the New Republic.* Boston: Little Brown.

Semprun, J. (1997) *Literature or Life.* New York: Viking.

Singleton, N., Meltzer, H. and Gatwood, R. with Coid, J. and Deasy, D. (1998) *Psychiatric Morbidity Among Prisoners in England and Wales.* London: Office for National Statistics, Stationery Office.

Toch, H. (2001) 'The future of supermax confinement', *The Prison Journal*, 81, 376–388.

Walters, R.H., Callaghan, J.E. and Newman, A.F. (1963) 'Effects of solitary confinement on prisoners', *American Journal of Psychiatry*, 119, 771.

Ward, D.A. and Breed, A.F. (1986) 'Consultants report on the United States Penitentiary, Marion, Illinois', in *Marion Penitentiary 1985 – Oversight Hearing before the Subcommittee on Courts, Civil Liberties and the Administration of Justice of the Committee on the Judiciary, House of Representatives* (Ser. no. 26). Washington, DC: US Government Printing Office.

Ward, D.A. and Carlson, N.A. (1995) 'Why successful regimes remain controversial (Study of the effects of long-term confinement under conditions of supermaximum custody)' *Prison Service Journal*, 97, 27–34, January.

Ward, D.A. and Werlich, T.G. (2003) 'Alcatraz and Marion: Evaluating super-maximum custody', *Punishment and Society*, 5, 53–75.

Chapter 6

The politics of confinement: women's imprisonment in California and the UK

Candace Kruttschnitt

Scholars in the US and elsewhere have drawn considerable attention to the rapid changes that have occurred in crime control, and especially penal policies, over the past decade. These changes have been variously referred to as the 'get tough' or 'penal harm movement' (Cullen *et al* 2000), the 'new penology' (Feeley and Simon 1992), 'penal modernism' (Garland 2001) and the 'new punitiveness' (Pratt 2000). The explanations for these shifts have been at least as wide-ranging as their appellations, referencing changes in public opinion and values that are increasingly intolerant of offenders and, concomitantly, tolerant of prison expansion (Jacobs and Helms 1996; Caplow and Simon 1999). Changes in the actual governance of convicted offenders has also been the subject of scholarly inquiry. Prison authority is thought to be increasingly centralised and encompassed in a new discourse that stresses risk and probability, identification and management, and classification and control (Feeley and Simon 1992; Simon 1993; Adler and Longhurst 1994; Irwin and Austin 1994).

We have argued elsewhere that the subjects of these changes – imprisoned offenders – have been largely ignored in this discourse, especially women prisoners for whom these changes have been particularly salient (Kruttschnitt *et al* 2000: 685). The rapid growth in women's imprisonment, particularly in the 1990s in the US and in England and Wales, combined with the trend towards gender equity in corrections, has meant that women offenders are increasingly encountering physical surroundings and disciplinary regimes that were once reserved only for their male counterparts (Kruttschnitt and Gartner 2003). In the research we conducted in two women's prisons in the mid-to-late 1990s in California, we attempted to unveil what these shifts in penal policy have meant for how women prisoners 'do time.' In so doing, we found that while the character and meaning of women's imprisonment have changed, the 'new penology' is far from complete or uniform in its application.[1] It is conditioned by institutional history and culture.

Specifically, our study examined women's imprisonment in California in three different contexts to provide insights into whether and how the discursive and technical shifts of the past several decades are reflected in their experiences. We began with a temporal focus, replicating some of the work that was completed at the California Institution for Women (CIW) in the early 1960s by Ward and Kassebaum (1965). Because we found that women's prison experiences at CIW in the 1990s could not be divorced from the ongoing shifts and expansion in the prison industry – particularly the addition of newer 'high-tech' institutions – we expanded our conceptual framework and included an examination of women's experiences at Valley State Prison for Women (VSPW), the newest prison for women in California. Based on interviews with 70 prisoners and surveys completed by 1,821 prisoners, we found that women respond to prison life in very predictable ways: by accommodation, by rebellion or by seclusion. Further, while these three responses appear to transcend prison environments, the particulars of these environments helped to shape how women are arrayed within them. It is at CIW, an institution that retains much of the rehabilitative temperament of the past, that we found a greater proportion of women effectively managing the contractions and tensions of the prison world and relatively fewer women openly rejecting the conditions and symbols of their confinement (Kruttschnitt and Gartner 2005). Our findings, then, resonate with the theories of Garland (1997) and others (O'Malley 1992, 1999; Hannah-Moffat 2001) who argue that we need to examine the diversity and incoherence of current penal regimes and the ways in which crime prevention policies and penal histories incorporate programmes from different eras in an uneven and negotiated fashion. They also suggest that the particular dispositions of power and practices of control have a greater impact on some prisons and their inhabitants than others.

In this chapter, I build on this earlier research by elaborating on the central question we initially posed in our research: *What can women's experiences of imprisonment tell us about punishment today?* This analysis, however, differs from the earlier work by explicitly examining how women's prison experiences in England compare with women's prison experiences in California. This cross-national comparison allows us to consider not only the lived reality of changes in penality in both nations but also the extent to which, as Sparks (2003: 20) argues, 'punishment is ineluctably both a political and cultural matter', or whether it is something that transcends political boundaries.[2]

The political context of the new punitiveness

In the United States, macro-level changes that have occurred in the social control of offenders have been well documented and include not only significant increases in the size of the prison population but also substantial shifts in the nature of who has been imprisoned. The dominant contribution to the growth in both the male and female prison populations has been the arrest and confinement of drug offenders (Blumstein and Beck 1999; Kruttschnitt and Gartner 2003). But, because of the enactment of various 'enhancements' to offenders' sentences – based primarily on prior record – increases in the time prisoners serve also has affected the size of the prison community (Zimring *et al* 2001). Perhaps the most infamous example of this is the Three Strikes Law in California but, as Zimring and colleagues (2001) demonstrate, it is the prosecutors' pursuit of second-strikers – increasing the certainty and severity of their sentences – that is, in the long run, continuing to swell the prison population. Finally, there also have been substantial changes in what the prison offers its charges. The prison's focal concern is no longer on rehabilitation but simply incapacitation. As Feeley and Simon (1994) have so aptly described, the emphasis is on providing a low-cost, no-frills environment that will keep criminal offenders, and parole violators, off the streets.[3] As we have shown elsewhere, all of these shifts in penal policy have touched the lives of both male and female offenders, but the effects have been particularly dramatic for women who have been swept into prisons for drug-law violations and parole violations in record numbers (Kruttschnitt and Gartner 2003).

Developments in English penal policy bear much in common with the developments that have occurred in the US, including, many have argued, the historical conditions that gave rise to what Bottoms (1995) refers to as a period of 'populist punitiveness' (Garland 2000; Downes and Morgan 2002).[4] Over the course of the 1990s, a number of acts and reports (The Crime (Sentences) Act 1997, Crime and Disorder Act 1998, The Halliday Report) focused attention on the sentences received by convicted offenders in the UK. As a result, pressure on judges to make greater use of custodial sentences and an increase in average sentence lengths swelled the prison populations in England (Langan and Farrington 1998; Bosworth 1999; Gelsthorpe and Morris 2002). Consistent with experience in the US, these changes in British policy had a disproportionate impact on women offenders in the 1990s, especially those who were arrested for drug-law violations. By the end of the 1990s, women convicted of drug-law violations comprised over one-third of the prisoner population in England and Wales, just as they did in the US. Finally, there also have been concerns about the prisons and a concerted effort to create a better managed prison system, one focused on a 'risk-assessed use of scarce resources' (Carter 2003: 34).

Despite the documented similarities in the factors contributing to the shifts in penal policies and their outcome both in England and the US, there appear to be some important and notable differences in the two prison systems ranging from the more visible distinctions based on, for example, size and average sentence length, to the more subtle distinctions which occur in official rhetoric and accountability. There were five women's prisons in California and, at the time we conducted our research, two of these prisons each held over 3,000 women; by contrast, the prison system for women in England and Wales is much more dispersed and encompasses nineteen institutions. The prison with the largest operational capacity (Holloway) holds roughly 550 women. These differences in scale are also matched by substantial differences in the amount of time women serve in prison. Despite the noted increases in the women's average sentence in the UK (Matthews 1999: 86), in 2000, 79 per cent of all females received into prison under sentences of immediate imprisonment were serving sentences of 'up to and including one year' (Gelsthorpe and Morris 2002: 286); by contrast, in the US, at year end 1997, only 5 per cent of the female prisoners in custody were serving sentences of one year or less (Bureau of Justice Statistics 2000).[5]

The official rhetoric around imprisonment in California and England and Wales also provides a striking contrast. Consider first the official mission statement for California Department of Corrections (CDC):

Our mission is to develop and implement effective and innovative correctional policy, create a coordinated correctional system which is responsive to the citizen's right to public safety and governmental accountability, and maintain a reputation for excellence and integrity.

The relevant equivalent (a 'statement of purpose') for HM Prison Service directs attention not only to the importance of public safety but also the humanity of those they are charged with imprisoning:

> Her Majesty's Prison Service serves the public by keeping in custody those committed by the courts. Our duty is to look after them with humanity and help them lead law-abiding and useful lives in custody and after release.

Several orders and rules, issued by HM Prison Service, ostensibly seem to suggest that the emphasis on treating prisoners with humanity may be more than just rhetoric. The Prison Service has a public statement on race relations that applies to both staff and prisoners and each prison is required to have a race relations management team chaired by the Governor or Deputy Governor of the prison. Similarly, the Prison Service issued a policy on 'bullying' in 1993 and they have subsequently updated the policy, providing that all establishments also have the anti-bullying strategy in place and an anti-bullying coordinator (HM Prison Service 1999). The attention directed towards self-harm and suicide by prisoners in England and Wales also exemplifies the way in which prison officials are more directly accountable for the well-being of their charges than are prison officials in California. Correctional officers are mandated to report both those individuals they deem may be at risk of harming themselves as well as actual incidents of self-harm. Although a proposal was put forward to mandate suicide-prevention programmes in the California prisons in 1999, it does not appear that this mandate was enacted (see California Code of Regulations, NCDR 1999, Section 3365, Title 15). Additionally, unlike the situation in England and Wales, inmate suicides, or for that matter what are classified as 'inmate incidents in institutions', are accorded relatively little attention by either the CDC or the public.[6] Finally, given the number of policies mandated by HM Prison Service, it is perhaps not surprising that their operations are overseen by three separate bodies: the Independent Monitoring Board, HM Chief Inspectorate of Prisons, and, most recently, the Internal Standards Audit Unit.

Do these apparent differences in rhetoric and system management – one, although morally toned, layered with a concern with effective management and administrative oversight – and the other devoid of passion, embodying a purer form of what has been referred to as post-modern penality – affect women's actual prison experiences? Women's imprisonment, while not impervious to distinct patterns of penal control (Rafter 1990), has always been replete with conflicting and competing messages. Assumptions about criminal women, and the ways in which their character contrasts with normatively feminine women, have changed relatively little over time. Despite political fads and fashions which resurrect notions of a new violent female offender and the drug-crazed addict (Faith 1993; Inciardi *et al* 1993), women prisoners are more often depicted as 'sick', 'emotionally disturbed' or 'troublesome' than as dangerous and threatening. While this has tended to soften women's prison regimes, it has also meant that they have been an afterthought in the development of penal policy. Their institutions, and the resources to which they have access in these institutions, are somewhat removed from the rest of society. As a consequence, women's experiences of imprisonment may be marked by a greater degree of continuity than men's experiences, increasing the likelihood that their penal experiences will transcend politics and the attendant penal developments. We turn now to explore this hypothesis and the counter-hypothesis which draws attention to the ways in which punishment reflects a particular cultural and political regime.

Data sources and methods

The data sources and methods used in our study of two prisons in California have been described extensively elsewhere (Kruttschnitt *et al* 2000; Gartner and Kruttschnitt 2004; Kruttschnitt and Gartner 2005). Accordingly, I note here only those data that are relevant to the cross-national work currently under way.

The California prisons

We conducted interviews with women in two prisons in California in the mid-to-late 1990s. The prisons present a contrast in architecture and regime that reflect their relative histories in the development of penal policy in California. One, the California Institution for Women (CIW), was the first prison for women in California. Opened in 1952 during the rehabilitative era, it exemplifies the campus style of prison architecture with a main administration building flanked by several long, flat housing units initially referred to as 'cottages'. Years of use, and several significant increases in the female prison population, have both worn down the edifice and produced additional layers of perimeter security. Although the prison was designed to hold approximately 900 women, by the time we conducted our research it had swelled to almost 1,800, resulting in women double-bunking in cells that were once designed to hold only one prisoner. By contrast, our second prison, Valley State Prison for Women (VSPW), emerged in the era of new penology. Opened in 1995, the prison was built to be used for male prisoners if the state's female prison population declined. It has the prototypical modular design that is typical of the new male facilities in the US, with multiple layers of perimeter security (electrified fences, foot and vehicle patrols by armed guards, and stadium light standards). Despite its newness, VSPW also suffered from overcrowding. Its design capacity of 2,500 had been exceeded by over 1,000 at the time we conducted our research and cells that were intended to hold only four women were holding eight.

Although these structural differences capture some of the cultural distinctions we observed between these two establishments,[7] they obscure the underlying similarities in the internal operations of the prisons that reveal much about penal life in the 1990s. Both prisons housed women of all security levels and in both institutions the women were governed by Title 15 of the California Code of Regulations, which specifies prisoners' behaviours, appearance and activities, along with their rights and privileges. Core features of women's day-to-day lives – for example, wearing prison uniforms, being subjected to multiple counts throughout the day, lining up for meals at the cafeteria at specified times and having their mail and telephone calls monitored – were invariant and served to soften some of the more obvious distinctions we observed between the two prisons. Further, because we found that the effects of the institutional context on women's responses to imprisonment were a matter of degree and not kind (where the effects of the new penology were more deeply etched into the experiences of women at VSPW), I draw on interviews from both California prisons in making our comparison to women's experiences of imprisonment in England.

The case of England

The interviews with women prisoners in England were conducted primarily in two prisons: Downview and Edmunds Hill. However, my fieldwork extended into other female establishments in the Prison Service (Eastwood Park and Styal), where I conducted selected interviews with staff and prisoners. Because this research is ongoing, this chapter reports only the initial findings, drawn from the research completed at Downview.

Downview, initially serving as a nurses' home for a hospital, was opened as a prison in 1989. It held male Category C prisoners until 2001 when it was 're-rolled', or converted, into a female facility. The prison is enclosed by security fencing and consists primarily of four separate wings, in addition to an administrative building and gatehouse; each building is enclosed by fencing and a locked gate.[8] The Prison Service lists its operation capacity at 343 but at the time I conducted interviews, the prisoner population was closer to 200 because part of C-wing was shut down due to a refurbishment project. Each woman has her own cell and all cells, except those on C-wing, have a standard size TV. The accommodations were not dissimilar to those I observed in other women's prison establishments in England; however, whether women were single- or double-bunked did vary by prison establishment and sometimes by unit within a given prison.

The prisoner interviews

The prisoner interviews I conducted in England were designed to replicate those I conducted in California. I obtained a list of all prisoners in Downview with their offence, date of release, race and location within the institution. From this list I selected women randomly for interviews while attempting to ensure that the group of interviewed prisoners would be representative of the prison population. Some of the women whom I selected could not be interviewed because of their work assignment or because they were not available for other reasons. Of those I was able to contact, only five refused.

The women who were interviewed were representative of the prison population in terms of length of time served on their current sentence and, generally, their race. The majority had served more than six months on their current sentence and were white British. About one-fifth of the interviewees were black, with slightly more being of African (12 per cent) than Caribbean (9 per cent) origin. The distribution of offences is also fairly representative of the types of offenders found in the prison's population, but the interviewed women slightly under-represent the proportion of women convicted of drug-law violations and over-represent those convicted of property offences. Because the different wings of the prison, at least in part, represent women at different stages of their prison careers (e.g. reception into prison on A-wing vs. 'super-enhanced' on D-wing), I also examined whether the interviewed prisoners were representative of these different areas of the prison.[9] Again, we find that the interviewed women are quite representative of the entire population, with the largest percentage being drawn from C-wing. Table 6.1 also provides, where possible, comparable data on the women we interviewed in California. The California prisoners are more evenly divided between whites and non-whites than the prisoners from Downview and they also include more women who have been sentenced to prison for violent crimes. Differences in the proportions of interviewees who were imprisoned for violent crimes reflect the relatively large proportion of women at CIW who have been sentenced to prison for life on a murder conviction.

The characteristics of the 33 women interviewed, and the entire prison population, are shown in Table 6.1.

Most interviews were conducted in the women's cells but a few were conducted in the recreation room on the wing; no prison staff were present during the interviews. All of the women agreed to have their interviews taped and I asked the women the same four questions

Table 6.1 Selected characteristics of the prison population and the women interviewed at HM Prison Downview and the women prisoners interviewed in California

| | Downview | | | | California | |
| | Prison Population | | Interviews | | Interviews | |
	N=210	%	N=33	%	N=70	%
Sentence length						
<6 months	38	18	5	15		
>6 months	169	80	28	85		
Unknown	3	1	0	0		
Race*						
White British	134	64	24	73	36	51
Black African	28	13	4	12	16	23
Black Caribbean	31	15	3	9	14	20
Other	17	8	2	6	4	6
Offence						
Violent	45	21	7	21	29	41
Property	67	32	14	42	21	30
Drugs	70	34	9	27	18	26
Other	25	12	3	9	2	3
Unknown	3	1	0	0	0	0
Wing						
A	42	20	7	21		
B	47	22	7	21		
C	83	40	13	39		
D	37	18	6	18		
Unknown	1	<1	0	0		

*The interviewed prisoners in California consisted of White, African Americans and Hispanics rather than the White British, Black African and Black Caribbean prisoners at Downview.

we asked of the women in California: (1) What are the most difficult aspects of doing time? (2) What are the specific problems of prison life for you? (3) What are the various types of prisoners and how would you characterise the relationships among prisoners? And (4) What is the nature of prisoner–staff relations? Because some of these questions require women to focus on the most unpleasant, and perhaps painful, aspects of prison life, we supplemented them with two other questions that were not systematically included in our California study: (1) Are there any good things that have come out of this experience for you?[10] And (2) If you had one piece of advice to give a new prisoner, what would it be?

Analysis

Each interview lasted between 30 and 60 minutes and each interview was transcribed and assigned to a separate computer file.[11] The interview questions were not meant to restrict the data being gathered from the prisoners but rather to provide openings for discussing how women manage both the significant and the more mundane aspects of prison life. I found, for example, that the women often spent time discussing how they got to prison, other prisons they had spent time in, and what they hoped their lives would be like when they were released from prison. In this regard, they offered important information on their personal biographies. As the classical sociological literature on imprisonment has shown (Irwin and Cressey 1962; Irwin 1970; Cohen and Taylor 1972), these background experiences are critical to understanding how prisoners do time and I draw on them in my attempts to distil how women relate to other prisoners and staff in the UK and in California.[12] This type of analysis is consistent with what Garland (1997: 201) refers to as 'grounded social analysis that tries to make sense of penal policy by examining how it operates' and how 'it is experienced by those who inhabit it'. As such, this work should be viewed as exploratory in nature, and more inductive than deductive in its approach.

Findings

The practices of imprisonment

As previously noted, prisons in California (male and female) are governed by Title 15 of the California Code of Regulations and the CDC has made clear its priorities in prison's major functions: custody, classification and case record management. Other prison services have a lower priority

(California Department of Corrections 1994: 11–12). The prisoners' time is generally well structured, and not so subtly enforced by a system of 'programming'. Programming is essentially filling your days with constructive activity – working or attending legally mandated education classes – which earns you half-time credits, or an earlier release date. The prisons vary in the types of work opportunities they offer prisoners, but most women were employed in jobs that can be considered aspects of institutional maintenance (food preparation, cleaning, record-keeping). The nature of the vocational programmes offered varies by prison, but both older and newer institutions offer non-traditional vocational opportunities for the women prisoners, including plumbing, auto mechanics, eyewear manufacturing, small-engine repair and welding. Consistent with the demise of rehabilitation, therapeutic programmes (drug rehabilitation, parenting classes) were in short supply and largely dependent upon the largesse of community volunteers.

The wardens who headed CIW and VSPW when we conducted our research differed in their approaches to imprisonment but, in the context of the neo-liberal penal rhetoric, their differences were based on degree and not kind. The warden of CIW believed that she was a role model for her prisoners, someone who had used life's adversities to make herself stronger. Her belief that 'it is all up to the individual' resonates with the notion of responsibilisation that has come to characterise prison life since the demise of rehabilitation (see Garland 1996: 452). The deputy warden had little concern with whether the women prisoners want to change themselves or improve their lives. Instead, his concerns were managerial. Classifying women offenders by security level, he thought, would be an important innovation for CDC, allowing prison administrators to run their institutions more effectively by sending women who were considered to be troublemakers to a more secure facility. The warden at VSPW was also not concerned with self-help or the possibility that women might be able to change their lives while they were in his charge. His focus, as we observed the staff's, was on their security and safety. He found the lack of spaces for all of the convicted female offenders the biggest problem facing the female correctional establishment in California. While this approach also exemplifies the managerialism that is thought to be characteristic of the criminal justice system (Loader and Sparks 2002: 87–8), this warden was critical of the system. Having worked for 20 years in men's prisons, he was quite concerned about how little is done to help women with their histories of drug and alcohol use and, as he saw it, given their lack of emotional and financial resources, it was to be expected that women would have high recidivism rates. The staff painted a similar, but perhaps less sympathetic, view of their charges.

While taking the issues of security and safety seriously, a message well articulated by the warden, most seemed to view women offenders as more troublesome and needy than truly dangerous or posing a serious risk to their own safety (see also Britton 2003).

HM Prison Service also sees the custodial management of convicted offenders as one of its primary duties but this management function is paired with a stated concern for the 'humanity' and future lives of their charges. In response to several very visible prison disturbances, which belied any notions of humanitarianism (see Liebling 2004: 3–50), a determined effort was made in the 1990s 'to professionalise prison staff and management practices and to deliver a value for money service' (McEvoy 2001: 310). In the process, successive plans issued by the Prison Service demonstrated an increasing concern with whether the standards and procedures for monitoring, for example, bullying and race relations are followed and whether each prison is meeting its Key Performance Targets (KPT) and Key Performance Indicators (KPI).[13] Consistent with at least one KPI, the prisoners' time is carefully scheduled, ideally to ensure they are spending enough time outside of their cells. Generally, this includes two hours out of their cells in the morning and the afternoon for work or classes. At least three days a week, they are locked into their cells from the dinner hour (4:30 pm) until the next morning. Despite the relatively high ratio of staff to women prisoners in HM Prison Service, prison officers indicated that staffing shortages explain why women are locked in for two hours at lunch and frequently in the evenings.[14] When the women are at work, it is frequently in the laundry, kitchen or garden or other institutionally required maintenance functions. But the prisoners are offered educational classes as well as some relatively gender-typical vocational training (e.g. hairdressing, interior design).

The governor of Downview had spent almost his entire working life with HM Prison Service and had considerable experience in female prison facilities, having served as both the governor and deputy governor of Holloway in the 1990s. His perspective on women prisoners and the state of the prison service mirrored the dual vision of the Prison Service. He pointed out that female offenders come to prison with many more problems than their male counterparts. He estimated that 80 per cent have drug and/or psychiatric problems and many have a wide range of health problems. Because of these problems, he believed that the courts frequently use the remand period just to stabilise women, but he also acknowledged that this is a 'bizarre' scenario which essentially entails opting to send people to prison for the help they should receive in the community. More broadly, he seemed to see the developments in the Prison Service in a positive light, noting both that the current extent of oversight, and in particular the audits, KPTs and KPIs, have created a separate bureaucracy within Downview, but that this extent of scrutiny is justified. As he put it, 'we are running our prisons on behalf of society; it is right that we are held to the amount of scrutiny we are.' His staff, however, may have a different view. Many seemed to be quite harried and meal times, when the prisoners were unlocked from their cells, were particularly chaotic. However, by comparison to the staff we encountered in California (and especially at VSPW), they seemed to be far less concerned about formal security and quite comfortable with my wandering throughout any given wing.[15]

Summary

While the strategies and rationales surrounding the imprisonment of women in California and the UK bear witness to much of the current discourse about the neo-liberal penal era, they do so in somewhat different ways. Based on official policy statements, and my observations, it appears that issues of control and regulation of the prison population and the safety of prisoners and the communities they serve are particularly central to the functioning of the women's prisons in California. While the Prison Service in the UK also acknowledges the importance of custody and protecting the communities they serve, they must balance custodial functions with accountability to the government. Greater governmental oversight has 'prudentialised' the Prison Service, making them responsible for managing their own prisons and assessing and measuring their outcomes in the context of maintaining a humane and decent environment for prisoners. However, as Hannah-Moffat (2001) noted in her analysis of federal women's prisons in Canada, whether such innovative strategies actually create a new regime of governing, or whether they simply reinforce pre-existing penal relations of power, often remains unclear (see also Carlen in this volume; and Ramsbotham 2003).

Despite these differences, interviews with prison officials concerning their assumptions about female offenders and the expectations they held for women prisoners reveal important continuities. Administrators in both California and the UK readily acknowledge how the system has failed women, and were quick to point out their many needs. Suggestions that the prison experience might actually benefit these women, or reduce their likelihood of recidivating, were clearly absent. Without explicitly stating it, then, they understood that, without more resources, there was little they could do other than temporarily contain these women and provide them with a respite from their street lives.

Women's experiences of imprisonment in California and the UK

Do the differences and similarities in penal objectives and prison administrators' philosophies in California and the UK affect women's carceral experiences? How do they view the prison and the most visible aspect of their confinement, the staff? How do they manage their lives, and their relationships with other prisoners, in these different carceral worlds?

The prison and staff

Perhaps the most consistent refrain we heard from women in both the California and the UK prisons was the difficulty they found being away from family, and especially their children. As Bosworth (1999) revealed in her study of women imprisoned in the UK, motherhood is a key identity point for female prisoners and they use various strategies for dealing with this obvious pain of imprisonment. Most often this involved filling their cells with cards and letters from family and pictures of their children and friends but sometimes it also involved the realisation that they cannot effectively parent from their cells. This response was more typical of the California prisoners who, generally speaking, were doing much longer sentences than the women in the UK. For many of these women, coping with imprisonment means acknowledging that loss of liberty is one's 'new reality', as opposed to the free life previously led. As one prisoner, told us:

> Doing time in prison … it's hard; it's very hard; very stressful. It's sorta' like when you do time you lose, you lose really all contact really, to me, with reality. Because your family members, or people who cared about you, or people you cared about, you don't see anymore, or you might see, say, once out of every two or three years. So it's very, very hard doing time. But then as you, go, you learn how to cope with it. You never really accept it, but you learn how to cope with it; because if you don't, it'll do you. You know, it'll do you, and that will only tear you down. It'll tear you down.

This seemingly prison-based approach to doing time also appeared among some of the foreign nationals in Britain who had a harder time maintaining contact with their families overseas. One prisoner from Jamaica characterised this well when she explained that while being away from her kids was the hardest part about being in prison, you have to adapt by 'getting on with your sentence':

I thought I couldn't survive in here. I thought God I am going to die and put my head down and scream. But after the sentence and then all the stress of worrying about what is going to happen to you, then eventually, you adapt. I can adapt; everybody can't adapt, but I can adapt. So, um, after being sentenced everything just fall in place and I start thinking about what courses I want to do and I just try to get on with my sentence.

Women in both prison systems were also acutely aware of some of the inherent contradictions in the regimes to which they were subject. In California, where there is a premium on behavioural conformity, women often complained not only about the extent of rules and regulations they were required to follow but also about the absurdity of some of the rules. For example, as one prisoner explained to us, the prisoners are forbidden to wear shower shoes into the dining room because they might slip and fall; and hair dye and makeup were banned to prevent women from assuming various disguises. In the UK, women were also quick to identify seemingly meaningless rules, as well as their inconsistent application. As one prisoner explained to me:

When I first come in here, I got told over on A-wing to press the emergency bell, yeah. You know, press it 'cause they couldn't hear you calling. So when I come on C-wing now, I pressed the bell and I got in trouble for it. Red writing in my book and I said, look I got told on A-wing they couldn't hear me knocking so to press the bell. And they said they shouldn't have told you that 'cause the rules are you don't press it unless it's a right emergency. So I got red writing. If you get three red writings, you're on basic which means [you] get £2.50 a week or something, but then I got nicked for smoking in the BCT building and I didn't know, yeah. I was stupid, but anyway...um...all the other officers let you smoke except this one officer and I never know that. Got caught smoking on there so I got nicked. I said to the governor that I don't think it's fair that all the other officers let you smoke and then this one won't let you smoke and I get nicked. And I didn't know that, that she don't let you smoke in there, do you know what I mean? So, she asked me my name and said I'm going on report and getting nicked. So I said, fuck you, I'm not going on report and I gave her a fake name, you know what I mean?

More generally, while the women in both prison systems acknowledged the presence of both good and bad staff, and were quick to attribute these qualitative judgements to the age and experience of particular staff members they had encountered, staff were seen in a more favourable light in the UK. Women often mentioned that staff permitted them to call them by their first names, they didn't have to address them as 'Sir' or 'Miss' or 'Madam' and they found some really cared about their problems and spent time talking with them. As one prisoner who had spent time in more than one prison described:

> This prison, and the other one, I could always talk to the staff about problems, which obviously, at the beginning I needed to. You know, they're there and you know … they have got a hard job. Cause I was talking to an officer at the other prison, and she said, people think that, you know, we haven't got any problems, but we go home with all your problems. So, you tell them that you are feeling low that day and haven't done something about it, they go home worrying all night, you know. So they have feelings as well. They're just like us, aren't they, really at the end of the day.

Such positive reviews were particularly unlikely to emerge in the context of women's experiences at Holloway,[16] where women often indicated that 'the officers haven't got the time of day for you'. These kinds of complaints were voiced more often by the prisoners we talked to in California, especially among the women at VSPW who recounted not only being dismissed by staff but also being treated in an abusive fashion. As one woman told us, 'they call us bitches; they refer to us as bitches, or fucking bitches'. Another prisoner at VSPW recounted not what particular correctional officers said but, instead, their demeanour towards the prisoners:

> You know they don't want you near them, they don't want to touch you in anyway. You're all trash; you know they talk to you like you're a dog. They really just don't have to say anything. It's just the way they approach you, the way they speak to you, and that gets to me. I don't do anything to deserve that. Yes I made a mistake, and I'm here and I'm paying for my time. If I was acting in an unordered fashion or like an animal, I would expect to be treated like that. But I'm not. I don't disrespect them, and they still want to treat you like that.

Relationships with other prisoners and managing prison life

Just as the absence of family and friends was a defining feature of life for women prisoners regardless of where they served time, so also were many of the basic features of their relationships with other prisoners. Women bemoaned the fact that it was difficult to make really close friends in prison and, in large part, this was due to the inherent distrust they felt toward their colleagues (see also Greer 2000). For some, as was the case for this prisoner from Downview, this distrust was born from experience:

> Yeah, I consider the girls amongst themselves to be close friends. But one wouldn't know, would we? How would you know? They seem very friendly towards each other, but then, you know, it's a prison. It's just an unnatural place to get a friendship. I don't know ... it's strange. Like for instance, I was in prison ... on a prison sentence a couple of years ago and I was on remand for a year. And I was really close to a girl, not in any way other than platonic, but I thought I knew her really well, but it turned out I didn't know her at all. She turned out to be something that I didn't think she was. So I don't know. How close you can be?

Similarly, a prisoner at VSPW told us:

> I've learned you have to want to stick to yourself unless, unless you sit back and you take a view at things and get to really know how people are. Because you can misjudge people and they're not what you think they are.

Distrust of other prisoners also seemed to emanate from the fear that prison friendships were largely based on commercial gain:

> Just keep to yourself. [Don't] tell too many people your business. Tell 'em what you've got, you know [and then] people know you've got this and they pretend they are your friends. Just do your sentence the best way possible. The best way you can. Keep your head down and you'll be alright.

Or as another Downview prisoner put it:

> We have a saying: 'liberty comes through carelessness'. I could come to you tomorrow and ask you to do something for me and

the next week it's like, oh, do you have something for me? And you just probably don't need to go there.

The same cautiousness was echoed in the women we talked to at VSPW, who described what was often behind women's seemingly friendly gestures:

> You have to be real careful. Sometimes people just are, you know … kiss you and act real, you know, kind with you and all that and actually, don't really care. You know it's they want, want, want things and when you don't have it, or you stop giving – they'll be gone.

The women we interviewed in California and the UK also described similar social distinctions among prisoners based on age and race. Middle-aged women saw younger prisoners as more disruptive and loud, and women with longer sentences were particularly bothered by seeing young girls 'coming in time after time' and, as they put it, wasting their lives. In both countries, women also readily acknowledged that, although they tend to 'stick with their own kind', racial hostility among the prisoners was largely absent. In the UK, the foreign national prisoners were quick to point out that while prisoners of different races have no problems associating with each other, women often prefer to be with prisoners from their country. As this Jamaican women describes it:

> I sit with the English girls. I prefer English girls' company but you tend to, especially on the yard, you tend to mix with your own. Even the Africans come to sit with us too. But you tend to have the black together and the white together and if they have white friends they will come and sit with you.

Elsewhere (Kruttschnitt *et al* 2000: 695–6), we have described this as the 'subtext' of social life in women's prison (see Owen 1998: 152), an aspect of the structure of prisoner relations but not one that is determinative of their interactions.

The most striking difference between the women prisoners in California and the UK may revolve around how they relate to doing time not just in the context of their relationships with other prisoners but also in the context of what the prison prioritised. Bullying was a central issue to the women in the UK and they described incidents of being harassed or seeing other women harassed over canteen items, tobacco, drugs and, as this woman describes, even their medication:

> People intimidate other girls for their medication, you know. The majority of these people in here, I wouldn't talk to them on the outside. They aren't on my level. I may be a drug addict as well, although I came in clean this time but I've always dealt in big amounts of drugs. Drugs are only a problem when you have a habit or when you have to do bad things to get them. I've never sold nothing. Always had plenty of work when I wanted and I would never take nothing off of nobody ... I was on this wing two months ago and I got a visit and my sugar daddy brought me a lot of things and a lot of drugs. And people knocking at my door, knocking at my door threatening, nasty, nasty things like that. I know it happened to another girl a few nights ago. She was that scared that she gave most of her drugs away.

The women also described incidents of self-harm and attempts at suicide, something we rarely heard about in California.[17] One woman told us that she knew the prison was worried about her, but she felt that her reactions to imprisonment were quite normal, considering that this was her first experience with imprisonment:

> I felt depressed, very low, you know and I still do sometimes. But, it's ok to feel low, you know, when you reach your limits. There's people out there that do care about you, no matter what you think, they do and you find out who they are when you're in here.

By contrast, some of the staff I talked to were more sceptical about the prisoners harming themselves and the procedures they were required to follow if they felt a prisoner was suicidal. One officer felt that since the 2052 system (which requires the reporting and monitoring of incidents of self-harm) had been introduced, there have been more incidents of self-harm. He also felt that some of the prisoners were manipulating the system by feigning suicide to obtain a transfer to another prison or another wing within the same prison. Another officer believed he could identify the women who really were 'having problems'.

Despite staff members' perceptions about the reality of a woman's ability to cope with her confinement, women prisoners in the UK were much more likely to look to the Prison Service for solutions to their problems than were women prisoners in California. As women in the UK explained it, being imprisoned was enforced detoxification, it meant 'being clean' for awhile, 'giving me a time out from outside ... time to look at, like, what I do want to do when I get out'. The women were especially concerned about the prison's ability to provide them with programmes that might address their problems with drugs. These comments were much less commonly heard among the women we interviewed in California. Perhaps because women in California had much longer sentences to serve, they drew less attention to how the prison might prepare them for life on the outside. But it was also clear that the California prisoners had accepted the fact that rehabilitation was something of the past and the prisons offered them fewer and fewer resources. They accepted the notion that if they wanted to change, it was their responsibility. One prisoner put it succinctly by noting that: 'How you do your time boils down to individual responsibility. You do have choices, even in here. You can make your time worth something. I think I have.' Another prisoner described how she does time by keeping to herself and the importance she places on individual responsibility: 'I don't worry about the mess and their thing, because I can't help 'em. Gotta' help their self, nobody can help.'

Summary

How women cope with doing time, in their interactions with staff and in their relations with other prisoners, reveals some consistent themes. For the women I interviewed in California and the UK, the absence of family and friends, the inherent distrust of their fellow prisoners, and the frustration in dealing with what seem to be arbitrary and inconsistent rules, are all defining aspects of prison life. As such, it is tempting to suggest that women's prison experiences are invariant. But, as I have pointed out, there also some important differences in how the women in each country characterised their interactions with staff and related to each other and their own solitude. These differences draw our attention back to the issue of the political context of penal values and cultures and their importance for understanding carceral experiences.

Conclusion

The new histories of crime control and punishment have provided important insights into the structural and 'cultural sensibilities' responsible for the emergent neo-liberal or post-modern penal era (e.g. O'Malley 1999; Garland 2001; Simon and Feeley 2003). However, the attempt to find the causal factors that can explain these developments in a select group of countries (principally in North America and Western Europe) has meant that variations between countries have been ignored, as have the individuals responsible for, and subject to, these new strategies of control (cf. Lynch 1998, 2000). This is especially true for female offenders who, as Howe (1994) suggests, have been systematically ignored in most historical and social accounts of the development of punishment.

Building on our earlier research on the effects of the neo-liberal penology on women prisoners in California, I have tried here to begin to situate women's carceral lives in a comparative framework, one which directs attention to the ways in which different political environments enact sanctions and penal outcomes. Using the UK as a basis of comparison for our research, a country whose recent strategies of crime control are frequently paired with those in the USA (e.g. Garland 2000), I found some important continuities in women's experiences of imprisonment. These include the wardens', the governors', and even the correctional officers' characterisation of the extent of problems women present to the prison system and the lack of resources for addressing them as well as women's own identification of what are the most difficult aspects of doing time. But perhaps what is of more interest are the differences that surfaced. Relative to women imprisoned in California, I found that the women prisoners in the UK had more favourable interactions with correctional staff and, in turn, these staff seem to accord greater attention to the prisoners' well-being.[18]

These differences may reflect the inherent inconsistency and volatility of modern penality (O'Malley 1999) or variations in the ways in which, and the extent to which, the new penality is being manifested.[19] Relative to the UK, the women's prisons in California appear to have abandoned any pretence of treating prisoners in a benevolent fashion and, as the mandates from the CDC demonstrate, the primary focus is on custodial management and security. If there are any remnants of rehabilitation left, they have been placed firmly in the hands of the prisoners themselves, what is now referred to as a process of responsibilisation. By contrast, in the UK we see a very different agenda, one where the notion of treating prisoners humanely has been subsumed into an actuarial form of managerialism. Although correctional officers may not be able to prevent acts of bullying and self-harm, or even ensure that women spend enough time out of their cells, they are charged with recording these facets of prison life in order to demonstrate the Prison Service's accountability. As I alluded to earlier, unlike the situation in California where responsibilisation has been shifted to the prisoners, in the UK it has been shifted to the Prison Service, exemplifying a process of prudentialism. The Prison Service has become the entrepreneur of its own development, assuming responsibility for, and managing, its own financial and human risks (see O'Malley 1992).

Why retain this rhetoric of decency and humanity if the Home Office is embracing change and imposing a new managerialism on the Prison System? Perhaps, as Lynch (1998) suggested in her analysis of parole in California, abandoning such rhetoric means failure, an acknowledgement that prisons can do no more than incapacitate individuals. More likely, it reflects the slow process of change. While correctional officers bemoaned the amount of time they had to spend on documenting various aspects of their job, as I alluded to, they were also quite willing to offer their own assessments of women prisoners' vulnerability. Their notions that experience and intuitive judgement are important to the jobs they perform suggests that they are a long way from the wholesale endorsement of the managerial discourse.

As this research is ongoing, the conclusions I draw here are some-what speculative. Accordingly, they should be seen as talking points, departures not only for future work that will result from this comparative research project but, hopefully, also for the work of others. Cross-national research in penology has much to offer us, potentially providing both a more reliable body of knowledge on which to base penal policy (Tonry 1999: 63) and one that can inform our understanding of the society context of gendered social control.

Notes

1 It is important to note that subsequent to Feeley and Simon's (1992, 1994) original treatise on the transformation in crime control, they have argued that the new penology does not constitute a 'fully realized vision of criminal justice or even a significant part of it' (Simon and Feeley 2003: 93).

2 Although California is often considered to be a 'bellwether state' in US penal policy (Clear 1994: 54), it is important to remember that the organisation, management and policies of the California Department of Corrections are not necessarily representative of those found in other states.

3 Parole violators constitute over one-half of the prison population in California (see Petersilia 1999).

4 In fact some scholars even argue that there has been a 'policy transfer' in crime control between the US and Britain. Newburn (2002), for example, points to several US innovations – 'zero tolerance', 'three strikes', private prisons and the employment of a drug tsar – which currently have a counterpart in UK criminal policy.

5 Comparable data are not available from the California Department of Corrections. They do report, however, information on the average time served on prison sentence. These data indicate that for felons first released to parole in 1998, the average time served for females was 18 months

(California Department of Corrections 1999a). Gelsthorpe and Morris (2002: 286) report that the average sentence for women received into prison from the Crown Court in 2000 was 23 months and from the magistrates court 3.5 months. But, according to the Criminal Justice Act 1991, those sentenced to between 12 months and under 4 years are released at the half-way point on Automatic Conditional Release. Thus, the average amount of time served for women sentenced in the Crown Court would be considerably less.

6   Inmate Incidents in Institutions include assault/battery, possession of weapons, suicide, attempted suicide, controlled substances use and/or possession. It excludes serious accidents and escapes (California Department of Corrections 2003).

7   See also Rock's (1996) examination of the reconstruction of Holloway prison.

8   Each wing holds a separate category of prisoners. A-wing holds women that have just been received into the prison. B-wing holds 'enhanced' prisoners as well as the prison's segregation unit. C-wing is the oldest wing and it has the fewest amenities; it houses 'basic-level' prisoners. D-wing is structurally unique, resembling a large separate house, and holds the 'super-enhanced' prisoners or those who are given the most freedom within the prison. This gradation of security within the prison is used in all facilities in HM Prison Service as a part of the Incentives and Earned Privileges (IEP) System (see Bottoms 2003).

9   The IEP system used to allocated women to spaces in the prison is not without problems. Because there is limited cell space in any one wing, women who should being living in an enhanced wing, because of earned privileges, may not be there. As such, the distribution of women in different wings is not completely reflective of institutional status.

10 I am indebted to Alison Liebling, and her use of the appreciative inquiry technique, for the addition of the question 'are there any good things that have come out of this experience for you?'

11 Consistent with our California study, I anticipate using Atlas/ti for developing a more complete coding scheming once all of the interviews have been transcribed.

12 For the time being, then, I have put aside questions about variations between prisons within a given socio-political context in favour of concentrating on the larger penal environments and their impact on women's views of other prisoners, staff and the prison experience itself. Additionally, focusing on the effects of specific institutional characteristics (such as the nature of the disciplinary regime, size and organisational objectives) on prisoners' reactions to institutional life may be more difficult in the UK than in California both because of the relatively shorter terms of time they serve in prison and their mobility among different prisons while serving one sentence. Ultimately, this may make discerning the impact of any particular carceral experience in the UK more difficult to tease out than it is in California.

13 Although audits, KPIs, and KPTs contribute to measuring how the prison is doing, albeit in different ways, there is serious scepticism about their purpose and effectiveness including whether they are capable of producing a more 'humane' prison environment (Sparks *et al* 1996; Liebling 2004).

14 The ratio of custodial staff to prisoners at Downview was almost two to one; by contrast, at the time we conducted our research at CIW it was almost five to one and at VSPW roughly seven to one.

15 Other incidents provide additional evidence of the more relaxed level of security found in the women's prisons in the UK. Upon entering the women's prisons in the UK, I have never been personally searched nor have they asked to search any of my personal belongings. The only query I have received is whether I am carrying a mobile phone. By contrast, in California we always had to pass through a metal detector and we always had our personal belongings searched. Additionally, as was true in California, my movements to and from various wings in Downview required a correctional officer's escort for locking and unlocking the gates to each wing. However, after a number of visits to Downview, I was asked by one of the correctional staff if I had my own set of keys. Interestingly, but perhaps the subject of another paper, a tour of the recently opened HM Prison at Bronzefield – the first private prison for women in the UK – provided a level of security comparable to what I experienced in the women's institutions in California.

16 Holloway is located in north London and serves as a 'feeder and allocation' prison for all the women's prisons. The majority of women at Holloway are unconvicted or unsentenced.

17 The California Department of Corrections (2003) reported that in 2002, there were no suicides among the roughly 9,700 women prisoners. HM Prison Service (2003) reported nine suicides during the same year among the 4,500 women prisoners they held.

18 It is important to remember that this observation is based largely on my interactions with prisoners and correctional officers in two women's prisons in the UK. It is not clear that I would have had the same results if I had examined male prisoners or a wider range of female establishments (see e.g. Liebling 2004).

19 We observed a somewhat similar outcome in our comparison of women's prison experiences at CIW and VSPW where the effects of the new penology on the prisons and prisoners lives were conditioned by the prison's culture.

References

Adler, M. and Longhurst, B. (1994) *Discourse, Power, and Justice: Toward a New Sociology of Imprisonment*. London: Routledge Press.

Blumstein, A. and Beck, A.J. (1999) 'Population growth in U.S. prisons, 1980–1996', in M. Tonry and J. Petersilia (eds) *Prisons, Vol. 26 of Crime and Justice: A Review of Research, Edited by Michael Tonry and Norval Morris*. Chicago: University of Chicago Press.

Bosworth, M. (1999) *Engendering Resistance: Agency and Power in Women's Prisons*. Aldershot: Ashgate Publishing.

Bottoms, A. (1995) 'The philosophy and politics of imprisonment and sentencing', in C. Clarkson and R. Morgan (eds) *The Politics of Sentencing Reform*. Oxford: Clarendon Press.

Bottoms, A. (2003) 'Theoretical reflections on the evaluations of a penal policy initiative', in L. Zedner and A. Ashworth (eds) *The Criminological Foundations of Penal Policy: Essays in Honour of Roger Hood*. Oxford: Oxford University Press.

Britton, D.M. (2003) *At Work in the Iron Cage. The Prison as Gendered Organization*. New York: New York University Press.

Bureau of Justice Statistics (2000) *Correctional Populations in the U.S., 1997. NCJ-177613*. Washington, DC: US Department of Justice, Bureau of Justice Statistics.

California Department of Corrections (1994) *Inside Corrections: Public Safety, Public Service*. Sacramento: California Department of Corrections.

California Department of Corrections (1999a) *Time Served on Prison Sentence. Felons First Released to Parole by Offence – Calendar Year 1998*. Sacramento: California Department of Corrections.

California Department of Corrections (1999b) Notice of Change to Directors Rules (NCDR) *California Department of Corrections. Section 3365, Title 15 of the California Code of Regulations*. Sacramento: California Department of Corrections.

California Department of Corrections (2003) *Inmate Incidents in Institutions, Calendar Year 2002*. Sacramento: California Department of Corrections.

Caplow, T. and Simon, J. (1999) 'Understanding prison policy and population Trends', in M. Tonry and J. Petersilia (eds) *Prisons, Vol. 26 of Crime and Justice: A Review of Research, edited by Michael Tonry and Norval Morris*. Chicago: University of Chicago Press.

Carter, P. (2003) *Managing Offenders, Reducing Crime. A New Approach*. London: Home Office.

Clear, T. (1994) *Harm in American Penology: Offenders, Victims, and Their Communities*. Albany, NY: State University of New York Press.

Cohen, S. and Taylor, L. (1972) *Psychological Survival. The Experience of Long-term Imprisonment*. Harmondsworth: Penguin.

Cullen, F.T., Fisher, B.S. and Applegate, B.K. (2000) 'Public opinion about punishment and corrections' in N. Morris and M. Tonry (eds) *Crime and Justice: An Annual Review of Research, vol. 27*. Chicago: University of Chicago Press.

Downes, D. and Morgan, R. (2002) 'The British General Election 2001', *Punishment and Society*, 4, 81–96.

Faith, K. (1993) *Unruly Women: The Politics of Confinement and Resistance.* Vancouver: Press Gang.

Feeley, M. and Simon, J. (1992) 'The new penology: Notes on the emerging strategy of corrections and its implications', *Criminology,* 30, 449–74.

Feeley, M. and Simon, J. (1994) 'Actuarial justice: The emerging new criminal law', in D. Nelken (ed.) *The Futures of Criminology.* London: Sage Publishing.

Garland, D. (1996) 'The limits of the sovereign state: Strategies of crime control in contemporary society', *The British Journal of Criminology,* 36, 445–71.

Garland, D. (1997) '"Governmentality" and the problem of crime: Foucault, criminology and sociology', *Theoretical Criminology,* 1, 173–214.

Garland, D. (2000) 'The culture of high crime societies', *British Journal of Criminology,* 40, 347–375.

Garland, D. (2001) *The Culture of Control: Crime and Social Order in Contemporary Society.* Chicago: University of Chicago Press.

Gartner, R. and Kruttschnitt, C. (2004) 'A brief history of doing time: The California Institution for Women in the 1960s and the 1990s', *Law and Society Review,* 38 (2) (in press).

Gelsthorpe, L. and Morris, A. (2002) 'Women's imprisonment in England and Wales: A penal paradox', *Criminal Justice,* 2, 277–301.

Greer, K.R. (2000) 'The changing nature of interpersonal relationships in a women's prison', *The Prison Journal,* 80, 442–468.

Hannah-Moffat, K. (2001) *Punishment in Disguise: Penal Governance and Federal Imprisonment of Women in Canada.* Toronto: University of Toronto Press.

HM Prison Service (1999) *Anti-Bullying Strategy.* Prison Service Order (Order Number 1702). London: Home Office.

HM Prison Service (2003) *Working with Women Prisoners* (edited by Bernice Ash). London: Women's Estate Policy Unit, HM Prison Service.

Home Office (2001) *Making Punishment Work. Report of a Review of the Sentencing Framework for England and Wales (July 2001) (The Halliday Report).* London: Home Office Communication Directorate.

Howe, A. (1994) *Punish and Critique: Towards a Feminist Analysis of Penality.* New York: Routledge.

Inciardi, J.A., Lockwood, D. and Pottiger, A.E. (1993) *Women and Crack Cocaine.* New York: Macmillan.

Irwin, J. (1970) *The Felon.* Englewood Cliffs, NJ: Prentice-Hall.

Irwin, J. and Austin, J. (1994) *It's About Time: America's Imprisonment Binge.* Belmont, CA: Wadsworth.

Irwin, J. and Cressey, D. (1962) 'Thieves, convicts, and the inmate culture', *Social Problems,* 10, 145–47.

Jacobs, D. and Helms, R.E. (1996) 'Toward a political model of incarceration: A time-series examination of multiple explanations for prison admission rates', *American Journal of Sociology,* 102, 323–57.

Kruttschnitt, C., Gartner, R. and Miller, A. (2000) 'Doing her own time? Women's responses to prison in the context of the old and the new penology', *Criminology,* 38, 681–718.

Kruttschnitt, C. and Gartner, R. (2003) 'Women's imprisonment', in M. Tonry (ed.) *Crime and Justice: A Review of Research, Vol. 30*. Chicago: University of Chicago Press.

Kruttschnitt, C. and Gartner, R. (2005) *Marking Time in the Golden State: Women's Imprisonment in California*. Cambridge: Cambridge University Press.

Langan, P.A. and Farrington, D.P. (1998) *Crime and Justice in the United States and in England and Wales, 1981–1996. NCJ 169284*. Washington, DC: US Department of Justice, Office of Justice Programmes, Bureau of Justice Statistics.

Liebling, A. (2004) *Prisons and Their Moral Performance. A Study of Values, Quality and Prison Life*. Oxford: Oxford University Press.

Loader, I. and Sparks, R. (2002) 'Contemporary landscapes of crime, order, and control: Governance, risk, and globalization', in M. Maguire, R. Morgan and R. Reiner (eds) *The Oxford Handbook of Criminology*. Oxford: Oxford University Press.

Lynch, M. (1998) 'Waste managers? The new penology, crime fighting, and parole agent identity', *Law and Society Review*, 32, 839–70.

Lynch, M. (2000) 'Rehabilitation as rhetoric: The idea of reformation in contemporary parole discourse and practices', *Punishment and Society*, 2, 40–65.

Matthews, R. (1999) *Doing Time: An Introduction to the Sociology of Imprisonment*. Houndsmills, Basingstoke, Hampshire: Palgrave.

McEvoy, K. (2001) *Paramilitary Imprisonment in Northern Ireland: Resistance, Management and Release*. Oxford: Oxford University Press.

Newburn, T. (2002) 'Atlantic crossings. "Policy transfer" and crime control in the USA and Britain', *Punishment and Society*, 4, 165–194.

Notice of Change to Directors Rules (NCDR) (1999) *California Department of Corrections. Section 3365, Title 15 of the California Code of Regulations*. Sacramento, California.

O'Malley, P. (1992) 'Risk, power and crime prevention', *Economy and Society*, 21, 252–75.

O'Malley, P. (1999) 'Volatile and contradictory punishment', *Theoretical Criminology*, 3, 175–96.

Owen, B. (1998) *In the Mix. Struggle and Survival in a Woman's Prison*. Albany, NY: State University of New York Press.

Petersilia, J. (1999) 'Parole and prisoner reentry in the United States', in M. Tonry and J. Petersilia (eds) *Prisons Vol. 26 of Crime and Justice: A Review of Research, edited by Michael Tonry and Norval Morris*. Chicago: University of Chicago Press.

Pratt, J. (2000) 'The return of the wheelbarrow men; or, the arrival of postmodern penality?' *British Journal of Criminology*, 40, 127–145.

Rafter, N.H. (1990) *Partial Justice: Women, Prison and Social Control*, 2nd edition. New Brunswick, NJ: Transaction Publishing.

Ramsbotham, D. (2003) *Prisongate: The Shocking State of Britain's Prisons and the Need for Visionary Change*. London: Simon and Schuster.

Rock, P. (1996) *Reconstructing a Woman's Prison: The Holloway Redevelopment Project, 1968–1988*. Oxford: Clarendon Press.

Simon, J. (1993) *Poor Discipline: Parole and the Social Control of the Underclass, 1890–1990*. Chicago: University of Chicago Press.

Simon, J. and Feeley, M. (2003) 'The form and limits of the new penology', in T.G. Blomberg and S. Cohen (eds) *Punishment and Social Control* 2nd edition. New York: Aldine De Gruyter.

Sparks, R. (2003) 'State punishment in advanced capitalist countries,' in T.G. Blomberg and S. Cohen (eds) *Punishment and Social Control*, 2nd edition. New York: Aldine De Gruyter.

Sparks, R., Bottoms, A.E. and Hay, W. (1996) *Prisons and the Problem of Order*. Oxford: Clarendon Press.

Tonry, M. (1999) 'Parochialism in U.S. sentencing policy', *Crime and Delinquency*, 45, 48–65.

Ward, D.A. and Kassebaum, G. (1965) *Women's Prison: Sex and Social Structure*. New York: Aldine.

Zimring, F.E., Hawkins, G. and Kamin, S. (2001) *Punishment and Democracy. Three Strikes and You're Out in California*. New York: Oxford University Press.

Part 2

Revisiting the Society of Captives

Chapter 7

Codes and conventions: the terms and conditions of contemporary inmate values

Ben Crewe[1]

The 'inmate code' represents one of the key empirical and theoretical terrains of prison sociology. Defined as the idealised model of inmate behaviour, the code has been discussed in relation to a range of phenomena, including inmate leadership (Sykes 1958; Sykes and Messinger 1960; Ohlin 1956), the processes of inmate socialisation and reintegration (Clemmer 1940; Wheeler 1961; Atchley and McCabe 1968), the alleviation of the pains of imprisonment (McCorkle and Korn 1954; Sykes and Messinger 1960) and the maintenance of order within prisons (Sykes 1958). The debate about whether the prison's internal value system is generated by imported factors (Irwin and Cressey 1962; Jacobs 1974) or by the structural deprivations of prison life (Sykes 1958; Sykes and Messinger 1960; Goffman 1961) is well documented, and requires little elaboration here. Few researchers now doubt that prison culture is determined by a combination of institutional and external variables. There may be little room for significant theoretical advances in this area.

The research literature on the content of the prison value system has highlighted a number of recurring themes (*inter alia*, Ohlin 1956; Sykes and Messinger 1960; Garabedian 1963; Mathiesen 1965; Welford 1967; Irwin 1970, 1985; Thomas 1977; Garofalo and Clark 1985; Einat and Einat 2000; Winfree *et al* 2002; Einat 2004). Put simply, these include prescriptions that prisoners should hold anti-authority views, be oppositional to the behaviour patterns expected by the official administration, and should fraternise as little as possible with officers and other representatives of the regime; that they should be loyal to fellow inmates – i.e. not exploit others, display honour and integrity

– and should not 'grass' upon or betray each other; that they should display emotional and physical fortitude, or 'manliness'; and that they should mind their own business, or 'do their own time'.

Much research has used these formulations as a starting point for analysis, gauging levels of 'prisonisation' or 'code adherence' in relation to their terms (e.g. Garofalo and Clark 1985; Leger and Gray Barnes 1986; Wilson 1986). The focus of such studies has tended to be general notions of inmate solidarity. However, by drawing on descriptions and 'attitudinal items' that are several decades old, such work has assessed what may be discarded notions of ideal behaviour. Inmate conduct may be being evaluated against a template that prisoners no longer deploy to judge each other and navigate their own actions. Prison researchers are in danger of losing sight of the shifts in the normative system that one would expect to occur during years of change in the society outside the prison walls and in the terms of penal administration.

Indeed, there are few detailed, contemporary descriptions of the everyday values of the inmate community. Recent accounts of prison argot have helped to illustrate certain aspects of prison culture, for example, changes in the nature of sexual hierarchies (Hensley *et al* 2003) and the role of drugs in the prison community (Einat and Einat 2000). Yet little explanation exists of how the code functions as a dynamic normative system and how its terms are interpreted and enforced in the daily world of the jail. This chapter seeks to elucidate some of these issues, focusing on three key areas of inmate conduct norms: views about 'grassing', relationships between prisoners and staff, and the terms of loyalty and solidarity.

The study

The chapter draws on emerging findings from a long-term, semi-ethnographic study of HMP Wellingborough, a medium-security UK training establishment. The general aim of the research is to provide a detailed description and analysis of the social life and culture of this prison. As Simon and others have noted (Simon 2000; Liebling 2000; Wacquant 2002), the inner life of the prison has almost disappeared as an object of enquiry, and we have relatively little sociological knowledge about the everyday social structure, values and practices of the modern prison in the context of late-modernity and a prison system that has undergone significant change in recent years (Liebling 2004).

Without aiming to be directly comparative, the study revisits many of the classic themes of prison sociology, and employs the same method of sustained immersion in the field that has characterised many of the discipline's benchmark studies (see Clemmer 1940; Sykes 1958; Mathiesen 1965; Carroll 1974; Jacobs 1977). This kind of prolonged empirical enquiry ensures that the prisoner value system can be seen *in action*, as a set of rules that are employed and negotiated in complex ways in the everyday social world of the prison; and *in context*, as one component of a prison social system shaped by a multitude of forces within and beyond the institution.

A ten-month fieldwork phase between October 2002 and August 2003 comprised three months of dedicated observation and informal conversation, and over 300 hours of in-depth, semi-structured interviews with prisoners and staff. Visits were made three or four days per week, including weekends and evenings, to all areas of the prison. At the time of the study, the prison held around 520 prisoners, on seven residential wings. These included a Voluntary Drug Testing Unit (VTU) housing around 180 prisoners and a wing dedicated to around 60 life-sentence and long-term prisoners deemed suitable for medium-security conditions. All prisoner interviews were conducted solely by the author, in an office on the prison's induction wing. Interviewees were a mixture of randomly selected prisoners and a number with whom relationships had already been established. Explicit questions about the 'inmate code' formed one section of the interview schedule, with prisoners probed on the informal rules of prison life. Responses to many other questions generated much of the material included in this chapter. All interviews were recorded, with the permission of the interviewees.

Solidarity, loyalty and the inmate code

Sykes was clear that the code he identified was 'an ideal rather than a description' of inmate behaviour (Sykes 1995: 82), but he emphasised that it had a direct and forcible presence in the prison. Regardless of their actual conformity to the maxims they espoused, prisoners were, he reported, 'vehement' in their assertions about appropriate conduct, and the code was verbally accorded 'almost universal allegiance' (Sykes and Messinger 1960: 9). Other researchers have concurred that, regardless of the realities of everyday prisoner activity and the lack of complete uniformity in views about idealised behaviour, the code is a powerful agent of socialisation which prisoners endorse relatively consensually and with which they 'must identify' (Einat 2004; Welford 1967). Akers *et al* state that 'as with any system [of norms] there are core participants, followers and isolates [who are] unaffiliated with the social system.

The only assumption is that the inmate system is pervasive enough to be recognised and that enough inmates participate in it that we may speak of a system which sets the tone and style for the entire inmate group'(Akers *et al* 1977: 528–9).

In informal conversation and interviews, prisoners in HMP Wellingborough commonly responded to initial questions about the inmate code either by stating that it resided 'elsewhere' – in higher-security establishments or in the past – or with summaries that rehearsed the conventional descriptions condensed above. However, further investigation quickly revealed that, in practice, everyday behaviour was regulated less by a system of highly idealised stipulations than by a set of *conventions* about appropriate action. For the significant majority of prisoners, absolutist principles of general solidarity and opposition to the prison regime bore little relation not only to what they observed in others, but also to what they expected of their peers and themselves felt obliged. The value system to which most inmates were effectively accountable and to which they declared normative allegiance was a much diluted version of the ideal code. In each of its areas, as this chapter illustrates, there were caveats, ambiguities and mitigating circumstances.

Prisoners commented consistently that there had been a decline in the importance and intensity of a shared value system of solidarity, mutual aid and opposition to prison staff. Three main explanations were provided for this development. Firstly, and most broadly, general changes in the culture and conditions of prison life had reduced the confrontational and depriving nature of prison life. These related to improvements in the physical environment, shifts in the attitudes of officers, and the introduction of a range of privileges, such as in-cell televisions and wing telephones, which had altered daily life inside prison in significant ways. Some prisoners regarded such developments as genuinely benign, and highlighted the decreased need for collective action in a system where basic rights such as telephone calls, showers and time out of cell were assured. More cynical prisoners viewed them as insidious but effective forms of control. In typical comments, one prisoner described television as 'visual mogadon' (Interview, March 2003), while another attributed the decline of 'the social prison' to the stultifying effects of in-cell entertainment:

> They're basically just sitting in their cell watching telly. Basically doing nothing ... That's how it's changed. At one time you would get a group of lads together and they'd be sitting talking about things, having a laugh, playing dominoes, going down to education.

I mean education used to be full at night time. Now you're lucky if you get 20 people.

(Interview, April 2003)

Secondly, the development in recent years of a culture of hard drug use in prison was also considered to have undermined inmate solidarity in a number of ways. Heroin, in particular, was blamed for encouraging debt-related violence and theft, reducing levels of trust, limiting many prisoners' concerns to the acquisition or distribution of heroin, and eroding the general dignity of the prisoner population (see Crewe forthcoming). A perceived rise in the frequency of informing was also attributed to cultures of drug-related debt: certainly, prisoners who requested protection to escape from debts were pushed by staff, in return, to reveal the names of drug dealers.

Thirdly, prisoners cited new mechanisms of penal administration, such as the Incentives and Earned Privileges (IEP) Scheme, and early and temporary release systems, including 'taggings' and home leave, as factors that had divided and individualised the inmate community and motivated prisoners to conform to institutional goals – as the following quotation illustrates:

Here, people don't really care. They don't want to stick together. Even though it would work in their benefit if they did stick together. But at the same time you think 'Well, if we stick together, [officers are] going to take my enhanced [status] off me, and I'm going to lose my job. Is it worth the risk just for a hot meal?' I don't think so. I'll do me fucking cold meal. I'd rather keep my enhanced and make life a little bit easier.

(Interview, January 2003)

Many of these mechanisms had particular salience in a category C establishment, where most prisoners were looking to progress through the system. Many insisted that one consequence of this was that prisoners were increasingly willing to inform on each other in order to prove their compliance, and obtain taggings or 'D-cats'. Likewise, prisoners maintained that their own and others' determination to 'get to the gate' or maintain their material standards had reduced the penalties for code violation:

In here, people really do wanna move on, and wanna get theirselves out. If you're lookin' at the next fifteen years in prison, then you've got nothing to lose to bash someone up, but in here, you do that, then you lose everything that you gained, so it doesn't really happen. People know who the grasses are, but they just pay 'em no mind.

(Interview, June 2003)

Since they brought in all this basic, enhanced, and piss tests and all the rest of it, everything's changed. The solidarity's gone. You've got nonces serving your food.

(Interview, May 2003)

Prisoners rumoured to be informers or sex offenders were often, therefore, grudgingly tolerated. Many prisoners recognised and resented their own reluctance to enforce the ideals of the inmate community: 'I'd like to do something, but I'd have more to lose than gain', said one prisoner, in reference to his parole application, after someone on the wing had slashed the pool table with a razor. 'I don't want no trouble, and he ain't causing me no trouble' was a typical refrain (Interview, April 2003).

Such expressions captured the ways that, in the category C estate especially, modern prison policy has successfully set personal goals at odds with the collective principles of the prisoner population. Certainly, among Wellingborough prisoners, declarations of general solidarity with the prisoner community were an exception. As the following quotation illustrates, commitments were more often expressed as limited and conditional.

Interviewer: Is there solidarity between prisoners?
Prisoner: [Laughs] Solidarity? Certain prisoners, there is certain prisoners that've got solidarity between them. But I myself personally haven't got any, because I don't need any at the moment, y'know ... Loyalty goes as far as individual groups of inmates. Four inmates may agree with something, you may get five, but there was a loyalty once when we argued about food, certain things [but now] it wouldn't be in my interest at all, and I don't think it would be in most people's interests. 'Cos when you're in a C cat, you come as an individual, and you try and get along with other inmates, and try and get each other to get along together [...] My loyalties are basically to myself. But I am loyal to other inmates in the sense of if he does something [for me] I'll do something for him, things like that. If you call that loyalty, being loyal, yeah, I do that every day.

(Interview, June 2003)

Instead, prisoners proclaimed their allegiances to themselves, their families, or to small prisoner sub-groups based on friendship, ethnicity, religion or geographical area. Where group loyalties existed, they provided informational, physical, material and social support (Harvey 2004). A prisoner with a regional or ethnic peer group could expect to socialise with his peers during association periods, borrow tobacco and phonecards from them without having to repay at 'double-bubble' (i.e. with 100 per cent interest), and count on them to 'watch his back' in the event of aggravations and arguments. Loyalties among certain ethnic and regional groups – the latter described by one prisoner as 'automatic connections' (interview, January 2003) – were particularly strong, and it was taken for granted that they were reciprocal.

Indeed, such expectations resulted in some individuals being pressed into activities they would rather avoid, such as storing and distributing illicit goods, or getting involved in fights on behalf of others. Prisoners recognised this double-edged nature of loyalty, especially when it was based on regional affiliations. Those from urban centres some distance from Wellingborough commonly expressed relief that, in being in a prison where their regional alignments were restricted, they could be socially anonymous and could avoid being pulled into other people's problems. The links to external cultures were critical here. The obligation to fulfil codes of local loyalty was founded partly on a recognition that reputation outside the jail (in one's neighbourhood, hometown or local prison) would be seriously undermined by any failure to 'back up' one's peers. Conflicts could therefore arise between a prisoner's self-interest and his commitment to his regional sub-group. In such predicaments, prisoners had to weigh up, and often explicitly negotiate, a number of factors:

> *Interviewer*: Would you be able to say, 'listen lads, I really don't wanna get involved, I'm out in four weeks'?
> *Prisoner*: They'd probably accept that, yeah, but if it was Derby lads, I wouldn't say that. Even if I was out in four weeks, I would get involved because ... if I ever come back to prison and something happened ... people might remember that, they might not be so quick to jump in and help ... you might not wanna get involved ... but you can't turn round and say 'pfff'. Like I say, they might accept it but they won't forget it ... say, in this jail, a week before I get out, somebody puts it on me in the TV room, I'm in a position here now where I can say 'hang on a minute mate, I'm not scared of you but at the end of the day, I'm out next week, so

I don't want no fuckin' trouble, so just leave it, yeah' and other people would probably say to the geezer, 'yeah, leave it, the man's out next week.' If I was in a prison where everybody knew me and somebody put it on me, I couldn't do that... I'd have to go for it, because I know if I don't, I'm gonna get slated out there.

(Interview, February 2003)

Interviewer: So what happens if one of [your friends] comes to you and says they want you to help them in a fight?
Prisoner: That's happened recently. But I managed to sort it out without having to fight. [A friend] was getting a bit of hassle off somebody else... And my mate was worried about it. And he says 'what's going to happen?' And I said 'you know I'm your friend ...', but I mentioned that I'd got home leave soon, and I says 'don't expect me to be fighting, because I'm not losing nothing for no-one.' And he said 'no, I wouldn't want you to do that'... The lads who I'm with know I wouldn't jeopardise anything – they know I wouldn't jeopardise another day in this shit-hole for anyone.

(Interview, April 2003)

As these quotations indicate, then, a prisoner's commitment to his primary group was not beyond negotiation. Prisoners generally accepted that there were limits to the loyalties that they should expect from, and be expected to display towards, others. The majority were focused on being released, and understood that others were in the same position. It was very common for prisoners to define the boundaries of their allegiances as the points where they might endanger or slow down their progression through the system. Being loyal to oneself, one's principles and one's family were accepted principles, and were stated in prisoners' deliberations over appropriate courses of action. Many reflected that their sentence was a punishment for personal failings, and should only therefore be conducted according to personal frames of reference. This discourse of personal responsibility was recurrent elsewhere in prisoners' testimonies (see below), and was often conveyed as a moral convention within a culture of mutual respect for individual values:

It seems to me the best way to take responsibility for your life is to make your own judgements and your own decisions, and not do what other people want you to do if you don't agree with it, so I think fundamentally a person's first loyalty has to be to themselves, to do what they think is right. But if somebody was being led down a garden path and I felt sufficiently close to that person, then I'd say, 'are you sure you know what you're doing 'ere?'; but I'd always leave it to other people to make their own decisions about things.

(Interview, May 2003)

In this context, to be staunch or self-sacrificial was seen as a positive virtue, but only up to a point, beyond which it was considered misguided. To be fiercely committed to prisoners who were not close associates was regarded as naïve, 'leaving yourself open to get hurt' (Interview, March 2003), and a gesture unlikely to be reciprocated. Prisoners rarely took risks for each other without immediate compensation or an expectation of reciprocity in the future; acts of pure kindness were uncommon, covert or were relatively minor forms of material provision; and emotional solidarity was highly circumscribed.

This is not to suggest that solidary and mutual respect were completely absent, in principle or practice, from the landings. Most prisoners suggested that they were more tolerant and respectful of others within prison than they would be outside it:

There's probably [only] about three or four lads on the wing that I'd go for a drink with out there. But I still show [others] respect. For instance there's a lad opposite me, he must be about four stone wet through. Every day he comes to my pad 'can I have a look at your telly guide?' or 'have you got a bit of sugar?' or a tea bag. And I'll give it him. I wouldn't give him the time of day out there.

(Interview, April 2003)

Displays of empathetic unity were also quite common. Prisoners often complained about perceived injustices and hypocrisies perpetrated on each other by the prison system. Likewise, sympathy and compassion were openly expressed after a suicide occurred in the jail. It was significant, though, that such declarations neither led to nor demanded collective action. Unity without commitment was also exhibited when prisoners warned each other of the imminent presence of an officer on a landing, and when they broke up fights to prevent others from being disciplined. Again, such actions appeared sensitive to preventing other prisoners from serving more time than was required, rather than any simple notion of 'solidarity'.

'Grassing'

Most commentators have noted that a central tenet of the inmate code is that one should not 'grass' on another prisoner (Clemmer 1940; Irwin 1970, 1980; Einat and Einat 2000). Sykes and Messinger defined grassing as the 'betrayal of a fellow captive to the institutional officials', and noted that 'in general, no qualification of mitigating circumstance is recognized' (1960: 7). However, among prisoners in HMP Wellingborough, definitions of what counted as grassing varied, and there was no firm consensus on why it was proscribed or the conditions under which it could be acceptable. Condemnations of grassing were rarely absolute.

Despite the general agreement that grassing was the most serious breach of inmate norms, there were certain scenarios in which it was considered 'understandable', even if not 'ideal'. The most clear-cut case was when a prisoner was being bullied or exploited, or when several prisoners on a wing were being victimised or agitated by a group of fellow inmates. In these scenarios, prisoners reported feeling entitled to make a collective approach to staff, in which they warned of the consequences if officers did not remove the offending prisoner(s) from the wing:

> If there's somebody that's trouble, and a nuisance on the wing... then they would say to the officers 'look, this guy's causing trouble. He hasn't just done it with one or two of us; if you don't get rid of him he's going to get seriously hurt. Get rid of him before he gets hurt. It would be an offence, a moral offence to us, for him to get hurt. We don't want it to happen. Get rid of him'. And they generally will.
>
> (Interview, April 2003)

While the insinuation of what might occur should officers fail to intercede was intended as a threat, the plea for intervention also indicated some basic level of empathy and shared identity between prisoners. Even where collective norms had been violated, prisoners placed limits on what counted as an appropriate response and sought to curb excessive consequences. As also suggested here, there was a perceived moral basis to what might be called 'collective grassing'.

The recognition that, under certain conditions, it was understandable for a prisoner individually to tell officers that he was being bullied, had similar ethical foundations. In such a situation, the ideal course of action was for him to take matters into his own hands, either by fighting or 'fronting up' to the aggressor.[2] This would generate respect regardless of whether he won or lost any subsequent fight, and prisoners claimed that anyone who stood up for himself was unlikely to be repeatedly victimised. A prisoner deemed capable of fighting in terms of his size and demeanour was expected to sort out any problem through these means. Someone seen as 'not a fighter' or who faced multiple perpetrators was encouraged to go for help either to friends or to influential prisoners on the wing. Prisoners reported that, in young offender institutions, bullying was a routine practice that was legitimised by a contempt for weakness and those who 'allowed themselves' to be victimised. In adult male prisons, by contrast, contempt was reserved for bullies, and there was sympathy for the vulnerable. It was passionately asserted that bullying was not tolerated and was 'sorted out' within the prisoner community, preferably without recourse to the prison officials. It was a display of bravery and power, and a mark of moral fortitude, to protect the victimised, and considerable credibility could be accrued from interventions of this kind. Although informing staff on behalf of another prisoner was less preferable than sorting out the problem oneself, it was not an entirely illegitimate course of action in certain circumstances:

> Say a little guy came up to me and he'd been bullied. If it was someone I could tackle myself, I would go and say something to him – 'leave him alone' – and if he wouldn't leave him alone I'd clump him. I've experienced that [bullying] when I was younger in prisons and Borstals, and things like that. It's a bad thing. It can cause major problems. And it's wrong. So I would help them if I could. But if I couldn't help them, say they were getting bullied by a great big 20-stone fellow I couldn't tackle, I would say something to the staff. Course I would ... You'd have to help them some way wouldn't you? You couldn't stand and watch it carry on, could you? ... It's wrong in outside society and it's wrong in here.
>
> (Interview, April 2003)

In situations where a bullied prisoner lacked the confidence or physical means to face up directly to his victimiser or seek support from other inmates, many prisoners reported that they would understand if he told officers about it:

> If you haven't got friends on the wing that are hard or you don't know 'em well enough to go and ask 'em that, then you can go and say to the screws: I don't think that's wrong. I hate bullying, you know ... I don't disagree with grassing for bullying in jail.
>
> (Interview, April 2003)

Interviewer: So if someone went to the officers in that context because they were getting badly done in, you wouldn't see that as grassing?

Prisoner: Not me, because I'd see him as a weak person. I'd think – he shouldn't have really said it, but at the end of the day the kid's frightened ... Some people are still looking at that as 'he shouldn't have gave his name' and they're still shouting 'you grass', [but] deep down the kid's frightened to death, somebody's been in and banged him.

(Interview, March 2003)

Thus, although this form of grassing remained partially stigmatised, most prisoners placed it within a sphere of acceptable practices. Other types of grassing were considered unjustifiable. Informing staff about other inmates' activities – for example, the brewing of illicit alcohol ('hooch') – without good reason, or to achieve personal gain at the expense of one's peers was indefensible. Prisoners differentiated between forms of grassing according to such distinctions, as the following quotations indicate:

Prisoner: The lad's getting bullied, and telling the officers he's just had enough. It's a cry for help, isn't it? He ain't doing it to benefit himself, you know, they haven't told him 'we'll get you D-cat, or we'll get you that job, or ...'.

Interviewer: That's when it's not acceptable, is it?

Prisoner: Course it is. Because you're using somebody as a stepping stone. And you're benefiting really from something that's none of your business.

Interviewer: What if somebody did it, and they weren't getting anything from it?

Prisoner: Spiteful. He's still a wicked bloke, isn't it? Why is he interested in what is none of his business? Let [an officer] find him, that's what he's getting paid for, isn't it? That's not for you to say, it's for him to catch him and then he gets his come-uppance. That's nowt to do with that bloke in the middle. Why has he got involved?

(Interview, March 2003)

If you was sitting in the cell smoking a bit of dope, who'd care? You're not bothering me, not bothering anybody else. If you were sitting in a cell gambling – you're not allowed to gamble, but you're not bothering me, you're not harming anybody else.

(Interview, April 2003).

Prisoners who informed on others in order to advance through or gain something from the prison system were deplored. Thus, one interviewee expressed his disgust at the behaviour of another inmate, a prison drug dealer, who was rumoured to have exposed the prison's main external drug supply route in return for securing his passage to open conditions:

> They've come to him and said, 'we know you're selling drugs. We can prove it from your phone calls alone' … He was a long term prisoner for violence … You don't let people like that who sell drugs [go to a D-cat] … straightaway you're in a Cat-B jail. Fuck your Cat-D, we're taking the Cat-D back, you're in a Cat-B jail. But because they wanted the staff more than they wanted him … two and two is four, simple as that. My man gets his Cat-D [because he] puts him in. And he was a Head.[3] He was a tasty lad. Shouldn't have done that. Just totally shouldn't have done it. I've got no respect for that geezer.
>
> (Interview, April 2003)

As also indicated here, it was particularly unforgivable for a powerful prisoner, or one who had benefited from the staunchness of others, to betray the inmate community.

There was little tolerance either for any prisoner who, having knowingly entered a material or social contract (for example, borrowed tobacco or started a conflict), informed in order to extricate himself from it. A first-time prisoner, unaware of prison interest rates, would be granted more sympathy if he turned to staff to escape his debts than a prisoner familiar with the rules of the informal economy. Equally, while it might be understood if the victim of an unprovoked attack took formal proceedings against his attacker, it would be considered illegitimate for the loser of a 'fair fight' (or anyone else) to tell officers who had beaten him up:

> Say you had a normal straightener with somebody, and you got done in and went and grassed to the screws, yeah you would get a fucking hard time like. You'd have to get off the wing … but if somebody's giving you a hard time, and then you went and grassed them up, no, some people would [think it was wrong]. But personally no, I wouldn't.
>
> (Interview, March 2003).

Where there was a risk of someone being seriously injured or sexually assaulted, many prisoners reported that they would have little hesitation in notifying staff, and would not expect to face the extreme reprisals from other prisoners that could result from less acceptable forms of grassing. There was also evidence that certain prisoners on Wellingborough's drug-free unit, particularly former addicts, considered it publicly justifiable to use staff channels to rid their wing of heroin.

Given that there were circumstances in which grassing was considered 'understandable', some discussion of why it did not happen more often may be merited here. Three different kinds of rationalisations were offered by prisoners as to why they did not grass in situations where they might want to. Some prisoners, mainly younger, less experienced criminals convicted of relatively minor offences, expressed their reasons for not informing in terms that were mainly instrumental and individualistic:

> I ain't telling no screws nothing. It's not my business giving chat to another man's business. But if anyone wants to do that, let them carry on. That's his business at the end of the day, I've got no qualms with it ... It won't affect me. Because if it affected me I'd do something about it myself. I wouldn't go running to a fucking officer. If it affected me I'd stand up for myself and – you know – but if it affected other people, I can't do nothing about it can I?
>
> (Interview, January 2003)

Other prisoners provided prudential explanations, recognising that the potential costs of informing outweighed the benefits:

> It would be silly to grass somebody up, it'd probably be better to take a kicking ... It would be a stupid move to get the label of a grass, gigantic ... You're going to make things worse for yourself by grassing, and at the end of the day, they aren't going to do nothing, they will put you on protection, the other person will get GOAD,[4] you know, and then what? You're going to spend the rest of your life on protection because you grassed somebody up.
>
> (Interview, March 2003)

Some accounts were both instrumental and prudential:

> [Officers] drop in little questions and I just laugh: 'I'm not telling you even if I knew'. It's not worth it at the end of the day. If they want to find [the hooch] it's their job to find it, I'm not going to make it easier for them ... At the end of the day it's a risk. [The officer] probably wouldn't say nothing to nobody but there's still

a chance that someone else will find out and then you get called a grass so it's not worth it at the end of the day because it'll just cause more trouble than it's worth ... If somebody finds out them officers aren't going to do anything for you, they're not going to give you anything for letting them know so what's the point? It's their job to find it, they get paid enough so why should you help them? You don't get nothing out of it so why should you help them?

(Interview, March 2003)

'Old-school' prisoners (generally older, more experienced, self-consciously moral and nostalgic for an era of clear divisions between 'cons' and 'screws') regarded such attitudes as deplorably individualistic or as regrettable expressions of vulnerability. They were more likely than other inmates to recognise the legitimacy of younger, weaker prisoners turning to staff. Yet they also insisted that grassing was normatively wrong, and that they themselves would never resort to such mechanisms. Such standpoints were consistent in their reflection of a broader commitment to a collective, mutually supportive orientation among prisoners. This orientation was encouraged by the *appropriate* application of the code. Thus, grassing was more pardonable when a prisoner was himself the victim of a code violation, for example, if he was being bullied or exploited.

Instrumental, prudential and normative explanations could all reflect 'imported' attitudes. Many prisoners had learnt from an early age that informing on others led to social ostracism (Irwin 1970):

If you opened your mouth it played against ya. You know. Regardless of what it was, you were just seen as a threat, 'cos you were somebody that had talked so you weren't allowed within certain things. 'Yeah, don't have owt to do with him he can't keep his mouth shut, he'll tell', you know. Whether it were like nicking bloody orchard apples, if you got caught and three got away, 'will he tell on ya?'

(Interview, January 2003)

For prisoners integrated into organised criminal cultures, or who were from close urban communities, social and professional reputation may always have rested on the ability to keep one's mouth shut (see also Parker 1970). Organised criminals were also more likely to associate prison officials with the police and other state agents. Grassing was therefore seen as a betrayal of an anti-authority morality, though not necessarily as a question of honour or solidarity *per se*:

It's nothing to do with a code of honour, it's 'they're the enemy'. It's nothing to do with solidarity. It's us and them and it's the 'us and them' mentality. It's not like, 'oh, lets protect the thieves, we're thieves, we're honourable.' No I don't believe that for one minute. No, there is no honour amongst thieves, they're all self-serving bastards.

(Interview, April 2003).

Ninety-nine percent of us in here are here because someone has grassed us up, maybe the victim or a witness, so we're in for someone grassing us up in the first place. The other thing is, if you're grassing someone up in prison you're helping out the screws...I'd prefer to get a kicking than grass, because that's just my morals...If you become a grass it's just as bad as the people who've put you in here and just as bad as the people who are holding you in here.

(Interview, July 2003)

However, it was a minority of prisoners who saw prison staff as 'the enemy' in such definitive terms, as the following section explores.

Relationships between staff and prisoners

Previous research suggests that conduct norms about staff–prisoner relations may vary considerably between prisons. Sykes and Messinger surmised that inmate rules forbade giving respect or prestige to officers, encouraged others to be suspicious of staff and to always side against them in disputes with prisoners, and prohibited commitments to 'the values of hard work and submission to duly constituted authority' (1960: 8). Irwin noted that American jail mentality involved an 'all pervasive' wariness of 'the man' (1985: 88), and 'a streak of defiance towards conventional society and its agents', especially agents of state control. Jacobs documented a highly politicised culture of confrontation and hostility between ethnic minority prisoners and the prison administration (Jacobs 1977; see also McEvoy 2001). However, studies in other countries (Mathiesen 1965; Akers *et al* 1977), women's prisons (Ward and Kassebaum 1965) and treatment-oriented establishments (Street *et al* 1966) have not always found cultures of solidary opposition to institutional norms.

HMP Wellingborough was known among prisoners as an establishment with a 'laid-back' atmosphere. The term was used repeatedly to describe a jail in which relations between staff and prisoners (and among prisoners) were relatively harmonious. Officers did not generally call prisoners by their first names (although nicknames were common) and were not perceived to be especially proactive in dealing with prisoner issues. Furthermore, the prison was considered to be quite tightly run compared to some other C-category jails: more of a 'screws' nick' than a 'cons' nick'. However, staff were generally regarded as friendly, and were thought not to overuse their power or harbour punitive attitudes. One prisoner commented that it was 'a different world compared to other jails... they speak to you like normal people' (Interview, March 2003). Many prisoners bantered and chatted comfortably with staff during evening association periods or when waiting to move off their wings. Certainly, there were limits to what most would discuss with members of custodial staff, not least, the daily politics of the inmate world. However, there was little stigma attached to having cordial relations with officers and outright hostility to uniformed staff was uncommon.

Experienced prisoners contrasted this state of affairs to relationships and attitudes in the past:

Now, it is different 'cos people'll stand there and speak to an officer. But at one time you never had that: 'Fuck off, don't speak to him, you're speaking to the fucking officers, fuck off you wrong'un'.

(Interview, March 2003).

There is still cons around who will, if they see you talking to them, try and make summat of it. But that's slowly dying out... Years ago, if you was talking to a screw you was thought of as a dodgy bloke. They'd think to themselves, 'What are you on about? You're grassing people up.' It was, literally, them and us.

(Interview, March 2003)

Several reasons were suggested for the development and acceptability of more friendly relationships between staff and inmates. Prisoners remarked that staff were generally younger, 'not so Prison Officers' Association orientated', more helpful, and more sympathetic to the realities of the lives that they led outside prison. Secondly, they noted that the introduction of the IEP scheme, and the expansion of early and temporary release schemes, had made prison life necessarily more interactive. Since all prisoners were reliant upon wing officers for reports and individual privileges, less suspicion was assigned to talking to them. As the following quotation also suggests, when officers were themselves more amenable, there was less reason to mistrust prisoners who were sociable with them:

> Years ago, if you was seen in the office, or hangin' around the office, you was a grass, you was no good. Nowadays, everyone's getting on with their own sentence, instead of doing someone else's. The staff that we've got, they are friendly and they are open, so if you're seen talking to them it's not misconstrued. People do their own thing. Lifers seem to have that mentality anyway, because they have to get on with certain people, [or] it can hold them back x amount of years.
>
> (Interview, June 2003)

Furthermore, the provision of greater opportunities for prisoners, in terms of work and education, provided a broad motivating factor for inmates to engage actively with prison staff and the regime they represented. Again, this was contrasted with an era in which prisoners were an undifferentiated mass:

> You was all in one big cauldron. Now there's a division, where if you toe the line in prison, if you are going along the lines of model prisoner, there is a better kind of life in prison ... If you're the sort of prisoner who respects himself, who wants to get up and do something for themselves, albeit not major, but to live a better way of life within the prison system, you can. Whereas before, you couldn't. You were just chucked in all together. There was no difference ... If you choose to take a good path in prison, doors will open for you now. If you're a decent person and you're liked by the staff and that ... Once you've settled down and you come to a category-C prison, where I am, I can find somewhere like the VTU [Voluntary Testing Unit], where I'm happy, I keep away from rogues, I keep away from drugs, I've found myself a job that I'm enjoying.
>
> (Interview, April 2003)

Changes in the flow, nature and deployment of power within the prison system have also had a significant impact on staff–prisoner relations. In previous years, prisoners were within a system founded on authority and confronted the bearers of that authority constantly. Officers had significant collective power and deployed it rigidly in the everyday life on the landings: as one prisoner recalled, they 'were gods. They had the power over life or death' (Interview, August 2003). In recent years, this power has been diminished and redistributed upwards, towards senior managers (Liebling 2004). It is at a higher level that the daily regime is determined, prisoners' rights assessed, and decisions made about home leaves, early and temporary release and other such motivating initiatives. Officers still have significant discretionary power at an individual level, but are responsible for far fewer of the issues that previously exercised prisoners at the collective level. As conditions have been improved and the mode of social control has been transformed, the late-modern, bureaucratic prison provides a different carceral experience. On the one hand, administrative decisions feel more out of reach and less negotiable to prisoners; meanwhile the IEP scheme has ensured that the system's grip on prisoners is tighter and its reach deeper (Liebling *et al* 1999): prisoners are no longer 'left to their own devices', and this can be experienced as a reduction of freedom. On the other hand, prisoners have more scope to 'take responsibility' for the terms of their incarceration, and there is less need for direct confrontation with the prison officials, as one prisoner articulated:

You don't exist right up against the authoritarian wall, you exist somewhere away from it, and there is a buffer zone in-between. If you start pushing for things, all of a sudden you hit up against that ... There are certain things that you're never gonna get, there are other things where you can undermine or erode that authoritarian block. But [mainly] you live in a buffer zone between it so you might not [hit it]. Then all of a sudden, bang, you will hit up against the wall ... You couldn't live with that shield or wall on you all the time because it would breed a greater resentment ... Back in the day the system was pure authority, there was no give in it. [You] were banging up against it, so you did get things like riots, you did get things that was problems, you did get the very us/them sort of division which has been eroded over the years to a certain degree. And I think that has been eroded because that shield has been removed slightly from your everyday contact with the prison, which makes it easier to cope with. It also makes it less likely to be able to kick off, because there are other ways round it. You have other recourses, you have other ways of retreating from hostilities as it were.

(Interview, February 2003)

All these changes have implications for the relationship between officers and prisoners. Officers can offer more and punish less (or, perhaps, just differently, since the privilege system and its use and misuse have created new ways of punishing prisoners); they are held less responsible for the failings of the institution; and although their reach into prisoner subculture has extended, they are – according to prisoners – more open than in the past to prisoner initiative and allowing prisoners minor deviations from the rules.

In this general context, there was considerable variation in the ways that prisoners related to officers. Experienced prisoners, lifers and many state-raised inmates tended to establish and recommend relationships which were detached but courteous, based on professional distance rather than outright hostility:

> They're doing their job, fair enough, but some of them try to act as if they're trying to be your friends. I'll speak to them, I won't be abusive, but at the end of the day I still know they're screws, so no matter how friendly they try and get with you or how friendly you think you've become with a screw, they're still going to nick you if you do something wrong, and still going to bang you up at the end of the day.
>
> (Interview, July 2003)

> I'm not becoming their friend, am I? I'm not going to knock around with them. I'm not going to sit in my pad with them. So it's a different relationship … At the end of the day, they're officers to do a job, and I'm a con. So there's only certain limits you can get to … I'm at the football level: when they're at the door, I'm 'Arsenal, phwoar, they've lost two more goals than Man U.' I'm at that level with them. To me, I don't dislike them.
>
> (Interview, March 2003)

Such prisoners made little effort to manipulate or ingratiate themselves with staff. Instead, they preferred to treat officers with a certain kind of respect that they expected to be reciprocated. Meanwhile, they were the prisoners most likely to condemn 'belligerence', rudeness or unjustified hostility displayed by other prisoners towards uniformed and civilian staff. This was often based on genuine sympathy, not just because such actions could have negative consequences for the prisoner community as a whole:

> Rogers threatened the officer and this officer I know was scared, and I felt sorry for the officer. [So] I said to the screw, 'listen, don't take that personal, he didn't have a thing against you, he just wanted to get shipped out the jail, and he knew if he threatened a

screw they can't take the risk that he'll carry that threat through, so he gotta go'. And the officer said to me, 'well, yeah, it's hard not to take it personal when it's done like that, I'm sure he could've found another way of doin' it'. Y'know, I felt for him and I went and said to him, 'listen, don't take that personal, you were just his ticket [out of the prison]. That's the way everybody else sees it as well, it weren't you, he just wanted out.'

(Interview, February 2003)

I do sometimes look at them and think it's a difficult job. And some of them are a bit soft. You do get cons that do try and take advantage of them. And the way they talk to them. But to me, and I could never say it, I think 'even though he's an officer, mate, there's no need to call him that down here in front of everybody'.

(Interview, March 2003)

As this second quotation highlights, prisoners were reluctant to stand up publicly for an officer against other prisoners. Nonetheless, in informal conversation, blanket criticisms of officers were uncommon and were rarely left unchallenged. There were always 'some good officers'. Only a small minority of prisoners – most notably, some Jamaican 'Yardies', and some lifers with particularly negative experiences of the prison system – regarded them with unadulterated disdain or presented the system and its custodians as illegitimate agents of state power. Opposition expressed in political terms was very uncommon, and self-declared 'non-conformists' recognised their minority status.[5]

Likewise, those younger prisoners who were more 'refractory' were, nonetheless, rarely oppositional in their stance towards officers and the prison system. Rather, they judged officers more as individuals than through any lens of collective judgement, and did not necessarily see the officer role as an all-defining identity. Whereas old-school prisoners accepted the official authority of prison staff and settled for respectful relations based on formal distinctions in role and status, younger prisoners were less inclined to recognise the symbolic authority of the officer position. This promoted the formation of relationships that were 'personal' as well as 'professional'. Officers were seen and judged as 'people' – and often as simply 'normal people doing a job' – rather than 'uniforms':

Some inmates don't even want to talk to any staff because they wear a uniform. To me, that's a bit pathetic really ... Some of the girls and the young male staff, I get on great with them.

(Interview, April 2003)

I find a lot of things weird about what people think [about officers]; like, I see a lot of the officers as just doing their job, you know ... I'm going to be here for a couple of years, and, I mean, I've already talked to a couple of officers ... I will get kind of a friendship with those sort of officers, it will happen, you know, I'm not just going to go through two and a half years here without making a friendship with an officer.

(Interview, March 2003)

In such relationships, deference and respect were never guaranteed (and had to be constantly renegotiated). While old-school inmates presumed to offer respect in order to receive it back, younger inmates expected it to be offered before they would return it. Once established, however, this form of personal respect could lead to much closer bonds than those formed by prisoners whose stance was one of professional detachment. It could generate relationships with officers that were more friendly *or* more hostile than those created by other inmates, according to how officers were regarded as particular individuals, rather than as representatives of a homogenous class.

Other prisoners were 'friendly' with staff in strategic and instrumental ways. They understood that manufacturing positive relationships with officers made daily life easier and improved their chances of getting what they wanted from the prison in terms of taggings, home leaves and parole applications:

If you want to play the system to your advantage you can ... I'll talk to all of them. Every officer in the jail ... There's some, obviously, that I won't like. But I'll try and get on with them. Just to make my life easier and to make his life easier. Mainly to make my life easier so he don't get on my back.

(Interview, January 2003)

One prisoner revealed in interview that his entire prison persona, including positive relations with prison staff, work on the prison's Youth and Community project and helping special-needs children in the prison gym, was a strategic identity designed to ensure that he was granted his parole. A small number of others revelled in having created false identities as former drug addicts in order to be seen as 'victims' that the prison system could 'restore' and therefore treat favourably.

However, of those prisoners who actively engaged in the prison regime, a high proportion were normatively committed to their own compliance, rather than just manipulating the system for their own ends. Like Irwin's (1970) 'gleaners', they participated in drugs courses, learnt a trade or took educational qualifications as genuine means to self-betterment, and resented implications that their compliance was feigned. Instead, their behaviour was presented as part of an exercise in personal reconstruction: 'for me, not for anyone else'. This discourse was particularly common among prisoners whose convictions were related to drug addiction. These were the inmates least likely to harbour anti-authority or non-conformist sentiments, and most likely to blame themselves rather than social forces for their offences. For former drug addicts, personal guilt was at least as important a pain of imprisonment as social rejection. It is thus unsurprising that, rather than mitigating the effects of incarceration through the anti-authoritarianism of the conventional inmate code, they instead denounced their former lives, renounced their former selves (cf. Maruna 2000) and often fixated on projects of personal reconstruction:

It doesn't matter how many people sit round and say 'oh, you should do this, you should do that', it's up to me. You can't make someone want to change. You've got to want to change yourself. And that change has come from within me. I've progressed. I came into prison nine stone, a crack and heroin addict. I was an habitual thief, living a terrible way of life, and because in my heart of hearts I came from a good home, I knew I was bad. I knew I was living a wrong, bad, existence. I don't care whether he's in a uniform or not. If someone's alright to me, I'm alright to him. If I wanted to buy drugs then no doubt I could go and find drugs if I wanted to. But that is a personal change with me, to distance myself with drugs but knowing I can go and get them if I want it. Not to go and get them, that's part of my personal rehabilitation. To keep myself away from drugs knowing that I can go and get drugs if I want.

(Interview, April 2003)

It is striking how neatly this discourse of personal responsibility matches recent Prison Service language about rehabilitation. The prisoner who interprets his commitment to the prison's official aims as a personal triumph, rather than acquiescence, represents the ideal, self-governing captive (Garland 1996, 1997).

To document the actual relations between staff and prisoners is not the same as describing the system of ideals that existed in regard to those relations. However, while prisoners acknowledged the vestiges of an ideal that officers should be shunned and disparaged, and recognised that getting too close to officers could still be dangerous, it was precisely because there was quite a broad tolerance for different ways of 'doing time' that prisoners could openly interact with staff without provoking actionable stigma:

> There's a lot of people that talk to officers and get on with officers and that and like some people, screw boys, whatever, I'm not bothered about that, if that's how you want to do your time you do it like that.
>
> (Interview, April 2003)

As this quotation suggests, this was not to say that there was no hierarchy of preferred behaviour. However, this was itself disputed, and many different modes of interaction with officers could be legitimated. Prisoners who developed 'strategic' relations with staff could boast of their skill in manipulating officers to their own advantage. And while those who cared too obviously about getting their tagging or parole were sometimes mocked, as suggested above, it was recognised that being released from prison as early as possible was an appropriate and universal ambition. Self-improvement and taking responsibility for one's criminality were rightful, even admired, objectives, and there was no *simple* conflict between the objectives of the administration and those of the inmate world (cf. Welford 1967: 198). Prisoners with families could certainly justify compliant behaviour through their loyalties to their wives and children. Those who developed close relationships with staff sometimes struggled to establish status within the prisoner subculture, but were accepted for 'doing their time in their own way'. Prisoners who purported to be 'big men' within the inmate community, but who compromised themselves to bend to the demands of the system, most risked losing credibility. In contrast, those who presented their compliance as a marker of strength and self-determination were by no means stigmatised. Again, then, being loyal to oneself, and forgoing the demands of general 'solidarity', was an accepted element of the inmate value system.

Discussion

One consequence of the contingent nature of the rules of inmate behaviour was that they were interpreted and enacted in specific ways within different parts of the prison. Prisoners on Wellingborough's VTU were more inclined than those on other wings to 'do their own time': the informal economy was less developed than on other wings, prisoners were less likely, and less expected, to intervene on behalf of both friends and strangers, and those suspected of being sex offenders or informers were less likely to face violent, summary retribution. The high proportion of addiction-related offenders on this unit also created a micro-culture in which much greater antipathy was expressed towards drug use and dealing, and prisoners were more absorbed in projects of personal reconstruction than on other wings.

Meanwhile, perhaps counter-intuitively, lifers were the inmates least likely to have strong ties to other prisoners. As well as making them less emotionally vulnerable, this rendered them less obligated to others, and therefore less likely to be drawn into the kinds of disputes that could jeopardise their progression to open conditions. In many other ways, the culture of protective loyalty on Wellingborough's long-termer wing was highly solidary. Stealing from cells was virtually unheard of (except in times when there was a high quantity of heroin in the prison); prisoners acted with courtesy and consideration towards each other (e.g. the wing was less noisy during 'quiet hours'); 'double-bubble' was generally viewed as exploitative rather than 'just business'; and prisoners were more inclined than on other wings to lend things to each other without entering into tight, contractual agreements. Furthermore, although their commitments towards 'friends' were often tentative and negotiable, lifers were more likely to enunciate moral solidarity towards strangers than prisoners on shorter sentences:

> I don't feel loyal to anybody on the wing. But if I seen an injustice, yeah, I'd be on the side of what I think was right, so I will step in in that sense...It just has to be what I believe in that's right or wrong...If somebody I knocked about with is coming from a standpoint I don't believe in, I wouldn't [agree] just for their sake, I'd tell them, 'no you're wrong, fuck off'...Even at the cost of friendship.
>
> (Interview, March 2003)

Thus, although in certain respects lifers were fairly atomised and self-interested, they also constructed a social environment which was more morally and materially solidary than existed on the prison's other wings. Indeed, by promoting a culture of abstract mutual support and respect, they discouraged the kinds of conflicts that could put each other's future release plans at risk. Elsewhere in the jail, it was proactive loyalty, based on the kinds of regional and racial ties I have discussed in this section, which could also lead to conflict and exploitation.

It has also been argued that, in recognising, for example, that not all forms of grassing were equally reprehensible, prisoners gauged the basic rules of their community (and how to respond to their infringement) by a further set of informal principles. One salient factor here was the position within the internal hierarchy that a violator occupied. Strong prisoners were most able to infringe certain norms, including those that warned against expressions of emotion and kindness: 'If you're a big, massive lad, if you've got muscles coming out of your neck, you can show as much weakness as you like and no one is going to say a peep to you' (Interview, July 2003). On the other hand, high-status prisoners who betrayed themselves and others were regarded with particular contempt:

> If you're supposed to be a Head, and you don't back it, you're a fucking faggot, and you're even worse than a faggot. Because you're trying to back it. You're trying to make out you're a Head, but you're not ... People will target you even more ... it irritates you even more ... Because you're trying to be something you're not. You're trying to rise up in the ranks and you ain't got it. And if you ain't got it, you're going to get punished. And people will go out of their way to do you in, because it's almost justified ... Like a weak person, a very weak person grassing on somebody – it happens. But, if you're a Head, you're getting done in.
>
> (Interview, March 2003)

As suggested here, weakness also mitigated the normal terms of the inmate code. While the display of weakness by most prisoners was generally stigmatised, it was rare that prisoners who were obviously highly vulnerable were ceaselessly exploited. Little status could be derived from victimising the defenceless, and many prisoners suggested that there were penalties for such acts:

> There was a lad, he's really timid and frail ... If I bullied that geezer, people would come and put it on my toes and say 'fucking leave him alone'. They would not stand for it ... If you do pick on somebody who everybody knows is weak, other Heads will do you in. Or people will get together and get you off the wing.
>
> (Interview, March 2003)

Paradoxically then, prisoners at the extremities of the inmate hierarchy were protected as well as potentially abused. Those who were not perceived as weak, or who were deemed capable of looking after themselves, but were unwilling to fight, were much less likely to be offered physical support.

As the first quotation above suggested, to put on fronts was also considered a violation of inmate values and justification for retribution. Under such terms, then, prisoners were encouraged neither to show weakness nor to bluff strength. This was one of several tightropes within the value system that prisoners were forced to walk (Bottoms 1999). Likewise, while prisoners who appeared to care too much about obtaining early release or home leave were derided, those who pretended not to be concerned about minimising their time inside were considered foolish and disloyal to their families outside. In such respects, few aspects of behaviour were regulated in the straightforward ways that descriptions of the inmate code as a set of uncompromising imperatives imply. Prisoners recognised in such refrains a highly idealised model of prisoner behaviour. Yet, in their daily interactions, they were guided by a far more complex and negotiable set of guidelines than is conveyed by simple maxims. That these guidelines also had moral dimensions (which were often consciously invoked by prisoners) challenges popular notions that the prison world resembles a Hobbesian state of lawless brutality and perpetual disorder.

Conclusion: 'Late-modernity' and the inmate code

A number of reasons have been offered by prisoners to account for the perceived decline in inmate solidarity. Alongside these observations, it is worth looking beyond changed conditions of incarceration and new technologies of penal government to account for the rules of the contemporary inmate community. The expanding literature on late-modernity (sometimes referred to as high- or post-modernity) is worth a brief reference here (Harvey 1990; Giddens 1991; Young 1999; Bauman 2000). While penal theorists (Garland 2001) and some empirical scholars (Liebling 2004) have begun to use this framework to account for shifts in penal culture and organisation, its heuristic lens has been little used in relation to the inner, everyday social life of the prison.

Among the characteristics commonly outlined by theorists of late-modernity are the following: a decline in the 'stable orientation points' (Bauman 2000: 7) and terms of reference by which life choices were previously guided and a diminished respect for moral absolutes and traditional forms of authority (Garland 2001); a culture of individualisation, immediacy and self-actualisation 'with the burden of pattern-weaving and the responsibility for failure falling primarily on the individual's shoulders' (Bauman 2000: 8); the 'compression' of time and space, such that geographic locality decreases in relevance; and a freeing of the lifespan from 'externalities associated with pre-established ties to other individuals and groups', particularly kinship relations (Giddens 1991: 147).

These features are notoriously hard to operationalise and verify, and, in relation to UK prison life, there is little with which to compare them meaningfully. However, they resonate in important ways with much of what has been observed in this chapter about inmate values and relations. Prisoners did not identify themselves as a unitary group and the criminal identity offered little in the way of shared status. I suggested above, for example, that those whose convictions were addiction related dealt differently with their sentences from other inmates. This did not go unnoticed by experienced prisoners, who frequently drew attention to a split within the inmate community between 'professional' criminals and those only incarcerated because of drug habits. Meanwhile, conventional markers of status within the prisoner hierarchy were reported to have declined in importance. Thus, prisoners claimed that, beyond sex offences, conviction categories had little independent impact on positions in the prisoner hierarchy or interpersonal respect. Personality and sincerity were deemed far more important characteristics, and many prisoners reported being disinterested in the lives, criminal careers and reputations of their peers. Likewise, for many younger prisoners, being an officer was not necessarily a role that dominated all other characteristics, and prison staff were judged by their personalities and orientations far more than by the uniforms that they inhabited. In relation both to the inmate world and staff, then, traditional sources of deference and authority appeared somewhat diminished.

Among prisoners, not only was there no single or consensual normative community, but a resistance to the implication that there was any external value system to which one ought to adhere. Although a hierarchy of preferred actions was discernible, it was neither rigid nor undisputed. Prisoners commonly expressed 'live and let live' attitudes about peer activities, and asserted their rights to define their behaviour within personal frames of reference. These were rooted not only in prudential concerns to stay out of other people's business, but also in a 'situational moral sensibility' (Garland 2001: 88) of mutual toleration and discourses of individual self-determination. Another expression of the latter inclination was that prisoners invoked narratives of personal responsibility far more often than those of structural deprivation, political oppression (cf. Jacobs 1977) or 'the raw deal' (Irwin 1985: 90–1). For a significant proportion of prisoners, the rehabilitative, pro-social ambitions of the prison system were not at odds with goals of personal reconstruction.

Finally, one can see reflected in inmate culture the more limited and conditional obligations to others that characterise life beyond the prison (Hobsbawm 1994). In part, as I have suggested, this relates to prison liberalisation and policies of penal administration which have individualised inmate interests. However, they also seem to signal a broader shift in the accepted relationship between the interests of the individual and that of the group. Yet those loyalties that did characterise prisoner society, many of which were rooted in commitments to localised spaces and relationships, are precisely those that theorists of late-modernity have claimed to be of declining importance. The strength of local loyalties within prison suggests that claims that, in contemporary society, 'place becomes phantasmagoric [...] does not form the parameter of experience; [and] becomes much less significant than it used to be as an external referent for the lifespan of the individual' do not apply to the lives of prisoners, both in jail and the community (Giddens 1991: 146–7). Prisoners' lives may be determined in all sorts of ways by the currents of late-modernity – in terms of patterns of employment, trends in criminal justice and the breakdown of structures of kinship and religion – but other aspects of their experience are not accounted for in broad theories of social change. It is only by continuing to delve into prisoner societies that the intricacies of their values, both within and beyond the institutional walls, can be properly appreciated.

Notes

1 This chapter is based on research funded by the Nuffield Foundation (award NCF/00076/G), to whom I am most grateful. Thanks also to Helen Griffiths and Sarah Tait for ongoing comments on the content of the chapter.
2 'Fronting up': preparing to fight, giving the impression of being ready to fight, or precipitating a fight.
3 A 'Head': a powerful or known prisoner; an inmate leader.
4 Good Order and Discipline: a disciplinary charge, used to segregate prisoners when there are 'reasonable grounds for believing that the prisoner's behaviour is likely to be so disruptive or cause disruption that keeping the prisoner on ordinary location is unsafe' (Prison Service Order 1700, http://pso.hmprisonservice.gov.uk).

5   Muslim prisoners were perhaps the most politicised members of the prison community, often railing against the role of the British government in world affairs. But while they sometimes came into conflict with the prison administration over how they were entitled to exercise their faith in the jail, such disputes reflected a relatively limited assertion of religious identity rather than a broad agenda of antagonism and opposition.

References

Akers, R., Hayner, N. and Gruninger, W. (1977) 'Prisonization in five countries: Type of prison and inmate characteristics', *Criminology*, 14 (4), 527–554.

Atchley, R. and McCabe, P. (1968) 'Socialization in correctional communities: A replication', *American Sociological Review*, 33, 774–785.

Bauman, Z. (2000) *Liquid Modernity*. Cambridge: Polity Press.

Bottoms, A. (1999) 'Interpersonal violence and social order in prisons', in M. Tonry and J. Petersilia (eds) *Crime and Justice: A Review of Research*, 26, 205–281.

Carroll, L. (1974) *Hacks, Blacks and Cons: Race Relations in a Maximum Security Prison*. Lexington, MA: Lexington Books.

Clemmer, D. (1940) *The Prison Community*. New York: Rinehart.

Crewe, B. (forthcoming) *'"The Only Loyalty Here is Heroin": The Society of Captives in the Era of Hard Drug Use'*.

Einat, T. (2004) 'Language, culture, identity and coping in Israeli prisons'. Paper presented at Cropwood Conference, 2004, The Effects of Imprisonment: An International Symposium, Robinson College, Cambridge, 14–15 April 2004.

Einat, T. and Einat, H. (2000) 'Inmate argot as an expression of prison subculture: The Israeli case', *The Prison Journal*, 80 (3), 309–325.

Garabedian, P. (1963) 'Social roles and processes of socialization in the prison community', *Social Problems*, 11 (Fall), 139–152.

Garland, D. (1996) 'The limits of the sovereign state', *British Journal of Criminology*, 36 (4), 445–471.

Garland, D. (1997) '"Governmentality" and the problem of crime: Foucault, criminology, sociology', *Theoretical Criminology*, 1, 173–214.

Garland, D. (2001) *The Culture of Control: Crime and Social Order in Contemporary Society*. Oxford: OUP.

Garofalo, J. and Clark, R. (1985) 'The inmate subculture in jails', *Criminal Justice and Behaviour*, 12 (4), 415–434.

Giddens, A. (1991) *Modernity and Self-Identity: Self and Society in the Late-Modern Age*. Cambridge: Polity.

Goffman, E. (1961) 'The inmate world', in E. Goffman (ed.) *Asylums: Essays on the Social Situation of Mental Patients and Other Inmates*. London: Penguin, pp. 13–72.

Harvey, D. (1990) *The Condition of Postmodernity*. Oxford: Blackwell.

Harvey, J. (2004) 'Transition and adaptation to prison life: A study of young adults aged 18 to 21'. Unpublished PhD thesis, University of Cambridge.

Hensley, C., Wright, J., Tewksbury, R. and Castle, T. (2003) 'The evolving nature of prison argot and sexual hierarchies', *The Prison Journal*, 83 (3), 289–300.

Hobsbawm, E. (1994) *The Age of Extremes: The Short Twentieth-Century*. London: Michael Joseph.

Irwin, J. (1970) *The Felon*. Englewood Hills, NJ: Prentice-Hall.

Irwin, J. (1980) *Prisons in Turmoil*. Boston: Little, Brown.

Irwin, J. (1985) *The Jail: Managing the Underclass in American Society*. Berkeley: University of California Press.

Irwin, J. and Cressey, D. (1962) 'Thieves, convicts and the inmate culture', *Social Problems*, 10 (Fall), 142–155.

Jacobs, J. (1974) 'Street gangs behind bars', *Social Problems*, 21/3: 395–409.

Jacobs, J. (1977) *Stateville: The Penitentiary in Mass Society*. Chicago: University of Chicago Press.

Leger, R. and Gray Barnes, H. (1986) 'Black attitudes in prison: A sociological analysis', *Journal of Criminal Justice*, 14, 105–122.

Liebling, A. (2000) 'Prisons, criminology and the power to punish: Or a brief account of the "state of the art" in prison Research.' Unpublished paper, presented at the British Criminology Conference, Leicester 2000.

Liebling, A. (2004) (assisted by Arnold, H.) *Prisons and Their Moral Performance: A Study of Values, Quality and Prison Life*. Oxford: OUP.

Liebling, A., Muir, G., Rose, G. and Bottoms, A.E. (1999) 'Incentives and earned privileges in prison', *Home Office Research Findings 87*. HMSO.

Maruna, S. (2000) *Making Good: How Ex-Convicts Reform and Rebuild Their Lives*. Washington, DC: American Psychological Association.

Mathiesen, T. (1965) *The Defences of the Weak: A Sociological Study of a Norwegian Correctional Institution*. London: Tavistock.

McCorkle, L. and Korn, R. (1954) 'Resocialization within walls', *The Annals*, 293, 88–99.

McEvoy, K. (2001) *Paramilitary Imprisonment in Northern Ireland: Resistance, Management and Release*. Oxford: OUP.

Ohlin, J. (1956) *Sociology and the Field of Corrections*. New York: Social Science Council.

Parker, T. (1970) *The Frying Pan: A Prison and its Prisoners*. London, Panther.

Simon, J. (2000) 'The "society of captives" in the era of hyper-incarceration', *Theoretical Criminology*, 4 (3), 285–308.

Street, D., Wintner, R. and Perrow, C. (1966) *Organization for Treatment*. New York: Free Press.

Sykes, G. (1958) *The Society of Captives: A Study of a Maximum Security Prison*. Princeton, NJ: Princeton University Press.

Sykes, G. (1995) 'The structural-functional perspective on imprisonment', in T. Blomberg and S. Cohen (eds) *Punishment and Social Control: Essays in Honor of Sheldon L. Messinger*. New York: Aldine de Gruyter.

Sykes, G. and Messinger, S. (1960) 'The inmate social system', in R. Cloward (ed.) *Theoretical Studies in Social Organization of the Prison*. New York: Social Science Council.

Thomas, C. (1977) 'Theoretical perspectives on prisonization: A comparison of the importation and deprivation models', *Journal of Criminal Law and Criminology*, 68, 135–144.

Wacquant, L. (2002) 'The curious eclipse of prison ethnography in the age of mass incarceration', *Ethnography*, 3 (4), 371–398.

Ward, D. and Kassebaum, G. (1965) *Women's Prison: Sex and Social Structure*. Chicago: Aldine.

Welford, C. (1967) 'Factors associated with adoption of the inmate code: A study of normative socialization', *Journal of Criminal Law, Criminology and Police Science*, 58 (2), 197–203.

Wheeler, S. (1961) 'Socialization in correctional communities', *American Sociological Review*, 26, 697–712.

Wilson, T. (1986) 'Gender differences in the inmate code', *Canadian Journal of Criminology*, 28, 397–405.

Winfree, T., Newbold, G. and Tubb, H. (2002) 'Prisoner perspectives on inmate culture in New Mexico and New Zealand: A descriptive case study', *The Prison Journal*, 82 (2), 213–233.

Young, J. (1999) *The Exclusive Society*. London: Sage.

Chapter 8

Revisiting prison suicide: the role of fairness and distress

Alison Liebling, Linda Durie, Annick Stiles and Sarah Tait[1]

A decent society is one whose institutions do not humiliate people.

(Margalit 1996: 1)

This chapter presents four main arguments. Firstly, most theories of prison suicide are vague and they take insufficient account of the differential nature of the prison experience. Secondly, insufficient thought has been given to appropriate methodologies to use in this complex field. Thirdly, a significant contribution to prisoner distress, and therefore suicide, is made by the uneven experiences of unfairness, disrespect and lack of safety. Fourthly, suicide prevention efforts should be informed by greater appreciation of the role of the moral climate of prisons, and (therefore) of prison officers in prison life as well as by individualised approaches to prisoner care. Particular attention should be paid to feelings of safety among staff and prisoners.

Although substantial international interest exists in the study of suicides in prison (for example, Biles 1991; Green *et al* 1993; Liebling 1999, 1992; Lester and Danto 1993; Dear 2000; Dear *et al* 1998; Dear *et al* 2001; Towl *et al* 2000; Blaauw *et al* 2001a, b), there are few systematic attempts to investigate which aspects of the prison experience might be most relevant to suicides and suicide attempts. Theories of prison suicide include *importation* models (that is, prisoners bring their elevated suicide risk into prison with them; Home Office 1984, 1986; Blaauw *et al* 2001b; and see Zamble and Porporino 1988; Zamble and Quinsey 1997), *deprivation* models (that is, suicide is caused by prison-induced distress; for example Kennedy 1984; Backett 1988), and *combined* models (that is, prisons expose already vulnerable populations to additional risk; Hatty and Walker 1986; Liebling 1995). Considerable evidence exists to support the third, combined model, although it seems that different types of prison suicide can be identified in which importation and deprivation factors play different roles (Liebling 1999). The specification of 'prison-induced distress' is often vague. There is a well-known 'prison effects' literature, although surprisingly little of it has historically considered distress or suicide as its main focus has been reconviction. There is a rich prison sociology literature which tells us much about the generalised pains of imprisonment, but which is striking for its avoidance of individual differences or the topic of suicide (see a review by Liebling 1992).

The most theoretically engaging work in the prisons field in recent years has been the work carried out by colleagues on legitimacy (Sparks and Bottoms 1995; Sparks et al 1996; Bottoms 1999). They too have avoided the problem of distress in what could be construed as a gendered approach to their subject.[2] In this chapter, we shall explore the relevance of certain aspects of theories of legitimacy to the study of prison suicide.

Prisons, legitimacy, order and well-being

Recent prison scholars, informed by theorists of justice and politics, have argued that fairness or legitimacy is empirically related to the reproduction of order, for good theoretical reasons (Home Office 1991; Bottoms 1999: 254–7). Theorists of the 'problem of order' have argued that common and stable expectations, shared meanings and norms, and power used carefully, 'make possible stable, recurrent, and cooperative social interaction' (Wrong 1994: 5; Beetham 1991). Tyler and colleagues have demonstrated that fair procedures, including respectful treatment, increase the perceived legitimacy of authority (Tyler 1990; Tyler and Blader 2000). They and others have shown that increased legitimacy encourages compliance with the law (Paternoster et al 1997).

Sparks, and others, have presented a plausible case that this legitimacy model is applicable to prison life. They have proposed that some prisons are more legitimate than others (Sparks 1994), and they have suggested the credible hypothesis that these differences will be empirically related to levels of and types of order found in individual establishments (Sparks et al 1996). Individual prisoners are more likely to comply willingly with a fairer form of authority and to resist less fair forms: such authority is represented, among other things, by the day-to-day actions of prison staff (Sparks *et al* 1996; Liebling and Price 2001). This link between legitimacy and order in prisons is of major importance. It has not, as far as we are aware, been subjected to detailed empirical scrutiny, using levels of order as an outcome or adopting a translation into operation of the complex concept of legitimacy (but see Ahmad 1996; Bottoms and Rose 1998; Liebling 2004).

Sparks and Bottoms define legitimacy broadly as encompassing 'considerations of fairness and respect' (Sparks and Bottoms 1995: 59), and fair actions as 'justifiable, comprehensible and consistent' (Bottoms and Sparks 1997: 22). There is clearly scope for more detailed deliberation on the precise meaning of these terms, and these authors offer that kind of deliberation at various places in their work (see Sparks *et al* 1996; Sparks and Bottoms 1995; Bottoms and Sparks 1997). It has been established that relationships, or the manner of one's treatment, are central to perceptions of fairness (Bottoms and Rose 1998). There will be some limits to this model of order because of the special conditions of the prison (Bottoms and Sparks 1997: 16).[3] Legitimacy is inherently limited in the prison, and some prisoners will resist penal authority because they find the experience excruciating and frustrating beyond endurance. Others will have psychological needs or drives that are fundamentally in conflict with what the prison requires. There will be other components of order in prison, such as routines, structural and physical constraints, incentives schemes and population characteristics (Bottoms and Sparks 1997: 24; Bottoms 1999: 257–61). Clearly legitimacy matters – it may also have some instrumental utility for those seeking to manage prisons.

So we have a fruitful agenda for further theoretical reflection: what limits are there to legitimacy in prison, and does the concept take us far enough? We also have a rich agenda for empirical research: what forms of fairness in the prison lead to how much order, of what kind? What is it to be treated with respect, or fairness in prison? Is trust relevant to perceptions of fairness, as we would expect it to be outside (e.g. Braithwaite and Makkai 1994)? How can staff use or under-use their formal and informal power in ways that communicate a will to legitimacy in prison?

We want to suggest that there is another route for legitimacy theorists to take. Giddens, Berger and other social theorists, as well as psychoanalysts, have suggested that human beings need order or ontological security (Giddens 1984; Berger *et al* 1977; Erikson 1995). Our claim, following their lead, is that legitimacy is empirically related not just to order and compliance but also to well-being. We want to suggest that human beings need fairness and respect: that is, they need to know that actions and decisions taken in relation to them are morally justifiable and to be in environments that treat them with dignity. Demeaning and careless treatment causes distress (as well as, or sometimes instead of, non-compliance or righteous anger).[4] MacIntyre proposes that vulnerable human beings need the virtues: that is, they require those qualities found within the best social practices and relationships, communities and the lives of individuals, such as justice, love, reason, courage, honesty, generosity and 'acknowledged dependence' (MacIntyre 1999; see also de Zulueta 1993). Others have argued that human flourishing requires freedom and justice (Paul et al 1999). Well-being is defined by Kant as 'satisfaction with one's condition' (Kant, in Paul et al 1999: 269). It is hardly surprising, then, that levels of well-being in prison are low (see Hill 1999: 157; see also Margalit 1996).

In prison suicide research, there tends to be an assumption that environmental demands or deprivations include factors such as isolation, inactivity, loss of freedom and autonomy, loss of safety and family contact, rather than the feeling of injustice. Clearly many of the above factors contribute to the experience of injustice. There are hints in the general effects literature about the importance of the psychological environment, for example:

> What do prisoners complain about? The 'psychological reality lying behind their incarceration' and the fact that they were not given clear criteria as to why they were placed in solitary, their review process was amorphous, and they were not certain as to how they could improve behaviourally so as to eventually leave. They claimed they were also gratuitously harassed in petty ways by the guards.
>
> (Gendreau and Bonta 1984: 474, discussing Jackson 1983)

The 'manner of one's treatment' may be more important than the physical environment (Porporino and Zamble 1984; see also Tyler 1990) and it is this aspect of prison life that varies most (Liebling 2004). Many autobiographical and qualitative studies of prison life suggest that lack of respect and fairness are frustrating and painful, but these ideas have rarely been empirically tested. Several sceptical commentators have argued, on the contrary, that prison life has little effect on the psychological well-being of prisoners overall (Walker 1987; Zamble and Porporino 1988; Bukstel and Kilman 1980).

We propose that levels of distress, and rates of suicide, in prisons will be, at least in part, demonstrably related to degrees of legitimate treatment – that is, to levels of fairness and respect in individual prisons.

This proposition stands in conflict with some well-being theorists, who suggest, among other things, that seeking security, safety and stability (let us say, security and order) is negatively associated with well-being, whereas seeking autonomy, self-direction and the welfare of others is positively associated with well-being (Sagiv *et al* 2000; Sagiv and Schwartz 2000). It is possible that more vulnerable individuals seek more security and order than others, or that the prison increases the need of individuals for security and order (see Grounds 2005). In any case, our argument assumes that legitimacy incorporates fairness and respect, and necessarily includes both considerations of safety and predictability, and considerations of individual autonomy. Our proposition, based on emerging research results, is that a careful balance between freedom and order is fundamental to human well-being, in or out of the prison, but that in the prison, these values are especially difficult to reconcile.

To formally develop this argument, we need to consider at greater length than we can offer here what legitimacy is, what fairness is, what respect is, what our term 'moral performance' has to offer, and to operationalise these terms (that is, translate them into measurable variables). We need to operationalise the terms 'well-being' and 'distress', and to explore whether these latter concepts have a significant relationship with institutional suicide rates. We cannot cover this in detail in one chapter, but we are working our way towards this agenda in a large longitudinal study. The study is aimed at the evaluation of a new set of suicide prevention procedures in five of ten prisons with high suicide rates, and an additional two prisons with low suicide rates included as a further control. We have included detailed measures of the quality of life – or moral performance – of each of the prisons as well as detailed data on levels of distress and suicide rates in each prison. The results from the baseline and outcome studies provide some support for the model we have developed.

Our use of the term 'moral performance' has its roots in a study of prison quality carried out with colleagues during 2000–01. In this study, we took seriously the complaints made by prison staff, and critics of the prison, that official measures of prison performance were inadequate, distorted and insufficiently related to things that matter. We tried instead to develop a set of measures based on what staff and prisoners told us comprised the most important dimensions of prison life. The methodology was highly participatory (we have reported fully on this elsewhere; Liebling and Arnold 2002; Liebling 2004). What we want to report here is simply that a consensus emerged about what the most important dimensions of prison life and quality were, from those who lived and worked in prison.

The dimensions that mattered were: respect, humanity, relationships, trust, fairness, order, safety, well-being, personal development, family contact, and the distribution of power. Staff and prisoners helped us, via a number of exercises and some qualitative and appreciative interviews, to identify the relevant dimensions, and then a series of statements or items that would reflect these dimensions in the prison setting. So the dimension 'humanity', for example, would be reflected by five statements distributed randomly throughout a questionnaire with which prisoners were asked to agree or disagree on a five-point scale. The statements in the dimension 'humanity', were:

1. [Statement 10] I am being looked after with humanity in here [.767]
2. [Statement 21] I am treated as a person of value in this prison [.761]
3. [Statement 29] Some of the treatment I receive in this prison is degrading [.758]
4. [Statement 47] Staff here treat me with kindness [.754]
5. [Statement 94] I am not being treated as a human being in here [.789]

The reliability for this dimension was .82. The answers were recoded so that all items were scored in a positive direction. We have used this technique to measure the quality of life or moral performance of numerous establishments, and we have found some interesting and significant differences as well as some departures from official visions of the prison provided by routine audit and performance data. We have used the term 'moral performance' to make the point that these dimensions reflect some serious normative reflection about what matters, as well as a current evaluation of how prisoners (and staff) feel treated in this environment. Several of the dimensions, particularly respect and fairness, reflect what we think legitimacy theorists are most concerned with.

There were interesting statistical relationships between the dimensions, so that a regression analysis with order and well-being used in turn as the dependent variables showed that evaluations of staff–prisoner relationships were highly correlated with perceptions of fairness, and that perceptions of both were highly correlated with perceived order and self-reported well-being. The relationship between perceptions of fairness and order was predicted by the available literature. What is less explicit in the literature is the finding that perceived levels of fairness and safety explained variations in levels of well-being. These results offer some support for the proposition that experiences of disrespect and unfairness are distressing and damaging for the individual: that as human beings we need to be in environments that acknowledge our dignity and permit our development (MacIntyre 1999). Prisons differ significantly in the extent to which they allow this.[5] Prison is experienced as punishing and painful by a significant proportion of prisoners. Levels of perceived painfulness vary more than levels of perceived punitiveness (see further, Liebling 2004).

In the version of the quality-of-life survey we have used in the study of suicide prevention, our original and positive emphasis on well-being became a more explicit concern with levels of distress. We shall report briefly on the methods used and on some of the findings from this part of our work in order to continue with our argument.

Methods and data

The methodology adopted in this evaluation study included a before–after quality-of-life survey of 100 randomly selected prisoners and 80–100 staff at Time 1 (Jan–Feb 2002) and Time 2 (Jan–Feb 2004) in each of twelve prisons. The prisoner survey included four sections: demographic and situational data (age, status, previous history); a list of 109 statements about prison life and quality which prisoners agreed or disagreed with on a 1–5 Likert scale; an open question asking prisoners to state 'the three best and the worst things about life in this prison'; and the General Health Questionnaire (GHQ-12) [12 items, .92, .92]. The 109 statements were used to form dimensions, following a factor analysis and guided by previous research. A detailed survey for staff was also conducted (not reported on here). Institutional data including performance data and suicide figures were made available to the research team on request. We included demographic and situational data, and detailed measures of aspects of the prison environment relevant to the care of individual prisoners, as well as the measures of 'moral performance' outlined briefly above.[6]

The prisons included in the study were all local prisons: accomodating prisoners on remand, and relatively short-stay sentenced prisoners. Ten of the twelve were selected on the basis of their relatively high suicide rates. A total of 1,301 prisoners completed the survey in 2002, and 1,307 completed it in 2004. The study also included a largely qualitative process study (based on observation and interviews) in each prison in the intervening period. The data drawn on in this chapter are taken mainly from the 'before' or baseline study, although the conceptual model has been developed using survey data from both the before and after the studies.

Imported vulnerability

There is an important contribution to prison suicide rates made by *imported vulnerability*. Our measure of imported vulnerability (which included previous suicide attempts, psychiatric treatment, self-harm and drug misuse) showed that levels varied between establishments of the same type (see Table 8.1). It is possible that populations from geographical areas with high psychiatric morbidity, drug dependence and prior suicide attempts bring more suicide risk into prison with them than populations from apparently less risky parts of the country. Some prisons may do a certain amount of 'weeding out' of the most at-risk candidates, sending them elsewhere on the grounds that better facilities exist there. A regression analysis showed that previous suicide attempts and previous self-harm were more highly correlated with distress than were either drug use or previous psychiatric treatment.

Distress in prison

We measured distress using the General Health Questionnaire (GHQ-12),[7] and a 16-item dimension of our own based on previous research, 'overall distress'. We had 1,240 usable GHQ questionnaires in 2002 (95% of the sample) and 1,213 usable questionnaires in 2004 (93% of the sample). The 'overall distress' dimension had fewer missing responses (99% usable data). These measures were highly related (they correlated at .74), so that prisoners scoring high in one tended to score high in the other, but they were also found (via a cross-tabulation) to tap slightly different aspects of distress in some individuals.

Levels of distress in prison were extraordinarily high. The average score on the GHQ-12 from the ten 'high-risk' establishments, for example, where a score of 12 or 13 is the threshold indicating significant disorder, was 16.78. Mean scores varied significantly between establishments (from 11.99 at one of the comparator prisons, to 18.87 at one male establishment). At eleven of the twelve establishments, the mean score was above the threshold used in most studies to indicate treatable illness. Some of the differences in levels of distress were related to individual circumstances, so the highest levels of distress were found among the unsentenced (18.82 > 14.86, p<.001), unemployed prisoners (17.99 > 15.27, p<.001), first time prisoners (17.23 > 15.87, p<.01), and those who were 'first time in this prison' (16.85 > 15.54, p<.05; see Table 8.2).

Table 8.1 Frequency of imported vulnerability per prison, 2002

			Vulnerability indicators			
Percentage of prisoners in each establishment	Attempted suicide	Psychiatric treatment	Self-harmed	Drug mis-use	All three indicators (suicide, psych treat, self-harm)	All four indicators
Winchester	25.0	22.0	16.0	41.0	9.0	8.0
Lewes	25.2	28.87	12.5	45.2	5.8	4.8
Eastwood Park	38.8	35.9	16.7	58.3	13.6	10.7
Styal	36.0	37.0	17.0	53.5	13.9	11.9
Leeds	12.3	22.8	9.6	57.0	5.3	3.5
Liverpool	11.9	21.4	6.0	55.6	2.5	1.7
Wandsworth	18.7	24.1	12.3	42.6	7.4	4.6
Manchester	13.1	20.4	7.1	38.4	5.1	4.0
Feltham	12.3	15.0	10.6	31.3	3.5	2.6
Glen Parva	8.4	17.6	7.6	47.1	3.4	2.5
Swansea	17.9	27.1	10.3	62.7	5.9	1.7
Forest Bank	6.9	18.8	6.9	48.5	4.0	3.0

Table 8.2 Key differences between groups of prisoners in levels of distress and vulnerability

	Mean score	Mean score	Difference
Anxiety & depression (GHQ) *(range 1–36, where higher is more distress)*			
Unsentenced v. sentenced prisoners	18.82	14.86	p<.001
Unemployed v. employed prisoners	17.99	15.27	p<.001
First time v. experienced prisoners	16.85	15.54	p<.05
First time in this prison v. the rest	16.85	15.54	p<.05
Distress on entry *(range 1–5, where 5 is high distress)*			
High imported vulnerability v. the rest	4.05	3.43	p<.001
Women v. men	3.97	3.44	p<.001
Unsentenced v. sentenced prisoners	3.64	3.45	p<.001
Black and Asian prisoners v. the rest	3.66	3.50	p<.05
First time in this prison v. the rest	3.44	3.25	p<.05
Imported vulnerability *(range 1–5, where 5 is high vulnerability)*			
Women v. men	2.47	1.93	p<.001
Experienced prisoners v. the rest	2.13	1.76	p<.001
White prisoners v. the rest	2.10	1.70	p<.001

The highest levels of *distress on entry* into prison were found among those with the highest levels of imported vulnerability (4.05 > 3.43, p<.001), women (3.97 > 3.44, p<.001), unsentenced prisoners (3.64 > 3.45, p<.001), black and Asian prisoners (3.66 > 3.50, p<.05), and those who were 'first time in this prison' (3.44 > 3.25, p<.05). The highest levels of *imported vulnerability* were found among women prisoners (2.47 > 1.93, p<.001), those who were repeatedly coming back to prison (2.13 > 1.76, p<.001), often to the same prison (2.18 > 2.02, p<.05), and white prisoners (2.10 > 1.70, p<.001). The most vulnerable prisoners reported the lowest levels of perceived physical safety (p<.001), family contact (p<.001) and personal development (p<.05), and the highest levels of drug use (p<.01). In other words, as Toch and others have argued before, the prison interacts with the person. There are vulnerable groups, and high-risk situations, in prison.

In general, we found the 'slow and gradual amelioration' described by Clemmer, Zamble and Porporino, and others (Clemmer 1958; Zamble and Porporino 1988; Sapsford 1983): that is, that levels of distress and dissatisfaction declined over time, with particularly high levels throughout the first month (see also Harvey, this volume).[8]

The relationship between distress and suicide rates

Our early analyses showed that two related but separate measures of prisoner distress could be devised and used in the prisons context. They had high reliability, seemed to be valid measures of the concept of interest, and they showed differences between prisons, taking into account differences in vulnerability. In order to use one or both of the above measures of distress as key outcome variables in this study more confidently, we explored whether there was any link between mean (aggregate) levels of distress in each prison, and recent suicide rates.[9] To do this, we confirmed calendar year average population figures for each prison (with the assistance of the Home Office Research, Statistics and Development Directorate (RDS). We also confirmed numbers of suicides (self-inflicted deaths) in each prison for each calendar year for the period 1991–2003. We calculated three-year moving averages for each prison[10] over a ten-year period. Correlations between suicide rates and mean distress scores for 2002 were explored. The results for the most relevant time period (2000–02 inclusive) showed that there was a statistically significant relationship between current mean GHQ scores, our measure of individual level distress, and institutional level suicide rates. Table 8.3 shows the main correlations of interest.

The correlations were strong and significant at p<.01. The Spearman rank correlations in column 3 of the table confirm the general patterns. Using the log scale for suicide rates gave slightly higher correlations than using raw scales (column 2). A scatter-plot for the log-scale correlations

Table 8.3 Main correlations between suicide rates and mean distress levels

	Pearson correlation with SID rate 2000–02	Spearman rank correlation with SID rate 2000–02	Pearson correlation with log scale (SID rate 2000–02)
Mean GHQ-12, 2002	.80	.78	.83
Mean distress, 2002 **	.73	.71	.78
% with GHQ-12 score 30 plus, 2002 (log scale)	Not calculated		.75
% with distress score over 4, 2002 (log scale)			.73

N=12 (establishments)
** negative correlations (due to scale direction) – sign not shown here.

showed a good approximation to a straight line. Alternative indicators based on percentage of prisoners scoring high on overall distress and GHQ did no better in the analysis than using mean scores (they were still significant). The correlations between these outcome measures and the adjacent moving averages (i.e. rates for 1999–2001 and 2001–3) were lower, so that as we moved further away from the survey period, the data were less related.

With certain caveats in mind (explored more fully in our project report, forthcoming), this series of analyses satisfied us that both 'overall distress' and GHQ scores could be used as valid and complementary measures of distress, and that in turn, these levels provided reasonable indications of levels of suicide risk in each prison over time. This assumption has the advantage of increasing the amount of data available for more detailed analyses of the effects of prison quality. Using levels of distress as a key outcome variable, rather than suicide rates alone (or levels of self-harm, which are notoriously unreliable and have an unclear relationship with suicide), allows for a more robust and detailed analysis of the relationships between aspects of prison life and quality, and outcomes for prisoners. Distress has a plausible theoretical significance, as well as some statistical significance, in this study. An exploration of the relationships between the dimensions in the study resulted in the following conceptual models (Figures 8.1 and 8.2).

Using our overall distress measure as the dependent variable, the measures of the prison environment that contributed most directly to distress were perceived physical safety, respect, relationships and fairness, dignity, frustration, clarity, security and order, and family contact.[11] Using the GHQ-12 measure as the dependent variable in a stepwise regression, the measures of the prison environment that contributed most directly to distress were prisoners' ratings of physical safety, personal development (and participation in offending behaviour programmes) and family contact. Many of these dimensions were also independently related to suicide rates. These relationships were stable over time (2002 figures are shown in plain font, 2004 figures in italics). Distress on entry into custody was highly predictive of distress generally.

Perceived safety was a key factor in explaining variations in distress, playing both a direct and 'mediating role'. As Haney argues, the prison is a high-threat, low-control environment (Haney 1997; see also Goffman 1961; Goodstein 1979). We can see in these models how perceived safety, fairness and care for the individual are crucial in minimising the distress caused by such an environment.[12] As de Zulueta argued, 'an unpleasant but predictable world is preferable to a chaotic one' (de Zulueta 1993:

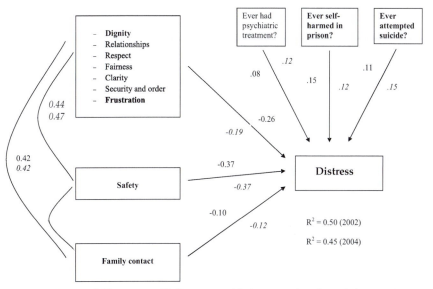

Figure 8.1 Modelling overall distress: with imported vulnerability: prisoner data 2002 and 2004

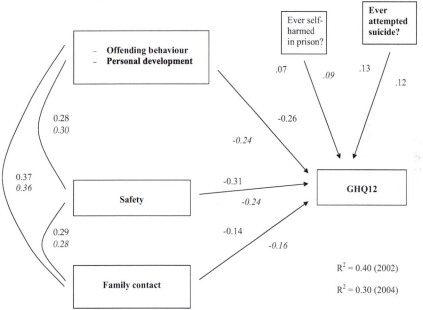

Figure 8.2 Modelling GHQ12: with imported vulnerability: prisoner data 2002 and 2004

In these figures, 'offending behaviour' represents involvement in offender behaviour courses, 'personal development,' in other constructive activities: 'safety' refers to perceived safety, and 'family contact' to satisfaction with the frequency and length of contact.

90). Respect and relationships are crucial to fairness (unfairness is, after all, an unsatisfactory relation between two people: one treats the other with insufficient consideration). The relational dimensions were highly correlated with perceived safety, suggesting that the experience of safety in prison has much to do with one's treatment, and with 'trust in the environment'.

So how satisfactory is the theoretical model we are developing? In the regression models, imported vulnerability measures contributed around 10 per cent of the explained variance in distress. Prison quality measures contributed between 30 and 40 per cent of the explained variance in distress. Together, these concepts (as we have measured them) accounted for around 45–50 per cent of the explained variance in distress. Some individual characteristics added to the model, as outlined above. Being highly vulnerable, first time in prison, early in the period of custody, unemployed in prison, and female seemed to significantly increase levels of distress.[13] Differences between prisons generally outweighed these factors, however, so that it was possible to be a highly vulnerable individual in a safe and respectful prison, and to experience relatively low levels of distress compared to other vulnerable individuals located elsewhere.

This is work in progress. The results so far tell us a great deal about the differences between prisons, the vulnerabilities of the prisoner population and the tendencies of prison environments to treat individuals in ways that are experienced as highly distressing.[14] We need a more precise and developed model of prisoner vulnerability, and a more developed theory of 'prison painfulness' in which attention is paid to the deployment of power, access to resources and the overall moral performance of individual prisons. We also need more developed theories of care, indifference and brutality by prison staff, and of the roles played by different staff groups in the experience of imprisonment. In the meantime we need to make sense of the qualitative (interview and observational) data we have been collecting, on and off, at each establishment throughout the evaluation.

Conclusion

Human beings are creatures capable of feeling pain and suffering not only as a result of physically painful acts but also as a result of acts with symbolic meaning.

(Margalit 1996: 8405)

Sparks and colleagues have demonstrated that order in prison is something that has to be worked at (Sparks *et al* 1996). Much of the skill of the professional prison officer is directed, consciously and unconsciously, at this end.[15] We suggest, given the findings outlined here, drastic increases in use of the prison, and elevated suicide rates, that further thought might be given to the relevance of extremely high levels of distress found in the prisons in this study. Further work is needed on possible variations in individual propensities to discern unfairness, lack of safety, and so on (see Piquero *et al* 2004), and the links between these variations and what we have called imported vulnerability (see further Harvey, this volume). Sufficient differences existed between prisons of the same type for us to argue that 'mean prisoner evaluations' reflected real differences in prison quality. It may be worth considering how and whether well-being might be accomplished, even in the prison, and if not, why not. The aspiration of much policy and practice is simply to reduce distress (see Figure 8.3). Ward and colleagues argue, similarly, that the aspirations of risk-reduction interventions to tackle offending behaviour are narrowly conceived. A more energetic concern with

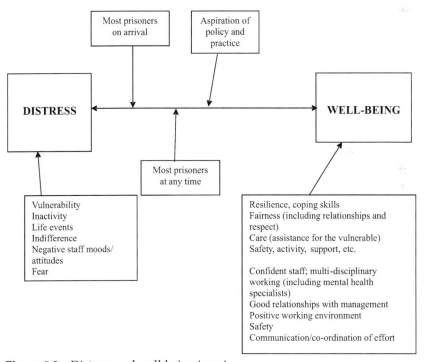

Figure 8.3   Distress and well-being in prison

promoting well-being, or human flourishing (in or out of the prison), might be relevant in both cases (see for example, Ward and Mann 2003; Ward and Stewart 2003).[16] This raises fundamental questions about the dual role of the prison, and whether, in the end, its punishment function must always dominate.

New claims are being made for the prison via a modernisation and performance agenda, and in a newly optimistic 'what works' climate. Our work suggests that we should be cautious, as well as more curious, about what the prison does. As Wormith said, taking issue with Cressey, it doesn't just 'sit there' (Wormith 1984: 427). The prison dispenses justice (Bottoms and Sparks 1997: 29), and injustice, and to the extent that it does the latter, it causes pain and distress, which in turn both constitute and generate apparently unintended consequences (see Haney 1997; Carlen 1994). Haney argues, after Christie, that the amount of penal pain accepted by a community is a question of standards, or values (Haney 1997). There is an important role for empirical knowledge in making value choices. The public, and many of those who work in and manage prisons, may underestimate how painful the prison experience is. In the light of these findings, are there 'limits to pain' (Christie 1993, 1981) and if so, should we not know more about how to set them?

Notes

1   We are most grateful to Joel Harvey for research assistance before and after his PhD (Harvey 2004), and to Gerry Rose for statistical advice, and for his assistance with the analysis. Early versions of the paper were delivered at the British Society of Criminology conference, and an American Society of Criminology Conference, both in 2003. We are grateful for useful comments and questions raised at these events as well as for the comments of three anonymous reviewers to whom the paper was sent in an early form. Others who have assisted in this work include Ben Crewe, Susanne Karstedt, Shadd Maruna and Helen Griffiths. We are also grateful to Jenny Shaw and her team for encouraging us to use the GHQ-12. The research has been conducted with the support of a grant from the Home Office.

2   That is, the focus is on order, and there is relatively little direct attention paid to emotion. This may be largely because the political-theoretical literature (on the problem of order) on which they draw takes this position. Tony Bottoms has recently suggested, in his discussion of research undertaken by the author and colleagues, that the emotion of *resentment* is significant in discussions of fairness and unfairness (Bottoms 2003: 176–7; see also Lucas 1980: 5–7 on the 'intense fury' and 'healthy indignation' aroused by injustice; and Barbalet 1998). None of these authors considers the less

healthy or active emotions aroused by injustice (like shame; see Ahmed *et al* 2001; depression or anxiety). However, see the recent work of Grounds on the effects of miscarriages of justice (Grounds 2004, 2005) and recent work by Crawley and Sparks on ageing prisoners (see e.g. this volume).

3   These include their punishment and 'segregative functions, their compulsory powers, and the unwillingness of their captive occupants' (Bottoms and Sparks 1997: 16).

4   Sparks and Bottoms argue that 'every instance of brutality in prisons, every casual racist joke and demeaning remark, every ignored petition, every unwarranted bureaucratic delay, every inedible meal, every arbitrary decision to segregate or transfer without giving clear and well-founded reasons, every petty miscarriage of justice, every futile and inactive period of time – is delegitimating' (Sparks and Bottoms 1995: 60). We want to suggest that the word 'delegitimating' is accompanied by the more emotive (and equally theoretically relevant) word 'distressing'.

5   Recent work by Adrian Grounds has provided support for the thesis that major injustices cause acute psychological trauma and lasting damage, including estrangement, loss of capacity for intimacy, moodiness, inability to settle, loss of a sense of purpose and direction, and a pervasive sense of mistrust towards the world (Grounds 2004, 2005; and Jamieson and Grounds this volume). The mechanisms involved include sudden dislocation from a previous life (loss), high levels of fear for one's safety, and unresolved feelings of bitterness (ibid.). As Grounds argues, his work is exploratory and relatively small scale, so far. Our thesis is that relatively minor (and not so minor) injustices and frustrations also cause trauma, distress and damage and that these experiences form a crucial, and differentially distributed, part of the prison experience. More work is needed on the mechanisms involved, including the important role played by perceptions of punishment, and of trust and mistrust in human and social well-being (see for example, Uslaner 2002; Misztal 1996; Hollis 1998; Braithwaite 1998).

6   The dimensions (with reliability scores in 2002 and 2004) included: Relationships [10 items, .89, .90]; Respect [5 items, .88, .88]; Fairness [7 items, .85, .86]; Clarity [2 items, .55, .58]; Frustration [6 items, .78, .79]; Order and security [4 items, .76, .79]; Dignity [6 items, .75, .73]; Personal development [8 items, .90, .88]; Family contact [3 items, .61, .59]; Physical safety [5 items, .67, .66]; Care and safety; [6 items, .70, .73]; Individual care; [4 items, .72, .71]; Assistance for the vulnerable [6 items, .78, .78]; and Distress [16 items, .92, .92].

7   Several studies have confirmed that the 12-item GHQ can be used as a short screening instrument for psychological disorders and minor (non-psychotic) psychiatric disorders. It produces comparable results to longer versions (Goldberg *et al* 1997). Its brevity makes it attractive for use in busy settings, and where it forms part of a broader survey. The results from GHQ studies have been shown to be unaffected by gender, age and educational level (Goldberg *et al* 1997). This method is particularly suited to comparing

levels of anxiety and depression within and between populations (Banks *et al* 1980); and to identifying change over time (Banks and Jackson 1982).

8 In our qualitative study of the implementation of new suicide prevention procedures and practices (ongoing), prisoners attributed their distress to continuing stressful life events (such as bereavement and relationship breakdown), frustration, shock and fear, lack of clarity and uncertainty about the rules, drug withdrawal, lack of support for major problems, lack of appropriate health care, indifference and lack of respect from staff, and worries about family.

9 NB. These figures are based on all self-inflicted deaths, not on deaths receiving suicide verdicts at inquests. They are collected by the Prison Service's Safer Custody Group.

10 This is a standard approach to smoothing trends that are unstable, and is common in studies of suicide rates.

11 The conceptual model was estimated using multiple regression. The objective was to build a model in which levels of distress were predicted by other variables, whether directly or indirectly. In order to control for establishment-level effects, dummy variables were created for the prisons (eleven dummy variables, with one establishment as the reference group). The dummy variables were entered into the model as predictors prior to adding any other explanatory variables. This ensured that the influence of prison-level variables would be removed. The dependent variable 'GHQ score' was predicted from a number of 'quality of prison life' dimensions, such as respect, relationships and fairness. A forward stepwise regression method was used in order to select the predictor variables from the set which would account for the most variance. Forward variable selection enters the variables into the model one at a time based on whether the variable contributes significantly. Using collinearity diagnostics, a cut-off point was determined so that the variables included in the model did not show high levels of multicollinearity (that is, where predictor variables are highly correlated; this is unfavourable because it suggests that the similar constructs are being measured). Condition indices were inspected and a condition index greater than 15 was seen to indicate a possible problem with collinearity. Once the predictor(s) of distress had been determined, the next step was to examine which variables would in turn explain variance in the predictors of distress. This was again estimated using a forward stepwise regression method.

12 Margalit argues that loss of control is experienced as a humiliation – an injury to self-respect (Margalit 1996: 19). She also proposes that 'humiliation ... is an emotion we may feel as a result of mere identification with others even if we are not the direct victims of the humiliation' (ibid.: 32).

13 Inevitably, given the focus of our research, the model is rather inward-looking. We have not attempted to take into account the continuing influence of negative life events during custody or the experiences of injustice and lack of safety prior to entering custody. These would be promising avenues to pursue.

14 We should note the inevitable limitations of quantitative data analysis here: we are omitting much that is significant, owing to individual differences and circumstances.

15 Developing the work of Sparks and colleagues further, it would be theoretically as well as pragmatically interesting to investigate what forms of order (e.g. social, situational) might be most directly related to well-being (see further Bottoms and Sparks 1997; Liebling 2004).

16 In the Good Lives Model of offender rehabilitation (a strengths-based model) emphasis is placed on increasing the individual's capacity to live a more fulfilling life, to seek primary goods (such as mastery experiences, autonomy, freedom from emotional turmoil and relatedness) via socially acceptable ways, and to achieve high levels of well-being. The model stresses the promotion of welfare as well as the reduction of risk (Ward and Mann 2003). As Margalit says, 'respecting humans means never giving up on anyone, since all people are capable of living dramatically differently from the way they have lived so far (Margalit 1996: 71).

References

Ahmad, S. (1996) *Fairness in Prisons*. University of Cambridge PhD thesis.

Ahmed, E., Harris, N., Braithwaite, J. and Braithwaite, V. (2001) *Shame Management Through Reintegration*. Cambridge: Cambridge University Press.

Backett, S. (1988) 'Suicide and stress in prison', in S. Backett, J. McNeil and A. Yellowlees (eds) *Imprisonment Today*. London: Macmillan Publishing.

Banks, M.H., Clegg, C.W., Jackson, P.R., Kemp, N.J., Stafford, E.M. and Wall, T.D. (1980) 'The use of the general health questionnaire as an indicator of mental health in occupational studies', *Journal of Occupational Psychology*, 53, 187–194.

Banks, M.H. and Jackson, P.R. (1982) 'Unemployment and risk of minor psychiatric disorder in young people: Cross-sectional and longitudinal evidence', *Psychological Medicine*, 12, 789–798.

Barbalet, J.M. (1998) *Emotion, Social Theory and Social Structure: A Macrosociological Approach*. Cambridge: Cambridge University Press.

Beetham, D. (1991) *The Legitimation of Power*. Basingstoke: Macmillan Publishing.

Berger, P.L., Berger, B. and Kellner, H. (1977) *The Homeless Mind: Modernisation and Consciousness*. Harmondsworth: Penguin.

Biles, D. (1991) 'Deaths in custody in Britain and Australia', *Howard Journal*, 30 (2), 110–120.

Blaauw, E., Kerkhof, A.J.F.M., Winkel, F.W. and Sheridan, L. (2001a) 'Identifying suicide risk in penal institutions in the Netherlands', *British Journal of Forensic Practice*, 3 (4), 22–28.

Blaauw, E., Winkel, F.W. and Kerkhof, A.J.F.M. (2001b) 'Bullying and suicidal behaviour in jails', *Criminal Justice and Behaviour*, 28 (3), 279–299.

Bottoms, A.E. (1999) 'Interpersonal violence and social order in prisons', in M. Tonry and J. Petersilia (eds) *Prisons, Crime and Justice: A Review of Research*, Chicago IL: University of Chicago Press, vol. 26, pp. 205–282.

Bottoms, A.E. (2003) 'Some sociological reflections on restorative justice', in A. von Hirsch, J. Roberts, A.E. Bottoms, K. Roach and M. Schiff (eds) *Restorative Justice and Criminal Justice: Competing or Reconcilable Paradigms?* Oxford: Hart Publishing, pp. 79–114.

Bottoms, A.E. and Rose, G. (1998) 'The importance of staff–prisoner relationships: Results from a study in three male prisons', in D. Price and A. Liebling (eds) *Staff Prisoner Relationships: A Review of the Literature*, unpublished report submitted to the Prison Service.

Braithwaite, J. (1998) 'Institutionalising distrust, enculturating trust', in V. Braithwaite and M. Levi (eds) *Trust and Governance*. New York: Russell Sage Foundation, pp. 343–375.

Braithwaite, J. and Makkai, T. (1994) 'Trust and compliance', *Policing and Society*, 4, 1–12.

Bukstel, L.H. and Kilmann, P.R. (1980) 'Psychological effects of imprisonment on confined individuals', *Psychological Bulletin*, 88 (2), 469–493.

Carlen, P. (1994) 'Why study women's imprisonment? Or anyone else's? – An indefinite article', in R.D. King and M. Maguire (eds) *Prisons in Context*. Oxford: Oxford University Press.

Christie, N. (1981) *Limits to Pain*. Oxford: Martin Robertson Publishing.

Christie, N. (1993) *Crime Control as Industry: Towards Gulags, Western Style?* London: Routledge.

Clemmer, D. (1958) *The Prison Community*. New York: Holt, Reinhart and Winston Publishing.

Dear, G.E. (2000) 'Functional and dysfunctional impulsivity, depression, and suicidal ideation in a prison population', *Journal of Psychology*, 134 (1), 77–80.

Dear, G.E., Slattery, J.L. and Hillan, R.J. (2001) 'Evaluations of the quality of coping reported by prisoners who have self-harmed and those who have not' *Suicide and Life-Threatening Behaviour*, 31 (4), 442–450.

Dear, G.E., Thomson, D.M., Hall, G.J. and Howells, K. (1998) 'Self-inflicted injury and coping behaviours in prison', in R.J. Kosky, H.S. Eshkevari, R. Hassan and R. Goldney (eds) *Suicide Prevention: The Global Context*. New York: Plenum Press, pp. 189–199.

Dear, G.E., Thomson, D.M. and Hills, A.M. (2000) 'Self-harm in prison. Manipulators can also be suicide attempters', *Criminal Justice and Behavior*, 27, 160–175.

de Zulueta, F. (1993) *From Pain to Violence: The Traumatic Roots of Destructiveness*. London: Whurr.

Erikson, E.H. (1995) *Childhood and Society*. London: Vintage Publishing.

Gendreau, P. and Bonta, J. (1984) 'Solitary confinement is not cruel and unusual punishment: People sometimes are!', *Canadian Journal of Criminology*, 26 (4), 467–478.

Giddens, A. (1984) *The Constitution of Society*. Cambridge: Polity Press.

Goffman, E. (1961) 'On the characteristics of total institutions', in D.R. Cressey (ed.) *The Prison: Studies in Institutional Organisation and Change*. New York: Holt, Rinehart and Winston Publishing.

Goldberg, D.P., Gater, R., Sartorius, N., Ustin, T.B., Piccinelli, M., Gureje, O. and Rutter, C. (1997) 'The validity of two versions of the GHQ in the WHO study of mental illness in general health care', *Psychological Medicine*, 27, 191–197.

Goodstein, L.I. (1979) 'Inmate adjustment to prison and the transition to community life', *Journal of Research in Crime and Delinquency*, 16, 246–272.

Green, C., Kendall, K., Andre, G., Looman, T. and Polvi, N. (1993) 'A study of 133 suicides among Canadian federal prisoners', *Medicine, Science and the Law*, 2, 121–127.

Grounds, A.T. (2004) 'Psychological consequences of wrongful conviction and imprisonment', *Canadian Journal of Criminology*, 46 (2), 165–182.

Grounds, A.T. (2005) 'Understanding the effects of wrongful conviction', in M. Tonry (ed.) *Crime and Justice: A Review of Research*, vol. 32. Chicago: University of Chicago Press, pp. 1–58.

Haney, C. (1997) 'Psychology and the limits to prison pain: Confronting the coming crisis in the eighth amendment law', *Psychology, Public Policy and Law*, 3 (4), 499–588.

Harvey, J. (2004) *Transition and Adaptation to Prison Life: A Study of Young Adults Aged 18 to 21*. PhD thesis, University of Cambridge.

Hatty, S.E. and Walker, J.R. (1986) *A National Study of Deaths in Australian Prisons*. Canberra: Australian Centre of Criminology.

Hill, T.E. (1999) 'Happiness and human flourishing in Kant's ethics', in E.F. Paul, F.D. Miller and J. Paul (eds) *Human Flourishing*. Cambridge: Cambridge University Press, pp. 143–75.

Hollis, M. (1998) *Trust within Reason*. Cambridge: Cambridge University Press.

Home Office (1984) *Suicides in Prison: Report by HM Chief Inspector of Prisons*. London: Home Office.

Home Office (1986) *Report of the Working Group on Suicide Prevention*. London: HMSO.

Home Office (1991) *Custody, Care and Justice: The Way Ahead for the Prison Service in England and Wales*. London: HMSO.

Jackson, M. (1983) *Prisoners of Isolation: Solitary Confinement in Canada*. Toronto: University of Toronto Press.

Kennedy, D.B. (1984) 'A theory of suicide while in police custody', *Journal of Police Science and Administration*, 12(2), 191–200.

Lester, D. and Danto, B.L. (1993) *Suicide Behind Bars: Prediction and Prevention*. Philadelphia: Charles Press.

Liebling, A. (1992) *Suicides in Prison*. London: Routledge Publishing.

Liebling, A. (1995) 'Vulnerability and prison suicide', *British Journal of Criminology*, 35 (2), 173–187.

Liebling, A. (1999) 'Prison suicide and prisoner coping', in M. Tonry and J. Petersilia (eds) *Prisons, Crime and Justice: An Annual Review of Research.* Chicago: University of Chicago Press, vol. 26, pp. 283–360.

Liebling, A. (2004) (assisted by Arnold, H.) *Prisons and their Moral Performance: A Study of Values, Quality and Prison Life.* Oxford: Clarendon Press.

Liebling, A. and Arnold, H. (2002) 'Measuring the quality of prison life', *Research Findings 174.* London: Home Office.

Liebling, A. and Price, D. (2001) *The Prison Officer.* Leyhill: Prison Service and Waterside Press.

Lucas, J.R. (1980) *On Justice.* Oxford: Clarendon Press.

MacIntyre, A. (1999) *Dependent Rational Animals: Why Human Beings Need the Virtues.* London: Duckworth Publishing.

Margalit, A. (1996) *The Decent Society.* Cambridge, MA: Harvard University Press.

Misztal, B. (1996) *Trust in Modern Society.* Cambridge: Polity Press.

Paternoster, R., Brame, R., Bachman, R. and Sherman, L.W. (1997) 'Do fair procedures matter? The effects of procedural justice on spouse assault', *Law and Society Review*, 31 (1), 163–204.

Paul, E.F., Miller, F.D. and Paul, J. (eds) (1999) *Human Flourishing.* Cambridge: Cambridge University Press.

Piquero, A.R., Gomez-Smith, Z. and Langton, L. (2004) 'Discerning unfairness where others may not: Low self-control and unfair sanction perceptions', *Criminology*, 42 (3), 699–734.

Porporino, F.J. and Zamble, E. (1984) 'Coping with imprisonment', *Canadian Journal of Criminology*, 26 (4), 403–421.

Sagiv, I. and Schwartz, S.H. (2000) 'Value priorities and subjective well-being: direct relations and congruity effects', *European Journal of Social Psychology*, 30, 177–98.

Sagiv, I., Schwartz, S.H. and Boehnke, K. (2000) 'Worries and values', *Journal of Personality*, 68 (2), 309–46.

Sapsford, R. (1983) *Life Sentence Prisoners.* Milton Keynes: Open University Press.

Sparks, R. (1994) 'Can prisons be legitimate?', in R. King and M. McGuire (eds) *Prisons in Context.* Oxford: Clarendon Press.

Sparks, R. and Bottoms, A.E. (1995) 'Legitimacy and order in prisons', *British Journal of Sociology*, 46 (1), 45–62.

Sparks, J., Hay, W. and Bottoms, A.E. (1996) *Prisons and the Problem of Order.* Oxford: Clarendon Press.

Towl, G., Snow, L. and McHugh, M. (2000) *Suicide in Prisons.* Leicester: British Psychological Society.

Tyler, T. (1990) *Why People Obey the Law.* New Haven: Yale University Press.

Tyler, T.R. and Blader, S.L. (2000) *Cooperation in Groups: Procedural Justice, Social Identity, and Behavioural Engagement.* Philadelphia: Taylor and Francis Publishing.

Uslaner, E.M. (2002) *The Moral Foundations of Trust*. Cambridge: Cambridge University Press.

Walker, N. (1987) 'The unwanted effects of long-term imprisonment', in A.E. Bottoms and R. Light (eds) *Problems of Long-Term Imprisonment*. Aldershot: Gower Publishing.

Ward, T. and Mann, R. (2003) 'Good lives and the rehabilitation of sex offenders: A positive approach to treatment', in P.A. Linley and S. Joseph (eds) *Positive Psychology in Practice*. Chichester: John Wiley and Sons.

Ward, T. and Stewart, C.A. (2003) 'Good lives and the rehabilitation of sexual offenders', in T. Ward, D.R. Laws and S.M. Hudson (eds) *Sexual Deviance: Issues and Controversies*. Thousand Oaks CA: Sage Publishing, pp. 21–44.

Wormith, J.S. (1984) 'The controversy over the effects of long-term incarceration', *Canadian Journal of Criminology*, 26 (4), 423–437.

Wrong, D.H. (1994) *The Problem of Order: What Divides and Unites Society*. New York: The Free Press.

Zamble, E. and Porporino, E.J. (1988) *Coping, Behaviour and Adaptation in Prison Inmates*. New York: Springer-Verlag.

Zamble, E. and Quinsey, V.L. (1997) *The Criminal Recidivism Process*. Cambridge: Cambridge University Press.

Chapter 9

Crossing the boundary: the transition of young adults into prison

Joel Harvey

This chapter sets out to understand the effects of early imprisonment. It examines the experiences of 70 young adults, aged eighteen to 21, who have recently made the transition into prison and have been in custody for three days. This research was carried out at HM YOI Feltham, a large remand centre in London, England.[1] I will begin this chapter with a review of the literature on this entry period into custody. I will then provide an overview of the transitional process and will examine the common themes that were evident from prisoners' description of their experiences at Feltham. These themes include uncertainty, losing control and freedom, separation and loss, and a preoccupation with safety. Although these were common themes, prisoners differed in the degree to which they experienced these aspects of transition and differed in the extent to which they felt distressed. I will conclude by examining what contributes towards psychological distress at this phase of imprisonment.

Literature on the transition into prison

Within the prisons literature there are a number of studies that have examined the transition from 'street to prison' (Goffman 1961; Ericson 1975; Gibbs 1982a, b; Zamble and Porporino 1988; Jones and Schmid 2000; Neustatter 2002: chapter 3). This entry phase of imprisonment has been found to be particularly distressing for prisoners and has been identified as a period of heightened vulnerability to suicide and self-harm (Esparza 1973; Heilig 1973; Fawcett and Marrs 1973; Beigel and

Russell 1973; Liebling 1999). Suicides occur disproportionately in the first month in custody. Between the financial years 1998/9 to 2003/4 a quarter of all self-inflicted deaths occurred within a week of arriving at an establishment, and half occurred within the first month (HM Prison Service 2004).

Gibbs (1982a) originally defined the entry period as one of shock: 'the early period of confinement, like death, may be reacted to with shock and disbelief when it does arrive' (p. 34). Gibbs examined this entry period in US jails and noted that prisoners entering reception were in a physical and psychological limbo. Indeed, 'the reception room is a discordant limbo. A man has just come from the street where he had some measure of control over his life and he has not yet been immersed into the daily routine of doing time. He is between worlds, and has mastery over neither' (Gibbs 1982a: 35). He identified four pains of jail confinement (withstanding entry shock, maintaining outside links, securing stability and safety, and finding activity) and argued that 'no group other than pre-trial detainees are exposed to high levels of stress from each of the four problem areas' (Gibbs 1982b: 99). Gibbs (1982b) found that this phase was marked by uncertainty and that individuals desired predictability (which, he argued, was a fundamental need for psychological survival).

Goffman, in his writing on total institutions,[2] argued that the arrival period involves several processes that mortify the self. The most general form of this process involves role dispossession, where the individual 'finds certain roles are lost to him by virtue of the barrier that separates him from the outside world' (Goffman 1961: 25). These roles include employment, education, and roles people play within relationships. More specifically, the admissions procedures are also identified as mortifying. The procedures at reception 'can be characterised as a leaving off and a taking on, with the midpoint marked by physical nakedness. Leaving off of course entails a dispossession of property, important because persons invest self feelings in their possessions' (Goffman 1961: 27). The individual suffers 'personal defacement' as he is 'stripped of his usual appearance and of the equipment and services by which he maintains it' (ibid.: 29). The individual entering a total institution also suffers from a loss of safety.

More recently, Jones and Schmid (2000) looked at the experience of first-time prisoners in a maximum-security prison in the US. Jones was a prisoner at the time and thus he employed the method of participant observation. Twenty interviews with first-time prisoners were also conducted, although it is not stated what stage these individuals were at in their imprisonment at the time of interview. These prisoners were not completely new to the *custodial* experience as they had spent time in county jails. Jones and Schmid argued that prisoners have three 'experiential orientations' to prison and their orientations change as their time in prison progresses. The three orientations are pre-prison, prison and post-prison. The pre-prison orientation was characterised by the prisoner being an 'outsider looking in'. The prisoner, at this stage, knows very little about the prison and can only rely on information that has been given to him through others he has met outside. The main concerns at this stage are violence and uncertainty and the dominant emotion experienced is fear. Individuals also have problems in preserving their pre-prison identity and they suffer from a great sense of loss. At this early entry period, the prisoner creates what they term an 'anticipatory survival strategy'. This strategy involves isolating oneself and 'can be described as an extreme version of "doing time"' (Jones and Schmid 2000: 45). Prisoners in their sample spent one week on induction and by the end of this week, not having moved onto normal location, 'still possessed only a vague, uncertain conceptualisation of prison life, and one that is dominated by the idea of violence' (ibid.: 54). At this early entry period prisoners were often unable to absorb information that was presented to them at induction classes. On being moved to a different landing after a few weeks, their strategy changed to 'territorial caution'. This strategy involved 'observing others, looking for behavioural clues, and then deciding on the safest course of action'. Prisoners gradually learned how they 'should act in various locations in the prison' (ibid.: 58). Within a few weeks tentative friendships began to be formed. This 'partnership' could 'provide a social relationship through which this interpretive process can take place' (ibid.: 63). The strategy of isolation had lessened and prisoners had begun to interact more with others. Central to their argument is the suggestion that prisoners engage in a recurrent self-dialogue, and that as time progresses, prisoners begin to understand the world they live in somewhat and modify their 'survival strategy' accordingly. The prisoner, at this stage, however, stills sees himself as different from the majority of other prisoners.

Ericson (1975) also argued that prisoners who have recently arrived in prison engaged in a self-dialogue. This study, conducted in the UK, examined the 'social work' that young adult prisoners carried out in response to their imprisonment. By 'social work', Ericson is referring to the way in which young prisoners deal with and react to the behaviour of others around them. A total of 46 first-time prisoners were interviewed between twelve and 72 hours of admission and in the final week before they left the prison (at approximately four months). A total of fifteen of the sample were followed up post-release in the community. Ericson argues that the 'new inmate tries to account for what happened in a manner which will be accepted both to himself and to the many social audiences he is concerned about' (Ericson 1975: 27). Prisoners are in a reflexive mood state. At the entry period there is an attack on the individual's personal identity and 'in order to overcome this, the new prisoner learns about the formal and informal social structures, and how to use them to best advantage' (ibid.: 51). Many of the participants were concerned with outside problems and these concerns were 'compounded by fears that one is out of place inside' (ibid.: 50). Uncertainty surrounds the new prisoner and this 'stems from the fact that he must confront the reality of a human myth creation; that others have told him about the detention in relation to how they wanted it to appear to him rather than how it would appear to him' (ibid.: 51). Ericson also notes that the newly received prisoner is withdrawn and does not engage much with others around him.

One of the most extensive studies to examine this entry period, and prisoners' subsequent adaptation, was carried out by Zamble and Porporino (1988). In their longitudinal study of prisoner adaptation in Canada, a total of 133 male prisoners were interviewed a few weeks following their reception into custody. Of these, 130 were followed up after four months and 98 after sixteen months. At the first time interval, prisoners were having a difficult experience. Zamble and Porporino concluded that, 'emotional disturbance is clearly a problem among inmates beginning a new term' (ibid.: 85). Over half of their sample had difficulties sleeping and the mean score on the Beck's Depression Inventory revealed mild depression; a further 8 per cent were severely depressed. On a more positive side, a total of 80 per cent of the prisoners said they had a goal to accomplish during their prison term. Using Irwin's (1970) classifications of approaches to imprisonment, the authors reported that 51.3 per cent were 'gleaners' (that is, the main aim was towards self-improvement), 39.4 per cent were 'doing time' (avoiding trouble but not gaining anything positive at the same time) and 9 per cent were 'jailing' (forgetting life outside prison and enjoying their time in side). The high proportion of 'gleaners' led to the conclusion that the initial entry period could be portrayed as a 'window of opportunity'.

Several problems were identified from interviews carried out after a few weeks in prison. These were coded into the following categories: missing family and friends, missing freedom, missing a specific object or activity, conflicts with other prisoners, regrets about the past, concern with the future, boredom, cell conditions, medical services, lack of staff support, concern with safety, and a lack of programmes or activities. The problem that seemed to surface the most for prisoners within their first two weeks was being apart from their family and friends. As Zamble and Porporino (1988) state, 'the great majority of subjects were troubled by the separation from loved ones on the outside, and for most of them the problem of missing someone ranked near the top of their lists' (p. 91). Gibbs (1982b) also noted the importance of family contact at this stage of imprisonment and argued that social support from outside ties could serve as an 'equilibrating' factor; aiding prisoner adjustment to their new social world.

In summary, studies that have examined this early transitional phase of imprisonment have concluded that this period is particularly distressing for prisoners. The majority of this research has been carried out with adult prisoners and there have been no recent studies examining this transition among young adult prisoners (except the Neustattar 2002 journalistic account; pp. 39–52). The research described in this chapter thus sets out to make a contribution to this area by examining the transitional experiences of young adults within one remand centre in the UK.

The transitional process into prison

I will begin by providing an overview of the transitional *process* that prisoners went through as they entered prison (and will present background and demographic information on the individuals that I interviewed who had been through this process). Most prisoners at Feltham began their transitional journey from the free world to prison at the time of their arrest.[3] Having been arrested by the police, they spent a night, or often a weekend, in a police station before being taken to court for their hearing. Most prisoners spent a full day at court and would wait for several hours in the court cells following their hearing, before being transported in the prison van to Feltham. For some prisoners this journey took less than one hour but for many the journey lasted up to four hours. Prisoners often arrived after 9 p.m. at the prison. On arrival at Feltham, prisoners were brought off the van and into the prison reception area. In reception they were asked various questions by the desk officer, they were strip-searched, and they had their property checked in. From reception, prisoners were brought over to the induction unit. There, it was standard practice for each individual to be seen by a nurse and to be interviewed on a one-to-one basis with both a prison officer and a link worker.[4] This interview took place in order to identify any immediate needs the prisoner may have had on his first night and to assess whether he was at risk of harming himself or others. This first-night interview was of particular importance, because this was the stage where family contact was facilitated (e.g. they might be given credit, or a free phone call). Following the interview they were issued with a 'first night pack'. They had the choice between a 'smoker's pack' or a 'non-smoker's pack'. In each pack was £2.00 credit for the telephone. Prisoners then ate their meal at a table in the 'association' area and were then allocated to a single or double cell.

The following morning, prisoners on Kingfisher unit (the induction unit) began their day by getting breakfast and then going outside for some 'exercise'. This involved standing or walking around a small yard for up to an hour. After this, prisoners attended an induction course given by prison officers and other members of staff. They met the chaplain on a one-to-one basis, and if need be they were seen by drug workers, voluntary workers and members of the outreach team. The induction programme took place over two mornings and in the afternoons prisoners attended association. It is at this point where they made a telephone call home if they needed to and took a shower. Generally prisoners remained on the induction unit for three nights and two full days. They were then moved off onto one of the residential units the following day.

Within a few days, individuals entering prison had been subjected to a number of different processes and transitions. There was the transition of moving from the outside world to the prison world. There were also smaller 'transition points': moving from the police station to the court, from the court to the van, moving from the van to reception and moving from the reception area to the induction unit and various changing locations within the prison.

Table 9.1 shows the demographic and background information of the 70 individuals interviewed, who went through this process. A total of 71.4 per cent were on remand (50 participants); 20 per cent were convicted but not sentenced (fourteen participants) and 8.6 per cent had received a sentence (six participants). A total of 41.4 per cent had never been in prison before (29 participants). As the table shows, the sample was ethnically diverse.

A number of individuals within the sample had also entered prison with 'imported vulnerability' factors. Of the 70 individuals interviewed, 10 per cent had received medication from a psychiatrist before coming to prison (seven participants), 10 per cent had self-harmed outside prison (seven participants), 15.7 per cent had self-harmed inside prison before (eleven participants) and 25.7 per cent agreed that they had a problem with drugs before entering prison (eighteen participants). Half of these were withdrawing from drugs on arrival (nine participants). Furthermore, 7.1 per cent self-harmed upon arrival into prison (five

Table 9.1 Descriptive characteristics of a sample of newly received prisoners

Variable		%	N
Legal status	Remand	71.4	50
	Convicted	20.0	14
	Sentenced	8.6	6
First time in prison		41.4	29
First time in Feltham		67.5	27
Ethnic group	White-British	41.1	29
	White-Other	15.7	11
	Black-African	12.9	9
	Black-Caribbean	15.7	11
	Black-British	5.7	4
	Asian-Indian	1.4	1
	Asian-Bangladeshi	7.1	1

N = 70

participants) and 14.3 per cent had current thoughts of suicide (ten participants).

Common elements of transition into prison

Having outlined the process of entering prison (and presented some background characteristics of the sample), I will now discuss the common themes that emerged from qualitative interviews with prisoners who underwent this transitional experience. To be received into custody was to begin to leave one world and to enter another; individuals within their first few days were occupying a place on both sides of a threshold or boundary. They were between two worlds and entered a liminal phase. As one prisoner recently remanded into Feltham explained:

> Yeah, the first few days, you're trying to get over your life and entering a new life and that's kind of hard to do. I felt really depressed. When you first come in you had plans for the next day. You had just done something recently and its one of those, 'Fuck! I could be on road' and you're not really into the whole bang-up issue there and then you are surrounded by people who you don't know and you'd rather not be around.

Prisoners presented themselves midway between two separate worlds, as they neither relinquished their hopes for the lives from which they had been torn, nor yet accepted their existence within a new enclosed order.

The idea of liminality was applied to rites of passage within the field of social anthropology (see also Jewkes, this volume). Van Gennep (1960) argued that there were three phases that constitute a rite of passage in different societies. These include separation, margin (or limen) and aggregation. Separation 'comprises symbolic behaviour signifying the detachment of the individual or group either from an earlier fixed point in the social structure, from a set of cultural conditions (state) or from both' (Turner 1969: 94). The liminal phase, on the other hand, is a period that is ambiguous where the individual passes through a cultural realm that has few or none of the attributes of the past or coming state (ibid.: 94). Finally the individual reaches a more stable state and because of this 'has rights and obligations *vis-à-vis* others of a clearly defined and structural type'. He is expected to behave in accordance with 'certain customary norms and ethical standards binding on incumbent social position in a system of such positions' (Turner 1969: 95) This process has relevance for individuals entering prison, particularly those who had never been in prison before. (To enter prison is to be separated from one world and moved into another.) Initial entry into prison may be characterised as a liminal state. In this phase the individual is 'neither here nor there, they are betwixt and between the positions assigned and arrayed by law custom, convention and ceremonial' (Turner 1969: 95). Finally, the prisoner may reach an equilibrium following the initial entry period. He may reach a more stable state once more.

Prisoners found it difficult to accept that this transition was taking place. Understandably, they did not want to accept that they were crossing a boundary from the outside world into the prison world. On the first night, accounts of their prison experience were characterised by disbelief that their incarceration had actually happened. As one prisoner stated:

> This isn't reality for me and I refuse to accept it as being so. This is not a way of life for me so I am very reluctant, maybe it will hinder my progress, but I am very reluctant to accept this situation to be reality and to be a way of life. Therefore I want to have minimal contact with the prisoners and just keep myself to myself.

Prisoners found entering this liminal zone a strange experience: one that did not seem real. One prisoner said:

> It feels strange and different. It almost doesn't seem real. I have to think about it. I'll be watching TV at one point and then I'll look and realise I am in the cell and then it kicks in again.

This was particularly the case for those who had never been in prison before. The sense of disbelief encompassed their transitional experience. I asked one prisoner:

> *Interviewer*: When you were walking through to the wing what was going through your head?
> *Prisoner*: I was thinking I see this on TV. I never thought I'd ever see myself walking down here going into a cell. I just thought I only see that on TV. I never thought it would come to this. I couldn't believe it basically.

During this liminal period of imprisonment a number of key common elements were identified that made it difficult. These included uncertainty, losing control and freedom, separation and loss, and a preoccupation with safety. Although prisoners differed in the degree to which they experienced these difficulties, most of these aspects of the transition could be identified in interviews with prisoners who had been in prison for three days.

Uncertainty

There were four main aspects of the prison experience that caused uncertainty and which elicited an array of negative emotions like being scared, anxious, frustrated, upset, confused, stressed, lonely, depressed and unsettled. Firstly, prisoners were uncertain about the prison itself. In particular, those who had never been to prison were not sure about their immediate future. Many were unsure what the prison would be like, what their cellmate would be like, what the staff would be like, whether they would cope, and whether they would be bullied. As one prisoner stated:

> The first few days I felt alone, like, I didn't know what to expect or nothing like that. I didn't know what to expect. I didn't know what the cell was going to be like. I didn't know what the staff were going to be like. I didn't know what the routines were.

Those who had been in prison before were more certain about the practical aspects of the prison, the rules and regulations, and the regime.

However, some had never been in Feltham before and others had been in Feltham before but had not been on the 'adult side' of the prison.[5] Even for those who had been in before, the social networks of prisoners had changed, staff had moved on, and the systems that were in place had altered.

Secondly, many prisoners felt uncertainty about their families and loved ones. This was true for both first-time prisoners and those who had been in before. Prisoners found it difficult to be away from their family and friends, and they were often concerned about the possible negative reaction of their families and also about their families' ability to cope with the situation the prisoner had created. Those with partners expressed anxieties about their partner's fidelity while they were separated, and if they had children, about whether they would be forgotten.

> They took my bail away and I just had to go downstairs and wait for the van. On my way to prison I was stressed out in that box. Basically I just wanted to cry. My eyes were hurting, my belly was hurting I was just thinking, driving, seeing people walking past, just thinking about my mum and my sister, how my family would be. If any of my family would phone from abroad and my mum would say I am in jail, how would they feel?... awe, I'm stressed out.

Imprisonment generated uncertainty in these relationships: Do they know I am in prison? What are they thinking now? Will my family disown me? Will my girlfriend leave me? Will she be faithful? So many questions remained unanswered during the first few days and remained problems for the weeks or months to come.

Thirdly, prisoners expressed uncertainty over their court case. They were mostly concerned about when they would be back at court, how long they would be kept in prison before possible sentencing (if they were on remand), and what the outcome of their court case would be. As one prisoner commented:

> I want to know what's going on. That's my main problem. I want to know what's going on with me. I don't know how long I am here for, em, I don't know when I'm going to court, I just don't know.

The difficulties of being in prison were here exacerbated by lack of knowledge. How would others control his fate outside prison? When would he be moving back from prison once again to the world outside? Uncertainty was felt over the prospect of being granted bail. Some believed that they would receive bail when next back at court. They desperately clung on to this hope; which was a false hope for many. The overall experience of being unsure how long they would be in prison was referred to as being 'on remand mode'. It altered their whole 'approach' to the situation they found themselves. As one prisoner commented:

> I'll be on remand mode. Going through the motions of remand. I'll get a bit used to it. I know at the moment I can't think of nothing. Got to go through it day by day. When I get sentenced I'll get used to it and get my mind sorted and that's it.

Finally, there was uncertainty over their short-term future. Prisoners were worried about what would happen to them when they got out of prison: concerns were expressed relating to accommodation, debts building up while inside, relationships breaking down, friends disowning them and losing their jobs. The prison experience was a severely disruptive one, a transition that affected most major facets of their lives.

Losing control and freedom

Along with uncertainty the transition into prison brought with it a loss of control and of freedom. One of the pains of imprisonment documented by Sykes (1958) was the deprivation of autonomy. Toch (1977) also identified autonomy as one of the main environmental needs prisoners had. Prisons are control-limiting, and freedom-depriving, environments. Goodstein *et al* (1984) identified three aspects of personal control that imprisonment may serve to reduce. These are outcome control (the ability of individuals to influence outcomes in their environment), choice (the opportunity to make choices in their environment) and predictability (knowing what will happen in their environment in the future). They argue that these three aspects of personal control are associated with one another and should not be viewed as separate (Goodstein *et al* 1984: 344–5). (Un)predictability is akin to (un)certainty, which has been discussed above. If individuals cannot (or perceive that they cannot) exert control over their world this may lead to 'learned helplessness' where the individual no longer uses their agency and becomes despondent (Seligman 1975).

Prisoners who had recently entered prison found it difficult to come to terms with a reduction in personal control and with being deprived of their freedom. This loss was felt in the court cells following the information that they were going to prison. One prisoner commented:

I was thinking about my freedom. I was thinking, 'please let me go home. I want to go home'. I was thinking about being locked up in a cell and being claustrophobic.

These feelings continued on their way to the prison, where many prisoners found the experience in the van particularly difficult. Often, being able to see outside but not being 'with the world' was very difficult to handle. The lack of freedom 'hits you', as one prisoner stated. They felt powerless when they saw the outside world, a world that was now out of their reach. I asked one prisoner:

Interviewer: What was it like coming in the van?
Prisoner: It was such a depressing feeling 'cause I knew I can't do nothing about it. You can see people are free and enjoying themselves. Even if they're not enjoying themselves at least they are free. And you are going to prison. Ah, that feeling is not a good thing.

The lack of freedom was most acutely felt when locked inside their cells. This was not only the case for first-time prisoners, but also for those who had been to prison before. One prisoner described his experience of being locked in his cell:

When they bang that door it is different. It is weird. Everywhere you turn you see the same thing. It is not like you can turn around and see a completely different part of the room or walk down the stairs and go into a different room. Everything is in the same room. It's like being trapped really. I can see why people harm themselves and try and kill themselves.

Many prisoners perceived that they had no control over their immediate situation due to the uncertainty that surrounded them and also due to the imbalance of power between staff and prisoners. This loss of control and freedom brought with it the desire to escape and rumination over what they could be doing 'on the out'. This was a change that many prisoners found difficult to accept. Moreover, many prisoners refused to accept the reality that had been forced upon them as this 'acceptance' served to reinforce the fact that their control and freedom had become limited.

Separation and loss

Separation and loss pervaded the thoughts of prisoners as they moved from one world to another. Prisoners felt they lost their whole 'life', their identities, and more specifically their relationships. Prisoners felt they had lost many aspects of their lives; there was a feeling of having 'thrown it all away'. Recalling his initial reaction to the news that he was coming to prison, one prisoner said:

> I thought 'fuck. I've lost everything'. This is the first time I have thought to learn to work and to do just, to go straight. I have enough of being in trouble, going to jail too many times. That is not the life no more. So I stopped smoking weed. I did stop. I've now come back to jail and lost my job.

They recalled that they felt their life had 'gone' and that they felt disconnected with the world they had just left. There was a feeling that their life was going on without them; they were no longer part of their own life. One prisoner commented:

> You feel like life has gone... You feel that your life is going on without you. You feel you want to be in the race but you've got a knee injury. You know what its like to sit on the side lines and watch the game and you say, 'if I had the ball right now I could have dodged this guy and gone through and scored', but you can't do it. You are close but you can't do it. You kind of feel away.

They felt that part of the 'self' was missing now that they had been brought to prison. This was associated with a sense of uncertainty and a fear of the unknown. One prisoner stated:

> There is confusion, there is a sense of uncertainty and you feel, it is hard to explain, it feels like there is a big abyss in your life. You standing on the end of this abyss and you know you can see something on the other side but you don't know how to get there.

Not only did part of the 'self' appear missing; there was a change in how they felt other people perceived them. Others perceived their social identity differently and this in turn made some prisoners question their identity and reassert themselves as they feared their identity was in the process of becoming lost. I asked one prisoner:

Interviewer: What could be done to make you feel more like a person?
Prisoner: Sometimes it's like you are a prisoner and society doesn't want you. You are a social outcast...I am still a person though. Because I did it doesn't make me a less of a person.

The most acute sense of loss, and separation, that prisoners experienced was from their loved ones outside the prison. When I asked prisoners to recall their experiences in the court cells, although their minds were flooded with thoughts about the prison, thoughts concerning separation from their loved ones also predominated. Many reported that they felt they had lost their families. As one prisoner stated:

My mind went blank. I was thinking – 'I've lost my family. What are my little brother and sister going to think?' I was thinking about my family and after that, what was going to happen.

This separation and perceived loss was difficult for prisoners to come to terms with at this transitional phase of their imprisonment. I asked one prisoner:

Interviewer: What was going through your head in the court cells?
Prisoner: I was thinking, 'oh my God. I am going to prison'. Like it was a shock. Cause the way things happened so quickly. I was thinking, 'oh my God. I am going to prison. I am leaving my mum, my girlfriend, and everyone I know'. I was thinking, 'I am leaving. I am gone. I'm by myself now'. Stuck in a little cell just thinking. Do you know what I mean? I was on my own in there.

Separation from loved ones was the biggest concern expressed by prisoners interviewed at this transitional phase. The most important ties individuals had were with their mother and their relationship partners. Many felt shame and guilt for what they had subjected their families to. At the same time, however, these relationships left on the other side of the boundary were often vital sources of practical and emotional support and it was difficult for prisoners to manage this aspect of their lives. As Toch (1977) stated, 'the absence of contact (outside) can create a psychological vacuum; its presence can be a mood modulator or safety valve' (p. 71). Most prisoners were motivated at this early entry phase to contact their families, friends and partners, and 62.9 per cent (44 participants) had done so within three days. Outside contact was fundamental to many prisoners' survival. As Toch (1992) wrote, in reference to jails in the US, 'some of the resources needed for psychological survival in the detention setting must be supplied by significant others in the community' (p. 182).

Preoccupation with safety

Although individuals varied in the extent to which they felt safe, most expressed some concerns over safety. Those who had never been in prison before had heard 'stories' from their friends outside prison that Feltham had a bad reputation. This was also a problem reported by Bartollas (1982) in his study on adolescent prisoners in the US. He found that reputation moulded their initial impressions of the institution. Many first-time prisoners in this research reported similarly. One prisoner said:

> I've heard you had to sing out of the windows. I heard you get your head kicked in; from mates who've already been in here.

Many were worried about bullying, wondering who they were going to meet in the prison.[6] One prisoner stated:

> I was just thinking, 'I am going to prison, I am going to prison'. That was it and I thought when I got there I was probably going to be beaten up or something.

Those prisoners who had been in before thought about who they might meet, thinking positively about meeting some friends 'from road'[7] but they also feared meeting their enemies. Some individuals had gang affiliations outside prison and, although this had some benefits when inside the social world of the prison, it could also be problematic if rivals of 'warring' gangs met within the prison gates.

Often initial fears were dispelled at this early phase. One prisoner expected a lot of fighting and for the prison to feel intimidating but he did not experience this. Others said their fears were confirmed, and these prisoners perceived the prison to be extremely large and overwhelming, frightening and daunting. Being in reception and being placed in different 'holding rooms' confirmed their feelings of powerlessness and helplessness. One prisoner said:

> I was feeling a bit scared like, knowing that I'm inside. I ain't on the outside world anymore.

Generally interactions at this transitional phase were defensive in nature. This self-induced ostracism made some prisoners feel even more uncomfortable and awkward. They felt that others were staring at them, and they did not know where to look. They were afraid to meet another's gaze, in fear of being victimised. One prisoner commented:

> You don't know them to speak to so you wouldn't go up and speak to them. If they want to speak to you, you let them come and speak to you.

However, concerns over safety tended to go beyond feeling afraid of being injured or threatened by others in the environment. Their perceived lack of safety encompassed the feeling that the world was an unpredictable place, a social context where uncertainty was rife:

> I don't want none of this. It doesn't feel a secure place. It feels like anything can happen at any time. I don't like it here.

To feel safe was to feel certain, to feel attached to the environment and to feel 'in control'; to feel unsafe was to feel uncertain, detached and 'out of control'.

Towards an understanding of prisoner distress during transition

Although the themes described above were evident in many prisoners' accounts of their transition into prison, this phase of imprisonment was not experienced in a uniform manner. Individuals at three days differed in the extent to which they experienced these problems and in their levels of psychological distress. This was clear from interviews with prisoners and from a self-completion measure of psychological distress. Table 9.2 shows the items that comprised the measure psychological distress used in the study and the percentage of participants who strongly agreed or agreed with each item.

The dimension scores ranged from 1 to 5. Scores on the dimension 'psychological distress' ranged between 1.36 and 4.82 (on a scale from 1 to 5 where a *higher* score indicates *higher* distress) with a mean score of 3.34 (SD = .82). Why did these individuals differ in their levels of distress? In order to explore this, I conducted a standard multiple regression analysis.[8] I had to limit the number of 'predictor' variables to include in the regression model due to the sample size of 70. Table 9.3 shows the regression model. Six 'predictors' were entered into the model. These

Table 9.2 Percentage of participants who 'strongly agreed' or 'agreed' with each of the statements measuring psychological distress

Statement	%
1. My experience of imprisonment in this particular prison has been stressful	54.3
2. I feel tense in this prison	52.9
3. I have experienced major feelings of distress in this prison	50.0
4. I often feel depressed in this prison	57.1
5. My experience in this prison is painful	40.0
6. I have many problems at the moment	65.7
7. I have problems sleeping at night	57.1
8. There is nothing I can do to relieve the distress I feel in this prison	52.9
9. My mental health is of concern to me	31.4
10. Life in this prison involves a great deal of suffering	54.3
11. I often feel aggressive and hostile in this prison	42.9

N = 70

Table 9.3 Summary of standard multiple regression analysis for variables predicting psychological distress (N = 70)

Variable	B	SE	β	T	Sign.
Past imprisonment	.145	.185	.088	.782	.437
Imported vulnerability	−.040	.173	−.025	−.245	.807
Locus of control	−.874	.193	−.517	−4.52	.001
Inside social support	.194	.116	.184	1.66	.101
Outside social support	−.139	.105	−.135	−1.32	.192
Safety	−.309	.108	−.302	−2.85	.006

Adjusted R^2 = .315

included past imprisonment, imported vulnerability, locus of control, inside social support, outside social support, and perceived safety.[9] The model was significant, $F (6,63) = 6.30, p < .001$.

A total of 31.5 per cent of the variance in psychological distress was accounted for in the model. The variables that significantly accounted for variance in psychological distress at three days were locus of control and perceived safety. I will therefore consider these two constructs below.

Rotter (1966) put forward locus of control as a construct within the framework of social learning theory and argued that individuals differed along a continuum on how they perceive control, differing in the extent to which they believe they are responsible for their own behaviour. Those with high internal control perceive reinforcements to be based on their own behaviour whereas those with high external locus of control perceive reinforcements to be based on chance or luck. This research has found that individuals who were more internal in their locus of control reported lower levels of psychological distress at three days. This finding is in line with previous research that has found that individuals with an internal locus of control adapted more successfully to prison life. Those with a high internal locus of control have been found to have lower levels of depression and anxiety (Zamble and Porporino 1988; MacKenzie *et al* 1987; Reitzel and Harju 2000). Goodstein *et al* (1984) argued that if individuals enter prison with a high internal locus of control, they 'find ways to maximise their choices, exert control over outcomes, and seek information to enhance the predictability of personally relevant future events' (p. 353). Indeed, it has been found that individuals with an internal locus of control are better at working towards desired ends (Wright *et al* 1980), and are able to seek out resources in their environment when they need them (Pugh 1993). They attempt to make environmental changes: they may create niches (see Toch 1992) or become active 'gleaners', for example (see Irwin 1970). As they feel they are able to control the environment, the environment has less of a controlling impact over them. Although losing control was a common element of the experience of transition to prison, it appears that individuals are able to deal with this differently. Despite the fact that prison limits control over outcomes, limits choices and the predictability of events, individuals who are internal in their locus of control may be able to find means to exert more control than those who are external. This, in turn, may enable them to feel less distressed.

Safety also appeared in the model as an important variable. Individuals who scored higher on the dimension 'perceived safety' reported lower levels of psychological distress at this early phase of imprisonment. Again, although concerns over safety were a common element in the transition to prison, individuals differed in the extent to which they felt safe. I also found a small, but significant, correlation between locus of control and perceived safety (r^2 = .28, p < .05). Edgar *et al* (2003), in their study of prison violence, found that safety consisted of five components, one of these being 'a sense of control over one's environment' (p. 90). This 'sense of control' may be enhanced when individuals 'import' with them into prison an internal locus of control. This, in turn, may help reduce their concerns over safety and alleviate their level of psychological distress. Due to the cross-sectional nature of the study reported here, and the small sample size, it is not possible to attempt causal modelling, but conceptually, the links between these constructs are of interest.

Conclusion

This study set out to explore the early 'entry' period of imprisonment and examined prisoners' experiences as they made the transition into the prison world. Many common themes emerged from interviews with prisoners. These included feelings of uncertainty, losing control and freedom, separation and loss, and a preoccupation with safety. Individuals differed in the degree to which they experienced these aspects of the transition to prison and in their level of psychological distress. The effects of imprisonment were not uniform. Despite the fact that everyone entered the same custodial environment, individuals differed in the transactions they had with this environment. Although levels of distress were generally high, some individuals felt more distressed than others. An individual's locus of control and their perception of safety helped to explain some of the differences in this regard. Crossing the boundary was a demanding task for young adults, one that required resilience in the face of adversity.

Notes

1 This research forms part of my PhD thesis 'Transition and adaptation to prison life: A study of young adults aged 18 to 21'. I employed an embedded multi-method approach using semi-structured interviews, quantitative self-report measures, observations, and social network analyses. The study described in this chapter is one component of this research. To carry out the fieldwork I was continually based at Feltham between July 2002 and May 2003.

2 Total institutions contained several features: 'All aspects of life are conducted in the same place and under the same single authority. Second, each phase of the member's daily activity is carried on in the immediate company of a large batch of others, all of whom are treated as alike and required to do the same thing together. Third, all phases of the day's activities are tightly scheduled, with one activity leading to a prearranged time into the next, the whole sequence of activities being imposed from above by a system of explicit formal rulings and a body of officials. Finally, the various enforced activities are brought together into a single rational plan purportedly designed to fulfil the official aims of the institution' (Goffman 1961: 17).

3 Five prisoners in the sample had court dates and were therefore more prepared for this experience. Eight were transferred from other prisons and therefore did not attend court before arriving at Feltham.

4 The link worker on the first night offered to make a telephone call to a family member or friend on the prisoner's behalf. These link workers were employed by the charity, The Foundation Training Company. The link worker's role was to provide connections between prisoners and their families and between prisoners and prison staff.

5 Prisoners at Feltham referred to the 'adult side' of the prison as the residential area that accommodated young adults aged eighteen to 21. The 'juvenile' side of the prison accommodated individuals aged fifteen to seventeen.

6 For a comprehensive study on bullying among young offenders, see Ireland (2002). Also see Edgar *et al* (2003).

7 This is a term often used by prisoners when describing life outside prison. The world beyond the prison gates is termed 'on road'.

8 'In the standard, or simultaneous, model all IVs [independent variables] enter into the regression equation at once; each one is assessed as if it had entered the regression after all other IVs had entered. Each IV is evaluated in terms of what it adds to prediction of the DV [dependent variable] that is different from the predictability afforded by all the other IVs' (Tabachnick and Fidell 1996: 149). Brace *et al* (2003) argue that 'if you have no theoretical model in mind, and/or you have relatively low numbers of cases, then it probably safest to use Enter [standard regression]' (p. 213).

9 Past imprisonment was 'dummy' coded: 0 = been in prison before, 1 = first time in prison. Imported vulnerability was a composite measure of a number of vulnerability factors that prisoners may have imported with them (self-harm history, psychiatric treatment, and a problem with drugs). The scale was coded 0 = no factors; 1 = one or more factors. A total of 37.1% (26 participants) arrived in prison with at least one vulnerability factor (self-harm, psychiatric treatment or substance misuse); 7.1% (5 participants) had two of the three, and 1.4% (1 participant) had all three of the vulnerability factors that I measured. As only six participants had more than one factor, including more levels in the data would not have added much to the analysis. The measure was thus coded 0 and 1. Locus of control was measured using Pugh's (1993) 20-item prison locus of control scale (Cronbach's alpha = .87) and outside social support was measured using items adapted from Singelton *et al* (1998). These items include: 1. There are people I know outside who do things to make me happy. 2. There are people I know outside who make me feel cared for. 3. There are people I know outside who can be relied on no matter what happens. 4. There are people I know outside who would see that I am taken care of if I needed to be. 5. There are people I know outside who accept me just as I am. 6. There are people I know outside who make me feel an important part of their lives. 7. There are people I know outside who give me support and encouragement (Cronbach's alpha = .85). Safety was measured using three items: 1. There is quite a lot of threats/bullying

in here. 2. I feel safe from being injured, bullied, or threatened by other prisoners in here. 3. Generally I fear for my physical safety (Cronbach's alpha = .41). Perceived support inside prison was measured using eight items: 1. I receive support from staff in this prison when I need it. 2. Staff help prisoners to maintain contact with their families. 3. I feel cared about most of the time in this prison. 4. I have been helped a lot by a member of staff with a particular problem. 5. Staff in this prison show concern and understanding towards me. 6. I feel I am trusted quite a lot in this prison. 7. I trust the officers in this prison. 8. This prison is good at delivering personal safety (Cronbach's alpha = .86). Cronbach's alpha for psychological distress = .87. These items were from Liebling's (2004) study on measuring the quality of prison life and some additional items from the Liebling *et al* (2005) study that evaluated HM Prison Service's new suicide-prevention strategy (the safer locals programme evaluation). The four measures (locus of control, outside social support, safety and perceived support inside prison) were recoded so a higher score denotes a more positive outcome; for psychological distress a higher score denotes a negative outcome.

References

Bartollas, C. (1982) 'Survival problems of adolescent prisoners', in R. Johnson and H. Toch (eds) *The Pains of Imprisonment.* London: Sage Publishing, pp. 165–180.

Beigel, A. and Russell, H.E. (1973) 'Suicidal behaviour in jail: Prognostic considerations', in B.L. Danto (ed.) *In Jail House Blues: Studies of Suicidal Behavior in Jail and Prison.* Orchard Lake, MI: Epic Publications, pp. 107–118.

Brace, N., Kemp, R. and Snelgar, R. (2003) *SPSS for Psychologists: A Guide to Data Analysis using SPSS for Windows,* 2nd edition. Hampshire: Palgrave Macmillan.

Edgar, K., O'Donnell, I. and Martin, C. (2003) *Prison Violence. The Dynamics of Conflict, Fear and Power.* Cullompton: Willan Publishing.

Ericson, R. (1975) *Young Offenders and their Social Work.* Farnborough: Lexington Books.

Esparza, R. (1973) 'Attempted and committed suicide in county jails', in B.L. Danto (ed.) *Jail House Blues: Studies of Suicidal Behavior in Jail and Prison.* Orchard Lake, MI: Epic Publications, pp. 27–46.

Fawcett, J. and Marrs, B. (1973) 'Suicide at the county jail', in B.L. Danto (ed.) *Jail House Blues: Studies of Suicidal Behavior in Jail and Prison.* Orchard Lake, MI: Epic Publications, pp. 83–106.

Gibbs, J. (1982a) 'Disruption and distress: Going from the street to jail', in N. Parisi (ed.) *Coping with Imprisonment.* London: Sage Publications, pp. 29–44.

Gibbs, J. (1982b) 'The first cut is the deepest: Psychological breakdown and survival in the detention centre', in R. Johnson and H. Toch (eds) *The Pains of Imprisonment*. London: Sage Publications, pp. 97–114.

Goffman, E. (1961/1991) *Asylums. Essays on the Social Situation of Mental Patients and Other Inmates*. London: Penguin.

Goodstein, L., MacKenzie, D. and Shotland, R. (1984) 'Personal control and inmate adjustment to prison', *Criminology*, 22 (8) 343–369.

Heilig S. (1973) 'Suicide in jails', in B.L. Danto (ed.) *Jail House Blues: Studies of Suicidal Behavior in Jail and Prison*. Orchard Lake, MI: Epic Publications, pp. 47–56.

HM Prison Service (2004) *Self-inflicted Deaths in Custody: Six Year Overview: 1998/9 to 2003/4. Safer Custody Group Research Briefing 5*. London: Safer Custody Group.

Ireland, J. (2002) *Bullying among Prisoners: Evidence, Research and Intervention Strategies*. Hove: Brunner-Routledge.

Irwin, J. (1970) *The Felon*. Englewood Cliffs, NJ: Prentice Hall.

Jones, R.S. and Schmid, T.J. (2000) *Doing Time: Prison Experience and Identity among First-Time Inmates*. Stamford, CT: Jai Press.

Liebling, A. (1999) 'Prison suicide and prisoner coping' in M. Tonry and J. Petersilia (eds) *Crime and Justice: A Review of Research, 26*. Chicago: University of Chicago Press, pp. 283–359.

Liebling, A. (2004) *Prisons and Their Moral Performance. A Study of Values, Quality and Prison Life*. Oxford: Oxford University Press.

Liebling, A., Tait, S., Stiles, A., Durie, L. and Harvey, J. (submitted 2005) *An Evaluation of the Safer Locals Programme: Final Report*. Home Office Report 2005.

MacKenzie, D.L., Goodstein, L.I. and Blouin, D.C. (1987) 'Personal control and prison adjustment: An empirical test of a proposed model', *Journal of Research in Crime and Delinquency*, 24 (1), 49–68.

Neustatter, A. (2002) *Locked In Locked Out. The Experience of Young Offenders out of Society and in Prison*. London: Calouste Gulbenkian Foundation.

Pugh, D.N. (1993) 'The effects of problem-solving ability and locus of control on prisoner adjustment', *International Journal of Offender Therapy and Comparative Criminology*, 37, 163–176.

Reitzel, L.R. and Harju, B.L. (2000) 'Influence of locus of control and custody level on intake and prison-adjustment depression', *Criminal Justice and Behavior*, 27 (5), 625–644.

Rotter, J. (1966) 'Generalized expectancies for internal versus external control of reinforcement', *Psychological Monographs*, 80 (full volume).

Seligman, M.E. (1975/1992) *Helplessness: On Development, Depression, and Death*. New York: W. H. Freeman and Company.

Singelton, N., Meltzer, H., Gatward, R., Coid, J. and Deasy, D. (1998) *Psychiatric Morbidity of Prisoners in England and Wales*. London: Office of National Statistics.

Sykes, G. (1958) *The Society of Captives.* Princeton, NJ: Princeton University Press.

Tabachnick, B.G. and Fidell, L.S. (1996) *Using Multivariate Statistics,* 3rd edition. New York: Harper Collins.

Toch, H. (1977/1992) *Living in Prison: The Ecology of Survival.* Washington, DC: American Psychological Association.

Toch, H. (1992) *Mosaic of Despair. Human Breakdowns in Prison.* Washington, DC: American Psychological Association.

Turner, V. (1969) *Ritual Process: Structure and Anti-Structure.* London: Routledge and Kegan Paul.

Van Gennep, A. (1960) *The Rites of Passage.* London: Routledge.

Wright, T., Holman, T., Steele, T. and Silverstein, G. (1980) 'Locus of control and mastery in a reformatory: A field study of defensive externality', *Journal of Personality and Social Psychology,* 38, 1005–1013.

Zamble, E. and Porporino, J. (1988) *Coping, Behavior and Adaptation in Prison Inmates.* New York: Springer.

Chapter 10

Brave new prisons: the growing social isolation of modern penal institutions

Robert Johnson

In America, more people are sentenced to more time in more prisons under more anachronistic conditions than at any time in recent memory. Prisons dot the American landscape, often opened and operated at the expense of schools, roads and social services. Most of these prisons are overcrowded, underfunded and located in remote areas, far from the urban centres from which most prisoners originate. The sheer number of prisons and prisoners is remarkable, creating what amounts to a parallel penal universe, a world surrounded by fortress walls or barbed-wire barriers that hold offenders at bay, away from the world, locked in a grim suspended animation.

Information about people, places and events is widely available in the outside world, by virtue of modern technology, but is sharply limited in prison. Information about the free world that is readily accessible to prisoners is conveyed primarily by television. Television, available in the cell for many American prisoners and in dayrooms for virtually all prisoners in regular prison housing, is a lifeline for many inmates, at once allowing them to escape (mentally) from the prison world, to establish familiar routines, and to feel some connection to the general culture that is shared by family and friends on the outside (televisions are generally not available in special housing units, most notably supermax prisons, which adds to the punitive, isolated character of these settings). Although on balance, television is a valuable commodity for prisoners, there is a downside, since television conveys what is at best a hazy, distorted view of the real world. Even 'media-rich' institutions, notes Jewkes (2002: 183), remain profoundly removed from the larger society. In some instances, TV may encourage prisoners to amuse themselves at the expense of other, more productive activities, such as reading, writing and participating in programmes that build social skills. TV may also be used as a means of controlling prisoners, further reducing the already limited autonomy that characterises their daily prison lives (see, generally, Jewkes 2002).

The image of prisoners watching television in their cells, moreover, may feed resentments held by many in the free world, who picture the prison as a haven of leisure time, a kind of country club for the lower classes. A self-defeating cycle might well ensue: prisoners confined in increasingly isolated institutions seek escape into the fantasy life of television. Politicians, pandering to vocal constituencies, rail for harsher, more restrictive conditions, including restrictions on television and anything else that smacks of leisure activity (like exercise, sports and even reading), adding to the social isolation of prisons and limiting the ways inmates might cope with the pressures of prison life. Modern information technology offers ways out of this impasse, notably by connecting prisoners and their families and by providing various types of 'distance learning', 'distance treatment' and even 'virtual treatment' (using virtual reality as a source of new learning environments),[1] but technology in prisons tends to be used for purposes of control, if not outright punishment, rather than reform.

Dead time

The deprivation of liberty, the first and arguably most profound pain of imprisonment (Sykes 1958), has grown dramatically in contemporary American prisons. Prison time, more and more, has become a species of dead time spent in empty activities carried out in isolation from the larger world. Meanwhile, the pace of life and productivity in the outside world have quickened dramatically. Free citizens live in what has been called an 'information age'. Information is generated and spread like wildfire by telephone and fax, computer and the Internet, disseminating ideas and linking people.[2] The technology of the information age, we are told, transcends time and space to make the world something very much akin to a global village built on the rapid exchange of information (Stix 2002).[3]

The amount of new information generated and stored in a single year is almost incomprehensible. In the year 2003, for example, five exabytes of new information were created, which is equivalent to (a) 'all words ever spoken by humans since the dawn of time', and (b) 'the information contained in half a million new libraries the size of the Library of Congress print collections' (Lyman and Varian 2003). This incredible figure does not include the information generated by mobile phones, which link people daily, expanding their social worlds almost to the four corners of the globe. Prisoners, essentially limited to television as the most modern technology readily at their disposal, are increasingly out of touch with the world as experienced by citizens of the larger free society. A new level of disconnection between prison and society has emerged, perhaps making prisons obsolescent as social institutions and certainly demarking a distinctive pain of modern imprisonment.

We sometimes speak of the outside society as the real world and the prison as an artificial world, even an unreal Alice-in-Wonderland venture marked by a topsy-turvy and largely dysfunctional way of life.[4] In this view, prison reform means bringing the free world to the prison, where possible, to reduce the pains of imprisonment and, more generally, to provide balance and perspective. If locking up people amounts to 'the deliberate infliction of harm', notwithstanding our hopes and aspirations for prisons, as Golash (2004) would contend, reforms that make prisons more like the real world reduce that harm.[5] Prisons that have been made more like the free world, moreover, allow for personal adjustments that are more likely to carry over into the free world. An inmate who takes a range of ameliorative programmes and otherwise adjusts well in such a prison should be better prepared for life on the outside, though problems of re-entry are great even in the best of circumstances (Toch 1992; Maruna 2001; Johnson 2002).

Regrettably, reforms that make prison more like the free world are increasingly a thing of the past in many American prisons. Visits, once a staple of American correctional systems, are now treated as matters of privilege, to be revoked at will and without explanation (Toch 2002). Furloughs and work-release programmes, once progressive features of correctional regimes, are in decline (Hill 2003). Compassionate leaves, once granted routinely to allow inmates to attend funerals of loved ones, are increasingly rare; in men's prisons, they are relics of a distant penal past. One wonders if many prison administrators today, particularly those who entered the field over the last decade or so, have even heard of a correctional policy featuring compassionate leave, let alone seen such a policy in action.[6] Telephone privileges have been extended to many inmates, and this is no doubt a lifeline for them, but one senses that it is the profitability of this endeavour that accounts for its availability rather than any concern for the welfare of offenders or their families. Prisons make money on telephones; if they didn't, calls might well be sharply restricted, no doubt for putative reasons of security. There is also some evidence that a minority of prisoners dominate telephone usage. These moneyed few (or their families) have the resources to pay, while most of their fellow prisoners do not (Hallinan 2003).[7]

The internal worlds of today's prisons often have a distinctively uniform and bland quality, as if they were designed by bureaucrats with time on their hands. This wasn't always the case. For much of the 20th century:

> Prisoners enjoyed considerable freedom to embellish their drab and monotonous prison life. For example, they decorated the walls of their cells, altered their prison clothing, acquired various pieces of furniture – such as rugs, chairs, and bookshelves – and kept birds and other small pets in their cells. These special touches enriched their lives with considerable comfort and individuality, which is very important in a world so marked by monotony.
>
> (Austin and Irwin 2000: 106)

Today's institutions, by contrast, offer fewer and fewer amenities and avenues for self-expression, once again making them less and less like the free world. Each year, survey evidence reveals, 'the list of curtailed or entirely eliminated privileges is longer' (Hill 2002: 8).

Some of these lost privileges include such human essentials as access to contact visits. New Jersey has recently 'implemented a zero-tolerance program for substance abuse infractions – a one-year loss of contact visits for the first infraction and permanent loss for a second violation' (Hill 2002: 8) Visits are a precarious commodity for prisoners as it is. Half of all prisoners no longer get visits or have never received visits. Others, in high-security housing, routinely endure sharp restrictions on visits (prisoners in some states, notably Texas, are denied contact visits as a matter of longstanding policy). Yet we know that 'visits under the best of conditions are difficult; under conditions of non-contact, a growing option today, we offer "anachronistic" and ultimately self-defeating policies' (Toch 2003: 28). A permanent ban on contact visits sends a dramatic message of social abandonment and virtually ensures that ties to loved ones will be compromised. For those who once looked forward to human contact with loved ones, the loss of contact visits would be devastating. For those who only dreamed of such visits, the message – that they cannot even hope for human contact – is no doubt devastating as well.

Other restrictions add to the social isolation and general discomfort of today's prisons. Prisoners in North Dakota, for example, can no longer receive personal property from outside (Hill 2002: 8). In Alaska, food is limited in quantity, not to 'exceed US military standards' (Hill 2002: 8).

Uniforms have made a remarkable comeback in recent years. As recently as 1998, 88 per cent of prisons allowed inmates to wear civilian clothes; that number has dropped to 'fifty percent or less', suggesting a dramatic rejection of the idea that prisons can be seen as 'normal', which is to say, as extensions of the real world (Hill 2002: 8–9). Books and magazines are increasingly limited in virtually all penal systems. Prison libraries, which have always had modest aspirations matched by modest budgets, are in recession as well, taking a seat at the back of a bus driven almost exclusively these days by security concerns.[8] In most prison systems, inmates have ready access to television, but are prohibited from viewing films with an '18' certificate (at least on those TV sets under the control of the officials) (Hill 2002: 8). One envisions glum denizens of an isolated world, bound by rules, dressed in uniforms, bereft of reading material and saturated by a 'PG 13' view of the world as presented in modern television sitcoms and, more recently, 'reality TV', an oxymoron if ever there were one. Neil Postman wondered if we were 'amusing ourselves to death' in modern America with a growing affection for, not to say addiction to, television (Postman 1985). It would appear that we may be willing to kill off our prisoners in this way.

The punitive thrust of modern prisons was captured in the title of a new book by a prisoner, *You Got Nothing Coming* (Lerner 2003) – nothing for free, not even punishment. Hence the trend to 'More and more fees … levied to defray the cost of services offered by correctional systems' (Hill 2002: 9). For those who can pay, over half of our prisons come with a room-and-board bill; upwards of three of every four prisons charge for medical services. 'Additional fees were mentioned for items such as TV service [cable only], destruction of state property, copying materials, ID cards and their replacement, emergency escorted visits, victim restitution or other court-mandated fees or fines' (Hill 2002: 9).

These various deprivations of amenities and internal freedoms make prisons more repressive, and less like the free world that surrounds them. Tightening budgets make matters worse, resulting in staff layoffs and programme cutbacks, which together make for a growth in idle time and associated problems of adjustment, notably violence.[9] As our harsh prisons become more crowded and dangerous, the focus of individual adjustment shifts to surviving one day at a time, which in turn adds to social isolation. Niches, so essential to individual adjustment and to retaining some semblance of normalcy in daily prison life, may be harder to create and sustain in these obdurate and unresponsive institutions (Toch 1992; see also Johnson 2002).

The design of penal institutions says something about the values they embody. The penitentiary, built during a hopeful time, 'was astonishingly grand, typically resembling a fortress or a chateau and often built on a hill, from which it could be seen for miles' (Hallinan 2003: xvi). When penitentiaries degenerated into human warehouses, they retained some of their grandeur. If nothing else, they and their immediate successors remained massive, serious undertaking. Today's prisons, in contrast, are typically bland and nondescript. 'The modern "correctional facility", has been described as "a concrete econo-box, low and bunkered and anonymous"' (Hallinan 2003: xvi). It is in the middle of nowhere; if you don't look hard, you could drive by one and hardly notice (for a brief time, new prisons built during the mid-20th century were located nearer to cities and towns, to make them more accessible to relatives and, one imagines, to community volunteers). Pollock (2003) suggests that we think of today's new prisons as low-rent 'self-storage units', places where things are left off and often forgotten, given over to the ravages of time and decay.

Storage, if not self-storage, seems increasingly to pervade our thinking about youthful offenders as well. California's Youth Authority, once considered a leader in the corrections field, now does little more than contain and constrain its young offenders. Confinement regimes even feature individual programme cages for kids. Called SPAs, a bizarre if unintended reference to the much-mythologised country-club prison, youthful offenders with a history of violence (many if not most of the current offenders) are placed in steel-barred cages during educational and counselling times. Started in 1998 as a temporary measure, the cages have become an accepted feature of the institution, justified, ultimately, as the only way the adults can protect themselves from the offenders and the offenders from one another.[10]

Making 'hard time harder' for all classes of offenders has become a cherished goal of many American politicians. This includes federal politicians, who passed the revealingly named 'No Frills Prison Act', limiting federal construction dollars to prison systems that cut back on a wide range of amenities and discontinued 'good time', a practice that rewarded prisoners for good behaviour by shortening their sentences (Johnston et al 1997). The federal courts have taken no explicit stand on this matter, in part because access to the courts has been sharply limited. Prisoners who get to federal court encounter an increasing tendency at the Supreme Court level to 'afford appropriate deference and flexibility to state officials trying to maintain a volatile environment'.[11] Something like the old 'hands-off' policy has returned, leaving prisoners at the tender mercies of prison administrators, who in turn face pressures from politicians and the general public to make prisons more restrictive (Johnston et al 1997; for a full discussion, see Pollock 2003).

Politicians live by the sound byte, which captures anger more readily than empathy and calls for action more readily than reflection. Politicians are tough on crime because it is popular; they are also tough on crime because this is a message they can readily convey by modern media. Political campaigns traffic in what amount to commercials driven by images and slogans (Postman 1985). Issues are secondary. A tough stand against criminals is readily presented. One could develop counter-commercials, with the idea that 'trying softer' can work, but that requires a story – the story of broken lives, inured to brutality – to put this contention in perspective. Not so with punishment: punishment is its own story. Bad people do bad things and we give them what is good for them: a taste of their own medicine. Good versus evil, with good triumphing in the end – the oldest story in the world, and one readily distorted to promote fear and reinforce calls for more repressive policies.[12] One can only imagine the hay that politicians might make with the fact that California prisons for the young feature SPAs.[13]

Super prisons

Supermax prisons are the culmination of the 'get tough on criminals' trend in America and are thought to 'set the tone for the rest of the system'.[14] The rigidity and isolation of today's prisons reach their zenith in supermax prisons, which have 'sprouted like mushrooms' across the American countryside (Toch 2003: 27). Supermax prisons are astronomically expensive, but that expense means profits for builders, jobs for local workers, an expanded tax base for the community and a sense of security (at least at the outset) for correctional personnel (Hallinan 2003). If any of the new prisons these days have pretensions to grandeur, it is the supermax prison, which stands as a monument to solitary repression. Any cost seems justified when one is told that these high-tech dungeons are reserved for the 'worst of the worst', which one supposes is a class dominated by bloodthirsty predators. And of course there are no amenities (and no TVs)[15] for monsters and virtually no human contact with others. Who makes the case for creature comforts and social support for the promiscuously predatory prisoner?

Hallinan toured a number of penal institutions during his 'travels in a prison nation', including several supermax prisons. Prisons, he found, produced the punitive beliefs necessary to sustain them. In prison town after prison town, residents bemoaned crime waves and took comfort in the protection afforded by prisons. Time and again, Hallinan discovered that none of these towns had crime problems. They had a belief problem:

> In every prison town I visited, people were eager to talk to me about crime – about how bad it was, about how something needed to be done. Brad Arvin, a Beeville community booster, told me crime was everywhere in his town – 'just as near as your morning paper', he said. But when I asked him whether he knew anybody who had been the victim of a crime, he couldn't think of one.
>
> (Hallinan 2003: xii)

Many prison systems turned to the supermax prison to control the violence within regular prisons. But as with crime, this violence was often more imagined than real. States like Virginia built two supermax prisons but did not have enough super-predators to fill the cells. In Virginia and elsewhere, the inhabitants of supermax prisons are all too often the most vulnerable inmates, the retarded, emotionally disturbed and even psychotic prisoners who simply can't cope with confinement and who, tragically, fall apart in the paranoid, isolated world of the supermax prison, often becoming more difficult to manage and control in the process (Haney and Lynch 1997; Toch 2001).

Supermax prisons were meant to be corrections' ace in the hole. The thinking was that officials had been dealt a bad hand. After Attica, prisons were seen as out of control, run by inmates with rights and comforts but no sense of right and wrong. Prison gangs were said to run rampant, stopping their mayhem only to file frivolous law suits (including one in which an inmate complained that barbed-wire fences might injure escaping felons). Supermax, long in coming, finally gave the authorities a winning hand by bringing back hard time with the force of modern technology. These 'state of the art' enterprises would wrest power away from convicts, including convict gangs, and give the reigns of control back to the keepers (see, e.g. Hallinan 2003: 129).

Supermax prisons have not lived up to their billing. Psychological breakdown and interpersonal violence occur on a regular basis in supermax prisons. Officers and inmates alike find the experience demoralising, even brutalising (Toch 2001; Rhodes 2004). The supermax prison has been described as a penitentiary without hope. Like a town without pity, a purely punitive penitentiary is a bleak and disheartening place. People are, in effect, buried alive, one day perhaps to be set loose upon the free world with few social skills, few social supports and limited familiarity with the world that awaits them. Some people are, in fact, released from supermax *directly* to the streets. One might think of this as a parable of modern prison practice: 'Punish, and ye shall be punished in turn by thy wayward brothers and sisters'.

Penitentiaries without hope

The supermax prison is a hopeless place in part because it spawns cavemen in an era of speed-of-light technology. There may have once been a demand for cavemen, but no more. (Officers in supermax prisons, for their part, are relegated to such modern caveman tasks as monitoring panels and pushing buttons. Though outfitted in impressive high-tech gear, sometimes looking like they just parachuted boldly into a combat zone, they spend much of their time delivering mail and food to their charges). By contrast, the original penitentiaries, though extreme in their own right, provided living and working experiences that were arguably more in step with the times than are our prisons today.

America at the birth of the penitentiary was a world dominated by work and worship, activities at the heart of the penitentiary regime. There was no formal social safety net in 19th-century America, so most people in the community either worked or starved. This was much the same in the penitentiary, only perhaps worse; in some institutions, offenders worked and starved. Whether the work undertaken in prison cells or workshops served as adequate preparation for work on the outside is a matter of dispute, but it is undisputable that prisoners of penitentiaries would readily recognise the world of work they returned to upon release from prison. This cannot be said for many released prisoners today.

Much of the public discourse in America in the time of the penitentiary was about religion, and of course religion was a central preoccupation inside penitentiaries as well. Printing presses in early 19th-century America produced books about religion more than about any other subject. Americans read a great deal, and much of what they read about dealt with matters of religion (Postman 1985; Noll 2002). The American postal service, then the envy of the Western world, produced a kind of early information explosion, yet the average American was much more likely to hear a sermon than to receive a piece of mail or a letter (Noll 2002: 200–01). Attendance at religious services was the norm in American communities of this time, as many records attest (Noll 2002: 167). A prisoner in a cell whose intellectual life was limited to sermons, interrupted by periods of solitary craft work or congregate factory labour, was living a life not unrecognisable to his fellow Americans outside the walls, where intellectual life, too, was dominated by religion and conveyed in sermons. Penance and repentance, staples of the penitentiary, were staples in the free community as well (Noll 2002: 439). Though prisoners spent time 'dead' to the society around them, they were mostly dead to the pernicious social forces that were thought to have corrupted them.

In their religious instruction and in admonitions to penance, penitentiary inmates grappled with issues central to their time. On such matters, notes Noll (2002: 439), 'hung nothing less than eternal life'. Rehabilitation was a part of the world view outside the penitentiary walls, and included concerns for redemption and reintegration into the saved community:

> Their seriousness about how God rescued humans from sin was matched by their seriousness about how rescued sinners might build a peaceful, prosperous, and yet benevolent life for themselves and their generation. They were not playing around.
>
> (Noll 2002: 439)

To be sure, the penitentiary degenerated into a brutal institution, and over time became a warehouse rather than God's house, but for a time, the penitentiary offered hope. It was a correctional formula that made sense in its time, even if it proved impossible to administer in a decent and sustained way.

No amount of sermons will bring the supermax or any other prison into line with the modern world. Churches and sermons have, for the common man, largely been replaced by television and commercials. Even TV evangelists cannot replicate the power of sermons in the 19th century. On TV, easy entertainment is the rule. Matters like remorse and repentance are never simple or easy, though they may be amusing to outsiders. Thus, in Huxley's *Brave New World* (2004), Mr Savage's bloody and sincere self-flagellation entertains the citizens, who call out, 'Do the whipping stunt. Let's see the whipping stunt'. The 'religion stunt' may capture the attention of offenders in their darkest hours, but these conversions are neither an enduring nor a reliable pathway to central values in modern America.

Brave new prison

Offenders in regular prisons today have ready access to television, described by some in corrections as 'the babysitter of choice' and by others in the field as 'electric Thorazine' that 'keeps the inmates tranquil' (Hallinan 2003: 11).[16] (Given the rise of mentally ill offenders behind bars, plenty of chemical Thorazine and other powerful drugs are deployed in prison as well.)[17] Like Thorazine, TV may in fact be addictive. A source no less credible than *Scientific American* recently devoted a feature story to that proposition. TV is, in any case, a cheap addiction for prison administrators to promote, if it is an addiction. TV is certainly a habit for many of us, and a hard one to break at that. In most prison systems, inmates, not the institution, bear the costs of TV viewing, from buying their own sets to paying monthly fees for in-cell cable service.

Television, as noted earlier, provides a link to American culture, reducing social isolation. Virtually all Americans watch TV, and most of us watch quite a lot. A TV in a barren cell is certainly to be preferred to isolation. Prisoners in unremitting isolation, such as provided in supermax prisons, tend to go mad (see Haney and Lynch 1997; Toch 2001). There is no evidence that TV, though sometimes numbingly boring, can accomplish this end. Indeed, TV is no doubt a respite from the rigours of prison life, just as TV is a break from the daily grind of life for many of us in the free world.

The difficulty is that television tends to monopolise free time wherever it is found.[18] The tendency of TV to capture time, moreover, may be exaggerated in American prisons, where limited programme and work opportunities leave a lot of time open to prisoners with nothing much for them to do. At the same time, many offenders enter prison with what might be called substantial TV habits. Thus, we know that African-Americans and persons of limited formal education are heavy viewing populations (Robinson and Godbey 1997: 148). Both groups are over-represented in American prisons.

The appeal of TV is that it entertains and distracts, typically at low cost, while demanding little from the viewer, who must bring no skills to the transaction and indeed can watch TV in a mildly comatose state. Many viewers routinely enter a 'sleeping awake' state that is part of TV's passive appeal (Kaufman 2002). There is evidence that watching TV saps drive. 'Survey participants commonly reflect that television has somehow absorbed or sucked out their energy, leaving them depleted. They say they have more difficulty concentrating after viewing than before' (Kubey and Csikszentmihalyi 2002: 76). This is not the case for mentally or physically active recreation, like reading or sports. A range of laboratory studies, including some monitoring brain waves, suggest that TV viewing 'may contribute to a shorter attention span, diminished self-restraint and less patience with the normal delays of daily life' (Kubey and Csikszentmihalyi 2002: 79). One anthropological study, conducted over 25 years ago with an isolated mountain community before and after the advent of TV, found that 'Over time, both adults and children became less creative in problem solving, less able to persevere at tasks, and less tolerant of unstructured time' (Kubey and Csikszentmihalyi 2002: 79).

Television took America by storm in the 1950s and is certainly here to stay. 'In 1950, barely 10 percent of American homes had television sets, but by 1959, 90 percent did, probably the fastest diffusion of a technological innovation ever recorded' (Putnam 1997: 18). TV viewing, in turn, has grown over each decade, with each subsequent generation beginning 'its life cycle at a higher starting point' in terms of hours logged in front of the set. 'By 1995, viewing per television household was more than 50 percent higher than it had been in the 1950s' (Putnam 1997: 18). Time diary studies reveal that TV has become more and more central to our daily lives while other activities, like reading, have declined. Since the 1960s, free time grew appreciably for Americans; remarkably, almost all of that new free time was devoted to watching television (Robinson and Godbey 1997). When all free time is examined, we find that the average American spends fully half of that time in front of the tube. Even what are called 'television-averse groups', the college educated and financially well off, spend fully one-third of their free time watching TV (Robinson and Godbey 1997: 149).

To put it simply, in America today most of us watch TV more, read less, get outside less, socialise less with others and generally initiate fewer activities. Again turning to time diary studies, we learn that 'people who watched television more worked less, but they also did less housework, did less shopping, and ate out less – and participated less in almost all away-from-home free-time activities: adult education, religion, cultural events, socializing and recreation' (Robinson and Godbey 1997: 144). TV watching is also associated with 'significant declines is use of radio, movies, and fiction reading' as well as 'declines in social life and in sleep and personal hygiene; laundry and yard/garden work ...' (Robinson and Godbey 1997: 165). Television is 'such an accepted way to spend time', note Robinson and Godbey, 'that we have encountered people who tell us they don't have any free time *because* they are watching television' (1997: 294). At the same time, and consistent with the literature on the addictive qualities of TV, these dishevelled, sleepy people are not entirely happy with their TV consumption. In fact, over the last few decades, people seem to enjoy TV less and less, though their viewing increases. As it stands, women rate TV viewing below housework. Men, in a remarkable finding, rate TV viewing as less satisfying than cooking (Robinson and Godbey 1997: 250).

One is tempted to see something sinister in the onslaught of TV into American culture and indeed the world.[19] In Orwell's *1984*, people were required to watch TV; we now know that people will watch TV without coercion, that they will watch more than they want, and that they will have trouble escaping its clutches. Once introduced into prisons, TV appears to have, without any coercion whatsoever, displaced reading and writing as recreational pursuits, pursuits that are thought to empower and even liberate rather than merely entertain.[20] The decline of San Quentin's fabled library, as well as a robust tradition of inmate writing, appear to have been casualties of television.

> In 1956, the San Quentin library had 33,420 books, and inmates read an astonishing ninety-eight books per man per year, or nearly two a week. Spector [the head librarian] also held group counselling classes of between three and ten inmates and co-sponsored an inmate self improvement class, 'The Seekers'. In conjunction with these he also ran therapeutic creative writing sessions, and these became wildly popular. San Quentin soon became a writer's colony, a criminal version of Yaddo. In 1947, inmates submitted 395 manuscripts for publication. In 1961, they submitted 1,989. So many inmates were writing books that in 1968 the California Department of corrections began charging a 25 percent agents' fee for each manuscript submitted.
>
> (Hallinan 2003: 80)

After TV was introduced, one inmate told Hallinan, 'respect for the library began to dissipate'. From 1978 on, after TV became widely available, 'the library really went down'. By 1990, the library held only 8,902 books. 'Three-quarters of the prison's library collection had disappeared. Inmates no longer read or wrote – they simply watched TV' (Hallinan 2003: 81).

Television sometimes has pretensions to higher educational ends, but research reveals that this medium simply does not train or socialise or even inform in a reliable way (Postman 1985; Kubey and Csikszentmihalyi 2002). Television, even educational television, cannot replace reading and writing as vehicles for learning in prison or in the free world. Critics of 'Sesame Street', for example, note that this much-praised show creates kids who love television, not learning. They go to school expecting entertainment, not work. TV, moreover, has been described as not merely a poor medium for learning but as antithetical to learning. By its very nature, TV typically presents a simple and unchallenging view of the world. In the words of Robert MacNeil, of the MacNeil News Hour, a happy exception to the general trend, 'the idea' of TV is to:

keep everything brief, not to strain the attention of anyone but instead to provide constant stimulation through variety, novelty, action, and movement. You are required ... to pay attention to no concept, no character, and no problem for more than a few seconds at a time ... [One learns] that bite-sized is best, that complexity must be avoided, that nuances are dispensable, that qualifications impede the simple message, that visual stimulation is a substitute for thought, and that verbal precision is an anachronism.

(quoted in Postman 1985: 105)

'The result', MacNeil observes, is that 'Americans are the best entertained and quite likely the least well-informed people in the Western world' (Postman 1985: 106). Neil Postman, a noted social critic, tells us that TV conveys a view of the world that is disconnected and even incoherent.[21] Ironically, this is most apparent on television news, where the broadcaster moves from event to event without connection or context, in effect, and sometimes literally, saying 'Now ... This ...'

'Now ... this' is commonly used on radio and television newscasts to indicate that what one has just heard or seen has no relevance to what one is about to hear or see, or possibly to anything one is ever likely to hear or see. The phrase is a means of acknowledging the fact that the world as mapped by speeded-up electronic media has no order or meaning and is not to be taken seriously. There is no murder so brutal, no earthquake so devastating, no political blunder so costly – for that matter, no ball score so tantalizing or weather report so threatening – that it cannot be erased from our minds by a newscaster saying, 'Now ... this'.

(Postman 1985: 99)

Adults are used to this discontinuity, indeed barely notice it, but the effect on those who rely on TV as their window to the larger world, notably children, may be quite deleterious. Most of us, it seems:

have become so accustomed to [television's] discontinuities that we are no longer struck dumb, as any sane person world be, by a newscaster who having just reported that a nuclear war is inevitable goes on to say that he will be right back after this word from Burger King; who says, in other words, 'Now ... this'. One can hardly overestimate the damage that such juxtapositions do to our sense of the world as a serious place. The damage is especially massive to youthful viewers who depend so much on television for their clues as to how to respond to the world. In watching television news, they, more than any other segment of the audience, are drawn into an epistemology based on the assumption that all reports of cruelty and death are greatly exaggerated and, in any case, not to be taken seriously or responded to sanely.

(Postman 1985: 104–5)

One could argue that convicts, marooned in isolated prisons, are a bit like children in the larger culture. They, too, might come to depend on TV for their 'clues' about the changing world outside the prison, and in turn learn that 'cruelty and death are greatly exaggerated' and 'not to be taken seriously or responded to sanely'. And since crime is a major source of entertainment, as is violence generally, this too can only minimise their appreciation for the seriousness of their own failings (crime shows are perennial favourites among prisoners). Perhaps feelings of victimisation will be produced, since the prisoners in the viewing audience are doing hard time for behaviour that is not, after all, so bad or consequential.

When convicts think about personal change, they may come to expect their problems to yield to easy solutions, like everything else on TV, most notably in commercials. 'The commercial asks us to believe that all problems are solvable, that they are solvable fast, and that they are solvable fast through the interventions of technology, techniques and chemistry' (Postman 1985: 130). Problems with sexual relations? Take X or Y and 'stay in the game', to quote a current ad for an erectile dysfunction medication. How your intimate team-mates feel about one's renewed vigour is not considered. Unhappy or easily upset? Tell your doctor about Z 'to get the mood you deserve', even if you have every right to be anxious or depressed (here I am borrowing from an ad for an antidepressant). Larger obstacles to success on release from prison, like racism and poverty, are duly minimised on TV, where 'virtual integration' and upward social mobility are norms (Steinhorn and Diggs-Brown 1999).[22] The real work required for personal change, and the substantial obstacles that must be overcome, may be all the more discouraging given these unrealistic expectations.

Research by Yvonne Jewkes suggests that the various problems raised by TV in the general culture apply to captive populations as well (Jewkes 2002). Jewkes's seminal work with English convicts reveals deeply felt concerns about wasting time watching television, about becoming addicted to television, and about losing interest in reading, writing and participation in programmes as a result of one's devotion to television. Life-sentence inmates feared that television would hasten

269

their deterioration into passive, compliant, zombie-like prisoners (Jewkes 2002: 91). Lifers and other long-term inmates were inclined to watch less TV than other prisoners, Jewkes notes, because they found it 'too painful to be reminded of a world they are longer a part of' (Jewkes 2002: 91). For prisoners facing big time, at least, social isolation was a relief, because it allowed them to focus on their daily prison lives, to live 'one day at a time' in the prison world, the only world open to them for the foreseeable future.

Jewkes's work is particularly instructive in pointing to the many *positive* uses of TV in the prison and, indeed, in the free world. TV may well come to dominate our lives, and certainly does so at a price, but television has appeal in considerable measure because it *helps* us cope with our daily lives. As with the unemployed or disabled or otherwise housebound, prisoners are particularly inclined to use the TV in service of a range of constructive personal ends: as a source of connection, however imperfect, to a world from which they are separated; as a vehicle to permit escapist fantasies about how life might one day be and to avoid painful introspection about what life could have been; as a way to create and confirm positive identities in a world that is hostile or indifferent; as a prop that makes the habitat – cell or room – more like home and the daily routine more like a familiar domestic experience; as a way to relate to others (watch shows with friends) and to find a private sanctuary (watching TV alone in the cell); as a possession that confirms one's worth as a person with resources and as 'company' that helps you pass the time; generally, as a multifaceted vehicle for the expression of moods, taste and autonomy. It would appear that we all use TV for these various purposes, in varying degrees, depending on the circumstances of our lives. In prison, an environment with limited options, TV is a particularly valuable resource, either on its own or as an adjunct to such traditional constructive endeavours as education or rehabilitation programmes.

TV, the carrier of images, has many images attached to it, including the notion that it is an addicting drug. The original image of the television portrayed it as a 'magic box', a view that is closer to how prisoners see television. From the confines a small, dark cell, as if by magic, a mere push of a button produces a miniature version of the living world, there on demand for one's entertainment. The word television – 'far-seeing' – captures the startling fact that TV lets us see far into the world from the security of our homes (or cells), a kind of magic when you think about it. Some people in the free world, perhaps speaking facetiously, claim that the appeal of that magic world is that it is simply more varied and interesting than the real world. As Andy Warhol famously said, 'When I first got my television set, I stopped caring so much about having close relationships'.[23]

A fair number of prisoners, we learn from Jewkes (2002: 21), find the world of television, even with a range of acknowledged shortcomings, more interesting, richer in colour and variety, and certainly safer than the prison world in which they find themselves, where close relationships are rare and even casual conversations can be precarious undertakings. On reflection, this depressing finding rings true. The typical offender lives in an impersonal and repressive institution located far from home, gets few or no visits over the course of his confinement, is marginally literate, has access to few ameliorating programmes of merit, and is surrounded by strangers, many of whom sport menacing facades and seem thin-skinned and prone to impulsive violence. Small wonder the world as mediated by television is as good as it gets for many convicts.

Time bandits: a thought on the roots of punitive attitudes today

Prisoners appear, from the outside, to have leisure time (as opposed to empty time) on their hands. It is no doubt jarring for the average citizen to consider convicts with ready access to television.[24] In the case of some high-tech prisons, there is also the image of a uniformed staff at the prisoners' beck and call, delivering meals and mail and perhaps even the TV guide to their doors. This would seem to be the stuff of country-club prisons; a myth, to be sure, but a myth that fuels a considerable anger at prisoners who seem to have it easy. Do we, in some sense, envy our convicts? What do we imagine they have that we don't? The answer may be time.

Americans think of time primarily in terms of work and efficiency, even approaching consumption of goods (and indeed time, at least time away from the TV) with a work ethic. 'Many Americans', notes Robinson, 'have become virtual walking resumes, defining themselves almost solely by what they do' (Robinson 1999). Prisons appear very much out of step with these values. Work and productivity do not figure prominently in popular images of prison, and in fact many American prisons don't have enough work to go around and don't produce much of value.[25] Treatment programmes, as we have noted, are in decline. Education classes are more common, but classrooms don't fit with popular perceptions of prisons and in any case only take up a few hours of a prison day.

Free citizens talk about prisons as though the cell blocks were populated with scruffy, tattooed convicts lollygagging in front of the TV for hours on end, when they are not jogging in the prison yard, pumping iron in the gym, or painting sunsets and writing verse in their cells.[26] Prisoners are *doing time*, to be sure, but they are *not pressed for time*. Most Americans, in sharp contrast, feel a 'time crunch'. Some even claim to value time over money, claim they are willing to *pay* for more time in their lives. The thought of prisoners locked up with their own TVs, often with cable service, when they are not out and about doing other ostensibly relaxing things with their time, may be more than some of us in the free world can bear.

In point of fact, Americans have a lot of free time, perhaps more free time than the convicts. We resent the free time convicts appear to have, I suggest, for two reasons. First, we feel pressed for time in part because we are unhappy with the way we fritter away free time watching television. (Some inmates, too, as we have noted, bemoan the unproductive time they spend glued to the tube; Jewkes, 2002: 103.) In any case, there is no indication to outside observers that prison operates at the frenzied pace of the free world, such that TV might plausibly be viewed as a safe haven from legitimate daily stresses.

Second, Americans only *feel* they have free time when they are on vacation. On vacation, time diary studies reveal, Americans escape their TVs and embrace a range of ways to relax and express themselves. Only on vacation, it would seem, do we achieve a 'leisurely' and enjoyable pace of life:

> there is a dramatic decline in television viewing, to less than 20 minutes a day. In its place, reading time more than doubles as does time in personal communication. Bigger increases are found in sports, walking, and other outdoor activities – nearly two hours. The increase in sleep and meal time, and the decrease in grooming time, also suggest a more leisurely pace…
>
> (Robinson 1999: unpaginated)

Can it be that we resent prisoners because their lives seem to us to be closer to vacation time than to work or even regular free time? We work and rush, measuring ourselves by our achievements and our possessions, labouring to shop, travel and even exercise in a way we view as efficient and productive. Prisoners, in an almost classic rendition of Leisure Man, appear to relax, read, reflect and exercise out of doors in the prison yard. By this reckoning, even rehabilitation programmes might offend harried free citizens, since programmes offer skill development that might enrich time while free citizens tend to see time as a burden they must manage or spend wisely, not a pleasure they might savour. One skill that permits a person to savour time is introspection, something one might well envy the convicts, who may in fact become more introspective when confined (Johnson 2002: 105). Ironically, prisoners often find introspection quite painful, while most Americans, who might enjoy and benefit from introspection, 'regard contemplation as simply a waste of time' (Godbey, White Paper #8).

Discontent with what we see as soft or congenial prisons may reflect deeper resentments that stem from unrealistic expectations about life. Americans, it seems, expect a lot from life. 'We have come to expect hassle-free personal relations, limitless material possessions, and a world unfolding to meet our personal agendas, time-wise and otherwise. We then feel more rushed than we would prefer when the world does not respond as we expected' (Robinson and Godbey 1997: 305). Feeling put upon by life, we in turn feel victimised.[27]

To be sure, our lives are quite complicated these days. We face daily a range of choices about how to live and balance obligations at home and at work. Ours is, moreover, a 'morally relative world', notes Robinson (1999), 'surrounded by choices about things that used to be matters of accepted doctrine', notably religious doctrine (our parents or at least grandparents, for example, did not have to grapple with the morality of abortion, homosexuality or gay marriage). Material options abound as well. Every commodity, it seems, comes in a range of shapes and sizes, each available for inspection. Choices big and small add pressure and shrink time (see Schwartz 2004). TV, which offers freedom from such choices, provides an escape, a major source of its popularity in the free world.[28] Prisoners, in contrast, seem to be *living a life of escape* – fed and clothed and spared difficult daily decisions, they even have TV for further escapist recreation.

Prisoners have always been scapegoats. An alien and devalued group, they can readily be made to bear the blame for disappointing aspects of our daily lives. If we are unhappy, as a consequence of our choices, prisoners can be made unhappier still, to validate our choices. The term 'scapegoat' originally referred to a goat that was marked and allowed to escape into the wilderness, carrying with it to oblivion the sins of the group. Our convicts escape the larger culture, only to enter the oblivion of prisons at remote outposts of civilisation, alone with their burden.

The future: two scenarios

Tough technology

One can easily envision a world in which technology renders prisoners useless. In this world, eerily reminiscent of the present, low-skills jobs are taken by immigrants willing to work like slaves and live without complaint in cramped quarters. Higher-skill jobs require advanced education and are increasingly subject to stiff competition across global lines. Computer engineers in idyllic places like Reston, Virginia, compete with their counterparts in rural India who can work for as little as one-tenth of their wages. As globalisation ameliorates some pockets of poverty in the Third World, America moves toward a two-tier society: the very rich, with good jobs and material wealth but limited time; and the working poor who serve the rich, cleaning their houses, raising their children and serving their fast food. A third group, criminals, prove disorderly and disruptive, and are kept on remote penal reservations under constant video surveillance. A panoply of punitive gadgets, like stun belts and full-restraint chairs, are available to keep the prisoners in line.

There are, of course, occasional escapes and periodic executions in this penal archipelago. There are also recurring waves of releasees emanating from these distant prisons, mandated by quaint human-rights laws from a past some remember with nostalgia. Yet as a practical matter, these offenders are metaphorically branded for life: they have a record, they cannot work at many jobs, they cannot live in public housing, they cannot get loans for higher education or to start small businesses, they cannot vote. They are monitored closely, not to help them but to control them. When they slip up, breaking a behavioural rule or violating a law, they are recycled back to the prison like dated commodities that have been duly recalled as defective or spoiled, useless to the larger society. Note that today, parole revocation rates are high and growing higher in America. In California, often a bellwether state, revocation rates approach 70 per cent; of this group, fully 80 per cent are sent back to prison for technical violations of a parole service that imposes surveillance but does not provide services or even link offenders to services (Petersilia 2003; Travis 2003: 18). Each return to confinement arguably limits their chances for successful assimilation into a society that had no room for them in the first place.

Tender technology

More difficult to picture is a world in which high-tech prisons take as their mission the reintegration of offenders. Prisons, especially high-tech prisons like the supermax, are frightfully impersonal, but some technologies can be used in these sterile settings to reduce social isolation and promote better adjustment.

Cells might be equipped with cell phones. Aside from the amusing play on words, such a policy would simply bring prisons into line with the rest of the world, where cell phones are ubiquitous.[29] Cell phones could be used as telephones, of course, making it easier for prisoners to stay in touch with loved ones (inmates now must wait for approved times and then get in line to use payphones. This requires staffing; fights occasionally break out over phone usage.) Cell phones also come with video capabilities. These video cell phones serve as camcorders, showing and recording live communications between parties to the call. These video cell phone visits could even be made available to prisoners in lock-down. Recordings can be stored and retrieved for viewing and reviewing at a later date. Cell phones can be used to send and receive email, providing another interactive link to loved ones. Finally, cell phones now get television reception, and could be used as inexpensive and highly portable miniature televisions that allow all prisoners, even those in close custody, ready access to television.[30]

Video-conferencing technology has been used in some institutions to promote what might be termed 'distance visiting'. This technology is used extensively for court hearings in confinement, and more recently for medical and psychiatric consultations, parole hearings, and pre-release placements.[31] Several American prisons are experimenting with video-conferencing visits. Typically, visitors sit in a room away from the prisoner, sometimes in a building outside the prison proper. Inmates are placed in a room in or near the prison visiting area. A live television monitor connects the rooms, so that visitors and inmates can speak to one another without having to undergo searches and without the risk of smuggling or other undesirable behaviour[32] (these security benefits accrue to cell phone visits as well). Work is underway today to create central visiting areas in selected major cities, so that a family with an inmate at a distant prison can go to a visiting centre near home and not have to travel to the prison. Experience suggests that these visits are an improvement over standard non-contact visits but are less appealing than regular contact visits.

Video conferencing has obvious programme applications, since the medium is interactive. One can use this technology for 'distance learning', as is done in many universities today, and for 'distance treatment' (e.g. counselling). Educational courses could be augmented by access to a 'digital library'. If we can't bring cart-loads of books to prison libraries or to individual cells, we can bring micro-chips and laptop computers, which are small and easily transportable. Again, even for people limited to cells, the world of books could be made available without the space and security considerations raised by normal library arrangements. One such concern is the fire hazard posed by a clutter of books and other reading materials. Digital books don't take up much space and they don't burn.

Down the road, virtual-reality technology may allow for virtual learning and treatment. Already, virtual-reality technology is used to help patients (mostly burn patients) deal with extreme pain. There have also been applications of this technology to persons who suffer from phobias and even post-traumatic stress disorder (Hoffman 2004). One can envision a time when we might immerse offenders in virtual prisons rather than real ones. In a matter of hours, one could expose offenders to realistic scenarios from prison life, either as a means of deterrence or, more positively, as occasions for rehearsing mature problem-solving strategies. By the same token, one could arrange virtual sequences that help offenders deal with everyday problems in more constructive ways. Scenarios could also focus on common sources of trauma, such as child abuse, traumas that we know contribute to a cycle of violence (Widom 1992; Widom and Maxfield 2001).

Modern technology may one day transform the cells of prisons, even supermax prisons, into the productive ameliorative enclaves envisioned in the original penitentiaries. The 'Good Book' would be supplemented by an almost unlimited range of good books, available on demand. Advisors, spiritual and therapeutic, would be beamed into these dark corners of our prison system, bringing the light of reason and hope with them. Virtual worlds would be fabricated to allow for rehearsals of coping strategies under conditions that allowed offenders to confront and resolve the hurt and anger that have driven their lives. Broadly speaking, technology would shine a bright light of inquiry into our prisons, providing all of us with more accurate images of prison life, images that may one day dispel myths about congenial prisons and contended prisoners.

Of course, technologies that connect the outside world and the prison world can also be used to control prisoners. So far, control has been the major use of technology in the prison, and it is the control possibilities that always loom large in the thinking of prison managers. In the coming years, we shall see how readily technology in the prison serves as a Big Brother or a Brother's Keeper.

Notes

1 See Hoffman, H.G. (2004) 'Virtual-reality therapy', *Scientific American*, August, 58–65.
2 The pace at which these technologies are spreading is remarkable. For example, in January 2004, seven out of ten US household had Internet access in their homes, up from a mere one in ten as recently as 1996. Minnesota Public Radio, Future Tense with Jon Gordon, 3 March 2004; www.publicradio.org/columns/futuretense/2004/03/03.shtml#000202.
3 The globalisation of many jobs is made possible by this information exchange. The 'convergence of a variety of software applications' together with the spread of personal computers 'made it possible to create global "work-flow platforms"'. These work-flow platforms can chop up any service job — accounting, radiology, consulting, software engineering — into different functions and then, thanks to scanning and digitisation, outsource each function to teams of skilled knowledge workers around the globe, based on which team can do each function with the highest skill at the lowest price. Then the project is reassembled back at headquarters into a finished product (Friedman 2004: 29).
4 In some segments of American society, nevertheless, imprisonment has come to be seen as a normal feature of life, something unremarkable, almost to be expected for young men and, increasingly, young women (Gonnerman 2004).
5 As Deirdre Golash has observed, 'Punishment, at its core, is the deliberate infliction of harm in response to wrongdoing … in the mistaken belief that it promotes some greater good … We would do well to ask whether the goods we seek in harming offenders are worthwhile, and whether the means we choose will indeed secure them' (Golash 2004).
6 Personal communication, Victor Hassine, 1 March 2004. Hassine notes that staff levels increased dramatically in Pennsylvania's prisons during the last decade or so, with personnel increasingly 'trained and socialized into a strictly punitive aversion philosophy'. Even as small steps are attempted today to reduce the punitive focus of the system, Hassine sees staff baulk because they 'simply do not know how' to operate in a less repressive system. There is no reason to suppose that the Pennsylvania system is unique in this regard.
7 Federal Bureau of Prisons Survey, March–April, 1998, Inmate Telephone Activity and BOP Practices. www.usdoj.gov/oig/special/99-08/table1.htm
8 See the Library Standards for Correctional Institutions, section on prisons: www.ala.org/ala/ascla/asclapubs/interface/archives/contentlistingbykey/prisonlib/prisonlibraries.htm
9 Staff cutbacks are especially problematic. 'The safety and security of facilities with lower staffing levels is a central issue, since financial cutbacks and limited resources inevitably present a heightened risk of victimization

for guard and inmates. Gang violence…is likely to increase…Prison disturbances pose a serious threat as overcrowding worsens and conditions of confinement deteriorate. Spares funding for vocational, educational, and treatment programs creates additional pressures for the staff as more and more inmates have idle time' ('Cutting corrections: Dwindling resources demand tough choices and creative solutions', *Criminal Justice Research Reports*, 4 (6) July/August 2003: 87–88).

10 See 'Profile: Conditions at a correctional facility in the California Youth Authority', 19 February 2004, 'All things considered' from NPR News. One correctional worker observed, 'These are not just your regular, cooperative, quiet, well-intentioned students who are getting in trouble. These are ones who have, time after time after time, demonstrated that the only thing that's important to them is getting back at the members of the other gangs. What can we do to protect these kids from the other gang members? We're just trying to protect them'.

11 *Sandin v. Connor*, 115 S. Ct. 2293 (1995) at 2293.

12 Politicians are key players in the generation of fear-driven policies but they are not alone. Advocacy groups often overstate crime and other sources of danger in the modern world, conveying their message in frightening, black and white terms.

13 Now it is true that, on reflection, people are often less punitive than politicians make them out to be. Surveys routinely tell us that citizens favour punishment *and* rehabilitation, though the constituency for treatment appears to be waning. A recent survey indicated that fully 74 per cent of respondents saw judges as too lenient. See Johnston *et al* (1997).

14 'Across the country, politicians began calling for harsher conditions of confinement. They wanted wardens to take away inmates' TVs, take away their weights, take away – although it was never quite put this way – their dignity. How else to explain the actions of Mississippi legislators who voted to put inmates back in striped uniforms? "When you see one of these boogers loose", promised the sponsor of the bill, "you'll say, I didn't know we had zebras in Mississippi"' (Hallinan 2003: xv).

15 Some supermax prisons have closed-access TVs in the cells. These TVs are used to send messages from the administration, for example, or as a source of in-cell programming. If anything, these communication systems, which allow staff to communicate with inmates but not vice versa, add to the eerie, controlling atmosphere of high-security cells.

16 This perception is common among English correctional officials as well (Jewkes 2002: 174).

17 See Kupers (1999).

18 Free time is defined in time-use studies as time not devoted to work, sleep, eating and grooming. See Robinson and Godbey (1997).

19 According to Stephens, 'television, which is less than a generation older than the computer, has already won over humankind…evidence indicates that almost three billion people are already watching television regularly,

for an average of more than two and a half hours a day' (1998: 6–7). Today, some six years later, one can only suppose that the figures for television watching in the world are considerably higher.

20 Librarians are periodically imprisoned in totalitarian countries like Cuba, not their colleagues in the audio-visual department. For a current example, see Hentoff, N., 'Cuba cages librarians', *Village Voice*, 5 March 2004.

21 Stephens (1998: 212) makes the interesting point that one might well think of the world as, much of the time, essentially disconnected and even incoherent. The order we impose on the world, he argues, is a product of printed words and the linear logic they impose. His view is that video images, especially rapid-cut video images, such as seen on MTV, are closer to reality as we see and experience it. Be that as it may, our discourse about the world is circumscribed by linear logic, and it is to the social world formed around that logic to which inmates must one day return.

22 Local news shows present a notable exception to these observations. Here, crime is portrayed as the province of young black men, adding to racial resentments outside the walls. But the local news is a small part of TV programming, easily overlooked or discounted by an inmate audience, except perhaps as it applies to their re-entry into these high-crime areas. To the extent that local news exaggerates crime, it will make these neighbourhoods look more threatening and less hospitable than they really are.

23 This quote is drawn from Stephens (1998: 128), who goes on to argue that as people watched more television and conversed less, conversation skills declined, making social situations less interesting and television, by comparison, more appealing.

24 Television has a special resonance in American culture. As things stand, no other society is as committed to this medium as we are, a fact partly related to our relative affluence (we can afford TVs, including fancy ones) and our general affection for consumption (TVs are often status symbols, in which size and appurtenances matter) (Robinson and Godbey 1997). Televisions in prison are thus a readily identifiable sore spot with Americans who are angry about crime and dissatisfied with the punishments meted out in our courts.

25 It is estimated by CRS Inc., described as 'a consulting firm for governments and the corrections industry', that between 30 and 40 per cent of prisoners 'do some sort of work, mostly maintenance jobs' (Boorstein 2004: C5).

26 Regrettably, corrections brought some of these misunderstandings upon itself. When once we promised rehabilitation, clamouring for indeterminate sentences, we couldn't deliver. At one point, group therapy in California prisons was conducted with up to 150 inmates, an obviously unworkable situation. Parole brochures promised ex-convicts that they'd 'live like millions', a promise no one could keep. Later, we tried to make prisons more normal, a laudable goal, but too often that amounted to providing amenities

rather than a world that in any way mimicked the ebb and flow of life and responsibility in the free world. Casual clothes and televisions did not a normal world make, though they did make for considerable resentment outside the walls. Today, we stand ready to correct, in the sense that we know a great deal about promoting personal change in prison environments. The trouble is that we now have more prisons and prisoners than we can reckon with, and we release offenders to a world that is indifferent or even hostile to their fate. See Johnson (2002) especially Part III, 'Prison reform'.

27 Americans live a life of considerable privilege, but appear not to appreciate it: 'The many ways in which our lives have improved economically are lost on the average American, particularly since new "entitlements" come to Americans in the form of services rather than in dramatic pay raises or price reductions' (Robinson and Godbey 1997: 295).

28 Interactive TV has not caught on in the American home because people don't want to be actively engaged by their televisions; interactive TV would require choice (Robinson and Godbey 1997: 312).

29 Joke of the future: Why do convicts like cell phones? Because they are used to bad reception.

30 See 'Phones, too, get TV time', *New York Times*, 29 January 2004, by David Pogue.

31 The Ohio Department of Rehabilitation and Correction uses video-conferencing for each of these purposes. The company that the Department uses, Tandberg, claims 'countless video-conferencing applications exist in the corrections sector' (Tandberg success stories, www.tandberg.net).

32 Tandberg offers a Visitation Package: 'The Visitation Package enables easier and safer administration of the visitation process. Through one simple touch panel, the administrator can instantly connect the inmate and the visitor and easily manage the length of the call. In order to ensure the rights of the inmate and visitor, the call is not initiated until the inmate reaches the visitation station and picks up the telephone handset on the video system – this allows the inmate and visitor to have the maximum amount of time for their visit' (Tandberg success stories, www.tandberg.net).

References

Austin, J. and Irwin, J. (2000) *It's About Time: America's Imprisonment Binge*, 3rd edition. Belmont, CA: Wadsworth.

Boorstein, M. (2004) 'Marking time, building futures', *The Washington Post*, 11 April: Metro Section, C5.

Friedman, T. (2004) 'Smaller and smaller', *New York Times*, Editorial, 4 March: Section A, Page 29.

Glassner, B. (2000) *The Culture of Fear: Why Americans Are Afraid of the Wrong Things*. New York: Basic Books.

Godbey, G. 'White Paper #8: The problem of free time: It's not what you think', www.academyofleisuresciences.org/alswp8.html (undated, unpaginated).

Golash, D. (2004) *The Case Against Punishment*. New York: New York University Press (in press).

Gonnerman, J. (2004) *Life on the Outside: The Prison Odyssey of Elaine Bartlett/* New York: Farrar, Straus and Giroux.

Hallinan, J. (2003) *Going up the River: Travels in a Prison Nation*. New York: Random House.

Haney, C. and Lynch, M. (1997) 'Regulating prisons of the future: A psychological analysis of supermax and solitary confinement', *New York University Review of Law & Social Change*, XXIII (4), 477–570.

Hill, C. (2002) 'Inmate privileges and fees for service', *Corrections Compendium*, 27 (8), August, 8–26.

Hoffman, H.G. (2004) 'Virtual-reality therapy', *Scientific American*, August, 58–65.

Huxley, A. (2004) *Brave New World*, new edition. London: Vintage.

Jewkes, Y. (2002) *Captive Audience: Media, Masculinity and Power in Prisons*. Cullompton: Willan Publishing.

Johnson, R. (2002) *Hard Time: Understanding and Reforming the Prison*, 3rd edition. Belmont, CA: Wadsworth.

Johnston, W.W., Bennett, K. and Flanagan, T. (1997) 'Getting tough on prisoners: A national survey of prison administrators', *Crime and Delinquency*, 43 (1), 24–41.

Kaufman, R. (2002) 'How television affects the mind': A review of The Tube – a film by Peter Entell. www.turnoffyourtv.com/reviews/tubemovie.html

Kubey, R and Csikszentmihalyi, M. (2002) 'Television addiction is no mere metaphor', *Scientific American*, February, 74–80.

Kupers, T. (1999) *Prison Madness: The Mental Health Crisis Behind Bars and What We Must Do About It*. San Francisco: Jossey-Bass.

Lerner, J.A. (2003) *You Got Nothing Coming: Notes from a Prison Fish*. New York: Broadway.

Lyman, P. and Varian, H.R. (2003) *How Much Information*. www.sims.berkeley.edu/research/projects/how-much-info-2003/

Maruna, S. (2001) *Making Good: How Ex-Convicts Reform and Rebuild Their Lives*. Washington, DC: American Psychological Association.

Noll, M.A. (2002) *America's God: From Jonathan Edwards to Abraham Lincoln*. Oxford: Oxford University Press.

Petersilia, J. (2003) *When Prisoners Come Home: Parole and Prisoner Reentry*. Oxford: Oxford University Press.

Pollock, J. (2003) *Prisons and Prison Life: Costs and Consequences*. Los Angeles: Roxbury.

Postman, N. (1985) *Amusing Ourselves to Death: Public Discourse in the Age of Show Business*. New York: Viking.

Putnam, R. (1997) 'Tuning in, tuning out: The strange disappearance of social capital in America', *P.S.*, December. Cited in Robinson, J.P. and G. Godbey (eds) *Time for Life: The Surprising Ways Americans Use Their Time*. Pennsylvania State University Press.

Rhodes, L.A. (2004) *Total Confinement: Madness and Reason in the Maximum Security Prison*. University of California Press.

Robinson, J.P. (1999) 'The irrelevance of time' fall, 1999. www.inform.umd.edu/CPMAG/fall99/irrelevance.html

Robinson, J.P. and Godbey, G. (1997) *Time for Life: The Surprising Ways Americans Use Their Time*. Pennsylvania State University Press.

Schwartz, B. (2004) *The Paradox of Choice: Why More Is Less*. New York: Ecco.

Steinhorn, L. and Diggs-Brown, B. (1999) *By the Color of our Skin: The Illusion of Integration and the Reality of Race*. New York: Plume.

Stephens, M. (1998) *The Rise of the Image and the Fall of the Word*. Oxford: Oxford University Press.

Stix, G. (2002) 'Real time: The pace of living quickens continuously, yet a full understanding of things temporal still eludes us', *Scientific American*, September, 36–39.

Sykes, G.M. (1958) *The Society of Captives: A Study of a Maximum Security Prison*. Princeton, NJ: Princeton University Press.

Toch, H. (1992) *Living in Prison: The Ecology of Survival*. Washington, DC: American Psychological Association.

Toch, H. (2001) 'The future of supermax confinement', *The Prison Journal*, 81 (3), September, 376–388.

Toch, H. (2003) 'Prison walls do a prison make: The untimely demise of visitation rights', *Correctional Law Reporter*, Volume XV No. 2, August/September, 17.

Travis, J. (2003) 'Parole in California, 1980–2000: Implications for reform', Testimony, *Public Hearing on Parole Reform*, Little Hoover Commission, 27 February 2003.

Widom, C.S. (1992) 'The cycle of violence', *Research in Brief*, National Institute of Justice.

Widom, C.S. and Maxfield, M.G. (2001) 'An update on "The Cycle of Violence"', *Research in Brief*, National Institute of Justice, 1–8.

Postscript

Pod People

Human husks wrapped in scorn
solitary figures, mute, forlorn
lay flat, unmoving, unmourned
arms crossed, faces slack
eyes half open, glazed, black
tortured on a modern rack

Buzzers beep, hum, a morning rite
inert figures come to life
a marionette review,
run in mime, lost in time

Over go pairs of feet,
thwack, thwack,
flat on the floor
Slowly rises each torso,
twisting, creaking,
turning gingerly toward the door
Carefully moves each form,
dragging, shuffling,
inching toward the murky light
Sepia-toned, heavy,
etched in grime, thick with blight
detritus of a long dark night

Each man, each day, in his way
goes the distance, makes his bones
traversing his cloistered world alone
touring his cell, his private hell
dancing with his demon
dreaming he's a free man

All this, yet no one knows
no one heeds these one-man shows
one puppet per stage, one prisoner per pod
one guard, on guard
unseeing, unseen
runs the supermax machine
a padded vest, hands gloved in gray
pushes buttons, shoves trays
recedes, a phantom, into the haze

People of the Pod,
pomanders and epithets
pressed to sweaty chests like amulets,
breathe deeply of the fetid air,
speak daily to God, Care
only that He use the Rod

The Effects of Imprisonment

"Punish me," they say, "for I am bad"
His Word redounds,
comes off the wall, off the page,
floats in space, feeds their rage
each cell a terminal stage
a killing cage, for men

stoned, dazed, left to fate
blinded by a bright white hate,
wallowing in delusion
stewing in corruption
yearning for direction,
to be a Somebody
not just some body

Robert Johnson
February, 2004

Chapter 11

'Soldiers', 'sausages' and 'deep sea diving': language, culture and coping in Israeli prisons

Tomer Einat

From the first moment of incarceration, the newcomer faces 'initiation rituals' (Kaminski 2003; Goffman 1961) and often humiliating trials that test his tolerance to physical and mental pain, self-confidence, mental strength, alertness, intelligence and humour. He is expected to lean norms and values of his new subculture rapidly and plan his strategies and goals patiently, acknowledging the domination of 'jungle law' in his new setting (Kaminski 2003; Johnson and Toch 2000). The prison environment socialises an inmate to behave in predictable ways. Very few actions are executed spontaneously and unpredictably in the prisoners' subculture. Injuries, violence, ambushes, humiliations and social isolation can be understood and explained as outcomes of carefully calculated acts.

The current study, the first of its sort to be conducted in Israel, wishes to open a window into a largely unknown world – the subculture of Israeli inmates. Its goals are two-fold: to have prisoners describe their everyday life in prison and to analyse how their code of conduct as well as the language they use ('ways of speaking') reflect the world views, beliefs and attitudes they hold about their existential condition.

The chapter contains six parts: the first part focuses on the Israeli Prison Service's (IPS) ideology and formal working objectives, and the second centres on the issues of 'pains of imprisonment' and Israeli prisoners' behavioural code. The third part relates to social and cultural meanings of the term 'argot' and examines the significant role of argot in the inmates' code of conduct. The fourth part concentrates on the methodology used in the research. The fifth part presents narrative, dialogues and phrases, as well as patterns of behaviour that describe, as accurately as possible, life in Israeli prisons. The final part of the chapter analyses the interaction between Israeli inmates' constraints, distresses and their world view, code of behaviour and argot, and discusses the potential conclusions that can be drawn out of it.

The Israeli Prison Service (IPS)

The IPS is a law-enforcement agency with a social duty. In collaboration with other government agencies and community organisations, IPS's formal mission is to enhance offenders' potential for successful integration within the community by ensuring their incarceration in a safe, secure and reasonable environment, respecting their dignity, accommodating their basic needs and assisting them in acquiring appropriate rehabilitative skills (Israel Prison Service 2003). Inmates engage in occupational settings inside and outside the prison, participate in supportive intake workshops and correctional programmes (often with their spouses and children), and have the opportunity to participate in a wide range of formal and informal education projects (Einat and Einat 2000; Wozner 1985a, b). The legal incomes received from these projects serve for purchasing varied products in the prison canteen, assisting their families and saving for release. In their final stage of incarceration, prisoners are relocated into 'rehabilitation wings' and participate in various treatment activities. These activities focus on inmates' needs, performances, familial relations and available sources of support in the community, establishing personal rehabilitative programmes and addressing community agencies for assistance. Practically, however, the IPS is also a security system emphasising safety, control, incapacitation and punitive objectives (Einat 2003). Most Israeli prisons are characterised by formal and structured contact between inmates and staff (Einat 1996). In order to fulfil its tasks, the IPS employs personnel in different security areas – in much larger numbers than in any of its other sectors[1] and exploits advanced and modern technologies in order to improve its security abilities (Israel Prison Service 2002). This security-punitive reality, combined with objective and subjective deficiencies and distresses ('pains of confinement'), creates an offensive-defensive position, and socialises Israeli inmates into a unique subculture that conceives society and its norms, values and modes of behaviour, as harmful and oppressive (Einat and Einat 2000; Timor 1998).

The 'pains of imprisonment'

Sociological literature has represented the power of total institutions – in general and prison – in particular, as cruel and harmful (Goodstein and Wright 1989; Goffman 1961; Sykes 1958). Three broad categories of incarceration were identified by these sociological studies and include (1) psychological and physical constraints of time organisation, deprivation of liberty, space distribution, etc.;[2] (2) official rules of the prison institution;[3] and (3) the norms of inmate subculture.[4]

Much that an inmate experiences in prison reminds him that he is regarded as an outcast, not only by prison officials and corrections personnel but by society as well. He is preoccupied with insults to his personal dignity and integrity by guards, staff, or official policies. The pains of imprisonment seriously hurt the prisoner's social status as well as personality, setting up a serious attack on his self-perception and self-esteem (Liebling *et al* 1999; Sykes 1958).[5] And 'however painful these frustrations or deprivations may be in the immediate terms of thwarted goals, discomfort, boredom, and loneliness, they carry a more profound hurt as a set of threats or attacks which are directed against the very foundations of the prisoner's being' (Sykes 1958: 78–9). Hence, it seems that the pain related to imprisonment is harsher than the clear evidence associated with it. These psychological and psychological pains of imprisonment stimulate inmates to create and adopt a semi-secret informal system of rules, roles and behavioural code (Kaminski 2003; Kalinich 1980).

The inmate code of conduct

The inmate's behavioural code contains informal duties, prohibitions, norms and structures of power that socialise prisoners into their new environment, and determine their actual behaviour and status (Einat and Einat 2000; Selke 1993; Sykes and Messinger 1960). Hence, for the inmate, the code is seen as representing a collective and functional stand for coping with the prison environment (Fisher 1990; Goffman 1961) and a means of alleviating the overall physical and psychological suffering of prisoners caused by the 'pains of imprisonment' (Farrington 1994; Toch 1992; Jones 1988). Inmates *must* identify with and obey the code. Violation of the code is perceived as 'treason' or 'collaboration with the enemy' and is, thus, punishable (Ross and Richards 2002; but see Crewe, this volume).

The idealised version of the inmates' behavioural code, which inmates externally endorse, consists of eleven Do's and eleven Don'ts, according to Ross and Richards (2002: 72):

Do:
1 Watch what you say
2 Play it cool
3 Volunteer as little information as possible about yourself and your personal life
4 Do your own time
5 Be loyal to convicts as a group
6 Mind your own business
7 Pay your debts
8 Be sharp
9 Be honourable
10 Be a man
11 Be tough.

Don't:
1 Break your word
2 Lose your head
3 Snitch on another convict
4 Exploit other convicts
5 Pressure another convict
6 Attract attention
7 Talk to prison staff without another inmate present
8 Collaborate with prison personnel
9 Initiate fights
10 Show weakness or back down from another prisoner
11 Do business with inmate merchants.

Argot

The fundamental means of learning and preserving the inmates' code of conduct is argot and communication proficiency (Kaminski 2003; Cardozo-Freeman 1984). Argot – originally defined as a language or jargon of thieves – is a particular form of prison slang (Einat and Einat 2000; Nielson and Scrapitti 1995; Maurer 1981). This type of language is 'a complete language, capable of describing the world from the prison perspective, using its own vocabulary while "borrowing" syntax and intonation rules from the source language' (Kaminski 2003: 103).

It has been argued that a prisoner lives, thinks and functions within the framework defined by the argot (Bondesson 1989). Experienced inmates use argot vocabulary fluently and can smoothly switch between regular terms and their argot counterparts. The degree of familiarity with the argot vocabulary is one of the most important symbols of group membership among prison inmates (Encinas 2001). Argot brings cohesiveness into prison life. The secrecy of communication among prisoners who share a separate language protects prisoners' privacy, even in the presence of intensive surveillance, and assists them in 'strengthening unity to counteract the threat from within' (Maurer 1981, in Cardozo-Freeman 1984: 570). Coded communication allows prisoners to define their relative status and rights, through words, whose meaning is known only to the initiated few; thus the group reinforces its shared identity.

The study method

In order to explore the way inmates experience their world and make meaning of that experience, a flexible design study was implemented (Briggs 1986). This approach allowed access to contents that were not anticipated *a priori* as well as exploration of the research topic from the standpoint of the research population (Silvermann 1993). Qualitative methodology and the phenomenological semi-structured interview were used to collect and analyse information from the inmate participants. The final stage of the analysis is the generalisation of the main trends that emerge from the findings (Stake 1995; Fisher 1990).

Implementation and population

The participants in the study consisted of 79 randomly selected Hebrew-speaking male prisoners serving long-term sentences[6] (minimum 6 years) in two medium- and maximum-security Israeli prisons. Based on general guidelines to ensure that all those being interviewed are subject to similar stimuli and, thereby, allowing for a common base for data analysis, the phenomenological semi-structured interview was found to be the most appropriate research tool to achieve the research's main objectives (Lofland 1971; Maruna 2001). In an effort to ensure some consistency across the interviews, the author facilitated each conversation. The design of the interview was tentative and modified in accordance with new findings – resulting from the flexible way of questioning (Rubin and Rubin 1995). This flexibility contributes to the quality and credibility of the interview (Suchman and Jordan 1990).

All interviews were tape-recorded with the consent of the inter-viewees.[7] The interviews were held in the inmates' personal cells during the morning and afternoon hours, each session lasting approximately two hours. Interviewees were encouraged to share their experiences with the interviewer in a setting conducive to a sense of interpersonal involvement.

Data analysis

Due to the essentially qualitative nature, the data were subjected to content analysis (Strauss and Corbin 1990), with the argot terms being divided into five main categories: (a) violence, (b) sexual relations in prison, (c) loyalty and informing, (d) drugs, and (e) miscellaneous.

Two measures were employed to assess the salience of the argot content areas:

- *attention*, provided by the frequency of words and expressions pertaining to a given category or topic
- *intensity*, assessed by the importance assigned to given a category or topic as reflected by its connotation and the number of terms assigned to it (Krippendorf 1980).

The analysis is, therefore, essentially thematic and based on the categorisation of content areas. The system serves to pinpoint the most salient norms and values of the inmate code and the thinking patterns that typify the research population (Maykut and Morehouse 1994).

Findings

The findings show that specific behavioural patterns as well as unique argot exist in Israeli prisons. Five areas of interest and over 500 argot terms were found, some 'endogenous' (Sykes and Messinger 1977; Tittle and Tittle 1965) and some 'imported' (Irwin 1985; Irwin and Cressey 1977).

Interpersonal loyalty and adherence to the code of conduct

The most important rule in the Israeli prisoners' code of behaviour, extensively documented in criminological studies, is: never, under any circumstances, snitch on a fellow inmate (Ross and Richards 2002; Einat and Einat 2000; Irwin 1970, 1980; Feld 1977; Clemmer 1940). This rule is public, simple and central in all Israeli prisons, and the fear of its violation is disproportionately greater than its violation *de facto*.

The centrality and magnitude of this norm stems from three major factors:

1 Feeling of self-revocation: Israeli inmates clearly feel as if no one respects them while they are forced to respect the ones who mock them (Einat and Einat 2000; Einat 1996). Hence, they convey strong feelings of rage and anger towards prisoners collaborating with prison staff.

2 Secrecy: Exposure of secret words and codes to prison authority disfunctionalises inmates' lives, their ability to communicate or deal with miscellaneous products on the sly, as well as their capacity to 'live their lives' in prison (Maurer 1981, 1955).

3 Mutual assistance among inmates encourages altruism, develops functional collectivism and enlarges the 'collective ego' (Ross and Richards 2002; Balvig 1998). Therefore, interpersonal disloyalty ('treason') is conceived as a dangerous pattern of behaviour. Sanctions for disloyal behaviour may include one's relegation to a lower caste, physical and emotional isolation, severe beating, or even death.

A significant number of argot expressions reflect the importance of loyalty and adherence to the inmate behavioural code. Argot expressions related to this aspect of the prison subculture were associated with high intensity: at least 20 different terms were used to describe informers (for a detailed list, including a verbatim translation into English, see the appendix to this chapter). This high intensity reflects the strong negative sanctions applied for infraction of this code (verbal and physical violence, social isolation, withholding food, withdrawal of commodities such as cigarettes and drugs) as well as the violators' weakness and inability to control their behaviour and destiny. To cite two inmates:

A prisoner who *sings*, becomes a *snitch*, and a *maniac* (informer/ collaborator) has to know that he will be treated as a *maniac*. He will be ambushed, knifed, his face will be cut ... so everybody will know who he is, and that they should never act like him.

These *maniacs* [informers/collaborators] are a bunch of *ahabals* [stupids]. They think that all of us are *dibels* [sillies] or *z'ilehs* [slow] and that we cannot see how they *sing* to the every *blue* [prison staff] or *moko* [prison employee]. They are behaving in an *abu-ali* [show-off] way, as like, no one can currently *blow* [hit/wound] them. But all inmates know about their actions and then, suddenly, a *little red riding hood* [ambush] is done to them, and their faces are marked with a small *Picasso* [face-cut/face-wound], so everyone will know that they are not to be trusted.

Equally, fifteen expressions were identified describing prisoners who adhere to the code and never betray their prison mates (see appendix). Such inmates (called 'right guys' and 'good guys' in American prisons; Irwin 1985) are characterised not only by loyalty to the code of conduct but also by their ability to stay 'cool', maintain their self-respect, never show weakness, and help other prisoners, irrespective of the severity of sanctions imposed on them by the custodial staff.

In view of their psychological and social benefits, these patterns of behaviour are significantly important for the inmate. Prisoners opposing prison policies, as well as adhering to the code of conduct, demonstrate high degrees of personal autonomy, are held in high esteem by their fellow inmates and, over the course of time, may become leaders or arbitrators. The status of these inmates is illustrated in the following example, which includes expressions such as *ustazim* ('leaders'), *rais* ('arbitrator'), *asli baldum!* ('what a man'), *do him Intifada* ('terrorise him'), and *do him kusa* ('cut him up'):

> You see prisoner A? He's out of our *austazim*. You can *sit with him face* [to face] and talk, tell everything and he, like, a living safe, will not *whistle* or reveal anything. Even if they put him in solitary, *do him a kusa* [cut him up/stab], threaten or *do him Intifada* [terrorise him], nothing will move him. He will never *open* [reveal] or lose his temper.

Violence

Inmate socialisation to life in an Israeli prison is mainly related to fear of being verbally and physically victimised. Constant tests of masculinity, especially in relation to ability and readiness to fight, physical violence and worry, affect the convicts' mental state and lead to cynicism, anger, stress, depression, resistance to authority and frequent extreme aggressive behaviour.

In addition, overcrowding[8] and boredom, which were found to be related to mental illness and violence (Toch 1992; Paulus *et al* 1985), are major sources of stress for the Israeli inmate. Many Israeli prisoners, especially those serving very long sentences and/or those who do not work, suffer from an inability to divide their time into significant portions and/or exploit it in a productive way (Gideon 2003). This situation is conducive to frustration, tension, and, in turn, outbreaks of violence (Johnson 1987; Goffman 1961).

Our data indicate that, in the general context of violence, Israeli prison violence can be divided into two main groups: (1) those who routinely dominate more submissive prisoners and (2) those that employ violence uncontrollably.

'Kings of their castles', 'real men', and 'cowboys' are powerful, assertive, independent inmates who exploit their power selectively. These inmates make use of their power against prisoners who violate the loyalty to the inmates' code and/or to their fellow inmates. 'Shoes', 'rabbits', 'invalids', 'dirties', and 'ass-openers', are argot terms use to describe a sub-group of weak, powerless and submissive inmates (Einat and Einat 2000). The more submissive sub-group is mainly composed of convicted rapists, attackers of children, and inmates who violently harmed the elderly, as well as prisoners who promised to provide drugs and goods to their peers but failed to fulfil their task. 'Loco`s' and 'chocho`s' make up the second group of extremely violent prisoners who harm fellow inmates frequently and rather unselectively, especially those who betray the code of behaviour.

Inmates' argot reflects power relations in prison, and assists in their construction. Nicknames given to violent/powerless inmates become symbols of status, and every inmate in each of the groups knows his social standing in accordance with behaviour and linguistic patterns addressed to him.

Sex in prison

Prisons are single-sex institutions. Deprivation of heterosexual relationships constitutes one of the most significant psychological and physiological pains of imprisonment (Hawkins and Alpert 1989), and their replacement (at least on a temporary basis) by homosexual relations has been widely documented (Kaminski 2003; Cordilia 1983; Toch and Johnson 1982).[9] Surprisingly, contrary to many studies focusing on homosexual relations in prison (Kaminski 2003; Irwin 1985; Cardozo-Freeman 1984), our data suggest that the incidence of homosexual intercourse in Israeli prisons may currently be rare. The Israeli code of behaviour emphasises 'normal' sexual behaviour and encourages inmates to act accordingly (Einat and Einat 2000). The few homosexual incidents that do occur inside Israeli prisons appear to relate to two situations: (1) extreme demonstration of power or harsh punishment of the disloyal; (2) initiative of a senior homosexual inmate.

Argot once used neutrally to describe homosexual relationships is now used derogatively to express negative sanctioning of such behaviour and/or contempt of disloyal inmates, regardless of their sexual preference or conduct. For example, prisoners who cooperate with the authorities during investigations are termed *'whores'*, and prisoners who submit to other inmates without a fight are termed *'cocksinelles'* (transvestites). Prisoners labelled by one of the humiliating sexual terms have two options: either to fight and defend their honour, thereby improving their social status, or to submit to constant and long-lasting contempt on the part of their fellow inmates.

Although many of the argot expressions in the sexual area have not changed significantly over many decades, their contextual meaning has: a total of 48 expressions (approximately 9.5 per cent) were related to sexual relations and homosexuality. Many of these are highly imaginative and, quite often, borrowed and adopted from everyday language for their argot use. For example, *'wallpaper'*, *'twister'* and *'sandwich'* are used to describe homosexual intercourse, *'scuba diver'* is used to describe oral sex, and *'muffler'* receives a sexual connotation due to its resemblance to the male sex organ. It thus appears that sexual terms in Israeli prison argot are formed in a three-phase process: (a) conventional words and phrases receiving new sexual connotations, (b) adaptation and re-definition of the 'new' words into social settings, and (c) conversion of words into status symbols.

Drugs

Prison inmates naturally seek out ways to compensate themselves for the pains of imprisonment (Kaminski 2003; Einat and Einat 2000); hence, drugs are the most highly valued commodity in the Israeli inmate economic system. Indeed, drugs are so central and dominant in Israeli prison life that it can be fairly stated that they form the backbone of inmate subculture. The high demand for drugs stems from the large financial profit to be gained from their sales, the fact that many inmates are regular drug users, and the tendency of many non-users to seek temporary 'escape' from the stresses and tensions of prison life by means of drugs (Gideon 2003).

Additional explanation for the centrality and importance of drugs in Israeli prisons is founded on the routine activities theory (Felson 1987) and the differential association theory (Sutherland and Cressey 1978: Ch.4). The former assumes that any delinquent act, including drug use, is an 'outcome of a situation where an opportunity to perform a crime occurs ... and one individual or more are motivated to commit it' (Gideon 2003: 12). The latter claims that delinquent behaviour, similar to any type of conduct, is learned by means of interaction with significant others in a communicative process, which includes, among other things, criminal techniques (Akers 1997). Since use of drugs is a normative learned process that functions as a principal criterion for membership in the Israeli prisoners' subculture, it is perceived as a rational act (Becker 1963).

The importance of drugs in Israeli prisons is expressed by a wide variety of argot terms: over one-quarter of the argot terms were related to the topic of drugs (149 out of a total of 503), and these terms can be grouped into seven subcategories: names of drugs, quantity of drugs, ways of use or administration, smuggling methods, craving, drug effects, and the state of the drug market (see appendix). Reinforcing the notion of importance, drugs in Israeli prisons often serve to overrule the dominance of inmate loyalty. A number of inmates reported that they would be ready to betray their friends and the inmate code of conduct for the sake of the drug (see also Crewe, this volume). Some stated that they would even be ready to harm a drug user who returned from leave without bringing back a drug supply. Words such as 'kriz' (withdrawal syndrome), 'atraf' (insanity), 'chocho' (crazy), and 'lezamer' (to inform) can be found in the following citations:

Believe me, all the gang see me as a good guy, as someone who will never betray them or inform on them to the *authorities* [prison staff] ... but sometimes when I get the *kriz* and I want to use drugs, I go really crazy and become *chocho* and then I *have no god* and I'm capable of doing anything, even *lezamer*. The main thing is that they should bring me the *staff* [drug].

One of the best ways to make a *buhta* [fortune] in prison is to be loaded with *grass* [marijuana]. It does not cost a lot of money [for the buyer] and since most inmates *starve* [desperately want] to *refuel* [use and enjoy] themselves with it, it is easy money.

It is all a game, like any other thing in prison. Play the game wisely and you'll win. *Yaeini* [meaning] you will not be *sanjered* [exploited]. You see, all of us are losers, that's why we are in prison. We understood and acknowledged it and learned how not to *fall* [get caught] again, once we are *outside* [free]. Trade wisely with drugs, work *solito* [independently] and succeed.

Miscellaneous

Of all the different factors that influence the development of a unique vocabulary in prison, humour, imagination, and cynicism are the most salient (Cardozo-Freeman 1984; Maurer 1981). Linguistic recreation and humour, which characterise inmate argot, are perceived as ways of coping with the harsh realities of prison life (overcrowding, excessive noise, lack of basic comforts) and achieving in-group cohesiveness (Andersson and Trudgill 1990; Partridge 1970).

Linguistic inventiveness and improvisation are clearly apparent in Israeli inmate argot. For example, the word *'bakbak'* (bed bugs) is used to describe tea leaves due to the widespread presence of bed bugs and their appearance. The parallel between ambushing an inmate and the trap that was set by the wolf in the 'Little Red Riding Hood' story led to the adoption of the term *'kipa-aduma'* for ambush. *Daeeg* (fishing) denotes a system for breaking into houses or cars by insertion of a stick or penetration of a little boy through a window. Accordingly, the burglar is nicknamed the 'fisherman'. In addition, 'Hilton' is the F Wing of one of Israel's largest prisons, and prison cells are 'hen houses'.

Table 11.1 summarises the number of words related to each of the main subject matters characterising the Israeli prison argot. As mentioned before, the number of words reflects, among other things, the significance of the area to inmates' lives.

Table 11.1 Distribution of frequency of argot terms

Subject matter	Number of words	Ratio of words in the subject matter out of all prison argot vocabulary (%)
Violence	71	14.11
Sex	48	9.55
Loyalty	73	14.51
Attitudes towards the custodial staff	29	5.77
Drugs	149	29.62
Miscellaneous	133	26.44
N	503	100

Discussion

The present study focused on the identification of different aspects of prison life and prisoners' subculture through their unique code of behaviour and argot. Systematic serfdom and deprivation of inmates, inability to physically and psychologically escape the pains of imprisonment, and lack of belief in revising their lives peacefully, accelerate the development of a system of norms, values and secret ways of behaving, that assist inmates in their everyday struggle (Sykes 1958). Communication and expression of the inmate code as well as definition of its rules and sanctions are accomplished through argot, the prisoner's own language (Bondesson 1989; Hebdige 1985). This code of conduct is the core of prison subculture (Kaminski 2003; Einat and Einat 2000; Irwin 1985); it provides its members informal ways of gaining power and status, and offers, by behavioural patterns of social interaction, rules, roles, and reinforcement of personal status and autonomy (Sykes and Messinger 1960).

The findings of the present study show that inmate subculture and argot clearly exist in Israeli prisons, and represent meaningful and rational actions on the part of inmates who make decisions subject to existing subcultural constraints. The findings also support the notion that inmates feel little obligation to adhere to codes and norms imposed on them by the prison authorities.

Qualitative analysis of the attention and intensity of the argot expressions reveals the importance and significance attributed to components of the code by the prisoners. The highest level of intensity was found for 'adherence to the inmate code and loyalty to fellow prisoners'. High levels of solidarity and unity characterise the Israeli inmates' subculture. Generally, a consensus exists in the inmates' society in regard to the definitions of normative and deviant and the benefits or sanctions imposed on inmates who support or violate the code of conduct. Violation of the code is compared to a fracture in a dam that endangers its stability; an imposition of a sanction against breaching inmates symbolises its repair. Collaborating with prison personnel and/or snitching on fellow inmates are regarded as the most severe violations of the code of conduct. Newcomers learn, from their first day of incarceration, that disloyalty carries a heavy price. Collaborators and informers are frequently victimised, socially isolated and linguistically stigmatised, and eventually made to act in accordance with their social status and role.

The study found that attention was highest for drugs, as indicated by the many argot terms related to this category.[10] Incarceration symbolises the inmate's loss of society's trust and status of citizenship (Liebling *et al* 1999). Its very existence in addition to the 'everyday pains of imprisonment' provides a significant source of stress for the inmate. Drugs, in this context, may be perceived as a means of reducing stress and a type of compensation and consolation (Napier *et al* 1983).

Violent behaviour and domination are also expressed through argot, and their terms and expressions may have significant effects on prisoners' status. Indeed, in many cases, not only do these terms describe the situation of an individual but they also serve to create it.

The most surprising finding of the present study is that, according to our respondents, homosexual relations, once commonplace in Israeli prisons, may now be relatively rare. Interestingly, however, the terms once used to describe it are now used to humiliate fellow inmates or to describe submissive or negatively sanctioned conduct. As for the relevance of argot terms in this area, it appears that they represent a twisted world of substance compared to the social-lingual norms that are accepted in the general society. Inmates developed black humour, mockery and paradoxical attitudes regarding homosexual relationships in prison. The 'scuba-diver', the 'muffler', the 'swallower' and their like, represent a caricaturist metaphor of conventional gender roles and social norms, while homosexual intercourse in the prison symbolically and perversely reflects prisoners' abuse (rape) by society. The state harms, injures and victimises inmates, and inmates, in return and as a symbol of coolness and masculinity, condemn homosexual conduct in prison and verbally and socially humiliate homosexual inmates and rapists.

Interestingly, the source of many of the negative terms in Israeli prison argot is the Arabic language (see appendix). It would therefore be interesting to examine whether the adoption of words and expressions from a minority language by inmate argot also exists elsewhere: for example, whether negative terms in American prison argot stem from Spanish words.

Notes

1   2,537 security personnel – 65.08%; 471 correctional staff members – 12.08: 884 release committees' employees – 22.63%; and six unassigned – 0.16%. 3,898 in total.

2   Boredom, deprivation of heterosexual relations, deprivation of material possessions, overcrowding and uncertainty and unpredictability (Einat and Einat 2002; Liebling *et al* 1999; Christopher *et al* 1994; Paulus *et al* 1985; Selke 1993; Toch 1992; Sykes 1958).

3   Prison hierarchy; isolation; deprivation of privacy; insults to personal dignity and integrity; etc. (Kaminski 2003; Walker and Padfield 1996; Sykes and Messinger 1960).

4   Initiation procedures and mortifying tests; sexual and/or violence; social isolation victimisation; lack of personal security; etc. (Kaminski 2003; Einat 1996; Irwin 1985; Goffman 1961).

5   It should be stated, however, that most studies were sociologically oriented, thus excluding psychological research or not validated by it (see Liebling *et al* 1999: 284–5).

6   The language criterion was applied to allow for efficient and fluent communication with the interviewers; hence, the exclusion of non-Hebrew-speaking inmates consisting mostly of Arabs and recent immigrants from the former Soviet Union and Ethiopia. Because proficiency in the inmate argot may develop as a function of time (Bondesson 1989), participants were selected from a group that had already served more than three years in prison, regardless of their offence, age, and socio-demographic characteristics.

7   Preference was given to recording rather than taking notes for the following reasons: (1) Taking notes efficiently can distract both researcher and interviewee and disrupt the conversation; (2) It is mentally exhausting to listen closely to everything that is said and take accurate notes; (3) It is important to keep data collection and analysis separate. Conclusions should not be drawn until all of the data are in, and taking notes by hand during the interview requires the researcher to make judgements about what is important and what is not during the interview; (4) Like any other research effort, it is desirable to keep the original data complete and intact so that the researcher and other interested researchers can refer to it if necessary (Doyle 2001).

8   2.6 square metres per inmate, per cell (Middle East Watch Report 1991).

9   Homosexual behaviour in prison is generally expressed in three major ways: (1) Consensual sexual relations – mutual willingness to execute homosexual relationships (Genders and Player 1989); (2) Coerced sexual relations – combination of sexual satisfaction and control. The assaulter demonstrates his superiority and power as well as the victim's weakness through coercion of sexual relations (Hawkins and Alpert 1989); (3) Sex for hire – having sexual relations for money and/or other benefits (i.e. drugs, protection, goods, etc.).

10   Note, however, that this may stem from the need for a large vocabulary to accommodate the wide variety of drugs and the need for terms to describe their transfer, sale, and so forth.

References

Akers, R.L. (1997) *Criminogenic Theories: Introduction and Evaluation*. Los Angeles: Roxbury Publishing Company.

Andersson, L. and Trudgill, P. (1990) *Bad Language*. Oxford: Blackwell Publishing.

Balvig, F. (1998) *The Snow-White Image: The Hidden Reality of Crime in Switzerland*. Oslo: Norwegian University Press.

Becker, H.S. (1963) *Outsiders: Studies in the Sociology of Deviance*. New York: Free Press.

Bondesson, U. (1989) *Prisoners in Prison Societies*. New Brunswick, NJ: Transaction Publishing.

Briggs, C.L. (1986) *Learning How to Ask: A Sociolinguistic Appraisal of the Role of the Interview in Social Science Research*. Cambridge: Cambridge University Press.

Cardozo-Freeman, I. (1984) *The Joint: Language and Culture in a Maximum Security Prison*. Springfield, IL: Charles Thomas Publishing.

Christopher, H., Winfree, L.T. and Mays, G.L. (1994) 'Processing inmate disciplinary infractions in a federal correctional institution: legal and extralegal correlates of prison-based decisions', *The Prison Journal*, 74 (1), 5–31.

Clemmer, D. (1940) *The Prison Community*. New York: Rinehart Publishing.

Cordilia, A. (1983) *The Making of an Inmate*. Cambridge: MAL Schenkman Publishing.

Doyle, J.K. (2001) 'Introduction to interviewing techniques', in D.W. Woods (ed) *Handbook For IQP Advisors and Students*. Massauchusetts: Worcester Polytechnic Institute.

Einat, T. (1996) *Argot as One of the Main Characteristics of Israeli Prison Subculture*. Jerusalem: The Hebrew University of Jerusalem.

Einat, T. (2003) 'Criminal fine enforcement in Israel: Administration, policy, evaluation and recommendations', *Punishment & Society*, 6 (2), 175–194.

Einat, T. and Einat, H. (2000) 'Inmate argot as an expression of prison subculture: The Israeli case', *The Prison Journal*, 80 (3), 309–325.

Encinas, G.L. (2001) *Prison Argot: A Sociolinguistic and Lexicographic Study*. Laham, NY and Oxford: University Press of America.

Farrington, D.P. (1994) *Psychological Explanation of Crime*. Aldershot: Dartmouth Publishing.

Feld, B.C. (1977) *Neutralizing Inmate Violence: Juvenile Offenders in Institutions*. Cambridge, MA: Ballinger Publishing Company.

Felson, M. (1987) 'Routine activities and crime prevention in the developing metropolis'. *Criminology*, 25, 911–931.

Fisher, S. (1990) *On the Move: The Psychology of Change and Transition*. Chichester: John Wiley.

Genders, E. and Player, E. (1989) *Race Relations in Prison*. Oxford: Clarendon Press.

Gideon, L. (2003) *Detoxification and Rehabilitation in Prison and Community Support Systems: Their Contribution in Reducing Recidivism and Drug Use Among Released Prisoners.* Jerusalem: The Hebrew University of Jerusalem.

Goffman, E. (1961) *Asylums.* Garden City, NY: Doubleday Publishing.

Goodstein, L. and Wright, K. (1989) 'Correctional environments', in L. Goodstein and D. Mackenzie (eds) *The American Prison: Issues in Research and Policy.* New York: Plenum Press.

Hawkins, R. and Alpert, P.G. (1989) *American Prison Systems.* Englewood Cliffs, NJ: Prentice Hall.

Hebdige, D. (1985) *Subculture: The Meaning of Style.* London: Methuen.

Irwin, J. (1970) *The Felon.* Englewood Cliffs, NJ: Prentice Hall.

Irwin, J. (1980) *Prisons in Turmoil.* Boston, MA: Little, Brown.

Irwin, J. (1985) *The Jail.* Berkeley, CA: University of California Press.

Irwin, J. and Cressey, D. (1977) 'Thieves, convicts, and the inmate culture', *Social Problems*, 10, 142–155.

Israel Prison Service (2003) 'Strategic mission statement', *Annual Report.* Jerusalem: Maor Wallach.

Johnson, E.H. (1987) *Handbook on Crime and Delinquency Prevention.* New York: Greenwood Press.

Johnson, R. and Toch, H. (2000) 'Living in prison', in R. Johnson and H. Toch (eds) *Crime and Punishment: Inside Views.* Los Angeles, CA: Roxbury Publishing Company.

Jones, B.L. (1988) *Legal Protection of Civil Liberties.* London: Butterworth Publishing.

Kalinich, D.B. (1980) *The Inmate Economy.* Lexington, MA: D.C. Heath.

Kaminski, M. (2003) 'Games prisoners play: Allocation of social roles in a total institution', *Rationality and Society*, 15 (2), 188–217.

Krippendorff, K. (1980) *Content Analysis: An Introduction to its Methodology.* Beverly Hills, CA: Sage Publishing.

Liebling, A., Muir, G., Rose, G. and Bottoms, A.E. (1999) *Incentives and Earned Priviledges in Prison.* Home Office Research Findings, 87.

Lofland, J. (1971) *Analyzing Social Settings: A Guide to Qualitative Observation and Analysis.* Belmont, CA: Wadsworth.

Maruna, S. (2001) *Making Good: How Ex-Convicts Reform and Rebuild Their Lives.* Washington, DC: American Psychological Association.

Maurer, D. (1955) 'Whiz mob?', *American Dialect Society*, 24, 313–329.

Maurer, D. (1981) *Language of the Underworld.* Lexington, KY: The University Press.

Maykut, P. and Morehouse, R. (1994) *Beginning Qualitative Research: A Philosophic and Practical Guide.* Washington, DC: Falmer Press.

Middle East Watch Report (1991) *Prison Conditions in Israel and the Occupied Territories.* New York: Human Rights Watch Publications.

Napier, T.L., Bachtal, D.C. and Carter, M.V. (1983) 'Factors associated with illegal drug use in rural Georgia', *Journal of Drug Education*, 13, 119–140.

Nielson, A. and Scrapitti, T. (1995) 'Argot use in therapeutic community', *Deviant Behaviour*, 16 (3), 127–129.

Partridge, E. (1970) *Slang Today and Yesterday*. London: Routledge, Kegan and Paul.

Paulus, P., McCain, G. and Cox, V. (1984) 'The effects of crowding in prison and jails', in D. Farrington and J. Gunn (eds) *Reactions to Crime: The Public, the Police, Courts, and Prisons*. New York: John Wiley.

Ross, J.I. and Richards, S.C. (2002) *Behind Bars: Surviving Prison*. Indianapolis: Alpha.

Rubin, H.J. and Rubin, I.S. (1995) *Qualitative Interviewing: The Art of Learning Data*. Thousand Oaks, CA: Sage Publications.

Selke, W.L. (1993) *Prison in Crisis*. Bloomington, IN: University Indiana Press.

Silvermann, D. (1993) *Interpreting Qualitative Data: Methods for Analyzing Talk, Text and Introduction*. London: Sage.

Stake, R.E. (1995) *The Art of Case Study Research*. Thousand Oaks, CA: Sage Publications.

Strauss, A. and Corbin, J. (1990) *Basic of Qualitative Research: Grounded Theory Procedures and Techniques*. Newbury Park, CA: Sage.

Suchman, L. and Jordan, B. (1990) 'International troubles in face-to-face survey interviews', *Journal of American Statistical Association*, 85, 232–241.

Sutherland, E.H. and Cressey, D.R. (1978) *Criminology*, 10th edition. Philadelphia, PA: J.B. Lippincott.

Sykes, M.G. (1958) *The Society of Captives*. Princeton, NJ: Princeton University Press.

Sykes, M.G. and Messinger, S.L. (1960) 'The inmate social code and its functions', *Social Science Research Council*, 15, 401–405.

Sykes, M.G. and Messinger, S. (1977) 'The inmate social system', in R.G. Leger and J.R. Stratton (eds) *The Sociology of Corrections*. New York: John Wiley and Sons.

Timor, U. (1998) 'Constructing a rehabilitative reality in special religious wards in Israeli prisons', *International Journal of Offender Therapy and Comparative Criminology*, 42 (4), 340–359.

Tittle, C.R. and Tittle, D. (1965) 'Structural handicaps to therapeutic participation: A case study', *Social Problems*, 13, 81–94.

Toch, H. (1992) *Mosaic of Despair*. Washington, DC: American Psychological Association.

Toch, H. and Johnson, R. (1982) *The Pains of Imprisonment*. Beverly Hills, CA: Sage.

Walker, N. and Padfield, N. (1996) *Sentencing: Theory, Law and Practice*. London, Dublin and Edinburgh: Butterworths.

Wozner, Y. (1985a) 'Institution as community', *Child and Youth Services*, 7 (3–4), 71–89.

Wozner, Y. (1985b) *Change of Behavior*. Tel-Aviv: Papirus.

Appendix

List of major terms in Israeli prison argot

Phonetic term	Translation	Meaning

Prisoner status (informers, inmate rank)

Informers

Awacs	Intelligence	Airplane informer
Antenna	Antenna	Stool pigeon
Wiseh	Dirty (Arabic)	Informer
Muzikai	Musician	Not to be relied upon
Patsooa	Invalid	Collaborator

Inmate rank

Ganoov	Stolen	Fool
Cochav	Star	Joker/clown
Klavim	Dogs	Inmates who obey the boss
Melech hata	King of the castle	Prison leader
Na`alayim	Shoes	Submissive inmate
Naknik	Sausage	An inmate who does not act by the inmate code
Ha`yalim	Soldiers	Inmates who obey the boss
Soos	Horse	Stupid
Shafan	Rabbit	Coward

Drugs

Gushim	Blocks	Ground grains of heroin
Glickstein	Name of an Israeli tennis player	Heroin (because of the 'white sport' and the colour of heroin
Duvdevan	Cherry	Opium
Lidfok	To knock	To inject drug
Galgalim	Wheels	Ball-shaped portions of hashish
Harman	Horny	Wants to use drugs
Telephone	Telephone	A tool to smoke hashish
Mizvada	Suitcase	An inmate who delivers drugs in his rectum
Efronot parsiim	Persian pencils	Persian cocaine
Pagaz	Shell (artillery)	Cigar filled with tobacco and hashish
Tarnegolim	Roosters	Drug portions wrapped for insertion in rectum
Shokolad	Chocolate	Hashish

Phonetic term	Translation	Meaning
Shvilim	Paths	Drugs arranged in rows
Tractor	Tractor	Drug addict
Narkis	Narcissus	Drug addict
Ekdah	Pistol	Injector
Hatsi herayon	Half pregnant	Half-way through the drug treatment process
Mitahat la'niar	Under the paper	Began taking drugs again
Metudlak	Fuelled	Stoned
Etsba	Finger	A piece of hashish
Nekevot	Female	Marijuana seeds
Seret	A movie	Stoned
Seret ra	Bad movie	Overdose
Shfecha	Tiredness	Feelings of sleepiness after taking drugs
Yeshiva	Sitting	The drug smoking ceremony

Sexual relations in prison

Exhauster	Muffler	Homosexual
Zonda	Intragastric tube	Homosexual rape
Tapet	Wallpaper	Homosexual relations
Sandwich	Sandwich	Homosexual intercourse
Tsolelim	Deep-sea diver	Oral sex
Shagrir	Ambassador	Homosexual

Violence

Kipa aduma	Little Red Riding Hood	Ambush
Madroob	Crazy (Arabic)	A violent prisoner
Picasso	Picasso	Face wound
Puntcher	Flat tyre	A stabbing
Krav hatoolim	Cat fight	Lots of noise without violence
Rien-rach	Zipper	Cuts
Intifada	Uprising (Arabic)	To terrorise
Kussa	Courgette (Arabic)	To cut up
Hanjar	Knife (Arabic)	Knife

Nicknames for prison staff

Shitonot	Authorities	Prison staff
Caftor	Button	Prison guard
Lool	Hen house	Prison cell

Phonetic term	Translation	Meaning
Columbia	Columbia (the country)	Prison full of drugs
Cachol meza'azea	Shocking blue	Patrol car
Malon	Hotel	Prison
Tsipor	Bird	Prison guard who cooperates with inmates
Abu-antar	Show-off (Arabic)	Prison staff
Wisach	Contaminated (Arabic)	Prison staff
Sharshuchot	Prostitutes (Arabic)	Prison staff

Miscellaneous

Indian	Red Indians	Arabs
Aron	Cupboard	Rifle
Yatsa letayel	Went for a walk	Was kidnapped
Poel	Worker	Drug dealer
Kufsa	Box	Brain
Shod be-tseva	Colourful robbery	Robbery with casualties
Shalach lo zer	Sent him a bouquet	Liquidated
Brara	Inferior fruit (Arabic)	The bottom of the criminal world
Halaka	Smooth	An impossible situation where an inmate tries to please everyone

Chapter 12

Forms of violence and regimes in prison: report of research in Belgian prisons

Sonja Snacken

This empirical study of violence in prisons in Belgium was commissioned by the Director-General of the Prison Administration due to fears that liberalisation of prison regimes was increasing the level of prisoner-on-prisoner violence, including rumours from some Belgian prison directors that certain prisoners no longer dared to participate in communal activities. In its report to the Belgian government following its second visit to Belgium in 1997, the Committee for the Prevention of Torture (CPT) also referred to inter-prisoner violence and resulting feelings of insecurity by prisoners in one of the visited prisons. Coupled with the question about the level of violence in Belgian prisons was the policy-related question about the necessity or desirability of reintroducing the special security units, which had known a turbulent history in Belgium and were closed in 1996 following judicial action (Snacken, 2001: 71; *infra* 5.7). The research was carried out by five researchers and two supervisors of the criminology departments of the two Free Universities of Brussels VUB (Flemish) and ULB (French) over a two-year period (1999–2000) (see Snacken *et al* 2000).[1]

Theoretical framework: explanations of violence in prisons

Two major models have emerged in the criminological literature to explain control problems and conflicts in prisons: the *deprivation model* (1950s–1960s) and the *importation model* (1970s–1980s). The deprivation model focused on the characteristics of prisons as total institutions and places of deprivation and scarcity (Goffman 1961; Sykes 1958), leading to coping mechanisms by prisoners that lie on a continuum between 'individualistic' ('lonely individuals': Mathiesen, 1965: 12) and the 'collectivistic' approaches (Sykes 1958: 107). The deprivations of prison life increase the risk of individual opposition or retreatism, self-harm and suicide, but also raise the potential for inmate solidarity and the development of an inmate subculture, riots and – coupled to long-term detention – institutionalism. The importation model, however, stresses that many aspects of inmate culture and behaviour are not peculiar to the prison but are imported from outside, reflecting demographic, social or political changes in society (Irwin and Cressey 1962; Irwin 1980; Jacobs 1977, 1983). Gang structures and conflicts, racial or political conflicts outside were hence imported into the prison. Subsequent research soon proved that aspects of both models were empirically detectable, thus suggesting an integration of the two models (Thomas 1977).

In the penological literature of the 1980s–1990s, violence in prisons is studied from a variety of perspectives, influenced by the increased attention to prisoners' rights and staff issues (see Jacobs 1977, and the 'post-authoritarian' prison), the renewed policy discussions on 'dangerous' prisoners, the analysis of major riots and escapes (e.g. Woolf Report, 1991), the work and standards of CPT on torture and inhuman and degrading treatment of detainees (Evans and Morgan 1999), and the emergence of the concepts of 'dynamic security' and 'dialectic of control' (Sparks *et al* 1996). This literature emphasises the importance of *prison regimes* and the interactions between *prisoners and staff*.

Policy discussions on tackling 'difficult' or 'dangerous' prisoner behaviour centre on the relative influence of personal characteristics versus the prison context. A survey carried out for the Council of Europe (Snacken 1997) led me to conclude that there are apparently two major policy tendencies in tackling the problem of violent prisoners:

1 Policies based on the assumption that problematic behaviour in prison is linked to individuals with certain problematic characteristics. This approach leads to the elaboration of more or less sophisticated prediction and classification methods, categorisation of prisoners and specific control techniques for 'high-risk', 'dangerous' or 'disruptive' prisoners (segregation, special security units, specific programmes, etc.).

2 Policies based primarily on the prevention of the emergence of problems in the general prison population through the provision of the same programmes and activities to all prisoners and the tackling of individual problems on an individual basis.

With regard to the latter approach, Justice Woolf's report (1991) analysing the origins of the major riot in Manchester's Strangeways prison has been influential in stressing the risks of overemphasising 'security' to the detriment of 'control' and 'justice'. However, I prefer Morgan's (1992) concept of equal priority and balance between 'custody, order, justice and care'. The distinction between security or custody and control or order is important from an analytical and empirical point of view. While 'security' or 'custody' refer to prison systems' duty to keep prisoners out of society as long as deemed necessary, 'control' or 'order' refer to prison systems' duty to ensure a safe and orderly execution of the imprisonment inside the prison, both for inmates and prison staff. The distinction between 'security' and 'custody', and between 'control' and 'order' is equally important, for it refers to the basic difference between the aim (custody and order) and *one* of the techniques to achieve that aim (security to achieve custody, control to achieve order). Another major distinction is made between *'passive security'*, resulting from the architecture, electronic devices, etc., and the *'dynamic security'* of high-quality staff–inmate contacts, relationships and communication, without which passive security cannot succeed (Marshall 1997).

Violence in prison is then seen as a problem of order. Order has been defined as 'any long-standing pattern of social relations, characterised by a minimum of respect for persons, in which the expectations that participants have of one another are commonly met, though not necessarily without contestation' (Sparks *et al* 1996: 119). Order can also, in part, be defined negatively as 'the absence of violence, overt conflict or the imminent threat of the chaotic breakdown of social routines' (ibid.). Control, on the other hand, refers to the 'use of routines and a variety of formal and informal practices – especially, but not only, sanctions – which assist in the maintenance of order, whether or not they are recognized as doing so' (ibid.).

How is order then to be obtained? Concepts such as Giddens' (1984) *'social agent'* or Debuyst's (1990) *'acteur social'* are important in understanding the development of the penological concepts *'dynamic security'* and *'dialectic of control'*. Prisoners are seen as *social agents*, who act upon their situation and respond to it not automatically but strategically (Sparks *et al* 1996: 79–84; Snacken 1990). The appearance of 'total power' by staff is diminished by the realities of the guard–inmate ratio (staff outnumbered by prisoners) and staff members' necessary reliance on prisoners' cooperation for the performance of routine tasks. Guards encounter a series of pressures to achieve some tolerable *modus vivendi* with prisoners through compromise. Order in prison then becomes a *'negotiated order'* (Sparks *et al* 1996: 42). Compromises may, however, constitute a slippery slope, where guards will at times have difficulty in maintaining even a semblance of control. Sykes (1958) viewed the recurrence of crisis and equilibrium in prison as the result of mounting pressures for staff to snatch back power. Others see it as a consequence of the fundamentally contradictory character of social relations in prison (Scraton *et al* 1991). Sparks and colleagues, however, object to the assumption of the periodic recurrence of the breakdown in order (1996: 44). Indeed, while some countries have known violent conflicts to reach catastrophic proportions (e.g., Attica in the US in 1972; Strangeways in the UK in 1990), others have gone for decades without anything approaching such an event, and not necessarily because their prisons are any more coercive (Sparks *et al* 1996: 36).

Control problems can take many forms and consist of unique, momentary crises or more endemic problems, such as interpersonal violence (from individual outbursts not necessarily seen as serious to conflicts between groups), the informal economy (which may lead to conflicts, debts and violent extortion) and different forms of protest, disobedience and abuse (which can be a means to assert one's selfhood and to negotiate the power relations within the prison) (Sparks *et al* 1996: 119–23). The strategies of staff to cope with such control problems present a range of possible modes of influence and will vary between prison systems and between prisons within one system, linked to the ethos, tradition or climate of a particular prison. New prisoners and staff members usually adapt to this local culture of interaction (ibid.: 103–7).

Order therefore does not refer to a situation of quietness, absence of antagonism or offending behaviour, but their containment into manageable forms (Sparks *et al* 1996: 181). It is increasingly acknowledged that care and justice are not only duties in themselves, but are also fundamental conditions to attain 'order' in prison. 'Care' refers to the provision of meaningful activities, health care, contacts, choices, etc., necessary to maintain or foster the physical and mental well-being of the prisoners. An active regime, with attractive incentives and adapted to local circumstances (flexibility), is an integral part of 'dynamic security' (Marshall 1997). 'Justice' in prison relates to fair treatment and consistent outcomes, effective grievance procedures, motivation and explanation of decisions by staff. The emphasis on justice also leads to the recognition that prisoners' goods and services are not to be regarded solely as privileges, awarded or removed by discretion, but that prisons must pay attention to the 'legitimate expectations' that prisoners have of their treatment (Woolf 1991: para. 12.129). A humane regime and fair procedures will reinforce the always fragile legitimacy of the prison for prisoners and will influence staff–inmate relations, local culture and institutional climate (Sparks *et al* 1996: 304).

The duties of custody, order, care and justice are thus equally important and prisons must strive to strike a balance between all four, which will, however, be a difficult task. The importance of 'dialectic of control' has also been recognised in policy documents, stating that violence in prisons cannot be solely understood, or limited to, a few violent persons, but that such behaviour must be seen as the result of interaction between persons and situations:

> Difficult prison behaviour is a function of many things in addition to the prisoner's own character, and it is generally recognised in the prison service that a man who presents intractable control problems in one establishment may be little or no trouble in another.
>
> (Control Review Committee 1984: 44)

This literature makes it quite clear that violence must be analysed in relation to the prison context (cf. deprivation model), while taking into consideration the personal characteristics of the prisoners and the broader social context (cf. importation model). Sparks and colleagues (1996), however, show that even risk factors such as age, offence (e.g. sexual offences) and ethnicity must still be seen in interaction with prison regimes and attitudes of prison staff. A more flexible, liberal regime reduces in principle the risks of institutionalism and resistance against the prison system or prison staff (individual aggression or riot). On the other hand, it increases the freedom of movement of prisoners inside the prison, which may increase feelings of (objective or subjective) insecurity with vulnerable prisoners. The risk of violence can be reduced by the fear of losing the advantages of a more liberal regime. This then presupposes a sufficiently high discovery rate, and the certainty that violent behaviour will be sanctioned by prison staff.

The Belgian situation

Belgian prisons vary to a great extent in several respects. As regards architecture, most prisons were built in the 19th century for a cellular regime; only a few were built recently and allow for more communal activities. Living conditions vary, with modern or renovated parts versus unrenovated parts. Most remand prisons suffer severe overcrowding, while prisons for the execution of sentences can impose waiting lists for the transfer of prisoners. The availability of work and activities will depend on local differences concerning the availability of external services and initiatives taken by local prison directors.

These local differences are also the result of the fact that the General Prison Regulations, laid down in a Royal Decree in 1965 and complemented by circular letters, allow a large discretionary power to the local directors and do not provide any formal rights for prisoners (with the exception of the freedom of religion and access to a lawyer). The prison system hence functions on the basis of privileges and sanctions. At the same time, for the last 20 years, a criminology degree was required for prison directors coming from outside the prison service, resulting in a whole generation of academically trained prison directors. This requirement has recently been widened to other academic trainings.

Belgium experienced, as many neighbouring countries did, a series of riots in the 1970s. This stimulated attention to the deprivations of imprisonment. From 1975 onwards a humanisation of prison regime was advocated and contacts for prisoners with the outside world were fostered. The concept of regional classification of prisoners emerged, to secure detention assignments as close as possible to the prisoners' social relations. The new federal structure of the country enhanced responsibilities and access of external community agencies inside the prisons.

These tendencies towards a more active regime were, however, countered by the growing overcrowding since 1983. As a result, 'regime' in many remand prisons was limited to one or two hours outdoor exercise and TV-watching in cell, and even the 'better' regimes in prisons were under pressure. Overcrowding led to more tensions for prisoners and staff alike, and ensuring a dynamic security and good relations with the prisoners became increasingly difficult. The regional classification was hampered by continuous transfers due to the overcrowding that resulted from the increase of long prison terms for violent, sexual and drug offences. Although offenders sentenced for a violent offence do not necessarily exhibit violent behaviour in prison (often on the contrary: cf. life-sentence prisoners), some may have limited communication abilities and may exhibit problematic behaviour in prison. An increasing length of imprisonment to be served and a growing uncertainty concerning early release is also known to constitute an important stress factor. The presence of illegal drugs in prisons may also entail a higher risk of violence, linked to the informal economy which results from drug trafficking.

The number of 'foreign' prisoners also increased in the same period, and these now represent 40 per cent of the prison population. The term 'foreign' here includes very different groups: second- or third-generation immigrants, illegal aliens, organised international drugs smugglers, trans-border criminals, etc. The population of 'foreigners' can also be subject to racist reactions, or create more problems themselves. Again, attitudes of prison staff are important, taking into account some racist tendencies in outside society.

Additional changes in the wider society also impacted on the prison system. In 1996, the Dutroux child sex scandal shocked the whole society, attacked the legitimacy of police and judiciary, increased the attention for victims of crimes and led to more repressive attitudes and measures, in particular towards sexual offenders. Parole legislation was reformed accordingly in 1998. The post-Dutroux climate may also induce prisoners to think that the victimisation of convicted sex offenders in the prison is condoned by public opinion, and may even influence staff attitudes towards such behaviour. The specialisation of several psychosocial services in prisons for expert advice on sexual offenders' parole possibilities has also increased the concentration and visibility of this population, their crime being thus more easily known by other prisoners.

Finally, in 2001, a draft Prison Act was submitted to Parliament, elaborating for the first time in Belgium a legal framework for the execution of imprisonment and reinforcing prisoners' rights. A first version of this Draft had been debated with prison staff (the Draft eventually became Act on January 12, 2005).

When we thus compared the Belgian situation with the international literature, it was obvious that several ingredients were present which could entail a higher risk of violence in prisons:

1 A liberalisation of some regime aspects, which probably reduce the risk of collective resistance or riots, and which may increase the risk of violence between prisoners due to the greater freedom of movement, but which may also have a preventive effect.

2 A changed profile of the prison population, with more risk groups staying for longer terms.

3 A changed social and political climate, with less tolerance towards some of these groups.

4 More uncertainty for prison staff, with more (and maybe more difficult) prisoners, more activities, higher expectations of their professionalism, and draft legislation aiming to ensure more rights for prisoners, which would reduce, in the future, the privileges they can decide upon.

None of these aspects had previously been researched in Belgium in relation to prison violence.

Research design

While the original concern of the Prison Administration was the possible link between liberalisation of regimes and inter-prisoner violence, we felt this to be too narrow, covering only part of the relationship between prison regimes and prison violence, and hence running the risk of partial and erroneous conclusions. Some measures may reduce the risk of inter-prisoner violence but enhance the risk of other forms of violence. Our proposal to broaden the scope of the research to all forms of violence and different types of regimes was accepted.

Within the framework of the 'dialectic of control', we decided not to start from a definition of violence, but to ask the actors in the field themselves what they considered to be violence. We assumed that the interactions within this dialectic would be determined by their *subjective* feelings and evaluations of certain behaviours or characteristics as violent ('what is experienced as real will be real in its consequences').

This inductive method proved valuable during the research. On the one hand, it led to the emergence of six forms of violence in prisons:

1 aggression by prisoners on staff
2 aggression by staff on prisoners
3 collective forms of prisoners' resistance
4 auto-aggressive forms by prisoners
5 violence between prisoners
6 institutional violence.

On the other hand, it also showed that similar behaviour was *defined differently* by staff and prisoners: verbal aggression was mentioned mainly by staff, institutional violence only by prisoners.

The topic of prison violence had never been researched in Belgium inside prisons before, and there is no central registration of violent incidents, with the exception of prisoner suicides. The research was hence carried out through a combination of quantitative and qualitative methods. During the first year, four prisons were selected to study the relation between prison violence and prison regimes:

1 Prison A was a large remand prison with an average population of 550 prisoners; around 250 prison officers, many of whom were new recruits who had a high turnover rate. There was no unit system (officers did not work in fixed units). The prison was officially classified as French speaking, but prisoners represented more than 60 different nationalities. The prison included a psychiatric unit.

2 Prison B was a large remand prison with an average population of 550 prisoners. Like prison A, many of the 300 officers were new recruits, and presented a large turnover. Guards had worked in a unit system since 1992. The prison was officially classified as Dutch speaking, but again prisoners represented more than 60 different nationalities.

3 Prison C was a small prison with an average population of 125 prisoners and around 100 guards who worked in a mixed unit system, which meant that each unit worked with one experienced guard. There was a small section for remand prisoners (10 per cent), but the prison was used mainly for the implementation of long sentences (more than five years), and included disciplinary transfers from other prisons. The prison was officially classified as Dutch speaking, which broadly reflected reality.

4 Prison D was a recently built large prison for implementation of long-term sentences, with an average population of 380 prisoners; there were around 250 guards, of which three-quarters were new recruits when the prison opened. There was no unit system; the prison was officially classified as French speaking, which broadly reflected reality.

Each of the four researchers involved in our project was assigned one prison. Integration in the prison was pursued through constant presence over a period of three months, leading to observations of daily routines, interactions, conflicts and their resolutions, outdoor exercise, and activities in the cell areas, the workplaces, during daytime and nights, and on weekdays and weekends. In order to avoid resistance or defensive reactions, the topic of violence in prison was presented within the larger framework of interpersonal relations in prison. Informal conversations with prisoners, guards, directors, psychosocial services, chaplains, etc., led to a better understanding of the local climate, ethos, culture, problems and solutions. Both formal incidents (overt conflicts and breaches) and informal problems (hidden tensions) were traced. On the basis of this first period, semi-structured interviews were then conducted over the following three months, totalling 187 interviews, each taking on average one hour to one hour and a half. A minimum of 20 prisoner interviews and 20 guard interviews was set for each prison, attempting to cover a variety of characteristics (professional experience, prison regime, job assignment for guards; age, nationality, offence, prison regime, prison experience for prisoners). Moreover, all disciplinary reports were analysed over a period of six months, totalling 3,012 reports, with special attention given to violent incidents and the use of disciplinary isolation. Preliminary results and conclusions were drawn concerning the relation between the varying prison regimes and the six forms of violence. Certain categories of prisoners or problems were also discussed: sexual offenders, juveniles, foreigners and drugs in prisons.

Finally, feedback of the results was organised in each prison studied, providing all levels of participants with a summary of the findings and asking them for advice, suggestions or critique. Reactions were collected either individually or through collective sessions.

Each of the methods and sources used had its advantages and limitations. Disciplinary reports only give an official view of the problems in each institution. Their reliability depends much on the topic studied. The observations and interviews make it clear that nearly all incidents of physical violence by prisoners on staff are registered in all prisons, as are attempted suicides. However, violence by staff on prisoners obviously is never mentioned in disciplinary reports, which cover only prisoners. For inter-prisoner violence, registration will depend on the visibility of the act, the presence or awareness of staff, and their reaction towards the incidents. Incidents during activities or outdoor exercise hence will be more easily registered than hidden forms of (sexual) violence committed in cell. The combination of methods used has proved to be important in understanding the exact meaning, not only of the quantitative results, but of prison reality in each of the institutions studied.

For each of the forms of violence studied, we will first look at the level of violence found and then at the factors influencing this violence, focusing more particularly on the prison regimes (prison context) and the personal characteristics of prisoners and staff (interpersonal context).

Violence by prisoners on staff

Level of physical violence by prisoners on staff

The quantitative analysis of the disciplinary reports indicates that the level of physical violence by prisoners on staff is rather low: between

1 per cent and 4 per cent of the reports in six of the eight prisons. The highest absolute numbers are, not surprisingly, found in the two largest prisons A (550 prisoners, eighteen incidents) and B (550 prisoners, fourteen incidents).

The majority of these incidents were not very serious: throwing a small object (e.g. table-tennis ball, thermometer), some pushing and pulling. Only fourteen out of the total 77 registered violent incidents entailed an intended aggression which could have resulted in serious injury (throwing a chair, attempt at stabbing). We assume these figures depict reality, as our observations suggested that all incidents of physical violence against staff were reported and sanctioned in all prisons.

Physical violence against staff is usually punished with disciplinary isolation between a minimum of one and a maximum of nine days. Sanctioning policy differs in the different prisons: while physical violence against staff always leads to the maximum penalty of nine days of isolation in a disciplinary cell in the remand prisons A and B, this maximum is seldom imposed in prison C, where the directors show greater tolerance towards the problems and irritations suffered by long-term prisoners.

Level of verbal aggression by prisoners on staff

The quantitative analysis shows that verbal aggression is more frequent than physical aggression and was to be found in a quarter to a third of the reports. Swearing, insults and threats are often labelled as 'psychological aggression' by staff in the interviews. Staff mentioned this form of violence more often than physical aggression as the origin of stress and feelings of insecurity. Verbal aggression by prisoners may, moreover, lead to escalating conflicts with staff, resulting in physical violence by either party.

Prisoners, however, tend to disregard this form of aggression and define it merely as 'street language'. The qualitative study shows that existing relations between prisoners and staff in the prison are very important in determining the reaction towards verbal aggression. Registration of this form of aggression hence appeared to depend more on the *'reporting culture'* of different prisons or sections than on the objective frequency of this behaviour. The lower number of reports in prison C (16 per cent) compared to prison A (31 per cent) again expressed a greater tolerance towards such behaviour, which is also found in the sanctioning policy. In C prisoners received a warning, demand for apology or loss of certain privileges for a few days, as opposed to disciplinary isolation in A.

Factors influencing physical and verbal aggression by prisoners on staff

Prison regimes

Prisons A, B and D have different sections with different regimes for prisoners who work and for those who do not: the first category also has more activities (education, leisure) and hence more freedom of movement. The frequency of violent incidents is systematically higher in the disciplinary sections and in the sections without work and with few activities. The lower frequency of incidents in the sections for 'workers' could be explained by the fact that interactions between staff and prisoners are based more on communication and dialogue; the fact that work and activities limit the pains of imprisonment; the risk for prisoners to be sent back to the lesser regime in case of trouble; the positive selection of 'calm' prisoners for the work sections; and the fact that activities foster the interpersonal relations between staff and prisoners.

Violent incidents by prisoners on staff in the disciplinary or security isolation sections occur during transfer from normal location to these cells: prisoners resist the isolation, kick out or throw objects. Other critical moments are disciplinary decisions, refusal or withdrawal of privileges (we reiterate that prisoners have almost no formal rights), and the opening or closing of cells. For mentally ill offenders, the uncertainty relating to the indeterminate sanction, the absence of adequate psychiatric treatment, and the lack of transparency of the decision-making concerning release leads either to institutionalism or to resistance. For sentenced prisoners, the uncertainties relating to the new parole legislation increase tensions. Reactions may then focus on the messenger or the person most present in daily prison life: the guard.

Characteristics of prisoners and guards

The quantitative analysis indicates that violence occurs more between certain prisoners and guards than with others. In prison A, most violent incidents happen at the psychiatric unit, although this group of prisoners represents only 14 per cent of the population. In prison C, violent incidents are also committed by individual prisoners who, although declared 'responsible', showed psychiatric problems.

The qualitative research interestingly shows that for many prisoners and guards alike, the risk to a guard being subject to aggression by a prisoner is dependent on his own attitude and behaviour towards

317

prisoners. For example, in prison A, one particular guard known for his aggressive behaviour has been assaulted three times by prisoners. In prisons A, B and D, respondents tell stories of guards reversing roles when reporting incidents: certain guards are known to commit violent acts against prisoners, but claim to have been the victim of a prior aggression by the prisoner.

Within this interpersonal context, the balance struck between security, order, care and justice appears highly relevant for both prisoners and guards. Questioned about what constitutes 'a good guard', prisoners emphasise mainly reliability and fairness: to hold ones promises, to explain ones refusals, to apply consistency and equality in the granting or refusals of requests, to respect the prisoner. This meant that 'justice' ranks high in the subjective evaluation by prisoners of the individual guards. However, flexibility and openness to individual needs are also felt as important ('care'). In general, older guards are more appreciated than younger guards, as their experience allows them a more flexible and relaxed attitude.

Guards appear particularly aware of the permanent conflicts which can arise between security and care, and of the difficulty in finding the right balance between these two at the right moment. In the more active regimes, guards have an even larger discretionary power (more privileges). In the absence of or delay in adequate training in Belgium, every individual staff member has to find his own balance and solutions.

Prisons A and D have a large number of young, inexperienced guards (50 per cent have less than two years' work experience), who are sent to the cell area without much training or support. Their feelings of uncertainty and insecurity lead either to a strict and restrictive attitude, without any flexibility in different circumstances, or to the other extreme of too much reliance on a social and flexible interaction.

Many older guards, however, refer nostalgically to 'the good old times, when guards decided and prisoners had to obey'. Questioned more deeply about the advantages and disadvantages of the evolution to a less authoritarian prison, most of them still conclude that the advantages outweigh the negative aspects, both for staff and prisoners. In particular, the level of physical violence between staff and prisoners, in both directions, was felt to have significantly decreased.

The research shows that staff's level of fear of prisoners' violence is also dependent upon their feelings about their job in general, about the particular prison in which they were working and about the other professionals working there. Fear is lowest where guards have a great deal of contact with the prisoners within a unit system, resulting in a better knowledge of 'their' prisoners. The trust in colleagues is also important in determining the level of fear: guards in several prisons remark that they feel safer in prison than outside. But solidarity between guards is not self-evident: different brigades may have different views ('military' versus 'relaxed' style in prison D), while younger guards reinforce a 'macho' attitude (prisons A and D). Staff policy by the prison director is also influential: in prison C guards feel that the director always sides with the prisoners, but concede that the high number of activities for prisoners improves relations with the latter. In prison B, staff absence and unrest have been tackled through a coherent policy by the prison directors of the introduction of a unit system, delegation of some decisions to the lower levels and guaranteeing of staff holidays (a problem in many prisons due to prison overcrowding).

Violence by staff on prisoners

This form of violence is more difficult to assess for several reasons. The use of force by staff may be legitimate in certain circumstances, e.g. to restrain an aggressive prisoner, to bring a recalcitrant prisoner to a disciplinary cell, or in self-defence. The problem is, then, to assess whether the use of force has been proportionate to the aim or excessive. Excessive violence is presumably not officially accepted, and hence more difficult to discuss with staff. In interviews, reports by staff and by prisoners about specific incidents may be contradictory. Finally, observation of such incidents is difficult, as staff may refrain from such behaviour during the research period or in presence of the researcher, and incidents may be of too short duration to be noticed by the latter.

The results of our inquiry showed a great variety between prisons, between prison sections with different regimes, and between staff groups.

Prison A (large, remand)

In the two sections for 'workers', both prisoners and staff say they have never witnessed physical violence by staff on prisoners. In case of a serious problem, a disciplinary report will be addressed to the director and the prisoner will lose his job and will be transferred to a 'non-workers' section with less privileges. Physical, verbal or psychological violence by staff on prisoners is almost nonexistent. Problems however, may arise when staff are transferred from other sections where relations are of a different nature.

In the two 'non-workers' sections, direct physical assaults by staff on prisoners are exceptional. However, verbal (insults) or psychological violence (false or one-sided disciplinary reports, wilfully 'forgetting' certain requests of the prisoner, unfounded refusals or limitations of certain privileges) is frequently observed. Our own observations and stories by staff and prisoners make it clear that certain guards resorted on purpose to this verbal or psychological violence, in order to provoke certain prisoners into a verbal or physical violent reaction. This then legitimises the use of physical violence against that prisoner, either by the guard himself, or through calling the 'intervention brigade'. The latter consists of ten guards sent to 'control the situation', which often implies inflicting blows and kicking. Such interventions are then condoned by the director as a reaction against alleged initial violent behaviour by the prisoner.

In the psychiatric unit, most guards work on the basis of dialogue with the mentally ill offenders. A few, however, again insult, provoke or assault prisoners unilaterally. As the unit is physically separated from the rest of the prison and as the directors are less present, such abuses remain more easily unnoticed by the hierarchy.

Prison B (large, remand)

Here too, prisoners refer to two groups of guards: the 'naturals' and the 'frustrated'. The first group, which constitutes the large majority, works in a human and social way. The latter, a small group of young and inexperienced guards, insults and provokes prisoners in order to legitimise their own reactions. These, however, seldom include direct physical violence on prisoners, which occurs mainly when placing a prisoner in disciplinary isolation (see 'Institutional violence' below).

Prison C (small, execution of long prison sentences)

All sources corroborate the fact that no incidents of violence by staff on prisoners occur in this prison. This situation seems mostly due to the policy of the director, supported by the head guard, who for many years now refuses to condone any such behaviour. Staff and prisoners know this. Guards hence realise that in the case of a violent act committed by them on a prisoner, the latter will certainly complain to the director, and the guard will be sanctioned. Even if there may be some small abuses or provocations by staff (impoliteness, delay in calling for a visit), they are generally seen as acting correctly.

Prison D (large, implementation of long-term sentences)

Physical violence by staff on prisoners is openly disapproved of in this prison, and no prisoner interviewed had personal experience of it. During the feedback session with guards, however, many referred to incidents of abusive or gratuitous acts of violence. Prisoners also referred to certain guards as 'rambos', 'cowboys' or 'sheriffs', provoking prisoners into disciplinary breaches in order to legitimise sanctions. Different senior guards and 'brigades' have conflicting views on how to maintain order in this prison, resulting in arbitrariness and uncertainty. Specific problems are linked to the fact that this long-term prison has opened recently (a year and a half at the time of the research) and that the majority of the guards hired are inexperienced. Pressed between the long-term prisoners, who demanded flexibility and maturity in handling order and security, and senior guards who impose a strict disciplinary approach, many inexperienced guards choose a strict application of the regulations and a repressive reaction to each breach, rendering each informal negotiation impossible and enhancing the risk of escalation. In its short history, this prison has known already several instances of collective resistance by prisoners.

Factors influencing violence by staff on prisoners

Prison regimes and the unit system

The level of violence is higher in sections for 'non-workers', where interactions between staff and prisoners are limited. These sections are much larger; prisoners remain in their cell for 22 or 23 hours a day; contacts are limited to control of cells and prisoner movements; staff attitudes are strict, distant and focused on security; the guards do not 'know' the prisoners in these sections. There is hence no dynamic security.

The situation is different in the prisons where a unit system has been introduced. The prisoners and a majority of the guards feel that the unit system improves interpersonal relations between staff and prisoners and facilitates the management of the section and of possible conflicts. Those guards who oppose a unit system (mainly to be found in prisons which have not yet introduced it) fear primarily that closer contacts with prisoners may increase the risk of corruption or inappropriate confidence.

The transfer of a prisoner to a disciplinary cell appears not only to represent a particular risk situation for violence by prisoners on staff, but also for violence by staff on the prisoner. Such transfer usually entails a large number of guards (ten in prison A, up to 20 in D) and may lead to the use of force against a recalcitrant prisoner. This large number enhances the risk of further escalation, either by increasing the resistance by the prisoner or by fostering the use of excessive force by the guards. The latter is observed more frequently in prison A, where violence may continue after the prisoner has been overpowered. Once in the disciplinary cell, incidents also happen during the requested complete undressing of the prisoner, often felt by the latter to be humiliating in front of such a large number of guards. Refusal by the prisoner may again lead to excessive force by staff.

Prisoners, guards and prison directors

Different aspects relating to the personal characteristics of the *guards* seem to influence the level of staff violence. Prisoners and staff hence refer to individual 'rambos' or 'sheriffs' as being more prone to use violence against prisoners. These guards represent a minority. They have a negative and stereotyped view of prisoners, to be found in expressions such as 'all prisoners are liars or manipulative', 'it's us or them', 'each contact can be abused', etc. They focus on the security aspect of their work, and more social aspects are considered irrelevant or dangerous. On the other hand, as the professional ethos and climate differ between prisons or prison units, guards sometimes ask to be transferred to a prison or unit which suits them better. For example, some guards who had previously worked in prison A and were then transferred, demanded to be sent back to prison A. Its more security-oriented climate was described as 'a prison where the prisoner does not rule yet, where the guard is still boss' (i.e. like the 'good old times').

Within this context, the attitudes of the prison directors appear to be of primary importance. In all prisons, the use of excessive force or plain violence by staff on prisoners is opposed by the directors and will be sanctioned through transfer of the staff member to another section, transfer outside the cell area or a disciplinary procedure. In prisons A, B and D, a certain tolerance exists, however, when the violent acts follow provocations or acts by prisoners. This is not the case in prison C, where staff are supposed to react in a professional, non-violent manner even in such instances.

In order to react, directors must be aware of the incidents, a knowledge that is easier attained in a small prison like C than in larger prisons like

A, B or D. It also implies that directors often visit the cell areas and know what is going on in their prison. Solidarity between guards may overcome the personal disapproval of such acts and hence hamper reporting or testifying to the director. A particular problem for the director lies with the evaluation of the exact circumstances of an incident in which the violent act by staff is described as a reaction against an assault or act by the prisoner. Confronted with two contradictory testimonies, directors may incline to follow the report by the guard, either because they fear to be seen as too pro-prisoner, or because prison guards are sworn official agents and hence have more legal credibility. Finally, prisoners themselves may not always dare to complain, fearing possible retaliation by staff when certain privileges have to be granted (decision on prison furlough, early release).

Inter-prisoner violence

Earlier sociological works on prisoners' reactions to imprisonment focused mainly on *collective aspects* (prisonisation, solidarity). More recent research (e.g. Matthews 1999: 55) emphasises *individual adaptations* to imprisonment: cooperation or colonisation (avoiding problems and conflicts), withdrawal (isolation, depression, self-mutilation and suicide), rebellion and resistance (riot and aggression or refusal to cooperate). Resistance can also imply participation in the informal economy or exclusion of and violence against certain categories of fellow prisoners (sexual offenders, informers) (Akerstrom, 1986: 10; Sparks *et al* 1996: 168). Analysis of inter-prisoner violence hence requires a variety of sources. Disciplinary reports are limited to incidents reported to or witnessed by staff, hence hidden forms of violence require long-term observations and building of trust with respondents. Interviews with chaplains, nurses and prisoners in separate semi-detention regimes have also been helpful in this respect. Our conclusions are based on the four prisons of the first year of research, the more prolonged and intensive presence of the researchers there having produced more reliable information. As verbal aggression between prisoners was seldom mentioned by them as 'violence', we will limit our analysis to *physical aggression*.

Level of physical aggression between prisoners

The same pattern of recorded violence is found for inter-prisoner violence as for aggression by prisoners on staff: of the four prisons studied, prison C has the highest incidence of disciplinary reports: 41 reports in six months for 125 prisoners (i.e. 33.6 per cent of the prisoners), versus 52 reports in A for 550 prisoners (9.6 per cent), 44 reports in B for 550 prisoners (7.2 per cent) and 24 reports in D for 380 prisoners (6.3 per cent). Again, however, this is only part of the picture.

Prisons A and B are large remand prisons, with few communal activities, and only a limited proportion of the prisoners work. Hence the large majority of prisoners stay in their cell 22 or 23 hours a day. Due to overcrowding, many of these stay with two or three prisoners in a single cell. One type of violent incident occurs mainly inside the cells, following conflicts related to the consequences of this overcrowding. Such incidents may go unnoticed by guards. A second type of violent incident occurs mainly during outdoor exercise, with conflicts resulting in fighting between individuals (e.g. accomplices) or groups (e.g. ethnicities). Such incidents have a much higher visibility.

Prisons C and D are institutions for the execution of long-term prison sentences and hence have more communal activities, a higher proportion of prisoners who work and can meet in the workshops and during movements to and fro. There are therefore more opportunities for violent encounters. Prison C seems to have the highest incidence of violent conflicts, prison D the lowest. This could be explained by the fact that prison C is known for its more 'difficult' population, including disciplinary transfers from other prisons and prisoners presenting psychiatric problems; or by the fact that C is a much smaller prison, and conflicts are hence more visible. Or by the fact that sanctioning policy is again different in prison C, where isolation for three days in the prisoner's own cell is the standard reaction, compared with the other prisons where isolation in the disciplinary cell is the rule. Indeed, the interviews indicate that *hidden violence* is almost non-existent in prison C, while the level of hidden violence is very high in prison D, as illustrated by the high number of prisoners who no longer dare to participate in communal activities or who request protection, mainly linked to drug trafficking.

Factors influencing inter-prisoner violence

Violence in an interpersonal context: prisoners' subculture?

Prisoners regularly refer to the decreasing solidarity between prisoners. Two factors are mentioned here. Firstly, the drug trafficking, which enhances dependency, extortion and violence between prisoners.

Secondly the individualisation of the execution of sentences (prison furloughs, early release), which fosters individualistic and instrumental behaviour. Some social groups may develop, based on regional origin, ethnicity or offence (e.g. sexual offenders). But solidarity between prisoners is mainly of a negative nature: a common animosity against certain groups of prisoners such as sexual offenders, informers, and to a lesser degree foreigners. Whether this negative solidarity or the drug trafficking result in violent incidents is, however, again influenced by prison regimes.

Prison regimes, drug trafficking and the 'zero-option'

In prisons B and D, violent incidents are more frequent in the units for 'non-workers' than in the units for workers. And although work enhances encounters and hence opportunities for violent incidents, these are very rare in the workshops. In the units for workers, conflicts between prisoners during outdoor exercise have been stopped by fellow prisoners, reminding the conflicting parties of the advantages they could lose by a disciplinary transfer to a 'non-workers' unit.

A particular area of inter-prisoner violence relates to the presence of illegal drugs in the prisons studied. Illegal drugs appear to be present in all Belgian prisons. About 50 per cent of the prison population in Belgium are estimated to be at least occasional drug users, of which 15 per cent inject intravenously. This is a consequence of the increase of drug use in the outside society and of sentencing policy, where drug use and drug-related offences more frequently lead to remand custody and prison sentences. On the other hand, the prison environment itself has also been described as amplifying 'maladaptive behaviours', such as drug abuse (Swann and James 1998).

The presence of drugs inside prisons is seen by the prison administration as one of the more negative consequences of the opening up of prisons since the 1980s, with increased opportunities to smuggle drugs inside prisons through visits, prison furloughs, semi-detention, etc. As a consequence, some prisons have introduced the so-called 'zero-option', prohibiting the introduction of any personal goods, clothes, gifts or packages through family or visits, obliging prisoners to purchase all these items through the prison.

In our research, the level of violence related to the drug scene appears directly related to three aspects: the level of organisation and concentration of power of drug traffickers, the 'zero-option' policy and the availability of prison labour as a lawful means to attain some income. In the remand prisons A and B, drug use is limited to soft drugs, drugs found inside the prison always represent a small amount, entrance of soft drugs into prison is usually meant for individual consumption. The high turnover of prisoners and the rather low average prison stay reduce the possibilities for developing stable and structured drug trafficking. Violent incidents in these prisons originate more from the problems of overcrowding than from the drug scene. In prisons C and D for execution of long-term sentences, drugs are more obviously present, including hard drugs (estimated at 20 per cent of the drugs in prison C and 50 per cent in D). But the scope of the problem is different in both prisons. In prison C, a small prison with an active regime, drugs do not constitute a pervasive problem; only two sections are known as 'drug sections', where problems between prisoners are also more frequent. The drug trafficking is fragmented between several individual prisoners and their couriers. Prison C applies the 'zero-option' policy, but the availability of prison labour for all prisoners guarantees some lawful income to purchase the desired goods. In prison D, however, the drug trafficking is organised through a pyramid structure, led by a small group of 'untouchables', who manage the provision, circulation and sale of drugs through their 'lieutenants' in exchange for protection or financial gain. The application of the 'zero-option', combined with a shortage of work (60 per cent of these long-term prisoners are without work), entices 'non-workers' to find an alternative income through acting as lieutenants.

Inter-prisoner violence linked to the drug scene then results from the spiral of debts, racketeering of prisoners to participate in the consumption or trafficking of drugs, retaliation towards prisoners who are seen as informers or who try to escape racketeering by informing staff. Such violence may take the form of beatings and threats on the prisoners inside the prison, or of pressures and blackmail on outside family members. Prisoners particularly vulnerable for such racketeering are drug users, sexual offenders, prisoners allowed prison furloughs, and prisoners employed in internal services, which allows them more freedom of movement. Some of these prisoners hence refuse to participate in outdoor exercise or communal activities, in order to escape such pressure. Referring back to the initial question of the Prison Administration, it is not the liberalisation of prison regimes that enhances inter-prisoner violence, but the presence of well-structured drug trafficking, coupled to a lack of work and lawful ways for prisoners to purchase goods.

Auto-aggressive forms of violence by prisoners

Four types of aggression usually fall under this concept: suicide, attempted suicide, self-harm and hunger strikes. In our results, we focus primarily on attempted suicide and self-harm as the two most frequent forms of auto-aggressive behaviour. No suicides occurred in the prisons studied during our research period, and information on hunger strikes was very scarce. The distinction between attempted suicide and self-harm is difficult, as the cutting of veins, for example, may be labelled as either.

International literature shows that the incidence of suicides is much higher in prisons than in outside society. Liebling (1992: 25), for example, found that for ten countries, including Belgium, the suicide rate in prisons was between two and fifteen times higher. This higher rate is usually explained in two different manners: either by the characteristics of the prisoners who constitute risk groups (e.g. age, marital status, nationality, psychological aspects), or by the deprivations and stress factors related to the detention. Liebling showed that both aspects are important: prisoners who attempt suicide share problematic characteristics with prisoners who do not attempt suicide (e.g. family violence, school drop-out, age at first sentence), but to a higher degree, and they have more difficulties coping with the deprivations of imprisonment (passive regimes with few activities, social isolation in and outside prison). This view was confirmed in our research.

The results of the disciplinary reports differ from official reports by the Prison Administration. While no suicide attempts for the whole year are officially mentioned by the latter for prisons A and B, and only two for prisons C and D, the disciplinary reports mention fifteen incidents of auto-aggression in A (2.7 per cent of prisoners), 33 in B (5.4 per cent), five in C (4 per cent) and twelve in D (3.4 per cent). Cutting of veins and hanging are the most frequent techniques used.

Factors influencing auto-aggressive violence

Risk groups and risk factors

As regards the prisoners, several risk groups have been identified:

- Prisoners who have previously attempted suicide: in the four prisons studied, several attempts were made by prisoners with a previous history of attempted suicide. In a later analysis of successful suicides, a similar result has been found.

- Remand prisoners: risk moments are the first days of imprisonment, appearance before the investigating courts, the anxiety preceding the sentence and the shock of the sentence.

- Prisoners presenting psychological problems: the incidence of attempted suicides is higher in the psychiatric unit of prison A and with drug abusers, especially at the start of their detoxification.

- Illegal aliens detained for administrative reasons: in prison B, 40 per cent of registered auto-aggressions are performed by this category of prisoners, linked to their social isolation and fear of expulsion.

- Sentenced prisoners: risk moments are transfers to other prisons, critical moments in the decision-making process towards prison furlough or early release.

A more general risk factor, mentioned by prisoners and guards alike, is the lack of support by the psychosocial service. This lack of support is linked partly to a shortage of staff, but also to the fact that since the new parole legislation of 1998 (following the Dutroux case) prison psychosocial services have been forced into a mainly diagnostic and advisory role in the parole procedure. This is especially felt in the prisons for implementation of sentences, where contacts with the psychosocial services only start in view of this preparation of the parole procedure, and where prisoners feel that 'everything they say will be used against them'.

Within the interpersonal context, the role of the prison guards is evaluated differently by the guards themselves. During interviews, guards in all four prisons said that confrontation with a successful suicide is – or would be – the most difficult experience of their work. Apart from this general feeling, two main attitudes can be distinguished. The first group of guards (the majority in prison B) considers prevention of suicides an essential aspect of their work. They feel that, through their daily contacts with prisoners, they should be able to assess warning signals of impending problems, and demand more specialised training in order to do so. A second group (more present in prison A) is convinced that persons who really intend to commit suicide would do so anyway, and that nothing can be done to prevent such acts. Prisoners who resort to self-harm or attempt suicide through cutting of veins are not seen as presenting a real risk of suicide. Such acts are seen as mere blackmail towards the guards or management, and should certainly not be taken into account to grant any request or privilege.

Prison regimes

The disciplinary records and the interviews show that auto-aggression occurs more frequently in units of non-workers with few out-of-cell activities, in units with a strict regime and in the disciplinary units. Contacts with the outside world are also an important regime element. Prisoners refer to the importance of external relations in explaining self-harm or attempted suicides. For example, when no visit was received or a visit developed negatively, when confronted with the loss of a partner or a family member, following a refusal by the prison administration to attend a birth or a funeral.

Suicide attempts, therefore, seem to be the result of an interaction between more vulnerable prisoners and a more difficult prison context: risk groups facing particular risk factors, coupled to the influence of prison regimes, contacts with the outside world and support by psychosocial staff and prison guards.

Collective resistance or violence by prisoners

Collective violence and riots have received much attention in the literature, as they embody the loss of control in a system where control is essential. Descriptions and explanations of particular events have led to several theories: collective violence and riots as instrumental tools or expressive events, as the work of a few troublesome or dangerous prisoners, as endemic risks or exceptional incidents (Matthews 1999; Montgomery and Crews 1998). 'Solutions' range from the penal pragmatism of recognising triggering events and sending armed troops or even robots (Sherman 1996) to fundamental questions of legitimacy and justice (Woolf 1991).

As stated previously, Belgium, like many other countries, experienced a wave of prison riots in the 1970s. The most important 'riot' happened in 1976 in a prison for long-term prisoners: a completely non-violent, well-organised and controlled movement of collective resistance, which led to the election of prisoners' representatives, the formulation of well-motivated requests (e.g. concerning the non-transparency of the parole procedure and the possibilities of allowing a liberal regime within a secure perimeter) and negotiations with the central prison administration. Eventually, this was crushed by police force under pressure from the guards' unions and the directors of other prisons, who feared the movement would spread further. It was still influential in liberalising prison policy in Belgium. That same prison, which houses mainly long-term and life-sentence prisoners, is now known for its active and open-door regime.

Massive and destructive prison riots have been almost nonexistent in Belgium since the 1970s. The last violent riots happened in the 1980s in prisons A and B,[2] so none of the prisons studied had any recent experience with riots. Several incidents of collective resistance, however, occurred in prisons B and D. The reasons for their emergence, and for their absence in prisons A and C, are again linked to some regime aspects.

Factors influencing collective resistance by prisoners

From individual frustrations to collective resistance in prisons B and D

In prison B, many prisoners used the interviews during the research as an opportunity to tell their personal stories and problems, often emphasising the difficulties they face in prison, and the impossibility of discussing such things with fellow prisoners or guards. This lack of trust in other prisoners may influence the uneasy development of collective movements. Collective resistance in prison B takes the form of refusal to re-enter the cells after the outdoor exercise. This happens mainly from April to October (due to weather conditions). The main complaints by prisoners relate to living conditions (overcrowding), food, poor ventilation when the weather was warm, and anxiety over the parole procedure for the sentenced prisoners. The justification of such collective resistance by prisoners is that 'it is the only way to see and to be heard by the director'. In fact, it developed a few years ago into a regular practice to see the director and express collective complaints (which were prohibited by the prison regulations), after which the prisoners would re-enter the cell areas. The current directors, however, feel this policy was amounting to rewarding resistance and was triggering more of such events. Policy recently developed into giving one warning to the prisoners before sending in the police forces. At the last incident witnessed during the research, the director even sent police from the very start of the collective refusal, leading to prisoners' astonished reactions of 'Why such repression? We only wanted to see the director.'

Such collective movements do not occur in the 'workers' unit and the unit with the more open and active regime. The regime here alleviates some of the frustrations, and dialogue with the guards is easier. The promise by the directors to increase regime activities and to introduce more sports in the other units had already decreased the conflicts and tensions there as well.

Prison D has, in its short history, already experienced three movements of collective resistance, usually refusals to re-enter the cells. One incident led to some material destruction. Whereas the directors minimise the incidents and explain them through the actions of a few agitators, prisoners refer mainly to the problems linked to the 'zero-option' policy and its influence on prison regime (inter-prisoner violence). Recent policy changes enhancing activities seemed to have subdued the collective movements.

Modus vivendi *in prison C*

Prison C has a strongly secured external perimeter, but the regime inside the prison is active and allows some freedom of movement. The long-term prisoners are rather individualistic, trying to serve their sentence with as many privileges and as little trouble as possible. Relations between prisoners and between prisoners and guards are quiet and tolerant, and the directors are easy to reach and spend much time listening to complaints and wishes. Recurrent complaints, for example about the food, may prompt a few prisoners to formulate a collective complaint, but it never leads to collective movements.

Deterrence in prison A

The emphasis on security and the strict disciplinary approach hamper communication with guards and directors and increase frustrations for the prisoners. The transformation of these frustrations into collective movements is subdued by the limited average period of stay, the focus of the remand prisoners on their judicial case and the fear of retaliation by staff. Guards who have also worked in other prisons state that the strict approach in prison A enhances order and quiet, but concede that the tensions are higher, and may eventually explode into violent incidents. Hence, collective resistance seemed to be mainly linked to the possibilities of communication with staff and directors and to certain regime aspects such as activities and living conditions.

Institutional violence

Institutional violence may be defined as the pressure exercised by the institution on its members through its mere existence. This is usually linked to the totalitarian elements of prisons as 'total institutions', described by Goffman, Sykes and others. In the recent literature, authors differ in their analysis of the remaining 'totalitarian' aspects of our modern prisons. Some see a decrease in totalitarianism through prisoners' rights, more activities, opening up of prisons and introduction of external services (e.g. Lemire 1991). Others think that the essence of the total institution has remained unchanged, i.e. control over the lives of its inmates (Rostaing 1996). The inmates remain completely dependent and subordinate to the institution (Chauvenet 1996), while the aim of the institution is to protect society against its inmates, not to foster their interests (Goffman 1961, 1968). We have used the analysis of Goffman on total institutions and of Sykes (1958) on the pains of imprisonment to determine the level of institutional violence of the prisons studied.

In all prisons studied, prisoners referred to the institutional pressure and to the five pains of imprisonment: deprivation of liberty, scarcity of goods and services, loss of privacy, autonomy and security. Complaints were generally about the daily limitations, the corporal searches, the lack of privacy, and the uncertainty of the eternal waiting. Some complaints were, however, much stronger in certain prisons than in others.

Factors influencing institutional violence: custody, order, care and justice

The main factors explaining the differences between prisoners' experiences of the level of institutional violence are the variations in living conditions, active versus passive prison regimes and liberal versus authoritarian regimes. The interaction between all these elements determines the level of deprivation felt by the prisoners.

Prison A (remand)

This is an overcrowded, only partly renovated old prison, where non-renovated parts still have 'slopping-out' and have no running water in the cells. Most prisoners do not have work, and the number of activities was low. In the non-workers' units, prisoners stay in their cells for 23 to 24 hours each day. Staff culture is focused on security and the strict application of the regulations. Activities and the introduction of external services are distrusted. Relations between staff and prisoners are limited and strained. The level of institutional violence is high, with bad living conditions and a passive and authoritarian regime. The situation is slightly better in the workers' unit. However, an increasing number of foreign prisoners live in serious social isolation: unable to speak French, they have no family or friends in Belgium, no communication with staff, no work or activities in the prison. The conclusion, then, is that it places emphasis on passive security, instils order through control measures, and exhibits a low level of care and justice.

Prison B (remand)

Prison B is also an overcrowded, only partly renovated old prison, where slopping-out still exists in non-renovated parts. Most prisoners do not have work, but many efforts have been made by the prison directors over the last four years to increase the number of activities for all prisoners: for example, education, sports and cultural activities. These are organised by external services, with the participation of some of the guards. Relations between staff and prisoners are more genial. Although the living conditions are also poor, the regime is more active and less authoritarian than in prison A. Foreigners are also an important group in prison B, but communication is better as a higher number of staff members speak different languages. The directors try to give foreigners some work in order to facilitate the purchase of goods. The conclusion, then, is that there is both passive and dynamic security, order through control and activities, attempts to provide some care, and that staff, overall, are attentive to issues of justice.

Prison C (execution of long sentences)

The level of comfort in prison C is satisfactory, and work and different types of activities are available. For a prison known for its difficult population (disciplinary transfers, psychiatric troubles), there is much emphasis on security through the external perimeter, but order inside the prison is attained through dialogue and communication. This policy is stressed by the directors and followed by most guards. The psychosocial care is, however, insufficient due to lack of staffing. This raises specific problems and tensions in relation to the parole procedure. The conclusion, then, is that prison C places emphasis on passive security outside, imposes dynamic security inside the prison, exhibits a high level of care and justice by guards and directors, yet receives insufficient support from the psychosocial services.

Prison D (execution of long sentences)

Prison D is a recently built prison with a good level of comfort. The emphasis on security through the introduction of the zero-option has had counter-productive effects on the internal order, however. Different brigades have different views on how to attain order. A difficult population of long-term prisoners, coupled with a majority of inexperienced guards, has led to control problems, in which a lack of flexibility and too strict repression alternates with loss of control. The lack of work and activities further fosters the importance of drug trafficking, increasing the level of insecurity inside the prison. Psychosocial care is insufficient for this population. In conclusion, in prison D there is an emphasis on passive security, problematic order, a low level of care, and varying levels of justice with different brigades of guards.

Conclusion

Prison violence is still relatively low in Belgium compared with some other countries: no violent riots have occurred since the 1980s, older guards agree that the level of violence between prisoners and guards has decreased over the years, and the majority of guards interviewed feel safe inside their prison. The decrease of authoritarianism, the introduction of more activities and the opening up of the prisons are generally recognised as having significantly contributed to this decrease in violence. That does not mean, however, that there are no problems in the prisons studied.

The institutional violence of the prison as a total institution is felt by all prisoners, although to a varying degree. The five pains of imprisonment described by Sykes are still valid, even in the modern or renovated, post-authoritarian prison. This institutional violence increases with difficult living conditions (overcrowding, slopping-out), lack of work or activities and lack of respect by staff. The stories told by the prisoners confirm the importance of the balance between custody, order, justice and care in their experience of the level of institutional violence and their reaction to it. The prisons studied show great variety in these aspects, both between the prisons and between different units of the prisons. Many prison directors and prison staff attempt to improve the situation as much as possible. It is also clear that the old-style authoritarian prison has not completely disappeared in Belgium, but lives on in the attitudes and behaviour of certain guards and directors of certain establishments. This perennial institutional violence is important to understand the interaction between the different forms of prison violence.

The variety between the forms of violence found in the prisons studied, coupled to the local climate and policy, indicates that prisons are like balloons or waterbeds. The deprivation of liberty and its consequences will lead to frustrations, tensions and conflicts. Prisons where this reality is accepted succeed better in channelling these tensions into manageable forms (cf. definition of 'order' by Sparks *et al* 1996: 119), while repression of a particular form of violence seems to foster the emergence of a different form.

Prison regimes cannot eradicate all the sources of tension, but they obviously influence them. More liberal, active and non-authoritarian regimes had more advantages than disadvantages for all forms of violence studied in this research. Relations between prisoners and between prisoners and staff are less strained in active and non-authoritarian regimes that have many activities, work or education, and more autonomy for prisoners. This results in a lower level of institutional violence, less collective resistance, less violence between prisoners and staff and less self-harm. The increased interpersonal contacts may lead to more arguments and discussions, and latent conflicts may come easier to the surface than in strict and authoritarian regimes. This certainly requires more support and training of staff to cope with such interactions in a professional way.

More strict, passive and authoritarian regimes hamper the development of a dynamic security. They may subdue the expression of frustrations and conflicts by prisoners in the short term, but they also lead to more hidden violence, to more violence by staff on prisoners, more collective resistance by prisoners and to escalation into violent incidents between prisoners and staff in the long run, either in prison or after release. Personal characteristics of prisoners, but also of prison guards and directors, are important too, as seen in the occurrence of violence between prisoners and staff or self-harm. But even these characteristics are mediated and influenced by prison regimes.

Referring to the initial question of the prison administration, we found no relation between more liberal regimes and an increase in inter-prisoner violence; quite the contrary. We have found great varieties in professional ethos between the different prisons, and sometimes between units or brigades. Individual staff members have different views of their jobs and the way in which to handle prisoners, which directly influence their interaction with prisoners. Staff training and policy are equally important, both locally and centrally. Communication and support by local prison directors are essential for the job satisfaction of the guards, and hence their willingness to make efforts at producing high-quality work with prisoners. We also found a great influence of a clear attitude of the prison directors towards forms of violence in prisons. Smaller prisons or unit systems facilitate knowledge and communication between directors and guards. They also enhance dynamic security between guards and prisoners, but not all guards are as yet convinced of its worth. And those guards who apply a 'dialectic of control' approach in their interactions with prisoners often reach its limits as soon as a prisoner stops 'behaving', e.g. during transfer to a disciplinary cell or when a prisoner is labelled 'dangerous'.

Here lies an important duty for the central prison authorities: to develop a clear policy based on dynamic security, and to train and encourage prison staff accordingly. The new Prison Act of January 2005 explicitly refers to the importance of dynamic security and of an active regime to attain order and security. If implemented, this Prison Act should further enhance the level of justice and care in Belgian prisons, by guaranteeing the continued opening up of the prisons to the external world, the introduction of more activities in the prison regimes and more formal prisoners' rights. Together with the small size of the majority of the prisons in Belgium, the quality of the (academically trained) directors and the commitment of the majority of the prison guards, these should continue to constitute preventive factors for violence in the prisons. In order to tackle the overcrowding of the remand prisons and some of the effects of the drug policy, however, will require a larger penal policy.

Notes

1 This paper could not have been written without the fieldwork and reporting done by the researchers Tom Bogaert, Peter Janssen, Hilde Tubex (researchers VUB), Juliette Beghin, Philippe Bellis (researchers ULB). Supervisors: Prof. S. Snacken (VUB) and Prof. Ph. Mary (ULB). The research report was written in French and Dutch (Snacken *et al* 2000).

2 These large remand prisons were suffering from serious overcrowding and bad material circumstances, amounting in the words of CPT to 'inhuman and degrading treatment'. The riots started after the Minister of Justice proudly announced in a TV programme that British hooligans, who were facing trial for the tragic events in a football stadium leading to 39 deaths, would be held in a completely renovated and spacious part of a prison for implementation of sentences.

References

Akerstrom, M. (1986) *Crooks and Squares: Lifestyles of Thieves and Addicts in Comparison to Conventional People*. New Brunswick, NJ: Transaction Books.

Bowker, L. (1977) *Prison Subcultures*. Massachusetts: Lexington Press, p. 173.

Chauvenet, A. (1996) 'L'échange et la prison', in C. Faugeron, A. Chauvenet and P. Combessie (eds) *Approches de la prison*. Ottawa, Montréal, Bruxelles: De Boeck Université, pp. 45–70.

Cohen, A.K. (1976) 'Prison violence: a sociological perspective', in A.K. Cohen, G.F. Cole and R.G. Bailey (eds) *Prison Violence*. Massauchusetts: Lexington Press.

Comité Européen pour la prévention de la torture et des peines ou traitements inhumains ou dégradants, *Rapport relatif à la visite effectuée en Belgique par le CPT*, CPT/Inf(94)15; CPT(97)75.

Control Review Committee (1984) *Managing the Long-term Prison System*. London: Home Office.

Debuyst, C. (ed.) (1981) *Dangerosité et justice pénale. Ambiguité d'une pratique*, Collection Déviance et Société. Masson, Genève.

Debuyst, C. (ed.) (1990) *Acteur social et délinquance. Une grille de lecture du système de justice pénale*. Pierre Mardaga, Liège-Bruxelles, p. 475.

Ditchfield, J. (1990) *Control in Prisons: A Review of the Literature*. Home Office Research Study No. 118, London, p. 183.

European Committee for the Prevention of Torture and Inhuman or Degrading Treatment or Punishment, *Second General Report*, CPT/Inf(92). Strasbourg, 1992.

Evans, M.D. and Morgan, R. (1999) *Preventing Torture: A Study of the European Convention for the Prevention of Torture and Inhuman or Degrading Treatment or Punishment*. Oxford: Clarendon Press.

Giddens, A. (1984) *The Constitution of Society*. Cambridge: Polity Press.

Goffman, E. (1961) 'On the characteristics of total institutions', in D. Cressey (ed.) *The Prison: Studies in Institutional Organization and Change*. New York: Holt, Rinehart and Winston Press.

Goffman, E. (1968) *Asylums: Essays on the Social Situation of Mental Patients and Inmates* (first published 1961). London: Penguin Books.

Irwin, J. (1980) *Prisons in Turmoil*. Chicago: Little Brown Publishing.

Irwin, J. and Cressey, D. (1962) 'Thieves, convicts and the inmate culture', *Social Problems*, 10.

Jacobs, J. (1977) *Stateville: The Penitentiary in Mass Society*. Chicago: Chicago University Press, p. 281.

Jacobs, J. (1983) *New Perspectives on Prisons and Imprisonment*. Ithaca and London: Cornell University Press, p. 241.

Keve, P.W. (1974) *Prison Life and Human Worth*. Minneapolis: University of Minnesota Press.

King, R.D. (1985) 'Control in prisons', in M. Maguire, J. Vagg and R. Morgan (eds) *Accountability and Prisons*. London: Tavistock Publishing.

King, R.D. (1994) 'Order, disorder and regimes in the Prison Services of Scotland, and England and Wales', in E. Player and M. Jenkins (eds) *Prisons after Woolf*. London: Routledge, pp. 46–65.

Lemire, G. (1991) *Anatomie de la prison*. Les Presses Universitaires de Montréal, Montréal.

Liebling, A. (1992) *Suicides in Prison*. London: Routledge.

Marshall, S. (1997) *Control in Category C Prisons*, Research Findings No 54, Home Office Research and Statistics Directorate. London, p. 4.

Mathiesen, T. (1965) *The Defences of the Weak*. London: Tavistock.

Matthews, R. (1999) *Doing Time. An Introduction to the Sociology of Imprisonment*. London: Macmillan Press.

Montgomery, R. and Crews, G. (1998) *A History of Correctional Violence: An Examination of Reported Causes of Riots and Disturbances*. Lenham: American Correctional Association.

Morgan, R. (1992) 'Following Woolf: the prospects for prisons policy', *Journal of Law and Society*, 19, 231–250.

Morgan, R. (1994) 'Thoughts about control in prisons', *Prison Service Journal*, 57–60.

Player, E. and Jenkins, M. (eds) (1994) *Prisons after Woolf. Reform through Riot*. London: Routledge, p. 278.

Research and Advisory Group on the Long-term Prison System (1987) *Special Units for Long-term Prisoners: Regimes, Management and Research*. London: Home Office, p. 69.

Rostaing, C. (1996) 'Les relations entre surveillantes et détenues', in C. Faugeron, A. Chauvenet and Ph. Combessie (eds) *Approches de la prison*. De Boeck & Larcier, pp. 101–125.

Scraton, P., Sim, J. and Skidmore, P. (1991) *Prisons Under Protest*. Buckingham: Open University Press, p. 181.

Sherman, D. (1996) *Preventing and Managing Riots and Disturbances*. Lenham: American Correctional Association, vols 1 and 2.

Snacken, S. (1990) 'Le détenu acteur social?', in C. Debuyst (ed.) *Acteur social et délinquance. Une grille de lecture du système de justice pénale*. Pierre Mardaga, Liège-Bruxelles, pp. 327–337.

Snacken, S. (1997) *Long-term Prisoners and Violent Offenders*, 12th Conference of Directors of Prison Administration (CDAP). Strasbourg, Council of Europe, November 1997, 43–73.

Snacken, S. (2001) 'Belgium', in D. van Zyl Smit and F. Dünkel (eds) *Imprisonment Today and Tomorrow. International Perspectives on Prisoners' Rights and Prison Conditions*, 2nd edition. Kluwer Law International, pp. 32–81.

Snacken, S., Mary, Ph., Beghin, J., Bellis, Ph., Janssen, P., Tubex, H. and Bogaert, T. (2000) *De problematiek van geweld in gevangenissen. La problématique de la violence en prison*, research report VUB/ULB. Brussels: Ministry of Justice.

Sparks, R., Bottoms, A. and Hay, W. (1996) *Prisons and the Problem of Order*. Oxford: Clarendon Press, p. 377.

Swann, R. and James, P. (1998) 'The effect of the prison environment upon inmate drug taking behaviour', *The Howard Journal*, 188–205.

Sykes, G.M. (1958) *The Society of Captives: A Study of a Maximum Security Prison.* Princeton, NJ: Princeton University Press.

Thomas, C.W. (1977) 'Theoretical perspectives on prisonisation: a comparison of the importation and deprivation models', *The Journal of Criminal Law & Criminology*, 68, 135–145.

Woolf, Lord Justice (1991) *Prison Disturbances*, April 1990. London: Home Office.

Part 3

Coping Among Ageing Prisoners

Chapter 13

Older men in prison: survival, coping and identity

Elaine Crawley and Richard Sparks

As a result of recent changes in sentencing and paroling practices (including the incremental extension of the life sentence, the increasing number of life sentences and the phenomenon of the 'natural life' sentence for certain prisoners), the number of prisoners over state retirement age has, over the past ten years, increased significantly on both sides of the Atlantic. In the UK, the relatively recent determination to pursue 'historic' (usually sexual) offences has been a significant contributor to the increasing numbers of men serving a first prison sentence late in life.

In England and Wales in the period 1992–2002, the number of males under sentence increased from 34,389 to 53,967 – a rise of just under 50 per cent. Over the same period, the number of males under sentence aged 60 years and above increased from 442 to 1,359 – almost exactly a three-fold rise (Home Office 2002; Prison Reform Trust (2003). This has significant practical and economic implications for establishments holding elderly prisoners, especially if those prisoners are suffering the more serious diseases and disabilities that often accompany old age.

Although the economic implications of this development (in particular the expanding cost of prison health care) have been recognised – prison governors are acutely aware, for example, of the strain community hospital 'bed watches' place on their prison budgets – the practical and policy responses to older prisoners' needs contrast markedly across jurisdictions. In the United States, the so-called 'greying' of the prison population is now an acknowledged consequence of mass incarceration. Moreover, the sheer scale of the problem has demanded that the Federal Bureau of Prisons turn its attention to developing programmes and regimes specific to the needs of its older prisoner population. Similarly, the Correctional Services of Canada (CSC) undertook, in 1994, a number of key research initiatives regarding the unique characteristics of older prisoners in order to develop a coordinated management approach for this specific population. In 1999 the CSC created an Older Offender Division tasked with elaborating a research programme and correctional strategy[1] for older offenders.

In the UK, in contrast, the longstanding presumption that imprisonment is 'a young man's game' continues to mask the dimensions of age at the levels of both policy and research. Almost five years on from the publication of a joint report by Her Majesty's Inspectorates of Prisons and Probation (HMIPP 1999), which recommended the development of a national strategy for dealing with ageing prisoners, the Prison Service of England and Wales still does not have such a strategy. In consequence, the Prison Service has made little progress in terms of the development of appropriate regimes for ageing and infirm prisoners, even for those serving a life sentence and for whom the need for palliative care is likely to become increasingly pressing. Neither has the Service developed a coherent resettlement strategy for elderly ex-prisoners. On the contrary, prison programmes, services, policies and, indeed, prison architecture, have generally been designed with younger offenders much in mind, and this inevitably poses difficulties and challenges in the proper[2] management of an ageing and ill prison population. We have also noted, from our conversations with uniformed staff, that training courses for working with the elderly are not yet available to prison staff.

While at the national level of the Prison Service of England and Wales the growing number of elderly and infirm prisoners remains an issue of remarkably low visibility (Crawley and Sparks 2003), our research demonstrates that at the *local* level (i.e. within certain individual prisons) the question of how best to manage this population is stimulating a range of practitioner-led adjustments and initiatives, despite the lack of additional resources.

Survival, coping and identity: Imprisonment in old age

As we noted in our research proposal to the Economic and Social Research Council (ESRC),[3] the notions of 'coping[4] with' or 'adapting to' imprisonment (and to the depth and duration of imprisonment in particular) were important concerns of prison sociology during its 'classic' mid-century phase (Clemmer 1940; Sykes 1958). Not since the 1970s, however, when Cohen and Taylor (1972) asked prisoners to describe their own experiences of long-term imprisonment, have the experiential, ontological and conceptual challenges of extreme and sometimes literally lifelong confinement received sustained analysis.[5] Even Cohen and Taylor's work, however, focused on the anxieties and fears of prisoners sentenced well before middle age, and, since most of them could expect to be released at some point, on their *anticipations* about life after prison. We realised that little was known about the experiences and survival strategies of men whose lives were likely to *end* in prison, nor about the men who *entered* the prison in later life. Our research provided us with the opportunity to revisit the problems of 'coping', 'entry shock', 'adaptation' and 'psychological survival' from the vantage point of this prisoner group.

Spoiled identity

The concept of 'spoiled identity' is also central to this chapter. In the prison setting, discrediting (and public) social attributes or stigmas – in this context stigmas of *character* (i.e. not only 'prisoner' but also prisoner as 'nonce', 'rapist', 'murderer' etc.) – have significant implications not only for how individuals and groups are treated by other prisoners and prison staff but also for the maintenance (or destruction) of the 'private' self. The problem lies in finding means of limiting, or even turning to some advantage, the damaging effects of the stigma. Throughout this chapter we explore the implications and possibilities for identity construction, identity preservation and identity loss in the prison setting, with particular reference to older men.

Research methods

This chapter draws from our two-year study of the implications of ageing in the prison setting. In addition to (1) a review of the sentencing trends which affect the age distributions of prison populations in Britain, the United States and Canada, and (2) a review of current policy developments, our research project – 'Surviving prison in later life'– had two key strands. The first strand comprised an intensive, qualitative engagement with a number of older[6] male[7] prisoners, in order to contribute to an enhanced understanding of their biographies, social relations and current problems and prospects. The second strand comprised a qualitative engagement with uniformed (and other) prison staff.

Our research entailed observations and interviews in four[8] prisons housing relatively large concentrations of prisoners over state retirement age. Approximately 60 in-depth interviews and innumerable informal conversations were conducted with prisoners aged between 65 and 84 years, along with months of sustained observations of prisoners' daily tactics, innovations and routines for survival, and for coping with the (often distressing) impacts of inappropriate prison regimes. We were able to identify a number of prisoner sub-groups. Some of our interviewees had grown old in prison as a result of lengthy sentences, whereas others were repeat offenders with prior prison experience. Many, however, had received their sentences late in life and had no prior experience of prison. Their sentences ranged from two years to life imprisonment for a variety of offences, including fraud, manslaughter, murder, war crimes and the sexual abuse of minors. Notably, many of the latter are 'historic' crimes, i.e. offences allegedly carried out two, three or four (and in one case, five) decades ago.

Our research had a number of key objectives. First, we wanted to explore the social, psychological and emotional impacts of imprisonment on older people, and to examine the coping and survival strategies which they adopt in coming to terms not only with the fact of custody but also with the cultures, routines, rules and practices of the prison. Second, we wished to explore how physical ageing (and the decline in physical effectiveness that accompanies it) is experienced in the prison setting, and to examine the day-to-day challenges that arise for uniformed staff working with this prisoner group. We also thought it important to identify and explore the social networks and sources of support which older prisoners enjoy (or lack), and their relation to prisoners' aspirations, hopes and fears – perhaps especially in preparing for release (see Crawley 2004b). Finally, we wanted to illuminate the resource, regime and policy implications of the confinement of older (sometimes very elderly) men.

Coping and survival: Imprisonment as catastrophe

The research demonstrates that the social and emotional impacts of imprisonment on men in their later years can be intense. We found that the prison 'neophyte' – the older prisoner unfamiliar with the cultures and routines of the prison – is likely to feel particularly anxious and depressed. Not only do these prisoners suffer 'relocation stress'[9] on entering such an alien environment, they are often unable to fathom how their lives have 'come to this' (this is especially true for those imprisoned for 'historic' crimes). For these men, the prison sentence represents nothing short of a disaster, a catastrophe, and, in consequence, they are often in a psychological state of trauma. Erikson (1985: 110) defines the individual (as opposed to collective) trauma as a 'blow to the psyche that breaks through one's defences so suddenly and with such force that one cannot respond effectively'. In our research we have drawn upon the work of Hodgkinson and Stewart (1991) who in their book, *Coping with Catastrophe*, use survivors' own words to provide a vivid and moving account of the experiences of survival in a variety of circumstances and conditions. Although their work is intended as a handbook for professionals working in the field of disaster management, we have found it useful in our exploration of how older men (perhaps particularly elderly men) respond to, and attempt to 'survive', a very personal type of disaster – that of being sent to prison, and the emotional turmoil[10] that accompanies it.

But what, exactly, *is* 'survival'? As Hodgkinson and Stewart (ibid.: 2) note, 'Survival is not just the difference between living and dying – survival is to do with quality of life. Survival involves progressing from the event and its aftermath, and transforming the experience'. The authors identify five central experiences borne by survivors, namely: (1) the 'death imprint' (indelible imagery of the encounter with death), (2) 'survivor guilt' (why did I survive and others not?), (3) 'psychic numbing' (a defensive manoeuvre preventing the survivor from experiencing the reality of the event), (4) 'nurturance conflicts' (suspicion of offers of help from outsiders), and (5) 'quest for meaning' (why did it happen?). Bearing in mind that our interviewees are not the survivors of the events we normally term 'disasters' – for example, plane crashes, earthquakes, explosions and so forth – when we use the term 'disaster' here we are referring to a prisoner's sudden recognition that through his own actions,[11] his life as he knew it has changed forever. For the long-term and life-sentenced prisoner, 'psychic numbing' and 'quest for meaning' are likely to be the most common post-disaster experiences. (We return to our discussion of trauma, coping and survival in prison in the illustrative prisoner comments presented below.)

Discussing her work on the nature of psychological response to the various components of disaster, Raphael (1986: 69) notes that one important factor is the powerful *human attachment* that people have for one another. It seems that for many long-term prisoners, however, emotional attachments can generate a great deal of suffering. In the 1940s, Maurice Farber (1944) described the problems of outside relationships in terms of the amount of suffering that the presence of such relationships produces for prisoners. He found clear evidence of prisoners who had cut off all contacts in order to reduce suffering. As a number of lifers commented during our own research, 'prison life is more bearable and easier to cope with if you have nobody to care about beyond the walls'. Many of our interviewees had wives who were into their later years and had been married for a very long time, and in terms of coping, these men seemed to fare worse than those with no spouse and little family. For Albert, who had been married for 52 years, being away from his wife (who was disabled and in the early stages of Alzheimer's) was the worst part of being in prison. He said simply:

> It upsets me. We'd never been apart before this. Sometimes I wish I could die. It [the sentence] broke our lives. It's the last part of our life and she's out there on her own and I'm in here.

Another factor important for survival is what Raphael terms the *attempt at mastery*. Attempts at mastery may take many forms. Review of past coping and survival is one form; indeed, for many of our interviewees, recollections of how they endured the brutalising environments of military life experienced in their twenties (or, for some, a childhood of institutional 'care') proved to be useful resources on which to draw in order to survive the deprivations and rigours of prison life and retain a sense of self. For others, an internal refusal to accept their 'prisoner' identity as a master status was evident from their determination, in each of our interviews, to steer the conversation to events, people and places *outside* the prison and *before* their personal disaster had taken place. These interviews were, in consequence, replete with enthusiastic descriptions and recollections of who they *really* were and the respectable things they had done: they were survivors of military service across the globe; loyal husbands and kind fathers; keen gardeners; DIY enthusiasts – in other words, hard workers and good providers, not simply 'prisoners'.

Our research demonstrates that a life change that is as dramatic as coming into prison can be devastating for men in their later years, and their imprisonment can have profound effects on family unity and stability. This is especially true for those whose offence arose within the family setting or is felt as shameful by other family members (as in the case of many sex offenders). As Cohen and Taylor (1972: 53) correctly observed, at *any* stage of life, extreme events (the death of a partner, prolonged illness, enforced separation from loved ones) can be 'literally and metaphorically shattering' (Cohen and Taylor 1972: 53). They also note that the predicament of long-term prisoners is similar to that of individuals in very different, but equally extreme situations. To fully understand the *meaning* of long-term imprisonment for those who must undergo it, they asked themselves how people *in general* manage to cope with massive disruptions in their normal lives. To answer this, of course, one must first appreciate the situation where there is no such disruption. At such times, life appears relatively orderly and meaningful to us; we act with a sense of purpose and with a reliance on specific domestic, social and occupational routines. When disturbances do occur we can usually resolve them with culturally approved modes of resolution: we speak of 'talking it through', 'waiting for it to pass over', etc. Occasionally, however, the problem is so extreme – so dreadful – that one's whole view of the world or sense of self is uncertain. Such experiences have disturbing consequences: we talk of 'going grey overnight', 'being scarred for life', of 'never being the same again'. Such shattering events, by disturbing the orderliness of life, may bring the meaning of life itself into question. But as Cohen and Taylor point out, at least after such events there is usually *something* of that world left and, gradually, meaning and significance return. This is because such events tend to occur in only *one part* of one's life, in *one domain*, and this means that other domains can be called into service to provide reassurance and re-establish credibility. The long-term prisoner, however, cannot play one domain off against another in this way. When he arrives in prison he has to come to terms with the fact that he is starting a new life: he has been given 'life' – a prison life – and somehow he must learn to live it. For Cohen and Taylor, it is this notion of the destruction and then the rebuilding of a life that captures the predicament of the long-term prisoner.

What, then, is the meaning of a long prison sentence to a man who is already old? How does the elderly first-time prisoner cope with such a dramatic disruption to his life – to the loss of status and respectability acquired over 50 or 60 years, to the almost total loss of privacy, loss of identity and loss of autonomy? Since the time of Cohen and Taylor's original formulation of the problem of 'psychological survival', the questions of autobiographical retrospection and the narrative construction of social identities have assumed much greater salience in methodological and theoretical debates and in substantive social research. We have therefore been able to draw upon a developing tradition of inquiry, and its associated methodological protocols and principles in our efforts to answer questions about the place of the personal past, the problematic present and the uncertain future in the constitution of older prison lives (cf. Freeman 1993; Bornat 1994; Chamberlayne *et al* 2000).

Pragmatism and acceptance

It was interesting to note that some of our interviewees took a pragmatic or accepting approach to their predicament. These men were largely those who had been in prison a long time but they also included one or two 'first-timers'. Of the latter, these men commented that once they had got over the disorientating and stressful 'entry shock' phase of their imprisonment (the high noise levels, lack of privacy, impoverished facilities, claustrophobic atmosphere, bewildering array of rules and routines and, on occasion, hostility from both younger prisoners and from uniformed staff) they had begun, with the help of some of their 'neighbours'[12] to settle into – or at least learn not to rail against – prison life. When asked how they had managed to cope, many of our interviewees said that at the entry-shock phase their ability to call upon previous depriving experiences – particularly the experiences they had endured during their (often teenage) induction into army life[13] or a childhood in 'care'[14] – had been central to their emotional and psychological survival. On reception into the prison, memories of national service and army life (including the 'beasting',[15] the rigidity and pettiness of military rules, the rigid timetable and the enforced company of often disagreeable others) had come flooding back, providing an appropriate blueprint for how to perform in the prison setting and a belief that this episode in their lives could also be endured.

Coping strategies

Many of these prisoners – some of them in their late seventies – had thrown themselves into a variety of coping, time-consuming activities, including campaigning, letter-writing and list-making. With regard to the latter, 'Andrew', a prisoner in his seventies, told us how he recorded, in various notebooks, virtually everything that he did and that happened, including the dates/destinations of letters he sent/received; details of the medication he was taking and when he was supposed to take it and every visit to the prison nurse. We were intrigued (and rather sceptical) when he told us that he lifted 'four or five tons a day', but it turned out that he got this figure by multiplying the weight of the bar (20 kilos) by the number of times he lifted it (he claimed that he lifted it 400 times per session). He also said that he lifted the end of his metal bed frame 200 times a day – 'two hundred times a day, no more, no less' – in his efforts at self-discipline. According to the weight-lifting columns in his book records, he had done '35,000 lifts of my bed frame since Christmas' (a period of six months). Despite this lifting, Andrew was not a muscular individual; on the contrary, he was relatively thin and had the physique one might expect of a man of 74. He was, nonetheless, relatively mobile for a man of his age and walked briskly about the wing. Andrew also made a note of every penny he had spent at the canteen, made lists of words he came across that he especially liked (e.g. 'decrepitude' and 'contemporaneous') and compiled scrapbooks of newspaper cuttings he found interesting. He also went to computing classes, had gained 30 certificates for various competitions and education courses and regularly assisted in the prison chapel. For Andrew, this apparently endless stream of activity, record-keeping and list-making was clearly a successful survival and coping strategy.

Other older prisoners also went to education, were engaged in light employment (see below), participated in various 'treatment' courses[16] or simply pottered around the wing and visited their 'neighbours'.[17] Others, for reasons of ill health and poor mobility, found they were much more restricted in what they could find to pass the time and, consequently, found it difficult to find a sense of purpose. Older prisoners tend to have an orientation to work, largely because they have usually worked all their lives. For this generation, work is a strong component of personal identity and once they are unable to do it, many older people feel bereft. Consequently, even when prisoners no longer *have* to work in prison, i.e. when they reach retirement age, most still choose to do so, even if they are not in the best of health, and they tend to do so for as long as they can. One of our prisons (HMP Wymott) had been successful in securing small-scale outside contracts involving light work (such as comb packing) which could be done sitting down. Such work enabled elderly prisoners to continue some degree of employment (and hence a work identity), to earn a little money and in the process, to chat and reminisce. This was clearly a beneficial development; indeed, we were struck by the extent to which formerly listless and despondent elderly prisoners, most of whom had previously whiled away the days sitting alone in their cells, became more animated and, to some extent, more active by their engagement in this activity. The flexibility of the work routine (infirm prisoners who needed to were allowed to take a rest in their cells and then return to work) meant that the vast majority of the elderly men on this unit could be involved in work to some degree if they so wished. At the end of each working day, usually around 3.30 p.m., the men returned to their cells to relax, listen to the radio or watch TV. With regard to the latter, it has been interesting to note, in our study of this older prisoner group, the benefits (and problems) of allowing in-cell television (for a wonderful analysis of television viewing in prisons, see Jewkes 2002; see also Johnson, this volume). At HMP Kingston, for example, permitting several televisions in one room (in this prison, rooms were shared by up to five men) led to innumerable arguments. This was perhaps unsurprising given that each man might want to play a different channel, at a different noise level (several prisoners were hard of hearing), at a different time of the day to his room-mates (those who found it difficult to sleep at night often watched television into the small hours – a practice which, on one occasion, led to a scuffle between two elderly prisoners and resulted in other prisoners pressing the alarm bell for staff assistance). On the other hand, we found that where only one television was available in a shared room, friction often developed over whose turn it was to choose the programme. At HMP Littlehey, where cells did not have sufficient power-points to permit the plugging in of a TV, prisoners could rent, for a pound a week, a small, battery-charged television. Unfortunately for those with poor eyesight, these televisions were very small (approximately four inches square); they also only ran for a period of approximately four hours until the batteries expired, so unless the prisoner had spare batteries, they were often unusable until new batteries arrived with the next canteen order. Those who could not afford batteries, i.e. those who were unemployed and only received a basic pensioner's allowance (approximately £3.50 per week), did without the television until the next 'pay day', while others with greater access to funds were able to buy a battery charger. Like the prisoners interviewed by Jewkes (2002), our elderly interviewees appreciated a variety of programmes, including horse racing, football, *The Antiques Road Show* and *Flog It*.

Adaptation and trepidation

Some of those prisoners who had grown old in the prison had lost touch with the outside world, lost touch with family and friends, doubted their ability to make independent decisions and, in many respects, viewed the prison as home (for a discussion of this in the US context, see Aday 2003). Some of these men could barely remember how long they had been in prison; one thought it was 'about thirty years', another thought he had come into prison when he was 'about forty' (at the time of our interview he was 62) and a third, an Alzheimer's sufferer, neither knew where he was, how long he had been there or what he was there for. Among our long-serving interviewees, the claim that there was 'nothing and no one to go out to' was not uncommon. Perhaps unsurprisingly, these men showed little interest in being released. One such prisoner (we shall call him Max) had served previous prison sentences. He came into prison on his latest sentence at the age of 61 years and at the time of our short and somewhat laboured conversation (he was not very inclined to talk) was 73 years old. He had a long, grey beard, wore shabby and stained prison-issue jogging clothing and shared a dirty, airless room[18] with three other men. When asked how long he had been in this particular prison, he said 'Three or four years – I'm not sure', then reflecting on his sentence, said that he 'got an eight to nine year tariff over ten years ago'. When asked, Max said that he had not been on a town visit (it was the practice on this wing for those with prospects of release to be taken into the local town two or three times a year for reintegration/resettlement purposes) but that he did not want to go on a town visit anyway. When asked why this was, he replied that he was 'not interested in what's out there'. We were also struck by the number of elderly men who, although not particularly wishing to stay in prison, nonetheless were anxious about release.[19] In some cases this was hardly surprising, given that, although only two or three weeks away from their release date, they had still not received confirmation from Probation as to where they were going to live or who would support them once they were out. For elderly, relatively frail men, fears of hostel life were often intense. Not only were they unsure if they could cope with the nature of hostel life and with the behaviour of other men living there,[20] they had no one to visit or to visit them. As one prison chaplain observed, this was indeed 'a tragic and lonely end to a life'.

Coping with thoughts of death and dying

Fear of physical and mental deterioration was significant among many of our interviewees, particular those on regular medication for chronic illnesses. Not only were the latter restricted in their movements (thus making access to, and involvement in, certain activities held in other parts of the prison (e.g. education, library, chapel, workshops) difficult or impossible.[21] As Cohen and Taylor (1972) noted more than 30 years ago in their interviews with much younger men, many long-term prisoners are obsessively concerned with signs of deterioration, and that 'the features of prison that provoke these concerns include the fact that prisoners frequently receive unfavourable labels'.[22] When people are chronically ill, they are forced to confront their own mortality. In the prison setting, where access to immediate medical help (especially at night) can be problematic, fear and anxiety about having a heart attack, stroke, asthma attack or a fall can be great. Another stressor of long-term confinement in later life is the possibility of a prison death. Indeed, common to each of our older prisoner groups was a dread of dying in prison. All recognised that a prison death was not unlikely given their age and the length of their sentence (several of our interviewees who were in their seventies had a number of years left to serve). Increasingly, older offenders are receiving sentences that will keep them imprisoned for the remainder of their lives. Sadly but perhaps unsurprisingly, several of our interviewees – all of them life-sentenced prisoners (one a 'natural lifer') expressed a deep yearning to die as free men and in the company of a loving family and friends. The growing numbers of elderly, frail prisoners can put medical staff – who are primarily interested in the (physical and emotional) comfort of their patients and in providing compassionate nursing care – at odds with the often rigid security concerns and procedures of the prison environment. Like their counterparts in the free community, dying patients in prisons also need mental and spiritual preparation to prepare them for the process of dying (Aday 2003: 166) and this is difficult to achieve in traditional prison settings. If the Prison Service of England and Wales accepts medical evidence that a prisoner has only three months or less to live,[23] prison medical staff can seek community hospice care for that prisoner. Those who do not meet the three-month criterion, but who nonetheless have serious medical conditions that are clearly exacerbated by the nature of the prison environment (e.g. high noise level, stairs, thin mattresses, slippery flooring, restricted bedding allowance), are generally expected to stay where they are.

Struggling to survive: Denial and distress

For some of our interviewees, prison life was a lonely, almost unbearable struggle. The oldest of our interviewees (we shall call him Thomas) simply could not come to terms with the fact of his imprisonment, nor with the knowledge that his last days will be spent in the prison. Like many of his fellow prisoners, Thomas felt bewildered and resentful that he had been imprisoned for crimes carried out so long ago; he felt that justice should be *swift* as well as fair; and from his experience, it was neither. It was only now – decades after the crime was committed and when he himself felt too old to cope with imprisonment – that he was being punished for these crimes. Feelings of resentment, desperation and panic were particularly intense for Thomas because he had been given, at the age of 79, a 'natural life' sentence for crimes that took place 57 years ago and which he steadfastly denies committing. Consequently, his conversations with us about his past, his present and his (ultimately bleak) future were often punctuated, much to our own distress, by suppressed sobs, streams of tears and cries of bitterness and exasperation. As Thomas put it, his sentence simply marked 'the end of everything'. He knew that for him, release – the light at the end of the tunnel that most prisoners do eventually get to see – would never come. Although the thought of death in confinement is, for most prisoners, simply appalling, for prisoners like Thomas and others like him it represents release:

> Every night I hope I don't see the morning because there is no life for me. I am depressed twenty-four hours a day, and I know I'm going to die in prison. I hope I don't wake up – there is no life for me.

With bitterness he reflected that for 60 years he had worked hard, he had raised a respectable son and he had lived a blameless life, yet it had counted for nothing:

> I never missed a day's work, not even when I was feeling unwell. I was never on social security and now when I deserve it [a restful and respectable retirement] I have to spend my life in the prison. Work and bed, work and bed, that's all I been doing all day all my life – and now look.

This prisoner's health problems (in addition to being hard of hearing, breathless and unsteady on his feet, Thomas was taking eleven types of medication for heart problems, poor circulation, water retention, arthritis and diabetes) restricted his access to prison activities and to a wider range of prisoners and staff beyond his own landing, and this increased his feelings of depression and isolation.

> I feel dizzy a lot – two or three times a week I fall down at the side of the bed. Sometimes I fall down somewhere else. I don't want people to see me like this.

Finally, we wish to comment on the prison life of 'Roberto', a man 80 years of age who was sentenced to five years' imprisonment in 2001 for sexual offences carried out 25 years ago. Like Andrew, Roberto eventually signed up to full-time prison education – computer studies, 'citizenship' and 'life skills'. At weekends he attended mass and, although he found it very difficult to get to certain locations outside of the wing (he was only able to walk with the aid of a stick), he was, at the time of our interviews, rehearsing for the prison drama and choral group as this allowed him to emphasise his former identity of 'a great voice'. Although not as intensive as Andrew's, Roberto's time-filling pursuits served the same purpose, i.e. they 'make the time go more quickly and take me out of myself'. For Roberto, a genteel, quiet, cultured individual, the prison was:

> An alien place … The [bad] language, the uncouth behaviour, the shouting … it's the first thing you hear in the morning and the last thing at night – some invective or other. Oh, so dreadful … so dreadful.

Reflecting, at my request, on his childhood, Roberto said that he:

> Had a great gift. I was a singer – a boy genius. I sang all over the country – Bach, Mozart, Schubert. And now … I just feel so sad that my life's had to come to an end in a place like this … [I've had] an unfulfilled life. Yes.

Reflecting on the pains he experienced upon reception into the prison:

> It was difficult for me [when I came in] because my life was so correct before these allegations. It's different for those who have been in prison before, they accept it. Me, I can't accept it. I live for the day I can walk through that gate. This is a world that is apart from me, even though I'm part of it.

For Roberto, prison life was 'polluting', and as such, he felt tainted by its effects. He said that he had struggled to keep his Catholic faith but, in his deepening depression, felt that 'sadly, even that seems to be dying now'. On his own wing, Roberto was comforted and supported by a small number of his neighbours – men of roughly the same age. Generally referring to him as 'poor Roberto', several of his neighbours told us that they found his ill-health and despondency upsetting, and that they did whatever they could to help.[24]

Elderly prisoners and the life review

We want now to turn to other psychological and emotional impacts on men given a prison sentence late in life. As we live out our everyday lives, we are all engaged – both consciously and unconsciously – in a complex process of identity construction, identity maintenance and identity performance. As we build, rework and develop, over the years, our sense of self and our place in the world, we embroider, tone down, 'forget', try out and ultimately weave together a 'pick-and-mix' selection of those events, recollections, friendships, experiences, endurances and achievements (and the emotions that accompany them) that are most significant and precious to us. As though through a kaleidoscope, we shake up and then refocus these pieces (the stories) of past and present; as we do so we attempt to re-present them as a coherent *narrative* of our lives, one which is 'designed to make sense of the fabric of the past' (Freeman 1993: 8). The narrative that we weave is one that we feel able to live with – it is usually one that generates the greatest sense of satisfaction and the least amount of guilt or emotional pain. It is to this life narrative that we turn when we undertake what Butler (1963) terms the 'life review' – a mental process that becomes more salient as we grow older and as we develop a greater sense of our own mortality. The life review – the tendency to look back over (and ultimately reassess) our lives is, for Butler, a normal developmental task of old age; as we realise there is limited time available to us we examine what kind of life we have lived and what kind of person we feel we have become. On the basis of this examination, we may ask ourselves whether we feel our life has been a success or a failure. Perhaps unsurprisingly, a positive evaluation is thought to enable us to deal positively with death; a negative evaluation, in contrast, can fill us with regret, anxiety and despair (on this see also Erikson 1959, 1985). Although we may wish to change what we are and what we have done, there is insufficient time left in which to do so and this can make the prospect of death difficult to endure. In such circumstances, the life review 'may involve the obsessive preoccupation of the older person in his past and may proceed to a state approximating terror and result in suicide' (Butler 1963: 269). In our view, it is this recognition that time is running out that makes the prison experience of elderly men different from that of men not yet in middle age. The latter have sufficient years left to try to remake (and rewrite) their life when they are released; the former know they do not.

When an elderly individual's life narrative is suddenly unravelled, he may feel that all life's meaning has been lost and that he has been cast adrift. Indeed, for those of our interviewees who had been convicted and imprisoned in retirement (usually for crimes committed in the long-distant past), the conduct of a life review was often traumatic. They realised that the narratives from which they had previously drawn satisfaction and pleasure in old age – in particular their relationships with family and friends and a 'respectable citizen' identity – had been 'erased', 'lost', 'rewritten', 'rubbed out'. With their personal family and social lives so drastically disrupted, most felt some degree of guilt, shame, regret, bewilderment and distress, either about the offence, the sentence or the implications of both for their families. Some felt that their social identities had been irreparably spoiled and that their lives – despite all they had achieved – had, in the end, been a failure. Those whose families and friends had abandoned them felt this particularly keenly.

Spoiled identity revisited: 'Proper' prisoners? 'Proper' prison officers?

Just as these men felt that their pre-conviction identities were all but lost, for elderly men, the construction of a new prison identity is also problematic. As we have noted elsewhere (see e.g. Crawley and Sparks 2003), the elderly man in prison is, compared to his younger counterparts, relatively compliant, dependent and quiet. As we indicated above, he is also likely to suffer from more chronic and acute illnesses and have more pressing needs for personal care. For these reasons, in the eyes of many staff the elderly man in prison is not seen as a 'proper' prisoner. Consequently, officers who choose to work with elderly prisoners are often seen by their colleagues as not doing 'proper' prison work, largely because the work is seen as too safe, too quiet and too predictable. The elderly prisoner, then, also blurs the boundaries of what it means to be a 'proper' prison officer. Indeed, working on a unit described by some officers as an 'old folks' home' because of the high proportion of elderly men living there is something to be resisted by many prison officers – not least because they perceive that much of the work to be done there represents a threat to professional status, in that it is dishonourable, domestic, 'women's work'. Consider this comment from a prison officer working with elderly men in HMP Littlehey:

> *Interviewer*: How much caring work would you be prepared to do with prisoners? Things like washing them, helping them to get dressed, things like that?
> *Prison Officer*: Well we are in no way nurses and we are in no way carers. We have a duty of care but we are not … I mean there's no way I'm going to do stuff like washing prisoners. We make sure there's clean sheets available, things like that, but if they need, say, nappies for incontinence things, that's health care. We try and keep a nice dividing line…

Concluding comments

Try as we may, we see no readily available solutions to the sorts of emotional, and indeed existential, troubles outlined in this chapter. To be sure, this account raises a host of practical implications on the levels of training, regimes, health-care provision, prison design and location, resettlement and palliative care and so forth, any of which could serve substantially to alleviate the predicament of older prisoners. There are also examples of practice elsewhere in the world – Canada is the case most familiar to us – which demonstrate that this issue can be made the subject of concerted policy attention, and to this extent rescued to some degree from its historic invisibility. Further attention is also urgently required to *explaining* the rapid growth in the number of older prisoners, not just in the UK but internationally (though not uniformly), both as a by-product of the more general phenomenon of mass incarceration and as a specific issue with its own particular dynamics in sentencing and paroling practices and, in turn, in contemporary political culture. Each of these issues are ones that we intend to explore much more fully in current and future work.

For the time being, in England and Wales at least, we stand at best on the threshold of this question becoming an explicit topic for policy. To date, most examples of innovation and recognition that we have been able to identify have been *improvisations* on the part of individual prison managers and indeed lower-level staff who have struggled to address a problem that has crept up on them unannounced and for which they often feel ill prepared. Although still quantitatively a minor issue within the overall contours of prison expansion, the issues are *locally* acute. Neither is there any reason on current projections to suppose that the issue will do anything other than increase in scale.

In the context of this still underdeveloped debate, the levels of distress that we have encountered in the course of our research propel us back towards first principles in the social analysis of imprisonment. We find ourselves, ethically as well as analytically, required to confront again the ethnographic moment of the research encounter and to attempt to render, almost as if for the first time, the strangeness and intractability of that world. It is perhaps notable that others currently also seem to be smitten by this mood of recovery. It seems timely and necessary to revisit the notions of 'the pains of imprisonment' and 'psychological survival' (see for example Crewe, this volume; Jamieson and Grounds, this volume) as well as to refresh these perspectives using other conceptual resources (Jewkes, this volume).

Reviewed in this way, the notion of the 'pains of imprisonment' seems less like a monument from the history of prison sociology and more like a pressing contemporary reality when we find those pains magnified by experiences of physical debility and emotional isolation. Similarly, the concept of 'psychological survival' (or indeed the somehow blander language of 'coping') appears in sharper relief when we are confronted by people who may literally not survive their sentence, or who at least have a credible fear that they will not. Our preliminary view, one which we intend to develop much further in subsequent work, is that the low visibility of the problem of elder imprisonment on the level of *policy* can also produce a certain inadvertence – what we have begun to think of as an 'institutional thoughtlessness' – on the level of *daily practice*, notwithstanding some outstanding local examples of sensitivity and care which we also wish to register and explore. Moreover, the peculiarly powerless and voiceless situation of older prisoners may also call for some rethinking of our understandings of prisoners' responses to the *legitimacy* of their position, given the very different conditions under which that discussion has previously been developed (cf. Sparks *et al.* 1996; Bottoms and Sparks 1995).

Thus the narratives of loss, disruption and anxiety that we have begun to record here seem to us to pose anew the question of how the experience of imprisonment intrudes upon the trajectory of any human life. For those who grow old in prison, and perhaps especially for those who enter prison for the first time in old age, questions of memory, identity, meaning and ultimately mortality, seem unavoidably to be entailed. Similarly there can be a loss of power, voice, esteem – even of having already been 'erased' – which small acts of thoughtlessness can painfully intensify. Equally, there can be instances of companionship, humour and generosity (whether from fellow prisoners or from staff) that markedly alleviate this otherwise bleak prospect. On one hand, these matters speak to much larger questions about ageing in contemporary Western societies and the strikingly divergent possibilities that open before us as we grow older (see, for example, Greengross 1985; Bernard and Phillips 1998; Phillipson 2000). On the other, they return us to the issue of what it is for any of us to spend a significant fraction of our life in confinement. We are only beginning to understand what results when these two sets of questions intersect.

Notes

1 In 2002, with funding from the Canadian High Commission Institutional Research Programme, a small-scale qualitative study by a UK research team which included one of the authors of this paper (Dr Elaine Crawley) was carried out with the aims of (1) examining the experience of the CSC with regard to older prisoners, most notably in the development of policies relating to custody (including the palliative care of the dying) and release, resettlement or community supervision; and (2) exploring the practical outcomes of these developments with a view to assessing their practical application in the UK (see Jamieson *et al* 2003).

2 Our use of the word 'proper' here does not indicate that we accept the *propriety* of imprisoning old people. Indeed, we are aware – and wish to explore further – that different countries in Europe already take divergent views on this. We intend to address this matter directly in subsequent papers.

3 We are extremely grateful to the Economic and Social Research Council (ESRC) for their financial support of this research project (Award No. R0000239840).

4 According to Folkman and Lazarus (1980), 'coping' is a mixture of thoughts and actions; individuals' coping styles and abilities can vary over time, and coping can be seen as a mediator of emotion.

5 Liebling's extensive work on prisoner coping (see e.g. Liebling 1999, 1992) does, however, cover some of the same ground. Jewkes (2002) is also concerned with coping, but here the emphasis is on the role of the media in the maintenance of the prisoners' sense of self.

6 We define as 'older' those prisoners who have reached the state retirement age of 65 years.

7 After much discussion we decided to confine our research to the experiences of older *men* in prison. This was largely for reasons of limited resources; while at each of our four selected prisons we were able to interview several male prisoners aged 65+ during each visit, we were not able to find sufficient numbers of women prisoners aged 65+ to interview during the same time frame. We felt that the experiences of women prisoners of the same age deserved more sustained investigation than we could have managed.

8 We have conducted interviews both in prisons where separate facilities for older prisoners are available (i.e. HMP Kingston and HMP Wymott) and in prisons where they are not. The prisons in which we carried out our research (these were selected on the basis that they housed relatively large numbers of older prisoners) were HMP Whatton (a Cat. C male in Nottinghamshire); HMP Wymott (a Cat. C male prison in Lancashire with a large VP Unit); HMP Littlehey (a Cat. C male prison in Cambridgeshire) and HMP Kingston (a Cat. B prison in Portsmouth). Although Kingston is a Category B prison, within it is a Cat C. wing for older prisoners (in this case those aged 50+).

9 Sieber *et al* (1993: 169) use the term 'relocation stress' to describe the feelings that elderly people are likely to experience when they have to move out of their familial home and into institutional care.

10 Like other prisoners, the elderly prisoner must not only cope with the initial impact of imprisonment, he may also have intense feelings of guilt, helplessness, hopelessness and loss. For the elderly man who has to leave an elderly, long-term partner to cope alone for several years (as one man put it, 'to fend for herself and with only half a pension'), feelings of loss and guilt can be overwhelming. Not only is he himself now dependent, his partner can no longer depend on him. Again, this is particularly true for those charged with historic crimes, when the disaster (i.e. the arrest) comes decades after the alleged offence and without warning.

11 That is not to say, however, that all prisoners are imprisoned because of their own actions. As we know, there have been numerous instances where innocent men and women have been wrongly imprisoned.

12 'Neighbours' were those in adjoining or nearby cells who provided company and support.

13 Most of our interviewees had done National Service and many had served in the Second World War.

14 When asked how he had managed to cope with prison life, one man remarked: 'I could cope 'cos I was in a children's home and then in the army. I've always been told what to do.'

15 In the Army, to be 'beasted' during basic training is to be forced by superior officers to endure a great deal of psychological and physical pressure. Beasting involves sleep deprivation, forcing 'squaddies' to run long distances carrying heavy packs (and to repeat the exercise if they are too slow) and verbal humiliation (see Hockey 1986). According to prison officers I interviewed in a study of prison work – all of whom claimed to having been beasted in a military fashion during basic training (see Crawley 2004a) – the aim of beasting is that recruits learn to obey orders (even unreasonable ones) without a second thought.

16 Participation in the Sex Offender Treatment Programme (SOTP) was compulsory for those sentenced for sex offences and who were keen for positive reports from psychology departments (and hence positive parole hearings).

17 Some of our interviewees told us that, each week, they took it in turns with a favourite 'neighbour' to buy a family-size cake from the canteen. This was saved until the weekend and they would then meet up in one or other's cell to have afternoon tea together.

18 Elaine Crawley's field notes record that her initial visit to this ground-floor room, located two floors down from the wing office, came as something of a shock. The linoleum floor was filthy and although it was two o'clock in the afternoon, two of the four prisoners living there were still asleep, entangled in bedding that was grubby and tattered and covered with tea, coffee and chewing-tobacco stains. It struck her as a room in which the men were left

almost totally to their own devices and into which staff barely bothered to look. In short, the elderly prisoners there seemed neglected. It is important to note, however, that during our more recent visits (spring 2004) plans were clearly under way to develop and improve the regime.

19   Anxieties about what release would bring were especially strong for those serving sentences for sexual offences against children. Several of our interviewees said that they had had to flee their homes, leaving all personal possessions behind, because of threats from neighbours to kill them or burn their houses down. In cases where offenders had expected to return home after the court hearing but had, instead, received a prison sentence, they had to rely on relatives or friends to retrieve personal possessions and this was not always possible. In numerous cases where the prisoner had been living in council-owned accommodation, it transpired that the housing office, upon hearing of the prisoner's conviction, had entered the property and thrown everything out, including personal papers and family photographs.

20   Reflecting the prison population as a whole, those who are released from prison to hostels are usually relatively young men. Many have histories of violence and problems of alcohol and drug abuse and, as such, are seen by elderly men as threatening.

21   The physical layout of all of our selected prisons included stairs and long corridors. Only one prison (HMP Kingston) had a stair-lift but this simply gave the less mobile access between floors of the wing in which they were housed. No stair lifts were available outside the wing. In none of our prisons was seating provided along the corridors to allow the less mobile to rest on their way to other parts of the prison.

22   There is insufficient space in this chapter to discuss this issue in any meaningful way. For this reason we reserve most of our thoughts on this issue, and the impact of labelling by staff, for a later paper.

23   In the prisons of England and Wales this criterion must be met by all prisoners seeking early release on medical grounds.

24   Like many of our interviewees, Roberto could simply not have managed certain tasks, e.g. carrying a meal tray, putting on his socks, filling his hot-water flask, fastening his buttons, cleaning his cell – without the help and support of his peers. Many did these tasks for no reward bar friendship; those formally recognised by staff as 'minders' of infirm prisoners could receive an additional £1.70 per week.

References

Aday, R.H. (2003) *Aging Prisoners: Crisis in American Corrections*. Westport, CT: Praeger Publications.

Bernard, M. and Phillips, J. (eds) (1998) *The Social Policy of Old Age*. London: Centre for Policy and Ageing.

Bornat, J. (1994) (ed.) *Reminiscence Reviewed: Perspectives, Evaluations, Achievements* Buckingham: Open University Press.

Bottoms A.E. and Sparks, J.R. (1995) 'Legitimacy and order in prisons', *British Journal of Sociology*, 46 (1), 45–62.

Butler, R.N. (1963) 'The life review: An interpretation of reminiscence in the aged', *Psychiatry*, 26, 65–75.

Chamberlayne, P., Bornat, J. and Wengraf, T. (2000) (eds) *The Turn to Biographical Methods in Social Science: Comparative Issues and Examples*. London: Routledge.

Clemmer, D. (1940) *The Prison Community*. New York: Holt, Reinhart and Winston, 1958; first published 1940.

Cohen, S. and Taylor, L. (1972) *Psychological Survival*. Harmondsworth: Penguin.

Crawley, E. (2004a) *Doing Prison Work: The Public and Private Lives of Prison Officers*. Cullompton: Willan Publishing.

Crawley, E. (2004b) 'Release and resettlement: Older prisoner perspectives', *Criminal Justice Matters*, 56 (Summer), 2004.

Crawley, E. and Sparks, R. (2003) 'Surviving prison in later life', paper presented at the American Society of Criminology Conference, November 18–22, Denver, Colorado.

Erikson, E. (1959) 'Identity and the life cycle: Selected papers', *Psychological Issues*, 1, 50–100.

Erikson, E. (1985) *The Life Cycle Completed*. New York: W.W. Norton.

Farber, M. (1944) 'Suffering and time perspective in the prisoner' in K. Lewin (ed.) *Studies in Authority and Frustration*. University of Iowa Press.

Folkman, S. and Lazarus, R.S. (1980) 'An analysis of coping in a middle-aged community sample', *Journal of Health and Social Behavior*, 21, 219–239.

Freeman, M. (1993) *Rewriting the Self: History, Memory, Narrative*. London: Routledge Press.

Greengross, S. (1985) *Ageing: An Adventure in Living*. London: Souvenir Press.

HMIPP (1999) *Lifers: A Joint Thematic Review by Her Majesty's Inspectorates of Prisons and Probation*. London: Home Office.

Hockey, J. (1986) *Squaddies*. Exeter: Exeter University Publications.

Hodgkinson, P.E. and Stewart, M. (1991) *Coping with Catastrophe*. London: Routledge Press.

Home Office (2002) *Prison Statistics England and Wales 2002*. London: Home Office, Research, Development and Statistics Directorate.

Jamieson, R., Crawley, E.M., Grounds, A. and Noble, B. (2003) *Final Report 'Older Prisoners in Custody and on Release: Lessons from the Canadian Experience'* to Canadian High Commission Institutional Research Programme (unpublished).

Jewkes, Y. (2002) *Captive Audience: Media, Masculinity and Power in Prisons*. Cullompton: Willan Publishing.

Liebling, A. (1992) *Suicides in Prison*. London: Routledge.

Liebling, A. (1999) 'Prisoner suicide and prisoner coping', in M. Tonry and J. Petersilia (eds) *Prisons*. Chicago: University of Chicago Press.

Phillipson, C. (2000) *The Family and Community Life of Older People: Social Networks and Social Support in Three Urban Areas*. London: Routledge.

Prison Reform Trust (2003) *Growing Old in Prison: A Scoping Study on Older Prisoners*. London: Centre for Policy on Ageing and Prison Reform Trust.

Raphael, B. (1986) *When Disaster Strikes*. London: Hutchinson.

Sieber, M.J., Gunter-Hunt, G. and Farrell-Holtan, J. (1993) *Coping With Loss of Independence*. San Diego, CA: Singular Publishing Group.

Sparks, J.R., Bottoms, A.E. and Hay, W. (1996) *Prisons and the Problem of Order*. Oxford: Oxford University Press.

Sykes, G. (1958) *The Society of Captives*. Princeton, NJ: Princeton University Press.

Chapter 14

Loss, liminality and the life sentence: managing identity through a disrupted lifecourse

Yvonne Jewkes[1]

> Being given a life sentence is like being told by a doctor that you're going to die, you know, like you've got a terminal illness. You feel as if your life's effectively over. And even when you've got your head down and started doing your time it doesn't get any better 'cos you don't know when you'll be able to start your life again, or even *if* you'll get that chance. It's every prisoner's greatest fear you know … that they'll be taken out of here in a coffin.

This was said to me by a life sentence prisoner who was in his sixteenth year inside during my earlier research on mediated identity and power in prisons (Jewkes 2002).[2] The quotation provides a context for this chapter and for an ongoing research study, the aim of which is to explore further some of the 'micro-aspects' of social life within a wider context of the organisational and institutional structures of the prison. Three themes run throughout the chapter. The first concerns the extent to which a life sentence seismically disrupts the lifecourse and forcibly suspends future expectations.

The chapter considers the ways in which – to continue the seismological analogy – the 'shock' of receiving the maximum penalty of life imprisonment and the 'aftershock' of entry into prison are experienced and managed in relation to the individual's sense of self and in relation to others. The second theme that underpins the chapter is the proposition that, for the 'lifer', loss of control over significant life events thwarts taken-for-granted assumptions about the lifecourse in ways that are comparable to the experience of chronic or terminal illness, especially when perceived by the patient as dying 'prematurely'. It will be argued that both indeterminate confinement and incurable illness are experienced as 'liminal' states. However, while liminality usually implies movement from one stage of life to the next, it will be suggested that a life sentence and a life interrupted by a diagnosis of chronic or terminal illness may be experienced as permanent or near-permanent liminal states.

The third and final theme will develop this analysis of the analogous relationship between life imprisonment and chronic or terminal illness with the aim of better understanding the ability of the human psyche to withstand extreme conditions. In brief, the chapter problematises the prevailing view that responses to both life inside prison and a life foreshortened by serious illness are predictable, inevitable and universally negative.

Managing a disrupted lifecourse

The term 'lifecourse' and its role in identity-making have received much attention in the social sciences in recent years. Although usually conceptualised as the period of human embodiment, it has been suggested that the term should be extended to embrace the notion of 'social' (as well as 'physical') existence and include life trajectories beyond the fixed moments of birth and death (Hockey 2003). Lifecourse transitions are the public rites of passage which usually involve a range of symbolic representations and rituals – from ultrasound scans through to post-mortems – and which validate the meaning of the event for the individual, the social group, and the wider society (Billington *et al* 1998). The notion of lifecourse implies not only a chronological order and pattern as we make the transition from one stage of life to the next, but it also connotes an 'ideal' whereby significant events and rites of passage – entry into the workforce, marriage or commitment to a long-term relationship, raising a family, retirement, decline into decrepitude – occur at the 'right time' (Exley and Letherby 2001). Of course, 'macro' economic, social and political changes have resulted in demographic fluidity and ideas about the 'right time' have become increasingly flexible and individualised. But nonetheless, events which interrupt the anticipated chronology of life may be experienced as profound assaults on the self and can create relationships with significant others that dramatically diverge from the 'ideal'. The ongoing impacts of lifecourse interruption can also result in negative effects. For example, the failure to experience certain 'expected' life events (e.g. marriage and raising children) or indeed to have unexpected events imposed with little sense of participation in or control over them (e.g. divorce or the death of a relative) may pose a serious and intractable challenge to an individual's self-identity. Consider these statements from two life sentence prisoners:

> I'm 34 but I feel 50. I'm going to be an old man by the time I get out of here … I'm terrified of losing Sharon. I'm lucky, I shouldn't be in here but she's stood by me. She's my wife, my lover, my best friend, everything to me really. But I get this little … 'belly feeling', I call it. Anxiety I suppose … When you hear guys in here saying they don't really know their families anymore … them and their wives are more like brother and sister … it's frightening to be honest with you.

> I like to think I have the resources to deal with anything, I've got the resolve to cope. But if a member of my family died I'd be spiritually broken. I'd recluse myself.

Focusing, then, on the effects of lifecourse disruption specifically experienced by those serving life in confinement, it is instructive to consider two aspects of living with a life sentence that illustrate the more general argument that the effects of imprisonment extend far beyond physical constraint. The two examples chosen are gendered lifecourse transitions that are highly bound by cultural expectations: women as mothers, and men as workers. In Western society, all women live their lives against a background of personal and cultural assumptions that they are or will be (and *want* to be) mothers. For women across all socio-economic groups, motherhood is proof of adulthood and a natural consequence of marriage or a permanent relationship with a man (Letherby 1994; Jewkes and Letherby 2002). But for a woman serving a life prison sentence, the issues of child-bearing and child-rearing are especially salient because losing control over time means potentially losing control over her fertility and her relationships with her children, both actual and as yet unborn (Walker and Worrall 2000). Despite recent technological developments and medical advancements, the 'biological clock' still has a much greater significance for women than for men. As one respondent in Walker and Worrall's (2000: 30) study of female lifers says, 'men can do a life sentence and come out and still have a family, but a woman can't come out at 40 or 50 and start a family'.

Involuntary childlessness may be experienced not simply as a life taking a different course from that which was anticipated, but as a 'failure' (i.e. failure to be a 'proper' woman), especially in an environment which reinforces ideals of femininity so pervasively, and where so many of the qualities of 'good' womanhood are synonymous with those of 'good' motherhood. Several writers have suggested that particular images and representations of femininity are central mechanisms in the social control of women (Smart 1976; Carlen 1983; Young 1990). Certainly, most women in prison endorse aspects of an idealised femininity and cherish the socially constructed ideal of motherhood, drawing much of their strength and sense of self from their roles as mothers, wives, girlfriends and daughters (Bosworth 1999). But when a life sentence is imposed, these roles may be forcibly suspended or even terminated, and future expectations – including motherhood – may have to be put on permanent hold. In a study of infertility, Houghton and Houghton (1984) suggest that when women discover that they are unable to have children they frequently grieve for the children and grandchildren they will never have, thus endorsing the proposition outlined above that the lifecourse has social as well as physical dimensions and extends beyond the physical period of embodiment. Such grief for unborn children is particularly hard to bear because there are no memories and the anguish is unfocused (Houghton and Houghton 1984, cited in Exley and Letherby 2001). It is likely that women in prison who are childless and who have had the opportunity to be mothers denied them because of the sentence they are serving, may experience a similar sense of loss and grief for the child they never had.

For men in confinement, one of the most salient deprivations is the restriction imposed on their ability to work. Many men serving life sentences are one-time offenders or – because of advances in forensic (notably DNA) technology – have received their sentences retrospectively, for crimes committed years, sometimes decades, before (Crawley and Sparks, this volume). Consequently, many have lived 'normal', 'respectable' lives prior to, or subsequent to, their offence, and a primary aspect of their identity is their trade or profession. For these individuals, prison is experienced as unemployment insofar as what passes for work in prison is usually repetitive, monotonous and fragmentary, and frequently more akin to occupational therapy (Sapsford 1983). Stripped of their work identities and concomitantly their status, men who are serving (especially indeterminate) long or life sentences may experience a loss of any marker by which to locate themselves within the social world (ibid.). Like the unemployed more generally, the loss of a clear time structure often chronically deprives them of meaning in their lives. Lacking the conventional resources to mark the transition from one time-band to the next (e.g. from work time to leisure time, or week to weekend), men in these circumstances may find that their sense of purpose, of feeling *in control* is diminished. This loss of temporal rhythm, combined with the lack of money with which to confirm one's status through symbolic consumption, can lead to an impoverished, passive and emasculated group (Bostyn and Wight 1987; Jewkes 2002).

Of course, it would be inaccurate and misleading to suggest that work has no meaning for women or that fatherhood is not an important aspect of male prisoners' identities. Women in prison may equally experience the loss of work-related status as an attack on their self-worth, and many men experience the separation from their children as one of the severest pains of imprisonment and work hard at maintaining their relationships with their families from inside prison. However, it is arguable that women and men do not feel the significance of these identities as much due to the social and cultural expectations that accompany such roles. Put simply, the statuses of male unemployment and non-motherhood are much more culturally meaningful and may therefore be more damaging for the individual than female joblessness and non-fatherhood.

Life and death

As the discussion above demonstrates, the sudden interruption of the lifecourse, and the realisation of what has been taken away, may be regarded as the ultimate sanction of life imprisonment. In denying individuals what could be contemporaneously considered to be basic human rights, indeterminate life sentence prisoners suffer more than a restriction of liberty: they are stripped of their fundamental sense of 'being' and may experience imprisonment as a kind of social death (Goffman 1961; Walker and Worrall 2000). The indeterminate life sentence may thus be experienced as a kind of bereavement for oneself; the loss involving lost worlds, lost futures and lost identities. When an interruption to the lifecourse occurs, expectations are put on hold, anticipated lifecourse transitions are experientially altered, and ceremonies traditionally and conventionally used to mark rites of passage (which help the individual to adjust psychologically to their new identity) are denied. Furthermore, while a 'real' bereavement usually involves public performance of grief, and rituals designed to alleviate emotional distress, the emotions felt by the life sentence prisoner, by and large, must be contained within, and manifested privately. As Walker and Worrall (2000) note, lifers have forfeited the right to grieve.

When considering the experiences of bereavement for oneself, striking parallels can be observed between being given an indeterminate life sentence and being diagnosed with chronic or terminal illness, especially when we consider them as frameworks for understanding and giving coherence to the disruption, disorder and dislocation that forcible suspension of one's routine brings. Changes within the self brought about by non-serious illness are usually assumed to affect our identity only temporarily as we adopt a 'sick role' (Billington *et al* 1998). That role is experienced as a mere interruption to other, more enduring roles or identities in the same way that a short-term prison sentence is often experienced as a blip in an individual's normal life and criminal career. But when illness is diagnosed as chronic or incurable, or when a prisoner has to come to terms with the indeterminacy of a life sentence, the self may be not changed, but lost. Studies of ageing and death suggest that perceptions of self and identity may be irrevocably altered as the body itself is transformed by degenerative illness. In a study of palliative care in hospices, Lawton (2000) notes that progressive disease can so undermine the body's integrity that claims to selfhood or social identity may be withdrawn, either by the patient or by their survivors. Although an extreme example, similar loss may be experienced by those who are spending a significant part of their life in confinement. The feeling of being in stasis while the world moves on around you only serves to intensify the experience of ageing and fears of physical and mental deterioration. In these circumstances prisoners place a high premium on pastimes that challenge the mind and exercise the body. But memory also becomes a crucial aspect of 'being', locating the self outside of the corporeal constraints of confinement and linking the individual with their former self no matter how different they may since have become (Lowenthal 1985; Jewkes 2002). The ability to remember allows us to be temporally extended in time and space. We transcend not just our present but our historical, socio-cultural and geographic location (Adam 1995). The faculty of memory shifts our sense of self from a painful present to a remembered past and can thus be an important aspect of living with a life sentence or with diagnosis of incurable illness. In both circumstances, memory permits the recovery of former identities and allows the individual to retain a sense of their 'true self'. Illnesses that rob the individual of their memory are viewed as especially cruel and dys-identifying, but in such circumstances the memories of a person that are held by their loved ones may similarly operate to keep alive the true 'essence' of the person's character.

The 'rational despair' brought on by the 'inherent uncertainty' of life imprisonment (Walker and Worrall 2000: 27) is mirrored in the literature on coping with being diagnosed with HIV or cancer. In both cases the individual is denied a self-determining future, and both conditions involve structuring knowledge and experience around time; specifically, an unknown and unknowable quantity of future time. In fact, while the linking of life sentence imprisonment with incurable illness around the 'problem' of time does not imply that the experience is precisely the same, the similarities may be greater than suggested at first sight. For example, it might be broadly assumed that the problem for an individual serving life is likely to be one of having *too much* time, whereas for the sufferer of chronic or terminal illness, there is likely to be an overwhelming sense of *too little* time. But as Jamieson and Grounds (this volume) imply, individuals serving very long prison sentences live their lives along two very different trajectories. In one sense, they do indeed have 'too much' time and the copious references to 'doing' time, 'marking' time and 'killing' time that underpin sociological prison research indicate the amorphous, monotonous, endless nature of temporality in prison just as effectively as the term given to a prison sentence in popular discourse – a 'stretch'. But while prison inmates must find ways of passing significant amounts of unstructured time and of adapting to being 'caged in a boring, regressive present' (Burman 1988: 139), they must simultaneously cope with a sense of their lives being foreshortened. Just as patients facing their own mortality might feel that their lives are ending before their allotted time, and may experience a profound sense of de-synchronicity, especially if they are outlived by their parents, life sentence prisoners frequently feel a profound sense of time being stolen from them. In their circumstances, it is not unusual for the passage of time to stultify their awareness of their growing maturity. As one prisoner in his sixties said to me:

> I haven't got a day older since being in prison. I'm still thirty … I wonder why I'm not getting anywhere with the female screws and then I look in the mirror and of course get a shock.

Other life sentence prisoners echoed these comments and remind us once again of the fear of one's own mortality that prison engenders:

> I was 27 when I came in. Now my body's saying I'm 45 but my brain's still 27. The minute you come into prison it's like your watch has stopped. Entry shock didn't hit me for seven years. I spent seven years kicking off, being angry – it made me survive. It was the injustice, the sheer cheek of the criminal justice system. I met the Guildford Four and all those and it just made me very despondent with the criminal justice system. When people in here try and commit suicide it makes me feel very sad. Very sad. But

that's good because I know it means I'm still in touch with my feelings. I don't get visits though. I said no visits. They used to wind me up. My biggest fear is dying in prison. Sometimes I lie awake at night not daring to go to sleep in case I don't wake up. And that's terrible because trying to get to sleep when you can't doubles your time.

Prison is a terrible waste of life. I sometimes look in the mirror and don't recognise myself. Your body changes, grows older, but emotionally you stay the same, you stay an adolescent. My sister's kids come to visit me and I find I relate really well to them. Daft really 'cos they're half my age.

This sense of existing in the 'wrong' time and being of a different generation to one's peers is even more pronounced if or when the individual is released from prison, particularly if – as is common – they still *feel* the same age as they did when they started their sentence (cf. Jamieson and Grounds, this volume).

Both life in confinement and chronic or terminal illness help to define us socially and have implications in terms of our place within the world and our relationships with those around us. In such states, the transition from being one identity to another frequently is imposed *upon* us and doesn't sit easily with our own sense of self (Billington *et al* 1998). Like admission to hospital as a patient, reception into prison can be experienced as disempowering and infantilising, and in both institutions, the entrant may be made to feel powerless and stupid on a continuing basis (Oakley 1984). Illness – once diagnosed – legitimately releases the individual from social participation and requires him or her to take on a new social role (Billington *et al* 1998). Similarly, it is common to find in the prison literature references to inmates 'leaving their identity' at the prison gate to be 'picked up' again on release – although, of course the indeterminacy of 'life' makes the 'pick-up point' a very unpredictable affair (Schmid and Jones 1991; Jewkes 2002). Both medical appointments and prison receptions become more than forms of ritual which serve practical or technical purposes. They have the effect of securing the recipient's consent to a specific set of procedures, norms and values and require him or her to relinquish responsibility to a higher authority. Successful induction into the culture of both institutions is achieved through symbolic manifestations of power (e.g. the doctor's white coat and the prison officer's dark uniform) and in both medical environments and prisons, encounters between active and passive parties are highly structured events that help to secure consent at a point when the individual may be unwilling or resistant to make such a transition (Billington *et al* 1998).

While in some cases a life sentence might be said to be anticipated (if an individual commits a crime that carries this sanction) in the same way that diagnosis of chronic or terminal illness might not be entirely surprising (if an individual makes lifestyle choices that put his or her health at risk), both are nonetheless experiences that most individuals concerned do not plan for. Although, as Giddens (1991) notes, individuals possess the capacity to react to such unexpected occurrences and incorporate them into the reflexive project of the self, they must still adjust to the disruption of certain taken-for-granted assumptions about their lives. Moreover, both life sentence prisoners and patients who face dying 'prematurely' might be said to be occupying marginal spaces. They are neither here nor there. A range of theoretical perspectives from sociology could be drawn on here (such as Simmel *et al*'s concept of the 'stranger' (1997), Goffman's 'territories of the self' (1959), or Becker's definition of the 'outsider' (1963)) but this chapter takes as its point of orientation the notion of 'liminality' which originated in the work of anthropologist Arnold Van Gennep (1908) and was developed by, among others, Victor Turner (1982) and Mary Douglas (1966).

Van Gennep argues that lifecourse transitions involve shifts between fixed points within social systems; for example, childhood, marriage and death. In moving between different social statuses, individuals are, temporarily, ambiguous in terms of their social identity (Billington *et al* 1998). Van Gennep uses the terms *separation*, *liminality* and *reintegration* to denote the stages through which a lifecourse transition is made. In other words, in order to change status (e.g. from child to adult, from single person to married partner, from worker to retiree, from healthy being to patient, or from 'free' citizen to prison inmate), the individual must be separated from their previous position within social structure; they must then occupy a liminal space which disengages them from both their past and future roles, before finally being incorporated into a new, relatively stable and well-defined position in society. The following quote from Turner may help to explain the idea of liminality:

> [A] period and area of ambiguity, a sort of social limbo which has few ... of the attributes of either the preceding or subsequent social statuses or cultural states ... In liminality, [everyday] social relations may be discontinued, former rights and obligations are suspended, the social order may seem to have been turned upside down.
>
> (Turner 1982: 24, 27)

Liminality can refer to physical spaces that act as a boundary zone where one group of individuals, or one kind of environment, is distinguished from another. The doctor's or hospital waiting room, the prison reception area and the holding bay for prison visitors all represent liminal spaces. As these examples demonstrate, passage through the liminal environment signifies uncertainty, vulnerability, chaos and danger because customary rules are upturned and normal codes of activity or behaviour are suspended. However, the intensity of the experience, often involving pain and humiliation, allows change to take place and new possibilities to arise (Billington *et al* 1998). For example, common in popular discourses are stories about people diagnosed with terminal illness (perhaps the ultimate state of liminality insofar as it positions the individual precariously between life and death) who, after an initial period of trauma, go on to find a renewed zest for life, defying medical professionals' predictions of life expectancy and, in many cases, finding previously undiscovered talents or enjoying a period of heightened creativity, allowing them to circumvent both medical and social ascriptions that label them pejoratively.

Similarly, in relation to life imprisonment, while the rippling shockwaves of being sentenced and incarcerated might be every bit as mortifying as much of the 'pains of imprisonment' literature suggests, the traumatising impact is not necessarily permanent or long-lasting. The self may be temporarily suspended, but may reassert itself at a later point as the initial feelings of fear and loss subside. Indeed, many prisoners serving life sentences find that, after a period of resistance and readjustment, they are able to reconstruct their narratives of self:

> I wasn't happy with my identity before I came in, I felt a failure. Now I need to prove I can do what I'm doing. I'm doing an Open University degree ... I read newspapers and watch TV, but select things that are a lot more intellectual than I would have before. It's all part of the re-invention of myself. I've matured more in the past five years than in the 34 years before. I'm studying Ancient Greek and I read proper newspapers. If I'd been put inside when I was sixteen, I might have turned out a better person. I was a wimp when I came in; now I'm much more assertive.

Education, body-building, religion, work and even, as the quotation above suggests, reading a 'proper' newspaper can all become integral to the creation of 'redemption narratives' (Maruna 2001): strategies of resistance and empowerment that allow inmates to form entirely new, 'unspoiled' identities independent of their past or present circumstances (Jewkes 2002). Such a strategy is reminiscent of Irwin's (1970) classification of 'gleaners' – individuals who have rejected some of their previous subcultural values and undergone something of a 'conversion'. But the point to emphasise here is that conversion comes from instability, vulnerability and confusion. It is only by becoming liminal that individuals are able to construct new narratives of self.

Liminality, then, can refer to states of being or states of mind, as well as physical spaces, as we pass from a period of stability to one of ambiguity or undergo some kind of transformation. Of course, individuals who are enduring some form of social exclusion – the chronically sick, terminally ill, and life sentence prisoners among them – may experience a permanent liminality in that they are not moving between established boundaries. Moreover, Douglas's (1966) suggestion that liminal spaces are often repositories for the fears and anxieties of the wider social group is particularly resonant in these examples: there are few groups who combine cultural manifestations of 'stigma' and 'taboo' to the extent that must be borne by life sentence prisoners and the terminally ill. However, as we shall see later, this does not necessarily imply that such individuals are cowed into a state of passivity and powerlessness.

Victor Turner uses the term 'liminoids' to describe individuals who inhabit liminal spaces ('-oid' meaning 'like' or 'resembling', rather than 'identical'). The distinction between liminal and liminoid is frequently blurred, but one linguist has distinguished them thus:

> [While] liminal practices tend to contribute to the smooth functioning of social systems, liminoid practices are often creative, containing social critiques and exposing wrongs in mainstream structures and organisation ... Similarly, liminality tends to involve symbols with common intellectual and emotional meaning for all members of the group, while liminoid phenomena tend to be more idiosyncratic, quirky, to be generated by specific named individuals and in particular groups.
>
> (Rampton 1997: 5; cf. Turner 1982: 54)

The concepts of liminality and liminoidity thus merge with a number of other themes that recur in discussions of late- and post-modernity. For example, they complement Foucault's (1977, 1978) notion of 'limit-experiences' and Giddens' (1984) theory of 'discursive consciousness'. To take each of these in turn, limit-experiences are activities laden with risk or danger (which in Foucault's work, and in his life, included anonymous sex, sado-masochism, drugs and AIDS – an inventory to which we might also add falling in love and madness) that explode the limits of consciousness, breaching the boundaries separating the conscious and unconscious, reason and unreason, pain and pleasure, and ultimately life and death (Miller 1993). Like liminal practices, limit-experiences push us to extremes and have a transformative, self-transcendent capacity (an idea that has recently been found, in a slightly different guise, in the emerging field of cultural criminology which views much criminalised activity in this way). Limit-experiences may be indulgent, delinquent and dangerous but they allow us to exercise control and take responsibility for our own destinies. Ultimately (and ironically) these dangerous, and sometimes deadly, pursuits give us a sense of aliveness. Although serious illness has been conceptualised in this way (Sontag 1978/2002), the notion of life imprisonment as limit-experience has yet to be explored.

While *liminality* bears some similarities to limit-experiences, Turner's conceptualisation of *liminoidity* echoes Giddens' notion of discursive consciousness; one of two levels of reflexivity in which social actors are continually engaged. While 'practical consciousness' refers to the 'doing' of social interaction and social life in a way that reproduces the structured, predictable properties of everyday social life, discursive consciousness denotes individual autonomy and agency. It also implies scrutiny and criticism, not just of the self and one's own actions, but of society and social institutions (Billington *et al* 1998). It is at this level of reflexive practice that individuals can 'make a difference' and affect social change. Giddens' theory thus helps us to understand how the social life of prisons is both patterned and ordered, and at the same time, dynamic and changing. In brief, Giddens argues that social structures are both constituted *by* human agency, and yet at the same time are the very *medium* of this constitution. Like people in all areas of everyday life, prisoners are subject to the patterns, discourses and logic of the organisational and institutional context in which they find themselves. But the reverse is also true, and life (in any sphere, but not least the prison), although immensely routinised and structured, only 'happens' because 'real-life, flesh-and-blood people make it happen' (Sparks *et al* 1996: 72). This 'duality of structure' (Giddens, 1984) should alert us to the dangers of assuming that a life sentence (or any other prison sentence for that matter) is experienced in the same way by all those who undergo it. On the one hand, structuration theory helps to explain why so many studies of the effects of imprisonment share similar themes, definitions and findings. The clear emergence of discernible patterns of behaviour among individuals undergoing similarly traumatic experiences suggests that, when it comes to the impact of confinement on the human psyche and the human spirit, the meaning of the prison has certain universal features. Little wonder, then, that common conceptualisations of the inmate code, prisoners' strategies for coping and adaptation, and the relationship between the self and the environment are to be found in the literature on imprisonment dating back over most of the last century.

On the other hand, it is important to underline that prison research does not stand still. For example, two recent studies that have sought to chart *transformations* in the normative experience of those who are confined, have noted – contrary to some of the 'classic' prison texts – the decline of solidarity among inmates and a growing sense of individualisation: a trend that is consistent with recent neo-liberal policy developments based on the idea of punishment being a social contract, but one which is at odds with notions of collective responsibility and the value of friendship in difficult circumstances (cf. Jewkes 2002; and Crewe, this volume). Similarly, counter to much of the so-called 'coping literature', several contemporary studies have highlighted the fact that many inmates simply do not cope and, in many cases, even fail to see *why* they should cope (Liebling 1992, 1999; Walker and Worrall 2000; Crawley and Sparks, this volume). So, while it is interesting to note the similarities between responses of inmates today and those whom Sykes (1958), Bettelheim (1960), Goffman (1961) and Irwin and Cressey (1962) observed nearly half a century ago, we should remain mindful that flesh-and-blood people do not experience events – even traumatising, stigmatising events – in an identical fashion. As McEvoy (following Matthews 1999) shrewdly observes, the inclination towards viewing certain behaviours as the *inevitable* response to the pains of imprisonment within closed institutions at times obscures 'important institutional dynamics' such as the way in which power is administered in prisons, and the ways in which internal flows of power interact with external political, economical, sociological and ideological forces (McEvoy 2001: 27). The extent to which this tendency homogenises differential responses to confinement, eliding personal, individual manifestations of power and resistance, is an emerging concern among prison sociologists. Even acts of suicide and self-harm in prison may be conceived as strategic and 'knowing' acts of resistance rooted in moral and political indignation rather than as passive admissions of defeat (Giroux 1983; Liebling and Krarup 1993).

Humanity and hope

Perhaps what unites the most successful sociological studies of confinement, then, is that they reveal what it means to be human; in terms of both the universal emotions and experiences that all individuals undergo when faced with potentially dis-identifying circumstances, and the particular, peculiar, idiosyncratic reactions that such circumstances can give rise to in any given time and place. It is this dual aspect of self that, in the current context, is most usefully served by comparisons with the literature on disruptions to the lifecourse brought about by incurable illness. Confinement within a diseased and degenerating body may be experienced as similarly dis-identifying as confinement within a prison cell (both incurable illness and life imprisonment may constitute a master status, subsuming all other personal identities), and both may be anticipated to give the individual a hyper-conscious awareness of self. Yet, even people who face the most dramatic lifecourse transition – from 'free' citizen to life sentence prisoner, or from healthy individual to chronically/terminally ill patient – are *agentic*: they are able to choose their response to their circumstances. For example, they can be willing victims, resigned fatalists or active resisters; they can take the view that their life scripts have been written for them long ago and that there is nothing they can do to change them, or they can reconstruct their own narrative, reclaim a sense of their personal identity and assert themselves as 'figure' against 'ground' (Burman 1988; cf. Maruna 2001).

One of the classic studies that most brilliantly captures the essence of being human (and illustrates the phenomenon that Giddens was later to term the 'duality of structure') is that written by Bruno Bettelheim about his experience of surviving two Nazi concentration camps in the Second World War. Describing the 'deep feeling impressions one receives in an extreme situation' (1960: 13), Bettelheim is also concerned (and here we find echoes of Turner's definition of liminality) to explicate the journey to self-realisation achieved within an environment that has the capacity to 'turn personality upside down' (ibid: 15). In this endeavour, he highlights the importance of autonomy – not 'rugged individualism' or 'noisy self assertion' but rather 'a quiet acting out of inner conviction' (1960: 72) – as fundamental to retaining a sense of self-determination and self-respect:

> To survive, not as a shadow … but as a man, one had to find some
> life experience that mattered, over which one was still in command
> … The two freedoms, of activity and passivity, constitute our two
> most basic human attitudes, while intake and elimination, mental
> activity and rest, make up our most basic physiological activities.
> To have some small token experiences of being active and passive,
> each on one's own, and in mind as well as body – this, much more

than the utility of any one such activity, was what enabled me and others like me to survive.

(ibid.: 147–8)

By way of illustration, Bettelheim highlights the twin themes of this chapter, pointing to the examples of a concentration camp inmate forcing himself to eat repellent food as a chosen act of freedom, self-imposed not SS-enforced, and a critically ill patient swallowing bitter medicine in an active desire to live. By contrast, he notes that it is the requirement to perform senseless tasks, the futility of present time, and the uncertainty of a future which made planning ahead pointless, that were deeply destructive:

> By destroying man's ability to act on his own or to predict the outcomes of his actions, they destroyed the feeling that his actions had any purpose, so many prisoners stopped acting. But when they stopped acting they soon stopped living. What seemed to make the critical difference was whether or not the environment – extreme as it was – permitted (or promised) some minimal choices, some leeway, some positive rewards, insignificant as they seem now.
>
> (ibid.: 148–9)

The prisoners who survived were those who came to realise what they had not perceived before; that they still retained the human freedom to choose their own attitude in any given circumstance:

> Prisoners who understood this fully, came to know that this, and only this, formed the crucial difference between retaining one's humanity (and often life itself) and accepting death as a human being (or perhaps physical death): whether one retained the freedom to choose autonomously one's attitude to extreme conditions even when they seemed totally beyond one's ability to influence them.
>
> (ibid.: 158–9)

For Bettelheim, the decision to remain alive or to die is probably the supreme example of self-determination (in much later life he killed himself by asphyxiation while living in a retirement home, an act that was entirely consistent with his views about personal autonomy in extreme situations). It also illustrates the extent to which the 'punishment effect' (Young 1998) of both imprisonment and, in a more tenuous sense, chronic or terminal illness, is limited. The patient can agentically choose not to take the medicine that might alleviate their pain and/or extend their life. But equally, the life sentence prisoner may define his or her own individuality in terms of cultural conformity or resistance to the prison regime. Whatever their circumstances, individuals are not mere bearers of structure but are complex amalgams of several influences, responding to their life experiences with greater or lesser degrees of compliance and confrontation. Whether chronically ill or incarcerated, the individual retains an area of control via the active self. Hence, even death, when precipitated or self-imposed, can be an act in which the unintelligible is made intelligible, thus challenging popular conceptions of death as 'point zero' where loss of control is total (Giddens 1991: 203).

Consider by way of example the following narrative. At the end of *The Informed Heart* Bettelheim tells the profoundly moving story of a group of naked prisoners about to enter the gas chamber. The commanding officer learned that one of the women prisoners was formerly a dancer and ordered her to dance for him. As she danced, she approached him, seized his gun and shot him, only to be immediately shot to death by another officer. Bettelheim reflects:

> Dancing, she was singled out as an individual...no longer was she a number, a nameless depersonalized prisoner, but the dancer she used to be. Transformed, however momentarily, she responded like her old self, destroying the enemy bent on her destruction, even if she had to die in the process...this one example, and there were several like her, shows that in an instant the old personality can be regained, its destruction undone.
>
> (ibid.: 265)

This moment of rapture seized by the prisoner as she danced in the face of death, is a powerful metaphor for the strangely intoxicating feeling that sometimes accompanies a journey into the unknown. Here, once more, the literature on serious illness provides a counterpoint to the 'pains of imprisonment' studies, and reminds us that mortification can be transposed into a seemingly much more positive emotion. For example, John Daniel describes his emotional responses to living with HIV. When his counsellor asked him how he felt on receiving a positive HIV diagnosis he said 'I feel exaltation'. 'Exaltation', said the counsellor as he began to look at the clock on the wall and then beseechingly at his patient, willing him to have other, more manageable feelings. 'That's a difficult one' (Daniel 1997).

Such responses to serious illness are far from uncommon:

> Exaltation was my initial response to breast cancer. I realised that a very complicated and at times empty life had become somehow simplified and somehow fuller. I really only had one thing to worry about. My illness.
>
> (Sontag, cited in Daniel 1997)

> I wouldn't say I'm glad HIV happened, but it sometimes feels like a terrifying mind-expanding drug that I would have been less of a person for not having experienced. Just wish like other such drugs I could give it up. At least life becomes a case of collecting your thoughts not your pension. Not necessarily a bad thing... philosophically.
>
> ('Jamie' in email correspondence to Ruth Picardie: Picardie 1998: 8)

Daniel – himself a professional counsellor – muses that the medical professions are unprepared or unable to redefine their emotional response to diagnosis of serious illness because to do so would require starting at a point in the emotional landscape that is unintelligible to them and threatening. So he began to draw his own map using Van Gennep's (1908) concept of liminality, recognising that liminal spaces are characterised by disorder and chaos, but that if one can create a path through them, they can affect positive change. He achieved this by learning to live at the borders and he describes his journey as one that has taken him from marginality (as a gay man who is a practising Catholic), through liminality (as a person diagnosed HIV positive), into 'active border living', which involves the 'shaping of a role which is different, distinct and separate from the cultural norm' but which allows the individual to live within the chaos of a destiny out of one's control (Daniel 1997). Again, Foucault's thoughts on limit-experiences may be recalled here. Acts of transgression allow us to traverse the boundaries of experience and find ways of being free (Foucault 1977). In showing up the limits of everyday life, they outline the trajectory of our very being. For Daniel, border living involves a certain solitariness but standing at the border he feels an equal, which is very different to the view from the margins where one is an outcast. Marking boundaries is an attempt to establish a new identity, to achieve self-determination, and to resist the feeling of helplessness that accompanies the unpredictability of permanent liminality. Like the dancer described above, those who live on the borders are making a conscious decision to honour the self.

Concluding thoughts

This chapter has highlighted some of the ways in which the experiences of life imprisonment and chronic or terminal illness each reveal how living under extreme conditions can open up new ways of understanding what it means to be human. The theoretical approaches outlined here will guide future empirical research, the aim of which is to shed light not only on the pains of indeterminacy, but also on the ways in which (gendered) patterns of coping emerge that enable life-sentence prisoners to reaffirm that life has a course and that the self has a purpose. It is hoped that the study will offer new insight into the ways in which social life is patterned and ordered and yet, at the same time, is dynamic and transformative. We get our roles 'off the peg' with cultural scripts attached (Billington *et al* 1998). But, at the same time, individuals are engaged in a continual process of rewriting their scripts.

The research objectives are to make a contribution to the ongoing discourse in criminological prison research concerning the effects of imprisonment, as well as to the debate on the comparative utility and justice of indeterminate sentences for men and women at a time when the rapid growth of the long-term prison population is causing concern. The research is located within a small but growing body of sociologically informed prison studies which recognise the value of critically analysing prisoners' subjective and experiential accounts – what Lyotard (1984) has called 'little narratives' – as a significant contribution to knowledge about prisons and imprisonment. One aim of the study is to explore the extent to which customary habits and culturally specific choices are transformed in liminal spaces. In *Captive Audience* (2002), I noted the ways in which personal routines and rituals – such as watching a favourite TV programme – change their meaning when experienced in a different context; for example, rather than being simply a reliable source of pleasure they become a symbol of loss or disconnection (Jewkes 2002). This new study will continue this line of inquiry but, instead of focusing on the meaning of media texts and technologies, it is anticipated that it will explore the culturally specific meanings attached to food, friendship, sex, health and illness, ageing and death within the context of loss and liminality. It also aims to underline the value of studying commonalities between prisons, the lived experience of imprisonment and prison research, alongside other institutions, social experiences, and bodies of literature in an effort to reach greater understanding of the effects of trauma on the human psyche brought about by a sudden and immense disruption to the lifecourse. However, the research will remain attuned to the personal responses of life-sentence prisoners to the pains of indeterminacy and their individual narratives of self. The extent to which life imprisonment can be conceived as a limit-experience will be an important theme, as will individuals' redemption narratives, their efforts to reinvent themselves, and their experiences of 'border living'.

As a final thought, this chapter has demonstrated that both the life-sentence prisoner and the chronic or terminally ill patient are required to negotiate their way through a world of 'nightmare uncertainties' (Sapsford 1983: 19). Yet there are three specific prison populations whose lives are overshadowed by the grim certainty alluded to in the lifer's comment quoted at the beginning of this chapter. They are individuals who are intent on taking their own lives in prison; those who are suffering degenerative or terminal illness while serving life sentences; and those who are serving 'whole life' tariffs. While the first group – those who have committed suicide – have been subject to attention from academics and policy-makers alike, and the second group – those suffering from (mainly) age-related degenerative illnesses – are the subject of renewed interest (see Crawley and Sparks, this volume), the third group – those consigned to imprisonment for the rest of their natural lives – are all but invisible in academic and policy discourses. In addition to recalling the narratives of life and death that underpinned my prison research in 1999, I am reminded of an individual whose story has, to some extent, haunted me over the intervening years. I interviewed Harry Roberts who, at the time of our meeting, had served 33 years inside. During the course of our conversation, we discovered that he had been sent down approximately three months after I was born, and we marvelled at the punitiveness of a judicial system that could keep someone confined for as long as I'd been alive – in fact, Harry seemed rather amused by the idea. I found him to be lively and engaging company as he described the furore surrounding his case and his recollections of leaving court in a Black Maria with police motorcycle escorts in tin helmets and garters, making a slow procession through crowds of Fulham football fans on their way to the match. Although in recent years sections of the British press have reported that Harry was handed a natural life tariff, in fact the Home Secretary was not successful in doing so. In 1997, when the Parole Board recommended that Harry should be transferred to an open prison, then Home Secretary, Jack Straw, failed to act on the recommendation for seven months, during which time he took legal advice as to whether he could increase the tariff to 'whole life' – a move that he was advised would be unlawful.

Despite the fact that his 30-year tariff had already expired three years prior to our interview, Harry epitomised the indefatigability of the human spirit. By his own admission a rule-breaker, he had attempted many escapes over the decades and had never decorated or personalised his cell on the grounds that 'it would institutionalise you to make it like home'. But now, at the age of 63, he was quietly looking forward to release, having been moved down the security classifications (to a low-security Cat. C prison at the time of our meeting) and taken on escorted visits to the nearest city to acclimatise him to life in the 'real' world. Shortly after our meeting in 1999, Straw finally accepted a Parole Board recommendation that Harry should be moved to an open prison and he was duly transferred to HMP Sudbury. However, this move was short-lived due to unfounded allegations including newspaper stories that he had made unauthorised visits to London, a set of circumstances which ironically coincided with a further recommendation that he was safe to be released. He has since been informed that more allegations have been made against him during his time in prison that are so 'sensitive' that they cannot be disclosed to either himself or his solicitor, and that the person or persons who have made the allegations have the right to remain anonymous. Moreover, a 'special advocate' was appointed to represent Harry's interests at his Parole Board hearing, but was not able to tell him or his solicitor what the evidence against him consisted of.

The decision to remove Harry from an open prison on the day his parole dossier was disclosed to him recommending his release, and the subsequent decision to keep the reasons for his move back to closed conditions 'secret', would appear to blur the distinction between a 'lawful' whole-life tariff and what effectively amounts to an 'unlawful' version of the same outcome. In July 2004, the Court of Appeal upheld the Parole Board's adoption of the special advocate procedure in order to protect its sources, thus authorising lawyers representing the current Home Secretary to use the secret evidence to argue against release. Harry Roberts' solicitor, Simon Creighton, believes the process to be a 'politically motivated farce' that will ensure that Harry remains in prison for the remainder of his life (private email correspondence). The unfairness of a system that detains a person indefinitely, prevents him from defending himself against unknown allegations that have come from a hidden source, and appoints a 'special advocate' to deal with the evidence at a private hearing – a measure designed by Parliament specifically for use against the threat of terrorism – is shocking to most liberal thinkers. The fact that Harry's crime was the murder of three unarmed police officers may explain the punitiveness with which he is being treated, but it does not make it seem reasonable, at least not to those of us who cannot recall the days of Black Marias and policemen in tin helmets and garters. For the police, this case occupies a powerful symbolic place in their history, but for the public – informed as we are by a popular media that considers only certain murderers suitable for sustained demonisation – the fact that this individual has served 38 years inside, and is now an elderly man of 68, does not trouble our conscience. Yet the much-quoted expression that the level of civilisation in a society is to be judged by how it treats its prisoners surely has never seemed so apposite. For those whose lifecourse has been frozen in another time, who occupy permanently liminal spaces, are denied the opportunity to reconstruct a narrative of self, and who – even in old age and decrepitude – are held in secure conditions because they are deemed to represent a danger to the public, the notion of civilisation must seem bleakly ironic.

Notes

1 Thanks go to Peter Young for commenting on an early draft of this chapter.
2 All the prisoners' quotations used in this chapter are taken from interview data collected during a period of research undertaken in 1999 in two Category C men's prisons in the English Midlands. Although written up and published under the title *Captive Audience*, most of the quotes in this chapter are cited here for the first time.

References

Adam, B. (1995) *Timewatch: The Social Analysis of Time*. Cambridge: Polity Press.
Becker, H. (1963) *Outsiders: Studies in the Sociology of Deviance*. New York: Free Press.
Bettelheim, B. (1960) *The Informed Heart: The Human Condition in Modern Mass Society*. London: Thames and Hudson.
Billington, R., Hockey, J. and Strawbridge, S. (1998) *Exploring Self and Society*. Basingstoke: Macmillan Press.
Bostyn, A.M. and Wight, D. (1987) 'Inside a community: Values associated with money and time', in S. Fineman (ed.) *Unemployment: Personal and Social Consequences*. London: Tavistock Publishing.
Bosworth, M. (1999) *Engendering Resistance: Agency and Power in Women's Prisons*. Aldershot: Ashgate Publishing.
Burman, P. (1988) *Killing Time, Losing Ground: Experiences of Unemployment*. Toronto: Wall and Thompson Publishing.
Bury, M. (1982) 'Chronic illness as biographical disruption', *Sociology of Health and Illness*, 4 (2), 167–182.
Carlen, P. (1983) *Women's Imprisonment: A Study in Social Control*. London: Routledge and Kegan Paul.

Daniel, J. (1997) 'The creative use of cognitive restructuring: From marginality, through liminality and beyond', in P.J. Barker and B. Davidson (eds) *Psychiatric Nursing: Ethical Strife*. London: Arnold. Available at: www.bendavidson. co.uk/professional_pages/publications/books/estrife/papers

Douglas, M. (1966) *Purity and Danger*. Harmondsworth: Penguin.

Exley, C. and Letherby, G. (2001) 'Managing a disrupted lifecourse: Issues of identity and emotion work', *Health*, 5 (1), 112–132.

Foucault, M. (1977) 'A preface to transgression', in *Language, Counter-Memory, Practice*. Ithaca, NY: Cornell University Press.

Foucault, M. (1978) *The History of Sexuality: Volume 1. The Will to Truth*, trans. R. Hurley. New York: Pantheon.

Giddens, A. (1984) *The Constitution of Society*. Cambridge: Polity Press.

Giddens, A. (1991) *Modernity and Self-Identity*. Cambridge: Polity Press.

Giroux, H. (1983) 'Theories of reproduction and resistance in the new sociology of education: A critical analysis', *Harvard Educational Review*, 53, 257–293.

Goffman, E. (1959) *The Presentation of Self in Everyday Life*. New York: Anchor.

Goffman, E. (1961) 'On the characteristics of total institutions: The inmate world', in D. Cressey (ed.) *The Prison: Studies in Institutional Organisation and Change*. New York: Holt, Rinehart and Winston.

Hockey, J. (2003) *Beyond the Womb and the Tomb: Towards a New Model of the Life Course*. Unpublished paper.

Houghton, D. and Houghton, P. (1984) *Coping With Childlessness*. London: Unwin Hyman.

Irwin, J. (1970) *The Felon*. Englewood Cliffs, NJ: Prentice-Hall.

Irwin, J. and Cressey, D. (1962) 'Thieves, convicts and the inmate culture', *Social Problems*, 10 (1), 142–155.

Jewkes, Y. (2002) *Captive Audience: Media, Masculinity and Power in Prisons*. Cullompton: Willan Publishing.

Jewkes, Y. and Letherby, G. (2002) 'Women in prison: Mothering and non-mothering identities', *Prison Service Journal*, (139) January, 26–28.

Lawton, J. (2000) *The Dying Process: Patients' Experience of Palliative Care*. London: Routledge.

Letherby, G. (1994) 'Mother or not, mother or what?: Problems of definition and identity', *Women's Studies International Forum*, 17 (5), 535–532.

Liebling, A. (1992) *Suicides in Prison*. London: Routledge.

Liebling, A. (1999) 'Prison suicide and prisoner coping', in M. Tonry and J. Petersilia (eds) *Prisons*, Crime and Justice, Volume 26. Chicago: University of Chicago Press.

Liebling, A. and Krarup, H. (1993) *Suicide Attempts and Self-Injury in Male Prisons*. Report for the Home Office Research and Planning Unit, September 1993.

Lowenthal, D. (1985) *The Past is a Foreign Country*. Cambridge: Cambridge University Press.

Lyotard, J.F. (1984) *The Postmodern Condition: A Report on Knowledge*. Manchester: Manchester University Press.

McEvoy, K. (2001) *Paramilitary Imprisonment in Northern Ireland: Resistance, Management and Release*. Oxford: Oxford University Press.

Maruna, S. (2001) *Making Good: How Ex-Convicts Reform and Rebuild their Lives*. Washington, DC: American Psychological Society.

Matthews, R. (1999) *Doing Time: An Introduction to the Sociology of Imprisonment*. London: Macmillan Press.

Miller, J. (1993) *The Passion of Michel Foucault*. London: Simon and Schuster.

Oakley, A. (1984) 'Doctor knows best', in N. Black, D. Boswell, A. Gray, S. Murphy and J. Popay (eds) *Health and Disease: A Reader*. Milton Keynes: Open University Press.

Picardie, R. (1998) *Before I Say Goodbye*. London: Penguin.

Rampton, B. (1997) 'Sociolinguistics and cultural studies: New ethnicities, liminality and interaction', *Working Papers in Urban Language and Literacies (4)*. King's College, London.

Sapsford, R. (1983) *Life Sentence Prisoners: Reaction, Response and Change*. Milton Keynes: Open University Press.

Schmid, T. and Jones, R. (1991) 'Suspended identity: Identity transformation in a maximum security prison', *Symbolic Interaction*, 14 (4), 415–432.

Simmel, G., Frisby, D. and Featherstone, M. (1997) *Simmel on Culture: Selected Writings*. London: Sage.

Smart, C. (1976) *Women, Crime and Criminology: a Feminist Critique*. London: Routledge and Kegan Paul.

Sontag, S. (1978/2002) *Illness as Metaphor and AIDS and its Metaphors*. Harmondsworth: Penguin.

Sparks, R, Bottoms, A.E. and Hay, W. (1996) *Prisons and the Problem of Order*. Oxford: Oxford University Press.

Sykes, G. (1958) *The Society of Captives: A Study of a Maximum Security Prison*. Princeton, NJ: Princeton University Press.

Turner, V. (1982) *Dramas, Fields and Metaphors*, 2nd edition. Ithaca, NY: Cornell University Press.

Van Gennep, A. (1908/1960) *The Rites of Passage*. London: Routledge and Kegan Paul.

Walker S. and Worrall A. (2000) 'Life as a woman: The gendered pains of indeterminate imprisonment', *Prison Service Journal*, 132, 27–37.

Young, I. M. (1990) *Justice and the Politics of Difference*. Princeton, NJ: Princeton University Press.

Young, P. (1998) 'The fine and auto-punishment: Foucault and the sociology of punishment', in P. Duff and N. Hutton (eds) *Criminal Justice in Scotland*. Aldershot: Dartmouth/Ashgate.

Part 4

Expanding the Prison Effects Debate Beyond the Prisoner

Chapter 15

The effects of prison work[1]

Helen Arnold

Like the prisoners they supervise, officers adapt to prison life in the context of both public and private worlds.

(Johnson 2002: 201)

Prisoners are not the only ones who 'do time'. Prison staff do as well, as when they talk about their 'sentence' as the time they've got to do until retirement... and the conditions of their work are exacerbated by their own type of isolation.

(Lin 2000: 160)

The aim of this chapter is to outline some of the effects of doing prison work. It is based primarily on a number of emerging findings from doctoral research currently being conducted on 'Identifying the high performing prison officer',[2] and will focus on the psychological and behavioural effects (as opposed to, for example, the physiological, sociological and occupational or cultural effects) of working in prisons on prison officers specifically, as a clearly identifiable group of staff who work closely with prisoners and who comprise the largest collective of employees within any prison establishment. Although the research objectives did not originally include reference to the *effects* of the job on prison officers, this issue has transpired to be a dominant and recurring theme throughout the fieldwork stages and data collection process, and has developed into a key factor with reference to the question of what it means to be, and perform as, a 'good' prison officer.

Following a brief summary of the research in progress, some important considerations in relation to previous research will be raised.

However, rather than reciting a lengthy review of the existing literature, or providing a detailed summary of the findings and conclusions from prior empirical studies, this chapter will present the data collected from focus group discussions, observations, interviews, and the shadowing of prison officers. The exploration of the views and perceptions of both new and qualified and practised officers, as well as the personal experience of undergoing the Prison Officer Entry Level Training (POELT) course, and that of others from the training cohort, suggest that the effects of prison work can be classified into three, inter-related, types: cognitive, emotional and behavioural. These are examined in turn. The chapter ends by offering some concluding comments about the consequences of working within a prison environment.

Instinctively, it feels not unreasonable simply to assert that prison officers are *affected* by the work they do, the people they deal with and the situations they encounter on a daily basis; that doing prison work can have an impact on officers, both individually and collectively. Arguably, as in the case of many prisoners, officers undergo some kind of process of adjustment or adaptation to prison life, in order to cope with the demands of the job and to survive in their working environment and offset the pains of imprisonment (see for example, Clemmer 1940; Sykes 1958; Toch 1977; Zamble and Porporino 1988; Adams 1992). As stated by Marquart and Sorensen:

> The prison guard is not subject to the same degree of deprivation as is the inmate. Nonetheless, it would be naïve to think that prison as a work environment does not impose its own unique set of pressures and characteristics on the officers and wardens that have been charged with maintaining smooth daily operation...
>
> (1997: 151)

The research project

The research on which this chapter is based explores two central questions concerning the individual performance of main grade prison officers: What makes a good prison officer? How can they be identified? It also considers the role of emotions within the prison context and 'emotion management' in the work of officers and in staff–prisoner relationships and interactions. The research consists of three studies: full participant observation of the (then) eleven-week new entrant prison officer training course; a small-scale longitudinal study of ten officers from this training cohort as they take up their posts; and a cross-sectional, observational and interview-based study of prison officers working in one prison.

The objective of the participant observation study was to gain a deep understanding of the core skills and competencies required to perform the job and to explore how these are developed through the content and delivery of the entry-level training course. The aim of the longitudinal study is to consider and assess any changes in individual officers' attitudes, professional orientation and personality characteristics over time in the light of their specific job-related experiences since completing the training course. This aspect of the research may contribute to an understanding of the apparent development of 'burnout' and cynicism, or conversely the contexts in which newly trained officers thrive. The main study is largely qualitative and exploratory, seeking to identify (through group discussions with staff and prisoners, interviews, observations and shadowing a sample of 'good' officers) what the key characteristics, abilities and qualities are that are shown by effective, 'role model', or high-performing officers. The aim is to develop a theoretical model, or typology, of prison officer performance, to be tested more systematically for its discriminatory power by means of a self-completion questionnaire comprising standardised measures of the identified key characteristics or concepts, such as empathy, resilience, professional orientation and emotional intelligence.

Previous research

There are a number of publications about the sociological nature of the work and role of prison officers or correctional staff that explore, for example, officer subculture and features of their relationships (for example, Thomas 1972; Colvin 1977; Jacobs 1978; Lombardo 1981; Kauffman 1988; Herberts 1998; Liebling and Price 1999, 2001; Stojkovic 2003; Crawley 2004). Many of these studies are based on qualitative interview data and include detailed descriptive information concerning the way officers do, think and feel about their job; the views they hold and the attitudes, perceptions and beliefs they have about their daily occupation and those they work with. These studies often rely on the presentation of retrospective accounts and the analysis of 'present-day' views, which renders it difficult to ascertain whether a cause-and-effect relationship actually exists between the work an officer does and the way an officer thinks, feels and behaves in response.

Other previous studies are mainly cross-sectional in design and generally comprise quantitative survey research that has sought to measure, by the use of self-report instruments, a number of concepts that represent some of the possible effects of doing prison work. A number of these are concerned with more 'occupational outcomes' or effects, or with attitudinal responses 'produced' by organisational factors such as the institutional climate, occupational culture and management style and practices. There has been a tendency to focus on, in particular: *stress and burnout* (Poole and Regoli 1980; Cheek and Miller 1983; Lasky *et al* 1986; Whitehead and Lindquist 1986; Launay and Fielding 1989; Triplett *et al* 1996; Lancefield *et al* 1997);[3] *job satisfaction* (Lindquist and Whitehead 1986; Lambert *et al* 1999); *role conflict and anxiety* (Hepburn and Albonetti 1980; Sharma and Sharma 1989); *employee turnover* (Wright 1993; Camp 1994); *occupational tedium* (Shamir and Drory 1981); *professional orientation* (Klofas and Toch 1982; Whitehead *et al* 1987; Whitehead and Lindquist 1989); and *alienation* (Toch and Klofas 1982; Poole and Regoli 1981; Walters 1991; see also Johnson 2002), as well as the measurement of beliefs and attitudes (for example, Shamir and Drory 1981; Jurik 1985; Farkas 1999).

There are a few published autobiographical accounts of working in prison as an officer or guard that have been written either by officers at an advanced stage in their career (Dickenson 1999) or upon retirement (Merrow Smith 1962; Papworth 2000). However, these again are primarily descriptive and journalistic, reciting various personal work experiences in a 'story-telling' manner and which generally tell us little of the impact that working in prison as an officer has on an individual. In addition, there also exists a small number of ethnographic studies conducted by 'outsiders' that employ participant observation as the main research technique (Colvin 1977; Marquart 1986; Fleisher 1989; Conover 2000), but they remain somewhat limited in explicitly addressing the effects of working in prison.[4] Marquart's (1986) article 'demonstrates that involvement in the prison as a prison guard, an insider, is a viable and needed form of participant observation' (p. 35) but his focus is on presenting the strengths, weaknesses, demands and ethical dilemmas of 'full participation as a research role' as opposed to any extended discussion of how it felt and what effect doing the job may have had on him personally.

In summary, what can be established about the effects of prison work from the existing literature is tentative and questionable. Studies are, in the main, rather narrow or subjective and often only indirectly suggest the consequences of prison officer work, or require inferential reading of the data presented. Although valuable attempts have been made to discover the relationship between certain occupational factors and individual outcome variables, insufficient research has been conducted to explore the process(es) involved in creating lasting change or effects. It remains the case that empirical research that purposely addresses the effects of working in prison for prison staff is relatively scarce.[5] As Crawley (2004) asks:

> … we know a good deal about the impact of prison on its prisoners, about the ways in which prisoners attempt to adjust to living in a prison and the ways in which they cope with (and sometimes are unable to cope with) the routines, demands and pressures of prison life. In contrast very little is generally known about the impact of the prison on uniformed staff. What psychological and emotional adjustments must ordinary men and women make in order to become prison officers? How do they adjust to the prison environment?
>
> (2004: xii)

There is a lack of knowledge as to whether the reported effects on, or changes within, prison officers can be considered to be exclusively work-related or role-specific outcomes that have evolved as occupational reactions, or whether they may have developed nonetheless, naturally, or originated from other sources. Arguably, in order to fully understand the consequences for the individuals employed in prison officer work, there is a pressing need for longitudinal research. A longitudinal design may provide a more valid means of determining *how* views and perceptions, personality and behaviours, attitudes, values and beliefs, coping strategies and working styles and practices modify, transform or endure over time, and in response to which influencing factors and personal experiences.

Initial effects: training as a prison officer

> The process of becoming a prison officer is a slow, difficult and sometimes painful one, involving a complex process of acculturation … While the formal training programme sensitises new recruits to the need for vigilance in security matters, it is interesting to note how unprepared most new recruits were for the emotional and domestic demands of prison work.
>
> (Crawley 2004: 65)

Participant observation of the initial training course for newly recruited prison officers provided a unique and valuable personal insight into what it 'feels like' to (learn to) become a prison officer in the modern Prison Service. This foundation experience meant I was able to draw upon my own subjective, practical, emotional and social experience throughout subsequent stages of the research. This has undoubtedly contributed to my understanding of what it is like to do the job of a prison officer and the effects this work may have. I attended the training course at the Prison Service College Aberford Road in Wakefield, and the 'gap weeks' at a high-security prison, during the spring of 2002. I graduated as an officer on 3 May that year.

It is noteworthy that there seemed to exist a prevailing 'assumption of change' that was acknowledged by the other members of the course. Other people readily expressed their expectation that undergoing the training would produce some kind of modification in our personalities. These thoughts were verbalised not only by the course tutors and staff at the prison in which some of the training programme took place, but also by close friends, relatives and colleagues, whether they were familiar with prisons or not. Implicit in their assumptions was that the job of a prison officer is in itself an unusual occupation and that it entails specific demands and the handling of situations that lie outside the realm of 'normal' social interactions.

Although I did not believe I would change in any enduring and significant way in response to undergoing the training, on reflection, and as a result of discussions with others, it appears that there were some noticeable effects in terms of differences in the way I felt and behaved. Some of these effects were negative, while others suggested positive adaptation. Some were more prevalent during the training, within the college and prison environments, while others spilled over into my private life and remained to a greater or lesser degree after the training course had finished. It became apparent, through the numerous and often in-depth conversations and discussions with many of the cohort during the course, that there were common themes and many parallels in the way in which the trainee officers described their experience of change and expressed the effects that the course was having.

In summary, the prevailing comments referred to the following effects: an increase in general self-confidence and assertiveness, the capacity to say 'no' more readily and the ability to 'look after' and protect oneself physically; a heightened sense of awareness of events within the immediate surroundings; and an enhanced suspiciousness about people generally and of prisoners in particular (alongside a raised consciousness of the potential for manipulation and 'conditioning' and an attentiveness to thought preceding speech, in anticipation of giving away personal information unnecessarily or unintentionally that prisoners might hear).

I also began to readily identify with, and have empathy for, prison officers as a cohesive group; I began to understand and have sympathy for their views, suggesting that being a prison officer had, to some degree, become part of my own social identity. I felt I gained a deeper insight into the motivations of others within personal interactions and the roles that I and others might play in social relationships. I learned to try to understand what other people might want from interpersonal transactions and to structure others' expectations, while recognising the importance of offering explanations for decisions and actions with prisoners.[6]

As mentioned above, there was particular consensus among the officer cohort that the training had served to increase their confidence. They also commented that many of their colleagues had become noticeably more self-assured. This was attributed to the Control and Restraint (C&R) training component of the course, where many individuals had originally felt the techniques were too complicated for them ever to be able to learn. One officer said:

> Personally, I don't have any fears working as a prison officer as I am a lot more confident after doing the C&R course. If there was any problem with violence I feel I could look after myself and others to the best of my ability.

New officers felt the pressure to succeed in this area more than any other and their fear of failure (as well as my own) was evident. In addition, the context in which C&R was taught meant that an individual's 'performance' was clearly visible to others and many felt obviously self-conscious. On passing the formal assessments, however (as all but one person of the 48 on the course did) and having reached a recognised level of competence, levels of self-efficacy among the officers had increased; they had developed a belief in their own ability to achieve (as well as in the value of teamwork), and felt proud. In this sense the training was considered to be character-building.

In addition to recognising the influence of the training process, as the course neared completion, the officers also seriously considered and reflected upon the effects that working as a prison officer may have, on both themselves and their colleagues, throughout their future careers. They had become aware of the potential impact that some experiences and aspects of the job may have on them. As one trainee officer stated:

> The only worry, or fear, I have is finding someone that has attempted or committed suicide. As I work in a YOI I worry what effect this will have on me due to the sadness that someone so young would want to do this.

As the period of the relative safety of training came to a close and the 'real world' of prison work approached, new officers articulated their personal fears and worries, and, for some, their previous self-confidence began to fade. Their most discernible concerns included: 'making a mistake' in the prison; making the wrong decision; being unable to remember what they had been taught; compromising security; 'not getting the routine right'; being too quiet ('I am sometimes I bit quiet when I first meet people, so it may take me sometime to have professional working relationships with prisoners') and not being assertive enough ('The role I might find difficult is being continually assertive'); being 'too nice'; not being able to deal with confrontation or violence effectively; being taken hostage; being 'conditioned' by prisoners ('Learning how prisoners can manipulate and condition you gives me cause for concern'); and being attacked or assaulted by prisoners ('There is always the notion of being attacked which I'm sure plays on everybody's mind'); or discovering or seeing a prisoner who had seriously self-harmed, died, attempted or committed suicide.

The confined, secure and structured environment of the college and the collective novel experience of undergoing training resulted in a level of enforced familiarity and intimacy, socially, domestically and emotionally, and meant that some close bonds had been established among members of the group. We had shared and become united by each others' anxieties, apprehensions and fears as well as personal triumphs and by the end of the course a genuine sense of cohesion and camaraderie had formed. The training course also began to shape the new officer's views towards management. As the course progressed, an anti-management attitude began to develop among the cohort, which served to reinforce the solidarity of the group (see Kauffman 1988). A mutual feeling of resentment towards the senior personnel started to grow and was cultivated by the hierarchy of rank (between student and tutor). The new officers often felt that their treatment was patronising and degrading and the imposed discipline and frequent collective reprimands for breach of what were often considered to be needless and petty rules and regulations resulted in a polarisation of officers and managers that, traditionally in the prison literature, is more commonly described as a 'them and us' position existing between staff and prisoners (see for example, Kauffman 1988).

It seems a plausible claim that the initial training course has an effect on those new officers learning the complexities of the job and developing into the role of a prison officer. Throughout the training, although the premise of maintaining a 'duty of care' was frequently alluded to, and the concepts of respect and decency were regularly cited when discussing professional working relationships and ways of dealing and interacting with prisoners, the security aspects of the work were emphasised over and above all else as a critical occupational norm. The need to maintain physical and dynamic security (through relationships) appeared to be intrinsically tied to (and led to) the increase in suspicion, mistrust, vigilance and an overriding concern for their own and others' safety reported by the new officers. This finding is echoed in the work of Crawley:

> Like police officers, prison officers are specifically trained to be suspicious; to be constantly on the look-out for potential, as well as actual, 'trouble'. For the prison officer, the ability to 'read' people and situations is crucial for the maintenance of order and indeed for his or her own safety, and the new recruit is taught during basic training not to trust any prisoner. New recruits are instructed to observe inmates carefully and constantly; to get into the habit of asking themselves, when supervising inmates: 'What is he doing?' 'Why is he doing it?' ... the development of a suspicious 'mindset' has certain knock-on effects for officers' relationships outside as well as inside the prison.
>
> (2004: 69)

Transitional effects: 'becoming' a prison officer

> In the first few days and weeks of being employed as a prison officer (the 'culture shock' period) the new recruit is likely to experience a range of emotions, including surprise, panic, confusion, anxiety and fear. While surprise, panic and confusion usually disappear entirely as recruits become more familiar with their surroundings and with the routines of the prison ... feelings of anxiety and even fear may well remain, although they usually diminish in intensity.
>
> (Crawley 2004: 77–8)

Following graduation from the initial training course, ten officers were interviewed after six months, and then after one year, at the end of their probation period. These officers were asked whether they had found it easy to adjust to the demands of the job; to what extent the training had prepared them for the 'realities' of prison officer work; whether they felt they had changed in any way; and if the job had altered their attitudes. Their responses suggested that, overall, confidence levels continued to grow as they became familiar with the prison routines and procedures, knowledgeable about the rules and regulations, and became practised and accomplished at conducting some of the common tasks (such as using the radio and unlocking cell doors) and security activities (such as searching). They also felt more confident about interacting with prisoners, saying 'no' to some requests, and more sure of their ability to deal effectively and appropriately with confrontation or difficult or spontaneous situations (such as breaking up a fight or responding to a self-harm incident).

Several of the new officers reported that they were learning to be, or had become, less judgemental about prisoners, and suppressed their personal views about some types of offenders; not letting them influence their behaviour. For example, one officer said:

> As a new officer an aspect of the job that did bother me was having to deal with sex offenders, for the simple reason that I have three beautiful nephews and I can't comprehend how people can do such things. So, at times I really had to try hard not to treat them like deep down I knew I wanted to. I was very professional but I wouldn't be honest if I said it didn't affect me.

They became more open-minded towards, and less afraid of prisoners, often coming to see and treat them as normal 'human beings' and individuals (see Johnson 2002), and treating them accordingly with empathy, respect and compassion, and adopting a helping role, while at the same time remaining wary of some prisoners' motivations, questioning their behaviour and not trusting them:

> I've got more hardened, and have a lot more confidence than I used to have; I'm more assertive and I try not to be judgmental. Even though there are paedophiles around, I try not to judge them for what they've done. You might be cuffed to one of them but I treat them the same as everyone else; they are still humans and deserve respect. At the same time the most valuable advice I had was never trust prisoners no matter how close you get to them.

A few officers had started to feel the frustrations of the job; in particular, what they felt to be their limited ability to help prisoners and meet their needs:

> I enjoy interacting with prisoners, but sometimes I feel like I'm not satisfying all their needs and it's a bit frustrating for me and for them. I feel disappointment because sometimes you can't give them an answer or a solution to their problem there and then, or they can't see the reason why. It's hard sometimes…

They also expressed some dissatisfaction with management, suggesting that there was a lack of support for officers; that managers were rarely seen around the prison, that the priority was the well-being of prisoners as opposed to landing staff and that there was too much prisoner appeasement. Perceptions about the purpose of imprisonment and the role of a prison became modified; often translating into a feeling that life inside was 'too easy', 'not disciplined enough' and 'not a punishment' for prisoners:

> I'm more open-minded now I have an insight into the prison world. My personal view is that they have it way too easy; it's not really a punishment. It should be more like a boot camp, so they never want to re-offend.

The nature of the job began to impact on life outside of the prison; the officers said they had become more security conscious (both around the home and when walking the streets – they were more observant and more suspicious of other people), and acknowledged that their friends and family often felt they had become more verbally aggressive and authoritative; they were often criticised for talking to others 'like prisoners'. One officer said:

> I think I used to be a bit sharp with my tongue with people; I'm more aware of that, but on the other hand I'm more assertive. My tolerance level outside is less. They appease all the time in here but when you go out you don't have to; do you know what I mean? I'm more confident in myself… to approach things and tackle things, because in here I have to.

One officer stated that his relationship with his children had improved:

My understanding and reasoning with my teenage kids has increased. I noticed this not long after the training course. I'm better at dealing with confrontation with them; my patience with them was limited but has now improved a lot. I listen to what they have to say ... and then explain why they can't do something!

After six months it appeared that the officers were learning to become more detached, or less emotional about their work, and to conceal their true feelings. This was sometimes the result of having to deal with a sensitive or upsetting situation (in one case, of needing to inform a prisoner of the death of a family member) or witnessing or consoling a prisoner in acute distress. At other times it arose as a need to mask their feelings of fear and to appear calm and confident:

> In the Segregation Unit we had to manhandle a bloke which kicked off the rest of them because they thought we'd hurt him. I was the youngest and concerned about my own safety ... It was quite a scary day ... I had to act cool when inside I was shitting myself – outside I was trying to stay calm ... It's almost all a front.

More often, however, it was a product of feeling constantly harassed by the daily demands of prisoners. They were recognising the need not to get too involved with prisoners' personal problems or situations, not to show their feelings and to be able to 'switch off' from the job and not 'take things home with them'. As one officer described:

> I've just got over not being able to switch off from work, probably only from last month. I would get home and have to sit in the garden for 5 minutes everyday to calm down and think over the day before going indoors. I'd just sit down and take my boots off. When I went straight in the door it was just too much, too demanding; three more people all wanting a bit of me and you've got this buzz in your head; people have been wanting a bit of you all day.

Another said:

> There was a guy who had a double death in his family, within 48 hours and I was trying to sort out compassionate leave for him ... He was distraught ... We've been told to show decency, respect and compassion but I was told that in this case I had got too involved; to stand back and take a look again ... You do take on

the emotions of a prisoner; I think you have to if you really want to understand them but I tend not to take things home with me, I've become quite good at switching off. It could really change your life if you did – when I'm at home my mind is not there, in the prison.

It was a common view that adjusting to the demands of the job had been straightforward and was facilitated by help and advice provided by other, experienced officers. However, 'survival' and adaptation were not as simple for some as for others. For one individual the strain of the job had become overwhelming. At interview six months after training he informed me:

I'm not enjoying it and I feel I have taken it out on my family. But they don't understand how hard it is; it's mentally hard. You're dealing with a whole cross-section of the community under one roof, and you have to deal with all kinds of people, all cultures, all races, all religions. My family can't appreciate what it's like inside ... I have different emotions now, a different personality. I'm not the happy person I was anymore ... I've got more hardened; I've had to act cool when inside I'm shitting myself – outside I'm trying to stay calm. I'm not the same person I used to be; I'm not as fun and happy-go-lucky, easy-going.

This officer did not feel safe within the prison environment and, when surrounded by groups of prisoners, was very aware of his own vulnerability, and fearful of the potential physical threat. He described how helpless he had felt when he dealt with a prisoner who had tried to hang himself and was lying on the floor. He regretted joining the job:

The hours we spend here; it seems like a lot longer than 39 hours a week. I find the job depressing. I am a bubbly person but it suppresses you. Staff shortages mean you sometimes have to do two people's jobs. The rest of the staff are depressed – that brings you down. I probably could be more assertive ... I have had sleepless nights and I've woke up worrying about coming to work. It was a warning sign. I've felt like I'm doing time myself. Once you go behind the walls you feel trapped. I find it weird when I'm going home seeing cars and buses ... In the back of your mind you don't know if there will be trouble. I find it depressing. I don't want to come to work. I can't relax at home or on my time off because I'm always dreading when I have to come to work next.[7]

However, this reaction was atypical and the majority of new officers seemed to have settled well into their role after a few months and were getting used to the shift work. They were gaining enjoyment and job satisfaction from the variety of the work, interacting with prisoners and helping to solve their problems, and working as a team with their colleagues. They were also learning to deal with some of the pressures of the job and felt that their past experiences and employment background had assisted in this:

Due to my background of being in the forces I found it quite an easy step to make…I think being young has helped me to adjust, like being open to ideas. I've not really found it demanding; sometimes it's a bit stressful but it goes over my head.

Dealing with confrontation can be demanding but my past experiences have helped me; I've had a good grounding…We were given a mentor and in the early stages for anything I needed I was running to her but you get less and less dependent on them … The shifts, the job and the people you get used to but in this job you've got the added problem of the cons. You've got an unknown quantity. You're trying to do a job that is variable; they know you are new and will test you out which gives added pressure. I am older than the other recruits though, so they do think you're more experienced; I've been around the block a bit. You're trying to do the job you did the training for and that is what is exciting and challenging about the job.

My partner says she can always tell when I've had a bad day but I do try not to take it home; everyone tries not to do that … I've not gone home and lay in bed thinking, or sat down and thought I can't handle that. My previous job was performance related, not like this, and it was a lot more stressful. I'm conscious of stress, like when you've been locking up and some [prisoners] have taken the piss but I don't feel I bottle it up.

It's a great job. You meet interesting people and its something different everyday; really rewarding. It has been a lot easier to adjust than I thought it would be, I think mostly due to the other officers on my wing who have been really helpful and supportive. They have been superb from the start; I've had no trouble with any of them!

The first year of becoming a prison officer represented a consolidating experience; a continued process of learning and habituation to prison life and the role of an officer within it. It reflected a gradual strengthening, through varied, first-time, and repetitive experiences, of the effects that first emerged during training. In particular, the new officers learned self-control; to manage their emotions and feelings (which generally meant reducing their sensitivity to their own and others' emotions) as well as their self-presentation. As an aid to survival, officers became accustomed to masking or suppressing their true feelings and often embraced a certain demeanour, such as acting tough, cool, calm and confident, for example, when persuading a prisoner to do something they didn't want to do; when dealing with an incident or breaking up a fight or an argument between prisoners; when explaining something or saying 'no' in response to a query; or just when supervising a large number of prisoners or being present on the landings. As one prisoner said in a focus group discussion about what makes a good prison officer:

> You don't want them to be too weak. They have to show that they can be confronted, and not show fear; they have to be confident and stand their ground otherwise the prison wouldn't run ... They don't really show their emotions.

By assuming an impression of hardness and a lack of emotion, officers produced a formal distance between themselves and prisoners, which served as a self-protection mechanism to help them cope with the stresses of the work (see Johnson 2002: 220) and to carry out their tasks effectively. As Kauffman wrote:

> The façade most officers adopt at prisons like Walpole is that of the 'Hard Ass', coldly indifferent to inmates ... We all change a little bit when we come in the front door for roll call. You ... assume a different disguise for eight hours a day ... You got to kind of knuckle down and be the tough guy. They seek to maintain that disguise regardless of the circumstances they are in or the company they are keeping.
>
> (1988: 244–5)

One officer I interviewed stated:

> You have to be resilient, towards all the comments and emotions, be thick-skinned and not take things personally. You need the strength

of character, and have to look confident and sure of yourself, even if you don't feel that way inside; your tone of voice, the way you stand, the way you walk. You can't be emotional; you couldn't do the job if you were.

Crawley (2004) demonstrates that the process of becoming a prison officer 'is inextricably tied up with the management of certain emotions – particularly anxiety, sympathy and fear'. She provides an in-depth discussion of the 'emotional and performative character of prison work', which are key aspects of the job, and highlights the importance of emotional labour and impression management in learning to survive as well as their relationship to officers' performance and professionalism. She states:

> It became clear to me that emotions are right at the heart of prison work. It also became clear that prison officers' emotions must be managed and that they must develop strategies for doing so.
>
> (2004: 43)

Enduring effects: 'being' a prison officer

> ...Each officer was affected by working in such a hostile environment. It was unavoidable. The extent of the changes in an officer's life depended largely upon his own beliefs, attitude, goals and support which he might have received ... Within the very best of circumstances, he would view the world differently. Any innocence once possessed had been wiped away, almost from the start.
>
> (Herberts 1998: 198)

Having explored some of the effects of undergoing training and doing prison work for officers in the early stages of their career, below is a summary of effects of the job as described by officers at a later stage in their career. Many of the comments included were offered by the officers I shadowed and held focus group discussions with by way of explanation for the way they carried out their daily tasks and duties; the way they treated and dealt with prisoners' problems and resolved conflicts; and the reasons for their decisions. There seemed to be three main ways in which the effects of prison work manifest themselves: cognitively, emotionally and behaviourally.

Cognitive effects

Survival techniques or traits learned and practiced inside often overlapped into Robby's personal life. At times, he found himself becoming cynical, almost sadistic in his thinking because of the hostility dealt with each day. Even within safe places within the community, Robby became just shy of being paranoid of all people. He became non-trusting and forever suspicious of being conned ... In the real world, that level of awareness or anticipation was not needed, nor was it healthy.

(Herberts 1998: 205)

In terms of cognition, prison officers seemed to adopt a more rational style of thinking and became less analytical; as the realism of the job set in they became more concerned with the pragmatic aspects of the job, for example, getting to the end of the day without any incidents or harm coming to anyone, and maintaining and accomplishing the daily routine. In the words of Lombardo:

For the prison guard going about his day-to-day business, it is the immediate present that matters, life as it is lived and passes within the prison community ... Faced with a work environment laden with fear, mental tension, uncertainty, isolation, inconsistency and boredom, correction officers are more motivated to develop strategies to cope with these conditions than to pursue management goals.

(1981: 55, 165)

With experience, officers learned to pay attention to different things as they became accustomed and oriented to the normalities of the prison environment. As one officer put it:

On association you have to know what is happening, you're all the time looking at the wing, checking the behaviour of the inmates, seeing how they're reacting, listening for raised voices or if it is too quiet on the wing. You're always watching, seeing the behaviour and if they are watching you. It's like a sixth sense, which comes with more time spent in the job. You learn to shift your attention. You don't really think about what you do, you have to constantly assess and be aware all the time of your environment, even when they are asking you questions – you do it without thinking.

There also appeared to be a shift in their motivations and expectations as to what they believed they could realistically hope to achieve or gain from their working lives. Their focus moved from a drive to 'making a difference' to concern for their colleagues and making the job 'easier' and more manageable. Officers' attitudes towards prison, prisoners and punishment altered. As with the novice officers, a frequently reported view was that there was a lack of discipline within today's prisons; that imprisonment neither rehabilitated nor deterred. This seemed to be a particularly prevalent view among officers working in local prisons, where after years in the job they consistently 'saw the same faces' coming back into custody time and time again. Officers often felt like prisoners; there was a prevailing view that they were also 'doing time' and they regularly measured their own 'time left to serve' before they could retire (see also Lin 2000; Crawley 2004).

Officers believed that the job of a prison officer was stressful, undervalued and misunderstood. This was evident from the outset of officers' careers; this 'fact' was verbally reinforced time and again during the training course by the tutors, and subsequently became confirmed in the minds of staff in light of their own and others' experiences. They also believed that it was a necessary and inherent part of being able to do the job competently to develop and employ methods of coping with the demands of the job; in particular, that it was imperative to have a sense of humour.

The use of humour served several purposes in the working life of a prison officer, most notably as a means of communication and a learned survival strategy (see also Crawley 2004: 49, 85). It manifested itself in many different ways (such as name-calling, day-to-day banter with prisoners and among staff, sarcasm, joking and practical jokes) and contexts (such as after a suicide) and was a technique that became ingrained in the thought processes and behaviour of officers in order to offset unwanted emotions such as distress, fear and anxiety, or even, at times, as a way of not being seen to display too much care, compassion and sympathy. Humour, although often described by officers as 'unique', 'black' and 'sick', was seen as an appropriate method of communication for resolving or diffusing potential conflict and lightening the atmosphere for both staff and prisoners:

> Yes, you do need humour – can you make light of a situation? But it's important to know when to use it. You need to know who will and who won't take it; you've got to be aware of respect. Most of the humour is not directed to prisoners but is amongst staff. You

need light-heartedness...Because it relieves tension and stress. After a serious situation a one-liner can just break it.

At the training college much of the humour found its expression in 'laddish' jokes and sexual innuendo, practical jokes and the assigning of nicknames; which were often derived from a 'mistake', or gaffs, some feature of a person's appearance, their place of origin, or a recurring behaviour.[8] If derisive, acceptance of the nickname was seen as an indication of whether you could 'hack it' and was a 'test' of character. While undergoing the training course I wrote the following on the role of humour in my fieldwork diary during the middle of the second week at the college:

> It seems that it is humour that has brought the section together as a supportive team – even if this means singling someone out as the brunt of the jokes. It is at the college where the culture and importance of prison officer humour arises and develops and makes for effective team working as well as trust. This environment is where the stressful role begins and I can now see clearly how it [humour] is a necessary part of coping – and where it all starts from.
>
> (Personal notes, 06/03/02)

Emotional effects

> I'm a completely different person now – I've sold my soul. I've become a lot more cynical. You need to for self-preservation.
>
> (Officer)

> I'm a lot less tolerant of people outside, like beggars and I don't give people the benefit of the doubt now, I tend to look for the bad in people now instead of the good.
>
> (Officer)

The emotional effects of doing prison work included an array of feelings such as anger, frustration, fear, guilt, sadness, tension, stress, upset, anxiety, tiredness, empathy, pity, relief and uncertainty. Officers experienced themselves, and encountered from prisoners, a number of these feelings in their daily working lives in prison:

> We come across all the emotions in prisoners: jealousy, frustration, anger...They try to embarrass you...humour, sad, happy,

superman-syndrome when they are on a high…depression, anxiety, quietness as well – everything. The emotions we experience are the same…Unexpectedness and uncertainty when you come into work because you don't know what might happen that day…Excited, upset, angry, empathise with their situation and talk sympathetically…

Many of the prisoners I spoke to in the focus group discussions agreed:

I have seen officers get angry and agitated … they show frustration at times because they want to sort something out but they are tied by rules and regulations and that gets their backs up. I've seen them upset…I've seen two of them cry, and show compassion and humanity.

(Prisoner)

In an emotional sense, the consequences of prison work can be considered to be generally fairly negative. Officers, in abundance, described themselves as having become hardened, cynical and detached, and anger and frustration were the most frequently cited emotions they experienced while doing their job. However, officers were somewhat reluctant to acknowledge that they responded in emotional ways to the people they dealt with and the situations in which they found themselves. Having and expressing emotions and feelings were perceived to be 'maladaptive' traits that hindered effective performance and signified unprofessional behaviour – being 'emotional' was undesirable (this was borne out by the fact that, when asked directly, they found it difficult to name the feelings, emotions and moods that they experienced, and commonly reported that they 'don't feel anything'):

You just can't get too involved, you have to be detached, that's the best word for it. It doesn't mean you're heartless and it does mean you can have sympathy. Like when you deal with a self-harm incident, you have to just focus on getting him sorted and doing the paperwork afterwards. Then you can just carry on and try not to dwell on it – manage and deal with the problem, just go in there and deal with the wound.

Officers most often talked about emotions in relation to the psychological reactions to incidents. To many people these incidents, such as serious self-harm, attempted suicide, violent assaults and cell fires, would be considered to be traumatising events. Officers recognised the potentially negative effect of these events, whether they were personally involved or not:

> I saw a prisoner die of a heart attack through the spy-hole in the cell door once. I'm not sure how I felt about it … I'm not sure if I ever dealt with it.

The way that officers responded to incidents could be said to be a 'test' of prison officers' survival and was a constant concern. The reason for this concern was the acknowledgement that experience of these types of incidents did not necessarily guarantee the effective and appropriate management of future incidents, even when of a similar nature. This led to a high level of psychological preparedness; not only because the incidents were unpredictable, but also because their own reaction, or that of others, was unpredictable. The next incident they may have to deal with may be the one that would have such an impact on them that they felt unable to continue in the job, or that in a cumulative sense led to unmanageable levels of stress and anxiety. As one officer said in relation to dealing with prisoners who self-harmed:

> You don't know if you will be able to deal with it next time. It might not be the more superficial cuts across their wrist … their throat might be cut with all the ligaments showing and blood squirting everywhere … you just don't think about the blood.

Another told me:

> I found a prisoner hanging in his cell, dead, on Christmas morning. It was worse because I just wasn't expecting it. I had checked on him only a few minutes before but was passing his cell again and thought I'd just look. It has affected me. Every Christmas day I think about him hanging there and see it in my mind, his face, like a flashback. It spoils my day every year.

Symptoms of stress, anxiety and depression were potential unwanted effects that could persist to a dysfunctional level. One of the adaptive processes that officers went through was therefore the numbing of feelings that led to these negative effects. They became immune and desensitised as a protective mechanism; their enforced detachment served to buffer their emotional discomfort. However, if this emotional state dominated and became part of their daily lives, this could be detrimental to the officers' psychological well-being. As Herberts (1998) described, in the case of one officer:

> While on the job, training had taught Robby to remain objective, not to take anything personal. But, with even more years of training in being a human being it was difficult to merely cast feelings aside, so that duties might be performed while staying unbothered, unaffected. A survival trait was to become hardened…However, in reality Robby knew this was also sacrificing a piece of his inner self. Looking at situations from two different extremes, it became evident why the job created such strong emotions which had to be suppressed…but the department had determined that a professional officer should handle those situations, as though no emotional factor was present.
>
> (p. 201)

Behavioural effects

Whereas the emotional effects of prison work seemed largely to stem from specific incidents, the behavioural effects seemed to arise from the repetitiveness of prison work and the daily routines and tasks. Much of this behaviour became habitual and more or less instinctual in some cases, crossing over into the personal lives of officers (such as unfailingly ensuring that doors were closed and/or locked behind them). The majority of these behavioural effects seemed to be connected to the security and supervisory functions of a prison officer.

To summarise their comments, experienced prison officers talked of how they became more alert and vigilant, found themselves assessing situations outside and were wary of the potential for, and escalation of, trouble. In social situations they placed themselves, or took up a position in such a way as to be able to survey their surroundings. They automatically counted the number of people in a room and described feeling a preparedness to intervene and manage confrontations in the 'real' world as they had to inside the prison walls. They described their sensitivity to sounds that were commonly found in the prison environment which signalled trouble, shifting their attention to noises akin to a buzz, a noise like a cell bell or alarm, and to (uncharacteristic) silence. An example from one officer was:

> Even when I'm in a supermarket, I can't help it, I get an adrenaline rush when I hear the beep at the start of a public announcement!

In their communications with others, officers said that since working as an officer they found, and were told by others, that they frequently talked to other people as if they were prisoners; explaining things in a straightforward and forceful or assertive manner. They reported that they were more willing and likely to express their dissatisfactions and complain in different situations where they felt their own needs or expectations were not being met (such as at poor quality food in a restaurant, or unsatisfactory service or goods).

It seemed to be the case that there were certain enduring effects associated with becoming and being a prison officer. One notion that could be used to draw the three strands of effects described above together is the concept of empathy.

Discussion and conclusion

> The fact of being a prison officer and working day-to-day behind the walls of prison with people who, on the whole, do not want to be there, appears to produce some common effects ... Everyday exposure to conflict (however subtle) and argument, to the claustrophobia and enclosed nature of a prison, to the various tasks involved in trying to 'achieve quiet' clearly has its effects.
>
> (Liebling and Price 2001: 150–1)

This chapter has attempted to show that there are various identifiable effects of doing prison work for prison officers, which begin to occur once training commences and which may persist and develop to varying degrees throughout the early stages of a prison officer's career. The presence at this point of such predominant effects as increased confidence and assertiveness indicates a process of learning and becoming; of adjustment to the primary demands and requirements in their new jobs of maintaining security, order and the provision of care in their relationships with prisoners. With experience, officers continued to develop coping strategies, such as the creation of emotional distance, detachment, vigilance and the use of humour, in order to offset their own 'pains of imprisonment' and to facilitate the effective management of incidents and relationships in prison. Many of the manifested effects also contributed to the officers' creation and maintenance of authority, which was partly derived from learning to manage their image and their 'style of presentation of self' (Lombardo 1981: 73). This included, for example, exuding an air of confidence, controlling and masking feelings, and 'standing their ground' both physically (such as when faced with a threatening or dangerous situation) and verbally (such as when firmly saying 'no' in response to prisoners requests).

Taken collectively, the responses of prison officers to working in prison suggest that there are three main types of effects: cognitive, emotional and behavioural, and that these effects of prison work can be located within three settings: in the workplace; in the personal and social lives of officers outside the prison; and more internally within the person. The effects of prison work are linked in that, in a positive sense, they usually represent 'enablers' for officers; they are part of the way in which officers adapt occupationally and they represent facets of survival for the individual and, in a broader sense, serve a functional purpose in helping to cultivate a better environment in which to live and work. However, the possible negative aspects of the effects of doing prison work over a prolonged period should not be ignored. There are potential human and environmental/organisational costs should some of the effects described become pervasive. Individually, how some officers change and adjust may well be adaptive in one context but maladaptive in other arenas of their lives, and there is a risk that physical health problems and detrimental psychological problems (such as dysfunctional levels of stress, anxiety and depression) could result. There are some dangers and important implications within the prison environment should prison officers become too detached and desensitised to carry out some of their tasks effectively (such as those involved in maintaining a safe environment). As recognised by Liebling and Price:

> The desensitisation produced by exposure to prison…is another important theme. Officers may become numbed to experiences which should trigger 'corrective' responses. Prison work demands of staff that they cope with brutality without becoming brutalised, that they experience feelings without being able to express those feelings legitimately or without the risk of being ridiculed or rendered ineffective.
>
> (2001: 152)

Kauffman (1988) interviewed a group of prison officers in the weeks before they began work and again four years later. In summarising the effects that the prison had on them, although arguably 'an extreme reaction to an atypical prison' (Liebling and Price 2001: 151), her findings highlight some of the negative afflictions the role of an officer can induce:

Most officers recognised the changes that had taken place in themselves and spoke of their changes with sorrow and bitterness in the interviews. Many of their young marriages were in trouble or destroyed. Some officers were so burnt out they could not go into supermarkets or take their children to the zoo. Others were so drug dependent that they had to get drunk before going to work on the 7 a.m. shift. Some were so angry and frustrated that they punched holes in the walls of their homes and abused those whom they loved. Most of all, they were desperately unhappy and despaired that life could ever seem so good again.

(1988: 212)

The demands on prison officers to provide or create a humane and caring environment (as well as a secure, safe and ordered one) may be more difficult than prison managers and policy-makers realise. It involves a delicate (cognitive, emotional and behavioural) balancing act by officers, and requires that, through emotional control and behavioural regulation, an equilibrium is reached between becoming too involved or too detached. As Goffman suggested:

The capacity of inmates to become objects of staff's sympathetic concern is linked to what might be called an involvement cycle that is sometimes recorded in total institutions. Starting at a point of social distance from inmates, a point from which massive deprivation and institutional trouble cannot easily be seen, the staff person finds he has no reason to refrain from building up a warm involvement in some inmates. This involvement, however, brings the staff member into a position to be hurt by what inmates do and what they suffer, and also brings him to a position from which he is likely to threaten the distant stand from inmates taken by his fellow staff members. In response, the sympathizing staff member may feel he has been 'burnt' and retreat ... Once removed from the dangers of inmate contact, he may gradually cease to feel he has reason to be wary, and then the cycle of contact and withdrawal may be repeated again.

(1961: 79)

Although not necessarily explicitly expressed by officers, this cycle remains a valid description of the relationships and interactions that officers today have with prisoners. As acknowledged in the prison literature (for example, Liebling and Price 2001), getting these relationships right is a crucial element of the job of a prison officer and

415

is arguably more difficult than it might seem:

> At the end of the day, nothing else that we can say will be as important as the general proposition that relations between staff and prisoners are at the heart of the whole prison system and that control and security flow from getting that relationship right. Prisons cannot be run by coercion: they depend on staff having a firm, confident and humane approach that enables them to maintain close contact with prisoners without abrasive confrontation.
>
> (Home Office 1984: para. 16)

One way in which officers need to achieve the right relationship with prisoners is in the demonstration and management of empathy and care. The cycle of involvement put forward by Goffman could be extended to incorporate these facets and could equally be applied to levels of sympathy and empathy, which officers do show and feel and which assist them in understanding and managing prisoners' motivations and behaviour. They want to care for prisoners, but without showing it, or without experiencing distress themselves on the one hand, or disapproval from others on the other.

As an effect of working in prison, learning to utilise, manage and control emotions, and particularly feelings of empathy, is a key area related to the effectiveness of a prison officer and one which officers said was an important and inherent component of their job. As with levels of involvement, though, a delicate balance had to be struck: feeling and showing some empathy was appropriate and needed, but in small doses. Too much empathy could be overwhelming, and could lead to an 'emotional flooding' that could obstruct cognitive processes such as perspective-taking, that was required in order to deal with some situations successfully. Too little empathy, and an officer could become so withdrawn and distant that they ceased to care and to perform their job properly. Empathy allowed an officer to 'do the job' but the stakes could be high if the balance was wrong and they could not manage the physiological and psychological effects of strong emotions.[9]

Whether cognitive, behavioural or emotional, the nature and extent of the effects of working in prison on prison officers are a legitimate and worthy course of enquiry. However, as discussed by Walker (1987) when exploring the reliability of some of the findings in relation to the unwanted effects of long-term imprisonment for prisoners, an important consideration is the durability and reversibility of any identified effects. Can we really say there are effects of doing prison work, if they do not result in lasting changes in personality? If they do not endure after officers have left the job and the workplace setting? Or if they do not go beyond modifications in thought and behaviour patterns that facilitate and explain how and why officers think about, and do/perform, their job in a particular way on a daily basis. As Walker suggested:

> Undesirable changes in a prisoner should be considered as deterioration only if they prove irreversible after his release ... Even if these men had experienced the changes found ... most of the changes seem to have been reversed. That is not to say that they are unimportant, or that no effort needs to be made to counter them: some of the changes which have been described have an undesirable effect on the 'quality of life' of long-term prisoners. What is quite unjustifiable, however, is the prevalent assumption that they persist for long periods after release, or are permanent.
>
> (1987: 193–4)

Robust empirical research about the effects of prison work is limited. There is a need for further and longitudinal research in order to measure, explore and understand the issues more fully.

Notes

1　This chapter is based on a paper presented at the Cropwood and Prisons Research Centre Conference: 'The effects of imprisonment: An international symposium', at Robinson College, Cambridge, 14–15 April 2004.
2　This PhD research is being carried out by the author at the Institute of Criminology, University of Cambridge. The study is funded jointly by the Economic and Social Research Council and the Prison Service as a CASE Studentship, and is supervised by Dr Alison Liebling.
3　See Schaufeli and Peeters (2000) for a comprehensive review of this literature.
4　Although Colvin's (1977) thesis does address the impact of the job upon prison officers' lives outside work.
5　Crawley's recent work (2002, 2004) explicitly discusses the impact of prison officers' work on their families and acknowledges that the prison can 'spill over' into personal and family life.
6　Prior to this research, I had conducted two research projects focusing more clearly on the experience of prisoners.
7　During the last communication I had with this officer, he was adamant he was going to leave the Prison Service and had conveyed this intention to his line manager and some senior managers in the prison, whom he said tried to persuade and encourage him to give it more time.

8   For example, one new officer was called 'The Rock' on account of his size and strength and ability at C&R. Another was called 'Scouser Two-Belts' after he arrived for the first time in the classroom adorning one belt for his trousers and another to hold the key chain and pouch. During one session at the college, when trainees were practising the locking and unlocking of cell doors, one member of the group sneaked into a cell to jump out on his unsuspecting colleague as he unlocked the door, taking him completely by surprise. The result was hilarious and tested his ability to resist any anger he felt in the face of shock and fear, and to take his humiliation in good humour.

9   For these reasons it appeared that officers distinguished between situational and emotional empathy; they understood and described much of their empathy in terms of a cognitive understanding as opposed to a feeling that they 'took on', or shared with the prisoner. Their method of problem-solving, then, in relation to prisoners, was more practical than emotional and they focused their helping and caring behaviour on the presenting problem, which would in turn alleviate or help with altering the prisoners' unwanted feelings.

References

Adams, K. (1992) 'Adjusting to prison life', in M. Tonry (ed.) *Crime and Justice: A Review of Research*, Vol. 16. Chicago: University of Chicago Press.

Camp, S. (1994) 'Assessing the effects of organizational commitment and job satisfaction on turnover: An event history approach', *The Prison Journal*, 74, 279–305.

Cheek, F.E. and Miller, M. (1983) 'The experience of stress for correctional officers: A double bind theory of correctional stress', *Journal of Criminal Justice*, 11, 105–120.

Clemmer, D. (1940) *The Prison Community*. New York: Holt, Rinehart and Winston.

Colvin, E. (1977) *Prison Officers: A Sociological Portrait of the Uniformed Staff of an English Prison*, PhD Thesis, University of Cambridge.

Conover, T. (2000) *Newjack: Guarding Sing Sing*. New York: Vintage Books.

Crawley, E. (2002) 'Bringing it all back home? The impact of prison officers' work on their families', *Probation Journal*, 49 (4), 277–286.

Crawley, E. (2004) *Doing Prison Work: The Public and Private Lives of Prison Officers*. Cullompton: Willan Publishing.

Dickenson, L. (1999) *The Keepers of the Keys*. Fort Bragg, CA: Lost Coast Press.

Farkas, M.A. (1999) 'Correctional officer attitudes toward inmates and working with inmates in a "get tough" era', *Journal of Criminal Justice*, 27 (6), 495–506.

Fleisher, M.S. (1989) *Warehousing Violence*. London: Sage Publications.

Goffman, E. (1961) *Asylums: Essays on the Social Situation of Mental Patients and*

Other Inmates. Harmondsworth: Penguin.

Hepburn, J.R. and Albonetti, C. (1980) 'Role conflict in correctional institutions', *Criminology*, 17 (4), 445–459.

Herberts, S. (1998) *The Correctional Officer Inside Prisons.* New York: Nova Science.

Home Office (1984) *Managing the Long-term Prison System: The Report of the Control Review Committee.* London: Home Office.

Jacobs, J. (1978) 'What prison guards think: A profile of the Illinois force', *Crime and Delinquency*, 24, 185–196.

Johnson, R. (2002) *Hard Time: Understanding and Reforming the Prison*, 3rd edition. Belmont, CA: Wadsworth Publishing.

Jurik, N. (1985) 'Individual and organizational determinants of correctional officers' attitudes towards inmates', *Criminology*, 23, 523–539.

Kauffman, K. (1988) *Prison Officers and Their World.* Cambridge, MA: Harvard University Press.

Klofas, J. and Toch, H. (1982) 'The guard subculture myth', *Journal of Research in Crime and Delinquency*, 19, 238–254.

Lambert, E.G., Barton, S.M. and Hogan, N.L. (1999) 'The missing link between job satisfaction and correctional staff behavior: The issue of organizational commitment', *American Journal of Criminal Justice*, 24 (1), 95–116.

Lancefield, K., Lennings, C.J. and Thomson, D. (1997) 'Management style and its effect on prison officers' stress', *International Journal of Stress Management*, 4 (3), 205–219.

Lasky, G.L., Gordon, B. and Strebalus, D.J. (1986) 'Occupational stressors among federal correctional officers working in different security levels', *Criminal Justice and Behavior*, 13, 317–327.

Launay, G. and Fielding, P.J. (1989) 'Stress among prison officers: some empirical evidence based on self report', *The Howard Journal*, 28 (2), 138–148.

Liebling, A. and Price, D. (1999) *An Exploration of Staff–Prisoner Relationships at HMP Whitemoor.* London: Prison Service Research Report No. 6.

Liebling, A. and Price, D. (2001) *The Prison Officer.* Leyhill: Prison Service Journal.

Lin, A.C. (2000) *Reform in the Making: The Implementation of Social Policy in Prison.* Princeton, NJ: Princeton University Press.

Lindquist, C.A. and Whitehead, J.T. (1986) 'Burnout, job stress and job satisfaction among Southern correctional officers: Perceptions and causal factors', *Journal of Offender Services, Counselling and Rehabilitation*, 10 (4), 5–26.

Lombardo, L.X. (1981) *Guards Imprisoned: Correctional Officers at Work.* New York: Elsevier.

Marquart, J.W. (1986) 'Doing research in prison: The strengths and weaknesses of full participation as a guard', *Justice Quarterly*, 13 (1), 35–47.

Marquart, J.W. and Sorensen, J.R. (1997) *Correctional Contexts: Contemporary and Classical Readings.* Los Angeles: Roxbury Publishing.

Merrow Smith, L.W. in collaboration with Harris, J. (1962) *Prison Screw.* London: Herbert Jenkins.

Papworth, R. (2000) *Key Man*. Derbyshire: Richard Papworth.

Poole, E.D. and Regoli, R.M. (1980) 'Role stress, custody orientation, and disciplinary actions', *Criminology*, 18 (2), 215–226.

Poole, E.D. and Regoli, R.M. (1981) 'Alienation in prison: An examination of the work relations of prison guards', *Criminology*, 19, 251–270.

Schaufeli, W.B. and Peeters, M.C.W. (2000) 'Job stress and burnout among correctional officers: A literature review', *International Journal of Stress Management*, 7 (1), 19–48.

Shamir, B. and Drory, A. (1981) 'Some correlates of prison guards' beliefs', *Criminal Justice and Behavior*, 8 (2), 233–249.

Sharma, S. and Sharma, D. (1989) 'Organizational climate, job satisfaction and job anxiety', *Psychological Studies*, 34 (1), 21–27.

Stojkovic, S. (2003) 'Accounts of prison work: Corrections officers' portrayals of their work worlds', in M.R. Pogrebin (ed.) *Qualitative Approaches to Criminal Justice: Perspectives from the Field*. London: Sage Publications.

Sykes, G. (1958) *The Society of Captives*. Princeton, NJ: Princeton University Press.

Thomas, J. (1972) *The English Prison Officer Since 1850: A Study in Conflict*. London: Routledge and Kegan Paul.

Toch, H. (1977) *Living in Prison: The Ecology of Survival*. Washington, DC: American Psychological Association.

Toch, H. and Klofas, J. (1982) 'Alienation and desire for job enrichment among correction officers', *Federal Probation*, 46, 35–44.

Triplett, R., Mullings, J.L. and Scarborough, K.E. (1996) 'Work-related stress and coping among correctional officers: Implications from organizational literature', *Journal of Criminal Justice*, 24, 291–308.

Walker, N. (1987) 'The unwanted effects of long-term imprisonment', in A.E. Bottoms and R. Light (eds) *Problems of Long-term Imprisonment*. Cambridge Studies in Criminology LVIII. Aldershot: Gower.

Walters, S. (1991) 'Alienation and the correctional officer: A multivariate analysis', *American Journal of Criminal Justice*, 16, 50–62.

Whitehead, J.T. and Lindquist, C.A. (1986) 'Correctional officer job burnout: A path model', *Journal of Research in Crime and Delinquency*, 23 (1), 23–42.

Whitehead, J. and Lindquist, C. (1989) 'Determinants of correctional officers' professional orientation', *Justice Quarterly*, 6, 69–87.

Whitehead, J., Lindquist, C. and Klofas, J. (1987) 'Correctional officer professional orientation: A replication of the Klofas-Toch measure', *Criminal Justice and Behaviour*, 14 (4), 468–486.

Wright, T.A. (1993) 'Correctional employee turnover: A longitudinal study', *Journal of Criminal Justice*, 21, 131–142.

Zamble, E. and Porporino, J. (1988) *Coping, Behavior and Adaptation in Prison*. New York: Springer-Verlag.

Chapter 16

Imprisonment and the penal body politic: the cancer of disciplinary governance

Pat Carlen[1]

A couple of months ago I met a 45-year-old woman who had been newly released from prison. She was totally depressed – 'unmotivated' was how she had been taught to describe herself by her 'key worker' at the hostel where she had been living for three months. When I inquired about her American accent, she told me her story. Briefly, her family had emigrated to the United States when she was two years old, and she had never previously returned to England. She had been a drug user since the age of seventeen, in and out of prison for various thefts and minor frauds committed to fund her addiction. After the last sentence of twelve months, during which she had undertaken several programmes designed to aid rehabilitation upon release, she, never having obtained American citizenship, had been taken straight from the prison with her few belongings and deported to England, which she had last seen 44 years before. At Heathrow she had stayed two nights in emergency accommodation and then the campaigning organisation Prisoners Abroad gave her the fare to the north London hostel where she had been ever since. During the same period, of course, other foreign nationals were going in the opposite direction, deported from English gaols to Jamaica, Nigeria, and elsewhere – while English prisoners were returning to their own wastelands of homelessness, addictions and unemployment. Same old story – new global twist.

Thinking about the global aspects of the contemporary penal body politic[2] and the burgeoning international prison business with its sale of programmes for prisoners, its costly (and lucrative) evaluations, and the repetitive reports of prison inquiries, and research studies (my own included) whose main claim to prowess is that they are extremely good at reinventing the wheel,[3] led me to wondering why there has been so much penal policy-making and so little penal progress in recent years in terms of reducing recidivism.[4] Additionally, and in obeisance to the ideology that one objective of imprisonment must be to turn prisoners into law-abiding citizens, there has been ongoing debate about what form of punishment is most successful at preventing recidivism (e.g. Bottoms 1983; McMahon 1992; Maruna 2002: 159–62); with some commentators claiming that 'nothing works' in relation to both custodial and non-custodial interventions into criminal careers (e.g. Martinson 1974); and yet others claiming that imprisonment can help reduce recidivism if the 'correct' forms of training are undertaken with persistent offenders (Social Exclusion Unit 2002: 38–9). 'What works' in terms of recidivism reduction has become the penologist's stone.[5]

And it seemed to me that, as we have on the one hand a myriad of studies of prisons and prisoners, of sentencing and penal policy, and, on the other, a cornucopia of cultural studies of globalism and risk in punishment, it might be a useful corrective in this chapter, to return to a more mundane and neglected concern (though one unflinchingly pursued by the recent Chief Inspector of Prisons for England and Wales 1992–1997):[6] the effective governance of the penal body politic itself.

One answer to why there has been so little progress in England in terms of reducing the recidivism of prisoners may indeed be that the reduction of prisoner recidivism cannot possibly be a prime function of imprisonment. For if one ignores the official ideology that implies that prisons are primarily for recidivism reduction via rehabilitation, it can be seen that on other criteria prisons are very successful indeed. For instance: first and foremost, penal custody provides harsh punishment in societies currently loud in their demands for the punishment of lawbreakers and a range of deviant 'others'; secondly, rising imprisonment rates can (ironically) be presented as a visible index of a government's determination to wage war on wrongdoers; thirdly, prisons continue to be important mechanisms in the management of poverty and marginality (Waquant 2001; Becket and Sasson 2004); and, fourthly, prisons protect the public from dangerous criminals – at least for the duration of their sentences.[7] Yet, while these four indices of prison success also help legitimate the continued existence of prisons at the same time as being icons of governmental probity in relation to both welfare and crime control, their success is the product of a tangle of mechanisms of restraint (disciplinarities[8]), many of which have not been developed primarily for the governance of prisons and prisoners, but which have, instead, been fashioned for the governance of prison legitimacy, penal knowledge and penal personnel. Unfortunately, however, regimes primarily organised to keep prisoners securely in custody and prison personnel (and prison critics) securely in their place are not those most conducive to assisting prisoners to see desistance from crime as being both desirable and possible. To address the wide-ranging psychological and social issues within which particular prisoners' criminal careers have been constituted, organisational creativity and management of innovation are required which, to be successful, would have to cut through the layers of disciplinarities of the labyrinthine but fragmented bureaucracies characterising today's penal body politic in England and Wales (see Burns and Stalker 1967). Nor is it any consolation that such a view is very conventional and, moreover, one with which many in the higher reaches of the Home Office and Prison Service would agree. It merely highlights yet another neglected dimension of today's penal body politic: that it is marked by a *consensus* about what needs to be done, a *hyperactivity* of directives, plans and programmes about how to do it effectively ... and then an almost absolute *paralysis* when it comes to actual implementation within both the prisons and the post-prison agencies which should, logically, be even more implicated in prisoner resettlement than the prisons could ever be expected to be.

In view of the foregoing, this chapter attempts to fill in just one tiny piece in the 'what works' jigsaw. It is not concerned with grand theories in relation to the 'penologist's stone'; and makes no claims about what prisons are '*really*' for. Instead, it merely focuses on what kind of institutional and organisational framework is best suited to realising the rehabilitation ideology which English governments have endorsed for so many years, and which has received renewed endorsement within the last four years (Social Exclusion Unit 2002). It is because of that very narrow focus that the (mildly) theoretical part of this chapter is not primarily about prisons, prisoners and rehabilitation. Instead, discussion centres on the vexed question of what type of organisational ethos is possible in both the penal body politic and its prisons – institutions which (because of their essential nature) have to employ restraining rules to constrain and keep prisoners in prison but which also (because of their legitimacy requirements) at the same time have to employ creative rules to prepare prisoners for release and a law-abiding life after prison.

The strategy employed for answering that question in the rest of the chapter makes a distinction between *creative rule-usage* for the *management of innovation* and *constraining disciplinary rule-usage (disciplinarities) for the constraint of managers of innovation*. That distinction is then employed to inform the following argument: that in recent years many imprisonment and official resettlement policies in England, and maybe elsewhere, have been continually blocked by, and left to rot in, the defunct layers of disciplinary baggage piled on them by successive governments. Because prisons have to fulfil contradictory objectives in environments where cultures of political opportunism and institutional recrimination infuse prison policy and management at every level (see Ramsbotham 2003 for illustrations of this), the present profusion of old and new management techniques is a main (though most probably not the only) reason for the continuing failure of English penal policy in relation to the rehabilitation of prisoners.

Although the theoretical part of the chapter is about rule-usage and disciplinarities, and not about prisoners and their ills, its domain assumption is that raising questions about how best to make a bonfire of the disciplinarities is directly pertinent to this book's focus on the 'effects of imprisonment'. For until both prisons and post-prison rehabilitation structures are organised for managing rules in such a way that they can employ constraints in the service of creativity, they may well be able to keep prisoners *in* but they certainly will not be able to prepare them to lead law-abiding lives upon release. Substantively however, the paper has a two-fold practical focus: first, on the corrosive effects of the sometimes inappropriate, sometimes redundant, and always 'too many' disciplinarities; and second, on how to reduce or 'disappear' them.

Argument

The central argument of the chapter is that the disciplinary governance which, as Foucault (1977) so brilliantly taught us, has characterised imprisonment from its inception, has, since the 19th century, so burgeoned and transformed itself that at the present time it is a cancerous growth obfuscating the essential nature of imprisonment and the deleterious effects it has on prisoners.[9] Concomitantly, it is also corrosive of attempts to address some of the worst effects of incarceration, and inhibitive of committed attempts to implement non-custodial responses to crime.[10]

The chapter is divided into three. The first section notes that three recent and parallel transformations in the disciplinary project have been: first, the shift from the *disciplining* to the *programming* of prisoners; and second, from the *empowerment* to the *disciplining* of penal personnel. Additionally, the new managerialism in society at large (of which managerialism in prisons is only one instance) has also had disciplinary effects in the universities and voluntary and campaigning sectors, which in turn have brought a new commercial ethos to bear on the work of academic penal theorists and campaigning groups. This play of old and new disciplinarities over the whole penal body politic has resulted in a strengthening of the disciplinary managerialism shaping prison policies, prison and probation managements[11] and penal knowledge. In the process, questions of both their penal probity and their relevance to prisoners' rehabilitative requirements have been subordinated to the inward-looking claims of managerialist audit, the seeming transparency of which, one suspects, may be nothing more than a conjuring trick to suggest that something is being done.

Yet rules are both necessary and inevitable. In the second section, therefore, a distinction is made between normal rule usage and pathological disciplinarities; and it is this distinction which is then used to inform the third section's discussion of possible strategies for arresting the excessive disciplinary trend in the administration of prisons and resettlement services.

Discipline, programme, audit

From discipline and punish to discipline and programme

In *Discipline and Punish*, Foucault (1977) argues that modern modes of social regulation function to create a disciplined citizenry which has so internalised the rules of disciplined behaviour that bodily constraints should fall into disuse. The continuous technology of mass discipline, rather than depending upon physical terror or pain, aims for psychological mastery. When, therefore, in a 1998 address to the Howard League in London, a government minister (the Home Secretary, Jack Straw) argued that prison could be made to work if the right programme were to be found to address the needs of each prisoner, one might have expected that this programming strategy would be no more (though no less) than a continuation of the disciplinary penality of the modernists, a penality functioning to re-programme the prisoner as a citizen and worker. And in many ways it is. Yet it is also different. The prison programming which Foucault (1977) described was seen to inhere in a seamless web of total social and cultural control within nation states. By contrast, however, today's prison programmes (especially the psychological ones) are the marketable outpourings from a global commodification of penal products (Christie 2000; Garland 2001; Jones and Newburn 2004).

Garland (1996) argues that the privatised penal market has come about primarily because states no longer appear to be able to satisfy demands for law enforcement. The resulting legitimacy threat has therefore been met by governments formally distancing themselves from policy and taking on the guise of indirect consumers of penal products via agencies operating to get the best deal for them and their electorates who nowadays have been taught to think of themselves more as *customers* of government agencies than as *participants* in government. For whereas, in England, government departments were previously responsible for all aspects of penal policy, the commodification of penal products ensures that nowadays parts of policies are 'delivered' piecemeal in 'packages' or as 'programmes' which have not been tailor-made for the local situation or as part of a democratically fought-over policy but have, instead, been developed by private businesses in other cultures and for prisoners with entirely different characteristics. Thus, although 'programming' in prisons today may at first sight appear to be a continuation of the 19th-century disciplinary trend as described by Foucault (1977), its genesis is different. Today's penal programming is not directed so much at being a total form of internalised control (Rose 1999). Rather, the promise of programming is that it will reduce recidivism by being a 'magic bullet' targeting individual (psychological) need (Kendall 2002). As Craig Haney points out in Chapter 3 of this volume, it is surprising that individualistic psychological explanations of crime are being used to inform in-prison programmes just at a time when psychologists of crime are promoting more context-based, social explanations.

However, although the promises of the programmers attempt to legitimate imprisonment by claiming that matching the right programme to a prisoner's criminogenic needs should reduce recidivism, the essential logic of imprisonment, that prisoners must be *kept in*, means that when this post-modern ideology of multiple programming is activated in custodial institutions, its coercive psychological programmes are implemented alongside all the old modernist disciplinarities of placing, normalising and timetabling, and against a backcloth of the even older pre-modern controls such as lock-ups, body searches and physical restraints, and often in the confused conditions which result from overcrowding. As a result, their possibilities for benign effect are largely neutralised (see Hannah-Moffat 2001). Moreover, whereas the *modernisers'* emphasis on discipline had the ideological advantage of sidestepping questions of punishment and legitimacy by giving primacy to a *disciplinary* mode of regulation seen to be equally desirable for all citizens, the *post-modernist* emphasis on the reconfigurability of all disciplines (to meet multiple but differentiated 'need') manages to convert even primarily material needs such as homelessness, sexual abuse and unemployment into the *criminogenic* needs of people defined by their crimes rather than by their citizenship (Hudson 2002). Thus, far from being fashioned to meet the individual needs of prisoners of society who will be returned sooner or later to that same society, programmes on sale in the penal marketplace have mainly been framed to meet governmental demands for a product selling itself as an antidote to essentialised, psychological and criminogenic tendencies. Perhaps this is why questions concerning the legitimacy of mixing psychological treatment (brainwashing) with penal incarceration appear to be raised less frequently nowadays than they were previously (see Kittrie 1971). Be that as it may, the build-up of disciplinarity upon disciplinarity in the treatment of prisoners at the beginning of the 21st century has certainly tended to obscure the 'fiasco' (Mathiesen 2000: 26) of contemporary imprisonment and resettlement policies in England and Wales in terms of their lack of success in reducing recidivism. And although there have been many penal personnel whose professional knowledge has told them that the rampant bureaucracy inherent in the new managerialism has been inappropriate to prisons and other agencies whose client needs are so complex that a more flexible governance of service delivery is required, few prison governors have been willing to stick their heads above the parapet because of the ways in which they themselves were disciplined out of a *professional* into a *compliance* culture during the last quarter of the 20th century (see Carlen 2002a).

From discipline and manage to discipline and audit

The shift (or not) from the disciplinary penality described by Michel Foucault (1977) to the post-modern penality analysed by David Garland (2001) delineates the conventional axes within which differing histories of contemporary penal and regulatory practice are constructed and deconstructed (see Shearing 2001; Kemshall and Maguire 2001). Both Bauman's modernist Nazis and Pratt's pre-modern wheelbarrow men can be framed within the ever-changing kaleidoscope which refracts the contradictions and continuities in modern/post-modern debates about the nature of discipline at different socio-penal conjunctures (Bauman 1989; Pratt 2002). For, as Foucault also reminded us in his *Archaeology of Knowledge* (1972), old discourses never die; they merely transmute and transform. Managing (though not controlling) those transformations is the business of the executive arm of the penal body politic: government departments, prison managements. Analysing (though not controlling) them is the business of the knowledge arm: government researchers, academic penal theorists and campaigning groups. As the quest for a populist legitimacy (realised in the public sector through structures of punitive 'accountability') increasingly absorbed British governments during the 1980s, the disciplinary arm of the penal body politic was forcefully extended to prison personnel themselves.

A determination to discipline the public service sector was central to the ideologies and strategies of governance favoured by the Conservative administrations of the 1980s and 1990s, and, under the rubric of 'accountability' a confetti of paper-audit has continued to pour down from governments ever since (see Power 1997). Auditing via key performance indicators has attempted to manage-out risk altogether – a fruitless objective in any vibrant organisation, but especially so in prisons where, although by definition prisoners necessarily have to be *kept in*, most, according to the government's own rhetoric also have to be prepared for *going out* (Blair 2000: 3). Yet, despite repeated restructuring (of prison service management), re-roling (of prisons) and reviews (by the Service itself and by the Prisons Inspectorate), the criticisms of this seemingly unwieldy gulag persist – one of the most frequent being that the gap between the proclaimed aspirations of paper policies and the actualities of prison practice is as big, and maybe bigger, than it has ever been (Ramsbotham 2003). Meanwhile, however, the rhetoric of managerialism's much-vaunted transparency functions to obscure the fact that there is nothing there. And a further irony is that, as a result of managerialism's over-management of management, prison managers themselves complain that in the new world of disciplinary audit they have been stripped of any professional, discretionary or leadership approach to prison management by an over-rigid emphasis on rule compliance and the fears of experiment and innovation which a culture of recrimination is bound to engender.

Bringing the academy to heel

During the same period that the English Prison Service was attempting to tighten up accountability within the Service, its firewall against academic and campaigning critiques was strengthened through the engagement of more and more academics in research where the terms of reference and the publication of results are controlled by the Home Office.

Since the 1990s, British university staff have themselves been disciplined into publishing more research and chasing more research grants, both by the research audit known as the RAE (research assessment exercise) and by financial restrictions which have meant that both their career prospects and their research opportunities have depended not so much on the quality of their research products but more on the amount of money they can raise from external funding (Morgan 2000). The Home

Office in England (see Sim *et al* 2004), and similar government agencies in other countries (Walters 2003) therefore, have been able increasingly to set the agenda for much of the funded research being done by the rapidly growing number of university criminology departments.[12] Meanwhile, more radical prison research tends not to be financed; and criminologists who have the confidence not to be tempted to engage in contracted administrative penology research appear to concentrate their best efforts on cultural studies of changing penalities or on writing books about other books. This is not surprising: the in-your-face theoreticality of essays in cultural, historical and 'chattering' criminology is widely believed to enjoy higher academic acclaim than critical, policy-oriented empirical studies of the criminal justice system and imprisonment.[13] Result? Between the Home Office's interest in large-scale quantitative research within its own terms of (criminogenic) reference on the one hand, and the cultural turn in theoretical criminology on the other, the old modernist construct of the classbound, gendered and/or discriminated-against prisoner seems to have been somewhat lost. Indeed, in the latest resettlement reports, discourses of stratification, race and gender are routinely supplanted by the New Labour language of 'social exclusion' (see for instance, Prison Reform Trust 2000; Social Exclusion Unit 2002). Yet, as every prison officer and probation officer knows, and notwithstanding the rhetorics and prejudices of programming and audit, prisoners today have the same social characteristics as of yesteryear, and many prison staff are puzzled as to the relevance of the proliferation of rules, regulations and audit to making prisoners' in-prison experiences less damaging and their post-prison careers more law-abiding (Social Exclusion Unit 2002).

But what is to be done? Certainly a world without rules would be a world without meaning and it is unlikely (and undesirable) that all aspects of today's organisational disciplinarities should ever be sunk without trace. Nonetheless, although all prison personnel I have ever spoken to insist that prisons must be highly rule-governed places, of late many of them have ventured the opinion that maybe one can have too much of a good thing – that accretions of rules and regulations may perhaps be deemed pathological when they function to obstruct institutional objectives rather than help realise them (cf. Sparks *et al* 1996). The next part of this chapter, therefore, first distinguishes between normal rule usage and pathological disciplinarities before arguing that one strategy for stopping the rot of disciplinary governance in relation to prisons and resettlement may reside in the development, cherishing and activation of some fundamental concepts of moral prison organisation and democratic rule-usage; and with the concomitant relegation of disciplinary governance to its proper place as a *means* to those ends, rather than as an end in itself. For at present, many British penal policy-makers, unable to see their way out of the mass of disciplinarities of their own making, seem to have reified all rules as being bureaucratic rules, deified them as being 'natural' and then vilified anyone who claims that those rules could be otherwise. Yet, as O'Donnell and O'Sullivan (2003: 57) point out, more detailed knowledge of local contexts can provide evidence that global trends are often bucked in specific jurisdictions; and they observe, in support of their argument, that by 2003 Ireland, for one, had not seen an 'emphasis on monitoring, audit, cost-effectiveness and performance' in its prisons.

Normal rule usage and pathological disciplinarities

Rules are prescriptive and, until revoked, binding guidelines for getting things done or for living. They can be used creatively to produce new knowledge, but they themselves remain open to question and debate.

Disciplines, as defined by Foucault, on the other hand, are pedagogic rules which bind because they have been internalised. They produce 'docile bodies' and, as their ties become more and more refined, disciplines become political anatomies of detail (Foucault 1977: 138). They govern the soul through their appearance of naturalness. However, it is agued here that too often, instead of remaining techniques of governance, rules are eventually cherished and embellished as being ends in themselves – at which point they become 'disciplinarities'. *Disciplinarities* thus become ideologies of governance and persons who question their relevance to the contemporary situation are not seen as being engaged in legitimate argument; rather, they are seen as being 'not sound' or even 'loose cannons'.[14]

Since the radical disciplining of the public sector by the Thatcher and Blair governments, the operation of many public services, including those constituting the penal body politic, appears to have been increasingly atrophied by the growth of untrammelled, unquestioned (and therefore pathological) disciplinarities. In some ways, this disciplinary strain towards totalitarianism in rule-usage is reminiscent of Weber's bleak vision of the totally bureaucratised society (Weber 1954: 341). But there is a distinction to be made between bureaucracy and discipline: bureaucratic rule remains rooted in the office of the office-holder; disciplinary rule targets the soul (Rose 1999). Combined, they produce an anarchic but despotic rule usage, unassailable because of its coherence in contradiction: for example, prison governors whose budget does not allow them to finance the implementation of Prison Service Orders can none the less be personally blamed for any failure to meet Key Performance Indicators (KPIs) which are presented by the Service's bureaucrats as having 'no financial implications' at all (see Carlen 2002a). No one appears to be responsible for ensuring that the money is there to meet the cost of attaining the target (see Ramsbotham 2003): the very existence of a KPI, it is implied, should be enough to constrain a 'good' manager to meet his target. Those who show that they have not internalised the logic of the KPI by questioning it are depicted as 'mavericks'.

Now, of course, the internalisation of some social rules is both a necessary and desirable facet of socialisation – whether it be into language, 'society' or any one of its constituent parts. Bureaucratic rule, moreover, can be both facilitative of justice as fairness and a protection against despotism. However, disciplines become pathological, and bureaucracies despotic when, because of their inherent tendency to constrain and detail, they are no longer questioned and, even if superseded by newer rules and disciplines, continue to clutter up, and eventually shut up, innovative debate with the dead weight of complacent tradition. This affects prisons and prisoners adversely because it results in a centralisation and ossification of penal knowledge which suppresses innovation (see Roberts 2002) and obscures the lack of overall strategy and leadership necessary to the governance of complex and vibrant social institutions such as the Prison Service and its penal estate.

To recap: the disciplinary transformations in the penal body politic have not supplanted the old disciplinarities designed to keep prisoners both docilely and securely in prison. Instead they have added even more layers to the already compacted layers of encrusted disciplinarities. These, the baggage of successive bureaucratic reconstructions, not only obscures the fact that imprisonment is a violent deprivation of liberty imposed as a severe and painful punishment but also eats away at the best attempts of prison staff to run minimally healthy regimes (HM Inspectorate of Prisons 1999). One way, therefore, of stopping the disciplinary rot presently atrophying rehabilitation attempts both within and outside the prison walls might be by having a clear agenda for the supersession of disciplinary governance by democratic rule-usage. The final part of the chapter considers how that might be achieved.

Contesting disciplinary governance

> Without a framework within which prison can be made to work, and a vision of how it should work, expensive, avoidable muddle will continue to be the best description of the administration of imprisonment.
>
> (Ramsbotham 2003: 245)

At the end of his book, *Prisongate*, David Ramsbotham (2003) outlines a very clear and detailed agenda for the reformation of the governance of the English Prison Service. Two of the concepts on which he focuses (leadership and strategy) will be discussed below, together with those of 'remoralisation', 'penal probity', 'recognition of cultural diversity', 'minimal carceralism' and 'social realism'.

Leadership

One of the most peculiar aspects of the continuing crisis of management in the English Prison Service is that despite the plethora of rules, directives and other disciplinary baggage that prison administrators have had to carry over the past few years, there has been a dearth of leadership about how they are to choose between competing budgetary priorities and contradictory objectives. Via KPIs and targets, the management of the Prison Service seems almost to have abdicated from any human leadership role, seemingly expecting the disciplinarities contained in tons of paper directives to do the job for them. However, as Ramsbotham (2003) notes, rule compliance does not tell us anything about outcomes, and only a clear leadership structure is capable of the creative rule-usage which produces desired outcomes rather than more and more rules about rules. Writing of the period 1995–2001, when he was Chief Inspector of Prisons for England and Wales, Ramsbotham repeatedly commented on this phenomenon:

> Prison management concentrated on exact compliance with rules and regulations, and the achievement of a myriad of targets and performance indicators. These were more to do with process in prisons than outcomes for prisoners.
>
> (Ramsbotham 2003: 218)

Strategy

In a large and complex public enterprise ostensibly dedicated to the rehabilitation of prisoners, democratic leadership (in terms of the creative use of rules in place of the slavish adherence to the disciplinarities of process) can only occur if there is a clear overarching strategy to which all the subordinate strategies contribute (cf. Ramsbotham 2003: 81). Yet the mushrooming bureaucracies constituting the penal rehabilitation business are often working to entirely different priorities and under different legal constraints as they compete for narrow budgets and resources. Departments in the Home Office, Prison Service Headquarters and Social Exclusion Unit (to name but three different bureaucratic sites) may all be working on overlapping rehabilitation 'strategies' and, too often, in my experience, only for the time that it takes a civil servant to get enough experience to move on elsewhere! A visible rationalisation, minimalisation and stabilisation of the Civil Service role in the governance of prisons and prisoner resettlement would also contribute to much-needed remoralisation of prison personnel.

Remoralisation of prison personnel

It has been argued that when states are unable to deliver the citizenship goods (such as law and order) which they have been elected to deliver, they tend to displace responsibility from themselves to citizens (Garland 1996). In the case of the Prison Service, Prison Headquarters has used the impersonal targets and KPIs to displace responsibility for prison ills from policy-makers and senior management (at Prison Service Headquarters) onto middle management (prison governors) and prison officers.[15] O'Malley (1992) calls this strategy of blame displacement 'reponsibilisation', and it was a prime mechanism of public-sector control used in the 1980s. On the one hand, it functioned to discipline prison officers into the 'blame culture'; on the other, it helped ram prison governors into their roles as deprofessionalised managers of management rather than professional managers empowered to use their discretion as to how best realise institutional goals and objectives.

However, to realise the outcomes conducive to prisoners' rehabilitation, a corporate and more *democratised* structure of decision-making is nowadays required, extending shares in the ownership and shaping of innovation to the prison staff who actually have to operationalise it. Thus, unlike the 'responsibilisation' strategies described by Garland (1996) and Hannah-Moffatt (2001) whereby the state *distances* itself from responsibility for crime control by making communities responsible for crime prevention, and prisoners responsible for their own reform and rehabilitation, a 'corporate moral community' approach would not only implicate state employees at all levels, it would also open up the way for them to sow the seeds of effective change from

433

within (cf. Marks 2000). Therefore, in terms of prison governance, the requirement is to move from a *responsibilisation* (of prisoners) strategy to a *remoralisation of staff*. Additional moves to minimalise the disciplinarities would be the development of democratic staff structures within prisons so that ownership of issues could lead to accountable but creative rule usage in place of blame-laden and stultifying rule compliance.

Penal probity

Once rule compliance is no longer seen as an end in itself, it will be time to bring morals back into official prison discourse,[16] so that instead of the measure of the 'good prison' being whether or not it has met all its targets and KPIs, it will be about the quality of the life for all members of the prison communities, while issues of penal probity (in terms of human rights) will supersede those of mechanical rule compliance.

There is no recipe for penal probity, of course. Indeed, in talking of the quest for penal probity I am talking about a desirable process – saying no more and no less than that a conversation must go on between everyone involved in the criminal justice system about how prisons can be run according to moral principles which do not seek to justify imprisonment by dishonestly arguing that prisons can do something that they can't – for instance, 'win the war on drugs', or 'reduce recidivism' – but instead aim to make prisons moral communities which limit the damage done to prisoners and the harm done to society. In order to maximise the benefits of a move from audit to probity, there will need to be an ongoing attempt to recognise cultural diversity and achieve minimal carceralism.

Recognition of cultural diversity

A cut-back in disciplinarities and an ongoing search for penal probity should also lead to greater diversity in prison organisation to allow for the cultural differences (of culture, age, gender[17]) which the normal prison organisation does not allow for, and in not allowing for them, causes additional pain to particular groups. The pains of imprisonment which discriminate against women in prisons designed and organised for men, or ethnic minority women in prisons which cater primarily for white people, have been well documented; but ageing women also find their specific needs neglected in prisons organised primarily for young women; and sometimes lesbian women's talk about partners and home problems outside prison are not taken seriously by prison staff. In prisons geared to damage limitation in the service of recidivism reduction through successful resettlement, the quest for penal probity would entail a constant questioning of the provision made for cultural difference of all kinds and the appropriate treatment of prisoners would be decided within a moral calculus of prisoner need rather than a contractual one of prisoner-desert. With a relaxation of centralised direction, staff in non-custodial programmes would be allowed to tailor programmes to the clients they actually have, rather than to some stereotypical constructs of white male programme designers from an alien culture. However, the replacement of threadbare disciplinarities with more creative and culturally relevant rule usage will not occur while prisons are the overcrowded shambles which many of them are today.

Minimal carceralism

At first sight the plea for minimal carceralism may appear to have little to do with the abolition of excess disciplinarities within prisons. But minimal carceralism refers not only to prison reductionism in sentencing but also to in-prison management. For as the essential nature of imprisonment necessitates that security is both the prison's defining characteristic and its management priority, minimal carceralism, as used here, refers to the desirability of an ongoing conversation questioning the security value-added of every prison practice that is justified in the name of prison order and security. The Canadian criminologist Kelly Hannah-Moffat (2002) has used the concept of *encroachment* to describe how pre-existing organisational norms frequently encroach upon and undermine and destroy the logic of innovation, even when their relevance to security may arguably be tangential. Nowhere is this more prevalent in custodial institutions than in relation to pro-security prohibitions and curtailments of innovations (Carlen 2002b). However, there should also be a minimal carceralism in terms of resettlement policies as attempts to impose excessive disciplinary controls may result in a trancarceralism that is counter-productive in terms of resettlement.

Social realism

And finally, back to the programming of prisoners and a plea for social realism in relation to prisoners' resettlement needs. There is widespread belief among the relevant professionals in England and elsewhere that there should be less emphasis upon prison-regime reforms and programming, and more on, first, resettling ex-prisoners in their own safe accommodation; and then, second, supporting them in struggles against addictions and other environmental pressures. And, of course, anti-prison campaigners have research evidence on their side: studies of desistance from crime suggest that what happens outside prison in terms of housing, jobs and personal relationships is much more important than any brainwashing attempts made via prison programming. None the less, in England and Wales, at least, instead of the coordinated community provision recommended by all previous inquiries and reports (and which requires local rather than central organisation), there has been too much concentration on the in-prison provision of 'cognitive behavioural' programmes which have been exported from Canada and which in England cost between £2,000 and £2,500 per prisoner (Kendall 2002). Overall, these programmes are most probably harmless, and, insofar as they help prisoners pass the time more pleasantly in prison, may even be beneficial; but their claims to reduce recidivism are unproven. More worryingly, however, there may well be a link between the increased numbers of offenders sentenced to imprisonment (together with a possible transfer of resources from community to prison for drugs programmes) and the increasingly contested claims that the various programmes based on 'cognitive behavioural' approaches can reduce recidivism. And while the evidence in relation to these programmes is mixed (Friendship *et al* 2002; Inspector of Custodial Services 2003), we have more consistent evidence that 'there is considerable risk that a prison sentence might actually make the factors associated with re-offending worse' (Social Exclusion Unit 2002: 7).

Conclusion

Most of what I have had to say about the cancer of disciplinary governance in the penal body politic has been written about many times before – and mainly in authoritative official reports (e.g. Lygo 1991; HM Prison Service 1997; House of Commons 2001). But the recommendations of those reports have not been effectively implemented (Ramsbotham 2003). In the analysis given here, I have argued that one reason for their non-implementation inheres in the disciplinary cancer which has got such a stranglehold on the penal body politic that only a determination to cut it out root and branch will allow a more coherent and productive system to operate in the interests of prisoner resettlement and the hoped-for associated reduction in prisoner recidivism.

But maybe, just maybe, in view of all the illustrious commentators who have made similar analyses over the years, the reduction in prisoner recidivism is not really what imprisonment is all about. For even if the death of the disciplinarities were to free up the penal body politic for a more creative rule-usage in the service of prisoner resettlement, it has to be remembered that one of the triumphs of creative rule-usage is that rules and ever-new discourses can be invoked to accomplish the very opposite to what they conventionally appear to be accomplishing (Rawls 1955; Chomsky 1971; Burke 1969). My own view is simply that prisons cannot plausibly claim to rehabilitate at the same time as their primary custodial function necessitates regimes which debilitate. The most that can be hoped for is humane containment. Even so, (and mindful too that moral governance is seldom seen to coincide with social and political interests[18]), in the name of penal probity more might be done to prepare prisoners for release, to foster communication between prison and outside rehabilitative agencies, and to provide released prisoners with the material and psychological wherewithal to settle down as law-abiding citizens, than is presently being done in the name of the KPIs, psychological programming and various forms of audit.

However, the main objective of the argument presented here has not been to put forward another blueprint for penal reform. It has merely been to persuade that ongoing diagnosis of the essential tendencies of the penal body politic to stifle change via its self-protective disciplinarities is a necessary precondition for the creation and sustenance of regionally fashioned institutional frameworks wherein prisoners' welfare and resettlement policies might, in the future, successfully do battle with organisational inertia and the penal hypocrisy born of political interest.

Notes

1 I would like to thank Kelly Hannah-Moffat, Ian O'Donnell and Joe Sim for helpful comments on earlier drafts of this paper.
2 Penal body politic: government departments, prison managements and government researchers; academic penal theorists and campaigning groups.
3 Of course, much of the time new inquiries into the state of the prisons have to repeat previous reports and recommendations because although accepted by governments, they have seldom been acted upon.
4 'Of those prisoners released in 1997, 58 per cent were convicted of another crime within two years. 36 per cent were back inside on another sentence. Eighteen to twenty year old male prisoners were reconvicted at a rate of 72 per cent over the same period; 47 per cent received another prison sentence' (Social Exclusion Unit 2002: 5).
5 See Nutley and Davies (2000) for a concise overview of 'policy papers' on what works.
6 See Ramsbotham (2003).
7 See Carlen (1994) for a longer list of prison successes.
8 Term used to denote those technologies of managerialist discipline (i.e. different modes of governance by a specific body of rules directed at limiting

discretionary rule-usage) which cease to be actualised only in terms of their declared objectives, but instead become ends in themselves and function to obstruct organisational innovation.

9   In Foucault's *Discipline and Punish*, 'discipline' has a double meaning: it embraces both a distinctive type of organisational knowledge – bureaucracy – (just as we sometimes talk of the 'discipline' of history or geography), and also discipline's other meaning, 'bringing under a rule'. In this chapter, too, both meanings are intended.

10 I refer mainly to the UK both because that is the area I know best and because I also hold the view that, as a corrective to the cultural turn in penality studies, which has focused on global trends rather than on the minutiae of cultural difference, more regional studies should nowadays be undertaken with a view to analysing how the global trends are being differently realised within specific jurisdictions (see also Hope and Sparks 2000, Tonry 2001 and O'Donnell and O'Sullivan 2003 on the need for regional analyses to balance the contemporary emphasis on 'global trends'). However, the analyses presented here do have some relevance to penal politics in other countries.

11 Probation is not discussed in this paper.

12 Garland and Sparks (2000) demonstrated that academic criminology in England has always enjoyed a close relationship with 'official' criminology. The point here is that, owing to changes in the governance of academic research, that relationship has recently been strengthened.

13 This is not a criticism of cultural, historical or 'chattering' criminologies, merely a suggestion about their possible effects.

14 Cf. the way in which English prison governors questioning the excesses of managerialism have been routinely called 'mavericks' by Prison Service Headquarters staff (Carlen 2002a).

15 See Narey (2001) for a prime example of blame displacement from the Director General of the Prison Service on to the Prison Governors. See Ramsbotham (2003: 214–16) for a further comment.

16 Discussion of moral issues has routinely characterised the unofficial discourse of penal personnel and Prisons Inspectorate: see, for instance, Liebling and Price (2001); and Ramsbotham (2003).

17 See Crook (2003) on children in prison; Wahidin (2003) on ageing women in prison; and Crawley and Sparks, Chapter 13 of this volume, on older men in prison.

18 Cf. Durkheim (1963/1933: 416): '[A] number of things are useful or even necessary to society without being moral'.

References

Bauman, Z. (1989) *Modernity and the Holocaust*. Cambridge: Polity Press.

Becket, K. and Sasson, T. (2004) *The Politics of Injustice*, 2nd edition. London: Sage Publishing.

Blair, T. (2000) 'Foreword', in Social Exclusion Unit, *Reducing Re-offending byEx-prisoners*. London: Office of the Deputy Prime Minister.

Bottoms, A. (1983) 'Neglected features of contemporary penal systems', in D. Garland and P. Young (eds) *The Power to Punish*. London: Heinemann Press.

Burke, K. (1969) *A Rhetoric of Motives*. Berkeley: University of California Press.

Burns, T. and Stalker G. (1967) *The Management of Innovation*. London: Tavistock Publishing.

Carlen, P. (1994) 'Why study women's imprisonment or anyone else's?', in R. King and M. Maguire (eds) *Prisons in Context*. Oxford: Clarendon Press.

Carlen, P. (2001) 'Death and the triumph of governance', *Punishment and Society*, 3 (4), 459–471.

Carlen, P. (2002a) 'Governing the governors: Telling tales of managers, mandarins and mavericks', *Criminal Justice*, 2 (1), 27–49.

Carlen, P. (2002b) 'Women's imprisonment: Models of reform and change', *Probation Journal*, 49 (2), 76–87.

Carlen, P. (2004) 'Risk and responsibility in women's prisons', *Current Issues in Criminal Justice*, 15 (3), 258–266.

Chomsky, N. (1971) 'Topics in the theory of generative grammar', in J. Searle (ed.) *The Philosophy of Language*. Oxford: Oxford University Press.

Christie, N. (2000) *Crime Control as Industry*, 3rd edition. London: Routledge Publishing.

Crook, F. (2003) 'Children in prison: Advocating for the human rights of young offenders', *Criminal Justice Matters* 54 (Winter), 24–25.

Durkheim, E. (1963/1933) *The Division of Labour in Society*. London: Macmillan, Free Press.

Foucault, M. (1972) *The Archaeology of Knowledge*. London: Taviststock Publishing.

Foucault, M. (1977) *Discipline and Punish*. Harmondsworth: Penguin.

Friendship, C., Blud, L., Erikson, M. and Travers, R. (2002) *An Evaluation of Cognitive Behavioural Treatment for Prisoners*. Findings 61. London: Home Office.

Garland, D. (1996) 'The limits of the sovereign state', *British Journal of Criminology*, 36 (4), 445–471.

Garland, D. (2001) *The Culture of Control*. Oxford: Oxford University Press.

Garland, D. and Sparks, R. (2000) 'Criminology, social theory and the challenge of our times', *British Journal of Criminology Special Issue on Criminology and Social Theory*, 40 (2), 189–204.

Hannah-Moffat, H. (2001) *Punishment in Disguise*. Toronto: University of Toronto Press.

Hannah-Moffat, K. (2002) 'Creating choices, reflecting on choices', in P. Carlen (ed.) *Women and Punishment*. Cullompton: Willan Publishing.

HM Inspectorate of Prisons (1999) *Suicide is Everyone's Concern: A Thematic Review*. London: Home Office.

HM Prison Service (1997) *Prison Service Review*. London: HM Prison Service.

House of Commons (2001) *Making Government Work: The Emerging Issues, HC 94*, Public Administration Select Committee. London: HMSO.

Hope, T. and Sparks, R. (2000) 'Risk, insecurity and law and order', in T. Hope and R. Sparks (eds) *Crime, Risk and Insecurity*. London: Routledge Publishing.

Hudson. B. (2002) 'Gender issues in penal policy and penal theory', in P. Carlen (ed.) *Women and Punishment*. Cullompton: Willan Publishing.

Inspector of Custodial Services (2003) *Cognitive Skills Programs in Western Australian Prisons*. Perth: Office of the Inspector of Custodial Services.

Jones, T. and Newburn, T. (2004) 'The convergence of US and UK crime control policy', in T. Newburn and R. Sparks (eds) *Criminal Justice and Political Cultures*. Cullompton: Willan, pp. 123–151.

Kemshall, H. and Maguire, M. (2001) 'Public protection, partnership and risk penality: The multi-agency risk management of sexual and violent offenders', *Punishment and Society*, 3 (2), 237–264.

Kendall, K. (2002) 'Time to think again about cognitive behavioural programmes', in P. Carlen (ed.) *Women and Punishment*. Cullompton: Willan Publishing.

Kittrie, N. (1971) *The Right to be Different*. Baltimore: Johns Hopkins Press.

Liebling, A. and Price, D. (2001) *The Prison Officer*. Leyhill: Prison Service Journal.

Lygo, R. (1991) *Report on the Management of the Prison Service*. London: Home Office.

Marks, M. (2000) 'Transforming police organization from within: Police dissident groupings in South Africa', *British Journal of Criminology*, 40 (4), 553–569.

Martinson, R. (1974) 'What works? Questions and answers about prison reform', *The Public Interest*, 35, 22–54.

Maruna, S. (2002) 'In the shadows of community justice', in D. Karp and T. Clear (eds) *What is Community Justice?* London: Sage Publishing.

Mathiesen, T. (2000) *Prison on Trial*, 2nd English edition. Winchester: Waterside Press.

McMahon, M. (1992) *The Persistent Prison*. Toronto: University of Toronto Press.

Morgan, R. (2000) 'The politics of criminological research', in R. King and E. Wincup (eds) *Doing Research on Crime and Justice*. Oxford: Oxford University Press.

Narey, M. (2001) *Director General's Address to HM Prison Service Conference*. London: Prison Service.

Nutley, S. and Davies, H. (2000) 'Criminal justice: Using evidence to reduce crime', in T. Davies, S. Nutley and P. Smith (eds) *What Works? Evidence-Based Policy and Practice in Public Services*. Bristol: Policy Press.

O'Donnell, I. and O'Sullivan, E. (2003) 'The politics of intolerance – Irish style', *British Journal of Criminology*, 43, 41–62.

O'Malley, P. (1992) 'Risk, power and crime prevention', *Economy and Society*, 21 (3), 252–275.

Power, M. (1997) *Audit Society*. Oxford: Oxford University Press.

Pratt, J. (2002) *Punishment and Civilization*. London: Sage Publishing.

Prison Reform Trust (2000) *Justice for Women: The Need for Reform* (The Wedderburn Report). London: Prison Reform Trust.

Ramsbotham, D. (2003) *Prisongate: The Shocking State of Britain's Prisons and the Need for Visionary Change*. London: Simon and Schuster Free Press.

Rawls, J. (1955) 'Two concepts of rules', *Philosophical Review*, 64 (3), 6–7.

Roberts, J. (2002) 'Women-centred: The West Mercia community-based programme for women offenders', in P. Carlen (ed.) *Women and Punishment*. Cullompton: Willan Publishing.

Rose, N. (1999) *Governing the Soul*, 2nd edition. London: Free Association Books.

Shearing, C. (2001) 'Punishment and the changing face of governance', *Punishment and Society*, 3 (2), 203–220.

Sim, J., Tombs, S. and Whyte, D. (2004) 'Leaving a stain upon the silence', *British Journal of Criminology*, forthcoming.

Social Exclusion Unit (2002) *Reducing Re-Offending by Ex-Prisoners*. London: Office of the Deputy Prime Minister.

Sparks, R., Bottoms, A. and Hay, W. (1996) *Prisons and the Problem of Order*. Oxford: Clarendon Press.

Tonry, M. (2001) 'Symbol, substance and severity in Western penal policies', *Punishment and Society*, 4 (3), 517–536.

Wahidin, A. (2003) 'Women, old age and the prison system', *Criminal Justice Matters*, 53, Autumn, 38–39.

Walters, R. (2003) *Deviant Knowledge*. Cullompton: Willan Publishing.

Wacquant, L. (2001) 'Deadly symbiosis: When ghetto and prison meet and submerge', *Punishment and Society*, 3 (1), 95-134.

Weber, M. (1925/1954) *On Economy in Law and Society* (edited by M. Rheinstein; translated by E. Shils and M. Rheinstein). Cambridge, MA: Harvard University Press.

Chapter 17

The effects of imprisonment on families and children of prisoners

Joseph Murray[1]

> Family is affected and involved in the prison sentence. It affects everybody close.
>
> (Anonymous prisoner)

Researchers have only begun to explore the far-reaching effects of imprisonment beyond prison walls. Unintended consequences highlighted so far include: the social disorganisation of communities (Clear *et al* 2001); reduced job opportunities for ex-prisoners (Holzer *et al* 2004); diversion of funds away from schools and universities (Hagan and Dinovitzer 1999); and psychological and financial burdens on families.

Families are an important influence on many aspects of prisoners' lives. Family and parenting variables are key predictors of criminal behaviour through the life-course (Farrington 2002; Loeber and Stouthamer-Loeber 1986). Loss of outside relationships is considered the most painful aspect of confinement for prisoners (Flanagan 1980; Richards 1978). Family contact is associated with lower rates of self-harm while inside prison (Harvey, this volume; Liebling 1992). Families are one of the most important factors affecting prisoners' rehabilitation after release (Social Exclusion Unit 2002).

Unfortunately, prisoners' families have been little studied in their own right. The effects of imprisonment on families and children of prisoners are almost entirely neglected in academic research, prison statistics, public policy and media coverage. However, we can infer from prisoners' backgrounds that their families are a highly vulnerable group. Limited research to date suggests that imprisonment can have devastating consequences for partners and children. As such, issues of legitimacy and fairness may be as important outside prison as they are inside (see Liebling, this volume). As Roger Shaw pointed out almost 20 years ago, if we do not attend to the effects of imprisonment on children, we face the possibility of punishing innocent victims, neglecting a seriously at-risk group, and possibly causing crime in the next generation (Shaw 1987).

This chapter reviews research on the effects of imprisonment on prisoners' partners as a context for a more detailed discussion of the effects on prisoners' children. Evidence on these topics comes almost entirely from cross-sectional studies using convenience samples, and without standardised measures, triangulation of sources or suitable controls. Therefore, only cautious hypotheses can be proposed about the specific effects of imprisonment on families and children. A general model is proposed of hypothesised influences on child adjustment during parental imprisonment. Explanatory factors are distinguished by whether they appear to have selection effects, or direct, mediating or moderating effects. To test the hypothesised effects identified in this chapter, we need large-scale, longitudinal studies of prisoners' children, with reliable measures and appropriate controls. Disentangling factors that influence prisoners' children's outcomes is crucial to improving our understanding of prison effects, and to implementing effective social policies to support this vulnerable population.

Hidden victims

There are no accurate, up-to-date estimates of the numbers of imprisoned parents, or children of imprisoned parents, in the UK. The last National Prison Survey in England and Wales reported that 47 per cent of female prisoners and 32 per cent of male prisoners had children living with them before coming to prison (Dodd and Hunter 1992). However, information was not collected on parenthood specifically in this survey. By contrast, in the US, inmate surveys have been conducted every five years since 1974, compiling detailed information on prisoners' children (Johnson and Waldfogel 2004). Mumola found that there were 1.5 million children with a currently imprisoned parent in the US in 1999; over half a million more than in 1991 (Mumola 2000). Ninety-two per cent had a father in prison. Parental imprisonment disproportionately affected black children (7.0 per cent) and Hispanic children (2.6 per cent), compared to white children (0.8 per cent). The extent to which children experience parental imprisonment may be hidden because we know less about the incidence of parental imprisonment than we do about its prevalence. Although the

UK Treasury stated that 150,000 children currently experience parental imprisonment every year (HM Treasury 2003), it is not clear what evidence this is based on. The last well-known surveys of the incidence of parental imprisonment in England and Wales were conducted in 1984 for fathers (Shaw 1987) and in 1967 for mothers (Gibbs 1971). Despite calls from lobby groups, no one regularly monitors the parental status of prisoners in the UK; there may be literally millions of unidentified children experiencing parental imprisonment.

The effects of imprisonment on partners of prisoners

... It is like someone had died.
(Anonymous wife of prisoner, quoted in Morris 1965: 166)

Imprisonment of a partner can be emotionally devastating and practically debilitating. Loss of income, social isolation, difficulties of maintaining contact, deterioration in relationships, and extra burdens of childcare can compound a sense of loss and hopelessness for prisoners' partners. Unfortunately, prisoners' families have been studied almost entirely with reference to male prisoners' partners and wives. Limited research suggests that the impact on prisoners' spouses is generally more severe than on parents (Ferraro *et al* and Bolton 1983) although parents and other family members can also suffer practical and psychological difficulties (McDermott and King 1992; Noble 1995).

By far the most comprehensive study of prisoners' wives was conducted by Pauline Morris, who interviewed 825 imprisoned men in England and 469 of their wives (Morris 1965). Morris found that imprisonment of a husband was generally experienced as a crisis of family dismemberment rather than a crisis of demoralisation through stigma or shame. Stigma was experienced almost exclusively by wives whose husbands were imprisoned for the first time, and then only at the initial stages of the separation. Among the most common problems reported, 63 per cent of wives said they experienced deterioration in their financial situation; 81 per cent some deterioration in their work; 46 per cent deterioration in present attitude to marriage and future plans; 63 per cent deterioration in social activity; 60 per cent deterioration in relationships with in-laws; and 57 per cent deterioration in relationships with friends and neighbours.[2]

Since Morris's early work, other studies of prisoners' partners and wives have found remarkably similar themes across the UK, the US, Ireland and Australia. Studies consistently report that loss of income is one of the most important difficulties faced by partners of male prisoners (Anderson 1966; Ferraro *et al* 1983; McEvoy *et al* 1999; Noble 1995; Richards *et al* 1994; Schneller 1976). Sharp and Marcus-Mendoza (2001) found that imprisoning mothers also caused a drastic reduction in family income. Loss of income is compounded by additional expenses of prison visits, mail, telephone calls (especially if prisoners call collect, as in the US) and sending money to imprisoned relatives. As one family member put it, 'it becomes so expensive, and the cost becomes so enormous that it takes away other things that you could be doing with your money ... I have to look out for my well-being and my children's well-being, because I'm the only source of income they have' (Braman and Wood 2003: 164).

Imprisonment of a partner can also cause home moves (Noble 1995), divorce and relationship problems (Anderson 1966; Ferraro *et al* 1983; McEvoy *et al* 1999) and medical and health problems (Ferraro *et al* 1983; McEvoy *et al* 1999; Noble 1995). Partners with children face single parenthood at a particularly vulnerable time (Peart and Asquith 1992). As well as having to deal with their own problems, partners are expected to support prisoners and to look after children, who are likely to be particularly hard to manage if their parent has been imprisoned (see next section).

Partners face other difficulties that are more intrinsic to the facts of imprisonment (see Irwin and Owen, this volume). Prisoners' partners can suffer because of a lack of information about the imprisonment, visiting, and contact procedures (Ferraro *et al* 1983). Maintaining contact can be fraught with difficulties such as busy booking lines, inconvenient visiting hours, a lack of transport, and the cost and distance of travel (Hounslow *et al* 1982). Exacerbating these problems, prisons are clearly not family-friendly places to visit. Poor visiting facilities and hostile attitudes of staff can put families off visiting, especially those with children (Peart and Asquith 1992).

Although prisoners' families often experience similar stresses, there is growing appreciation that families and partners of prisoners are not a homogenous group. Even within cultural and penal contexts, prison effects on family members are likely to differ according to prior relationships, offence types, social support systems and other socio-demographic factors. Light (1994) found that black prisoners' families endure additional harassment in the English penal system. Richards and colleagues found that families of foreign nationals in British prisons face particular difficulties (Richards *et al* 1995). For some, a relative's imprisonment will offer relief from violent or difficult behaviour at home.

We need to identify how prison effects on families vary over time, as well as between individuals. McDermott and King (1992) distinguished between the traumatic experience of arrest, the overriding uncertainty during remand and trial, and the distinct experiences of families coping with different sentence lengths. However, little is known about prison effects on families over time. Particularly little is known about the effects on partners after prisoners are released. Partners often worry about adjusting when prisoners come home (Noble 1995) and studies of prisoners suggest that the reality of reunion can present profound difficulties for prisoners and their families (Jamieson and Grounds, this volume).

In summary, qualitative accounts have detailed the financial burdens, psychological traumas and practical difficulties that can accompany a relative's imprisonment. However, reliable measurement over time is almost nonexistent in studies of prisoners' families, making it hard to disentangle putative causes and effects.

The effects of imprisonment on children of prisoners

> I was very upset and shocked at first. Over three years I have come to terms with it but I had to develop a 'hard streak' and grow up quickly.

> (Anonymous boy with father in prison,
> quoted in Boswell 2002: 18)

Prisoners' children have been variously referred to as the 'orphans of justice' (Shaw 1992), the 'forgotten victims' of crime (Matthews 1983) and the 'Cinderella of penology' (Shaw 1987). Children can suffer a range of problems during their parent's imprisonment, such as: depression, hyperactivity, aggressive behaviour, withdrawal, regression, clinging behaviour, sleep problems, eating problems, running away, truancy and poor school grades (Boswell and Wedge 2002; Centre for Social and Educational Research 2002; Johnston 1995; Kampfner 1995; Sack *et al* 1976; Sharp and Marcus-Mendoza 2001; Shaw 1987; Skinner and Swartz 1989; Stanton 1980). It is commonly cited that up to 30 per cent of prisoners' children suffer mental health problems, compared to 10 per cent of the general population (Philbrick 1996). However, there appears to be no documented evidence to support this claim. In Morris's study,

49 per cent of prisoners' wives reported adverse changes in children's behaviour since their husbands' imprisonment (Morris 1965). Friedman found that children of jail inmates were more often rated below average in the school world on social, psychological and academic characteristics compared to controls (although subjects were not well matched on ethnicity) (Friedman and Esselstyn 1965). These studies suggest that parental imprisonment is a risk factor for mental health problems among children. However, to determine the actual increase in risk for mental health problems associated with parental imprisonment we need studies with representative samples, well-validated measures and appropriate comparison data.

An important question for sentencing is whether parental imprisonment causes antisocial behaviour and crime in the next generation. Anecdotal evidence suggests that children are at risk of antisocial reactions to parental imprisonment (Johnston 1995; Sack 1977; Sack and Seidler 1978). One boy in Morris's study was discovered by a policeman tampering with car locks and the boy declared his intention of joining his father in prison (Morris 1965: 91). It is frequently stated that children of prisoners are six times more likely than their peers to be imprisoned themselves. However, there appears to be no documented evidence to support this claim (see Johnston 1998, cited in Myers *et al* 1999). Only one study has prospectively examined later-life criminality among children who experienced parental imprisonment. Murray and Farrington (in press) found that, of London-boys who were separated because of parental imprisonment between birth and age 10, 48 per cent were convicted as an adult, compared to 25 per cent of boys who were separated for other reasons. However, these results need replication, especially for girls, and in other social contexts.

The assumption that parental imprisonment causes psychosocial difficulties for children is pervasive in the literature. Although it is a reasonable hypothesis that parental imprisonment causes adverse reactions in children, studies have lacked the methodological sophistication to distinguish the effects of parental imprisonment from the effects of other influences on children. Identifying which factors cause prisoners' children's outcomes is critical to developing the most effective solutions to their problems. I argue that four types of factors should be included in a model of parental imprisonment and child adjustment: selection effects preceding the imprisonment, and direct, mediating and moderating effects following the imprisonment. I explain the meaning of these terms below.

What are selection, mediating and moderating effects?

Selection, mediating and moderating effects occur when extraneous variables influence the relation between an explanatory variable (in this case parental imprisonment) and an outcome variable (in this case child adjustment). A *selection effect* occurs when a pre-existing extraneous variable is associated with the explanatory variable and causes the outcome variable. Selection effects reduce, or eliminate, the association between the explanatory variable and the outcome variable. In other words, selection effects are confounding effects, which can render the association between an explanatory variable and an outcome variable spurious. For example, if parental antisocial behaviour is associated with parental imprisonment and also causes child maladjustment, then parental antisocial behaviour has a selection effect, 'explaining away' the relationship between parental imprisonment and child maladjustment. A *mediator* 'represents the generative mechanism through which the focal independent variable is able to influence the dependent variable of interest' (Baron and Kenny 1986: 1173). In other words, a mediator represents an intervening causal mechanism between the explanatory variable and the outcome variable. For example, if parental imprisonment affects children's adjustment indirectly through a loss of family income, then family income is a mediator in the relation between parental imprisonment and child adjustment. A *moderator* 'is a variable that affects the direction and/or strength of the relation between an independent or predictor variable and a dependent or criterion variable' (Baron and Kenny 1986: 1174). In other words, a moderator changes the effect of an explanatory variable on an outcome variable. For example, if the effect of parental imprisonment on children depends on whether the child is a boy or a girl, then the child's sex is a moderator of the relation between parental imprisonment and child adjustment.[3]

Selection effects before imprisonment

> The damage was done before I came to prison.
> (Anonymous prisoner, quoted in Healy *et al* 2000: 23)

Selection effects occur when pre-existing differences between prisoners' children and their peers account for their difference in outcome. Selection effects are likely to exist because parental imprisonment does not occur randomly in the population. Compared to the general population, prisoners are more likely to have been unemployed, to be of low social class, have multiple mental health problems, marital difficulties, and to have their own experiences of abuse and neglect (Dodd and Hunter

1992; Singleton *et al* 1998). Many of these and other conditions associated with parental imprisonment are risk factors for mental health problems in children (see Johnson and Waldfogel 2004).

A notable absence in the literature is consideration of the effects of parental criminality on prisoners' children. Prisoners, by definition, must have at least one criminal conviction (except those on remand). Parental criminal convictions, regardless of the sentences that follow, are a strong independent predictor of children's own criminal and antisocial behaviour in later life (Farrington *et al* 1996). It is possible that the association between parental imprisonment and children's own antisocial and delinquent behaviour is largely explained by parental criminal convictions. If this were the case, parental criminal convictions would have a selection effect on the relationship between parental imprisonment and children's adjustment.

It has been suggested that prisoners' children are also likely to be at genetic risk for antisocial behaviour and mental disorders, even before their parent is imprisoned. In a retrospective study of prisoners' children, Crowe (1974) found that adopted children whose birth mothers were incarcerated were more likely than other adopted children to have been arrested, incarcerated and have a psychiatric record at the age of 25.

If selection hypotheses were true, analysing children's outcomes using suitably matched controls would reduce or eliminate the relationship between parental imprisonment and child maladjustment. Stanton (1980) compared jailed mothers' children with children of mothers on probation in an attempt to control for some pre-existing factors. Jailed mothers' children still performed less well on a number of academic variables compared to probation mothers' children. However, jailed mothers and probation mothers also differed on previous criminal convictions and employment and education histories, which might have confounded the results. In their analysis, Murray and Farrington (in press) found that the association between parental imprisonment and child maladjustment was reduced, but was not eliminated, by controlling for parental convictions and other childhood adversities.

In summary, although pre-existing factors associated with parental imprisonment are risk factors for child maladjustment, we need further evidence on how much they explain the relationship between parental imprisonment and child maladjustment.

Direct prison effects

My six-year-old couldn't sleep. She was a real wreck. After a while

> I figured out what the problem was – she thought her father was
> having to live on bread and water.
>> (Anonymous mother, quoted in Hounslow *et al* 1982: 23)

Most research emphasises the direct effects of parental imprisonment on children. There are three intrinsic features of imprisonment that might directly cause psychosocial difficulties for children. First, there is the experience of separation and enduring loss. Attachment theory predicts that rupturing of parent–child bonds through separation causes psychosocial difficulties for children (Bowlby 1973). Hounslow *et al* (1982) and Richards (1992) emphasise that parental imprisonment can also be experienced as desertion or abandonment, which can compound distress for children. However, the available evidence on the effects of separation among prisoners' children, and the effects of other forms of parental absence on children, suggests that the separation itself is not likely to be the most salient characteristic explaining children's outcomes (Gabel 2003).

Second, parental imprisonment might cause antisocial behaviour in children if they identify with their parent's criminality and imitate their parent's behaviour. In Sack's (1977) clinic study of eight boys with fathers in prison, some of the boys mimicked their fathers' crimes. Third, parental imprisonment involves uncertainty about how parents are treated while inside prison: children might suffer from fear about their parent's welfare.

Two hypotheses can be drawn from the supposition that imprisonment directly causes difficulties for children. First, one would expect a dose–response effect, with longer sentences and multiple imprisonments being associated with worse outcomes for children. Second, one would expect that positive parent–child contact during the imprisonment would mitigate the effects of separation and uncertainty for children. However, visits also can involve strains of long-distance travel, prison search procedures, a lack of physical contact during visits, and difficulty leaving parents at the end of a visits (Brown *et al* 2002; McDermott and King 1992; Peart and Asquith 1992). Therefore, it is possible that visits might actually cause further difficulties for children. Given the theoretical and policy importance of contact between prisoners and families, the issue is discussed in more detail in the section 'Prisoner–child contact' later in this chapter.

Despite a general assumption in the literature that parental imprisonment directly affects children, there has been little theorising on this subject. We also lack adequate empirical tests of whether parental imprisonment directly affects children independently of the effects of parental crime, arrest, conviction and other risk factors.

Mediated prison effects

The ways in which parental imprisonment can affect children are probably as varied as the range of parental influences on delinquency.

(Hagan and Dinovitzer 1999: 147)

Mediators represent mechanisms through which parental imprisonment indirectly affects children. Prison effects on prisoner–carer relationships, family income, children's care arrangements, home and school moves, and carers' well-being are also likely to have knock-on effects on children (Centre for Social and Educational Research 2002; Hounslow *et al* 1982; Sack 1977). In particular, three influences are likely to mediate the effects of parental imprisonment on children. First, children can face multiple care changes during parental imprisonment, and carers themselves are likely to experience emotional distress and practical difficulties (Stanton 1980). Therefore, it is likely that many children will face a decrease in stable, quality parenting following their parent's imprisonment. Lowenstein reports that mothers' personal and familial coping resources actually had a greater impact on children's adjustment following parental imprisonment than the separation itself (Lowenstein 1986).

Second, explanations given to children about their parent's absence are likely to mediate the effects of the imprisonment. Two studies report that approximately one-third of children are lied to about the whereabouts of their imprisoned father; one-third are told a fudged truth; and one-third are told the whole truth (Sack and Seidler 1978; Shaw 1987).[4] Richards *et al* (1994) found that in less than half of prisoners' families all the children knew about their mothers' or fathers' imprisonment. Carers often tell children that their parent is in hospital, or in the army, navy, or other work to try to protect them (Centre for Social and Educational Research 2002). However, researchers and prisoners' families' support groups commonly argue that children are better off knowing the truth about their parent's imprisonment, rather than experiencing confusion and deceit.

Third, parental imprisonment can lead children to experience stigma, bullying and teasing, which might mediate prison effects on children (Boswell and Wedge 2002; Sack 1977; Sack and Seidler 1978; Sack *et al*

1976). A problem for research is that families experiencing stigma are also more likely to practise deceit (Lowenstein 1986). Further, parental imprisonment might have an official labelling effect on children, making them more likely to be prosecuted for their crimes.

Indirect prison effects might be as important as direct effects on prisoners' children, and ought to receive considerably more research attention.

Moderating effects

> The child's reactions will obviously vary considerably with age, sophistication, and the previous relationship with both parents...
>
> (Schwartz and Weintraub 1974: 23)

Assuming that parental imprisonment does cause child maladjustment, factors that interact with this effect are called moderators. Moderators can help to understand why some prisoners' children fair better than others. For example, children are likely to react differently to parental imprisonment at different developmental stages (Johnston 1995). Sack (1977) suggested that boys aged six to twelve are the ones most likely to become aggressive in reaction to parental imprisonment. As well as age and sex, individual factors that might moderate children's reactions are: previous experiences of parental imprisonment, race, IQ, temperament and locus of control. However, there is no more than anecdotal evidence on the moderating effects of individual characteristics on children's reactions to parental imprisonment.

Parent–child relationships and parenting practices prior to imprisonment are likely to be important moderating influences on children's reactions. One would expect that if children experienced positive involvement with their parent prior to imprisonment, they would be more adversely affected by the loss. Conversely, children who have experienced abusive relationships might even benefit from parental imprisonment. One study suggests that imprisonment of mothers affects children more acutely than imprisonment of fathers (Richards et al 1994), which is likely to be because fathers are less often primary caregivers to children prior to imprisonment (Healy et al 2000). Before entering prison, 64 per cent of imprisoned mothers lived with their children, compared to 44 per cent of imprisoned fathers in the US (Mumola 2000).

Children's reactions to parental imprisonment might also vary depending on background levels of social support, parental antisocial behaviour, the type of crime committed by the parent, and possibly by neighbourhood context. Schwartz hypothesised that in neighbourhoods with high imprisonment rates, children can be more open about their situation, and feel less social stigma (Schwartz and Weintraub 1974). However, stigma might be especially high in neighbourhoods with high imprisonment rates because many victims of crime also live in these neighbourhoods (Braman 2004).

To date, we lack adequate evidence on moderators of prison effects on children, partly because of the difficulties of conducting prospective studies of prisoners' families. In summary, studies have documented a number of possible causes of maladjustment among prisoners' children. However, robust evidence on these effects is slim. Figure 17.1 shows the selection effects, and direct, mediating and moderating effects that are

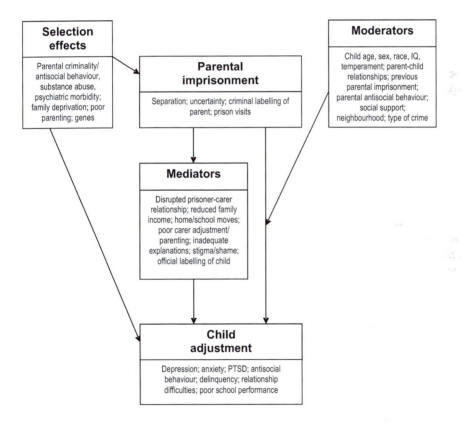

Figure 17.1 The relationship between parental imprisonment and child adjustment

hypothesised to explain the relationship between parental imprisonment and child adjustment. Other interaction effects are possible, for example between moderators and mediated effects; however, these are not shown in Figure 17.1 for simplicity.

Prisoner–child contact

> I would make sure people get visits which in turn would keep calmness and closeness.
>
> (Anonymous prisoner)

The Prison Service might reduce the negative effects of parental imprisonment on children by helping prisoners maintain regular and good contact with their children. However, visits are often considered a privilege for prisoners, rather than a right for families, and prison visiting has declined in recent years in the UK (Brooks-Gordon, 2003). Recently, Action for Prisoners' Families (UK) surveyed 134 imprisoned men and 68 imprisoned women in England about their family ties. Notwithstanding relatively low response rates[5] and the location of the men's prison,[6] these previously unpublished surveys suggest that prisoners and families can face a number of practical difficulties in maintaining contact. Eighty-one per cent of men reported that family contact was extremely important to them, but only 55 per cent of imprisoned fathers were visited by their children. Ninety-five per cent of women reported that family contact was extremely important to them, but only 67 per cent of imprisoned mothers were visited by their children. The absence of visits appeared to relate to practical difficulties of travelling, distance between prison and home, the cost of travel, and visiting times.

Most imprisoned parents and their children try to keep in contact by mail and telephone calls as well as by visits. In Mumola's study, 43 per cent of state inmates and 73 per cent of federal inmates had at least monthly contact with their children by telephone (Mumola 2000). In the surveys conducted by Action for Prisoners' Families, the main factor associated with prisoner–family telephone contact was the cost of calls.

Prisoners who talk with their children adjust better to the prison environment (Carlson and Cervera 1991). Children might also adjust better during the separation if they have more contact with their imprisoned parent. Although practitioners and researchers often stress the importance of contact for prisoners' children, recent evidence suggests children can be negatively affected by involvement with an antisocial father (Jaffee *et al* 2003). In the context of divorce, what is important for children is contact involving authoritative parenting and close relationships (Amato and Gilbreth 1999). In the prison context, active, close parenting is extremely difficult to achieve. Adolescents report mixed experiences of visiting, as they feel there is no time to talk individually, visiting can be frightening, take too long, involve unpleasant searches, and facilities tend to be physically uncomfortable (Brown *et al* 2002). Children can find visits confusing, frightening and upsetting (Richards *et al* 1994). Morris (1965) found that closed visits (behind glass) were regarded by wives as horrific: children tended to experience them with bewilderment and fear. Nevertheless, children generally seem to like having contact with their imprisoned parent (Boswell and Wedge 2002) and most adolescents say that contact is extremely important to them (Brown *et al* 2002). Children's visits and all-day family visits, although rare in the UK prison system, are seen much more favourably by visitors than normal visits (Lloyd 1992).

Only three studies have examined the effects of parent–child contact on child adjustment specifically in the prison context. In their clinic study, Sack and Seidler (1978) found that children were less disruptive after making initial visits to see their fathers in jail. Stanton (1980) found that *satisfactory* visits between children and jailed mothers appeared to lower a child's anxiety about their mother's absence, although 'satisfactory' visits were not defined in the study. Fritsch and Burkhead (1981) found that inmates who had more contact with children actually reported their children had more problems. However, results from this study are ambiguous because prisoners with more contact might just have been more aware of their children's difficulties.

To test the effect of parent–child contact on children during parental imprisonment, future studies should measure child well-being using different sources, control for parent–child relations prior to imprisonment, and devise sensitive measures of different types of contact.

Methods for studying prisoners' children

Understanding child adjustment during parental imprisonment requires separating out a complicated series of selection effects, and direct, mediating and moderating effects. The general model of child adjustment proposed here reflects, in several ways, well-known models of prisoner adjustment. The hypothesis of selection effects parallels importation models of prisoner adjustment. The hypothesis of direct and mediated prison effects parallels deprivation models of prisoner adjustment.

Including both selection effects and prison effects parallels combined models of prisoners' adjustment. Research on prisoners also highlights the importance of understanding individual differences. Reflecting this concern, the model proposed here emphasises moderating effects on children's reactions to parental imprisonment. Research on prisoners also shows the need for sophisticated and sensitive research design to disentangle 'imported' from prison-caused outcomes, and to protect an already vulnerable group. Similar requirements apply to research on the effects of parental imprisonment on children.

To date, research on prisoners' children has been hampered by methodological weaknesses (Gabel 1992; Hagan and Dinovitzer 1999). Among 43 studies of prisoners' families and children that I have found, only thirteen included any direct interviews with prisoners' children; only ten used standardised instruments or official records to measure children's outcomes; only seven reported using a longitudinal design; only one followed up prisoners' children for more than one year; and only ten used any sort of control group to try to isolate the specific effects of imprisonment on children. Most studies have used convenience samples from clinics, visitors' centres or prisoners' families' support groups, with attendant biases. No study researched prisoners' families prospectively (starting before the imprisonment took place).

It is not surprising that research on prisoners' families has been methodologically weak. Prisoners' families are a neglected group, which makes research practically very difficult (Hounslow *et al* 1982). Recruiting a random sample of prisoners' families in the UK is virtually impossible because no statutory agency holds their contact details. The best way, in practice, of trying to obtain a random sample of prisoners' families is by first interviewing prisoners. However, prisoners are often (understandably) unwilling for researchers to contact their families, and it is well documented that prisoners' families are reluctant to respond to official or independent enquiry (Johnston 1995).

The challenge for future research is to establish tight causal links between variables highlighted by previous qualitative research. Experimental designs are the best designs for testing causal hypotheses. However, the nature of imprisonment implies that, at best, research is likely to be quasi-experimental. A good quasi-experimental study of the effects of parental imprisonment on children would have a prospective, longitudinal design. It would include many at-risk children, and reliable measures of many background variables, including adjustment of children before, during and after parental imprisonment. It is rare that existing large-scale studies of child development have collected information on parental imprisonment. The *Fragile Families and Child*

Wellbeing Study (Princeton University 2004) is the most promising current study for the investigation of the effects of imprisonment on families and children. Although children in the study are still young, the *Fragile Families Study* has over-sampled high-risk families at the time of children's births, and has collected detailed information on family background and parenting measures, as well as parental criminal and imprisonment histories. We must hope that this, and similar research, attracts the resources to rigorously identify the impacts of imprisonment on families and children.

Conclusion

Prisoners' families and children can experience profound social, psychological and economic losses as a result of their relative's imprisonment. Researching the impact of events such as imprisonment through the life-course requires use of quantitative and qualitative data (Sampson and Laub 1993). However, to date, practically all studies of prison effects on families and children have been small, qualitative investigations, and have rarely included longitudinal follow-up. Four important questions remain:

1 What is the actual risk associated with parental imprisonment for children's mental health problems and antisocial behaviour?

2 Is parental imprisonment merely a 'risk marker', or is it a cause of child maladjustment?

3 If parental imprisonment is a cause of child maladjustment, what are the mechanisms by which it affects children?

4 Which interventions or policy changes could prevent the effects of parental imprisonment on children?

To help identify possible mechanisms, a model has been proposed here which separates out selection effects, direct and mediated prison effects, and moderating effects. What we need now are large-scale research projects to properly investigate prison effects on children and families through the life-course. Children experiencing other forms of separation from parents have attracted huge research projects leading to sophisticated understanding of children's adjustment, following divorce for example. Prisoners' children deserve the same research attention and, in all probability, deserve at least similar resources of support. Despite an impressive awareness of prisoners' rights, no statutory body, in prisons or in the community, is charged with responsibility for supporting the families of prisoners in the UK (HM Treasury 2003). Without serious efforts at research, intervention and support, prison will continue to punish these 'forgotten victims', and may contribute to increased levels of crime in the next generation.

Notes

1 I am grateful to Adrian Grounds for support of my work on this topic, David Farrington for thoughts on particular sections of this chapter and to the ESRC for funding the research
2 My calculations from Morris's results. I have combined all levels of deterioration, defined by Morris as 'slight', 'substantial' or 'serious' (see Morris 1965: 215–24).
3 See Kraemer *et al* (2001) for a good description of mediators and moderators, and other ways risk factors can work together.
4 But see McEvoy *et al* (1999) for different estimates in Northern Ireland.
5 Approximately 27 per cent for men and 85 per cent for women.
6 HMP Camphill is on the Isle of Wight off the south coast of England.

References

Amato, P.R. and Gilbreth, J.G. (1999) 'Nonresident fathers and children's well-being: A meta-analysis', *Journal of Marriage and the Family*, 61, 557–573.

Anderson, N.N. (1966) *Prisoners' Families: A Study of Family Crisis.* Minnesota: University of Minnesota.

Baron, R.M. and Kenny, D.A. (1986) 'The moderator-mediator variable distinction in social psychological research: Conceptual, strategic, and statistical considerations', *Journal of Personality and Social Psychology*, 51 (6), 1173–1182.

Boswell, G. (2002) 'Imprisoned fathers: The children's view', *The Howard Journal*, 41 (1), 14–26.

Boswell, G. and Wedge, P. (2002) *Imprisoned Fathers and their Children.* London: Jessica Kingsley.

Bowlby, J. (1973) *Attachment and Loss: Vol. 2, Separation: Anxiety and Anger.* London: Hogarth Press.

Braman, D. (2004) *Doing Time on the Outside: Incarceration and Family Life in Urban America.* Ann Arbor: University of Michigan Press.

Braman, D. and Wood, J. (2003) 'From one generation to the next: How criminal sanctions are reshaping family life in urban America', in A. Travis and

M. Waul (eds) *Prisoners Once Removed: The Impact of Incarceration and Reentry on Children, Families, and Communities.* Washington, DC: The Urban Institute Press, pp. 157–188.

Brooks-Gordon, B. (2003) 'Contact in containment', in A. Bainham, B. Lindley, M. Richards and L. Trinder (eds) *Children and their Families: Contact, Rights and Welfare.* Oxford: Hart Publishing, pp. 313–334.

Brown, K., Dibb, L., Shenton, F. and Elson, N. (2002) *No-one's Ever Asked Me: Young People with a Prisoner in the Family.* London: Federation of Prisoners' Families Support Groups (now Action for Prisoners' Families).

Carlson, B.E. and Cervera, N. (1991) 'Inmates and their families: Conjugal visits, family contact, and family functioning', *Criminal Justice and Behaviour*, 18, 318–331.

Centre for Social and Educational Research (2002) *Parents, Children and Prison: Effects of Parental Imprisonment on Children.* Dublin: Dublin Institute of Technology.

Clear, T.R., Rose, D.R. and Ryder, J.A. (2001) 'Incarceration and the community: The problem of removing and returning offenders', *Crime and Delinquency*, 47 (3), 335–351.

Crowe, R.R. (1974) 'An adoption study of antisocial personality', *Archives of General Psychiatry*, 31, 785–791.

Dodd, T. and Hunter, P. (1992) *The National Prison Survey 1991.* London: HMSO.

Farrington, D.P. (2002) 'Families and crime', in J.Q. Wilson and J. Petersilia (eds) *Crime: Public Policies for Crime Control.* Oakland, CA: Institute for Contemporary Studies Press, pp. 129–148.

Farrington, D.P., Barnes, G.C. and Lambert, S. (1996) 'The concentration of offending in families', *Legal and Criminological Psychology*, 1, 47–63.

Ferraro, K., Johnson, J., Jorgensen, S. and Bolton, F.G. (1983) 'Problems of prisoners' families: The hidden costs of imprisonment', *Journal of Family Issues*, 4, 575–591.

Flanagan, T.J. (1980) 'The pains of long-term imprisonment: A comparison of British and American perspectives', *British Journal of Criminology*, 20 (2), 148–156.

Friedman, S.E. and Esselstyn, T.C. (1965) 'The adjustment of children of jail inmates', *Federal Probation*, 29, 55–59.

Fritsch, T.A. and Burkhead, J.D. (1981) 'Behavioural reactions of children to parental absence due to imprisonment', *Family Relations*, 30, 83–88.

Gabel, S. (1992) 'Behavioral problems in sons of incarcerated or otherwise absent fathers: The issue of separation', *Family Process*, 31, 303–314.

Gabel, S. (2003) 'Behavioral problems in sons of incarcerated or otherwise absent fathers: The issue of separation', in O. Harris and R.R. Miller (eds) *Impacts of Incarceration on the African American Family.* New Brunswick, NJ: Transaction, pp. 105–119.

Gibbs, C. (1971) 'The effect of the imprisonment of women upon their children', *British Journal of Criminology*, 11, 113–130.

Hagan, J. and Dinovitzer, R. (1999) 'Collateral consequences of imprisonment for children, communities and prisoners', in M. Tonry and J. Petersilia (eds) *Crime and Justice*, Vol. 26. Chicago: University of Chicago Press, pp. 121–162.

Healy, K., Foley, D. and Walsh, K (2000) *Parents in Prison and their Families: Everyone's Business and No-one's Concern*. Queensland: Catholic Prison Ministry.

HM Treasury (2003) *Every Child Matters* (Green Paper). Norwich: The Stationery Office.

Holzer, H.J., Raphael, S. and Stoll, M.A. (2004) 'Will employers hire former offenders? Employer preferences, background checks, and their determinants', in M. Pattillo, D. Weiman and B. Western (eds) *Imprisoning America: The Social Effects of Mass Incarceration*. New York: Russell Sage, pp. 205–246.

Hounslow, B., Stephenson, A., Stweart, J. and Crancher, J. (1982) *Children of Imprisoned Parents*. NSW: Ministry of Youth and Community Services of New South Wales.

Jaffee, S.R., Moffitt, T.E., Caspi, A. and Taylor, A. (2003) 'Life with (or without) father: The benefits of living with two biological parents depend on the father's antisocial behavior', *Child Development*, 74, 109–126.

Johnson, E.I. and Waldfogel, J. (2004) 'Children of incarcerated parents: Multiple risks and children's living arrangements', in M. Pattillo, D. Weiman and B. Western (eds) *Imprisoning America: The Social Effects of Mass Incarceration*. New York: Russell Sage, pp. 97–131.

Johnston, D. (1995) 'Effects of parental incarceration', in K. Gabel and D. Johnston (eds) *Children of Incarcerated Parents*. New York: Lexington Books, pp. 59–88.

Kampfner, C.J. (1995) 'Post-traumatic stress reactions in children of imprisoned mothers', in K. Gabel and D. Johnston (eds) *Children of Incarcerated Parents*. New York: Lexington, pp. 89–102.

Kraemer, H.C., Stice, E., Kazdin, A., Offord, D. and Kupfer, D. (2001) 'How do risk factors work together? Mediators, moderators, and independent, overlapping and proxy risk factors' *American Journal of Psychiatry*, 158, 848–856.

Liebling, A. (1992) *Suicides in Prison*. New York: Routledge Publishing.

Light, R. (1994) *Black and Asian Prisoners' Families*. Bristol: Bristol Centre for Criminal Justice.

Lloyd, E. (1992) *Children Visiting Holloway Prison: Inside and Outside Perspectives on the All-Day Visits Scheme at HMP Holloway*. London: Save the Children.

Loeber, R. and Stouthamer-Loeber, M. (1986) 'Family factors as correlates and predictors of juvenile conduct problems and delinquency', in M. Tonry and N. Morris (eds) *Crime and Justice: An Annual Review of Research*, Vol. 7. Chicago: University of Chicago Press, pp. 29–149.

Lowenstein, A. (1986) 'Temporary single parenthood – The case of prisoners' families', *Family Relations*, 35, 79–85.

Matthews, J. (1983) *Forgotten Victims*. London: NACRO.

McDermott, K. and King, R.D. (1992) 'Prison Rule 102: Stand by your man', in R. Shaw (ed.) *Prisoners' Children: What Are the Issues?* London: Routledge Publishing.

McEvoy, K., O'Mahony, D., Horner, C. and Lyner, O. (1999) 'The home front: The families of politically motivated prisoners in Northern Ireland', *British Journal of Criminology*, 39 (2), 175–197.

Morris, P. (1965) *Prisoners and their Families*. Woking: Unwin Brothers.

Mumola, C.J. (2000) *Incarcerated Parents and their Children*. Washington, DC: Bureau of Justice Statistics.

Murray, J. and Farrington, D.P. (in press) 'Parental imprisonment: effects on boys' antisocial behaviour and delinquency through the life-course', *Journal of Child Psychology and Psychiatry* doi:10/1111/j.1469-7610.2005-01433.X

Myers, B.J., Smarsh, T.M., Amlund-Hagen, K. and Kennon, S. (1999) 'Children of incarcerated mothers', *Journal of Child and Family Studies*, 8, 11–25.

Noble, C. (1995) *Prisoners' Families: The Everyday Reality*. Ipswich: Ormiston Children and Families Trust.

Peart, K. and Asquith, S. (1992) *Scottish Prisoners and their Families: The Impact of Imprisonment on Family Relationships*. Glasgow: Centre for the Study of the Child and Society, University of Glasgow.

Philbrick, D. (1996) *Child and Adolescent Mental Health and the Prisoner's Child.* Paper presented at 'The Child and the Prison', Grey College, Durham.

Princeton University (2004) *The Fragile Families and Child Wellbeing Study.* Accessed at http://crcw.princeton.edu/fragilefamilies/

Richards, B. (1978) 'The experience of long-term imprisonment', *British Journal of Criminology*, 18 (2), 162–169.

Richards, M. (1992) 'The separation of children and parents: Some issues and problems', in R. Shaw (ed.) *Prisoners' Children: What Are the Issues?* London: Routledge Publishing, pp. 3–12.

Richards, M., McWilliams, B., Allcock, L., Enterkin, J., Owens, P. and Woodrow, J. (1994) *The Family Ties of English Prisoners: The Results of the Cambridge Project on Imprisonment and Family Ties*. Cambridge: Centre for Family Research, Cambridge University.

Richards, M., McWilliams, B., Batten, N. and Cutler, J. (1995) 'Foreign nationals in English prisons: I. Family ties and their maintenance', *Howard Journal of Criminal Justice*, 34 (2), 158–175.

Sack, W.H. (1977) 'Children of imprisoned fathers', *Psychiatry*, 40, 163–174.

Sack, W.H. and Seidler, J. (1978) 'Should children visit their parents in prison?', *Law and Human Behaviour*, 2, 261–266.

Sack, W.H., Seidler, J. and Thomas, S. (1976) 'The children of imprisoned parents: A psychosocial exploration', *American Journal of Orthopsychiatry*, 46, 618–628.

Sampson, R.J. and Laub, J.H. (1993) *Crime in the Making: Pathways and Turning Points through Life*. Cambridge, MA: Harvard University Press.

Schneller, D.P. (1976) *The Prisoner's Family: A Study of the Effects of Imprisonment on the Families of Prisoners*. San Francisco: R and E Research Associates.

Schwartz, M.C. and Weintraub, J.F. (1974) 'The prisoner's wife: A study in crisis', *Federal Probation*, 38, 20–27.

Sharp, S.F. and Marcus-Mendoza, S.T. (2001) 'It's a family affair: Incarcerated women and their families', *Women and Criminal Justice*, 12, 21–50.

Shaw, R. (1987) *Children of Imprisoned Fathers*. Bungay, Suffolk: Richard Clay Publishing.

Shaw, R. (1992) 'Imprisoned fathers and the orphans of justice', in R. Shaw (ed.) *Prisoners' Children: What Are the Issues?* London: Routledge Publishing, pp. 41–49.

Singleton, N., Meltzer, H., Gatward, R., Coid, J. and Deasy, D. (1998) *Psychiatric Morbidity Among Prisoners in England and Wales.* London: The Stationery Office.

Skinner, D. and Swartz, L. (1989) 'The consequences for preschool children of a parent's detention: A preliminary South African clinical study of caregivers' reports', *Journal of Child Psychology and Psychiatry*, 30 (2), 243–259.

Social Exclusion Unit (2002) *Reducing Re-offending by Ex-prisoners.* London: Social Exclusion Unit.

Stanton, A. (1980) *When Mothers go to Jail.* Lexington, MA: Lexington Books.

Afterword

Chapter 18

Reinventing prisons

Hans Toch

Thirty-plus years ago, a working group called the Citizens' Study Committee on Offender Rehabilitation submitted its final report to the then Governor of Wisconsin, in the mid-western United States (Wisconsin Council on Criminal Justice 1972). The group suggested to the governor the phasing out of Wisconsin's prisons over a five-year period. In support of this no-nonsense proposal, the group argued that:

> No amount of resources, however great, can enhance a convicted citizen's chances for productive re-entry to a democratic society when that citizen has been confined in an institution too large to provide individual services, too geographically remote to provide vital life contacts, and too regimented to foster self-esteem.

To dramatise the contention that the abolitionist solution they were advancing was 'compelling', the task force members posed a rhetorical question to the governor. They asked:

> If you were required to live in a cell with few facilities, little privacy, limited contact with other persons significant to you, limited access to employment, and a high degree of authoritarian regimentation, how might you fare upon re-entry into the broader and more competitive society, there to be greeted with the stigma of having been 'away'?
>
> (cit. Board, 1973, p. 451)

The argument might have sounded persuasive to the governor, but not the implications for action that one could draw from it. This disjuncture was brought home to me 26 years after the 1972 report was filed, when I was invited to a staff conference of the Wisconsin prison system (Wisconsin Department of Corrections 1998), plaintively entitled 'Managing the masses'. At this point in time, reliable extrapolations showed the Wisconsin system facing the largest percentage increase of prisoners in the country. The inmate population had grown from 12,340 to 16,000 in two short years, and was confidently expected to total 21,000 in another two years. Coincidentally, Wisconsin also ranked second-highest among 49 states on measures of overcrowding, and had to reinvent transportation to deal with this problem. One of every five of the state's prisoners had been shipped to other states, to languish at insuperable distances from home, under indefensibly substandard conditions.

The staff members of the system had been surveyed in advance of their conference for choices of topics to be covered. The top nominations – in order of predilection – were 'Managing the disturbed inmate', 'Crisis management' and 'Adequate rehabilitative resources'. This triad struck me as painfully revealing, given the course of Wisconsin's then-recent history. Because of an unmitigating and relentless press of blind punitiveness, the salient problem with the system was no longer that of the sterility and unproductiveness highlighted a quarter of a century earlier. At this juncture, we were no longer invited to ruminate about the ineffectiveness of prisons, but instead were enjoined to talk about indices of their destructiveness.

Even here, we were not entirely free of continuing pressure. A key document – the *Directive Governing Disciplinary Action in Wisconsin Prisons* – had been slated for revision. One provision to be deleted had required disciplinary hearing officers to consider 'whether the inmate was actually aware that he or she was committing a crime or offence at the time of the [prison] offence'. This requisite had made Wisconsin's virtually the only system of the period showing formal hesitation about punishing disturbed prisoners for acts that were clearly products of their mental illness. The relevant provision was being slated for deletion at the precise juncture at which the proliferation of stressors in the system and the consequent exacerbation of mental health problems was leading to the control and management crises the staff wanted to discuss.

With the mental health problems of prisoners reinforced by runaway custodial policies, the Wisconsin staff was being asked to define the problem as one of behaviour management, to facilitate additional custodial responses. Moreover, the forces that were promoting this situation were not about to be appeased with halfway measures. The political pressures in Wisconsin were to culminate, in short order, in the creation of a total-segregation, administrative-confinement facility. This prison's regime was calculatedly draconian and eventually inspired successful litigation (discussed during my last visit in Cambridge – see Toch 2002) on behalf of disturbed inmates whose problems were ignored or exacerbated through solitary confinement. The legal suit ended in a Settlement Agreement which ameliorated some of the more damaging features of the supermax regime. The problem of custodial overkill, however, remained to be addressed in Wisconsin, as elsewhere. It was no longer safe to assume that eloquent pleas to abolish prisons within five years would be taken seriously.

The real goal – behaviour control

For better or worse, every year I teach graduate seminars on the topics of 'prison reform' and 'prison environments'. In the final session of one such module last December, a diffident student who had said nothing for fifteen weeks decided to pose a question. 'This "prison" we have been talking about all semester', he asked, 'this entity – with its bars and cells and guards and walls or razor wire – who invented this?' He offered no further clarification, so I inferred that he wanted either a roster of historical minutiae or my ruminations about the evolution of societal institutions. From the expression on his face, he wanted neither.

After answering what I thought I had been asked, I had the belated revelation. I concluded that what that student had really been after was an answer to the question, 'what would some malevolent genius who set out to invent maximum-security prisons be trying to accomplish?' The implication was that there could be no conceivable function that such a design would be intended to serve. But if that was his point, I do not really believe the young man was right. I think there is in fact a continuing agenda that is related to the way prisons look and the way they are run, and the way they have always looked and have always been run. I think that what prisons are designed for is to effect physical behaviour control. Simply put, the assumption of the mythical inventor of prisons is that one can govern human behaviour in a tailor-made setting by obsessively squelching misbehaviour – and that one can do this without concern for, or interest in, the motives underlying the behaviour, or the occasions for it.

Of course, deep in our contemporary hearts we know that physical behaviour control of this sort is unachievable. To attempt it breeds resentment and a sense of injustice. Worse, we know that efforts at behaviour control tend to promote a jungle-like social milieu. Experience tells us that behaviour control inspires subterfuge and evasion. It provokes angry responses that lead to escalating conflicts that can be ugly and unseemly. It is also obvious to us that no matter how much one fine-tunes the control-oriented custodial approach, its hurtful impact is indiscriminate, spreading beyond its targets, penalising the innocent and injuring the vulnerable.

Yet, the 'inventor of prisons' has been far from alone in his preconception. The notion of behaviour control colours most people's view of prisons and their mission. I have encountered the premise daily, among my students. I meet no objection if I talk of parolees as 'ex-offenders', but my students will steadfastly deny the prefix to prison inmates. In their view of the goal of prisons, prisoners are unregenerate miscreants, which is the reason they are imprisoned. What we need and what we get is a setting that is designed to curb the predatory predilections of its denizens.

The most starkly stereotypic of our prisons most closely live up to the prescription. They do so by inviting their staff to buy into the obsessively custodial definition of their mission, and to act out the role that it prescribes. The stance provides us with the ideal-type prisons that we depict in the prison literature, because the mandate is self-fulfilling. There is no surer way to nurture a textbook inmate culture than to treat prisoners as presumptive malefactors. Playing cops and robbers as a managerial strategy creates the familiar caste system of keepers versus kept. It destroys chances of any positive encounters between inmates and staff, no matter how redolent with programmes our prisons may be, or how conscientiously we may observe due-process niceties, such as boilerplate explanations for sanctions or pro-forma avenues for appeals.

The control-oriented prison has come to be regarded by most of us as fated or pre-ordained. We have embodied the inevitability of the design in our scientific reports, including those of our classics, such as the Stanford prison experiment (Zimbardo *et al* 1974; Haney and Zimbardo 1977) and the observations of deprivation theorists (Clemmer, 1940; Sykes, 1958). The insights we have derived from these studies let us understand the dynamics of the institution that the inventor of prisons had in mind, but it may also have led us to assume that these dynamics are built in. It is possible that we may thus be according to the apocryphal inventor of prisons more credit and staying power than he or she might otherwise deserve.

Ameliorative settings

Many years ago, a planning process in which I played an ancillary role led to the creation of some prison units for moderately disturbed prisoners. These settings were called 'intermediate care programs' (ICPs) because they were, in fact, intermediate – each being a correctional setting, run by correction officers, with mental health staff input and involvement.

In New York State, ICP units have now been operating for decades, but were recently reviewed in the context of a survey of mental health services in the state's prisons (Correctional Association of New York 2004). There were many unflattering observations in this report, but the researchers had the following to say about officers in the ICP units:

The staff we met in ICP units tended to be among the most compassionate employees we encountered in the state prison system…ICP correction officers we interviewed said they bid on the posts because they wanted to be part of a rehabilitative environment, where they felt they could make a difference. In speaking with officers, we were struck by the extraordinary level of care and commitment they showed toward inmate-residents and their high level of job satisfaction, (p. 33).

The report pointed out that officers in ICP units work closely with mental health staff, and participate in joint treatment decisions, arrived at via case conferences. The officers intersect with prison personnel outside the units to arrange for placement and programming for residents, so as 'to identify appropriate jobs for the inmates and discuss with general population officers how best to work with them'. According to testimonials in the report from fellow staff members, 'our COs here become such great advocates for the guys…they go out of their way to help them reintegrate into general population' (pp. 33–4). Unsurprisingly, the report found that the prisoners 'value the role officers play in guiding the program' and that 'inmate–officer relations were among the most positive we have seen' (p. 34).

In alluding to the ICP officers, the survey staff wrote that they 'exemplify what is possible'. I believe that they illustrate that the conflicting roles we have assigned to inmates and staff in our conception of prisons are far from engraved in stone. ICP officers gain rewards and personal satisfaction from work-related achievements that transcend inmate supervision and control, and their prisoners benefit from the care they thus receive. As counter-intuitive as this may sound, we envisage the inmates leaving the prison with a sense of gratitude and nostalgia.

If this point were reduced to the argument that one can run unprisonlike units in conventional prisons, it might not be worth reiterating. Prison exceptions cannot disprove prison rules, because even total institutions must provide leeway in order to survive (Goffman 1961). In running a confinement facility, one must make accommodation for the halt and the lame and their equivalents. The easiest way to do this is to operate special ameliorated settings with appropriate remedial services. For the sake of consistency, one can argue that the halt and lame rarely pose security risks, though this argument is circular because it presupposes an environment that does not crowd the inmates by taxing their coping capacities. In the absence of ameliorative provisions, emotionally disturbed or intellectually challenged prisoners as a group tend to be disproportionately disruptive, because they often cannot negotiate rigidly structured, control-oriented regimes (Toch and Adams 2002).

Any special settings can also become innovation ghettos, ignored by the rest of an institution, and classed as strange but irrelevant aberrations. The inventor of prisons could happily subsist with Mother Teresa as unit manager, provided that her operation was suitably compartmentalised and she kept her mushy opinions to herself. In theory, an ICP unit or its equivalent can become an innocuous addendum to a prison. Where such a programme is administered by outsiders (mental health staff), for example, it cannot impinge on the operation of its host. The most likely result of such guest-room cohabitation could be to reinforce the control-oriented predilections of the more cynical clinicians in a programme.

The ICP happens to be a mainline correctional programme, and it is not a compartmentalised one. Its staff intermingle with other prison staff, as do most of the residents. The programme is inclusive, designed to retain and reintegrate its inmates. The object of the game is to import professional expertise rather than export prisoners, and the expertise enhances the sophistication of local, prisoner-management skills. These skills are people-management-oriented. While the ICP programme does not highlight control, it also does not abrogate the objective of behaviour improvement. ICP prisoners are carefully supervised, and they are subject to the same disciplinary process as other prisoners. The difference is that staff members in the programme know the prisoners and can consider the antecedents of their behaviour and the ramification of dispositions contemplated in response. The latter flexibility matters, because the most egregious harm that is done by prisons relates to the draconian punitiveness of disciplinary and administrative sanctions.

Beyond physical control

The control design that we see as salient in prisons has been with us since their inception, but so have some humane strategies for attenuating the destructive impact of the design on prison inmates and staff. These strategies are practised here and there in progressive prisons around the world. They include, but are not limited to, the following hypothetical courses of action:

- As prison administrators, one can provide officers with responsibilities and job definitions that transcend custodial functions.
- One can encourage officers to get to know individual inmates.
- One can promote teamwork and group activities linking prisoners with staff – placing officers in autonomous charge of such activities.
- One can organise programmes around face-to-face inmate communities that centre on program-related concerns.
- One can involve civilians and outsiders as members of inmate–staff communities.
- One can encourage prisoners to participate in making informed decisions about their own prison involvements.
- One can consider staff skills and predilections in making or creating challenging work assignments.
- One can institutionalise the use of compassionate discretion in defining behaviours that justify formal sanctioning.
- One can operate one's prison on the assumption that bad people can become good people given the benefit of the doubt and appropriate support.
- One can avoid the use of collective punishment when one does not know who is responsible for a problem.
- One can instruct officers to discontinue power contests with inmates over trivial issues.
- One can deploy disciplinary sanctions in strict moderation, always as a means to an end.

- In responding to prisoner infractions, one can consider the perspective of all incident participants, and take contextual information into account.

- In assessing inmate behaviour, one can keep in mind that mental health and mental non-health are a continuum rather than easily differentiated categories.

- In taking any significant action, one can try to share one's thinking and underlying assumptions with inmates.

This list can be easily expanded, but ultimately, *enlightened leadership matters*. To attenuate a control-oriented prison one needs sophisticated managers who try not to be rule-bound and are willing to take risks and push the envelope in considering innovations. In this respect, I am always reminded of the Stanford Prison Experiment, which claimed to have dehumanised not only its inmates and guards, but also the Experimenters who administered the 'prison'. One experimenter, Craig Haney, recalled that 'I pressed on without reflection. After all, we had a prison to run and too many day-to-day crises and decisions to allow myself the luxury of pondering the ultimate wisdom of this noble endeavour that had already started to go wrong' (Haney 1999: 227). This admission came from Haney as overworked prison administrator. But it was the same Haney, acting as a compassionate night-time prison governor, who accorded to the first disturbed 'inmate' in the programme an unscheduled early release. In doing so, Haney as reformer deliberately broke a rule, destroyed the experiment's control-oriented design, and saved the programme.

References

Board of Directors, National Council on Crime and Delinquency (1973) 'The nondangerous offender should not be imprisoned: A policy statement', *Crime and Delinquency*, 19, 449–456.

Clemmer, D. (1940) *The Prison Community.* New York: Holt, Rinehart and Winston.

Correctional Association of New York (2004) *Mental Health in the House of Corrections* (Final Report). New York: Correctional Association of New York.

Goffman, E. (1961) *Asylums: Essays on the Situation of Mental Patients and Other Inmates.* New York: Doubleday (Anchor).

Haney, C. (1999) 'The Stanford Prison Experiment and the analysis of institutions', in T. Blass (ed.) *Obedience to Authority: Current Perspectives on the Milgram Paradigm.* Hillsdale, NJ: Erlbaum, pp. 221–237.

Haney, C. and Zimbardo, P. (1977) 'The socialization into criminality: Becoming a prisoner and a guard', in J. Tapp and F. Levine (eds) *Law, Justice and the Individual in Society: Psychological and Legal Issues*. New York: Holt, Rinehart and Winston, pp. 198-223.

Sykes, G.M. (1958) *The Society of Captives: A Study of a Maximum Security Prison*. Princeton, NJ: Princeton University Press.

Toch, H. (2002) 'Opening Pandora's Box: Ameliorating the effects of long-term segregation conditions', *Prison Service Journal*, November, 144, 15–21.

Toch, H. and Adams, K. (2002) *Acting Out: Maladaptive Behavior in Confinement*. Washington, DC: American Psychological Association (APA Books).

Wisconsin Council on Criminal Justice (1972) *Final Report to the Governor of the Citizens' Study Committee on Offender Rehabilitation*. Madison, WI: Wisconsin Council on Criminal Justice.

Wisconsin Department of Corrections (1998) *Managing the Masses: Second Annual Psychological Services Conference*. Fontana, WI: November 17 and 18.

Wisconsin Department of Corrections (undated) *Administrative Directive regarding Disciplinary Action, DOC 303.83 Sentencing Considerations, No.6*. Madison, WI: Wisconsin Department of Corrections.

Zimbardo, P.G., Haney, C., Banks, C. and Jaffe, D. (1974) 'The psychology of imprisonment: Privation, power and pathology', in Z. Rubin (ed.) *Doing unto Others: Explorations in Social Behavior*. Englewood Cliffs, NJ: Prentice Hall, pp. 61–73.

Appendix

Conference participants

Helen Arnold	University of Cambridge
Keith Bottomley	University of Hull
Julian Broadhead	Cropwood Fellow, University of Cambridge
Pat Carlen	Keele University
Leonidas Cheliotis	University of Cambridge
Andrew Coyle	King's College, University of London
Elaine Crawley	Keele University
Ben Crewe	University of Cambridge
Deborah Drake	University of Cambridge
Tomer Einat	Jordon Valley College
Colette Godfrey	Keele University
Adrian Grounds	University of Cambridge
Mark Halsey	University of Melbourne (AU)
Craig Haney	University of California, Santa Cruz (US)
Joel Harvey	University of Cambridge
Paul Hirschfield	Rutgers University (US)
John Irwin	San Francisco State University (US)
Ruth Jamieson	Keele University
Yvonne Jewkes	University of Hull
Robert Johnson	American University (US)
Helen Johnston	University of Hull
Helen Jones	University of Hull
Hans-Jürgen Kerner	University of Tuebingen (GER)
Roy King	University of Cambridge
Candace Kruttschnitt	University of Minnesota (US)

Alison Liebling	University of Cambridge
Juliet Lyon	Prison Reform Trust
Alastair MacDonald	Scottish Prison Service
Shadd Maruna	University of Cambridge
Kieran McEvoy	Queen's University Belfast
Joe Murray	University of Cambridge
Tim Newell	Cropwood Fellow, University of Cambridge
Ian O'Donnell	University College Dublin (IRE)
Barbara Owen	California State University, Fresno
Coretta Phillips	London School of Economics
Peter Scharff Smith	Danish Institute of Human Rights (DEN)
Joe Sim	Liverpool John Moores University
Sonja Snacken	Vrije Universiteit Brussels (BEL)
Richard Sparks	University of Keele
Hans Toch	University at Albany (US)
Jason Warr	Affiliate, Prisons Research Centre

Index